LARGE
PRINT
EDITION

RANDOM
HOUSE

Heading home after his first game
in the majors, April 15, 1947

JACKIE ROBINSON

A Biography

Arnold Rampersad

Published by Random House Large Print
in association with Alfred A. Knopf, Inc.
New York   1997

Library of Congress Cataloging-In-Publication Data

Rampersad, Arnold.
Jackie Robinson : a biography / Arnold Rampersad.
p.   cm.   ISBN 0-679-77433-5
1. Robinson, Jackie, 1919–1972.
2. Afro-American baseball players—United States—Biography.
3. Brooklyn Dodgers (Baseball team)—History.
4. Large type books.
I. Title
GV865.R6R35   1997   96-48648
CIP

Random House Web Address: http://www.randomhouse.com/
Printed in the United States of America
FIRST LARGE PRINT EDITION

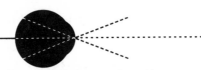

This Large Print Book carries the
Seal of Approval of N.A.V.H.

for
Luke Rampersad
who loves baseball—and books

You opened the door for me and others who followed you and when you opened it you threw it wide open.
                                                      —Brooks Lawrence (1957)

The word for Jackie Robinson is "unconquerable." . . . He would not be defeated. Not by the other team and not by life.
                                                      —Red Smith (1972)

He could beat you in a lot of ways.
                                                      —Yogi Berra (1972)

Contents

x *Contents*

JACKIE ROBINSON

Prologue

1962

Now everything is complete. . . .
—Jackie Robinson (1962)

ON THE MORNING of Monday, July 23, 1962, in the pretty and historic village of Cooperstown in upstate New York, a young white man awoke nervously in the darkness just before dawn, dressed himself quickly, and was out of his hotel, the Cooper Inn, just after six o'clock. The previous evening, he had left his home in Brooklyn, boarded a bus at the Port Authority terminal in Manhattan, and traveled some seven hours through the gathering darkness to be in Cooperstown in good time to witness the events of this day. Outside his hotel, he found the air more than a shade nippy for a midsummer morning; the sky, heavy and sodden with moisture, hung in thick shrouds that hid the sun. This was poor weather for the events he had come such a long distance to see. Later that morning, at ten-thirty, the Baseball Hall of Fame would induct four men into its ranks. Then, at two o'clock in the afternoon, two teams, the New York Yankees and the Milwaukee Braves, would meet in a memorial game played annually near the spot where—all facts to the contrary—baseball was said to have been invented by Abner Doubleday in a cow pasture in 1839, when the nation was young.

By seven o'clock, hours before the ceremony, the young man, Ron Gabriel, twenty-one years old and on summer vacation from his university, had eagerly claimed a seat in the front row of some two thousand chairs set out on Main Street before the official rostrum. This wooden dais stood on the lawn in front of the brick building, rich in baseball memorabilia, that housed the museum that was the Baseball Hall of Fame. Neither the chilly air nor the menace of rain could temper Gabriel's excitement: "I wanted to see everything!" Born and reared in the Flatbush section of Brooklyn, Gabriel had come above all to witness one event: the induction of Jack Roosevelt "Jackie" Robinson into the Hall of Fame. Since his days as a boy haunting Ebbets Field, the aged ballpark that the Brooklyn Dodgers called home, Gabriel had admired Robinson. But his interest in the ceremony ran deeper. Four years before, in 1958, the Dodgers had quit Brooklyn and moved to Los Angeles. Soon, to make way for an apartment complex, a wrecking ball had reduced Ebbets Field to rubble.

To Gabriel, as to his parents and thousands of other fans, Brooklyn and its old, sweet ways had begun to die the day the Dodgers left. Gabriel's grandparents had come to the United States from Russia and Austria, in the long river of migration that had brought millions of foreigners to New York. Almost as much as any other single force, the Brooklyn Dodgers had helped to make the children and grandchildren of many of these migrants truly American. With the departure of the Dodgers, that vision of old Brooklyn would live thereafter mainly in memory and legend, and most vividly in thrilling recollections of the baseball team of which Jackie Robinson, between 1947 and 1956, had been one unforgettable part.

When the ceremony at last started, every seat before the rostrum was taken, and all eyes were on the four men being inducted. Two were old-timers, chosen by a special committee: Edd Roush, sixty-eight years old and, in the seasons just before the ascendancy of Babe Ruth and the mighty home run, one of the premier hitters in the game; and Bill Mc-Kechnie, seventy-six, mediocre as a player but a paragon among managers. The other two inductees were stars of the recent past, selected by a far more exacting process. One was Bob Feller, forty-three, a flame-throwing pitcher from an Iowa farm whose 266 wins included three no-hitters and a dozen one-hitters. He had been, as one reporter put it, "supreme, a model athlete cast in the heroic mold, as a boy wonder who became a national sports idol." The other was Robinson, also forty-three years old. Robinson's complex fate had been to be the first black player in the major leagues of baseball in America in the twentieth century.

For all four men, as for virtually all baseball players, entry into the Hall of Fame was the crowning achievement of their lives. The white-haired McKechnie, breaking down at the podium, could not finish his remarks. More poised, Robinson was also deeply moved by the significance of the moment. "What I remember above all," Gabriel recalled, "was how absolutely radiant he looked. He wore a dark suit and a dark tie and his skin was very dark, too. But his hair was thick and a glowing white and his eyes were sparkling because he was obviously very proud and very, very happy." When it was his turn to speak, he did not hide his joy. "I feel inadequate," he confessed. "I can only say that now everything is complete."

Quickly, Robinson turned to include others in his moment of triumph. "I could not be here without the advice and guidance of three of the most wonderful people I know," he declared. One was a bulky, bushy-browed white man, Branch Rickey, eighty years old, "who was as a father to me." In 1945, as general manager of the Dodgers, Rickey had made up his mind to attack Jim Crow in baseball, and with many men to choose from in the Negro baseball leagues had summoned a rookie shortstop on the Kansas City Monarchs to walk point. The second was Robinson's mother, Mallie McGriff Robinson, seventy-one. Once a sharecropper's wife in rural Georgia, then a domestic servant in California, to which she had fled in 1920, she had also been the single most influential person in her son's often troubled youth, urging him on toward a clean, God-fearing life and whatever success he could wrestle for himself in a world hostile to blacks. The third was his wife, Rachel Robinson, whom he had married in 1946, just as his baseball ordeal was beginning, and who had shared with him most of the grief and the glory of the years since then. These three people "are all here today," Robinson said, "making the honor complete. And I don't think I will ever come down from Cloud Nine."

In January, five years after retiring, when he had become eligible for the Hall of Fame following a rule instituted in 1954, he had expected to be ignored. That month, according to a secret ritual, 160 members of the Baseball Writers' Association of America had each nominated ten eligible players for the Hall of Fame. (A separate, smaller committee chose from among old-timers, executives, and the like.) To enter the Hall, a player first had to appear on 75 percent of these ballots. The standards for nomination were in part subjective; the writers were often unpredictable. In the history of the Hall, no one had entered in his first year of eligibility since its opening in 1936, when the selectors tapped five immortals: Ty Cobb, Babe Ruth, Walter Johnson, Honus Wagner, and Christy Mathewson. In 1939, his last season, Lou Gehrig had entered by acclamation, because everyone knew that the "Iron Horse" of baseball was dying. But Rogers Hornsby, said to be the finest right-handed hitter ever, had waited six years; and Joe DiMaggio, lauded by Robinson himself as the finest player of their era, had waited two. Since 1956, the writers had not chosen any players.

Judged by the statistics of his career, Robinson's chances were strong but not overwhelming; judged by the many controversies of a career born in raw controversy, they were slim. Robinson himself thought he had no chance. "I'm positive I won't be accepted this year," he had told a reporter. "Maybe someday. But regardless of what some of my achievements were, many writers are going to disregard this because of Jackie Robinson, Negro outspoken."

"Negro outspoken" he had been as a player and in the five years since his retirement, which had coincided with the deepening crisis across the nation over civil rights for blacks. Putting his immense prestige at risk, he had almost recklessly thrown in his lot with the Movement. As a fearless competitor with the Dodgers, he had also clashed often with sportswriters; and the men who ran baseball, with one clear exception only, had both opposed his right to play the game with whites and turned their backs on him when he retired. "If I had been white with the things I did," Robinson offered sourly, "they would never have allowed me to get out of baseball." But he also commanded respect from many of the people who disliked him for stirring up antagonism. "He has a talent for it," one writer shrewdly judged. "He has the tact of a child, because he has the moral purity of a child. When you are tactless, you make enemies." Still, he concluded, "I am confident that Jackie's non-friends will sweep him into the Hall of Fame." "The aggressive Robbie carried a chip on his shoulder," another newsman declared, "and inspired among writers and fellow players little of the warm affection they lavished on such as Roy Campanella and Willie Mays. Yet he unmistakably won their admiration. What a whale of a competitor he was! . . . Jackie rates the Hall of Fame on merit and merit should be color-blind."

But color had to do with so much in Robinson's career. An incident on a cold, windy morning in Manhattan in January had poignantly underscored that fact. He was stepping briskly on his way to his office on Lexington Avenue when a black man, a stranger, stuck out his hand. "Jackie," the man said, "I know you are going to be elected into baseball's Hall of Fame. And when you are, it will be the happiest day of my life." Stunned, Robinson walked slowly away, musing on the man's words. "I was greatly moved by what that fellow said and the way he said it. Imagine him saying it would be the greatest day of his life if I made the Hall of Fame! It meant more to me than anything I can tell you."

In January, sure enough, merit was sufficiently color-blind for Robinson to garner 124 votes, or four more than he needed for admission. With congratulations pouring in, he had passed the months since his selection keenly anticipating this historic moment in Cooperstown. Three days before his induction, on the evening of July 20, he had sat in a golden haze of glory when some nine hundred admirers, led by the governor of New York, who hailed him as "a hero of the struggle to make American democracy a genuine reality for every American," honored him with a testimonial dinner at the Waldorf-Astoria Hotel. In an evening rich with praise, three messages stood out. One was from Richard Nixon, the former Vice-President of the United States, whom Robinson had firmly supported in the 1960 presidential election. "There are days when I feel a special pride simply in being American," Nixon had written Robinson when the news first broke, "and Tuesday, January 23, 1962, was certainly one of them." The second was from John F. Kennedy, who tuned out the persistent drumbeat of Robinson's opposition to his presidency to offer a glowing tribute. "He has demonstrated in his brilliant career," President Kennedy declared, that "courage, talent and perseverance can overcome the forces of intolerance. . . . The vigor and fierce competitive spirit that characterized his performance as an athlete are still evident in his efforts in the great battle to achieve equality of opportunity for all people."

The most eloquent tribute had come from Dr. Martin Luther King Jr., the central figure in the civil rights movement and the inspiration behind the testimonial dinner. King, like Kennedy and Nixon, was absent on July 20; he was in Albany, Georgia, caught up in perhaps the most explosive crisis of the Movement to that point, as a coalition of liberal organizations confronted one of the worst strongholds of segregation, about sixty miles from the place where Robinson himself was born on a plantation in 1919. Spelling out the meaning of Jackie Robinson's example, King defended Robinson's right, challenged by some observers who saw him as a faded athlete perilously beyond his depth, to speak out on matters such as politics, segregation, and civil rights. "He has the right," King insisted stoutly, "because back in the days when integration wasn't fashionable, he underwent the trauma and the humiliation and the loneliness which comes with being a pilgrim walking the lonesome byways toward the high road of Freedom.

He was a sit-inner before sit-ins, a freedom rider before freedom rides. And that is why we honor him tonight."

Praised by friend and foe alike, a hero to the heroes of a struggle inspired in many ways by his own achievements in baseball, Robinson felt a profound sense of satisfaction in what he had accomplished and was helping to accomplish. Now the vice-president of a successful company, living with his handsome family in a fine home in a wealthy Connecticut town, he seemed the epitome of success. "You are the richest man I know," a friend wrote to him a few days later, "because you have *everything;* who could ask for more?"

Now, at Cooperstown, Robinson set aside his bad memories and acknowledged the inner truth about his relationship to the game that had transformed his life even as he had helped to transform the game. "I'm a tremendously fortunate individual," he told the assembled guests. "I gave baseball all I had for ten years and baseball has given me everything I've got today."

When the simple ceremony was over, Gabriel beat the crush of spectators storming the stage and offered congratulations to Robinson, and Branch Rickey, too. "I thanked Rickey," he recalled, "for being the man behind this great moment. He liked what I said, I could tell that. I could also see that only Robinson was paying him any attention. He seemed far on the sidelines for a man who had helped to make the history we were witnessing." Standing a few feet away, Gabriel watched as photographers snapped pictures of the two men together; then he trailed them as they toured the wall of plaques, now ninety altogether, that was the heart of the Hall of Fame. He listened closely as writers peppered Robinson with questions about his dramatic entry into white baseball, his pact with Rickey to endure abuse and not strike back while the game and the nation absorbed the shock of his black presence. "The one question that stood out for me," Gabriel said, "was whether he was proud to have been the first black in major league baseball. And I heard him say, 'Yes, that's something I can really feel proud about. I will always be proud of that particular fact.' I could tell that his answer came from his heart, that he was not boasting but was really terribly proud that he had done that particular thing."

And yet the Hall of Fame plaque bearing Robinson's likeness said nothing about his black skin—or his ordeal. In the Hall of Fame, each man was finally the same color: bronze. But Robinson's color was central to his story. "Later his name would appear on two other plaques," Gabriel said, "and then you had a hint of what he had gone through. But not on his own plaque. I always thought that a pity." Under the heading "Brooklyn N.L. 1947 to 1956" Robinson's plaque read only: "Leading N.L. batter in 1949. Holds fielding mark for second baseman playing in 150 or more games with .992. Lead N.L. in stolen bases in 1947 and 1949. Most valuable player in 1949. Lifetime batting average .311. Joint record holder for most double plays by second baseman, 137 in 1951. Led second basemen in double plays 1949–50–51–52." Those numbers did not tell the whole truth, Gabriel knew. "To see Robinson's career in numbers," Roger Kahn would write, "is to see Lincoln through Federal budgets and to miss the Emancipation Proclamation. Double plays, stolen bases, indeed the bat, the ball, the glove, were only artifacts with which Jackie Robinson made his country and you and me and all of us a shade more free."

Leaving the museum, Robinson, Rickey, and others in the main party went on their way. After a quick meal alone, Gabriel strolled over to the venerable Otesaga Hotel, where he knew most of the honored guests were staying. Easing himself near a doorway that opened onto the glittering dining room, he had no trouble finding Jackie Robinson once more. "Again, Robinson was like a vision," he recalled. "He and his mother and his wife and their three children stood out because they were all dressed up, beautifully dressed up; but they were also the only black family in the entire room. Jackie couldn't keep still; he was talking to waiters, moving around his table, making sure everything was fine for his family. It was truly a beautiful thing to see.

"But it was also heartbreaking, too. I asked myself, are they the first black family to sit in that dining room? Somehow, it looked that way. Jackie seemed very much at ease and yet also a stranger, a man inside and yet, at the same time, apart. But he had earned his place, his right to be there. I thought, gee, this is really wonderful, this is what America is all about."

Fifteen minutes before game time, the skies opened and cool rain began to drench the village. For the first time in the history of the ceremony, officials had to call off the game. Disappointed, but musing still on the significance of all that he had seen, Gabriel boarded a bus for the long ride home.

— 1 —

In Pharaoh's Land:
Cairo, Georgia

1919–1920

Yet we did not nod, nor weary of the scene;
for this is historic ground.
    —*W. E. B. Du Bois (1903)*

NEAR SIX O'CLOCK on the evening of January 31,
1919, Jack Roosevelt Robinson was born somewhere near the town of Cairo in Grady County in
southern Georgia, a few miles north of the Florida
state line. Precisely where he was born is open to
question, although only two answers make sense. In
one place, a crumbling brick chimney is all that remains of the dwelling. In the other, two brick chim-
neys rise now above burnt-out ruins. The first place
was a rough cottage, the home of Jack's parents,
Jerry and Mallie Robinson, on a plantation just
south of Cairo owned by a white farmer, James
Madison Sasser. The other site, not far away, was a
somewhat more pleasant house sitting among whis-
pering pine trees on the edge of Hadley Ferry Road
near Rocky Hill, also to the south of Cairo. There,
Mallie Robinson's parents, Washington McGriff and

Edna Sims McGriff, lived on twelve acres owned at
that time by Edna.

Of these two places, the more plausible is the cottage on the Sasser plantation. Later, Mallie spoke of
giving birth at a farmhouse with about five big
rooms. With her were a doctor, her husband, her
brother, and a brother-in-law. A major flu epidemic
was raging, she noted; there were no women around.
The physician, the first doctor to attend Mallie in her
five birthings, was a white man, a Dr. Reynolds.
Almost certainly he was Dr. Arthur Brown Reynolds,
a University of Georgia medical school graduate who
had come to practice in the area around 1910. The
epidemic was the "Spanish flu," which in 1918 and
1919 killed millions of Americans.

Mallie had given birth to a healthy boy. In choos-
ing his middle name, his family intended to honor
Teddy Roosevelt. As President, the patrician Roosevelt had inspired many blacks because of his outspoken disdain for racism, especially during his first
term in office, before white supremacist power made
him retreat into conservatism. He had condemned
lynching and had also attacked the system called
peonage, which had emerged as the new slavery in
much of the rural South. Working with the premier
black leader of the age, Booker T. Washington of the
Tuskegee Institute in Alabama, Roosevelt had
appointed several blacks to high office. He had also
tried hard, if with little success, to forge a political
coalition of Southern whites and blacks under
enlightened white leadership. Roosevelt, a bitter
critic of the sitting President, the segregationist

Woodrow Wilson, was widely expected to run again for the White House in 1920. But on January 6, 1919, he died. When Mallie's son was born later that month, she named him after the twenty-sixth President of the United States.

Mallie had wanted a girl; now she had four sons, but only one daughter. She also knew that Jack's birth would not help her marriage, which was doomed. She and Jerry had been separated at least three times. Every patching-up had meant only false hopes and another child.

Marrying for love, Mallie McGriff perhaps took a step down. Jerry's father, Tony Robinson, had crossed over the state line from Florida to rent and farm land on the Sasser plantation. Jerry, most likely the eldest of eleven children, had labored all his life for the Sassers; tied to the soil, he could neither read nor write. Mallie had known a different life. The seventh of fourteen children, she had grown up on land owned by her parents and gone to school up to the sixth grade—no small feat for a black girl in rural Georgia. Born slaves, Wash and Edna McGriff had pressed education on their children; when Mallie was ten, she repaid her father by teaching him to read his beloved Bible. The McGriffs had brought up their children to fear God but also to plan for the future, and Mallie had learned those lessons well. For her, hope was essential. Everywhere around her, she could see history weighing heavily on the lives of blacks and whites alike.

Slavery had defined, and continued to shape, the culture of the region. Before the Civil War, the fertile

"Black Belt" across the middle of Georgia comprised
the densest population of blacks anywhere in the
United States. Most were slaves, who lived and died
on rich cotton plantations in what one observer mordantly called "the Egypt of the Confederacy." The
region where the McGriffs and their relatives lived
was well to the south, but was usually seen as part of
the Black Belt because it, too, was fertile and home
to many blacks. Taking in Grady County and the
adjoining Thomas County, this area rolled on as far
south as Tallahassee, the hilly capital of Florida.
Compared to northern Georgia, the region was isolated, and home mainly to striving small farmers.
Striving was part of its history. Needy white pioneers, many coming from the Carolinas, had helped
to drive the native Seminole Indians from their
ancestral grounds. Most of the territory that in 1909
would become Grady County, with Cairo as its seat,
was given away in the land lottery that followed, in
1820. The architect of the overthrowing of Indian
sovereignty was undoubtedly Andrew Jackson, later
President of the United States, who profited enor-
mously from this wanton theft and destruction.

Slaves had been essential to the growth of the
region; slave labor had cleared its primeval forests,
nurtured and harvested its crops. After the Civil War,
which saw little destruction in this part of Georgia,
blacks like Wash and Edna McGriff had looked forward to enjoying the fruits of their labor and freedom. Instead, Reconstruction became for them, in
the words of a local historian, "a period of broken
promises, abject poverty and crushed dreams." By

1900, because of the punitive use of devices such as the poll tax and stringent literacy requirements, few blacks could vote, and Jim Crow laws and customs also harshly shut off even the most common avenues to prosperity, especially jobs.

White hostility took even more violent forms. Between 1890 and 1902, when about 200 lynchings made Georgia the worst state in the Union in this respect, six took place in Thomas County. The years between 1909, when Jerry and Mallie were married, and 1918 saw more than 125 lynchings of blacks across the state, often for flimsy reasons and always unpunished. Mob violence was a daunting feature of black life in Georgia, with the most harrowing single episode the Atlanta riot of September 1906, when four leading blacks were killed by whites, who also looted and burned black homes and businesses. The effect on blacks of so much repression was widespread poverty, disease, and crime, as well as cynicism and despair. For many, freedom had actually been a step down from slavery. "Although there were white people in Thomas County," it was noted, "who believed that blacks should have a chance to have freedom on a par with whites, most local white leaders opposed black advancement at every turn."

Still, some blacks managed to rise. A chronic labor shortage made black people, no matter how poorly paid, necessary to white self-interest. In the 1880s, local blacks also benefited when tourism became important, as well as a new plantation culture that brought rich Northerners, including those with names such as Whitney, Vanderbilt, and Rockefeller, to acquire estates in the region. Attracted by the sunny climate, stunning landscapes, and rock-bottom prices after a plague of bankruptcies, the newcomers began to transform decrepit estates according to their fanciful notions about the Old South in its golden age, before the Civil War. Blacks were essential to this fantasy, which also encouraged not only prosperity but new standards of civility as well. In 1904, the region ardently supported the charming Tom Watson as the Populist candidate for the U.S. presidency. Nevertheless, white supremacy was the first rule of life. In 1910, when the local Board of Trade published a brochure designed to attract new businesses to Grady County, it offered as one inducement "the interesting fact" gleaned from the last U.S. Census that "the rural South is becoming white with the coming in of farmers from the Central West" to buy cheap land in Georgia. Cairo, the brochure boasted, "is the Diamond Stud on Grady County's Snow-White Front."

In southern Georgia, as elsewhere, some blacks seized on almost every passing chance, every loophole in the logic of Jim Crow, to build as best they could. Family, the land, and the church became central to their lives. Clearly the McGriffs, Mallie's family, were part of this group; clearly, too, they prospered. When Wash's sister Eliza McGriff married Jerry Walden Jr., her former teacher at the black school in nearby Beachton, the McGriffs became even more deeply rooted in the community of landed black farmers who believed in family pride, education, the accumulation of property, and

God. (Walden was a Morehouse College graduate whose family owned several hundred acres of land.) In the region south of Cairo, with its fertile red clay soil and rolling, pine-covered hills, black families like the McGriffs, the Waldens, and their relatives the Hadleys (whose patriarch, Richard Hadley, owned four hundred acres by the 1870s) endured and, now and then, even flourished. Prolific in off-spring and intertwined in marriage, they forged this union despite the resentments of most of their white neighbors; the black families bought land that their descendants would own tenaciously a hundred years later. Raising livestock and planting fields of corn, cotton, sugar cane, peanuts, and garden veg-etables, they were able both to feed themselves in times of grave financial hardship, which were not infrequent, and also to save a little money toward the future.

Religion was important. Breaking away from white churches, where they were unwanted, blacks dipped into their meager resources to build and maintain more than thirty churches in the region by the turn of the century. Mallie's people, generous in their support of religion, worshiped at churches like the Evergreen Congregational Church in Beachton, built on land donated by the Waldens; or the Rocky Hill African Methodist Episcopal Church, which the McGriffs attended; or Ochlocknee Baptist, important in Hadley family history. Mallie's faith in God was linked to her keen sense of family, and both were blended with her belief that family and God were the main defenses against the evils of the unjust world

into which she had been born as a black in the Deep
South.

Mallie no doubt would have remained in Grady
County, a devoted wife and mother, but for her husband's philandering. Handsome and virile, Jerry
Robinson had first flashed his teeth at her during a
party at Christmas, 1906. He was eighteen years old,
she only fourteen. Taking her home, he promised to
call on her on Sunday and escort her to church.
Incensed, Wash McGriff put a stop to that: Mallie
was too young, he insisted. Almost certainly, he saw
that Jerry Robinson was a shabby prospect; instead,
McGriff had in mind for Mallie an upstanding young
man, originally from South Carolina, whose family
lived in the best tenant house on the Sasser plantation. But Mallie, pretending to be scared of strange
South Carolinians, ignored him and encouraged
Jerry. On Sunday, November 21, 1909, about three
years after their first meeting, she and Jerry Robinson were married.

At first, Mallie was happy with Jerry in their
cabin on Jim Sasser's plantation; but Sasser's terms
and conditions soon disturbed her. To her dismay, she
found out that his tenants had to beg him for any farm
produce they wanted, from collard greens to turnips.
Hog-killing time that Christmas brought a further
shock; Mallie was stunned to hear that Sasser
allowed his black workers only scraps—he reserved
even the neckbones and backbones. When Jerry, bor-
rowing against his next year's salary of twelve dollars a month, gave Mallie five dollars to make the

season merry, she found the sum inadequate; further-more, Sasser expected her to spend it all at his plan-tation store. Farming here smelled like slavery, and Mallie said so. A bold young woman, she set about changing their life. She made Jerry insist on share-cropping status with Jim Sasser rather than monthly wages. Sasser was not happy about the request, but agreed to it. In the usual arrangement, he provided housing, the land, fertilizer, and seed in return for half of whatever Jerry Robinson grew.

Mallie then threw her energies into making sharecropping pay, and their life improved dramati-cally. Soon the Robinsons owned their own fat hogs, chickens, and turkeys as well as the cotton and peanuts, sugar cane, corn, and potatoes that were some of the staples of the Sasser plantation. But prosperity worked poorly on Jerry; with money in his pocket, his eye began to rove. "We were just living as I wanted to live," Mallie declared sorrowfully some forty years later; "only his love [was] drifting away." Dazzled by the lights of Cairo, Jerry wanted to move to town, but Mallie could not be swayed. Fed up, Jerry tried to put her out, but she refused to leave. He left, then returned; she forgave him. He left again, and came back again; she forgave him once more. Meanwhile, their children came—Edgar in 1910, Frank in 1911, Mack in 1914, Willa Mae in 1916; and Jack in 1919.

By this time, Mallie knew that her husband was romantically involved with one of the married daughters of a respected black family, the Powells,

who owned a large tract of land across the road from
the Sasser place. ("It's true," Olin Faulk said some
seventy-five years later; "my grandmother Fannie
Powell's sister was having an affair with him. The
family often talked about it.") Deeply hurt by the
knowledge, Mallie turned increasingly to God, who
warned her in a dream that Jerry and his lover were
about to run off together. When Jerry announced too
casually that he was going to visit one of his brothers
in Texas and would take little Willa Mae along,
Mallie replied just as casually that Willa Mae could
not go. On July 28, 1919, Jerry said goodbye to his
wife and children and went down to the railroad station in Cairo. Someone saw him skulking around one
end of the station; then he climbed aboard a local
train heading north—a curious way to go to Texas.
Next, Mallie heard that he was working at a sawmill
and that the woman was with him.

When Jerry's money and luck ran out, he was
back on her doorstep. But she was moving now in a
different direction. Jerry's departure had put her on a
collision course with Jim Sasser, who once told her
to her face: "You're about the sassiest nigger woman
ever on this place." Powerfully built, "a tall, rawboned man, who scared a lot of people," according to
one person, Sasser ran his farm with a mailed fist. A
county commissioner, he was widely respected as
perhaps the most enterprising farmer in the region,
but he was also rightly feared as one of the toughest.
When he found out that Mallie had actually helped
Jerry, perhaps his best worker, to leave, he was livid.

But Mallie stood up to him. When Sasser sought to bring the sheriff into the matter, to compel Jerry back into the marriage and onto the plantation, she refused to go along. When he tried to hire her as cook for his household, she declined the honor. Sasser struck back after one of Jerry's brothers offered to bring in the crops for her. "You might as well go," Sasser advised her. "I ain't gonna give you nothing."

To accommodate new tenant farmers, he evicted her and the children out of her house into another one, less spacious, then into yet another, which she found barely habitable. Still, when Mallie tried to take a job elsewhere, Sasser blocked the way. Finally she found work with another white family, who treated her kindly. But Georgia and the South itself had become a dead end. As Mallie tried to gauge the likely future for herself and her five children, she saw mainly poverty, humiliation, and possibly worse. In the preceding five years, race relations had become bleak. On Thanksgiving night, 1915, at the behest of the same Tom Watson who had tried to lead blacks and whites under the Populist banner, the Klan was reborn in a ceremony atop Stone Mountain, Georgia. In 1919, when whites lynched seventy-six blacks in the United States, Georgia preserved its record as the most violently antiblack state in the Union. In April, three months after Jack's birth, an incident in a church in Millen, eastern Georgia, led to the death of two white policemen; whites then killed five blacks and burned seven black churches and lodge halls. On May 10, a race riot broke out in Charleston in neigh-

boring South Carolina. Early in September, in incidents across Georgia, a number of black churches
and schools were burned down. Between the
Charleston riot and the epidemic of arson had come
the "Red Summer," which witnessed at least two
dozen race riots across the country, most notably in
Chicago, brought on by bitter postwar competition
between whites and blacks seeking jobs and housing.

A way out for Mallie came with a visit to Grady
County by Burton Thomas, her half-brother, who
had emigrated to southern California. (He was Edna
McGriff's son by a previous marriage, to Monroe
Thomas.) Elegantly garbed and exuding an air of settled prosperity, Burton expounded to one and all on
the wonders of the West. "If you want to get closer to
heaven," he liked to brag, "visit California." Slowly
and secretly, and apparently with the aid of some
whites among Mallie's employers, a circle of relatives began to plan an exit. Mallie would take her five
children with her. Her sister Cora Wade, two years
younger, would also move, with her husband,
Samuel, and their sons, Ralph, who was three, and
Van, an infant. Mallie's brother Paul McGriff also
planned to go. Eventually, about thirteen family
members formed the party migrating to Los Angeles.

On May 21, 1920, Mallie commandeered a
buggy, loaded her children and possessions on it, and
headed for Cairo. There, preparing to leave, she and
the children stayed briefly at the home on Adams
Street (later called Seventh Street) of her half-sister
Mary Lou Thomas Maxwell, forty-two years old and
the full sister of Burton Thomas. Unhappy with her

husband's ways, Mary Lou intended to follow Mallie and Cora to California.

Summoned by an indignant Jerry Robinson, as Mallie herself recalled, the police caught up with her at the small train station near the middle of town. To many white Southerners, migrating blacks were an insult and a threat: an insult to the myth that the South was perfection itself, especially in the harmony of its races; and a threat in that it meant the loss of some of the South's cheapest labor. Local Georgia police routinely saw it as part of their responsibility to curb black migration. In 1916, in Macon, Savannah, and elsewhere in Georgia, officers mounted specific actions, including the vigorous policing of the black section of Jim Crow train stations, to prevent blacks from leaving. Typically, they tore up train tickets or intimidated blacks into turning back. In Macon, the city council approved the purchase of forty rifles by the police to deal with a perceived threat from blacks angry over this issue. About fifty thousand blacks abandoned Georgia that year.

At the Cairo train station, some white policemen truculently checked train tickets, churlishly kicked at suitcases and boxes. But they did nothing to stop Mallie's party from leaving.

"In those days," Charles Copeland, a family friend, later recalled, "six trains passed through Cairo every twenty-four hours. I was young, but I remember the day the sisters left with their children, the commotion at the train station. I had never seen anything like it. It was a big thing for us, everyone was so excited." Around midnight, the number 58 train pulled into the station. The band of travelers wept, said their goodbyes, and climbed aboard. Almost certainly, Jack Roosevelt Robinson, only one year and four months old, was in his mother's arms as the train pulled slowly out of Cairo to start the long journey across the continent.

— 2 —

A Pasadena Boyhood

1920–1937

I might have become a full-fledged delinquent.
—Jackie Robinson (1972)

ON A WARM JUNE night in 1920, Mallie Robinson and her band of migrants from Georgia at last reached Los Angeles, California. After a sometimes dreary, more often absorbing ride across the continent, the first vista of the city dazzled her; it was, she wrote home, "the most beautiful sight of my whole life." The next day, passing through orange groves and winding upward toward the land under the San Gabriel Mountains, the train bearing the party reached its final destination, the city of Pasadena, about a dozen miles from Los Angeles.

The California weather and scenery were spectacular, the city of Pasadena impressive—but the Georgia migrants started their new life in a shabby cold-water apartment of three small rooms, with a tin tub serving as a kitchen sink, near the railroad station. The next morning, Mallie resolutely began her search for work; except for three dollars sewn into the lining of her petticoat, she was broke. Soon, however, she had landed a job as a maid with a white Pasadena family, on terms she liked: eight dollars a week, and her working day ended in the late afternoon, not into the night as in Georgia. When her employers moved away suddenly, she lost this job; but she soon found another, also with a white family, the Dodges, whose trust and respect she quickly earned. Twenty years later she was still working for them.

After a few weeks in the cramped apartment, the Robinsons and the Wades moved with Burton Thomas into a roomy house with an ample backyard at 45 Glorieta Street, in the tree-lined northwestern section of the city. Like all of Pasadena, this area was mainly white; but it also formed the center of Pasadena's small black population.

Late in the summer, Edgar and Frank Robinson, ten and nine years old respectively, started school at Grover Cleveland Elementary School nearby; Cora Wade, who was too frail to take a regular job, was in charge of Mack, Willa Mae, and Jack as well as her own children while her husband and Mallie worked. This arrangement worked well for the Robinsons and the Wades, less happily for Burton. Uncle Burton was "really very much a loner," Willa Mae later recalled, "and he definitely wasn't used to children." In 1922, after about two years in Pasadena, Mallie and Sam pooled their money and bought a house at 121 Pepper Street, on an all-white block just to the north of Glorieta. The 1921–22 Pasadena City Directory listed Sam Wade as owner and "Mattie" Robinson as a fellow resident there, but they were co-owners. According to family legend, a black real estate agent employed his light-skinned niece to buy the house, then sold it to Mallie and Sam. However, the county tax assessor's records indicate only that the property was bought in 1905 by two men, Charles R. Ellis and William H. Harrison, who then sold it in 1922 to Mallie Robinson and Sam Wade.

Two years later, in 1924, the Wades moved into their own home a few blocks away, at 972 Cypress Street. Mallie then became the sole owner of 121 Pepper Street, where Jack would live until he left home in 1941. In 1939, Mallie would also buy the property next door, 133 Pepper Street, at what was then the corner of Pepper Street and Navarro Avenue (years later, Navarro Avenue would be filled in at that point). In 1946, she acquired a third adjoining lot, at 1302 Navarro Avenue.

PEPPER STREET IN 1922 was a working-class district, but the black migrants from rural Georgia now lived in the wealthiest city in the United States, judged according to the size of its population. Twenty years later, despite the ravages of the Great Depression, Pasadena still ranked as "the richest city per capita in America." Its main thoroughfare, Orange Grove Avenue, adorned by impressive mansions and effulgent gardens, was commonly called "Millionaires' Row"; and signs of affluence and taste were everywhere to be seen. An educated black visitor passing through the city shortly before the arrival of the Robinsons in 1920 wrote admiringly of "a civic pride running through all the town," as well as other features that made Pasadena unmistakably "a city of beauty and harmony."

In some ways, its story is a familiar American tale; in other respects, it is more or less original. Familiar enough is the conquest by whites of the Gabrielino Indians, whose unusually pale skin led some people to believe in a race of white Indians but did not save that race from extinction. Their lands, dominated to the north by the stone-faced San Gabriel Mountains and embracing the fertile San Gabriel Valley, then passed from the hands of the Church to a succession of secular owners, who presided over great ranches once a part of Mexico. Where the Gabrielinos, feeding on acorns and squash, used to roam freely, profitable grape vineyards and orange groves, often the property of eastern financial interests, began to flourish in the balmy climate. Then, in 1873, a group of Indiana citizens, sick of midwestern winters, took steps to acquire a California home in the region. By the end of the year, a model community was in the making. Wanting a quaint Indian name for their settlement, in 1875 the founders came up with "Pasadena," which in a Chippewa dialect is said to mean "the valley," or "of the valley." The new community formally adopted this name.

The founders set lofty civic goals for themselves. They divided the land in a spirit of harmony, built roads with a respect for the natural features of the land, and planted thousands of fruit trees, which led to the area being celebrated as a kind of Eden. The warm, dry climate encouraged sanitariums and hotels and a steady flow of tourists, many of whom returned to stay. Spurning heavy industry, Pasadena wooed the rich and the educated. The city, making the most of its mountains and clean air, factors conducive to geology and astronomy, established what became the major science school in the west, the California Technical Institute, or Caltech. "Sophisticated and wealthy patrons fostered the arts," one historian has noted, "and Pasadena became an important center for distinctive architecture, painting and sculpture, music, literature and science."

For a while, Pasadena was a liberal community, proud of its Indiana abolitionist roots and its civic ideals. The city openly welcomed, first as visitors, then as settlers, Jason and Owen Brown, sons of John Brown, the martyr of the action at Harpers Ferry, in which Owen had fought. But the main test of its liberalism came from its servants and their descendants, of whom there were many. Pasadena was famous for its profusion of private gardens, the most famous of which was that of the beer magnate Adolphus Busch, formerly of St. Louis, Missouri. With its shimmering pools and fountains, winding paths, mossy stone walls, verdant lawns, and quaint little cottages out of Grimm's Fairy Tales, Busch Gardens became a magnet for visitors to the town. Built by the rich, such gardens depended on cheap labor. As with the faux plantations of southwestern Georgia, the fantasies of the white rich became a boon to the colored poor.

At first, the Chinese dominated, until the Exclusion Act of 1882 did its work; then the Japanese, less objectionable to whites, filled the vacancies. By

1920, when the Robinsons and the Wades arrived, blacks comprised the largest single minority group in Pasadena, although they numbered only about eleven hundred. The black presence dated back to 1883, when a Negro teamster, after driving a herd of cattle out from Nebraska, bought a vineyard and settled down with his family. Other blacks quickly followed in search of work in the homes and gardens of whites. Churches were founded and families took root, in relative peace. This period before the end of World War I came to be seen as their golden age by Pasadena blacks, who during the war found jobs for the first time in factories, mills, lumberyards, and other light industries. But with the end of the war came bitter clashes between them and returning white soldiers. If the war marked "the beginning of the transition in the economic livelihood of the colored people," as one scholar noted, it also marked "the start of more intolerance, prejudice, and persecution" than had ever been known in Pasadena.

In fact, Jim Crow had been a feature of Pasadena almost from the start. In 1900, the growing presence of blacks, Japanese, Chinese, and Hispanics led officials to zone the city according to race, a practice stopped only when the United States Supreme Court ruled against it in 1917. When blacks built a new African Methodist Episcopal church in 1909, whites attempted to burn it down. On July 4, 1914, came the issue that would symbolize more vividly than any other the mean and divisive spirit of Jim Crow in Pasadena. On that day, when city officials opened the sole municipal swimming pool, the Brookside Plunge in Brookside Park, they also restricted its use to whites only. After a storm of protest, the city instituted "International Day" at the pool—one day each week when anyone could use it. At the end of this day, they promised, the plunge would be drained and refilled with clean water.

Justice was not unknown for blacks in Pasadena. In 1918, after two black women filed a lawsuit against a local theater that charged them more than whites for admission, a superior court judge awarded them one hundred dollars in damages. But similar acts of race prejudice persisted, as whites sought to turn the screws on blacks and other minority groups, to keep them out of all but menial jobs and bar them from as many public places as possible. In 1919, appalled by local conditions, some blacks founded a chapter of the then-militant National Association for the Advancement of Colored People. That year, the local correspondent for the main black-owned newspaper in the region, the *California Eagle,* challenged African-Americans "to come together and agitate for the things necessary for their betterment, and circulate propaganda for the guidance of the race in this, the greatest crisis of the Nation's progress and reconstruction."

Meanwhile, white Pasadena leaders glowed understandably with a sense of accomplishment. In 1922, the city constructed the Rose Bowl, which served annually on New Year's Day as the venue of a nationally renowned battle between college football teams, as well as the terminus of the famed Pasadena Parade of Roses. Between 1927 and 1932, the city

completed an ambitious Civic Center, including a
new city hall and an imposing main library. Pasadena
saw the construction of the first freeway in the
nation, the imaginatively landscaped Arroyo Seco
highway, free of billboards, which linked the city to
Los Angeles. About this time, Henry L. Huntington
also committed himself to endowing the world-
famous library and art gallery that would bear his
name into posterity. The Pasadena Community Playhouse gained national fame, especially after its world
premiere in 1928 of *Dynamo* by Eugene O'Neill.

If Pasadena could now claim to be the Athens of
southern California, its white citizens increasingly
saw only one flaw in all this perfection: the presence
of blacks. Crime was not an issue; black crime was
insignificant. But Negro residents on any street drove
down property values, as Pasadena whites looked
with envy on nearby communities such as Eagle
Rock, South Pasadena, and San Marino—but especially on Glendale, which had had the foresight not
to employ blacks as domestics and now boasted that
not a single Negro lived within the city limits. As one
of Jack's friends remembered about Pasadena in the
1930s, the boundaries for most nonwhites were
strictly drawn, although there were also scattered
exceptions: "You couldn't live east of Fair Oaks. You
couldn't live north of Washington Boulevard. And
you couldn't live west of Lincoln Avenue."

Far more devastating were the restrictions on
where blacks might work. By 1940, a year before
Jack Robinson's departure from Pasadena, the city
had not yet hired, as one editorial indignantly put it,

"a single [black] policeman, fireman, regular day-time school teacher, meter-reader, or any other type of employee for the utilities; no, not even a janitor or an elevator boy in the City Hall." Pasadena employed some blacks in the park, street, and refuse departments, and then only as laborers, never as clerks. At some point, the post office began to hire blacks, and a county office gingerly broke the Jim Crow rule; but most businesses did not, and all trade unions scorned blacks as members. The result was chronic unemployment and poverty and a growing despair. In 1924, after the city rebuffed a petition to appoint a black policeman (by then Los Angeles had a black detective and several black patrolmen and firemen), the *Eagle* summed up its concern: "The condition of affairs surrounding the racial issues in Pasadena is nothing less than nauseating."

The white house at 121 Pepper Street, once the site of a local post office, was large; with five bedrooms and two baths spread over two floors, it offered for the first time a measure of comfort and privacy to the Robinsons and the Wades. Within the Robinson family it came to be known as "the Castle," not least of all because it was their fortress against an often hostile world. The lot was shady with a variety of fruit trees. "We had apples, oranges, peaches, and figs," Willa Mae recalled, "just about six or eight different kinds of fruit trees, and my mother put up cans of fruit during the summer that lasted us through the winter." Mallie also put in a large garden. She planted bright-blooming flowers to make the house beautiful, but in addition raised vegetables, "things we could go out in the garden and pick and eat." As in Georgia, Mallie also raised, at one time or another, turkeys, chickens, ducks, rabbits, and even a flock of pigeons.

Even so, the Robinsons were relatively poor and sometimes hungry. Late in life, Jack would write of his boyhood as marred by stretches of real hunger: "Sometimes there were only two meals a day, and some days we wouldn't have eaten at all if it hadn't been for the leftovers my mother was able to bring home from her job." He also recalled "other times when we subsisted on bread and sweet water." But Jack's earlier interviews about Pasadena apparently never mentioned such extreme poverty, and his sister, Willa Mae, denied it. She blamed the emphasis on poverty on the desire of writers to foster a rags-to-riches myth once Jack had become a star. Perhaps the truth is in between, but the Robinsons doubtless struggled to earn money in the 1920s, despite the purchase of their "Castle," and continued to struggle throughout the Great Depression.

Jack and Willa Mae disagreed about hunger but not about bigotry on Pepper Street. "We went through a sort of slavery," she recalled, "with the whites slowly, very slowly, getting used to us." At first, angry whites tried to buy out Mallie and Sam Wade; but Mallie's kindness won over the only person on the street with the means to buy her out, Clara Coppersmith, a widow who lived alone next door. After Edgar Robinson, at Mallie's behest, did various chores for her without pay, she gave her vehement support to her black neighbors. Still, resentment remained deep. Someone burned a cross on the front lawn. Down the street, an elderly white couple scurried indoors in terror if any Negroes approached. The police responded to complaints about the children, especially Edgar and his noisy roller-skating. "The police were there every other day," according to Willa Mae, "telling my mother that she had to keep us in the yard." Refusing to give up, Mallie also tried to look on her foes with charity. "My mother never lost her composure," Jack later wrote. "She didn't allow us to go out of our way to antagonize the whites, and she still made it perfectly clear to us and to them that she was not at all afraid of them and that she had no intention of allowing them to mistreat us." Once, when he and some friends, in retaliation against a white man on Pepper Street, spread tar on his lawn, Mallie ordered them to repair the damage; she supervised the job as they cleaned the lawn with kerosene and rags and carefully snipped blades of grass with scissors.

The worst episode on Pepper Street touching Jack directly occurred when he was about eight years old. One day, he was sweeping the sidewalk when a little girl from the poorest house on the block, almost directly across the street from the Robinsons', began to taunt him: "Nigger! Nigger! Nigger!" Incensed, Jack answered in insulting kind. Her father, a surly, shiftless fellow, stormed out of the house to challenge Jack. Soon stones were flying between boy and man until his wife came out to scold him for fighting with a child.

Eventually the Robinsons were accepted on Pepper Street, in large part out of respect for Mallie.

At one point, she even made the Robinson home a kind of relief center. On Saturday evenings, a bakery nearby allowed her boys to take away leftover baked goods; and daily, at the end of the milkman's run, he gave what was left to the "Robinson Crusoe" household, as he called it, rather than let it spoil. Generously, Mallie included her neighbors in distributing this largesse. "My mother divided with them because it was too much for just our family," according to Willa Mae, "so all the neighbors— even the one that was throwing rocks and fighting— they got some too. And then we got to be real friends and all in the neighborhood. They found out we were human, too; the color didn't do anything to them."

To many people, Mallie's job as a domestic servant, along with her black skin and her gender, fully defined her. In fact, she had a keen imagination and a radiant spirit, as well as abilities and interests that sometimes surprised even her children, who had not known her when she was a young woman starting out, with the world before her. As one of her daughters-in-law recalled, "Mallie loved to sit on her porch with people about her and spin stories endlessly. She would act out the various parts, the different characters, in an animated way, and she had a really vibrant sense of fun and pleasure." Her son Mack was astonished one day to see her impulsively climb up on a horse and happily gallop off sidesaddle with a skill and confidence he never expected. For all this whimsical aspect, Mallie also had her stern side. "We knew that we had to do what we had to do," Willa

Mae recalled, "or we got spanked, punished; she would pick a switch and come after us." She worked hard to instill in them the key values she herself had learned growing up in Georgia, about the importance of family, education, optimism, self-discipline, and, above all, God.

Tenaciously, Mallie tried to preserve her family ties to Georgia even if it meant helping several relatives and friends there escape to California. In 1927, following the death in Georgia of her father, Wash McGriff, Mallie welcomed her mother, Edna Sims McGriff, who lived for a while with Mallie, then with her son Burton, and finally with her daughter Cora. Near seventy in 1927, gnarled and feeble, she made a vivid impression on her grandson Jack. "I remember sitting by the flickering light of an oil lantern," he would recall, "and watching her face, which had a thousand wrinkles in it." Far more than Mallie, it was Edna McGriff, born a slave, who embodied for Jack the fearsome aspect of his Southern heritage, including the legacy of slavery. "I remember she told me once," he said, "that when the slaves were freed they wanted no part of freedom. They were afraid of it." Years later, at one of the most perilous moments of his life, when his future hung in the balance with his military court-martial, he would also recall what his grandmother had told him more than once about the word "nigger," and her insistence to him that no matter what ignorant whites said, he was not one. On July 25, 1933, when Jack was fourteen, Edna Sims McGriff died at Cora Wade's home at 972 Cypress Street. She became one of the first of the Georgia migrants to be buried in the Mountain View Cemetery in Pasadena.

Family was vital to Mallie, but God was supreme. For her, as she tried to make her children see, God was a living, breathing presence all about her, and she seeded her language with worshipful allusions to the divine. "God watches what you do," she would insist; "you must reap what you sow, so sow well!" Faith in God meant not only prayers on one's knees each night, and Scott United Methodist Church on Sunday, but also a never-ending sensitivity to God's power, an urge to carry out the divine will as set out in the Bible, and a constant appeal to Heaven for aid, comfort, and guidance. Through all his years living with Mallie, Jack was witness to his mother's unshakable attachment to religion, the entirely willful way she delivered herself and her fortunes to God without becoming fatalistic or withdrawing from the world. If anyone questioned the durability of the link between prayer and belief, Mallie had a forthright answer. "Prayer," she often told her children, "*is* belief."

CRAVING HIS MOTHER'S COMPANY, Jack as a small boy slept downstairs at 121 Pepper Street with her and refused to leave her bed. When she offered him a quarter a week to move out, he turned her down. Finally, after Jack dreamed one night that an intruder had climbed in through the window, he then fled upstairs to the large bed his older brothers shared.

With Mallie at work, Jack passed his early childhood mainly in the care and company of his sister, Willa Mae. "I was the little mother," she recalled; "I was Jack's little mother." Jack agreed: "When I was eight years old and she was ten, you would think she was a hundred the way she could talk to me when everything was blue." In his childhood, Willa Mae bathed, dressed, and fed him almost every day. Prompted by Mallie, who had no choice in the matter, she even took Jack with her to her school. There, sympathetic teachers allowed him to play in a sandbox outdoors while Willa Mae sat in class and watched him through a window.

He was a handsome, charming child. A boyhood photograph of him at four or five, perhaps his earliest portrait, caught him relaxed and insouciant, sitting on a rocking chair with a leg drawn up. Evidently he was more than a little mischievous. His lifelong friend Sid Heard remembered the day in 1925 when he first met Jack. It was Sid's first day at Cleveland Elementary School, a red brick building a few blocks from 121 Pepper Street. Sid and a friend, Timothy Harrison, were standing outdoors, waiting for their mothers, when they felt something hitting them. At first, they thought that acorns were falling from a tree arching overhead—"but it was only this little young guy, sitting on the edge of the sandbox, shooting small acorns like marbles at us, and smiling. That's how I met Jack."

His teachers, too, seemed to like him. Starting out at Cleveland Elementary in 1924, he was lucky in his first two teachers, Bernice Gilbert in kindergarten and Beryl Haney in the first grade. (All his teachers were white.) On some days, he recalled, he and Willa Mae "would get to school so hungry we could hardly stand up, much less think about our lessons." But Miss Gilbert and Miss Haney "always had a kind word for us—and a couple of sandwiches." According to Willa Mae, Jack and these teachers formed "a deep, embedded friendship" that lasted the rest of Jack's life, long after he became famous. This affection existed despite the fact that the idea of white supremacy was entrenched in the school system. In a confidential survey of Pasadena schoolteachers (still all white) in 1940, almost half would express a preference for schools with no black students at all; not surprisingly, more than ninety percent of the black parents in the same survey believed that their children were not treated fairly in the schools. Eleanor Peters Heard remembered that while Lincoln Elementary School, which she attended, had been fully integrated, in Washington Junior High "they put all of the blacks together."

After two years at the Cleveland school, Jack transferred in September 1926 to another elementary school, Washington Elementary, still only a stroll away from home. This change followed a rezoning of the Pasadena school districts when a rise in the black and Hispanic population in northwest Pasadena threatened to leave some schools with white minorities. Then, in 1931, at twelve, he left Washington Elementary and enrolled, as expected, in Washington Junior High School, which shared the same city block. His official transcript at Washington Elementary shows grades of B and C over the years, but with a decline in quality between the fourth grade and the sixth grade, his last year there. The transcript also includes a simple note made by a school official about his likely future occupation: "Gardener."

Jack's precociousness as an athlete undoubtedly helped him to negotiate the traps of racism early in his life. "He was a special little boy," his sister recalled, "and ever since I can remember, he always had a ball in his hand." Whether the game was marbles or soccer, he wanted to win, and usually won. Why he needed to win so early in his life is impossible to say, but the desire to surpass and the discipline to achieve this goal were there. "We used to play a game in the schoolyard with everyone in a circle, and you had to dodge the ball thrown at you," Sid Heard recalled. "Jack would always be the last one left. They'd have to stop the game." Whites as well as blacks bowed to his gifts; indeed, most of Jack's classmates seemed able to like and accept one another easily, without much anxiety about differences in race or social standing. He and other gifted young athletes in Pasadena, black or white or Asian-American, competed against one another without allowing race to drive a permanent wedge of hatred or resentment between them. After the democracy he had known as a boy among boys and girls in Pasadena, nothing could convince Robinson that Jim Crow in any sport—or in any other aspect of American life, for that matter—was right or natural.

Not the least of his good luck was the accident of growing up in northwest Pasadena, which was a paradise for sports lovers. An easy walk from home was the cliff looking down on the natural wonder of Arroyo Seco. Within its expanse was the only public golf course in Pasadena, laid out in 1928, when Jack was nine. There, too, was Brookside Park, with its fine array of sporting facilities for baseball, basketball, tennis, and swimming, with only the Brookside Plunge restricted by Jim Crow. Crowning Arroyo Seco like a trophy was the Rose Bowl itself, the most storied arena in California football. Early, Jack began to hone the skills that would make his phenomenal local reputation not simply as an individual star but as a team player. "When I was in third grade," he later recalled, "we got a soccer team together that was so good we challenged the sixth grade and beat them. After that, we represented the school in matches." Completely accurate or not, the story will do to mark the rise of his local reputation as a sportsman, of gifts both physical and mental, from which all the important achievements of his life would flow in time.

But sports could not save him from all distress. He entered his perilous teenage years at the lowest point of the Great Depression. Black Pasadena, including the household at 121 Pepper Street, felt its pain at once. Few white people could now afford to keep servants, and then seldom at the old pay; moreover, Mallie was now the only reliable wage earner in the household, since white men were snapping up jobs they once had left in disdain to blacks and other colored folk. To Jack's dismay, Mallie also insisted on trying to help other people. Living with her at 121 Pepper Street, in addition to her five children and Frank's wife, Maxine, and their two children, were her niece Jessie Maxwell, the young daughter of Mallie's sister Mary Lou Thomas Maxwell, who had died prematurely soon after migrating from Cairo. Other relatives and friends came and went, drawing on Mallie's strength and kindness, often moving on without much of a thank-you, as Jack saw it.

To help her, he took whatever jobs he could manage. He had a paper route, mowed grass for neighbors, and sold hot dogs at ball games in the Rose Bowl. None of these jobs lasted a long time. Young Jack Robinson was not lazy, but he did not like such work; all his life he would not enjoy manual labor. He also began to neglect his studies. For a while, he had loved reading; years later, veteran staffers at the La Pintoresca branch of the Pasadena Public Library would remember him as "a constant user." But Willa Mae recalled that by junior high school he began to rush into the house after school, drop his books on a table near the telephone, and hurry out to play. The next morning, he would pick up the books, unread, on the way out to school. By Jack's high school years, as a star athlete, he was coasting as a student, as his friend Ray Bartlett recalled, perhaps too severely: "I used to be a pretty good student. Jack wasn't a good scholar at all. He wasn't worth a damn. They just carried him through." In time, Jack would regret this inattentiveness to his studies and try to make up for the lost opportunity.

In other ways, too, he began to change. Despite his success in sports and the adulation it inspired, as he grew older he became less and less open. Outside of his tight circle of close friends, his boyish charm cooled uneasily with adolescence into a sometimes awkward shyness, which he covered more and more with a show of truculence. Now, at a time when many boys of his age were warming to girls, he wanted nothing to do with them. "I guess I was a little afraid of my ability to cope with women," he would recall at thirty. "I can't tell you for the life of me why I worried about it so much." When the prettiest girl (or so he thought) at Washington Junior High, Elizabeth Renfro, approached him, he rebuffed her. "I was too bashful to start conversations," he would recall, with some embarrassment. "All I did the first time she talked to me was tell her to go jump in the lake! Imagine that!" In his late teens, Jack had become an adolescent mixture of, on the one hand, overweening confidence reinforced by rare exploits as an athlete and, on the other, fragile self-esteem.

His nagging self-doubt probably had much to do with the way he was living. Jack knew he was poorer than most of his friends, and fatherless, and the knowledge hurt. Almost all of his black friends, and some of the whites and Asians, were poor; but nearly all had a father in the house, and most homes had fewer mouths to feed. Jack tried to strut and pretend that money didn't matter, but "to tell the truth, I think that behind all this sort of pride was the knowledge that we were very poor." His cousin Van, the son of Sam and Cora Wade, sensed that Jack "didn't have the things that normal families had." Because Mallie was out all day at work, her household had at best an erratic routine. "We had a dinner time, a breakfast time," Van recalled; "I don't think he had that. We got new clothes at Christmas, on birthdays, Easter, when school started, that sort of thing. He didn't have that. But I think he was really unhappy because he didn't have a father, and his mother did day work."

In 1921, according to one account, word had reached Mallie that Jerry Robinson had died, somewhere in the South. Later came reports that, like a black Kilroy, he had been here or there; but Jerry never surfaced. Resigned to the failure of her marriage, Mallie made no attempt to learn the truth, but tried hard not to speak ill of Jerry at home. According to Willa Mae, Mallie once explained that she held back "because some of us children might decide to take after him; we might figure, Well, that is what my Daddy did, I want to be like my Daddy. So my mother decided not to talk about him." From Edgar, however, Jack heard about nasty whippings Jerry had given him back in Georgia, and for mere trifles. "Edgar didn't like our father," Willa Mae knew; "he said he didn't want to remember him." As a child, Jack also saw contempt for Jerry in the attitude of the other boys, Frank and Mack. "We didn't know him," Mack said, "and we did not recognize him or ever consider him being a part of the family." Willa Mae, too, had closed her heart to Jerry Robinson. "I just didn't have a father," she said. "And when I heard about him, I didn't need him. I didn't need a father."

Like Mack, Jack would later deny having had the slightest interest in knowing his father, who was a phantom from the dark, forbidding South that was now forever behind them. But Jack's character and psychology were undoubtedly shaped in part by this loss and its denial. At least once, late in his life, Jack could be philosophical about his pain. "My father's will and spirit," he reasoned, "were slowly broken down by the economic slavery imposed upon him, the exorbitant costs of food and rent and other necessities." More typically, however, he was angry and unforgiving about Jerry Robinson and what he had done: "I could only think of him with bitterness. He, too, may have been a victim of oppression, but he had no right to desert my mother and five children."

Mallie herself set aside any thought of marrying again, according to Willa Mae, because "she wasn't going to have any man whipping her children." Over the years in Pasadena she had one male friend, known to her children only as "Mr. Fowler," with whom she was on intimate terms. But he never moved into the house, and she seemed to have no desire to marry him. "As far as I can remember, he was the only man in her life after we came out here."

As Jack struggled into his teens, his brothers were crucial to him, but not always much of a help. He looked at them and imagined he saw his own future, but the sight was not entrancing. His eldest brother, Edgar, was eccentric at the very least, or a mystery. Although he was "somewhat sickly sometimes," according to Jack, Edgar did amazing physical feats on his roller skates and bicycle. Speed fascinated him. Once, police ticketed him for skating at an excessive speed; he was known to terrify onlookers by jumping in his skates over the hoods of cars; he also could outrace the bus from Pasadena to the Santa Monica Beach, some thirty miles away. He started riding a motorcycle, but so recklessly it was taken away from him. Intellectually, Edgar was also a puzzle. He had no formal schooling past the sixth grade, and mainly one intellectual interest—the Bible, from which he quoted chapter and verse with ease. However, to one of Jack's friends, "Edgar was mentally retarded. He talked strangely, and he had difficulty with words, getting them out. He was definitely retarded."

Edgar, who would live to be eighty-four, never married. He lived mainly for his religion, and he died alone, surrounded by sagging shelves of books and recordings about his beloved Bible. To Jack in his youth, his eldest brother was a sometimes friendly, sometimes disturbing presence. "There was always something about him that was mysterious to me," Jack declared in 1949. "Maybe it was the way he'd get angry once in a while and lose control of his temper. Something like the way I do."

Frank was far more mild and sweet-tempered; Jack remembered that he was "tall and thin and the girls liked him." Of the three older brothers, Frank alone showed a subtle concern for Jack, who loved the fact that "he was always there to protect me when I was in a scrap, even though I don't think he could knock down a fly." And unlike young Jack, Frank was a smooth talker. "He could never be forcibly brutal," Jack recalled, "and could talk *me* out of any trouble." In other ways, however, Frank's life was anything but a model for his younger brother. Frank had done his best in school but then was stopped dead by Jim Crow in Pasadena. He couldn't find a decent job; around 1936, when he was twenty-five, he finally landed a position as a tree trimmer with the city. By this time he was a married man and a father, but he still was living at his mother's home.

Despite Frank's open love of Jack, it was their brother Mack, four and a half years older than Jack, who dominated the youngest child and became his idol, particularly when Jack was in the middle of his teenage years. A star athlete in Pasadena while Jack was still a growing boy, Mack was Jack's intimate introduction to the glory and the glamour of sports. "I remember going to track meets with him," Jack remembered, "and watching him run and listening to the crowd yell." Unlike Jack, Mack excelled not at team sports but in track and field. He was a sprinter with dramatic speed, especially over 200 meters or 220 yards, where he often started slowly but closed almost any gap with a supercharged rush; he was also a champion broad jumper. In 1932, when Jack was thirteen and the Olympic Games took place in Los Angeles, with some aquatic events contested at the Brookside Plunge, Mack committed himself to a relentless campaign of training. A diagnosis of heart trouble almost ended his career prematurely, but Mack pressed on until he won a place on the U.S. Olympic team in 1936. That summer, in Berlin, as the entire Robinson household heard the crackling radio broadcast of the race from Europe, Mack placed second to Jesse Owens in the 200-meter dash.

After a triumphant post-Olympics tour on the Continent, in which he set a world record in one race, Mack returned to Pasadena. Expecting a hero's welcome, he got nothing of the kind. Pasadena had a way of ignoring its many sports heroes, black or white. In 1938, a Pasadena *Post* columnist would list several Pasadena sports stars—including Ellsworth Vines, then the world's top tennis player; Charles Paddock, a white Olympic gold-medal sprinter; and Mack and Jack Robinson—and declare: "In many places they would be given the key to the city. Here we take them in stride, for granted. Never have they received their just due, from their own home citizens."

Unquestionably, racism played a big role in what happened to Mack after Berlin. When he applied for a job, the city treated him like any other Negro; it gave him a pushcart and a broom and the night shift as a street sweeper. Mack then irritated a number of white people by sweeping the streets decked out in his leather U.S.A. Olympic jacket. Some saw this act as provocative, but he brushed off the criticism: "When it was a cold day, it was the warmest thing I owned, so I wore it." He stayed on the job, unhappy but with few options, for about four years. A handsome man, Mack was said by a few people to be sometimes sullen and difficult; certainly he lacked his mother's calm in facing racism. Her faith in religion never took hold of him. Mack's relationship with Jack was also troubled. Mack encouraged his brother but perhaps saw him at times as competition to be crushed. Here, again, he was to be disappointed. As a runner, Jack never had Mack's great speed, but his legs were at least as powerful. Eventually, Jack would soar past Mack's best distance in the broad jump. Still later, his baseball fame would overshadow Mack's silver strike at the Olympics. Eclipsed, Mack tried to be gracious but could not hide his sense of hurt. "I think he thought Jack got some breaks that he should have had," a friend guessed. Mack himself denied ever being jealous; whatever a family member went through, "we was right there pushing for them, pushing for them and rooting for them to get along." Jack, he said, "learned by being the youngest of the family to fall into the line of being an individual who was, I guess, following after his brothers."

In 1940, Mack's wife, Grace, gave birth to their second son, Phillip. Because of either a congenital defect or a childhood illness, Phillip was mentally retarded and never learned to speak. When his family moved to put the boy into an institution, Mallie stopped them. "I will take care of him," she announced—and she did, until she died. Within a few years of Phillip's birth, Grace Robinson was dead. In his own days of triumph, Jack would speak cryptically of events in Mack's past that had "soured him on life completely, I guess." That way was not for Jack himself. "I sort of look back at my brother's experience every once in a while," he said in 1949, "and resolve to make the best of things."

In the turmoil of his adolescence, Jack unquestionably felt more and more guilty about his relationship with his mother. He felt guilty that she worked so hard and in such menial jobs to support him and so many others. Then and later he was often impatient with her; he found some of her ways hard to accept: her almost compulsive generosity to relatives, friends, and even strangers; her incessant talking about God; and perhaps other things. At some point in her life Mallie had lost the use of her right eye. Some people said one of the older children (no one knew which one) had poked it out by accident; in any event, it gave her at times a fearsome aspect. As a teenager, Jack understood as praiseworthy many aspects of his mother's moral heroism, but that heroism came clothed in a shabbiness that seemed unlikely to end, when he himself wanted to have more. Jack's sense of discomfort, his mixture of affection, guilt, and perhaps even a degree of shame, did not mean that he failed to love his mother, only that he was young, a boy striving to understand the true nature of the pact Mallie had made with the world. Decades later, just after her death in 1968, he would look back on her with a lifetime of experience and open eyes: "Many times I felt that my mother was being foolish, letting people take advantage of her. I was wrong. She did kindness[es] for people whom I considered parasites because she wanted to help them. It was her way of thinking, her way of life." In her life, he came to understand, "she had not been a fool for others. She had given with her eyes as open as her heart. In death, she was still teaching me how to live."

Whatever his reservations about his mother, she offered him unstinting maternal love and encouragement. In 1935, when he graduated from Washington Junior High School, her pride and joy at his achievement brought tears to his eyes. "Through some miracle" (as he put it) Mallie had managed to secure for him as a graduation gift something he badly wanted—his first dress suit. "I remember I cried a little when I saw it," Jack wrote. As always, Mallie gave all credit to God for everything. "My mother said she always believed the Lord would take care of us," Jack went on. "Right then and there, I never stopped believing that." This was not literally true. Jack's real religious awakening would come about three years later. But the way to his rebirth as a believer had been paved assiduously throughout his life by his remarkable mother.

As HE GREW OLDER, Jack turned naturally for his closest companionship away from his older brothers to neighborhood boys nearer his own age. These included youngsters like his cousin Van Wade, a powerful hitter who was often a teammate in baseball; Sid Heard, from his earliest days at the Cleveland School; the brothers Woodrow and Ernest Cunningham, who lived only a block away; and Ray Bartlett, who would play sports with Jack from kindergarten to college and beyond. In addition, Jack's circle included Japanese-Americans, like the brothers George, Frankie, and Ben Ito, and Shig Kawai, an excellent football and baseball player; Tim and Bill

Herrera, who were Mexican-Americans; and such white pals as George Spivak and Danny Galvin, a little fellow, younger than Jack, who was one of the most relentless scorers in Pasadena basketball.

Ernie Cunningham remembered that while Jack took a particular liking at one time to him and Ben Ito, Jack himself was not always liked. "At that time," he claimed, "Jackie wasn't a very likable person, because his whole thing was just win, win, win, and beat everybody." Some, but not all, of these friends resolved themselves at one point into what passed into local lore as the "Pepper Street Gang." Exactly when, and for how long, the gang operated is not clear—or even how democratic it was. "Our gang was made up of blacks, Japanese, and Mexican kids," Jack wrote just before his death; "all of us came from poor families and had extra time on our hands." But others, such as Eleanor Peters Heard, who lived near the gang's favorite street corner, would recall white members, including Danny Galvin. Another white friend of Jack's, Warren Dorn, who later became an influential political leader as mayor of Pasadena and a Los Angeles County commissioner, also claimed to have been a member of the gang.

Only its harshest critics thought the gang dangerous; for a city of its size, Pasadena's juvenile delinquency rate was well below average. "There was no drugs, no smoking, no liquor, no beating up anybody, nothing of that nature," recalled Ray Bartlett, who knew everyone in the Pepper Street Gang but was forbidden by his mother to be a member. "We never got into vicious or violent crime," Robinson insisted, but indulged instead in pranks and petty theft. They threw "dirt clods" at passing cars, "snatched" balls on the golf course and often sold them back to the players; "swiped" fruit at produce stands; "snitched what we could" at local stores. Such activity was enough to make some parents wary, and to bring Jack into direct contact with the police. His first, but not his last, brush with the law came when he was once "escorted to jail at gunpoint by the sheriff" for taking a swim in the city reservoir, which he felt justified in doing because of the rules at the Brookside Plunge. In fact, partly because of his local fame as a schoolboy athlete, the Pasadena police came to know Jack fairly well; at one point, he seemed likely to become, as he himself said, "a full-fledged juvenile delinquent."

"Hardly a week went by," Jack wrote, "when we didn't have to report to Captain Morgan, the police-man who was head of the Youth Division." Given the degree of racism and segregation in Pasadena, he was lucky in having to deal with Hugh D. Morgan. "About nine feet tall," as Ernie Cunningham remem-bered him, the burly, cigar-smoking former football player from Louisiana State University had migrated to Pasadena and joined the force in 1924. A student of juvenile delinquency control at the University of Southern California, Morgan relied on psychology and diplomacy rather than threats or brute force. "He was always ready to give us advice," Jack wrote in 1949, "and maybe a dollar or two if he thought we hadn't had any breakfast that morning." Willa Mae remembered Morgan coming to the house often, but not only to scold Jack; Mallie recalled going down to his office "often" to bawl him out, as she put it, when she thought he was too hard on the boys. "I think he did a good job at really keeping things in hand," Ray Bartlett judged (he would become Pasadena's second black police officer), "and actually pointed kids in the right direction." Despite a bad habit of quietly urging members of each ethnic group to avoid members of the other ethnic groups as being beneath them, he carefully avoided showing racial prejudice. In 1939, as protests grew over Jim Crow at the Brookside Plunge and segregation in housing, he publicly defended young blacks in Pasadena against the charge that they posed any special problem as delinquents.

Morgan was one of several male figures of authority, especially his coaches, to whom Jack responded well, as a good son might to his father, even as he muddled through his adolescence. Another such person was a black man named Carl Anderson, who challenged Jack to move beyond the inanities of the Pepper Street Gang. "He made me see," Robinson later wrote, "that if I continued with the gang it would hurt my mother as well as myself. . . . He said it didn't take guts to follow the crowd, that courage and intelligence lay in being willing to be different. I was too ashamed to tell Carl how right he was, but what he said got to me." Only seven years older than Jack, Anderson worked as a car mechanic near the intersection of Mountain and Morton, where members of the Pepper Street Gang often loitered. As one of the unofficial leaders of the local black community, he tried hard to undo the psychological damage done to black youngsters by Jim Crow. When the local Boy Scouts refused to integrate their units, Anderson founded the first black troop in northwest Pasadena. "He also organized a special group for us kids, that he called the Friendly Indians," Sid Heard remembered. "We'd go over to his house every Friday night and listen to him tell stories and the like. He really liked young people."

With each passing year, the cheering Jack heard at football and baseball games contrasted poorly with the pain of knowing what it meant to be black in Pasadena. At first, as a boy, he took Jim Crow in his stride; then he began to see and feel more intensely. "I always thought Pasadena was a great place," he recalled, "until I got more experience of life." One episode involved the YMCA, which had fine sports facilities but refused blacks as members, and stalled and frustrated Jack when he applied for membership. Another was the Brookside Plunge: "During hot spells, you waited outside the picket fence and watched the white kids splash around. I honestly think the officials didn't think the Negroes got as warm and uncomfortable as white people during the Pasadena heat." Jim Crow dogged him in the movie houses, where blacks were forced to sit in one section only. At the Pasadena Playhouse, empty seats, if available, quarantined black patrons from whites. "At the Kress soda fountain, you could sit at the counter and wait and wait and no one would serve you," one friend would recall. "The same thing at Schrafft's. You could work in the kitchen, but you couldn't eat there, at least not without a hassle."

The veteran Los Angeles *Times* sports journalist Shav Glick, who as a fellow Pasadena Junior College student would cover Jack's exploits for the Pasadena *Post* for some years in the 1930s, wrote in 1977: "The Robinson the world came to know, competitive and combative, aggressive and abrasive, impatient and irascible, was tempered on the streets, the school-grounds and the playing fields of Pasadena." But Glick stressed that this process of tempering went on inside, and was kept inside, by Robinson. The face Jack presented to the world, especially after high school, was on the whole calm. And then, as well as later, he almost never brought his anger home, as Willa Mae and others would attest. Jack could not and would not use profanity in his mother's home, or rebel against her or his sister and brothers. "The only curse word he would ever use," Sid Heard recalled with amusement, "was 'Dadgummit!' When he said that word, that was it. Yessir, 'Dadgummit!' Then he'd go and beat your brains out!"

EARLY IN 1935, in the middle of the school year, Jack finished at Washington Junior High and enrolled at the John Muir Technical High School, where Mack and Willa Mae were also students (Mack would graduate in June). Once a vocational school, Muir Tech was now in every sense a typical high school, one of Pasadena's two public high schools, with a full range of academic courses. Muir offered first-rate facilities, with handsome buildings designed in the local California Mediterranean style,

and landscaping that made the most of its fine location, within sight of the San Gabriel Mountains. In
addition, by 1935 Muir Tech had developed an outstanding regional reputation as a sports powerhouse.
It would provide the backdrop for Jack's first emer-
gence as a star school athlete.

Before the summer of 1935, he had established
himself as the most versatile of the Muir Terriers. He
also sang in the glee club, but sports were his mainstay. Light but nimble at 135 pounds and with excellent, even uncanny, hand-to-eye coordination, that
spring he nailed down a spot on the baseball team as
a shortstop in what one enthusiast called an "exceptionally good" infield. He then shone for Muir Tech
as a star at the annual regional baseball tournament in
Pomona, when the Muir Terriers went to the finals
before losing to Long Beach. Despite conflicts with
baseball and little time to train, he also earned honors
that spring in both the broad jump (or long jump), in
which Mack also competed, and the high jump. Even
his casual efforts left him far ahead of most competi-
tors. As he later recalled, he particularly loved the
broad jump: "You [toe] the line and spring forward
with all your strength. Then you jump—you really
try to jump off the earth and your legs churn the air
like you wanted to reach the moon. Then you come
down to earth in soft sand and you have to remember
to fall forward so that there are no marks behind the
back of your heels."

In the fall of 1935, he went out for Terrier football but, still a lightweight, had to bide his time on a
brilliant team that was dominated by the brothers Bill

and George Sangster, two white youths who were among the finest athletes in Pasadena history; the Terriers went undefeated that year. (In all of Jack's schools, most of his teammates were white, just as all the student bodies were predominantly white.) Late in the season Jack saw some action as quarterback, running and passing the ball, and showed "much ability," according to one judge. When the football season ended, he switched at once to basketball, where Jack's speed and deftness in ball handling, his aggressive play under the basket on both defense and offense, as well as his unselfish style, made him an outstanding guard and a "mainstay." Contending all season for the league championship, the Muir Terriers lost it in the last game of the season.

From basketball, he cycled back into baseball and track to establish his athletic routine of the next few years. In 1936, having lost several lettermen, Muir Tech had a mediocre baseball season, but Jack excelled despite moving from shortstop to catcher for the team's sake. That year, he earned a place on the annual Pomona tournament all-star team, which included two other future Hall of Fame players: Ted Williams of Hoover High in San Diego and Bob Lemon of Long Beach's Wilson High. In track, where the Terriers also struggled much of the season, Robinson was one of seven athletes hailed as "the nucleus of the squad." He went out again for the broad jump but also competed for Muir in the pole vault. Not surprisingly, so much versatility led at times to inconsistent results. In the broad jump, for example, he won the Southland Class A title with a superb leap of 23 feet 1 inch. A week later, however, he failed to place in the California state championships.

On September 6, 1936, just after Mack's Olympic Games success, the legend of Jackie Robinson as a sports prodigy gained new life when he captured the junior boys' singles championship in the annual Pacific Coast Negro Tennis Tournament. Jack played tennis only sporadically. His game was unorthodox; he relied on speed and guile and on his fierce will to win. Playing mixed doubles with his ambidextrous childhood friend Eleanor Peters, he refused to accept defeat easily. "Jack was always very competitive," she said, "but of course we were all very competitive. Our parents all wanted us to achieve, to do something more with our lives." Jack's competitive fire helped her when she nervously faced the women's singles champion in another Pacific Coast tournament. "Jack said, 'You can play with her, you can do it,'" she recalled. "And I said, 'No, I can't.' But he pushed me and pushed me, and I started to believe in myself. I didn't win, but I gave her a run for her money. That's what Jack was like."

Ray Bartlett, too, recalled the amazing drive Jack showed even in junior high school. "He was a hard loser," Bartlett said. "By that I mean that he always played his best and did his best and gave all he had, and he didn't like to lose. He liked to be the best, and he would be unhappy at school the day after we lost. He took losses very hard. The rest of us might shrug off a loss, but Jack would cry if we lost."

In the fall of 1936, as his young body developed, Jack's football skills reached new heights. Although the Terriers started the season with almost every star of the previous year gone, they ran Muir's record to eighteen consecutive league victories before losing in the last game of the season to Glendale, who won the league championship. Playing in the backfield on offense, Jack emerged as the star of the team. In the first game, before five thousand captivated spectators in the Rose Bowl, the "snake-hipped" quarterback (as the Pasadena *Post* called him) scored a rushing touchdown in the last minutes of the game to earn a tie against powerful Alhambra. In the third league game, against the Hoover High team from Glendale, he returned the opening kickoff fifty yards, then scored later as Muir won. Taking note, the Pasadena *Post* surprised its readers with a large picture of Jack, poised to hurl a football, on the front page of its sports section. Against Fullerton, "dusky" Jack Robinson scored the first touchdown as he "sped around right end" and "outraced the entire Fullerton team to cross the goal line standing up." Against Pomona High, Muir Tech was down by thirteen points in the first half. "Then the fun started as the second half opened," the *Post* reported. The Terriers struck back with a touchdown by Robinson to begin a rally that ended in a Muir victory.

In its final game, however, against Glendale, the Terriers fell apart. Early—and perhaps according to a plan—Robinson was brought down, then "three Glendale boys piled on." With cracked ribs, Jack staggered off the field and out of the game. His injury sickened the other Terriers, who proceeded to fumble the game and the championship away. Still, Muir

Tech had enjoyed an excellent season, and Jack had established himself as a sensational quarterback and all-around football player, one of the finest prospects in talent-rich southern California.

When his ribs finally mended, he rejoined the basketball team. Again, the loss of several stars made Terrier fans expect little for the new season; experts picked Muir Tech to finish fourth or fifth in its league. But the Terriers won almost all of their games and ended in second place. Closer now to his full height, which was just shy of six feet, Robinson started at forward instead of guard; he also began the league season as acting captain. In the first game, against the elite Hoover High team, he led the Terriers to an upset victory that set the tone for the rest of the season. Not only was Robinson Muir's most reliable and prolific scorer, but his precocious sense of the importance of team play and his fearless desire to win also made everyone around him a better player. In the last sixty seconds of a crucial game against South Pasadena, Jack led a furious charge that brought Muir from behind to win the game. Leading his team's scoring, he tallied 20 of his team's 49 points.

On January 29, 1937, he played perhaps his most dominating basketball game ever for Muir Tech; he was like a man possessed in a league encounter with archrival Glendale. Much was on the line. His Terriers entered the game with a tenuous hold on first place; but it was also the last scheduled game of Jack's high school career. Rising to the challenge, he went all out for victory. "Robinson was all over the floor," the *Post* marveled, "and when he wasn't scoring points he was making impossible 'saves' and interceptions, and was the best player on the floor." His unselfishness stood out. "Many times," according to the *Post,* "he fed the ball to teammates, giving them setups. And there were few times Glendale, even with a decided height advantage, could snatch the ball away from Robinson off the backboard." The Terriers won, to tighten their grasp on first place.

The day of the game against Glendale was Jack's last at Muir High. Whatever his misgivings about Pasadena, he clearly loved his teammates and his high school and cared deeply about its fortunes and the nurturing role it had played in his life. As an athlete, he had given Muir Tech everything he had to offer, and knew how much he had profited from the giving. His efforts had been recognized even by those who took no pleasure in doing so. Even the powerful Pasadena *Star-News,* usually frigid to blacks and begrudging in its praise of his exploits, conceded finally that Jack Robinson "for two years has been the outstanding athlete at Muir, starring in football, basketball, track, baseball, and tennis."

Two days later, on January 31, 1937, he celebrated his eighteenth birthday. The next day, he enrolled as a student at Pasadena Junior College, across town. In the next two years, Jack would take his local fame to new heights. Through his amazing exploits in his four top sports, he would also bring himself, for the first time, to the attention of the wider world. But in these two years, he would also come close to disaster in his conflicts with himself and white authority, especially the police. He would come to the brink of killing the hopes his mother had nursed for him, and that he had been nurturing for himself during his boyhood in Pasadena.

— 3 —

Pasadena Junior College

1937–1939

It was there that I lost most of my shyness.
—Jackie Robinson (1972)

ON FEBRUARY 1, 1937, when Jack Robinson made his way out to Colorado Boulevard to register for classes at Pasadena Junior College, he found a campus in a state of serious disrepair. Instead of green lawns and ivy-covered walls, he saw raw dirt that turned to dust under the hot sun or to mud in the rain; the bare walls of three unfinished buildings dominated the bleak scene. Robinson had come to enroll near the end of the four-year "tent era" of campus history, a time of reconstruction and makeshift facilities in the wake of the destructive Long Beach earthquake of 1933, which had rocked Pasadena. However, even as Jack arrived, workmen were finishing the construction of three gleaming white buildings that would form the heart of the new PJC.

For Robinson and other students of his time, attending the junior college after leaving high school was fully expected; the local public school system was designed to lead them to PJC. Pasadena

High School was part of its campus, as its lower division; and the following year, 1938, Muir Tech itself would become the lower division of a new western campus of PJC. Some students attended PJC in order to qualify for entrance into a four-year college or university; others sought simply to complete the first two years of college. The Depression made PJC a deal that few could resist; for the poor, like Robinson, it was a godsend. Tuition was free; and with no dormitories, most students lived at home. With teachers said to be first-rate, a lively student body, and a tradition of excellence in sports, PJC enjoyed a local reputation as one of the finest junior colleges anywhere.

Important for Jack and the sixty or seventy other blacks in a student body that numbered about four thousand, PJC was also among the more liberal institutions in Pasadena. All classes and facilities, including the swimming pool, were open to all students; blacks could attend official school dances without hindrance. Only in dance classes was the color line openly drawn; blacks could enroll only as couples, not as individuals. On the whole, PJC offered a friendly, relaxed environment, where Jack saw many familiar faces from his earlier schoolboy days.

Already known as an athlete, Jack nonetheless arrived at PJC decidedly in the shadow of his brother Mack, who was also enrolled that semester. Following Jesse Owens's decision to turn professional, Mack Robinson was now the premier amateur sprinter in the United States; on campus, he was almost a god, although he was only a sometime student, concerned almost exclusively with sports. Since leaving Muir Tech two years previously, he had spent only one semester at PJC, in the spring of 1936, just before the Berlin Olympics. But Mack had stamped his name on PJC athletic history as the college's "iron man," who carried the school flag in at least five events—the two elite sprints (100 and 220 yards), the sprint relays, the low hurdles, and the broad jump. No one expected Jack ever to rival Mack's record. The younger Robinson, slender and wiry in the winter of 1937, weighed little more than 135 pounds—hardly the body of a champion athlete. Still, as Jack settled in at PJC, he set his sights on stardom in three team sports: baseball, probably his first love; basketball, which appealed above all to his passion for team play; and football, which offered the best chance by far for glory. In addition, he expected to compete, with and against his brother, in the broad jump.

That spring semester, Jack quickly made the baseball team, which played in the Western Division of the Southern California Junior College Athletic Association. With his flashy fielding, steady hitting, and aggressive base running, he soon became a favorite of the Bulldog coach, John Thurman, who had helped develop Jack's skills the previous summer in a city-sponsored baseball school in Brookside Park. In addition to playing shortstop, Jack was his team's leadoff batter. Lacking home-run power, but showing a remarkable eye for the strike zone as well as unusual patience, he seldom struck out; one way or another, he usually found a way of getting on base.

Once there, in what would become his bedeviling trademark as a player, he was a constant threat to steal bases and induce paranoia in opposing pitchers.

The Bulldog season started slowly; then momentum began to build. PJC crushed the freshmen of the University of California. The Bulldogs lost to Modesto Junior College, the champion junior college team in northern California; in the third inning, however, Jack Robinson "created a sensation" among the spectators, according to the Pasadena *Post,* which also ran Jack's picture with the story, when he stole second, third, and home to score a run for Pasadena.

In April, Robinson came into his own. Against the elite University of Southern California freshman team, he went three-for-four at the plate; he went five-for-six and also stole two bases in a defeat of Glendale Junior College. In the next game, against Los Angeles Junior College, he singled four times in five at-bats and stole a base as the Bulldog winning streak reached fourteen games. The streak ended there. In the following game, in a loss of form, Robinson went hitless, committed three errors, and failed to steal a base. Against Compton Junior College, a wild throw by Jack helped Compton to win the championship. But Robinson was now widely recognized as the premier shortstop in the league and a major contributor to what the *Post* called "one of the most successful baseball seasons in the history of Pasadena Junior College."

In the first semester at PJC, Jack also established himself as the college's second best broad jumper, after "Iron Man" Mack Robinson. Dogged by injury at the start of the season, Mack stormed back late in March to tie the national junior college record in the 220-yard dash against UCLA; he also won the 100-yard sprint, the low hurdles, and the broad jump. In the broad jump, Jack lost every time to Mack, even when Mack jumped well below his best. Steadily, however, Jack's leaps improved; by the end of the season he reached 23 feet 9½ inches. Spurred on, perhaps, by this rivalry, Mack enjoyed his best season ever as a jumper. At the famed Drake Relays in Des Moines, Iowa, he set a new national junior college record with a leap of 25 feet 5½ inches. Returning to a hero's welcome on the campus, he led the Bulldog team to the West Coast Relays at Fresno, California, widely regarded as the unofficial state collegiate championships. There, Mack won two individual races, helped in two relay victories, and also won the broad jump. Once again, his brother Jack took second place.

If this rivalry and these defeats caused Jack any discomfort, he admitted none. Losing to his older brother was no dishonor, and he loved sharing in Mack's glamour and traveling with him. What Mack himself thought of the rivalry is also unknown; probably he had no firm idea about Jack's potential. In any event, Jack was proud and happy about his small share of the glory in what the *Star-News* saluted as "the greatest athletic season in Pasadena Junior College history."

AS JACK SETTLED in at PJC, he made one friend for life, a sprinter named Jack Gordon, who quickly became his best friend. They were an unlikely pair in some respects. Although both young men were handsome and athletic, Gordon was small in stature compared with Jack; his skin was a light brown compared with Jack's ebony; and he was as voluble and outgoing as Jack was reserved, especially with women. "Jack was kind of shy at times," Gordon would recall. "I guess he didn't have the personality to get along with most people. He didn't talk much; he wasn't really outgoing. He never pushed himself on you." Left to Robinson, they might never have become friends. Gordon was standing in the middle of a motley group of black students when "I asked everybody and nobody in particular, 'Is anybody around here going to have some waffles?' Nobody said anything. And then Jack Robinson spoke up: 'Did I hear you mention waffles? Let's go!' And that was it. From then on it was Little Jack and Big Jack."

Gordon and Robinson were not strangers. Playing football for McKinley Junior High against Marshall one day, Gordon had run back a punt some eighty or ninety yards for a touchdown. The next day, aglow with his success, he was holding court near a water fountain, chatting with some girls after choir practice, when Robinson walked up. He barely glanced at Gordon. "I hear you got lucky yesterday," he said suddenly. "You won't do that against us." Stunned, Gordon opened his mouth to answer, but Robinson was gone. Robinson was right; his team beat Gordon's, 6–0. The next time they met, Gordon was taking part in a track meet for which he was ineligible. No one noticed but Robinson, who walked up and got right to the point: "What are you doing participating in this meet? You're still at McKinley." Gordon started to explain, but Robinson was gone. "He was the greatest person in the world for just walking away," Gordon recalled, "just the greatest person at walking away. The guy had such confidence. I don't think he knew how much confidence he had in himself. And it *was* confidence."

For Robinson, however, it was Gordon who had true confidence. "I remember he used to be a spokesman for me," he recalled. "He would go with me every place. Through him I met my first girlfriend. . . . I don't think I had enough courage at that time to go out on a date with a girl alone." Actually, Jack and the young lady had already met; she was Elizabeth Renfro, the girl Jack had told to go jump in a lake. Bessie and her sister Mabel were close friends of Bernice Burke, Jack Gordon's girlfriend (and later his wife). Soon Robinson was dating Bessie and enjoying it, especially when they went on double dates with Gordon and Bernice, whose nickname was Rudy. A date usually meant a movie, with popcorn, at the Park Theater or Farrell's, which cost ten or fifteen cents, or sometimes they splurged at the posh United Artists cinema, where a ticket cost as much as thirty-five cents.

Gordon saw Robinson's mischievous side, which some people at times mistook because in those days it had a slightly manic edge. "Say we are at the movies," he recalled, "and Jack saw one of our friends eating a snack. He might go up and knock it out of his hand and not say a thing about it. He was just devilish that way. Or he might toss a firecracker and scare some people, and laugh. He was just a devilish guy. But he wasn't belligerent or anything like that. He was definitely not a bully. He wasn't picking a fight, and he never looked for trouble. He didn't avoid trouble, but he didn't look for it, either. Everything was a lot of fun to Jack."

Some people, Gordon knew, disliked Robinson: "Someone told my mom, You'd better stop your son from running around with that Jack Robinson, he's going to get into trouble. My father told me so. But I paid them no mind. Jack just didn't appear that way to me." Their friendship deepened. In 1946, when Robinson married, Gordon would be his best man; a few years later, he would move to New York with his wife and their son to work with Robinson and continue a friendship that obviously meant a great deal to both men. Eventually, Jack would see PJC as the place where he shed some old, rough skin and healed some wounds, including, no doubt, a few that were self-inflicted. "It was there," he said, "that I lost most of my shyness that had always made my early life miserable." Undoubtedly, Jack Gordon was an essential part of this process of healing.

Over the summer of 1937, Jack enrolled again in John Thurman's baseball school in Brookside Park. At night, he also played shortstop for Floracube, a commercially sponsored team in the popular city-run Owl League (softball played with baseball rules) in Brookside Park. Floracube was made up of members of the black North Pasadena Athletic Club. Against this opposition, Jack ran wild. His base running was so astonishing that the *Post* sports columnist Rube Samuelsen reported in July that "in almost every game" Robinson had stolen second, third, and home at least once. "It's practically a habit," Samuelsen marveled. "That isn't stealing. It's grand larceny." Before thirty-five hundred fans in the all-star game that closed the season, Robinson singled twice in two at-bats, then thrilled the crowd further by stealing third base after each hit. He was also thrown out twice at home.

In September, he returned to a transformed PJC. The "tent era" was over; set among what one school official touted as "the most beautiful of college grounds in Southern California," with freshly planted lawns and flowering plants and a serene reflecting pool, the three new buildings gleamed white as the "reconstructed" PJC opened its doors at last. The college, blessed with nothing less than the "last word in modern facilities for both academic and technical training," would now begin a "new era in higher education."

But Jack's mind was mainly on football. Football defined athletic excellence at PJC and almost everywhere else on the American college scene. The Bulldogs had a new, young head coach, Tom Mallory. A former football star at Pasadena High School and at USC (class of '32), Mallory had just arrived from Oklahoma City, where he had been coaching high school football. Several Oklahoma players, all white and with no experience playing with or against blacks, had followed him to PJC; about ten of them enrolled near the start of the season. Mallory's black players were few and homegrown. At least three were expected to start: at quarterback, Jack Robinson; his boyhood friend Ray Bartlett, a sensational pass receiver; and Larry Pickens, also a talented end. Other blacks hoped to make the team as substitutes.

On September 13, at the first scrimmage, Robinson was clearly the most brilliant player on the field. "Jack Robinson, the dashing quarterback from Muir, stole the show," according to the PJC *Chronicle.* "Time and again Robinson broke loose from the defense with his spectacular style of running." But the next day, disaster struck. In the middle of the scrimmage, Jack limped off the field with a wrenched ankle and what was diagnosed as a chipped bone in his right leg. The leg required a cast; he would be out for at least a month.

On October 9, after PJC sustained four consecutive losses, Jack's cast was cut off and he returned to the practice field. The next week, in Phoenix, Arizona, against Phoenix Junior College, he entered the game as a substitute and scored the third touchdown in what proved to be an easy victory. In the next game, at home before fifteen thousand fans against PJC's archenemy, Compton Junior College, he again did not start. When he was inserted, however, his first rush was a thing of beauty that gained twenty yards. Then, stung by the interception of one of his passes, he raised the crowd to its feet with the longest Bulldog run of the day, a dazzling trip of thirty-four yards. With his rushing and passing, and aided by brilliant catches by Bartlett and Pickens, Robinson starred in two long drives against the Compton squad. The game ended in a scoreless tie, but he was now poised to assert himself as a football Bulldog.

Jack shone again in the next game, against the Loyola University freshmen; intercepting a pass, he ran it back ninety-two yards for a touchdown in an easy win. Against Chaffey Junior College, Jack added a new page to his already storied season. Playing at safety on defense, he caught a punt on his own 22-yard line, "fumbled the ball, picked it up on the 20, and behind some of the finest downfield blocking by Pasadena all year, ran 80 yards to a touchdown, standing up." In the final game of the season, against a weak Caltech team, and before a crowd of eighteen thousand in the Rose Bowl, Jack was masterful again. A young white sportswriter noted of the "dark-hued phantom of the gridiron" and his "brilliant running and passing" that "it would have been a far different story if the Negro quarterback had not been in the game last night." Scoring one touchdown, Jack also passed for another. The writer, Shav Glick, caught something of Robinson's astonishing body control, his uncanny ability to run at a blazing pace, shudder suddenly to a stop, change direction, then swiftly accelerate past befuddled opponents. On one defensive play against a pass, "Robinson reared up, took the ball out of the air in midfield, cut toward the west sidelines, and just as he was about to be forced out of bounds, he sidestepped a Caltech man and raced on to a touchdown. A twisting change of pace which Robinson used baffled the Caltech defense into several errors."

With such inspired playing, Jack ended the season a hero to the student body and to much of Pasadena. Almost by himself he had helped to rescue the Bulldog season from ignominy, and he had done so with amazing flair. Nevertheless, on December 7, before a festive crowd of about four hundred citizens at the annual banquet of the Pasadena Elks at the Altadena Golf Club, his teammate Bill Busik won the Most Valuable Player award. Robinson had hoped for the prize; Busik had carried the team in his absence, but not to victory. "I had found out earlier that Busik was going to win," Jack Gordon recalled, "and I told Jack about it. Jack got very quiet. I thought he was upset. I told him, Well, Busik played well, he carried the team for a long time. Jack didn't say anything. Then he sort of shrugged and that was the end of it." He was present at the Altadena Golf Club when Busik was handed a "gold" football and lauded in a ceremony that apparently made scant reference to the other Bulldog quarterback. Jack probably laughed as loudly as everyone else when, according to a newspaper report, "the three colored players, Jack Robinson, Ray Bartlett, and Larry Pickens, came in for their share of kidding about incidents of the past season."

On December 17, 1937, Hank Shatford, a student journalist who had praised Jack all season, reported tersely in the *Chronicle* that "Pasadena will lose Jackie Robinson's football talents next year. He intends to enroll at Oregon State in September." Whether this plan had anything to do with the award or the ceremony is unclear. With Mack Robinson's two years of junior college eligibility gone, he had decided to accept a scholarship to the University of Oregon, in Eugene. Perhaps Jack had decided to leave with him. Finally, however, Jack decided to stay in Pasadena, where he was now out from under the shadow of his celebrated brother.

AT PJC, JACK'S STOCK rose with his amazing feats on the football field. On the whole, he moved easily if quietly among the students, black and white, but stayed mainly within the small group of blacks. The junior college had no student union or other convenient gathering place, but black students had their favorite spot, which was near the swimming pool and a short-order food shop. Often Jack could be found there. Openly associating with the other black students, he nevertheless had misgivings about their tendency to cling together and hang back in the company of whites. Neither Jack nor Ray Bartlett had much use for the Armulites, the all-black society. "I wouldn't join it," Bartlett said. "I wouldn't think of doing that." And Jack Gordon remembered Robinson urging other black students to give up their habit of sitting in the back of the balcony at school assemblies; he wanted them to spread out more. But Jack and Bartlett responded differently to the ways of most of their fellow blacks. "They used to call me all sorts of names because I wouldn't loaf with them all day," Bartlett recalled, "but Jack would spend time there, hanging out with them. I would be at the library. I don't think I ever saw Jack at the library."

At some point, however, Robinson, Gordon, and another black student became the first blacks elected to the Lancers, a service organization with policelike duties at assemblies, tournaments, and other gatherings of students. "We wore our official black sweaters," Gordon recalled, "and were your big men on campus, giving orders. Jack liked that." Certainly Jack managed to maintain some links with whites, especially his old friends. When Warren Dorn, a sweet-natured boyhood friend and self-professed admirer of the Pepper Street Gang, stood for a school election, Jack jumped in to help. "I remember we had a lunchtime rally at PJC," according to Dorn, "and Jack just got up before everyone and made a fine, rousing speech about why it was important that Warren Dorn should be elected. Everybody listened, too; it definitely helped me." (Also speaking up for Dorn at that noon rally was another friend and fellow student, and a future movie star, William Holden.) As for trying to date white women, Jack drew the line there; deliberately he squelched any overtures that may have come his way with his sporting success. Again Bartlett was different: "Sure, I socialized with Caucasian girls, especially the ones that hung around the athletes. I sat with them in class, talked with them. Not Jack, though. He kept his distance. Jack was always kind of slow with the girls. He was always bashful."

Jack was popular, but racial hostility was real. Shig Kawai, an outstanding athlete who had joined him on an all-star southern California high school baseball team in 1935, also played basketball and football at one time or another with Jack for the Bulldogs. "A lot of the time you would hear 'Get that Jap' and 'Get that nigger,' " he recalled. "We had to hear these other teams making racial remarks all the time. Of course, that only made us fight a little harder. And we usually won!" For all Bartlett's sports success and his striving, he too felt the sting of exclusion. "I felt left out," he conceded. "I felt that because I was a Negro I was being passed over, not considered, for many things. All the clubs were white. You can look through all the old yearbooks and see that so clearly."

On a trip north to Sacramento, Robinson and Gordon were flatly refused service in a restaurant. "You can't eat in here," a woman told them. "Why not?" Gordon asked. " 'Because you're colored.' That was the whole conversation." He also remembered that the entire track team, except for one Oklahoma "jackass," then walked out in a show of solidarity. The Bulldog football trip to Arizona was marred for Robinson and the other blacks when the team hotel in Phoenix refused to accept them. Such episodes enraged him, but Jack tried to curb his anger. At a junior college picnic once, he would recall, a white student made "a slurring remark to me about my race." When Jack angrily challenged him to a fight, the fellow "sort of snapped out of it." He hadn't meant the insult, the student explained; "he said it was just a bad habit. . . . I accepted his apology and we shook hands in a very friendly way."

He was starting to discover the truth of his mother's lesson that doing good often brought good in return, that the dangers of idealism were outweighed by its benefits. Nowhere was this more evident than in generosity to teammates; in his intense desire to win, Jack was both a nonpareil star, burning with individual brightness, and the unselfish team player. Perhaps his major test at PJC came with Coach Mallory's Oklahoma players, who tried to freeze out the black players, or some of them. Gordon remembered one day finding Robinson, Bartlett, and some other black players sulking on the sidelines. "The Oklahoma boys don't want to play with us," they explained. "So we just walked off the field." Robinson himself offered two versions of the episode. In one, the Oklahomans had treated him, Bartlett, and Pickens fine but slighted the other blacks: "I called a little harmony session, urging that we either get together or go elsewhere and play football. . . . After that, we had real teamwork." In another version, Jack recalled going to Tom Mallory and threatening to transfer to a rival school. In any event, Mallory put down the rebellion decisively— and Jack learned a lesson both about the value of protesting injustice and about using his market value as an athlete to fight against it. "Coach Mallory laid down the law and the Oklahoma fellows became more than decent. We saw that here was a case where a bit of firmness prevented what could have grown into an ugly situation."

He also learned another lesson, apparently. He recalled: "I decided that Bartlett and I had a responsibility to do something to make the Oklahoma fellows feel that they had nothing to fear from Negroes—that they were just as valuable to the team as we were." As quarterback, Jack said, he went out of his way to spread the scoring around to include the Oklahoma players who blocked for him and the other backs but were never expected to score. In gratitude, they returned the favor by blocking for Jack with a vengeance. "That convinced me that it was smart to share the glory," Jack said, "that in the final analysis white people were no worse than Negroes, for we are all afflicted by the same pride, jealousy, envy and ambition."

Consciously or not, Jack was acting as his mother Mallie had done in winning over Pepper Street, when she saw that some whites were mainly prisoners of their ignorance and had to be treated accordingly, with a measure of understanding. Drawing both on religion and on her practical sense of the world, Mallie had responded calmly to them, as one might treat children, and she had won out, in her own way, over racial prejudice. Now Jack, younger and impetuous, and in a milieu about which she knew nothing, and which seemed to breed rage and violence, was striving to do the same.

The football season had barely ended before Jack showed up for practice with the Bulldog basketball team under Coach Carl Metten. Like Mallory, Metten was an alumnus of Pasadena High School; at Oregon State he had lettered in football and basketball. The PJC basketball team labored under two handicaps. The first had to do with its arena, which was little more than a shed, with one side exposed to the elements, so that fans shivered on chilly nights, or fled the rain. The other handicap was the team itself; its average height was only about six feet.

With Robinson and Bill Busik at forward and Ray Bartlett (also about six feet) at center, the Bulldogs started the season with two victories, but soon fell to earth. In a virtually all-white league, with all white officials, the Bulldogs believed they were being mistreated. At an early tournament, Jack's spirited play and team-high scoring were offset by questionable calls, as PJC saw them, including a technical foul against Jack. A string of losses followed, including one in Sacramento when Jack left the court with bruised ribs; Busik, too, was hurt. These injuries were no accident. By this point, the league-leading scorer Jack Robinson was a prime target of blows. In turn, Jack was hardly bashful about hitting back, if he could do so surreptitiously. Gordon remembered a game in which an opponent hacked at Jack repeatedly without a foul being called. Robinson waited patiently for his chance. "Jack had the ball," according to Gordon, "and he had his head sort of down. All of a sudden he comes up with the ball. He just ripped the guy, right up the front. Blood went everywhere. But no foul. After that, he had no problems in that game."

On January 22, with the Bulldogs in their barn against Long Beach Junior College, where black students were not welcome, tempers flared. An explosion was expected, apparently; Jack's brother Frank arrived at the barn with a concealed tire iron. Jack found himself locked in an ongoing struggle with Sam Babich, a substitute guard and "the stormy petrel" of Long Beach; according to the *Chronicle,* Babich "started a one-man campaign against Robinson as soon as he was inserted in the game." With the final whistle, Babich walked over to Robinson and punched him. "The next moment," according to a *Post* reporter, "Babich was lying on the floor of the gym, with Robinson on top of him." At that point, "nearly all the people in the gym began swinging at the nearest person, friend or foe." This "riot" involved "about 50 players, subs, coaches and spectators." Later, the Long Beach student body president apologized to Jack and the Bulldogs, who had won both the fight and the game.

The rest of the season saw the team record decline, although Jack remained a feared player. PJC finished third in the conference. He ended in second place, by one point, in the race for individual scoring honors in the Western Division of the Southern California Junior College Athletic Association. By this time, he was also in deep trouble.

Within a few days of the Long Beach game riot on January 22, Jack spent a night in the Pasadena city jail. His arrest had nothing to do with the riot. He and a friend named Jonathan Nolan were coming home from seeing a movie when Nolan began to sing a wildly popular song of the day called "Flat Foot Floogie." They passed a policeman, who felt insulted by the song and decided to challenge Nolan and

Robinson. One thing led to another, and Jack ended up in jail. He spent the night in custody; no one at the station bothered to call his mother.

On January 25, at a hearing, Robinson was sentenced to ten days in jail. However, bowing no doubt to the fact that this was Jack's first arrest, and that he was a football star, the judge suspended the sentence on condition that Robinson not be arrested for two years.

Although the incident apparently did not make the newspapers, it probably became common knowledge in Pasadena. The myth began to take shape of a Jack Robinson in frequent conflict with the police, young Jack Robinson as jailbird. In 1987, fifteen years after his death, a *Star-News* reporter would write: "There is a story that during his junior college career, Robinson frequently was tossed into jail on a Friday night only to be released for Saturday's game." Jack's brother Mack, openly bitter at Pasadena, either wanted to lend credence to the story or was made to appear so: "All that left a lot of scars," Mack said in response to this "story." "This town gave Jack nothing."

The "story" is almost certainly false, and part of the myth of an antisocial, violent Jackie Robinson that arose, ironically, even as he struggled to assert himself against racism in the major leagues. The myth would often involve tales of Robinson punching white men in the mouth, especially smashing their teeth, as the would-be mythmaker pressed into service the embodiment of black male heroism, Jackie Robinson, against centuries of slavery, segregation, and racism. Even Mack endorsed the myth, as in avowing elsewhere that Jack "had busted many a white boy in the mouth if he was out of line with him," or in boasting that he and Jack and their brothers had "kicked some white ass" in their youth. "Kids aren't so tough when you can knock them down with a punch."

Undoubtedly there were fistfights now and then between Jack and young whites, but probably nothing like the legend of Jack's brutal aggressiveness. Ray Bartlett remembered Jackie as having a far worse temper than Bartlett himself but being much less willing to fight on the football field. "We didn't have face masks in those days—your bare face hung out," Bartlett said. "Jack would see a little blood, and I would see it, and it would make me angry, but Jack wouldn't react that way. Jack really didn't fight back like I thought he should have. I didn't see him as being a real fighter. I've always said that what made him such a good runner was that he didn't want to get hit. You couldn't get away with anything against him, but he was not dirty and he was not one to start a fight."

Robinson's eagerness to talk back to the police became mixed up in legend with the fact of his raw physical power and then became conflated into a habit of brutality when in fact he drew a line early between protest and violence. Hank Shatford of the PJC *Chronicle* in Jack's time, later a lawyer and superior court judge in Pasadena, found out what the police thought of Jack. "They didn't regard Jack as a rabble-rouser," Shatford related. "Not at all. It's just that Jack would not take any stuff from them, and they knew it. Frankly, some of them were bigots then. Jack never wanted to be regarded as a second-class citizen. He rebelled at any thought of anybody putting him down, or putting any of his people down. He wanted equality. And he had a temper. Boy, he could heat up pretty fast when he wanted to! When he felt he was right and the other guy was wrong, he didn't hesitate. He was in there. But he also had an extremely warm side to him that I saw all the time."

In any event, on January 25, 1938, Jack acquired a police record, as well as a jail term hanging over his head. Before his probationary period was over, he would come before a Pasadena judge again as a defendant.

At almost precisely this time, in a stroke of rare good fortune, Karl Everette Downs entered Jack's life. Earlier that month, Downs had arrived in Pasadena to assume the pastorship of Scott United Methodist Church on Mary Street, where Mallie worshiped. He was then only twenty-five years old. Robinson and some friends were loitering at a popular street intersection when a tall, razor-thin black man, stylishly dressed in a tailored suit, white shirt, and a tie sharply knotted, stopped his car and called out: "Is Jack Robinson here?" When no one answered, he left a message: "Tell him I want to see him at the junior church." In their small community, no one had to ask what he meant or guess for long who he was. Sometime later, Jack delivered himself to the church and began a relationship that lasted only a few years but changed the course of his life.

Born in 1912 in Abilene, Texas, the son of a Methodist district superintendent, Downs had attended public schools in Waco, Texas, then earned degrees at black Samuel Huston College in Austin, Texas, and Gammon Theological Seminary in Atlanta, Georgia, before going on to Boston University. Downs arrived in Pasadena determined to transform Scott United Methodist. In a short time he put in place an amazing number of services and facilities, including a day nursery, a social service department, a toy and book lending library, a skating rink and a basketball court, folk dancing, a young married couples' fellowship, a Sunday-afternoon radio program, a program of interracial teas, and a celebrity night that brought a variety of speakers to Scott Methodist, from the Harlem activist Adam Clayton Powell Jr. to the Nobel Prize–winning scientist Linus Pauling. Above all, he emphasized the importance of young people and the need for change.

According to Robinson later, "elder members objected to Reverend Downs's program. They felt tradition should be maintained." But while the elders objected and debated, Downs quickly won over the youth. "He looked half his age," Eleanor Heard recalled (he officiated at her marriage), "and yet he was a serious man that you had to respect and admire." Downs was cosmopolitan but also race proud; he was mature and yet challenged the old ways. Two years before coming to Pasadena, he had published a fighting article, "Timid Negro Students!," in *Crisis,* the magazine of the NAACP. Calling on black and white students alike to fight social injustice, he demanded "fearless, rational, comprehensive and cooperative ventures of both the Negro and white students." He warned that injustices like the Scottsboro case and lynchings in the South would continue "until *the Negro student substitutes courage for his timidity and sacrifice for his comforts.*"

To Downs, Robinson evidently was someone special who had to be rescued from himself and the traps of Jim Crow; to Robinson, Downs was a revelation. "He really was a sort of psychiatrist," Ray Bartlett thought. "I'm not sure what would have happened to Jack if he had never met Reverend Downs." Downs led Jack back to Christ. Under the minister's influence, Jack not only returned to church but also saw its true significance for the first time; he started to teach Sunday school. After a punishing football game on Saturday, Jack admitted, he yearned to sleep late; "but no matter how terrible I felt, I had to get up. It was impossible to shirk duty when Karl Downs was involved." The young minister, with his love of athletics and his easy manner, was also a pleasure to be around. "Karl Downs had the ability to communicate with you spiritually," Jack declared, "and at the same time he was fun to be with. He participated with us in our sports. Most important he knew how to listen. Often when I was deeply concerned about personal crises, I went to him."

In his last autobiography, *I Never Had It Made,* Robinson then mentions only one problem or crisis that he brought to Downs: his relationship to his mother, her long hours of menial work, and his own inability to help her end this cycle of toil. "When I talked with Karl about this and other problems," he wrote, "he helped ease some of my tensions. It wasn't so much what he did to help as the fact that he was interested and concerned enough to offer the best advice he could." The relationship between his minister, his mother, and Jack himself was crucial. As a young man, vibrant, educated, articulate, and brave, Downs became a conduit through which Mallie's message of religion and hope finally flowed into Jack's consciousness and was fully accepted there, if on revised terms, as he himself reached manhood. Faith in God then began to register in him as both a mysterious force, beyond his comprehension, and a pragmatic way to negotiate the world. A measure of emotional and spiritual poise such as he had never known at last entered his life.

Looking back in 1949 on his youth, Jack would point out as a major turning point in his life his relatively late understanding of the crucial role his mother played in it—that "there was somebody else in this world beside little me." The turning point had come "all of a sudden in junior college. . . . It made me realize there was somebody battling and pushing us along. With a mother like that a fellow just had to make good." Acknowledging at last the moral victory Mallie had made of her life despite her dreary job and country ways, Jack came to see the strength from knowing "that I had a lot of faith in God. . . . There's nothing like faith in God to help a fellow who gets booted around once in a while."

Downs also gave Robinson his first inspired sense of a reliable future vocation. From about this point in his life, Jack knew that when the cheering stopped, as he understood it would, he would seek to become a coach, or to serve in some other intimate capacity with young people, especially young black people, to try to shape their lives as his life had been shaped by his mother and by Karl Downs.

WHEN THE BASEBALL SEASON STARTED, Jack was now an established star of the Bulldogs. His hitting was assured; his fielding was brilliant; his base running set him apart from all other players. In one play that astonished a sportswriter, Robinson found himself apparently trapped by fielders between second and third base; but when he saw the shortstop drop the ball, "instead of stopping at third, the dusky flash, noting that home was uncovered, went all the way to score." Early in April, riding a thirteen-game winning streak, PJC climbed atop their division. In the process, Jack had made his mark. On May 1, when he was named to the All-Southland Junior College team, he was also selected as the Most Valuable Player in the region. The next day, he celebrated by going five-for-six and stealing two bases against Los Angeles Junior College.

On May 7, the sporting legend of young Jackie Robinson grew even more imposing. Arriving late for a vital division game against Glendale Junior College in Glendale, Robinson had one hit and stole a base in a PJC victory. But he had a good reason to be tardy. Earlier that day, in Pomona, about forty miles away, Jack jumped 25 feet 6½ inches on the last of his three allotted tries at the Southern California Junior College track meet to set a national junior college record. In the process, he erased his brother's mark, which Mack had set one year before at the Drake Relays in Iowa.

The legend grew some more on May 17 in a game against Pomona, when Coach Mallory tossed the ball to Jack in the third inning for his debut as a pitcher. Hurling the remaining innings, Robinson gave up five hits, walked five batters, hit one, and uncorked one wild pitch. Nevertheless, the Bulldogs won, 12–1, and he gained official credit for the win. Two days later, the Bulldogs demolished Compton to take the divisional title. Playing in twenty-four games, Jack had batted .417 and scored forty-three runs; scoring in all but three of the games, he struck out only three times and stole twenty-five bases. The PJC *Chronicle* pronounced him "the greatest base runner ever to play on a junior college team," as well as "one of the most sensational fielders in the business."

This was surely the moment for a major-league club to sign Robinson and begin grooming him. In March, in a game that pitted a Pasadena youth nine against the Chicago White Sox (in town for spring training), Jack's brilliance had been clear. After his second hit of the game, he stole second base almost impudently against the White Sox catcher Mike Tresh. In the next inning, after his superb stop of a smash by Luke Appling, the American League batting champion, he started a brilliant double play to snuff out a White Sox threat. A reporter heard Jimmy

Dykes, the White Sox manager, declare: "Geez, if that kid was white I'd sign him right now."

Signed by a major-league organization, Jack would have joined a group of young and still developing baseball players—such as Ted Williams, Joe DiMaggio, Ralph Kiner, Bob Lemon, and Bob Feller—he would meet later either in the majors or in the Hall of Fame. But in 1938, the prohibition against blacks in major-league baseball was like iron. The years from about this point in 1938 until 1946, when he took the field for the Montreal Royals of the Brooklyn Dodgers organization, would be in effect the lost baseball youth, never to be recovered, of Jackie Robinson.

In 1937, Jack had entered PJC a wiry fellow, with a sinewy yet undernourished body; one sportswriter in 1941 would recall him as having been in 1937 "a rather skinny kid." Another writer, much later, remembered that "what struck me then was how thin and fragile he looked and how suddenly he could be the man who wasn't there when tacklers attempted to down him." By the time Jack played his last football game for the Bulldogs, however, his body had changed; benefiting from football team "training tables," his weight had jumped from around 135 pounds to nearly 175. By the fall of 1938 Jack's shoulders were visibly broader and denser with muscle, his thighs were thick for a person with his relatively modest frame, and he had achieved his top height, just under six feet. Now in his twentieth year, he stood at the peak of his physical perfection.

With his broad-jump record as well as his amazing football, baseball, and basketball exploits, he had emerged completely from his brother Mack's dominance. Neither brother seemed entirely comfortable with the change. "I couldn't get over it, breaking Mack's record," Jack recalled. "Mack had always been my idol, making the Olympics and all that, and here I'd broken his record." Again using his college or university mainly as an outlet for athletics, Mack finally enrolled in the spring at the University of Oregon. In June, on a visit home, he let the press know how pleased he was by Jack's record jump. But the Pasadena press now needed no prompting to sing Jack's praises or to see him as a greater athlete than Mack. When the PJC *Chronicle* named Jack its athlete of the year, Hank Shatford saluted him as "the greatest all-around athlete ever to attend P.J.C." And that month, to help raise funds to send Jack to the National Amateur Athletic Union's big track-and-field meeting in Buffalo, New York, Rube Samuelsen of the *Post* paid tribute: "It is doubtful if Pasadena ever has had a greater all-around athlete and that is saying a lot in a city where champions are produced as regularly as the years roll by."

The Buffalo meet, on July 3, promised a dramatic clash of the Robinson brothers in the broad jump. But Mack, who won the 200-meter race after being eliminated in the 100, decided late to withdraw from the event. Jack himself placed third. At the end of the summer Mack did not return to Oregon. Instead, he stayed in Pasadena to work for the city, sweeping streets. Some people wondered how he, a college man, could work at such a job. "I never did understand those people," Mack remarked later. "I had to take whatever I could get."

The late spring and summer of 1938 found Jack once again playing some tennis and golf at Brookside Park, but challenged mainly by the nighttime softball Owl League. Again he played on a team made up of young black men from northwestern Pasadena, including his cousin Van Wade in center field and Ray Bartlett in left. Their sponsor this year was Pepsi-Cola, which provided uniforms and some equipment.

Typical of his brilliance was a game against Jones Barber Shop, which ended in a tie "mainly because the barbers were unable to stop Jackie Robinson." Playing shortstop, Jack "made two singles for his team's only hits, stole five bases and scored his club's two runs. Jack also sparkled in the field by engineering a brilliant double play." Again and again, Jack was the difference between victory and defeat. He and his team began to attract crowds never before seen at softball games at night in Brookside Park; in early August, five thousand fans turned out for a league game involving the Pepsi-Cola team. On August 17, when Pepsi-Cola played its last regular game of the season, with Ray Bartlett the star that night, the team accorded Jack the honor of pitching the last inning. He retired the side in order. Pepsi-Cola then rolled through the playoffs to take the title.

The fall brought a return to PJC and to football, and a magnificent season for the Bulldog team and Robinson in particular. Santa Ana arrived boasting a twenty-two-game winning streak; it left town with its streak snapped in a game that saw Robinson "directly responsible for each and every Pasadena touchdown." Against Ventura, Jack gave "another scintillating exhibition of broken field running" when he took a lateral at the 40-yard line, "streaked down the north sidelines until he was trapped on the 10, where he suddenly cut diagonally across the field to score." After five games, the Bulldogs were undefeated. Although Jack had missed one game with an injury, his 61 points scored was thought to be the second highest by any player in the country that fall. In the Rose Bowl, an assembly of some thirty-eight thousand saw Pasadena smother Los Angeles. One run by Robinson was unforgettable; "after squirming out of the arms of four would-be tacklers, the Negro sensation went down the south sidelines to a touchdown."

An even larger crowd, about forty thousand—thought to be the largest to that date in junior college sports history—saw undefeated Pasadena crush hated Compton. A "phenomenal" Jack Robinson was involved directly in all of the Bulldogs' twenty points. Duke Snider, the future baseball star, then a young spectator from Compton, recalled a play when Robinson caught the ball after a kickoff, "reversed his field three times, and returned it for a touchdown. It was as dazzling a piece of broken-field running as you could ever hope to see." "Have you ever seen anyone, anywhere, play better 'heads-up' football than Robinson?" Rube Samuelsen asked his Pasadena *Post* readers. "He is an opportunist of the first water. He thinks out there. He can evade a tackler with rare finesse. He has athletic sense, in doing the right thing at the right time as few sports stars do. He is a 'natural' athlete in the fullest sense."

In San Francisco, before a huge, expectant crowd, Jack disappointed no one. On his first carry, he sped 75 yards for a touchdown. On another play, he humbled a defensive end with a feint that left the player sprawled on the turf, then sped 55 yards to score. After a punt return that rocked the stadium, he fired two deft passes for touchdowns. Robinson left the game to an ovation seldom accorded a visiting player. He was superb again on Homecoming Day in November before a huge crowd of loyalists in the Rose Bowl against Glendale. On the last play, with victory assured but his team anxious to preserve its scoring average of 33 points per game, Jack took off on an astonishing 85-yard sprint that made the final score 33–6. In the next game, his last as a Bulldog, Jack said farewell with a masterpiece. Setting up behind his own goal line in punt formation, he gathered in the hiked ball, then raced 104 yards for a touchdown against a muddle of disbelieving Caltech players.

After a season of eleven wins and no losses, in which he scored 17 touchdowns and 131 points, Jack was showered with adulation; along with Ray Bartlett of PJC, he was named to the all-Southland first team by the Kiwanis Clubs of Southern California. He was the center of attention when the Associated Women Students of PJC sponsored their annual football banquet for the Bulldog team. Coach Mallory, awarding nicknames to his departing seniors, dubbed Jack "Gift from Heaven." And on December 6, he won the honor that had eluded him in 1937, the Most Valuable Player of the Year award given by the Pasadena Elks. Proudly Jack accepted a "gold" football and a year's stewardship of the trophy. His popularity among the Bulldogs was clear when the team itself, in a surprise, awarded a custom-made trophy to Coach Mallory. On the trophy, high on a pedestal above tiny statues of the rest of the Bulldog starters, was a taller statue of Jack, dynamic in a broken-field running pose.

As JACK'S ATHLETIC accomplishments mounted, so did interest in him among those colleges and universities willing to recruit and start a black player; he himself recalled "a number of colleges putting out feelers, offering athletic scholarships." Jack Gordon remembered Fresno State, in central California, offering Jack all sorts of inducements, including a set of new tires for the ancient car that had come into his possession. Jack recalled that the college with "the most attractive scholarship" was "very far" from Pasadena. Probably this was the University of Oregon; but Jack knew by this point that Mack was probably not going back to the Ducks, and he also was less than enchanted with the rain and cold he associated with the town of Eugene.

Several top schools, committed to Jim Crow, were out of the question. A Stanford alumnus, according to

Robinson, offered to pay his college expenses any-where as long as he did not attend a school in Stan-ford's conference; attending Stanford itself, of course, was out of the question. The University of Southern California, located in Los Angeles, as pres-tigious as Stanford but with an even greater sports program, sometimes took blacks. Its acclaimed foot-ball coach, Howard Jones, had praised Jack lavishly at the Elks banquet. But Jack heard Jones's eulogy with mixed emotions. "We all knew USC had the best athletic program and the best teams," Ray Bartlett recalled. "They were *the* team in almost every sport in southern California. But we knew we would just sit on the bench over there. Howard Jones was a good coach, but he was a very prejudiced man." Hank Shat-ford recalled that USC offered Robinson "a real good scholarship," with "some benefits that he probably wouldn't get at UCLA." But he, too, knew that the Trojans had only "token blacks" who seldom got to play, "which was disgusting."

Helping Jack make this important decision was his loyal, loving brother Frank, "my greatest fan." Frank loved to scout opposing teams for Jack, to warn him about this or that player, help him plan his attack or defense, and loudly cheer him on during games. To the two brothers, UCLA made the most sense. The institution was young and its sports pro-grams on the whole weak. But its coaches seemed eager to have Robinson enroll and genuinely deter-mined to use him. Tuition was free, the annual administrative fee only a token sum, and Jack could continue to live at home while commuting to the village of Westwood, the site of the campus. Above all, Frank would be near, and "I didn't want to see Frank disappointed."

On December 1, UCLA became even more attractive to Jack when the school announced that Edwin C. "Babe" Horrell would be its new head football coach. The name Horrell was almost synonymous with sports in Pasadena; the main playing field at PJC was Horrell Field, named after Babe and his brothers. All had been outstanding Bulldogs; after starring in even more sports at PJC than Jack, Babe Horrell had gone on to become an all-American center at the University of California, Berkeley, on its celebrated 1924 "Wonder Team." Horrell was "high class, cultured and civilized," according to one of his black players. "He always dressed right; he always talked right." Another family member, Jack Horrell, a top sprinter on the current Bulldog track team, had given money publicly to help send Jack to the NAAU track meet in Buffalo. By Christmas, Jack's mind was made up. On December 13, Rube Samuelsen reported on a visit by the Oregon head coach to the Bulldog campus but warned his readers in the *Post:* "Don't bet any money that Jackie will NOT go to U.C.L.A. At this writing the Bruins are Robinson's No. 1 choice and I can tell you straight that Jackie would be welcomed on the Westwood varsity next fall."

Jack would leave PJC at midyear, but not before one last round in basketball. Now well known statewide, he was lionized at a state tournament in Modesto. "He made a decided hit with tournament fans," according to a reporter, "who cheered his every move. The versatile Negro youth was hailed as the best sportsman and the sensation of the event." With the Bulldogs reaching Christmas undefeated in conference play, Robinson was a stifling defender, a constant threat to score, and a determined fighter. In a key game against Compton, when PJC trailed at halftime for the first time all season, "Compton's old bugaboo in every sport, Jack Robinson, was the man that brought about the Compton loss." When the winning streak ended and a PJC victory over Los Angeles Junior College became essential, he stepped up again. Before a howling crowd that included his brothers Frank and Mack, Jack sank a free throw with twelve seconds remaining to give the Bulldogs a victory. Scoring 26 of his team's 49 points, he also broke his own record for the most points ever by a Bulldog in a game. "The phenomenal Negro athlete," the *Post* reported, "played one of his best games, dropping shot after shot as the bewildered Cubs attempted to guard him." Winning its next two contests, PJC took the conference crown.

On February 4, against Glendale, Jack played the last game of his two-year career as a Bulldog. Just before he left the campus, he gained one more significant honor: induction into the junior college's most respected honor society. On January 27, before the assembled student body, Jack and nine other students received a gold pin to mark their acceptance into the Order of Mast and Dagger; each semester, Mast and Dagger tapped a few students who had performed "outstanding service to the school and whose scholastic and citizenship record is worthy of recognition." A group picture of the chosen students, including Jack, made the front page of the Pasadena *Post*. While Jack's sporting exploits had won him this honor, his induction also showed an appreciation by his peers at PJC of his strength of character. On the campus, to the mass of students, Robinson was a respected figure, acclaimed and yet modest, as the journalist Shav Glick (also tapped that day) recalled almost forty years later: "To them he was a quiet, capable student who became a superstar on the athletic field."

Away from the campus, however, life was another matter. The cheering crowds and his honors and awards could never make up completely for the humiliations that came with being a young black man in a city hostile to people like him. On January 2, Jack had further painful proof of where blacks stood in Pasadena when his oldest brother, Edgar, was beaten by two policemen, then charged with resisting arrest and violating a city ordinance. The ordinance barred individuals from placing chairs along the annual Tournament of Roses Parade without a license (the chairs were then rented out for four or five dollars each).

According to Edgar, two policemen accosted him about the rental of certain seats. When he reached into his pocket to retrieve a license (for which he said he had paid four dollars on December 30), one officer knocked him down. Next followed, according to a newspaper report based on Edgar's statement, "a free-for-all scuffle, in which his eye was blackened, his arms twisted and bruised." Denied medical treatment or a chance to call home, Edgar pleaded guilty to the charges and paid a ten-dollar fine. At the city hospital, the staff refused to treat him. Edgar then went to the office of the chief of police to lodge a complaint. "Before he had an opportunity to say anything," according to the newspaper, "he said he was ordered out, 'before you are clubbed on the head,' these words reputedly said by the chief himself."

Apparently, the police also robbed him. He was carrying $60 when arrested, but at the station only $36.55 was counted out as belonging to him. The two policemen vanished from the record; they might have come from Los Angeles, Edgar thought, because he had to direct them to the local police station and because (so he said) they told him at one point that "we don't allow Negroes in Los Angeles to make this kind of money." Protests against the police proved a waste of time. The Pasadena branch of the NAACP passed a resolution of protest to the city police department and offered it documents detailing other accusations "of flagrant discrimination and brutal treatment of colored citizens in Pasadena by the police." The NAACP was ignored. Apparently, the only newspaper to mention its move, or Edgar's arrest, was the black-owned *California Eagle*.

This incident, and other episodes like it, eventually made Jack loathe Pasadena. Some of his childhood friends, including Sid and Eleanor Heard, who never left the city, became reconciled to its faults. But Jack's final response was different. "If my mother, brothers and sister weren't living there," he declared, "I'd never go back." His resentment went deep. "I've always felt like an intruder, even in school. People in Pasadena were less understanding, in some ways, than Southerners. And they were more openly hostile."

Early in February, just past his twentieth birthday, Robinson took his first bold steps away from home when he began to commute daily between Pasadena and Los Angeles to attend classes at UCLA. In the next two years, he would grow in maturity in many ways, but he would also be forced to endure even more embittering incidents that led him to resent the city of his youth. As always, however, he looked with hope to the future; and in the winter of 1939, the future for Jack Robinson was UCLA and its promise of national glory.

Blue and Gold at UCLA

1939–1941

I certainly hope that Friendship continues on and on.
— *Jackie Robinson (1941)*

O<small>N</small> F<small>EBRUARY</small> 15, 1939, ending "the wild rumors that have been running rife regarding his future plans," Jack Robinson drove his 1931 Plymouth from Pepper Street in Pasadena to Vernon Avenue in downtown Los Angeles to begin his formal association with UCLA by enrolling at the Extension Division of the university. There, he would complete the requirements for full entry to the university in Westwood in the fall.

At UCLA, where its new football coach, Babe Horrell, saluted Robinson as "one of the greatest open-field runners I have ever seen," the student newspaper added its endorsement. Quoting the PJC track coach to the effect that Robinson was the state's "outstanding all-around athlete," the *California Daily Bruin* also foresaw no academic problems for the recruit, although his transcript showed deficiencies in algebra, French, and geometry. "Judging by his previous scholarship record," the *Bruin* declared,

"Robinson should have little difficulty in making good in Extension Division." But Jack himself then shook up reporters—and, no doubt, at least two coaches at UCLA—by announcing that he would no longer strive to be a "four-star" athlete. Instead, he would compete in football and the broad jump only, because the strain of competition in four sports was too great. "And besides," he added, "I think I should study. That is why I chose UCLA. I don't intend to coast so that I can play ball."

Jack's decision meant only one thing, really: he had set himself the goal of following in Mack's footsteps and making the U.S. Olympic team in 1940. Already some experts were hailing him as the finest broad jumper in the United States. With time now to train for the event, he was expected to earn a spot on the team easily.

For Robinson, the next few months were a respite from the intense athletic activity of the previous two years. In the spring, he stuck to his promise and emphasized his studies. Taking courses in English, French, physiology, and physical education, he also finished work in algebra and geometry started at Muir Tech. If he attended spring football training in Westwood in March, he did so as a spectator. He also played no basketball for UCLA. However, suiting up for an Alpha Phi Alpha team in a statewide league of Negro fraternities, "the Black Panther," as the *California Eagle* dubbed him, scored 25 points in leading the Alphas to a victory.

The spring passed quietly, if with one major change on Pepper Street. His mother completed the purchase of the house and land at 133 Pepper Street, next door to 121 Pepper Street. With this purchase, Mallie moved into 133 accompanied· by her niece Jessie Maxwell; she left 121, the larger house, to an assortment of family, including Jack, Willa Mae, Edgar, and Frank and Maxine and their children. The summer began well, with yet another sports triumph for Jack when, over the Fourth of July weekend, on the tennis courts at La Pintoresca Park near his home, he won the men's singles and doubles titles in the tenth annual championship tournament of the black Western Federation of Tennis Clubs. Opponents crumbled before what one observer called "his wickedly unorthodox style, characterized by lightning speed and uncanny judgment." In the men's singles final, faced with his "devilish placements, speed, and a merciless little cut, used in net play," his veteran opponent "quietly folded up." Teaming with a friend, Jack then took the doubles title. In the entire tournament, neither he nor his doubles team came close to dropping a set. "The amazing thing about Robinson's performance," the observer marveled, was that although he "only plays tennis in the summer vacation months . . . [he] nevertheless ran rough shod over players who are devoted to the sport year round and for years on end."

But within days of these victories came the worst blow of Jack's life to that point. At about 6:25 p.m. on July 10, his brother Frank was riding his motorcycle along Orange Grove Avenue in Pasadena when a woman driving a car in the opposite direction turned across his path to enter a service station. Frank braked hard and swerved to avoid the car, but its left front fender snagged his machine. Frank, along with a passenger behind him, went flying. They struck a parked car so hard that the impact left a huge dent in its body. With only bruises, his passenger walked away; Frank was knocked unconscious. An ambulance sped him to Huntington Memorial Hospital, where doctors found that he had fractured his skull and broken several ribs as well as a leg and a thigh. The accident had also ruptured his liver, spleen, and kidney and punctured his left lung.

Jack was playing cards at the home of a friend when he heard the news. Rushing to the hospital, he heard to his horror that Frank was near death. In tears he called home and broke the news to his sister, Willa Mae. "Mama was living next door then on the corner," she recalled, "and I hollered out the window. I didn't think what I was doing, so the whole neighborhood heard and everybody came running." Fleeing the hospital, Jack went home and fell sobbing into bed. Frank, who had regained consciousness, lingered for several hours. Jack Gordon remembered him cursing in his pain, and Mallie recalled his deep groaning as he begged her to turn him over so he could die in peace. A few minutes after midnight, he was gone. On July 14, he was buried in Mountain View Cemetery. "I was very shaken up by his death," Jack wrote later. "It was hard to believe he was gone, hard to believe I would no longer have his support."

Jack sought relief from sorrow in sports—mainly tennis, golf, and baseball. Playing for the Pasadena Sox, a racially mixed team made up of past and present PJC players and sponsored by the Chicago White Sox, he helped to lead his team to victory in the California State Amateur Baseball championship. Near the end of August, in the championship game in Brookside Park, Jack scored his team's first two runs, stole four bases, started one double play, and had five assists. On this team Jack was one of three black starters, and probably the outstanding player on the field—a fact hardly lost on the major-league scouts who attended the game. At one point, the *California Eagle* called the play of the three, and their easy acceptance by the many white spectators, "the biggest argument for the participation of the Negro in major league baseball."

But even as this mixed team advanced smoothly, a harsher spirit prevailed elsewhere. In a fight that would last nine years, NAACP lawyers finally took on the city over segregation at the swimming pool in Brookside Park. That year, a superior court judge, setting aside arguments by the city that "swimming offered the opportunity of certain intimacies like marriage and that the races should be separated," placed the NAACP petition on the court calendar. The legal battle was joined. (Later that year, a court ruled against the plaintiffs, but on the basis of a legal technicality. When the plaintiffs appealed and, years later, won their case, the city closed the pools to everyone.) This legal battle was of more than passing interest to Jack. Either at this point, or after some other protest about the city pool, Mack and all other recently hired black workers were fired in revenge by the city manager. The summer of 1939 also saw the founding of the Pasadena Improvement Association. On July 1, the association, endorsed by every important business and real-estate organization in Pasadena, was incorporated. Its explicit goal was to restrict the "use and occupancy of property" in the city of Pasadena "to members of the White or Caucasian Race only."

As racial discrimination in Pasadena took this nasty turn, Jack himself became caught up in yet another dangerous episode involving the city police. On September 5, he was in his aging Plymouth, coming home from a softball game in Brookside Park, with Ray Bartlett and other friends riding playfully on the running boards, when he pulled up at the corner of Mountain Street and Fair Oaks Avenue. Although Jack would tell the story somewhat differently, Bartlett remembered clearly that a car driven by a white man came up alongside, "and the man said something about 'niggers' to us, and I popped him with my glove, slapped him in his face." When the man shot his car forward and pulled over, Jack pulled up behind him. "I thought me and this guy were going to have a fight," Bartlett recalled. "But Jack got right in the middle of it, as usual." Out of nowhere, according to Jack, a crowd of young blacks quickly gathered. When the white man saw the youths, "he turned pale and backed away, saying that he didn't want to fight or even start anything in this neighborhood."

Just then, a motorcycle policeman, John C. Hall, pulled up. By this time the crowd had grown, according to a police report, to "between 40 and 50 members of the Negro race." Scared not so much of the police but of his strict mother, Bartlett decided to slip away. "So I withdrew," he recalled. "But not Jack. He just wouldn't back down. He was just stubborn." When Officer Hall tried to make arrests, his "suspects" kept melting away into the crowd. Suddenly he drew his gun on Robinson, who alone refused to run or hide. "I found myself up against the side of my car," he said later, "with a gun-barrel pressed unsteadily into the pit of my stomach. I was scared to death."

Charged with hindering traffic and resisting arrest, Robinson was hauled off to jail, where he spent the night without being allowed to make phone calls. Finally he was able to reach John Thurman, his old PJC baseball coach. The next morning, before an acting police court judge, he pleaded not guilty to both charges. His case was set for September 19. After paying bond in the amount of twenty-five dollars, he was set free.

The charges took on added seriousness because of the suspended ten-day jail sentence hanging over Jack's head since January 1938 on condition of good behavior for two years. Most likely, he would have to appear before the same judge who had sentenced him the previous year.

At UCLA and within the Pasadena court system, Babe Horrell and other Bruin loyalists swung into action; Robinson had to be saved for UCLA. Someone described in the press only as "an attorney prominent in sports circles in the state" sent a petition to "city officials" urging that Robinson be allowed to forfeit bail, enter a plea of guilty, and depend on the mercy of the court. On October 18, the case was finally heard. Jack, who understood it was to be continued, was absent. On his behalf, one of his friends ("another Negro youth of about his age") so informed the court, which proceeded to settle the matter. Judge Herbert Farrell of Alhambra, filling in for the police court judge, Kenneth C. Newell, who had sentenced Robinson in 1938, accepted the advice of the prosecutor and allowed a change of plea from not guilty to guilty, along with the forfeit of Jack's bail. Asked by a puzzled reporter about the suspended sentence, the prosecutor ventured the opinion that "the police court had no right to suspend a sentence for longer than six months." Without comment, the *Star-News* revealed that the deciding factor had been the prominent sports attorney's request "that the Negro football player be not disturbed during the football season."

Jack understood what had happened: "I got out of that trouble because I was an athlete." He remembered being fined fifty dollars in absentia and that UCLA paid the fine; he also recalled that he got back his forfeited bail of twenty-five dollars, presumably from UCLA. "I understand, and was told as fact," Ray Bartlett recalled fifty-six years later, after a career in the Pasadena police force, "that Babe Horrell got ahold of Kenny Newell, the judge, and told him what the situation was, and Kenny Newell handled it from there." But the change of plea, offered without his knowledge, rankled Jack. Also disturbing to him was the vivid reaction of the press: "Didn't the newspapers come out with a big blast and paint it up pretty, though!" As a result of this bad publicity, Jack recalled, his first few weeks as a full-time student at UCLA were uncomfortable; the suggestion that he was a sort of thug persisted for a long time: "This thing followed me all over and it was pretty hard to shake off."

Later, Jack would call this episode "my first personal experience with bigotry of the meanest sort." Blocking traffic and resisting arrest were not the worst charges that could be leveled at a young man, but to him they stemmed from a white policeman's hostility to blacks—not to mention a white motorist's casual contempt for young black men having fun. Some press accounts treated the matter humorously, but Jack did not laugh. These accounts exploited the stereotype of the lawless, shiftless black buck, which further offended and hurt him. Finally, he knew that he was lucky to have had powerful whites willing to speak up for him—or lucky to have physical gifts that these whites prized. With that sad knowledge he registered for classes at UCLA.

UCLA WAS YOUNGER THAN Jack himself. In 1919, the University of California, Southern Branch, had opened on Vernon Avenue as a two-year school; its four-year program started only in 1924. In 1926, the permanent campus in Westwood was dedicated on land that once was home to the Shoshone Indians and still possessed much of its pristine beauty. Wild chaparral covered the hills, sycamores and live oaks gave shelter in its leafy canyons to timid black-tailed deer and jackrabbits, and a charming stream flowed through from Stone Canyon on its way to the Pacific Ocean. The next year, the school changed its name to the University of California at Los Angeles. UCLA had then expanded at an amazing rate, but in 1939 the campus consisted mainly of five handsome, commodious buildings set amidst rolling fields. Workmen paved the first parking lot at the university in 1940.

In 1939, the student body stood at about ninety-six hundred, almost all of them undergraduates. "There were really two UCLAs," Hank Shatford, the PJC sportswriter who also enrolled there in 1939, recalled. "The bigger UCLA was a commuter school, with kids living all over the greater Los Angeles area. Then there was the other UCLA, much smaller, made up of students like myself who lived in Westwood and could take part in the evening life. For us, it was really wonderful." As a commuter, Jack belonged to the first UCLA; as a "colored" student, he also belonged to a third UCLA, inhabited by a handful of black students, perhaps no more than fifty in all, as well as a group of Asian-American students, who were hardly more welcome than the Negroes.

Although racial barriers were unknown officially at UCLA, a small wave of self-examination that fall in the pages of the *Bruin* exposed some injustices. Behind this self-scrutiny were an enlightened *Bruin* editor, the University Religious Conference, and the respected president of the University Negro Club, Tom Bradley, a Bruin track star in the half-mile and a future mayor of Los Angeles. A Japanese-American student complained that students like him despaired of ever being included in the social life of the campus. Jewish students also knew a degree of ostracism; Shatford remembered friends in Pasadena taunting him about going to "JewCLA." As usual, blacks had it the hardest. They could not live in the village of Westwood; they also were not expected at any "socials," or student parties, except those put on by the black club, the Sphinx; and certain jobs, such as work in the campus bookstore, were also denied them. No black had ever been admitted to the advanced course in military training at UCLA. And there was no black professor or instructor at the university, as the *Bruin* itself noted.

Still, in comparison to many other places UCLA was a friendly place for the black student, and the gifted black athlete was welcome. Eager for fame, the university placed a premium on athletics; but in several sports UCLA was the doormat of its conference, which included USC, Stanford, and Oregon as well as its parent institution, the University of California in Berkeley. Out of zeal to close this gap, but also because the young university was on the whole more democratic, UCLA reached out to black athletes when other universities turned their backs on them. "UCLA was the first school to really give the Negro athlete a break," according to Ray Bartlett, who also enrolled in 1939. "In the 1930s, the minority population was all pro-UCLA."

Going out for football, Jack joined a UCLA squad coming off its most successful year ever, having played in its first postseason bowl game. On that team, and returning for the last season of his glorious four-year Bruin career, was the most beloved player in the school's history, the halfback Kenny Washington. A Los Angeles native, Washington would become the first UCLA all-American. Another black star was the tall receiver Woody Strode, whose magnificent, statuesque body (he competed also in the shot put and discus events) would eventually take him into the movies. The heralded Robinson became the third member of what the press quickly dubbed the "Gold Dust Trio." Under a large photograph of Jack filling out his registration forms aided by two assistant coaches, the *Bruin* spelled out his promise: "Pasadena and Westwood faithfuls pin great hopes on Jackie and predict great things of his passing and elusive running that have made him the greatest open field runner in junior college circles."

On the night of Friday, September 29, before about sixty-five thousand spectators in the Los Angeles Coliseum, the major stadium of the 1932 Olympics and UCLA's home field, the Bruins took the field to open the season. Their opponent, the all-white Texas Christian University, was expected to win; the TCU Frogs were the top-ranked team in the nation in 1938. But UCLA prevailed, 6–2. The Texas players freely admitted that Washington and Robinson were something else. "We've never run into anything like them," the TCU center conceded, "and I hope never [to] again."

The next week, the Bruins scored another upset, defeating the University of Washington, 14–7, in Seattle; this time also Jackie Robinson, as the press was now calling him, lived up to his star billing. Down by seven points in the third quarter, the Bruins rallied behind Jack's magnificent 65-yard punt return to the Huskies' 5-yard line, which one dazzled reporter called "the prettiest piece of open field running ever witnessed on a football field." According to the *Bruin,* the Washington players "were unanimous in their statements that Robinson is the greatest thing they have ever seen. He twisted, squirmed, refused to be stopped." The Washington fans, too, showed their admiration, and their own class. When Robinson, battered and bruised, limped from the field at the start of the fourth quarter, "the fans rose as a man and gave him a greater ovation than any Washington man received that day."

Robinson's fighting spirit surged again the following week in Palo Alto against Stanford and its great quarterback Frankie Albert. Jack's brilliant 52-yard run had led to the sole Bruin touchdown; with only six minutes left, UCLA faced almost certain defeat after Albert's second touchdown pass of the game. "Three thousand Bruin rooters gave up the ghost right then," one reporter noted, "but Mr. Jack Robinson was there, and Mr. Jack Robinson saved the day." When Albert rashly tried another pass, "Jackrabbit Jack jumped fully three feet off the ground, grabbed the ball and hot-streaked it 50 yards upfield to the Red 20." Robinson made "a phenomenal catch of a rifle toss" by Washington, and then the Bruins scored with a plunge over the goal line. On the extra-point try, the hike was poor and the ball sailed high before the holder brought it down; but

Robinson, "never lifting his eyes, booted it through the uprights." The game ended in a tie, but for UCLA it was the same as a victory.

Against Montana, Jack did not carry the ball once. Coach Horrell's strategy was to use him as a decoy to set up passes or slashing runs by Kenny Washington and another gifted back, Leo Cantor. This time the strategy worked; Washington scored all three touchdowns in UCLA's victory. One moment of glory for "Jackrabbit Jackie Robinson—El Bruin's greatest threat"—came with a 33-yard punt return. The next week, Robinson dominated in a win at home over powerful Oregon. In a play that covered 66 yards, he caught a pass from Washington, then humiliated two defenders: "Mr. Robinson took the ball on the Oregon 23, sent [the defenders] flying on their faces with a series of hip-jiggling feints, and trotted over for the touchdown." On another run, Robinson "swung wide around left end, then cut inside the end—and broke wide again for the side-lines. This time he didn't do any feinting—no tricky work—just speed, blinding speed that left a flock of Webfoots in his wake."

Now Jack was being hailed locally as "the great-est ball-carrier in the nation." Even more remarkably, this praise came when, with Coach Horrell's decoy system, he had carried the ball only ten times in the five Bruin games. Jack had lived up to all expecta-tions. Thus, on November 1, when he was knocked down in a Bruin practice and lay motionless on the grass, his coaches saw their season's hopes in sudden jeopardy: "Bruin stock went all the way up and down the fluctuation scale," as one sportswriter put it. The team doctor determined that "the boy who has brought the Bruins out of hot water in every major game this year had turned his right knee."

Jack missed the next two games. Then, used sparingly against Oregon State, he stirred the crowd with one of his specialties, a reverse around left end, for 31 yards. Next, against the Cougars of Washington State, Robinson was back at full speed. With the game tied in the fourth quarter, Robinson caught a pass, "snaked his way down the sidelines and then into the center of the field, evading four Cougars on the way and going over for the touchdown standing up." He sparked another touchdown drive with dramatic runs of 29 yards and 32 yards; cleverly, "Jackie was well past the scrimmage line before the harassed Cougars woke up to the fact that he had the ball."

UCLA was undefeated (but with two ties) when they played their final game of the season, against USC, for the Pacific Coast Conference championship and a place in the Rose Bowl. The record crowd of 103,352—said then to be the largest crowd ever at a football game—witnessed an epic struggle in the Coliseum that ended in a scoreless tie. At one point, USC seemed certain to score. Its all-American Grenny Lansdell raced "past our secondary before we knew what happened," a Bruin recalled. "Then suddenly Jackie Robinson came flying out of the corner." Robinson hit Lansdell so hard that the Trojan fumbled away the ball for the first time that season. The teams ended the season tied for first place—but USC, with fewer ties, went to the Rose Bowl.

Playing in a system that limited his use as a running back, Robinson had managed to compile some amazing statistics. Kenny Washington had carried the ball 141 times for an average run of 5.23 yards; on only 40 carries, Robinson had averaged an astonishing 11.4 yards. Had Robinson not missed two games, UCLA almost certainly would have gone to the Rose Bowl. But despite their success on the field, both Washington and Robinson were slighted in postseason honors. Jack was only a junior; but Washington, a senior commonly regarded as the finest football player in Bruin history, was left off many all-American teams. He was also not included in the nationally prestigious annual East-West benefit game for the Shrine Hospital for Crippled Children on January 1 in San Francisco; no black player had ever been invited to the event.

Among a few teammates, Jack's success inspired some resentment. After the *Bruin* published a story by Hank Shatford entitled "Jack Robinson—Better than Grange" ("his open field running has been likened to that of Red Grange and nearly every other historic ball carrier"), a white football player confronted the writer. " 'White man, you're a black man,' he told me," Shatford recalled. "I said, 'I don't care what you say. What I wrote in the column is truth.' " A few days later, Jack sustained his knee injury in practice. To Shatford, the injury was no accident. Robinson had clearly pulled up at the end of a play when "this guy came over and hit Jack on the side. He hit him on the leg, just dove in with his shoulder pads. He did it on purpose, no question in my mind. I knew the guy well. The coaches were furious. There were some players on that team who weren't fans of Jack Robinson."

Throughout the fall, despite his success, Jack remained sensitive about his arrest and its effect on his reputation. Rumors spread about his alleged bad behavior. In one story, he and Kenny Washington had a fistfight in an alley, in a clash of titanic egos, or two black bucks. The story had no foundation; Washington was sweet and easygoing, and Robinson joked that he was too smart to pick a fight with a man of Washington's size and strength. At least twice that fall Robinson lauded "the Kingfish" or "King" Washington to reporters. In the *Eagle,* he asserted that "Kenny is a really great player and if the rest of us in the backfield give him 100 per cent support he's going to get the honors he deserves." And in the *Bruin,* he praised Washington as "the greatest athlete he has seen." Still the rumors persisted—not simply about Robinson and Washington, but about Robinson in particular.

Woody Strode, who left UCLA that year, remembered Robinson as somewhat unhappy at UCLA. "Jackie was a very intelligent and good-looking young man," Strode wrote, who had "steely hard eyes that would flash angry in a heartbeat." Jack was "not friendly" and seemed "very withdrawn. Even on the football field, he would stand off by himself. People used to ask me, 'Why is Jackie so sullen and always by himself?' " A proper answer would have had something to do not only with his arrest but also with his brother Frank's tragic death. In addition, the fact that Jack did not drink liquor or chase women, and was religious, made him an oddball to many men. Among the bevy of young black women in Westwood, he saw no one he really cared for; and at UCLA, as at PJC, he was cool to the friendly overtures of white coeds.

Despite Strode's observations, other students saw him as well adjusted to Westwood. As a reporter traveling with the Bruins, Hank Shatford sometimes roomed with Jack on the road and found him affable: "It was a real treat to be with him, to be in the same room with him, to talk about the game and one thing or another. At PJC and at UCLA he was very popular. Gee, all my crowd thought the world of Jack. I never heard a nasty word from my friends about him." Several people tried to make life easier for the handsome, likable football star. UCLA offered no formal athletic scholarships, but friends or "boosters" of the football team and other teams found ways of helping players meet their expenses and have a little extra money to spend. For example, Jack now commuted to and from Pasadena not in his aged Plymouth but in a Model A Ford of more recent vintage that somehow he had managed to acquire. Later, such arrangements would have come under the scrutiny of the governing body of collegiate sports; but in 1939, young UCLA was only doing what older schools had been doing for years.

He held at least two part-time jobs that year. Along with other varsity athletes, he worked as an assistant janitor in Kerckhoff Hall, the center of student activities at UCLA. Jack's other main job was at

Campbell's Book Store, which specialized in used textbooks, on Leconte Avenue in Westwood. Its owners, Robert and Blanche Campbell, were transplanted Nebraskans who had become major boosters of Bruin athletics by hiring Bruin athletes, including blacks, at their store. The future Nobel Peace Prize–winner Ralph Bunche had worked at Campbell's when he was a star basketball player on three championship teams before graduating summa cum laude in 1927; Kenny Washington and Tom Bradley also worked there. The Campbells had even helped to scout Robinson in Pasadena for UCLA.

To the Campbells, Robinson was a dependable, charming young man. He "was always eager to cooperate," according to Bob Campbell. Before the season was over, Jack and the Campbells were good friends; the couple helped provide a bridge to the adult white world of Westwood and beyond. Ray Bartlett believed that the Campbells had arranged for Jack to get his Model A Ford ("They had loaned me twenty-five dollars, interest-free and without security, to help me buy mine, and when I paid them back, they were shocked"). At the annual Bruin football banquet in the spring, which Jack's mother attended, she sat with the Campbells at their invitation.

Other people, including various coaches and administrators, obviously liked and respected Jack; they would still be enough in his life seven years later to attend his wedding, just as Bob Campbell, more than thirty years later, would fly overnight from Los Angeles to New York in 1972 to attend the funeral of his former young employee. By the end of the fall of 1939, Jack's intense grieving for his brother Frank and his outrage at his treatment by the Pasadena police had begun to subside. Not only his success on the football field but also his mother's lessons about striving onward and upward, in addition to his religious faith, especially as stimulated at Scott United Methodist Church by Reverend Karl Downs, had seen him through.

ROBINSON'S RESOLVE TO compete only in football and the broad jump did not last long. He was now much less interested in the broad jump. His dream of going to Helsinki for the 1940 Olympiad had ended on November 30, when the Soviet Union invaded Finland as the war in Europe started by Nazi Germany raged on. The 1940 Olympic Games were canceled. Moreover, the Bruin basketball coach, Wilbur Johns, badly needed help: coming into the season, the Bruins had lost twenty-eight consecutive conference games. Johns had seen Robinson lead PJC to an amazing upset of the USC freshmen. "When the Headman saw Robinson almost single-handedly cause the defeat of S.C.'s terrific frosh five," the *Bruin* noted, "he was sold on the boy."

Although Johns admired Robinson, coach and player soon clashed. Johns's system of play, patient and stationary, was ill suited to Jack's physical gifts. Early in January, after UCLA struggled in two games, the *Bruin* noted tartly: "Jack Robinson, who is nothing more than a wasted robot in a set-up offense, knows the game and would really utilize his speed and deceptiveness in a fast break." Perhaps Jack himself had whispered this criticism to the *Bruin;* at some point he challenged Johns by skipping practice. According to Bob Campbell, Johns thought Jack "a very willing worker" who was "trying to do too much." Summoning Robinson to his office, Johns laid down the law. Thereafter, the two worked well together, and Robinson would later praise Johns as one of his best coaches ever. "He encouraged me a lot," Jack recalled, "and praised me when I needed it most."

In mid-January, conference play started with a two-game visit to Palo Alto to play Stanford; the result was two losses but an improving Bruin team, which now sported a fast-breaking style. "Easily the best man on the floor," Jack scored 23 of his team's 28 points in the first game and 12 of the Bruins' 36 in the second. Soon, the Bruins ended a 31-game losing streak at Berkeley. As the season progressed, Robinson became locked in battle with Ralph Vaughn of USC, hailed by *Life* magazine as the best player in the country, for the individual scoring title in the nation. In another game against UC-Berkeley, according to one reporter, Jack turned in "the best individual performance ever seen in the Bruin gym." Above all, his style fascinated watchers, as he eschewed static play in favor of dazzling drives to the basket for layups. Reporters marveled at his unusual blend of speed, sinuous body control, and deception. "On one series of individual maneuvers," one puzzled writer noted, "Jack tried no less than three series of feints to get a set-up." Nibs Price, the Berkeley coach, offered his opinion: "Robinson has more natural talent, speed, and spring than any man in the conference, including Ralph Vaughn. Furthermore, if he had played the amount of basketball that Vaughn has, Robinson would probably outscore the S.C. forward twofold." (Price then proceeded to leave Robinson off his all-conference team. Admitting "the speed and shooting ability of the Bruin Negro," and conceding that "Robinson is a great natural athlete," he chose another player in his place on the basis of "basketball ability alone.")

Jack ended the season with 148 points to Vaughn's 138, but he was clearly far more concerned with what the Bruins accomplished as a team in their finest season in many years. Late in the season, at home against Stanford, with the crowd yelling at Jack to shoot, shoot, he had patiently frozen the ball and sacrificed points for himself in order to prevent a Stanford rally. "Schools cannot teach that type of sportsmanship from a textbook," Wilbur Johns would declare. "I wonder if we can teach it at all."

On March 10, with very little practice, Jack joined Ray Bartlett and the other players for his first baseball game at UCLA. His debut was a triumph. "The phenomenal Negro athlete made a terrific impression on the fans," a reporter wrote. At shortstop, Jack was flawless; at the plate, he got four straight hits; and he stole four bases, including what the reporter called "a sensational steal of home." The reporter summed up Robinson's start: "The amazing rapidity with which he got his batting and fielding eye speaks well enough for his ability as a base-baller."

Unfortunately, this turned out to be the high point of Jack's season. Two days later, Bruin baseball descended into farce, with Jack in a leading role. On the brink of a defeat, and with an icy gale blowing and the sun sinking fast, he came in to pitch against visiting Berkeley. "I can't see the plate!" Robinson screamed to the umpire, as he fastidiously threw wild pitches while the irate Bear players howled in protest. The ploy worked; the game was called, and defeat averted. But the gods had their revenge: Jack sank into what seemed to one observer "a permanent batting slump" (even as Ray Bartlett emerged as the leading Bruin batter). Once, the *Bruin* even referred to a certain weak team's hitting as "colder than Jackie Robinson's batting average." But his fielding remained steady, and his intrepid base running helped the Bruins win more than once. Against USC in April he broke up a double play so decisively that a fight almost broke out; an admirer called it "the kind of a behind-the-scenes play that you don't hear about now, but means plenty at the time." More often than not, however, UCLA went down to defeat. On May 1, the season ended with a loss to USC, in what the *Bruin* called "a long, sad afternoon" for the hapless team. When the season ended, Jack had a dismal average of .097. With a teammate, he shared the lead for the most errors committed by a Bruin.

In February, Jack had let it be known that he would not go out for the track team. But in April, as baseball ended, he teased his fans by filing an application to take part in a triangular track meet. He did not participate; then, casually, he jumped 23 feet 4 inches in practice. The Bruin coach was impressed, but cited Jack's lack of commitment in leaving him off the UCLA team to the important Fresno Relays in May. Two weeks before the Pacific Coast Conference championships near the end of May, he announced that Robinson would be allowed to compete "provided he met the regular training schedule." Forced into a jump-off against three Bruin regulars, Jack won a spot. At the championships in the Coliseum, he then soared to a new conference record of 25 feet (only one American jumped farther that year). In June, jumping indoors because of rain in Minneapolis, Minnesota, he won the NCAA title.

Jack now became the first UCLA student ever to letter in four sports in the same season. (Some would call him the second; in 1923–1924, when the school was known as the University of California, Southern Division, Burnett "Cap" Haralson lettered in the same four sports.) A banner headline in the *Bruin,* "'I Do Not Choose To Run!'—Jackie Robinson," proposed Robinson for the Presidency of the United States. The story, based on a mock interview of Robinson by Lenny Safir, the droll satirist at the *Bruin* (and the brother of William Safire), sent Robinson up as Superman, whose gifts knew no limits.

JACK ENDED THE SCHOOL YEAR solidly installed as a student. At a time when a C average was more than enough for graduation, in his first semester he earned C's in courses in education, geology, and history (two courses); in the second semester, he earned C's in two more history courses, in Spanish, and in military science. He earned two A's that year, in physical education.

Relaxed and reassured, he enjoyed the summer of 1940. On weekends he played golf and tennis, but he also made some money. Probably through Bill Ackerman, the powerful graduate manager at UCLA who had overseen his recruitment in 1938, he found a lucrative job in the property department at the Warner Bros. film studio. For the first time in some years, he played neither baseball nor softball in Brookside Park. Perhaps he was eager to rest after nine months of physical stress; perhaps he was bored by his old Pasadena routines.

Toward the end of August, he returned to the UCLA campus in eager anticipation of the fall football season. He was back barely a month or so when he found himself falling in love with a seventeen-year-old freshman from Los Angeles, Rachel Isum.

Jack had seen her first in the milling cluster of brown students in their chosen corner of Kerckhoff Hall, and now and then in the parking lot on sun-drenched mornings when she drove in from West Los Angeles with her carpool of girlfriends in her old Ford V-8. Five feet five inches tall, she somehow seemed even taller; her face was brown, with rounded cheeks, her hair long and worn usually in carefully massed curls. Her smile was open and friendly, but she was studious; he often saw her poring over her books on a bench in the sunlight. For a while, Jack admired her from afar but did nothing about his feelings. For one thing, he was still going with the tall Pasadena beauty Bessie Renfro. Finally he confided his interest to Ray Bartlett, who had never met Rachel but needed no formal introduction to any young woman. "He talked about this girl and how nice she seemed," Bartlett recalled. "And so one day I said, 'Haven't you met her yet? . . . No? Well, come on! You'd better meet her before classes really get going and she disappears.' And I introduced him to her."

Rachel Annetta Isum, just past seventeen and a June graduate of Manual Arts High School in Los Angeles, lived at home with her parents and a younger brother, Raymond, at 1588 36th Place; sometimes an older half-brother, Charles Williams, also stayed there. In many respects, her parents were unusual. Her father, Charles Raymond Isum, a second-generation black Californian, had been a bookbinder with the Los Angeles *Times* for more than twenty years. A former sergeant in the U.S. Infantry, he had retired from the *Times* with a severe heart condition brought on after he was gassed by the Germans in France in November 1918. After his retirement, his wife, Rachel's mother, had been forced to find work for herself. Now Zellee Isum was a self-employed caterer, with clients in Beverly Hills and Hollywood; on Saturdays she also worked in the huge employees' cafeteria downtown at the Los Angeles Public Library.

Both parents were children of the West and the Southwest. Zellee's father, C. T. Jones, had come from Atlanta; her mother, Annetta Garza Jones, was from Houston. They had lived as pioneering entre- preneurs in the Southwest, where Zellee grew up; at one point, C. T. Jones had apparently owned the largest café, a pool hall, and a theater on the main street of Nogales, on the Mexican border, as well as many acres of land thought to be rich in silver. Zellee had grown up well-to-do in Arizona and, for a while, Mexico; she spoke Spanish fluently. For two years she had studied at Tuskegee Institute in Alabama. Then the family businesses began to fail. About this time, Zellee eloped with a man who turned out to be worthless, except for the birth of her first child, Charles Williams. After C.T.'s death, his widow, Annetta, moved to Los Angeles to be near her daugh- ter and her new family.

Rachel's charm and drive had everything to do with the way her parents had brought her up. "My father was sick for a long time," she recalled. "He could do very little without being exhausted, which was hard on a man who had been a sportsman, gre- garious, really popular. He was often near death. But he was tender and loving, and seemed to favor me over my brothers." Her mother, too, loved her, but set lofty goals and strict standards for her daughter. In preparing for her career as a caterer, she asked Rachel to assume many tasks in the house, including cleaning, cooking, and shopping. "My mother wanted a lot from me, but she also gave me a lot," Rachel said. "She had impeccable manners, and when she spoke she was articulate and very careful about what she said; she was proper, always proper, and she expected the same of me." Rachel learned about the importance of personal grooming, from meticulous coiffure to garments that aspired to elegance rather than flash. In addition, she had to be self-sufficient. Her first job outside the home was at the public library, where her mother provided food. "By the time I was ten," Rachel said, "they had me in a black uniform with a little white organdy apron. I got fifty cents every time I helped. I liked helping, but I also loved the fifty cents. I think that was the whole point."

At home, she washed and scrubbed and polished to meet the meticulous standards set by her mother. Zellee also assigned her the task of taking care of both her younger brother and her father, so that drudgery and love came together, arm in arm. An electric bell alerted her when her father, who had his own bedroom, was in trouble: "He needed me so much that I felt I was like his guardian angel. I watched him and watched over him all the time." At times she felt oppressed, but she seldom rebelled. She and her mother became close. Zellee loved to cook, and she taught Rachel her secrets. They also loved music, both at home, where Rachel had her upright piano and the treasured violin someone had sold to her mother's father as a Stradivarius (it was not), and at Saturday concerts of the Los Angeles Philharmonic. Once, gloriously, they heard there the contralto voice of Marian Anderson.

As Rachel became a woman, her mother had watched her vigilantly, and especially when boys were around. "She had nothing to worry about with me," Rachel later insisted, "but she worried. I had a boyfriend named Eddie, tall and sweet, who arranged his classes so he could walk me to school and come home from school with me. We would talk on the phone for hours or sit on my steps. My mother watched from all sorts of doors and windows. But I gave her nothing to worry about. I let Eddie kiss me only when he had met my two terms: I had to be six-teen, and he had to join my church. I was sixteen, and he joined Bethel AME on 35th Street, so I let him kiss me. That's what I was like in those days!"

Rachel also had the residue of a nagging adoles-cent unhappiness about her body. She had been too tall; towering over boys in elementary school, she had felt unfeminine. Her cheeks were too round, not hollow like those of the reigning beauties. Her breasts were too large too soon, so that she walked on campus with her books pressed against them. Her hair was too thick, too stiff: "All my sorrows were there in my hair, the endless trouble and grief"—the hot straightening comb, the burns. Her skin was too brown, according to the perverse color-and-caste thinking of the day: she was darker than her mother, who was darker than *her* mother. Once, the mother of a pale-skinned boy down the block almost closed her front door on Rachel, who never went there again. Also hard had been her mother's insistence that Rachel play the violin in public as a small child. "Encouraging me to appreciate and love music and to play, that was fine. But making me perform at six and seven, before I was ready—that was traumatic. I was a very shy child. Still, I was happy and loved, and self-confident in many ways."

Rachel, more winsome now than shy, knew who Jack Robinson was; in high school, she had seen him play football. She had thought him conceited then, because he stood in the backfield with his hands on his hips, all too nonchalant in awaiting the violence at hand; then she found out that this was only a style and had little to do with his character. She never forgot their first meeting, and Ray Bartlett introducing her to Jack. "I remember the awkwardness of the moment. What I liked about Jack was his smile, and a kind of confident air he had about him, without being cocky in person." She also noticed then that Robinson wore white shirts almost exclusively. A snow-white shirt against a sable skin: "I thought to myself, Now why would he do that? Why would anybody that dark wear a white shirt? It's terrible!" But Jack seemed not to care. "He wore his color with such dignity and pride and confidence that after a little while I didn't even think about it. He wouldn't let me. He was never, ever, ashamed of his color."

Soon Jack and Rachel were seeing each other every day. "I was the aggressor, no doubt about it," Rachel confessed. "I would sit in my car and wait for him to drive into the parking lot. He was always running late, but I would wait. I would find a dozen excuses for walking through Kerckhoff Hall to see if he was pushing his mop." Then they would sit and talk and learn about one another. The differences were clear. "Intense" about her studies and accustomed to excellence, Rachel would have tried for medical school (following a cousin in Texas, who was herself a doctor) if Zellee had not counseled a career in nursing, the easier for Rachel to marry and start a family. Now she was enrolled in the five-year Bachelor of Science degree course in nursing at the university. Jack confided to her that he wanted to be a coach, which seemed reasonable enough. To Rachel, he seemed to have no interest in his studies: "I even thought he was being coached by faculty to get through his courses. His mind was very much on athletics. I could see he was intelligent, but I never thought of him as a student at all."

Rachel brought Jack home to the house on 36th Place, where he found a detached frame bungalow that her father had bought years before. A devoted gardener, he had planted so many roses, camellias, dahlias, and hydrangea bushes that the house stood out in the neighborhood. Jack immediately won Zellee over; she saw him from the start as a gentle person, a gentleman, serious and religious, as well as handsome. "He was Zellee's dream guy from the start," according to Rachel. "She was far more sure about him than I was." But her father was not smitten with Jack. As with all of Rachel's boyfriends, "my father was jealous of Jack, tremendously jealous. What was this big star athlete doing with his little daughter, just a freshman? He sulked and rumbled. He took it hard. But my mother never budged, and my mother had the last word in our household." Jack's sister, Willa Mae, declared: "Rachel's father didn't like Jack because he was too black—and Jack understood that very well." But Willa Mae never met Rachel's father, who was known in the community for his race pride. "Jack's color would not have been an issue for him," Rachel insisted. In any event, her father's hostility had little or no effect on the way Jack felt about Rachel.

In turn, Jack took Rachel home to Pepper Street. She would remember a rocking chair on the porch, crochet doilies on the upholstered furniture, and lots of family photographs on the walls. The house was simply furnished but clean and neat. The Robinsons were all friendly. Edgar was sweet, but he was also strange, with his averted glances and halting speech. Mack's infant son, Phillip, was sadly retarded. What was wrong here? On the other hand, she liked Mack and Willa Mae, who seemed perfectly fine. Most important of all, Jack's mother, Mallie, was a woman one had to respect and like. "Mallie was very gracious and kind to me," Rachel would say, "and right from the beginning I could tell that there was no competition or conflict with her. She thought of me the way my mother thought of Jack: Here's a girl in the church, she doesn't drink or smoke, a good student, going into nursing, no other boyfriends. Everything that she would have wanted for Jack—that was me. And I could relate to her very well, in her own struggle, what she had gone through just to be there."

For their first date, Jack sealed his romance with Rachel in October when he invited her, not Bessie Renfro, to the homecoming dance on November 2 at the premier hotel in Los Angeles, the Biltmore. Nervous and excited, Rachel bought a stunning black dress and a chic matching black hat with fox trim; escorted by Jack in his one suit, she set out for the Biltmore wrapped in the black broadtail fur coat that was her grandmother's pride. Both because they were black and because of Jack's fame, they found them- selves the focus of some attention; but they also felt a tension that had everything to do with their awareness of each other's bodies, still unknown. "The evening was fun but never completely comfortable," Rachel said. "It was stilted. Jack was a little awkward, I was confused." She was a very good dancer; less adept, he was unwilling to venture beyond a two-step even for a waltz. Still, they tried to relax to the orchestral strains of Hoagy Carmichael's "Star Dust" and Duke Ellington's "Mood Indigo" and all the other haunting tunes that young people danced to in the peaceful autumn of 1940 in America.

When Jack and Rachel returned to her home, he said goodbye quickly. "I was excited and happy and full of anticipation, wondering on the ride home whether he would kiss me," she remembered. "I wanted him to; I really wanted him to kiss me. He pecked me on the cheek. That was all. I was disap- pointed." Their deepening feeling for one another was shot through with a bracing sense of propriety. For both, a sexual relationship at this point was out of the question. Scrupulous and shrewd, Rachel would never have consented; the almost equally self- disciplined Jack had no desire to press hard, if he pressed at all. Undoubtedly he was already thinking of her as possibly his future wife, and accordingly had placed her on a pedestal, the better to worship her. So much was uncertain about their lives, even as they grew more certain of their love for one another. Jack and Rachel would know one another, and be committed to one another, for more than five years before they finally consummated their romance, and they would do so only within a week or so of their wedding day.

AT UCLA, THE 1940 football season opened on a note of high expectation, with Robinson at its center. His "colossalness," the *Bruin* enthused, "is almost universal knowledge among football fans all over the country"; he was "beyond doubt the Coast's No. 1 candidate for all-American honors." His sensational running behind the new UCLA line would make the Bruins "the greatest drawing card in the nation."

Nevertheless, the season turned out to be a disaster for the Bruins even as Jack shone as an individual. In the opener against Southern Methodist University, UCLA suffered a narrow loss; its sole touchdown came when Robinson gathered in a punt on his own 13-yard line, raced straight ahead, swerved dramatically left, "and went all the way by himself as the Mustangs stood petrified." The only Bruin win (against nine losses) came in mid-November against Washington State in "a wild and woolly, free-scoring orgy" in which Robinson turned in "one of the most amazing performances ever witnessed in the Coliseum." Passing for one touchdown, he ran 60 dazzling yards for another, then sealed the victory with a 75-yard ramble to score in the final minutes.

For the season, Jack finished second in the conference in total offense. His running average dropped
from the heights of the previous year to only 3.64
yards per carry, but he averaged 21 yards on his punt
returns, when he was most free to improvise, to set a
national record. He was also the third leading passer
in California football. However, with the Associated
Press calling UCLA the biggest disappointment of
the season, he earned only honorable mention as an
all-American.

At this point, with his football eligibility used up,
Robinson was surely tempted to walk away from
UCLA. As a student, he was now in sharp decline.
He would earn an A, a C, and a D in three courses in
physical education. He would earn a C in geology
but end with a D in history and an E in military science. He was starting to fall behind.

One reason for him to stay was Rachel's presence, although they had gone on no dates after the
event at the Biltmore. They saw each other on campus, where they were now recognized as a pair, or
Jack visited Rachel at her home. Jack's reluctance to
arrange dates bothered Rachel a little, but she
adjusted to his quirks of personality, his mixture of
nice manners and mannish roughness, his silences,
his passionate but also self-disciplined way of being.
"A lot of it," she said, "had to do with his sense of
himself as an athlete, the idea that he couldn't abuse
his body. One thing he was always harping on: he
had to be home and asleep by midnight. His body
demanded it, his training as an athlete demanded it.
He would never lose that sense of himself as in train-

ing, or having to be in training even if he also didn't like to exercise. That idea definitely got in the way of a lot of fun!"

He decided to sign on for another basketball season with Coach Wilbur Johns, who believed that were it not for his devotion to football, Robinson might have become "the greatest of all basketball players. His timing was perfect. His rhythm was unmatched. He had the valuable faculty of being able to relax at the proper time." Above all, Jack "always placed the welfare of his team above his chance for greater stardom." His right hand injured, Jack for a while shot the ball with his left but still managed to be a scoring threat. Nevertheless, the Bruins struggled in almost every game. Jack also had to contend with constant rough play. Once again vying for the individual scoring title, he was an obvious target; in one game at Berkeley, the *Bruin* complained, he was "viciously treated." At home, however, he was a hero. Early in March, when Coach Johns took him out of the last game of the "long, weary basketball season," Robinson received a thunderous ovation that acknowledged his heroic efforts on behalf of the Bruins over the preceding two years.

Once again, with 133 points, Robinson won the individual league scoring title. Once again, however, top honors eluded him. "Robinson Fails to Make All-League Cage Team," the *Bruin* protested; "Prejudice 'Rumored' to Have Played Major Role in Selection." Placing every Stanford starter on the all-conference first team, most of the coaches relegated Robinson to the second. (But Nibs Price of California, who had lauded him the previous year, now failed to vote for Jack on the first, second, or third team. In vain, *Bruin* sports editor Hank Shatford railed against this "flagrant bit of prejudice" that "makes our blood boil. . . . It's more than a miscarriage of justice.")

Now, although he was still eligible to compete in baseball and the broad jump, Jack was ready to leave UCLA. Where he would find work was a good question. His almost matchless sports record counted little. On February 28, as the basketball season drew to a close, Shatford had reported that Robinson had received job offers from the semipro Broadway Clowns, a basketball team, and from a Mexican baseball club. Unfortunately, the offers were poor; professional sports seemed to be out of the question. No blacks, not even all-American Kenny Washington, played now in the National Football League. (Woody Strode had just made his debut as a professional wrestler.) Also all-white were the National Basketball League and other forerunners of the NBA. Major-league baseball and its farm systems were forbidden.

But despite arguments against leaving UCLA by most of his coaches and by Rachel, Mallie, and Karl Downs, Jack was determined to go. "I was aghast," Rachel recalled. "I tried to talk him out of it. He was so close to finishing. He put it all on Mallie, that he wanted to help her financially, because she was still working very hard. But I think he would have left in any case. He had had enough."

Near noon on March 3, Jack strolled into the registrar's office. There, he made arrangements that would allow him to leave the university with an "honorable dismissal," instead of dropping out casually, without an official blessing. By the end of the day, he was gone.

In the spring, at the annual Bruin football banquet, he was absent, working in a small town up the California coast, when the UCLA Alumni Association gave him its coveted yearly award for outstanding service to the university. Jack sent what an official called a "very fine letter" of thanks, which elicited "a great burst of applause" when it was read to the assembled guests. "I was indeed serious about the friends and other things I mentioned in the letter," Jack later assured the official in another letter. "It really is something to know you have friends like the ones I made while attending UCLA. I certainly hope that Friendship continues on and on."

Jack's words were stiff and artless, but sincere. So was his hope that some lasting link could be preserved between himself and his two brilliant UCLA years, when roaring crowds shouted his name and he strode the campus in glory. But even as he wrote these letters, his future had begun to seem dim, even dingy, and the memory of his sporting triumphs at the university in Westwood was fading away.

— 5 —

Jack in the World at War

1941–1944

I am a negro, but not a nigger.
—Jackie Robinson (1944)

IN APRIL, ROBINSON REPORTED to the job that had helped him decide, against all advice to the contrary, to leave UCLA. "I had offers to join professional football teams," he later recalled, but had quickly turned them down. This job paid little and lacked glamour, but it offered to train him for what he was now sure would be his life's work. "I could see no future in staying at college," he would write, "no real future in [professional] athletics, and I wanted to do the next best thing—become an athletic director. The thought of working with youngsters in the field of sports excited me."

Despite his failure to graduate, Robinson was now a far more mature and polished young man than he had been when he entered UCLA in 1939. The adulation showered on him for his amazing athletic feats had not left him vain and self-indulgent; his core moral values, learned from his mother and reinforced by Karl Downs, among others, remained firmly in place. Despite his quick temper in the face of injustice, especially racial discrimination, he lived on the whole a life of discipline, restraint, and self-denial; he thought of himself and his future in terms of moral and social obligations rather than privilege and entitlement. Jack had hardly taken full advantage of UCLA as a center of learning, but he was much more comfortable now than in the past with the world of ideas and books. Welcomed by his coaches and professors as well as by the student body as a whole, he now had an even more inclusive sense of his country and a brighter confidence in his future as a black citizen—although the maddening contradictions of American democracy were everywhere around him, clouding his sense of possibility.

On the campus of the California Polytechnic Institute in San Luis Obispo, some six hours north of Los Angeles, Robinson signed on as an employee of the National Youth Administration to work at its training camp a few miles away, at Atascadero. Founded by Presidential order as a Depression measure in 1935, the NYA sought to provide jobs, job training, and relief for young people between sixteen and twenty-five years of age. The Atascadero facility took students up to the age of eighteen, and trained about one hundred at a time. Jack was hired as an assistant athletic director, at $150 per month, to help organize sports activities for these trainees; his job was to help make sure, as he put it the following year, "that their free time was well spent."

Because he was black, his appointment was news. An NYA official offered solemnly that the agency was "fortunate, indeed, to secure the services of this outstanding athlete." This was mainly a pre-emptive response to people who would question the wisdom and propriety of putting a black man in a position over whites, even white teenagers.

Buckling down to the job, and drawing on his rich experience as an athlete, he quickly set up a number of regular events and programs, including calisthenics, for the youngsters; he also played short-stop on the camp's baseball team. But learning to supervise and interact with the youths, who came from various ethnic groups and creeds but were almost all poor and from broken homes, was the real challenge. At first, he was not very happy; he could say of his job only that it was "something that I have wanted to do but it is not quite what I would like." The sometime delinquent was now a figure of authority, and had to learn to face youngsters from that unaccustomed position. In their young lives, he wrote with sympathy, many of the youths had had it "pretty tough," and some "don't know anything about anything"; but while "most of them are really swell guys," he also faced the fact that "there is that few that you always find in a large group that is bound to cause trouble."

His concern for young people and his passion for sports saw him through; "the biggest kid of all come recreation time was yours truly, Jackie Robinson." The star athlete put on no airs: "I realized that I had been no different than many of these kids, who would make good if given half a chance." The color of his skin didn't seem to matter to the white kids, who made up most of the number. Jim Crow reared its head only once. Trying to attend a camp dance at the urging of a friendly fellow employee named Lippman Duckat, who played second base on the camp team, Robinson was politely but firmly turned away by a doorkeeper. Duckat and Robinson left quietly.

Apart from this incident, Jack "loved and appreciated" his NYA job. Then, around July, the camp began to disband. In the wake of the Nazi conquest of Belgium, the Netherlands, and France, and following the Battle of Britain, American entry into the conflict seemed more and more a certainty. The previous September, 1940, the President had signed into law the Selective Service and Training Act, which called for the registration of all men between twenty-one and thirty-five, and the drafting of eight hundred thousand recruits. The NYA was now superfluous. Nominally Jack remained an employee at the work camp until September, but by the end of July he was finished at Atascadero as the Army moved in and took over the NYA buildings.

Early in August, with no new job in sight, Jack arrived in Chicago for three weeks of football practice before playing in the nationally renowned annual charity game sponsored by the Chicago *Tribune*. The contest pitted an all-star college team against the Chicago Bears, the reigning champions of the National Football League. Although Jack had received more than seven hundred thousand votes in a *Tribune* poll to secure one of the sixty-six places on the college squad, some people undoubtedly questioned his right to be on a team with stars such as Tom Harmon of the University of Michigan, who had won the Heisman, Maxwell, and Walter Camp trophies to capture the finest collegiate honors. However, as one reporter noted, "it took one scrimmage to establish the Negro boy's rightful place among the All-Stars." Pictured as "a soft-spoken, dark-skinned kid with a flash of illuminating white teeth," the versatile Jackie Robinson was "the Jim Thorpe of his race." Jack enjoyed both the three-week camp, with all expenses paid, and the game itself, which took place on the night of August 28 before a crowd of more than ninety-eight thousand fans at venerable Soldiers Field. For three quarters, the collegians gallantly battled the Bears, before three touchdowns in the last quarter sealed Chicago's victory. From Jack's point of view, the highlight undoubtedly came when he caught a 36-yard pass from Charley O'Rourke of Boston College for a touchdown. "The only time we worried," a Chicago defensive end said, "was when that guy Robinson was on the field."

From Chicago, Tom Harmon and other stars moved to begin their lucrative NFL careers; Robinson headed home. The following month, September, when he made his professional football debut, it was a one-shot deal in a setting far inferior to the NFL. Before a crowd of about ten thousand at Gilmore Stadium in Los Angeles, Jack started for the racially mixed but mainly white Los Angeles Bulldogs against a similar team, the Hollywood Bears, which included his old Bruins teammate Kenny Washington. Jack's debut was not a success. In the second quarter, he pulled up lame; not for the last time, the right ankle he had injured in his first PJC football season in 1937 let him down. He watched the rest of the game from the sidelines. A week later, however, he accepted an offer to join the Honolulu Bears (formerly the Honolulu Polar Bears) in the semiprofessional Hawaii Senior Football League. Along with Ray Bartlett, Jack was hired by F. J. "Brick" Brickner, the Bears' team director and a former California college player himself. Brickner offered Robinson tough terms: $150 as an advance payment against his salary, a payment of $100 for each game he played, and the promise of a bonus if the Bears won the league championship (as they had done the previous year). The deal also included a construction job near Pearl Harbor. "The construction job was a very important part of the package," Bartlett recalled. "We could use the extra money, because we were both trying to help our mothers. But because the construction job involved defense, it also meant we wouldn't be drafted—at least, not yet."

Sailing on the *Matsonia* with Bartlett, Jack arrived in Hawaii a celebrity. His full-length picture adorned a page of the Honolulu *Advertiser,* where a banner heralded the arrival of the "Century Express," Jackie Robinson. An advertisement urged football fans to come and "See the Sensational All-American Half-Back Jackie Robinson." Soon Jack was installed with Ray Bartlett in a duplex apartment in the Kaimukai district, near St. Louis College. They reported to their construction job by day and then to the practice field at night, when the regular games would be played because of the Hawaiian heat. According to Bartlett, Jack did not make a good laborer. Their jobs were with an outfit called Hawaiian Constructors, under a foreman who had attended college in Berkeley. "When he found out that Jack and I were from UCLA," Bartlett recalled, "we were pretty much in. But Jack didn't like to work. I'll never forget the scene. He'd pick up one board, maybe eight or ten feet long, about six inches wide—not heavy—and put it on his shoulder, and carry it over to the carpenter. Finally the foreman said, 'Jack, in the future, I want you to pick up two boards at a time, okay?' Jack didn't last long on the job. Either he quit or was fired."

He was more of a hit playing football. Immediately he boosted his local reputation, and the sale of tickets, with a brilliant performance in an exhibition-game victory over a seasoned team from the 35th Infantry of the U.S. Army. But his success had one adverse effect on the Bears: their top running back of the previous year, Charles "Babe" Webb, formerly of New Mexico State University, allegedly stormed off the club after being passed over. Webb's rebellion proved to be only a token of the club's lack of discipline, which showed at once when the six-game league season started. A record crowd of twenty thousand paid to see the first game, but the Bears lost badly to the veteran Healani Maroons. "Robinson, almost entirely on his own, reeled off some brilliant runs," one newspaper reported, "but faltered in his passing, many of his attempts being intercepted." In other games, Jack was electrifying at times, then injured his right ankle once again. Playing hurt, he performed poorly. By early December, the luster was gone from the league. On December 3, fewer than six hundred persons paid to see the Bears lose.

Unhappy with his season and homesick, Jack hurried to leave Hawaii. On December 5, bidding goodbye to Ray Bartlett and Brick Brickner, he boarded the *Lurline* for passage back to California. On December 7, he and some other men were playing poker when they noticed the ship's crew painting the windows black. Soon the captain ordered everyone on deck and broke the news that Japanese airplanes had attacked Pearl Harbor, north of Honolulu, with massive destruction of American lives and ships. The United States and Japan were now at war. To thwart any lurking Japanese submarines, the *Lurline* would travel home stealthily, with lights out at night, slipping in and out of regular sea lanes. Jack watched and waited anxiously until the California coast came into sight.

Back in Los Angeles, he quickly found a job with Lockheed Aircraft in nearby Burbank. Normally the aircraft industry was hostile to blacks, but the suddenly vital need for military equipment and supplies following Pearl Harbor had cracked the racial walls. The previous June, responding to pressure from black leaders such as the labor organizer A. Philip Randolph and Walter White of the NAACP, as well as to the threat of a massive civil rights march on Washington, D.C., President Roosevelt had reluctantly signed Executive Order 8802, which sought, through the Fair Employment Practices Commission

(FEPC), to end "discrimination in the employment of workers in defense industries or government because of race, creed, color, or national origin." Most white employers still evaded the order, especially if it meant putting blacks and whites together in intimate working conditions. But after Pearl Harbor, more blacks were hired than ever before. Jack found work as a truck driver, for which he earned $100 a month.

Once again he was living on Pepper Street, but able now to contribute to his share of the expenses, which was important to him. Too many people, he believed, still depended on Mallie Robinson. Willa Mae had just married, but she and her husband, Lewis Walker, a laborer; her brother Edgar; Frank's widow, Maxine, and their children; and Mack and his wife and children lived in one or another of the two houses Mallie owned on Pepper Street and looked to her for help. "If Jack and his mother had any consistent conflict," according to Rachel Robinson, "it was about the number of people she took in out of the kindness of her heart, including those he thought were simply exploiting her." Jack hated to see how some of her grandchildren conducted themselves at Mallie's house on Pepper Street, which he believed should have been her sanctuary. Instead, they were "running in and out and raiding her refrigerator and taking her spare change and things like that, and Jack was furious." Being able to give his mother money instead of taking from her was a most important milestone in his life.

He continued to see much of Rachel, who was now a sophomore at UCLA. From Atascadero and

Hawaii, Jack had sent her a shallow but persistent stream of brief letters, mainly to let her know that she was often on his mind. Without the prospect of a good job, he could hardly do more. Besides, Rachel had her own plans, which centered on staying in school until 1945, when she expected to earn her B.Sc. in nursing from the University of California and qualify as a registered nurse. She would not give up college for love. "I wasn't thinking necessarily about a career or graduate school or anything like that," she would say. "It was just that I had a sense of boundaries and goals, of tasks that had to be finished. I had seen too many women, good students, fall into marriages after a year or two. I couldn't be like that." A dropout himself, Jack fully supported her desire to graduate; he liked the fact that she excelled at school. He was also content that their relationship remained chaste. While he was at Atascadero, she had made no attempt to visit him. "That was out," she recalled. "I never went anywhere to see Jack, although he would come to see me. Visiting him just wasn't done. I wouldn't have thought it proper, and he wouldn't have thought it proper, either. We had no conflict there. In those days, Jack was at least as much into propriety as I was."

Bringing them closer that year, if tragically, was the death on March 6, 1941, of Charles Raymond Isum. Although her father had come close to dying several times, his passing devastated Rachel; the intensity of her mourning amazed Jack. "Rae's deep grief had a profound effect on me," he wrote later. "In this time of sorrow we found each other and I knew then that our relationship was to be one of the most important things in my life no matter what happened to me." Ray Isum's death gave Jack an opportunity he might not have had otherwise. "My father's death," Rachel saw eventually, "gave Jack an opening where he could at last be the man, the main man, in a family of his own. On Pepper Street, he had been fatherless, the last child, loved from a distance, almost on the periphery. With the Isums, it was different. My mother adored him. My younger brother was crazy about him. I loved him. Jack could step right into the center of us all and take possession of his own family—at least in his mind. I think it had a profound appeal for him."

At some point, more than a little awkwardly, Jack sent her a gift to signify his commitment to her, short of a formal engagement. Into an envelope, without much of an explanatory note, he stuffed a heavy charm bracelet made up of miniature pieces of sports equipment—footballs, basketballs, and the like— that he and other varsity athletes received at the end of the season, and sent it through the regular mail. "It's a wonder it ever reached me," Rachel said; "when I got the envelope, the charms had broken through the corners. It could easily have been lost, or stolen. Still, I was thrilled to receive it—it was just the sign of commitment and love I wanted at the time. I wore it proudly." She was wearing it when Jack returned home in December 1941.

Hovering now over their relationship, and Jack's life, was the military draft. Before Pearl Harbor, Jack had not been eager to enlist. Registering at Longfellow Elementary School in Pasadena, he had struggled with the local board over his hope for an exemption. Throughout the South, ironically, draft boards worked hard to keep blacks out of the services, in the name of segregation; in Pasadena, the draft board often seemed too eager to take blacks and spare whites. "Like all men in those days I was willing to do my part," Jack later declared; but before Pearl Harbor he had at least three reasons for wanting to stay out of the Army. First, eager to have his mother stop working, he had put himself down as her sole means of support. Second, he doubted that his bad ankle could withstand the rigors of infantry training, much less combat. Last of all, his patriotism was sorely tried by the humiliations facing blacks in the military.

Not surprisingly, after Pearl Harbor the draft board rejected his application for exemption out of hand. On March 23, 1942, his "Order to Report for Induction" was issued by the President of the United States. The order arrived almost on the day that Robinson, along with another black player, Nate Moreland, a pitcher, was teased and tantalized by an opportunity to work out in Brookside Park with the Chicago White Sox, in town once again for spring training. Pressed by a reporter, the White Sox manager, Jimmy Dykes, solidly endorsed the idea of racially integrated baseball. "Personally," he declared, "I would welcome Negro players on the Sox, and I believe every one of the other fifteen big league managers would do likewise. As for the players, they'd all get along too." Robinson, he said, was easily worth fifty thousand dollars to any major-league club. But on April 3, as ordered, Jack presented himself at the National Guard Armory in Pasadena with the specified three days' worth of clothing. From there, he was taken to the induction station at Fort MacArthur in San Pedro, near Los Angeles. After a doctor declared him in excellent health, he was given his first set of vaccinations and dispatched for thirteen weeks of basic training at Fort Riley, Kansas.

Two or three years before, Fort Riley had been a relatively sleepy Army reservation of some thirty-five hundred souls, known mostly for its fabled role as a cavalry post defending the wagon trains of white adventurers and settlers heading west on the Santa Fe Trail; the monument to the Battle of Wounded Knee, in which many Indians were slaughtered, stood on its grounds. Fort Riley had also functioned as the only cavalry school maintained by the Army; it was home, too, to the only all-black cavalry regiment in the military. Now, in 1942, it had become a major staging area and training ground for U.S. infantry divisions heading overseas.

For black recruits entering the armed forces in 1942, the first enemy was probably Jim Crow. Increasingly, black Americans saw two wars taking place. One conflict was with the Axis powers; the other was being fought out at home and overseas with white American notions of racial supremacy. In 1939, fewer than four thousand blacks served in the Army, and most were in service occupations; only five blacks, including three chaplains, were regular officers. In the Army Reserve, Jim Crow rules called for white officers to lead black men in their segregated outfits, no matter how distasteful whites found the job or how bitterly some blacks resented them. In 1940 the secretary of war, Henry L. Stimson, deriding the record of blacks in World War I, insisted on segregation as a permanent feature of Army life; an official memorandum argued that segregation "has been proven satisfactory over a long period of years and to make changes would produce situations destructive to morale and detrimental to the preparations for national defense." Another memorandum insisted: "There is a consensus that colored units are inferior to the performance of white troops, except for service duties."

Outside the Army, the record was even worse. After World War I, when ten thousand blacks served in its ranks, the Navy first barred blacks altogether, then accepted them only as mess attendants, to wait on whites. In its grand history dating back to the American Revolution, the all-volunteer Marines had never accepted a black into its ranks. The Army Air Force barred blacks until 1939, when it herded them into segregated units for training. In a final humiliation, the Red Cross bowed to military pressure by refusing blood plasma prepared from the blood of blacks "on the score that white men in the service would refuse blood plasma if they knew it came from Negro veins." The irony of the fact that the major scientist behind the development of blood banks, Dr. Charles Drew of Howard University Medical School, was himself an African-American was lost on the Red Cross.

And yet 1942, when Jack entered the Army, also marked a turning point in race relations in the military. The number of African-Americans in the Army soared. The Navy and Coast Guard began accepting blacks for general service, albeit hemmed in by often humiliating restrictions, and the Marine Corps ended its ban on African-Americans with the formation of segregated units. At Fort Riley, caught between Jim Crow ways and the first glimmerings of change, Jack, like countless other black men, accepted the evil of segregation and buckled down to basic training.

Quickly he separated himself from the pack. On the gunnery range, he scored 196 with an M-1 rifle and was designated an "expert" marksman. His character was also rated as "excellent." With his basic training accomplished near mid-July, Jack's crisp intelligence, his steely self-discipline despite his flaring temper, his excellent record in sports, and his four years of college should have made him a prime candidate for Officer Candidate School (OCS). But when he applied for OCS, he was summarily refused, without explanation. "The men in our unit had passed all the tests for OCS," he recalled. "But we were not allowed to start school; we were kept sitting around waiting for at least three months, and we could get no answers to our questions about the delay." Instead, while many whites with less aptitude and education moved toward their commissions, he was assigned to help take care of horses in the stables at Fort Riley. His most complex challenge was learning to keep the horses' heads still during their vaccinations. Secretary of War Stimson himself had stated the Army's core reason for denying almost all blacks a chance to be officers: "Leadership is not imbedded in the negro race yet and to try to make commissioned officers to lead men into battle—colored men—is only to work a disaster to both."

Jim Crow was in charge even on the playing field. When Jack went out for the baseball team, he was stopped. Apologetically, a white player mumbled to him that the officer in charge had laid down the law: "I'll break up the team before I'll have a nigger on it." Even games between all-black and all-white teams were discouraged. But Jack's athletic fame could not be ignored completely; two years later, a book on racism in the armed forces would report that "Negro athletes such as Joe Louis, the prizefighter, and Jack Robinson . . . are today greatly admired in the army." Fortunately for him, Robinson and Louis found themselves thrown together by fate that year, 1942, at Fort Riley, where Louis also went through basic training. Becoming firm friends, the two athletes played golf and went out riding together regularly; Robinson also joined Louis in some of his special training sessions as a boxer. Louis's attentions flattered Robinson. Louis was then at the peak of his national fame, which had soared with his first-round victory in 1938 over Max Schmeling of Germany, in a match widely seen as a showdown between democracy and fascism. In the days after Pearl Harbor, Louis's popularity reached new heights when he announced that proceeds of a coming title fight would go to the Navy Relief Society; then, the next month, he voluntarily joined the Army. "We gon do our part," he assured an American public still shattered by the disaster of Pearl Harbor, "and we will win, because we are on God's side."

Many blacks criticized Louis for supporting the Navy despite its contempt for blacks, and for invoking God on the side of America while Jim Crow flourished. Robinson did not join the critics, although in several ways he was the antithesis of Joe Louis. Compared with Jack, Joe was poorly educated. Jack seldom looked twice at women; Louis pursued them obsessively. Jack was frugal; Joe "was the quickest fellow I ever saw in reaching for a check," according to Robinson, "and whenever I'd try to pick up one, he'd snatch it away and say with a scowl, 'Jackie, be yourself, man!'" But Jack admired Louis for more than his generosity; Louis had "one of the sharpest minds I have ever encountered." Robinson would recall playing poker with Louis one long evening while a radio in the background offered periodic reports about elections. Although Louis had seemed absorbed in his playing, to Jack's surprise he was able to give precise tallies for a number of candidates according to the last report.

Jack also liked the fact that Louis was humble. Passing through Los Angeles that November, Louis telephoned Rachel. "I got this telephone call from a Joe Barrow," she remembered, "who said he was an Army buddy of Jack and he was going to come by and 'honk at' me." Rachel, who did not care to be honked at, was in the bathtub when her caller arrived. "My mother came flying through the door," she remembered. " 'You won't believe who's on the front porch. Joe Barrow is *Joe Louis!'* I was stunned, embarrassed, but most of all thrilled. . . . It was the modesty and simplicity of it which impressed me." Robinson liked the way Louis enjoyed his fame and money, and the adulation of both white and black America, while remaining true to himself. Within four years, Jack himself, and Rachel also, would be caught up as principals in an even more complex drama involving the sometimes harmonious, sometimes conflicting needs and desires of black and white America. As different as the men were, Louis's lessons of modesty and humility would not be lost on Robinson.

"I'm sure if it wasn't for Joe Louis," Jack would insist, "the color line in baseball would not have been broken for another ten years." At Fort Riley in 1942, Louis used his prestige to try to help the young black men, including Robinson, who wanted to be officers, although exactly what he accomplished is open to question. According to Louis's old friend Truman K. Gibson, an attorney who was then an assistant to William Hastie, the black civilian aide to the secretary of war, Louis telephoned him about Robinson's plight. Gibson then flew to Fort Riley to investigate conditions there. At a meeting organized by Louis, he met with Robinson, Louis, and other blacks to hear their grievances. On another occasion, Gibson pointed out that the wheels were already in motion to take those men toward OCS. What is certain is that after waiting in limbo for about three months, Jack and a small group of other blacks at Fort Riley were accepted into OCS. Around November 1, and after

Jack had served for some time as a squad leader, they began their thirteen weeks of training in a class of just over eighty candidates.

The candidates were from all over the United States; more remarkably, they included both whites and blacks. For the first time in Army history, OCS was integrated. Suddenly, whites and blacks studied, worked, ate, trained, and were billeted together, in the middle of an otherwise viciously segregated world. Integration did not free black officers altogether; for some time, Army rules would continue to forbid any black officer from outranking a white officer in the same unit. The integration of OCS at Fort Riley was bound to cause trouble, and gave rise to a story with Jack Robinson at its explosive center. According to Truman Gibson again, Jack was on a drill field when a white officer denounced a black soldier as a "stupid nigger son of a bitch." Robinson intervened: "You shouldn't address a soldier in those terms." The white officer turned on him: "Oh, fuck you; that goes for you too!" Jack, who had "an explosive, terrible temper," erupted in a rage: "He almost killed the guy." Summoned by Joe Louis, Gibson went with him to see "the commanding general" about the incident. After Louis presented the general with "some very expensive gifts," Robinson was "permitted to finish officer candidate school."

Almost certainly, this episode never took place. (But it would be accepted as truth in an important biography, Chris Mead's *Joe Louis,* and transmitted even deeper into history by other writers quoting from that biography.) In another telling, Gibson identified the gifts: "Joe gave the general some bottles of Roederer Champagne and a gold watch. That took care of that." It represents an aspect of Robinson's eventual reputation, after his bold integration of white baseball; he would emerge as an icon of raging black manhood, and be refashioned by some people, black and white, into a figure not only of racial triumph but also of racial revenge. Conditions at Fort Riley were no doubt trying, but Jack was capable of holding himself in check to avoid such a gross violation of the military code. In contrast, a white writer, Ruth Danenhower Wilson, gathering material for her study of blacks in the wartime military, *Jim Crow Joins Up* (1944), would report that "at Fort Riley the faculty of the Officer Candidate School felt that the Negro all-American Football Player—Jack Robinson—had been better liked than any other Candidate in the school."

In any event, on January 28, 1943, following Army custom, a fellow graduate ceremonially pinned the gold bars signifying the rank of second lieutenant on Jack Robinson, and he signed the oath of office that marked his commission as an officer in the cavalry of the U.S. Army. For Jack, who had graduated from neither Pasadena Junior College nor UCLA, his Army commission was probably the most significant public accomplishment of his life to that moment outside of sports.

In March, on leave and decked out in his dashing cavalry officer's uniform, Jack headed for California. His old friend Jack Gordon, now himself in the Army, was in Blythe, California, when Robinson arrived without notice. "I was at headquarters," Gordon recalled, "in a room where all the black officers used to hang out, when the door opened and who should walk in but Jack Robinson. He was an absolute sight, just beautiful to see! He had on his cavalry outfit with the riding breeches and the dark jacket and the wide-brimmed hat with the chin strap and the high polished boots and everything. Folks just stopped talking and looked at him." But Jack's final destination was San Francisco, where Rachel now lived in the nurses' dormitory of the University of California Hospital on hilly Parnassus Avenue. Because UCLA had neither a medical nor a nursing school, she had moved north for the last three years of her program, which involved both academic and clinical work at the hospital.

When they were at last alone together, Jack presented her with an engagement ring, complete with a tiny diamond. She accepted the ring, and they were formally engaged. Rachel was happy to be engaged, but she was still in no hurry to be married. Jack had only a limited sense of the reasons for her reluctance; and Rachel, too, was in something of an emotional fog. "I had come to realize," she would say, "how dominated I had been by my family all my life, how they had shaped my thoughts, my goals, my very being. Now I was in nursing school, which was terribly demanding and regimented. I could see that marriage was going to be another force, maybe even more powerful, keeping me in place, with me trying, striving hard, as usual, to be the best wife I could be, just as I had tried to be the best child, the best young lady, the best student I could be. I could see marriage suffocating me, and I really was not eager to rush into it."

Rachel knew that Jack and her mother were quite different people; but she also sensed that he would want her to be the woman her mother had groomed her to become, and the thought sometimes oppressed her. This was all a little too complicated for Jack, who could not imagine why Rachel would not want to be that woman. "Jack began to get just a little edgy about my hesitating. Still, I held onto him, because I loved him. And he had my mother totally on his side, and my mother pretty much had me." (Once, Zellee had consulted a psychic about her daughter. "Tell her," the medium advised, "to either marry a certain man or stop riding around in his Buick." Zellee's mouth dropped open; Jack was then driving a Buick.)

Rachel knew exactly what she wanted as a wedding present from Jack: a sable fur coat. Jack, who probably still owned only one suit, agreed to the purchase but with some reluctance. Although he had no interest in buying fine things for himself, he expected his wife to know and want them; still, a fur coat seemed a bit much. A little reluctantly, he went with Rachel to one of the fanciest fur shops in the city. "Do you have a sable coat to show me?" Rachel asked, with as much confidence as she could muster. "The poor salesman was stunned. 'Oh yes, lady, I can show you one. But I want you to know that only Bing Crosby's wife owns one, as far as I know.' " Standing behind Rachel, Jack snickered; she heard him distinctly. However, "I was not about to acknowledge the defeat. I drew myself up and asked the man, 'Well, if not sable, is there something else you can suggest?' He told me: 'I have a very nice dyed ermine.' He brought this little piece of fur out. I looked at it. It wasn't what I had in mind, but I knew by this point that I was in over my head." Jack, chuckling, put a down payment on the ermine. The fur coat caper was something they would both laugh about in the coming years.

RETURNING TO FORT RILEY, he found himself assigned to a provisional truck battalion. In addition, he was appointed morale officer of his company. The men respected his sports knowledge and skills and also understood that he could and would speak up for them, in his fluting, high voice that showed hardly a trace of his mother's Southern drawl. Certainly he knew their racial troubles at Fort Riley from personal experience. Once again, for example, whites barred him from the baseball team. At least one witness to the episode, ironically, would later play with him on the Brooklyn Dodgers. "One day we were out at the field practicing," Pete Reiser would recall, "when a Negro lieutenant came out for the team. An officer told him, 'You have to play with the colored team.' That was a joke. There was no colored team. The black lieutenant didn't speak. He stood there for a while, watched us work out, and then he turned and walked away. . . . That was the first time I saw Jackie Robinson. I can still see him slowly walking away."

Jack was barred from the baseball team, but it appears that either this year, 1943, or the next, he competed in and won a table tennis competition that made him the champion player in the U.S. Army, in a sport he had played only sporadically over the years. (In October 1944 a USO director in the Fort Riley area tried to match Robinson against Miss Jini Boyd O'Connor, said to be the current Middle Atlantic champion, "because we know of his ability as a ping-pong artist.")

But sports provided only respites from the boredom of life at Fort Riley, as Jack and the other black officers and men watched and waited for something significant to happen. The overwhelming question was whether blacks would be allowed a chance at combat. Summer brought news of massive shipments of black soldiers overseas, but the Army was shunting most of them into service units, where most whites contemptuously thought blacks belonged. Early in 1944, the black 2nd Cavalry Division, after two years of zealous training, would be turned into a service unit and denied the chance of battlefield glory. Morale also suffered with the multiplying acts of violence against black soldiers by whites, to whom the sight of a black man in uniform, and especially an officer, was often an affront. In Little Rock, Arkansas, a white policeman killed a black sergeant on a city street. In Centerville, Mississippi, a sheriff nonchalantly ended a dispute between a white MP and a black soldier by shooting the soldier dead. Incidents such as these, emblazoned on the pages of newspapers such as the Chicago *Defender,* the Pittsburgh *Courier,* and the New York *Amsterdam News,* scarred the image of the military in the eyes of blacks. About this time, the only African-American general in the U.S. Army, Benjamin O. Davis, testified to the mournful truth that black Americans "had lost confidence in the fairness of the Army to Negro troops."

Frustrated in his role as morale officer, Jack himself refused to give in to cynicism or despair. This refusal often meant friction between himself and whites, or worse. His most dangerous episode came after some soldiers complained bitterly to him about conditions for blacks at the post exchange, where they often waited and waited for the few seats assigned to blacks while "white" seats went unused. Determined to intervene, Jack telephoned the provost marshal of the base to complain; at the very least, he wanted more spaces assigned to blacks. With the provost marshal, a Major Haffner, unaware that Robinson was black, the conversation became more and more heated as Robinson developed his points. Finally, Major Haffner came to the point: "Lieutenant, let me put it to you this way. How would you like to have your wife sitting next to a nigger?" Jack was livid. "Pure rage took over," he admitted. "I was so angry that I asked him if he knew how close his wife had ever been to a nigger. I was shouting at the top of my voice. Every typewriter in headquarters stopped. The clerks were frozen in disbelief." On the advice of a warrant officer who had overheard Jack's words, he made a full report of the conversation to the battalion commander. The incident ended fruitfully. Additional seats became available for blacks, and Major Haffner himself, in later encounters with Robinson, was polite and even helpful. One thing remained constant, however: segregation.

Jim Crow at Fort Riley was only a token of racism in America, and the sweltering summer brought bizarre news of major civil disturbances across the country even as the United States fought abroad in order to uphold and restore democracy. Early in June, rioting started in Los Angeles when Mexican-American youths living under dismal conditions clashed with white sailors and soldiers who had flooded the city in search of the usual wartime pleasures. On June 16, two blacks were killed when a white mob fomented a mass disturbance in Beaumont, Texas, sparked by the rumor, later disproved, that a black man had raped the wife of a white serviceman. In Detroit on June 20, far more destructively, marauding mobs clashed in various parts of the city and left twenty-five blacks and nine whites dead. On August 1, Harlem exploded in a riot that took six lives, injured some three hundred persons, and cost millions of dollars in property damage. Appropriately enough, the spark was a report, erroneous, that a white policeman had shot and killed a black soldier.

News of the civil disturbances made life at Fort Riley even more difficult for blacks there. Thus Jack was in no mood to comply when, in August, he was asked to join the football team at the fort. Finally, he decided to practice with the team. However, the season was to start with a game against the University of Missouri when he suddenly found himself given two weeks' leave to go home, although he had not applied for leave. Before long he recognized the reason: Missouri had "made it quite clear to the Army that they would not play a team with a black player on it. Instead of telling me the truth, the Army gave me leave to go home." Angry at the deception, Jack left Fort Riley on September 4. When he returned to duty on September 17, he reported to the team not to resume practice but to resign his place: "I said that I had no intention of playing football for a team which, because I was black, would not allow me to play in all the games." The colonel in charge of the team reminded Robinson that he could order him to play. "You wouldn't want me playing on your team," Jack replied, "knowing that my heart wasn't in it." Although no one ordered him to play, "I had no illusions. I would never win a popularity contest with the ranking hierarchy of that post."

Jack had another reason for not playing. His right ankle, the Achilles heel of his splendid body, was now a constant source of pain. Just after his return from California, Jack had twisted it badly on an obstacle course. In October, he hurt it again during a softball game. The pain was so intense that on October 21, and again on November 15, he had the ankle X-rayed. He was almost ready to think himself healed when a routine platoon training exercise left him badly hobbled. Christmas found Jack laid up in the dispensary at Fort Clark, Texas. Yet another X-ray showed a large number of bone chips floating in the ankle joint; his medical record described his condition as "arthritis, chronic, nonsuppurative, moderately severe, right ankle." The history of the injury was noted, starting with the fracture in Pasadena in September 1937, at the start of his first season with PJC, and its refracture in Hawaii in 1941.

The decision was made to send Jack for further treatment to Brooke General Hospital at Fort Sam Houston in San Antonio, Texas, where he was admitted on January 5, 1944. Following yet another examination, on January 28 the Disposition Board at Brooke met and endorsed the findings of the doctors at Fort Clark. The board then recommended that Jack Robinson be declared "physically disqualified for general military service, but qualified for limited service." It further stipulated: "He is not qualified for overseas duty at this time." It was also stipulated that he should be carefully placed so that "he will not encounter calisthenics, marching, drilling, or other duties requiring strenuous use of the right ankle." The board further recommended that Jack be examined again after six months.

As annoying as this injury was, it was not nearly as disturbing to Jack as the heartbreak he felt early in 1944 when his engagement to Rachel Isum faltered and then collapsed after a furious clash of wills. From San Francisco, Rachel had written to say that she had decided to join the Nurse Cadet Corps, a student organization loosely affiliated with the Army. Although members had no obligation to the armed forces, Jack was appalled. "I shook with rage and youthful jealousy," he later wrote, "as I read the letter far away in Kansas." To Jack, joining the corps was just about the same as starting a life of sexual promiscuity; women who served in the war were easy prey for unscrupulous servicemen. But Rachel's reasons were both innocent and pragmatic. Without serious temptation, she watched the endless stream of virile young men pass in and out of her dormitory and the hospital. Once, in the lobby of a San Francisco hotel, a renowned bandleader, the friend of a close friend, invited her up to his room for a tryst. "I told him I was engaged to be married," she recalled, "and would only have sex with my future husband. I didn't tell him I'd never had sex with anyone." She joined the corps because "I was broke as a student. I had no money, and I could earn none in the usual student ways. When I was not working in the hospital I was in class; there was no time. The corps paid a stipend of twenty dollars a month." Another reason was almost frivolous, except for the cool San Francisco weather. "I also liked the big, warm flannel coat that they gave you; I really wanted that heavy coat." Yet another reason may have been patriotism. More so than Jack, Rachel believed in military service. In World War I, her father had sacrificed his health for his country. In this war, her beloved older brother, Chuck Williams, was now listed as missing in action after his plane had been shot down somewhere over eastern Europe. Under the circumstances, joining the Nurse Cadet Corps was the least Rachel could do.

Nevertheless, Jack delivered an ultimatum: leave the Nurse Cadet Corps or end their engagement. To his astonishment, Rachel chose the latter. At Fort Riley one day, he opened a tightly wrapped, carefully insured package from Rachel and found his ring and bracelet nestled inside. His shock hardened into pride; their relationship was over: "Stubbornly I vowed to forget her." (Perhaps Jack operated with a double standard, or he felt himself freed by his breakup with Rachel to seek sex with other women, or he had a momentary lapse of loyalty. On February 29, he was treated at a Fort Riley dispensary for a case of " 'New' Gonorrhoea, Acute.")

A few weeks later, on April 13, he and more than a dozen other black officers at Fort Riley received the news they had been waiting for: they were to proceed immediately to Camp Hood, Texas, and report there to the headquarters of the 761st Tank Battalion, which was scheduled to go overseas and into combat later in the year. Jack and his fellow officers reached Camp Hood with some foreboding. If Southern camps had a poor reputation among black soldiers, among the more notorious was Camp Hood, a massive new military installation carved out of about 160,000 acres of lonesome farmland in the Texas heartland in direct response to the war. The success of the German blitzkrieg, spearheaded by Panzer tank divisions, had spurred the development of U.S. antitank technology and antitank forces, which needed a vast area of land to explore the complex lessons of blitzkrieg. A month after Pearl Harbor, the Army announced that its new Tank Destroyer Technical and Firing Center would be located in central Texas. Nine months later, Camp Hood was activated; by 1944, when Robinson and his friends arrived, it was easily the largest military facility in the United States.

To the military, Camp Hood was a triumph that helped dispel the myth of Panzer invincibility. The proud Tank Destroyer insignia featured a black panther crushing a tank between its jaws, encircled by the fighting motto "Seek, Strike, and Destroy." To the sixty thousand servicemen stationed there in 1944, Camp Hood was often a horror. The hot land crawled with rattlesnakes, tarantulas, black widow spiders, and scorpions, and the humid air buzzed with mosquitoes and other sniping insects. In addition, black soldiers and civilians had to deal with raw aspects of Jim Crow (the Army had named the camp after a Confederate hero, General John Bell Hood, a West Pointer who had commanded a brigade of Texans against the Union). Black soldiers, quartered in the least desirable part of the camp, in makeshift housing, lived segregated lives at every turn, with a separate USO and a separate officers' club; venturing off the base, they faced a hostile, narrow-minded local population backed by stringent Jim Crow state laws and customs. "Segregation there was so complete," a black officer said, "I even saw outhouses marked *White, Colored,* and *Mexican;* this was on federal property."

Jack quickly found out that his lieutenant's bars meant little to whites at Camp Hood. A soldier recalled: "One day Jackie was on his way to town when he realized he didn't have enough money. He stopped at the white officers' club to get a check cashed and they barred him at the door; he wasn't allowed across the threshold. Jackie became very bitter about this." Fortunately, the 761st Tank Battalion,

Company B (to which he was not assigned but only attached), was an oasis in this desert of human relations, not least of all because of its leader. Activated in 1942 and now part of the armored forces in training at Camp Hood, the 761st was commanded by a white fellow Californian, Lieutenant Colonel Paul L. Bates, a thirty-four-year-old former star football player and graduate in economics at Western Maryland College. Among the black men under him, Bates had a reputation as a white man who appreciated their troubles but who was also determined to mold them into a powerful fighting force. He set high standards, from personal hygiene and dress to battlefield efficiency. "Our boots were shined like you couldn't imagine," Bates remembered; "our men would go out of their way to salute officers and to look them straight in the eye." He also channeled the racial indignation of his men into a desire to succeed as no black U.S. outfit had succeeded before. Of the battalion's later military success in Europe, which was substantial, he would say with satisfaction: "I believe they fought against Germans not as Germans so much as against the white man."

Jack and the other Fort Riley officers were each assigned to head a platoon. For Robinson, this spelled trouble. At Fort Riley, some officers had trained in mechanized cavalry, but he had been a genuine horse soldier and knew nothing about tanks and tank warfare. The M-4 medium tank (the General Sherman) used by the 761st was a mystery to him. Rather than pull rank and bluff his way through, he decided to confess his ignorance openly and rely on the goodwill of the men under him. He recalled his first meeting with his platoon. "Men," he recalled saying, "I know nothing about tanks, nothing at all. I'm asking you to help me out in this unusual situation." A "deep and impressive silence" followed. He turned to a veteran sergeant standing beside him and allowed that the sergeant, not Lieutenant Robinson, was in charge of the platoon. Evidently, Jack's candor and humility had an energizing effect on the men: "It turned out to be one of the smartest things I ever did."

A white fellow lieutenant, David J. Williams, a Yale graduate who later wrote a book about the 761st, captured a graphic snapshot of Robinson as army officer: "He was kind of aloof, very straight, dressed really sharp, didn't swear much, was religious. He was a really good person, but he was never close to anyone." Although Robinson was a friend, Williams never really knew him: "He was a very private person." No doubt, Jack's toughness and asceticism offended a few men. One veteran would recall him as someone "who tended to pick on people who were smaller than he was or who he felt were less important than he was." Under oath, however, Colonel Bates would testify that Robinson was held "in very high regard," especially by the enlisted men but also by Bates himself: "I tried to have him assigned [not simply attached] to the battalion because of his excellent work."

Despite Jack's bad ankle, Bates asked Robinson to consider going overseas with the battalion as morale officer. (On June 9, the War Department had alerted the 761st that it would soon be heading for

Europe and combat. The advance party would leave on July 20; the rest of the men were to follow about three weeks later.) Not only had Jack done an outstanding job with his platoon; his leadership in the battalion in sports, especially in organizing baseball and softball teams, had boosted the morale of the men. Clearly Bates's request pleased Jack. To go overseas, however, he would have to be examined again and sign a waiver releasing the Army from any financial claim or benefit in case of reinjury to his ankle. "I said I'd be willing to do that," Jack later recalled. On May 25, a thorough hospital examination was requested by the adjutant of the 761st "to determine the physical qualification for overseas service of 2nd Lt. Jack R. Robinson." But Jack's status could not be changed without an appearance before an Army Retiring Board. Accordingly, on June 21 he reported to the Army's McCloskey General Hospital in the nearby town of Temple for an examination to see the "type of duty, if any, that he may be physically qualified to perform." To doctors there, Jack reported no improvement in his condition. After every baseball game, his ankle became swollen. Every day, at odd times, the ankle joint would lock up; a few kicking motions released it. Although this examination found no swelling or cramping of motion, X-rays revealed "a bony mass distal to the medial malleolus," as well as "several smaller pieces of tissue of osseous origin anterior to the ankle joint": in other words, bone chips.

Five days later, on June 26, the Disposition Board at the hospital declared Robinson still unfit for general duty but "fit for limited military service." It recommended "that this officer appear before an Army Retiring Board for consideration of reassignment to permanent limited military service." The board concluded: "This officer is fit for overseas duty."

Robinson was now ready to acquiesce to Colonel Bates's wishes and go overseas with the 761st Battalion. But on July 6, he became entangled in a dispute that threatened to end his military service in disgrace. Around 5:30 p.m. that day, still a patient at McCloskey Hospital in Temple, Jack boarded a city bus that took him to Camp Hood, about an hour or so away. There, he took a camp bus to the colored officers' club, located on 172nd Street in the camp. He reached the club around 7:30 p.m. About three and a half hours later, or around eleven in the evening, he boarded a Camp Hood bus to begin the return journey to the hospital in Temple. He started to move to the rear when he saw a young woman he knew, Virginia Jones, sitting in the middle of the bus. Virginia Jones, the wife of First Lieutenant Gordon H. Jones Jr. of the 761st Tank Battalion, lived in nearby Belton. Jack sat down beside Mrs. Jones. After going five or six blocks, the driver, a white man named Milton N. Renegar, turned around in his seat and ordered Robinson to move to the back of the bus. Robinson refused. The driver then threatened to make trouble for him when the bus reached the station. Robinson again refused. By this time it had probably occurred to him that the driver believed that Virginia Jones was white; she was not.

On the ride from Temple to the camp, Robinson had obeyed Texas law requiring Jim Crow seating on the bus. But he also knew that the Army now forbade segregation on its military bases. The previous month, after the killing of a black soldier by a white bus driver in Durham, North Carolina (a civilian jury soon acquitted the driver), the Army had proclaimed its new policy. Robinson also knew about the widely publicized refusals by Joe Louis and Sugar Ray Robinson to obey Jim Crow rules at a bus depot in Alabama.

Exchanges between Robinson and Renegar grew more heated. When the bus reached the crowded central bus station at the camp, another passenger, Mrs. Elizabeth Poitevint, who worked in the camp kitchen, let Robinson know that she herself intended to press charges against him. Her intervention, as a white woman, brought the incident close to a flash point. According to Robinson's statement, which was taken down by a white stenographer he considered hostile to him, "I said that's all right, too, I don't care if she prefers charges against me. The bus driver asked me for my identification card. I refused to give it to him. He then went to the Dispatcher and told him something. What he told him I don't know. He then comes back and tells the people that this nigger is making trouble. I told the driver to stop fuckin with me, so he gets the rest of the men around there and starts blowing his top and someone calls the MP's."

Renegar, the driver, had asked the dispatcher, a man named Bevlia "Pinky" Younger, to call the military police, and Younger had promptly done so. The first MP to arrive was Corporal George A. Elwood. The police escorted Robinson to the military police guard room, where Robinson encountered a sergeant and also a private, Ben W. Mucklerath, he would accuse of calling him a nigger. The police then summoned the officer of the day, Captain Peelor Wigginton, who was also the camp laundry officer. Turning first to Mucklerath, Wigginton set out to question him about the incident. When Robinson interrupted the private to dispute what he was saying, Wigginton ordered Robinson outside.

Next to arrive on the scene was an assistant provost marshal, Captain Gerald M. Bear, who was also commander of the military police. According to Robinson, he was following Bear into the guard room when Bear rudely turned on him: "Nobody comes into the room until I tell him." Since Robinson could see Mucklerath in the room, he protested at being kept out while the white private was allowed in. Bear repeated his order, and Robinson left the guard room.

In his own statement, Bear declared that when he arrived, Robinson was inside the guard room. He then asked Robinson to step outside the guard room and into the receiving room while he, Bear, heard a report from Captain Wigginton. However, instead of obeying, "Lt. Robinson kept continually interrupting Captain Wigginton and myself and kept coming to the Guard Room door-gate. I cautioned and requested Lt. Robinson on several occasions to remain at ease and remain in the receiving room." Furthermore, "in an effort to try to be facetious, Lt.

Robinson bowed with several sloppy salutes, repeating several times, 'OK, sir, OK, sir,' on each occasion." According to Bear, he ordered Robinson "to remain in the receiving room and be seated on a chair, on the far side of the receiving room. Later on I found Lt. Robinson on the outside of the building. . . . Lt. Robinson's attitude in general was disrespectful and impertinent to his superior officers, and very unbecoming to an officer in the presence of enlisted men."

Robinson would soon vehemently dispute this version of the episode. To him, Bear on arriving seemed "not polite at all" and "very uncivil toward me." The heart of the matter for Robinson was that Bear "did not seem to recognize me as an officer at all. But I did consider myself an officer and felt I should be addressed as one."

After taking statements from all the whites involved, Bear at last allowed Robinson to speak. Jack could not help noticing that he was made to stand while "they asked that private [Mucklerath] to sit down." For the statement, Bear employed a stenographer, a white woman named Wilson. The presence of yet another white woman, as well as Robinson's refusal to efface himself before her, added to the tension. Robinson remembered her asking him sharp and, to him, totally inappropriate questions as a civilian: "Don't you know you have no right sitting up there in the white part of the bus?" Robinson would also testify that after he objected to a part of her transcript, she snapped, " 'If you had completed your statement it would have made sense'

and I told her that if she had put down Captain Bear's
question, it would have made sense; and she then
picked up her purse and said, 'I don't have to make
excuses to him' and she went out, and Captain Bear
went outside to her and talked awhile." (Bear would
deny under oath that there had been any friction
whatsoever between Wilson and Robinson.)

At some point, against Jack's wishes, Bear
arranged to have military police drive the black lieutenant back to the hospital in Temple. Robinson
protested that he had a pass that was good until eight
in the morning and should be free to go where he
wanted. Repeatedly he asked if he was under arrest.
Bear finally told Robinson that he was under "arrest
in quarters," which meant that he was not being taken
into custody but that he would be considered under
arrest at the hospital, although without a guard.
Robinson was then taken to the hospital in a police
pickup truck.

At the hospital, a white doctor who knew Jack
warned him that a report had come in about a drunken
black lieutenant trying to start a riot; the doctor
advised him to take a blood alcohol test at once. The
test proved he had not been drinking. He also
informed Colonel Bates about the episode. Bates
quickly discovered that Captain Bear intended to
bring Robinson up on a court-martial. When Bates
refused to endorse the charges, Bear moved to have
Robinson transferred to a battalion with a more com-
pliant commander. By this time, his superiors at the
camp understood that the Jackie Robinson case could
bring trouble for all concerned. On July 17, in a tele-

phone call to another colonel, Walter D. Buie, chief of staff of the XXIII Corps, Colonel E. A. Kimball, commander of the 5th Armored Group, advised: "This is a very serious case, and it is full of dynamite. It requires very delicate handling. . . . This bus situation here is not at all good, and I am afraid that any officer in charge of troops at this Post might be prejudiced." Nevertheless, on July 24, Robinson was transferred to the 758th Tank Battalion, where the commander signed orders to prosecute him.

Also on July 24, military police placed Robinson under arrest. On that day, he wrote to the NAACP in New York "seeking your help and advice. I feel I am being unfairly punished because I wouldn't be pushed around by the driver of the bus. . . . I am looking for a civilian lawyer to handle my case because I know he will be able to force the truth with a little technique." He had refused to move "because I recalled a letter from Washington" barring segregation on Army posts; the statements against him were "a pretty good bunch of lies." (The NAACP did not reply until the day after the trial: "We will be unable to furnish you with an attorney in the event that you are court martialled." However, if he was convicted, the association would write on his behalf to the Adjutant General in Washington.) Other messages urged the NAACP to intervene; an anonymous writer warned that "this incident is only one of many which have seen Negro officers and enlisted men intimidated and mistreated in Camp Hood, and the surrounding towns." Someone in Los Angeles contacted both U.S. senators from California, Sheridan Downey and Hiram W.

Johnson, who then wrote to Secretary of War Stimson inquiring into the matter. Several black newspapers, including the Pittsburgh *Courier,* also spread the story.

Although the coming trial worried Jack, it did not intimidate him. Even as his fate hung in the balance, he took up the challenge of supporting another black officer, who had been found guilty of buying tires on the black market. Sure that a white officer in a similar circumstance would have been treated differently, he wrote to Truman Gibson, now civilian aide to the secretary of war, asking him to help the man. Jack's composure under fire had a great deal to do with his faith in God; he still said his prayers on his knees at night before going to bed, as he would for many years to come. To Rachel, brought up in the church but less devout, Jack was possessed by the deep sense, instilled by his mother, "that God would take care of you. You are a child of God, made in God's image. Because God is there, nothing can go wrong with you. You can allow yourself to take risks because you just know that the Lord will not allow you to sink so far that you can't swim. An ordeal like the court-martial was a sign to Jack that God was testing him. And Jack just knew that he would respond well, he would come through, because he was a child of God. His faith in God was not very articulate, but it was real, and it did not allow for much doubt."

At 1:45 in the afternoon on August 2, the case of *The United States* v. 2ND LIEUTENANT JACK R. ROBINSON, *0-10315861, CAVALRY, COMPANY C, 758th Tank*

Battalion, began. Nine men would hear the case. One was black; another had been a UCLA student. Six votes were needed for acquittal.

Robinson's defense attorney—nominally, at least—was Lieutenant William A. Cline, a thirty-year-old native Texan who had served in North Africa before being assigned to Camp Hood. Listed as assistant defense counsel was First Lieutenant Joseph C. Hutcheson of the 635th Field Artillery Battalion. However, the trial record indicated yet another defense lawyer: "The accused stated he desired to be defended by regularly appointed defense counsel, assisted by 1st Lt. Robert H. Johnson, 679th Tank Destroyer Battalion, as his individual counsel." Although his role may be lost to history, Lieutenant Johnson, not Cline or Hutcheson, was probably crucial to Robinson's fate at the trial.

Jack had started out with deep reservations about his appointed counsel. Lieutenant Cline, from the small town of Wharton, Texas, was not comfortable defending a black in such a case, and candidly told Jack so. Robinson "told me the NAACP had offered to provide him with a lawyer," according to Cline fifty years later. "I told him I thought that was a pretty good idea because I came from just about as far south as you could go." In addition, Cline had little courtroom experience. "I was a general country lawyer," he recalled. He and his father, also a lawyer, "had a title business. I didn't engage in much adversary stuff."

Not hearing from the NAACP, Robinson returned to Cline. According to Cline, "I never asked him why he changed," but went on to defend the accused. However, in his autobiography *I Never Had It Made,* Robinson related that his first lawyer, a Southerner, pleaded prejudice, then yielded to "a young Michigan officer who did a great job on my behalf." Robinson was probably referring to the work of Lieutenant Johnson; but the trial records do not indicate which part any individual played in his defense in the courtroom. For the record, Cline was his defense counsel. (Fifty years later, interviewed for an article in the *National Law Journal,* Cline gave no indication that anyone else had helped him defend Robinson.)

Jack faced two charges. The first, a violation of Article of War No. 63, accused him of "behaving with disrespect toward Capt. Gerald M. Bear, CMP, his superior officer." Robinson had incurred the charge "by contemptuously bowing to him and giving him several sloppy salutes, repeating several times 'OK Sir,' 'OK, Sir,' or words to that effect, and by acting in an insolent, impertinent and rude manner toward the said Captain Gerald M. Bear." The second charge was a violation of Article No. 64, in this case "willful disobedience of lawful command of Gerald M. Bear, CMP, his superior." It alleged that Robinson, "having received a lawful command . . . to remain in a receiving room and be seated on a chair on the farside of the receiving room, did . . . willfully disobey the same."

Three other charges had been prepared, then abandoned. The first accused Robinson of disrespect toward the officer of the day, Captain Wigginton, by saying to him: "Captain, any Private, you or any

General calls me a nigger and I'll break them in two, I don't know the definition of the word"; and by speaking to Wigginton "in an insolent, impertinent and rude manner." Why this charge was dropped is not clear. The other two charges involved civilians and perhaps were seen as manifestly ill advised. One charge accused Robinson of using "abusive and vulgar language" toward the bus driver "in the presence of ladies." He had said, according to the charge, " 'I'm not going to move a God damn bit,' or words to that effect, and 'I don't know what the Son-of-a-Bitch wanted to give me all this trouble,' or words to that effect." The third charge, also dropped, accused Robinson of telling Elizabeth Poitevint, the white woman who entered the dispute: " 'You better quit fuckin with me' or words to that effect."

Dropping those charges actually hurt Jack's defense, to some extent; the defense could no longer link what had happened on the bus to what had gone on with the white soldiers, although a common thread was an utter disrespect for him as an officer and a human being. The defense then decided to try to show that Robinson had not been insubordinate to Captain Bear but rather that Bear had managed the entire matter poorly. The defense could not dwell on the subjective area of Bear's racism, but it could hammer away at any weakness in his execution of his authority. "The provost marshal [Bear] didn't know how to handle it," Cline would recall. "It had developed into a kind of personal matter."

The cross-examination of Bear (by Cline, Hutcheson, or Johnson) sought to exploit the likelihood that Bear, rudely brushing aside Robinson on arriving at the guard room, had not given him specific instructions about where to wait; that Bear probably had become incensed when Robinson insisted on correcting the transcript of his statement as typed by Bear's stenographer; that Bear had declined to answer when Robinson had asked repeatedly if he was under arrest; and that Bear's decision to send Robinson back to the hospital in a police vehicle under guard was unwarranted. Skillful questioning of Bear and other prosecution witnesses brought out inconsistencies about his handling of Robinson that night, and especially about what he told Robinson to do in sending him out of the guard room—except that Robinson was supposed to be "at ease," which gave Jack's lawyers latitude in defending his behavior.

Clearly, almost all of the whites involved were genuinely mystified that Robinson disliked being badly treated. The white private, Ben Mucklerath, denied that he had called Robinson a nigger, as Robinson charged; but Corporal Elwood, the first MP on the scene, testified that Mucklerath "came over to the pick-up and asked me if I got that nigger Lieutenant. Right then the Lieutenant said, 'Look here, you son-of-a-bitch, don't you call me no nigger.' " The bus dispatcher, "Pinky" Younger, who had summoned the military police, asserted that when Corporal Elwood asked him what was going on, "I told him that the trouble was with a nigger Lt. The nigger Lt., hearing the remark, resented being called so." The bus driver, Milton Renegar, swore that Elizabeth Poitevint had explained aloud: "I don't mind waiting on them all day, but when I get on the bus at night to go home, I'm not about to ride all mixed up with them."

One white witness only, Mrs. Ruby Johnson, gave an account of events on the bus almost exactly as Robinson related them. Ironically, she was a friend of Mrs. Poitevint and had been sitting with her on the bus. According to her statement, when the bus became crowded, the driver asked Robinson to move to the back. "The Lt. said, 'No, I'm going to sit here, I'm not going to move to the back of the bus,' he said that in a very forceful voice, and [t]hen he told the driver, 'You had better sit down and drive the bus wherever you are going.' He told the bus driver that twice, and the bus driver told the Lt. that he would wish he had gone to the back of the bus when they got to the Central Bus Station." Mrs. Johnson reported no obscenities spoken by Robinson to anyone, including her friend Mrs. Poitevint. (Mrs. Poitevint herself swore that he had told her, " 'You better quit fuckin' with me.' He said that three or four times, after we got off the bus, and all that profane and obscene language he used could have been heard by anyone around there, and there was a big crowd there too.")

At last Robinson himself took the stand, although he was not obliged to do so. Full of suppressed passion and eager to be heard, he had to be cautioned more than once to speak more slowly for the stenographer's sake. (Ironically, this same swiftness of speech had irritated Bear and Wilson during his sworn statement.) He allowed that, yes, he had used obscene language once after being provoked, but not to Mrs. Poitevint. He denied behaving in a mocking and contemptuous fashion to any officer. The most poignant moment was perhaps when he explained his angry reaction to being called a nigger. In an inspired gesture, he then movingly invoked his memory of Mallie's mother, Edna Sims McGriff, who had died in Pasadena in 1933, and who had often talked to Jack and the other children about being born a slave in Georgia in 1858, before the Civil War. To the question "Do you know what a nigger is?" Robinson replied: "I looked it up once, but my grandmother gave me a good definition, she was a slave, and she said the definition of the word was a low, uncouth person, and pertains to no one in particular; but I don't consider that I am low and uncouth. I looked it up in the dictionary afterwards and it says the word nigger pertains to the negroid or negro, but it is also a machine used in a saw mill for pushing logs into the saws. I objected to being called a nigger by this private or by anybody else. When I made this statement that I did not like to be called nigger, I told the Captain, I said, 'If you call me a nigger, I might have to say the same thing to you. . . . I do not consider myself a nigger at all, I am a negro, but not a nigger.' "

The defense also called a series of character witnesses. Captain James R. Lawson and Second Lieutenant Harold Kingsley of the 761st Battalion testified, as well as Colonel Bates himself. Bates was evidently so eager to support Robinson that more

than once the prosecution tried to rein him in. He testified about Robinson that "particularly with the
enlisted men, he is held in high regard"; that his general reputation was "excellent"; that his ability as a
soldier was "excellent"; that he, Colonel Bates, had
tried to have Robinson assigned, rather than merely
attached, to the battalion "because of his excellent
work"; and that, yes, he would be satisfied to go into
combat with Robinson under him.

In summing up, the defense insisted to the panel,
as Robinson later wrote, that the case involved no
violations of the Articles of War, as charged, "but
simply a situation in which a few individuals sought
to vent their bigotry on a Negro they considered
'uppity' because he had the audacity to seek to exercise rights that belonged to him as an American and
as a soldier."

The trial lasted more than four hours. Robinson
secured the necessary two-thirds of the votes (secret
and written) for his acquittal. He was found "not
guilty of all specifications and charges."

Although it ended in his exoneration, Robinson's
court-martial would add further to the legend of his
brutality and his suffering. His white fellow officer
David Williams would write of seeing Robinson
restrained in a manner Jack never mentioned anywhere: "He was handcuffed, and there were shackles
on his legs. Robinson's face was angry, the muscles
on his face tight, his eyes half closed." According to
Williams, Jack had rebelled after the driver decided
to dump his black passengers short of their destination. "It was alleged that Robinson, who possessed a

quick temper and much pride, had roughed up the driver." And Truman K. Gibson, who told Joe Louis's biographer Chris Mead the unlikely story of Jack beating up an officer at Fort Riley, also placed a violent Robinson at "Camp Swift" in Texas. Here, a white bus driver pulled a pistol and ordered Jack to move to the back. "Jackie said, 'That's a fatal mistake. . . . You're gonna eat that son of a bitch.' So Jackie took it and broke every tooth in the guy's mouth, and they discharged Jackie for the good of the service. That's the Jackie Robinson story." This false story, published innocently in Mead's authoritative *Joe Louis,* was quoted from Mead's work in another important book on Joe Louis—by his son, Joe Louis Barrow Jr.—and then again by Woody Strode in his memoir, *Goal Dust.* Contrary to fact, the legend of Robinson as a violent man continued to grow.

ACQUITTED, JACK RETURNED to the 758th Battalion at North Camp Hood. Later that month, on August 24, he was formally reattached to the 761st. But by that time the battalion had already left Camp Hood and was on its way to Europe. The day before his trial, an advance detachment had left Texas on its way to Britain. On August 9, the main body (36 regular officers, 2 warrant officers, and 676 men) had departed for Camp Shanks, New Jersey, to embark for England.

On October 10, the 761st would land at Omaha Beach in Normandy as part of General Patton's Third

Army and as the first black armored unit ever sent into combat. On November 7, led by Colonel Bates, with five other white officers and thirty black officers, the 761st went into action. Fighting for 183 consecutive days, the battalion captured some thirty towns in France, Belgium, Holland, Luxembourg, Germany, and Austria. More than three hundred of its soldiers would receive the Purple Heart; the first person wounded was Bates himself, shot by an enemy patrol on the first day of combat. In November, twenty-two of its men were killed and eighty-one wounded on the field of battle. The 761st Tank Battalion would also help to liberate the Buchenwald concentration camp.

Later, Robinson never stated any regret about staying at home while the 761st Battalion went overseas into battle. His court-martial had probably killed his desire to continue in the Army. But that desire was documented. On July 21, after his arrest but just before his court-martial, he had appeared before the Army Retiring Board meeting at McCloskey Hospital in Temple and expressed a desire to remain on active duty, but on a limited service status. Asked if he wished to retire from the service, he answered, "No." Asked if he considered his disability "permanent," he also replied, "No."

On August 21, he was reassigned to the 659th Tank Destroyer Battalion at North Camp Hood. What the Army intended by this move is not clear, but he wanted no part of it. Four days later, Jack broke regulations, bypassed the regular chain of command, and sent a sharp letter, air mail special delivery, to the Adjutant General in Washington, D.C. He had sought a position, he wrote, with the Special Service Division (in the area of recreation), but "I was told there were no openings for Colored Officers in that field. I request to be retired from the services and be placed on reserve as I feel I can be of more service to the government doing defense work rather than being on limited duty with an outfit that is already better than 100% over strength in officers."

Jack was still uncertain of the outcome of his appeal when orders came on September 19 for Robinson (along with nineteen other "colored" second lieutenants) to leave Camp Hood and report to Camp Breckinridge, to be assigned to the 372nd Infantry Regiment. Given his physical problems, this transfer made little sense. On September 29, writing again to the Adjutant General, Jack pointed out that infantry service "would only further aggravate my injury. . . . Being an Infantry Officer requires a man that is physically fit and since I have been informed that I would be responsible for any further injury, I feel I would not give the government the services that are required of an officer." Again he pressed his request for "inactive status."

The end was now in sight. In late September, the Adjutant General's office in Washington had informed the Eighth Service Command in Dallas, Texas, that "inasmuch as Lieutenant Robinson does not desire to be retained on active duty in a limited service capacity, it is desired that orders be issued relieving him from active duty. . . . It is desired that the relief orders include the phrase 'by reason of physical disqualification.' " On October 17, he was ordered to transfer to Camp Wheeler, Georgia. However, he was also given leave of one month and three days, effective October 21, before reporting to Camp Wheeler. Precisely at the end of his leave, he would "revert to an inactive status," as the Special Order put it. In other words, for all practical purposes his service was now over.

Back in Pasadena, he made no move to call Rachel in San Francisco, but could hardly stop thinking about her. Finally, after his mother begged him to do so, he placed a call to Rachel and found her eager to patch up their quarrel. Racing to San Francisco by car, he offered her the engagement ring once again. The charm bracelet, alas, was gone; he had impulsively given it to a young woman at Fort Riley. In 1949, Jack would tell a ghostwriter that he had been on the verge of marrying this unnamed woman; "I had almost made up my mind to marry the other girl." But seeing Rachel again, he realized "really that she had more kindness, understanding and was more womanly than anybody I had ever known. . . . We became engaged again."

Rachel herself was in a happier mood: her brother Chuck was alive. Shot down over Yugoslavia, he had found shelter with a civilian family, then was arrested and jailed in a German prison camp. According to the Red Cross, he was badly wounded in one leg but otherwise was in good health. In fact, he was on his way back to the United States.

On November 28, 1944, Robinson was "honorably relieved from active duty" in the U.S. Army "by reason of physical disqualification." Almost certainly, he was at home in California when the end came.

His stint of almost three years as a soldier was over. So was his ordeal as a black officer in the mainly Jim Crow army of the United States. The war was a time of sacrifice for countless Americans, but for Robinson it had been deeply frustrating. With the potential to become an excellent soldier and a leader of soldiers, he had been barred from making something substantial of his talents; the Army had come close to destroying him. In the process, however, he had learned more about life. As 1944 drew to a close, he was a more seasoned and mature individual than when he had entered as a raw recruit in April 1942. He was far more deeply invested now in a personal commitment to the ideal of social justice, especially for blacks. But he had paid a stiff price in the process.

As he approached his twenty-sixth birthday, he was a man still moving largely in the dark. Prodigiously gifted as an athlete, with a fierce will to succeed, he was yet without a vocation or a profession or a skill that could be marketed easily in a nation deeply divided by race and indifferent or hostile to its black citizens and their dreams. Robinson was still drifting, drifting, still largely at the mercy of fate and the whims and wishes of whites, even as he also continued to nurture the faith that he yet might be destined by God for something great.

A Monarch
in the Negro Leagues
1944–1946

Why is Mr. Rickey interested in my arm?
Why is he interested in me?
—Jackie Robinson (1945)

NOVEMBER 1944 FOUND Robinson fresh out of the Army and with only the prospect of a job. The prospect had come casually enough. One day, passing by a baseball field at Camp Breckinridge in Kentucky, Jack noticed a black man snapping off some impressive curves. The player turned out to be Ted Alexander, now a soldier, but previously a member of the Kansas City Monarchs in the Negro National League. Suddenly it occurred to Jack that this might be an avenue worth pursuing. The war had left the Negro leagues short of talent; at the same time, they were attracting some of the largest crowds in their history. On Alexander's advice, Robinson sent a letter of inquiry to Thomas Y. Baird, who owned the Monarchs along with their founder, J. L. Wilkinson. Answering promptly, Baird offered Jack $300 a month—if he made the team. Robinson countered by asking for $400. Conceding, Baird ordered Robinson to join the team for spring training the following April in Houston, Texas.

By Christmas, however, Jack was already living in Texas. Early that month, perhaps in response to news from Robinson himself about his offer from the Negro leagues, Reverend Karl Downs, now the president of Samuel Huston College in Austin, Texas, sent a telegram to Jack inviting him to teach physical education there. Eager to work, and even more eager to repay his debt to Reverend Downs, Jack promptly accepted his offer.

The year before, when Downs left Pasadena to go to Samuel Huston, he became reputedly the youngest college president in the United States. From Camp Hood, Jack had gone to Austin at least once to visit Downs, who had counseled him during his court-martial ordeal. "I believe that my father had even gone up to Camp Hood and tried to help Jackie," Downs's daughter, Karleen, later offered. "He and my mother had such great respect and affection for him." When the athletic director of the college suddenly quit his job in the fall, Downs had turned to Robinson and begged him to come as a replacement.

Jack certainly did not go for the money. In 1945, Samuel Huston College, a black United Methodist Church school founded in 1876, was an institution in deep financial distress, its meager resources reduced further by the war, its student rolls shrinking. Enrollment teetered now at just over three hundred students, of whom only about three dozen were men. "The college was a ghost," a newspaper recalled some years later, "and it was Downs's duty to give this dead institution life and meaning in the community and the state." Downs had responded vigorously; aided by his local congressman, a onetime schoolteacher named Lyndon Baines Johnson, who believed—in part as a segregationist—in the importance of historically black colleges, Downs had launched a building program that soon added five new buildings to the campus. "Bringing Jackie Robinson to the campus was vintage Karl Downs," a friend of Downs's would recall. "It was the same spirit that led him to put in a visiting artists program that brought in all sorts of celebrated musicians, and that in turn made some very influential local whites take note of our little college. Nothing like that had ever happened before Karl came."

In sports Downs gave Jack a free hand, which he needed; Samuel Huston College had nothing that might be called an athletic program. Jack also set about installing the first physical training regimen in the college's history. To inspire the students, he also put on display most of his many medals and trophies. The response seemed enthusiastic; but when he made a public call for basketball players, only seven students showed up—and not all of them knew the game. Nevertheless, Jack threw himself into coaching the team, which played a sporadic schedule in the Southwestern Conference against other black colleges, such as Grambling and Southern of Louisiana; Bishop, Wiley, and Prairie View in Texas; and Arkansas A&M. The highlight of the season was undoubtedly Samuel Huston's upset of the defending league champion, Bishop College, 61–59.

At the end of March, a popular figure now on the Samuel Huston campus, Jack moved on to Houston for the start of spring training with the Monarchs. He reached Houston both excited at the prospect and with some reservations about the Negro leagues. In 1937, in Pasadena, he and his friend Nate Moreland had been promised twenty dollars each to sub for a barnstorming "top team from the Negro leagues." The two youths played their hearts out, only to be stiffed for their pains. "That night," according to Jack, "we went to a cheap hotel where the team was staying to collect our money. We never could find the man who was supposed to pay us. I decided then and there that Negro baseball was not for me." Up to April 1945, Robinson had probably never seen an official Negro league game. The Negro National League concentrated on play in the East, the Negro American League in the Midwest; California was not on the schedule. Nor would he have been romantic about the all-black leagues. Robinson's race pride led him to demand integration, not to glory in separation. His three Army years had only reinforced his contempt for Jim Crow.

Nevertheless, Jack knew that the Negro leagues gave blacks a chance that white baseball denied them. Behind the letters to him from Tom Baird was a controversial but also glorious history arising from the purge of blacks from organized baseball in the late nineteenth century. The decade that saw the U.S. Supreme Court rule that railroads could maintain "separate but equal facilities" for blacks and whites, thus sanctioning segregation, also saw a revolt by white players, officials, and fans against black athletes in baseball. Led mainly by Adrian "Cap" Anson, a star with the Chicago White Stockings, the revolt closed the roster of blacks in the major leagues after several had played since 1872. For some years, efforts to found a separate black league had come to nothing. Then, in 1920, the visionary Andrew "Rube" Foster, a former pitcher, assembled a group of owners and sports reporters from the black press who laid out a league structure to mirror organized white baseball. With a constitution setting the rules of the National Association of Colored Professional Base Ball Clubs, league play soon followed. By 1945, despite many struggles and disputes over the years, the Negro leagues had become for many blacks a cherished fixture of their segregated lives. The leagues were more stable than ever, with better attendance and higher earnings than at any other time in their history.

In joining the Kansas City Monarchs, founded by the only white owner in the Negro leagues, J. L. Wilkinson, Robinson entered black baseball at the top. Respected by most blacks, Wilkinson was perhaps the most generous and farsighted of the owners. The Monarchs traveled in such style as Jim Crow permitted; at home in Kansas City, they enjoyed the support of most of the black leaders and strivers and often outdrew the white club, the Kansas City Blues, with which they shared a stadium. Over the years, their roster of stars included the incomparable pitcher Leroy "Satchel" Paige; the famed base stealer James "Cool Papa" Bell; and the versatile player, then admired manager, John "Buck" O'Neil. For young black fans, the Monarchs were the height of baseball fashion; Hilton Smith, a pitcher, would claim that "everybody, *everybody*—anybody that played baseball wanted to play with the Monarchs." The Monarch players liked to think of themselves as gentlemen. Although boozing and fisticuffs were natural to professional sports, the Monarchs aspired to the high road, as befit aristocracy. According to O'Neil, "a Monarch never had a fight on the street. A Monarch never cut anybody. You couldn't shoot craps on our bus. . . . This was the only way to 'open the door.' "

But if the Monarchs were the best of the Negro leagues, Robinson found them wanting. He was disillusioned before he played his first game. No doubt remembering his youthful fleecing by a Negro league team, "I inquired about my contract and was promptly informed that the letters I received constituted all the contract I needed. This seemed rather strange to me." The letters were indeed a contract of sorts, but they spelled out few details. The next jolt came on his third day, when he found himself and the team on a bus heading for San Antonio and a game, without any practice, against Kelly Airfield there. "Spring training," Jack found out to his dismay, "consisted of actually playing baseball games rather than getting prepared for the coming season."

Thereafter, with the regular season opening on May 6 in Kansas City against the Chicago American Giants, Jack's experience as a Monarch continued to mix the bad with the good. The long rides in uncomfortable buses left him groggy and cranky at the start of games; he hated, too, the cheap Jim Crow hotels, where "the rooms were dingy and dirty, and the restrooms were in such bad condition that players were unable to use them." The umpiring was generally poor, and even the scorekeeping unreliable. He would recall a "lopsided game" in Baltimore when the Monarchs scored five runs in one inning. However, "only two showed on the scoreboard. We looked for the official scorer to straighten it out, but he had disappeared. He got bored with the game and went home early." With no team curfew, some players slept only a little, if at all, before a game, and drank far too much—which offended the abstemious Robinson. Such habits prevented fans from "seeing the best type of ball of which the players were capable of playing. In my opinion the lack of rules, or the failure to enforce the rules, hurts the caliber of baseball and certainly cuts down the interest."

Still, Jack knew a rare opportunity when he saw it, and tried to fit in. Sammie Haynes, an easygoing center fielder who sometimes roomed with Robinson, recalled: "Jackie was able to say, 'Look, I'm here to learn. I know I don't play the brand of baseball you guys play. But help me. I'm here to learn.' " On an overcrowded bus heading to New Orleans, when extra chairs were set up in the aisle, Jack caught everyone's attention by sitting in the stairwell. "This is my seat," he insisted, according to Haynes. "I'm a rookie. This is my seat. I don't even want a chair." With such humility on display, the team took to him "very warmly"; he became "one of the guys."

Jack's modesty made sense. Five years after his last competitive baseball season, at UCLA in 1940, he could hardly be sure about his ability to make the team. Later, in fact, some Monarchs would question his skills. A veteran, Newt Allen, claimed to have been assigned to evaluate Jack on the San Antonio trip. Robinson, who ran the bases and picked up signs well, was "a very smart ball player"; but Allen decided at once—or so he said—that Jack "can't play shortstop." He could not range far to his right, then gun the ball all the way to first base. Hilton Smith also remembered Robinson as only "an average fielder." "He didn't have that strong of an arm," according to Sammie Haynes, but "he had developed a quick throw, quick release of the ball." Nor was it at first clear to all, apparently, that Robinson could hit. The veteran pitcher Willie "Sug" Cornelius of the Chicago American Giants, it was said, had Jackie mumbling to himself by throwing him all sorts of junk "instead of the outside fastball that his stance seemed to call for and that Robinson hit so well."

Nevertheless, Jack not only became the Monarchs' shortstop when injury forced out the incumbent, Jesse Williams, but also went on to become in the major leagues what one expert has called "perhaps the best curve-ball hitter of his generation." Years later, when Robinson's success in the majors would help to destroy the Negro leagues as an attraction, the role of black baseball in his own rise would be controversial. Fueling the argument would be Jack's open criticism of the leagues, despite his praise of stars such as Paige and Josh Gibson. "All the time I was playing," he would write in 1948, "I was looking around for something else. I didn't like the bouncing buses, the cheap hotels, and the constant night games." In turn, some former teammates, irked by his ingratitude, would recall Robinson as being specially tutored by various Negro leaguers, who somehow knew early that he would be chosen to integrate baseball. "Quickly," according to one authority, "the old-time baseball men pulled together in an effort to teach Robinson the trade in as short a time as possible." The former Monarchs manager William "Dizzy" Dismukes is said to have asked Cool Papa Bell to "give Robinson a base-stealing exhibition because the Negro leaguers were not impressed with Robinson's tagging ability." Once, sliding safely under Robinson's tag, Bell schooled him. "See that? They got a lot of guys in the major leagues slide like that. You can't get those guys out like that."

In certain quarters, the later criticism of Robinson went further. "He did not fit in very well, and his combative nature resulted in several nasty exchanges" with other players, according to the writer Donn Rogosin. "He was not a popular player in Kansas City." Allegedly, when word came that his UCLA teammate Kenny Washington might become a Monarch, Robinson "quietly passed the word that there was room on the Monarchs for only one ex-UCLA star." But such a mean response would have been unlike Robinson, who respected Washington; and reports of special coaching are probably exaggerated. Excellently coached from his youth, Jack had shown all the elements of his mature baseball skills long before he reported to Houston: his inventive, daring base stealing; his sensational fielding at shortstop; his ability to bunt and to hit in the clutch; his sense of the importance of team play; and his unquenchable passion for winning. Whatever his teammates taught him he must have learned very quickly; at mid-season he was chosen to start at shortstop in the annual East-West All-Star game on July 29 in Chicago. In 1940, he had hit a hopeless .097 for UCLA; in 1945, with five years of rust, he batted a team-high .345 with the Monarchs— although, as Jack wrote disdainfully, "I could never figure out my batting average because so many games did not count in the league statistics.... Nobody knew for sure." In fact, in 1945 the Monarchs probably played 62 league games (and won 32); the team also played about 40 more nonleague games. Playing in 45 league games, Jack hit ten doubles, four triples, and five home runs.

In criticizing loose behavior on the Monarchs, Jack no doubt seemed priggish to some of his teammates. But his sense of self was tightly wound around core values of dignity and self-discipline, and he believed in God and the Bible. Absurdly or not, he drew a line in the dirt between himself and sin, and tried hard not to cross it. Thus, no doubt to the genuine bewilderment of some teammates, he showed little or no interest in easy sex on the road. Women were to be respected; sex had a moral element. One evening, according to Sammie Haynes, Jack broke up a promising little party with Haynes and two eager young women when he threw a glass of whiskey into a lighted fireplace, to demonstrate how lethal Scotch could be. At another point, Haynes became tired of hearing Jack talk about the virtues of Rachel Isum. "Well," Haynes asked, "have you been to bed with the woman?" Jack told the truth. "He said, 'No.' I jumped up. I said, 'Man, are you going to marry somebody you haven't been to bed with? Are you crazy?' He said, 'Sammie, this is the lady for me. I don't have to go to bed with her.' And I said, 'Man, this thing's crazy. You're crazy!' "

To some black players, Jack doubtless seemed to be from another world, a world of colleges, California, and a troubling familiarity with white people almost unheard of in Jim Crow America; at times, he himself felt like an outsider. But in the end Robinson owed a huge debt to the Negro leagues, even if he seldom looked back on the 1945 season sentimentally. One reason for his coolness was perhaps his loyalty to the Brooklyn Dodgers, who brought him fame and fortune when the Monarchs could give neither; another reason was his suspicion of segregated institutions, black or white. Yet another reason, however, might have been Jack's sense that the events that led him to the Monarchs, and then to the Dodgers, suggested that Providence was at work in his life, and that Providence deserved all thanks. A modest man, he believed nevertheless that God was behind his life, guiding it, and intending him for some important purpose.

Whatever that purpose was, in 1945 it seemed to have nothing to do with baseball. That April, in his first month with the Monarchs, Jack was again teased by white baseball, and again rejected. On April 16, the day before the Red Sox opened their season and the day after the burial of President Roosevelt in Hyde Park, New York, Robinson, along with two other Negro leagues players, strode into Fenway Park in Boston for a tryout before club officials. With him were Sam Jethroe, an outfielder with the Cleveland Buckeyes, and Marvin Williams, an infielder from the Philadelphia Stars. Watching them were two top Red Sox scouts and, from a secluded spot, the Red Sox manager, Joe Cronin.

Behind the tryout was the action of a Boston city councilman and Harvard College graduate, Isadore H. Y. Muchnick. In 1944, seeing his constituency change steadily from mainly Jewish to mainly black, Muchnick had joined the ragtag band of critics fighting Jim Crow in baseball. His main weapon was the annual threat by the Boston City Council to bar professional baseball on Sunday; wielding it, Muchnick pressed the Red Sox and the Braves, the city's two major-league teams, to allow at least one black player to try out. In 1944, the Red Sox general manager, Eddie Collins, had replied in writing that blacks did not wish to play in the big leagues (because, he claimed, they made more money in their own leagues). In 1945, when Muchnick pressed him again, Collins agreed to a tryout.

Encouraging Muchnick was Wendell Smith, a crusading sports journalist of the black Pittsburgh *Courier,* who then set about finding the players. At noon on April 16, with expenses paid by Smith's newspaper, the trio arrived at Fenway Park with Smith and Muchnick. They met a chilly reception but were allowed to enter. This was Jack's first time in Boston, much less in the historic ballpark with its massive and storied green left-field wall. Also on hand were a dozen or so high school prospects, all white, and most of them pitchers; but the three black players commanded attention. "I was in the outfield and the other two were in the infield," Jethroe remembered. "We fielded, threw to bases, ran and hit." Even with five years off, Robinson was ready; all reports called him the most impressive of the three. "I'm telling you, you never saw anyone hit The Wall the way Robinson did that day," Muchnick said in 1959. "Bang, bang, bang: he rattled it." Jethroe agreed: "Jackie hit balls over the fence and against The Wall." Even the Red Sox were impressed. "What a ballplayer!" the chief scout and a former star hitter, Hugh Duffy, is said to have exclaimed. "Too bad he's the wrong color."

After an hour or so, the session came to an end. Muchnick remembered meeting Cronin, who seemed taken with Robinson: "He said to me, 'If I had that guy on this club, we'd be a world beater.' " But after they filled out applications, their exit was as frosty as their entrance. Jack returned to Houston expecting little from the Red Sox beyond the courtesy of a reply—which never came.

But he had gained an important ally in Wendell Smith. Once a gifted pitcher, Smith had one day won an American Legion championship game with a shutout, then looked on in disbelief as the famed Detroit scout Wish Egan invited Smith's catcher and boyhood friend Mike Tresh (later of the White Sox), as well as the losing pitcher, to a tryout. "I wish I could sign you, too, kid," Egan told Smith. "But I can't." Smith's widow recalled: "He went home and cried that night." Joining the *Courier* after college, Smith had enlisted with a vengeance in the sporadic campaign to end Jim Crow in baseball. In the black press, he found allies in men like Frank Young of the Chicago *Defender,* Sam Lacy of the Baltimore *Afro-American,* and Joe Bostic of the Harlem *People's Voice,* who fought consistently against segregation. The most vigorous efforts came from the Communist press, including picketing, petitions, and unrelenting pressure for about ten years in the *Daily Worker,* notably from Lester Rodney and Bill Mardo. In the mainstream press were men like Ed Sullivan and Damon Runyon, Westbrook Pegler of the Chicago *Tribune,* Shirley Povich of the Washington *Post,* Jimmy Powers of the New York *Daily News,* and Dave Egan of the Boston *Record.* Surveying the long list of downtrodden peoples of the world uplifted by the United States, Egan once asked: "Could we, by any chance, spare a thought for the Negro in the United States? Do we, by any chance, feel disgust at the thought that Negro athletes, solely because of their color, are barred from playing baseball?"

Meanwhile, white baseball claimed that no ban existed. In 1942, Judge Kenesaw Mountain Landis, the commissioner of baseball, made it clear that "Negroes are not barred from organized baseball by the commissioner," and "no rule in organized baseball" prohibited their entry. In the South, segregationist laws barred interracial teams and competition, but nothing stood legally between blacks and the major leagues. Many factors were cited to explain why the majors included no blacks. No blacks wished to play in the majors—the Eddie Collins argument. No blacks were qualified to play—an argument routinely diminished by the record of black teams and individuals against their white counterparts outside the majors. White players, especially Southerners, would revolt if blacks tried to join their ranks; a 1942 New York *Post* column warned that white Southerners would "brandish sharp spikes with intent to cut and maim Negro infielders" and throw "murderous bean-balls" at their heads. However, a 1938 *Courier* poll told a different tale: most white players would accept a black among them. In 1939, Wendell Smith, the celebrated performer Paul Robeson, and other leading blacks had met with Landis to explore the issue. "Frankly," Smith recalled, "we were met with silence."

This silence was the silence of contented lions. But in 1943, in the middle of the war, a dissenting voice began to be heard. At the Brooklyn Dodgers' headquarters on Montague Street in Brooklyn Heights, the new president, Wesley Branch Rickey, proposed a daring response to the wartime shrinkage in talent. Instead of cutting back on scouting, as other teams had done, the Dodgers would intensify their efforts and be poised to dominate the market when the war ended. Rickey had another, related idea. In the course of this expanded scouting, a superior Negro player or two might materialize; perhaps the Dodgers would sign them. Approached first, George V. McLaughlin of the Brooklyn Trust Company, which provided the Dodgers with their financial base, had responded positively: "Why not? You might come up with something." Rickey had then found further support among other key members of the Dodgers family, including his main rival for control of the club, Walter O'Malley.

Now past sixty years old, Branch Rickey was a man to follow. In addition to a highly successful reign as general manager of the St. Louis Cardinals in the 1930s, he had invented or perfected several staples of modern baseball, including the farm system of minor-league clubs nurturing talent for the big leagues. A moralist some people found insufferable, Rickey was a dedicated, Bible-loving Christian who refused to attend games on Sunday. He was also a master of rhetoric, a grandiloquent speaker whose high-flown locutions overwhelmed most opposition and often obscured or embroidered key facts; reporters called his office the Cave of Winds. Personalizing the evil of Jim Crow in baseball, Rickey told of an incident that happened in South Bend, Indiana, in 1904, when he was coach of the Ohio Wesleyan baseball team and had gone there to play Notre Dame. A hotel manager had tried to bar the only black team member, Charles Thomas, from the hotel. Then, following Rickey's strong protests, Thomas was allowed to share Rickey's room. Rickey had returned to find Thomas, distraught, trying to peel the flesh from his hands. "Damned skin . . . damned skin!" he muttered. "If I could only rub it off." "That scene haunted me for many years," Rickey would write, "and I vowed that I would always do whatever I could to see that other Americans did not have to face the bitter humiliation that was heaped upon Charles Thomas." The story begged comparison to another, lodged in American lore, about Abe Lincoln going down the Mississippi and seeing slavery, and vowing to see it end one day. Indeed, a portrait of Lincoln hung in Rickey's office.

In twenty years with the Cardinals, Rickey had done little or nothing about racism in baseball. On this question, he argued, Missouri was stony soil: St. Louis barred blacks from the grandstand. However, arriving in Brooklyn in 1942, he began to move. After two seasons, he had become familiar with the pool of "colored" talent available not only in the United States but also in such baseball-loving lands as Cuba, Puerto Rico, the Dominican Republic, and Mexico. At some point, he decided not to take the easy route of hiring Latin players of African or Indian descent but to turn instead to the pool of bona fide African-American athletes whose inclusion would confront Jim Crow head on. The Negro leagues were no mystery to major-league baseball; many of the black teams, in renting white-owned stadiums, provided significant revenue to white clubs. The truly gifted black players, such as Paige and Gibson, were well known. But Rickey had to sort through the lot to find the player or players who would satisfy, in Rickey's mind, the complex requirements of his experiment.

Although Rickey and his publicists, formal and informal, would assert that pragmatism—the desire to win games and to profit from these victories—and not the ideal of social justice played the central role in his decision (a position shared, ironically, with cynics of various persuasions), Rickey's thinking clearly went beyond pragmatism. A man of grand gestures, already lampooned as "the Mahatma" by ridiculing scribes, but also a man of some vision, especially in contrast to other leaders of baseball, Rickey saw a chance to intervene in the moral history of the nation, as Lincoln had done. Aware of the dangers, he moved cautiously. However, he also saw history on his side. With the war, the logic of Jim Crow had been set back as never before. The 1943 Harlem riot, smashing the image of New York City as a haven of democracy, encouraged passage in 1945 of the Ives-Quinn Bill, establishing the State Commission Against Discrimination (even as Congress gutted its Fair Employment Practices Commission by declining to fund it). In the spring, at a joint meeting of the major leagues, Rickey agreed to serve with Larry MacPhail of the Yankees and two black leaders (to be selected) on a four-person committee to investigate the issue of the ban on black players. When Mayor Fiorello La Guardia, organizing a ten-person panel to work against discrimination, appealed to baseball to allow his committee to supplant its own unit, Rickey and MacPhail agreed to do so.

Despite such moves, Rickey camouflaged his ultimate aims. On April 6, 1945, he reacted angrily when Joe Bostic of the Harlem *People's Voice* showed up at the Bear Mountain, New York, training camp of the Dodgers to demand a tryout for two veteran players,

Terris McDuffie, a pitcher with the Newark Eagles, and Dave "Showboat" Thomas, a first baseman with the New York Cubans. Although Bostic got his tryout, Rickey was incensed both by the surprise nature of the attack and by the fact that the *People's Voice* was a Communist publication. At a press conference, he attacked the Negro leagues and the Communists. Accusing the leagues of being dominated by gamblers and of condoning shoddy business practices, he praised the new all-black United States League, founded in January mainly by Gus Greenlee, a former president of the Negro National League and the owner of the Pittsburgh Crawfords, which Greenlee had withdrawn from that league. Rickey then announced that he would put together his own team, the Brooklyn Brown Dodgers, to play in the new league. This team would use Ebbets Field when the white Dodgers were away.

Many blacks resented Rickey's remarks. In the Pittsburgh *Courier,* Cumberland "Cum" Posey, a pillar of the Negro leagues, denounced the Dodgers and Red Sox tryouts as "the most humiliating experience Negro baseball has yet suffered from white organized baseball." In the Chicago *Defender,* Frank Young ridiculed Rickey for "trying to assume the role of an Abraham Lincoln"—a charge Rickey would hear with increasing frequency and perhaps some satisfaction. However, the myth of the Brooklyn Brown Dodgers now freed Rickey to deploy the main Dodger scouts, Tom Greenwade, George Sisler, Clyde Sukeforth, and Wid Matthews, to gather information on black players openly. The list of prospects began to shrink. Over the years, Rickey had evolved three key questions about any prospect: Can he run? Can he throw? Can he hit with power? Emerging at the top was Jackie Robinson, who had been identified to Rickey by Wendell Smith as perhaps the most promising prospect. Shrewdly, Rickey sent three scouts at different times to observe Robinson, with none knowing what the others were doing, and with Robinson unaware that he was being watched. To Sisler, only Robinson's throwing arm was less than superb; Greenwade called him the finest bunter in baseball; and Matthews noted that Robinson protected the strike zone better than any rookie he had yet seen. When all three reported independently—if Rickey's later statements are to be believed—that Robinson was the one, "the ideal Negro star to lead the invasion of organized baseball," Rickey then made inquiries himself in California about Robinson's character. The news that Robinson was known to resent segregation, far from dismaying Rickey, encouraged him.

(The scouts also reported favorably on Sam Jethroe and an even younger prospect, the hard-throwing future Dodgers star Don Newcombe of the Newark Eagles. From the start, Rickey intended to sign not one token black player but several players, and thus quickly change the complexion of baseball. Because of certain circumstances, the spotlight would fall on Jackie Robinson. By the end of 1947, however, the Dodgers organization would have signed several black players, the fruit of Rickey's intense scrutiny of the Negro leagues over the previous three years.)

Now Rickey made his intentions clear to members of his family and other trusted advisers. When he brought the matter up casually at a card game, with seven other persons present, not one supported him. His wife and his son, Branch Rickey Jr., wanted integration but feared that the ensuing storm would hurt him badly. The Dodgers' traveling secretary, Harold Parrott, counseled that the team was poised to win the pennant; why risk almost certain success? (Parrott's job was to travel with the team and make all living arrangements. "I knew most of the problems would be mine if we brought in a black player. Ebbets Field would embrace a Negro, or even a Chinaman in a pigtail, if he could drive in runs for the Dodgers. But road games would bring up many headaches.") Nevertheless, toward the end of August, Rickey ordered Sukeforth, who had not yet scouted Robinson, to go to Chicago, where the Monarchs were to play the Lincoln Giants in Comiskey Park, and bring in Jackie Robinson.

BY LATE AUGUST 1945, Jack was pretty much fed up with life as a Monarch. Having threatened once to quit, he was ready to make 1945 his last year in professional baseball, with a barnstorming venture after the end of the regular season. He would then seek a job as a high school coach, marry Rachel Isum, and settle down in Los Angeles.

In June, Rachel had graduated, with honors, from the University of California. In a secret ballot, the students and faculty at her hospital in San Francisco

had also given her the Florence Nightingale Award as
the outstanding clinical nurse in the graduating class.
She then returned home to Los Angeles, where she
quickly found a job in the nursery of Los Angeles
General Hospital. With her mother's graduation
present of $100, plus whatever else she could save,
she planned to travel to New York in October with
her college roommate, Janice Brooks, and live there
for a few weeks. Then Rachel expected to return
home and settle down with Jack.

The trip to New York was very important. She
and Jack had set the date—February 10 of the following year, 1946—but their future seemed tightly
circumscribed. Setting the date seemed like surren-
dering to the ordinary. "My concern was that I was
going to get stuck in California and never get out of
there," she recalled. "I was getting ready to marry a
man who didn't really have a job, and we didn't
know what our future held. So I needed that adventure in New York."

On August 24, at Comiskey Park, Jack was out
on the field, but nursing a sore shoulder, when a
white man called out his name and beckoned. Jack
went over. The man introduced himself as Clyde
Sukeforth, which meant nothing to Robinson. Then
he said he was there on behalf of Branch Rickey of
the Brooklyn Dodgers. Now he had Jack's attention.
Mr. Rickey was starting a team, the Brooklyn Brown
Dodgers. He wondered about Jackie's arm strength;
could Jack throw a few balls for Sukeforth? The
Dodger scout would remember Jack listening "care-

fully, and when I was through he spoke right up—
Jackie was never shy, you know."

"Why is Mr. Rickey interested in my arm?" Jack
asked. "Why is he interested in *me?*"

Sukeforth convinced Robinson to meet him after
the game at the Stevens Hotel, where the scout was
staying, and where he bribed a bellman two dollars to
allow Jack to use the passenger elevator, from which
blacks were normally barred. Eventually Jack arrived
and began to pepper Sukeforth with questions. One
thing above all intrigued both men. Mr. Rickey had
made it clear, as Sukeforth informed Jack, that if
Robinson would not come to him, he would come to
Robinson. Both Jack and Sukeforth now suspected
that something more than a place on the Brooklyn
Brown Dodgers might be at stake.

The men agreed to meet in Toledo, where Sukeforth had to observe another player, then take the
train to New York. Sukeforth then sent a wire to
Rickey telling of Jack's injury ("Player fell on shoulder last Tuesday. Will be out of game a few more
days"). On Sunday night, after the white scout convinced a ticket seller that, yes, he intended to share
quarters with the black man, they left Toledo. On the
morning of August 28, after spending the night in
Harlem, Jack met Sukeforth outside 215 Montague
Street in Brooklyn. On the fourth floor, a receptionist
waved them toward an office door. In a darkly pan-
eled office, an illuminated fish tank glowed in a corner, and on a wall were four portraits, including the
one of Lincoln and another of the Dodgers' field

managers, Leo Durocher. On another wall, a black-
board held the names of all the baseball personnel at
every level in the Dodgers organization. Behind a
mahogany desk was the bulky white figure of Branch
Rickey. Light gleamed off his spectacles; his bushy
eyebrows flared above oddly expressionless eyes;
between his pudgy fingers was a cigar. The room
pulsed with summer heat, but he wore a jacket and a
bow tie. He listened as Sukeforth glided through an
introduction.

"Hello, Jackie," Rickey offered. Then he seemed
to lose consciousness of everything but Jack's face
and body, as if forty years of fantasy had in the twin-
kle of an eye become flesh. "He just stared and
stared," recalled Sukeforth. "That's what he did with
Robinson—stared at him as if he were trying to get
inside the man. And Jack stared right back at him.
Oh, they were a pair, those two! I tell you, the air in
that office was electric."

"Do you have a girl?" Rickey asked suddenly.

"I'm not sure," Robinson replied, taken aback.
He was sitting now, in an overstuffed leather chair
that barely eased the tension. Perhaps he was not sure
which answer Rickey wanted to hear; but Jack
explained quickly that with all his traveling and the
uncertainty of his employment, he was not sure he
should count on any girl, or that any girl should count
on him.

Rickey made it clear that Robinson should marry,
if he had found the right woman. A dangerous challenge was at hand, in which Robinson would need
the support of a good wife.

"Do you know why you were brought here?" Rickey demanded.

To play on a new colored Brooklyn team, Jackie replied.

"No," Rickey corrected him. "That isn't it. You were brought here, Jackie, to play for the Brooklyn organization. Perhaps on Montreal to start with, and—"

"Me? Play for Montreal?"

"If you can make it, yes. Later on—also if you can make it—you'll have a chance with the Brooklyn Dodgers."

"I was thrilled, scared, and excited," Jack would recall. "I was incredulous. Most of all, I was speechless." Silent before Rickey's revelations, Jack listened in wonder as the Dodgers' general manager, with rhetorical flourishes, revealed his hand. "I want to win the pennant and we need ball players!" he thundered, whacking his desk. "Do you think you can do it?"

Clyde Sukeforth would remember that "Jack waited, and waited, and waited before answering. . . . We were all just looking at him."

"Yes," he finally replied.

Rickey made it clear that Jack's ability to run, throw, and hit was only one part of the challenge. Could he stand up to the physical, verbal, and psychological abuse that was bound to come? "I know you're a good ball player," Rickey barked. "What I don't know is whether you have the guts."

Jack started to answer hotly, in defense of his manhood, when Rickey explained, "I'm looking for a ball player with guts enough not to fight back."

Caught up now in the drama, Rickey stripped off his coat and enacted out a variety of parts that portrayed examples of an offended Jim Crow. Now he was a white hotel clerk rudely refusing Jack accommodations; now a supercilious white waiter in a restaurant; now a brutish railroad conductor. He became a foul-mouthed opponent, Jack recalled, talking about "my race, my parents, in language that was almost unendurable." Now he was a vengeful base runner, vindictive spikes flashing in the sun, sliding into Jack's black flesh—"How do you like that, nigger boy?" At one point, he swung his pudgy fist at Jack's head. Above all, he insisted, Jack could not strike back. He could not explode in righteous indignation; only then would this experiment be likely to succeed, and other black men would follow in Robinson's footsteps to make a living reality of Rickey's unspoken promise to Charlie Thomas forty-one years before.

Robinson sat, transfixed but also stirred. "I had to do it for several reasons," he now knew. "For black youth, for my mother, for Rae, for myself. I had already begun to feel I had to do it for Branch Rickey."

Turning the other cheek, Rickey would have him remember, was not proverbial wisdom but the law of the New Testament. As one Methodist believer to another, Rickey offered Jack a copy of an English translation of Giovanni Papini's popular *Life of Christ* and pointed to a passage quoting the words of Jesus— what Papini called "the most stupefying of His revolutionary teachings": "Ye have heard that it hath been said, An eye for an eye, and a tooth for a tooth: But I say unto you, That ye resist not evil: But whosoever shall smite thee on thy right cheek, turn to him the other also. And if any man will sue thee at the law, and take away thy coat, let him have thy cloke also. And whosoever shall compel thee to go a mile, go with him twain."

Thus, cannily acting out of both religious faith and a sympathetic grasp of political history, the Mahatma invoked the Christian counterpart of the ancient Hindu philosophy of *satyagraha,* or active nonviolence, which Mohandas K. Gandhi, the original Mahatma, had adopted in his long struggle for Indian independence from British imperialism. Within three years, in 1948, India would be free— and Gandhi would be assassinated. Within less than a generation, black and white Christian ministers, led by Martin Luther King Jr., would themselves invoke Gandhi's philosophy of nonviolence to bring down the walls of segregation across the South.

More than two hours after he entered the dark office on Montague Street, Jack stumbled out into the Brooklyn sunshine. He had just signed an agreement, dictated by Rickey, that bound him to the Brooklyn Dodgers organization. On signing a player's contract he would receive a bonus of $3,500. His salary would be $600 a month. Until Rickey gave the word, Robinson must keep the arrangement a secret. Finally, according to the agreement, he would be signed, probably by the Dodgers' Montreal club, on or before November 1. This stipulation suggests strongly that Rickey was thinking about the city and state elections in early November and the impact the news of this signing might have on both.

Returning to the Monarchs, Jack looked on the team with an eye now hopelessly alienated; he could hardly wait to leave. He told no one on the team about Rickey's invitation. Even with his mother he only hinted at the news; she had no real idea what he was talking about. He was also guarded with Rachel: "On the telephone, he would tell me only that something wonderful had happened that would affect us both. He said he couldn't tell me, but that I'd know soon enough. He was excited, but he wouldn't give it away. He never mentioned Branch Rickey or the Dodgers."

A few days later, Jack proposed to the Monarchs that he be allowed to play until September 21 only, then go home. But the club, displeased by his sudden, unexcused trip to New York, and fearing the new league and the Brooklyn Brown Dodgers, laid down the law; "I was told I would have to play all the games or none." This threat was delivered in front of other players probably by Richard Wilkinson, the son of J. L. Wilkinson, who "gave me a lecture about my trip to New York and assured me that if I left the club I was through; that I could play no place outside of the Negro National League, and he was sure that Kansas City was the only team with which I could play." Seizing on this provocation, Jack left the Monarchs and returned to California.

By this time, some of his excitement about the Dodgers had worn off. Despite the signed agreement, little might come of the electrifying meeting in Brooklyn. Thus he presented the news to Rachel when he saw her. Still, Rickey had impressed him deeply. When he hinted at the news to family and friends—Mack and Willa Mae, Sid Heard and Jack Gordon—he found an unwillingness to listen, because they could not believe it. The white world was unreliable, even treacherous. But Jack's attitude was different. He had pride and anger, but because of his skills as an athlete he had been too deeply involved with white authority, with white coaches and administrators, who depended on him even as he depended on them, not to know that Rickey was, at the very least, credible. He understood that if something wonderful was to happen to him, as was now promised, a white man would almost certainly be central; and Rickey was more than a plausible white man. In their relatively brief meeting, Rickey had probably shown more concentrated personal fury and passion on the question of race and sports than Jack had ever seen in a white man. Within months, at least one black writer would call Branch Rickey a modern-day John Brown, the brooding, vengeful, God-haunted martyr of Harpers Ferry in 1859. Robinson's sensitivity and intelligence begged him to submit to this force.

In October, Jack and Zellee saw Rachel and her roommate Janice Brooks off to New York on their adventure. Then, having agreed to travel with a black barnstorming team in Venezuela, it was now Jack's turn to head east to join the team. He was in New York City when the call came from Branch Rickey. On October 7, Rickey had written to Arthur Mann, his publicist, indicating that he was thinking of extending the deadline for signing Robinson to January 1. Then he would sign several blacks "and make one break on the complete story"; also, he did not want to sign Robinson with other, "possibly better" players unsigned.

However, as the New York City mayoral election campaign drew to a close, the issue of blacks and the three city teams—the Yankees, the Giants, and the Dodgers—flared up. On the defensive, and coveting the black vote, Mayor La Guardia was eager to announce that his progressive racial program was yielding results. La Guardia wanted the teams to sign a formal pledge to uphold the spirit and the letter of the Ives-Quinn state law forbidding discrimination in hiring, and he wanted formal assurances that blacks would soon be hired. But the last thing Rickey wanted was to seem to be succumbing to local political pressure to hire a black. He decided to act preemptively, and to do so not in New York City but in Montreal, where Robinson would be playing.

On October 23, in the presence of the head of the Dodgers' farm system, Branch Rickey Jr., and the president of the Montreal club, Hector Racine, Jack Robinson signed a contract to play with the Royals. The terms were exactly those set forth at the August 28 meeting in Brooklyn.

For all the agitation by the politicians in New York, the news shocked many listeners, including the reporters present. They surged forward to hear what Robinson had to say about his hiring. Jack met the press calmly but said little. "Of course, I can't begin to tell you how happy I am that I am the first member of my race in organized baseball," Robinson said. "I realize how much it means to me, my race, and to baseball. I can only say I'll do my very best to come through in every manner." Branch Rickey Jr., who sought to make it clear that the search had been thorough and expensive (scouting Robinson had cost the Dodgers $25,000, he revealed), tossed in a note of defiance. Racine and his father "undoubtedly will be criticized in some sections of the United States where racial prejudice is rampant. They are not inviting trouble, but they won't avoid it if it comes." No doubt, the decision would cost the organization some support, but the Dodgers would not turn back. "Some players now with us may even quit, but they'll be back in baseball after they work a year or two in a cotton mill."

Support came quickly for Rickey's decision. Horace Stoneham, president of the New York Giants, calling it "a fine way to start a program," promised to look for black players next year. In Boston, Eddie Collins recalled Robinson's workout for his Boston Red Sox and warned that "very few players can step into the majors from college or sandlot baseball," but gallantly wished "more power to Robinson if he can make the grade." Satchel Paige, the best-known and most admired player in black baseball, was the soul of grace even as he was passed over for the role of ending Jim Crow. "They didn't make a mistake by signing Robinson," Paige said. "They couldn't have picked a better man." But there was also opposition. The commissioner of minor-league baseball, Judge

William Bramham, conceded that he was legally bound to approve Robinson's contract. However, he ridiculed Rickey as a whiteface version of the black religious charlatan Father Divine. Worse, Rickey was a carpetbagger: "It is those of the carpetbagger stripe of the white race, under the guise of helping but in truth using the Negro for their own selfish interests, who retard the race."

The most unkind cuts came from whites who opposed the ban but saw Jack as the wrong choice. In the New York *Daily News,* columnist Jimmy Powers declared that with the flood of returning talent Robinson "will not make the grade in the big leagues next year or the next if percentages mean anything. . . . Robinson is a 1000-to-1 shot to make the grade." The future Hall of Fame pitcher Bob Feller, who had played in one exhibition game against Jack, "couldn't foresee any future" for him; a football player, Robinson was "tied up in the shoulders and couldn't hit an inside pitch to save his neck. If he were a white man I doubt they would even consider him as big league material." (In fact, Robinson had doubled once in two at-bats against Feller in a barnstorming game earlier that year.)

The Monarch owners threatened to fight the signing as a violation of Jack's contract with them. "We won't take it lying down," J. L. Wilkinson fumed to the Associated Press. "Robinson signed a contract with us last year and I feel that he is our property." Wilkinson, who had previously attacked Rickey for venturing into black baseball, snapped again:

"Rickey is no Abraham Lincoln or FDR and we won't accept him as dictator of Negro baseball." Standing up in support of the property rights of the Negro leagues owners were the venerable owner of the Washington Senators, Clark Griffith, and the Yankee general manager, Larry MacPhail, both of whom profited mightily from renting their parks to black teams. "The Negro league is entitled to full recognition as a full-fledged baseball organization," Griffith declared.

But when the black press rallied behind Robinson and the Dodgers, the Monarchs backed off. Rickey himself gave no quarter: "There is no Negro league as such, as far as I am concerned." Without contracts, and with several eastern clubs in the hands of numbers kings, the leagues "are not leagues and have no right to expect organized baseball to respect them." He then created a further sensation in New York by revealing that his scouts had turned up some twenty-five Negro players who, as the press reported, could play in either the major or minor leagues, "and who are being lined up by the Brooklyn executive to play with the Dodgers or their farm clubs." "I have never meant to be a crusader," he insisted, "and I hope I won't be regarded as one. My purpose is to be fair to all people, and my selfish objective is to win baseball games." A day or so later, under severe pressure from other blacks, the president of the Negro American League, J. B. Martin, lauded Rickey to the skies: "I feel that I speak the sentiments of 15 million

Negroes in America who are with you one hundred per cent, and will always remember the day and date of this great event."

With the barnstorming tour of Venezuela delayed by its organizers, Jack remained in New York. There, he saw much of Rachel, who was rooming with Janice Brooks in Harlem next door to the YMCA on 135th Street. The room was in an apartment rented by a family long known to Rachel's mother. But Rachel's adventure was not going well. The family treated the girls like roomers, not friends; they were included in nothing. They also had to eat out. Looking for work as a nurse, Rachel had been asked to sign a one-year contract; instead, she took a job on the East Side at a fancy restaurant that exotically used young black women as hostesses. Teetering on high heels and wearing a slinky silk dress, Rachel escorted customers to their tables. The job soon lost its appeal, especially after she found out that the restaurant would not serve blacks. Rachel then signed on to work at the Hospital for Joint Diseases, but also made time to shop for her trousseau. At Saks on Fifth Avenue she had found something really nice—a hammered-satin gown sewn by hand from prewar fabric; a matching ivory-tinted veil adorned with seed pearls; and a pair of dyed shoes. To her surprise, Saks allowed her to pay for all this treasure on layaway.

These weeks shared by Rachel and Jack in Manhattan were invaluable; the city brought them closer together. But they saw it with different eyes, especially when they looked around Harlem. With his Army and Negro leagues experience, Jack had often known blacks en masse; to Rachel, the sheer vitality and depth of the Negro community on the teeming streets and the crowded subways were a revelation. She found such human density inspiring but also daunting; Jack moved more easily in the volatile mix. As a fellow Californian, he understood her sense of distance from this scene, but it was important to him that they both bridge the gap between themselves and the mass of black people, with whom Jack readily identified despite their differences.

This difference was not the sort of thing they talked about. Rachel lived and relived in her imagination her reactions to the world. Jack would not talk about his feelings, or even analyze them aloud, for her to hear. But he had a strong sense of knowing who he was, of being unassailable, invulnerable, especially where the color of his skin was concerned. He was satisfied with his constant anger at injustice, although also satisfied that he could control it. Rachel began to think of them as complementing one another. Her identity was fluid; his was a rock. He was impulsive, she was organized and practical. They could help one another; they did help one another. What they needed was a chance, and this was what Rickey and white baseball were offering, although neither Jack nor Rachel knew for sure what lay ahead.

Late in the autumn, now the best-known black baseball player in the world, Jack left for Venezuela. Apart from his quick trip to Montreal, this was his first journey outside the United States. He needed to make some money for his coming wedding, but above all he needed to hone his baseball skills for the coming challenge. In the latter task, his barnstorming teammates certainly could help him. A brilliant group, they included the catcher and outfielder Roy Campanella of the Baltimore Elite Giants (who was quietly signed by the Dodgers on his return from Venezuela); the first baseman Buck Leonard; Jesse Williams at second; Parnell Woods at third; the catcher Quincy Trouppe; and one of Jack's partners in the Fenway Park farce, Sam Jethroe. The pitchers included the talented Roy Welmaker of the Homestead Grays and Verdell Mathis of the Memphis Red Sox. In addition, the team included such stalwarts as Felton Snow, Marvin Barker, and Gene Benson of the Philadelphia Stars. Their schedule called for twenty-four games, played mainly in the capital, Caracas.

Jack was now the center of attention, with almost every move magnified both by the hopes and dreams many people invested in him and by the envy and resentment he stirred in others. Reaching down like a white God among the Negro leaguers, Branch Rickey had picked—a rookie! The fact that the rookie was almost twenty-seven years old mattered little. Hilton Smith echoed the sentiments of many players when he declared spitefully about Robinson that "it all came down to this, he had played with white boys, he had played football with white boys." These older Negro leaguers had good reason to be bitter. Soon, the leagues would be finished, destroyed by integration. "We'd get 300 people in a game," Buck Leonard would say. "We couldn't even draw flies."

Jack found himself caught in a tight place. He had immense confidence in his athletic skills, but hardly wanted to make enemies of people who sought to help him. Inevitably he did, at least according to a few observers. One writer about the Negro leagues would describe the strenuous efforts of his teammates on the Venezuelan tour to help Robinson but also declared that he "did not like being tutored by the self-made Negro leaguers." Quincy Trouppe recalled: "One day Felton Snow tried to talk to Jackie, about the right way to handle a certain play at shortstop, and Jackie really talked to him bad." However, Jack's roommate on the tour, Gene Benson, offered a far more favorable picture. Robinson was "just a swell person. I had been told he was controversial and used to get involved in fisticuffs all the time. But when we started rooming together, I didn't see any of that."

On January 4, after about ten weeks in Venezuela, Jack returned by airplane to Miami, then took a train north to New York City and a reunion there with Rachel. He also visited Branch Rickey in the hospital, where he was confined with heart problems. The following Thursday, January 10, Jack and Rachel boarded a train and left for Los Angeles. His preoccupation now was the coming wedding, for which he had flubbed his first assignment. He had gone to Venezuela with Rachel's design for her ring; losing the sketch, he had come back with a botched version that left her almost in tears. On his own, he had bought her an alligator-skin bag. Rachel beamed with delight, but her most charitable thought was that, given time, it yet might become fashionable. Last of all, Jack offered a wooden jewelry chest, hand carved. This gift she genuinely liked.

In California, they found preparations for their wedding in high gear. Zellee Isum had married twice, but never in a traditional ceremony. Now, with her own mother's help, she was making up for her lost chances. Bypassing her Bethel AME Church as far too small, she secured the Independent Church of Christ across town, reputedly the largest black church in Los Angeles. "It was my mother's show from start to finish," Rachel would admit. "Jack wanted a small, intimate wedding, and so did I. What she had in mind was much more like a pageant, an extravaganza. I was glad to make her happy in this way. She chose my silver, my crystal, my china. She wanted me to have all these fine things she had never had. I didn't fight very hard. I guess I wanted them too."

On Sunday afternoon, February 10, Jack and Rachel were married by the Reverend Karl Downs, who had come from Austin to perform the ceremony. The church was packed with family and friends. Ray Bartlett, who had introduced the couple in the late summer of 1940, was away, still in the Army; but on Jack's side of the church, in addition to his mother and other members of his family, were his best man, Jack Gordon, and Jack's wife, Bernice, who had eloped to Yuma, Arizona, in 1942. There were Sid and Eleanor Heard, who had been married by Karl Downs before he left Pasadena. UCLA was well represented by a group including Jack's old football coach Babe Horrell, the graduate manager Bill Ackerman, and Bob and Blanche Campbell.

As Jack, decked out in his rented formal wear, waited for Rachel to arrive, he was visibly nervous, restless and tightly strung. At last the organ sounded for the bride's entrance and Rachel entered, escorted by her older brother, Chuck Williams, who was now fully recovered from his war wounds. As Rachel drew near, Jack's nervousness reached a fever pitch. Holding Jack Gordon's hand tightly in his own, he looked around, caught a glimpse of Rachel in her veiled satin splendor, then did a double-take that made the church erupt in laughter. Rachel was mortified. And then Jack Gordon couldn't find the ring! Finally he located it, and Karl Downs finished the ceremony by pronouncing Jack and Rachel man and wife. "It was a lovely wedding," Bob Campbell recalled.

Now Jack's nervousness fell away, and with it whatever sense of nuptial etiquette he had brought to the church. Halfway down the aisle, he abandoned Rachel to exchange whoops and hollers with his old friends from Pasadena. Angry but determined, Rachel completed her walk down the aisle alone.

At the reception and dinner at Rachel's home, when the time came for the couple to slip away, their car could not be found: Gordon and his cronies had hidden it. Finally, after several hours, Jack and Rachel were allowed to leave.

Across town, they attempted to check in, as planned, at the Clark Hotel on Central Avenue, the only black hotel in Los Angeles. A reservation? What reservation? Jack Gordon had forgotten to make one.

They were shown to a room in the annex of the hotel. Inside, Rachel looked expectantly for a bouquet of flowers, but found none. She could have sulked; instead, she found herself laughing, and happy to be there, at long last, with her husband. "I could feel all my resistance to marriage falling away. I could feel all my anxiety about sex falling away." A few days before, they had finally had sex together. But Jack had little experience and Rachel none, and the event had left her so upset she had gone to see a doctor.

"But now, suddenly, my fears seemed to have no foundation. It suddenly felt so right to be there, with Jack in that room, knowing we would now be together all the time, forever and ever. Really, when the door closed, I felt that all my troubles had melted away, and that a wonderful new life was beginning for Jack and for me."

— 7 —

A Royal Entrance

1946

I just mean to do the best I can.
—Jackie Robinson (1946)

THE DAY AFTER THEIR wedding, Jack and Rachel left Los Angeles for San Jose, just south of San Francisco Bay, to spend what they hoped would be a quiet, blissful honeymoon at the home of one of Rachel's aunts, who would be away. But their stay turned out to be less than idyllic, although they were deeply in love and happy to be alone together at last. When neither Rachel nor Jack could master the wood-burning stove, her plans for elegant little meals for two fell apart; "I also compulsively spent more time washing and cleaning than having fun." Nervous about his coming ordeal, Jack was restless. San Jose was too quiet for his taste; when some pals from Pasadena showed up suddenly, he welcomed them. The couple took in a Harlem Globetrotters basketball game in San Jose, then crossed the bay to Oakland to visit Maxine Robinson, Frank's widow, who was now living there with their children. Then Jack and Rachel cut short their honeymoon and headed back to Los

Angeles to prepare for the biggest challenge of his life—and Rachel's, too. At Rickey's insistence, she would be the only wife allowed in the Dodgers camp in Daytona Beach, Florida, that spring.

At first, the Robinsons were to travel by train. Then they decided to fly, via New Orleans and Pensacola, Florida. The deadline for reporting to camp was firm: midday on March 1.

Jack faced his coming challenge with a mixture of confidence and foreboding. His confidence came from three sources mainly. In the first place, whites were no mystery to him, as they might have been to a young black player plucked from a rigidly segregated background and thrust among people foreign and hostile to him. Second, Jack had enormous faith in his versatile ability to meet almost any physical or mental test in sport; he had been the best of the best so often that he had virtually no doubt now that he would succeed as a player. Third, he had already begun to believe not only in Rickey's integrity but also in his wisdom and foresight. Robinson's foreboding came mainly from his vivid personal experience of humiliations in the South, especially in his court-martial. But he also believed finally that destiny was on his side, that the hand of God was visible in the strange circumstances that had brought him to this moment, and that he, and Rickey, would emerge victorious from the coming ordeal.

Late on February 28, after Jack played a round of golf in Los Angeles, a small, excited group of friends and family, including their mothers, gathered at the Lockheed Terminal in Los Angeles to see the couple off. To Rachel's mortification, Mallie, who had never flown, pressed on them a smelly shoebox of fried chicken and boiled eggs for the airplane ride. Rachel was dressed to kill; she wore the dyed three-quarter-length ermine coat that had been Jack's wedding present to her, a matching black hat, and the brown alligator-skin handbag he had bought for her in Venezuela. Although the weather hardly called for fur, "that piece of ermine was my certificate of respectability," she would admit. "I thought that when I wore it everyone would know that I belonged on that plane, or wherever I happened to be."

She flew out with twin fears: a dread of the Jim Crow South and a dread, also, of what Jack's defiant spirit, and perhaps even her own, provoked by unaccustomed Jim Crow, might cause. "I couldn't be sure what was going to happen," she would say. "I worried that something might happen, some incident, and we would be harmed, or killed." But the first leg of the journey went smoothly; they reached New Orleans around seven o'clock in the morning. Strolling through the airport, Rachel now saw Jim Crow signs for the first time in her life. With Jack looking on uneasily, she decided to make her own small protest. "Very deliberately, I drank from a water fountain marked 'White.' Nothing happened. I wasn't killed. So then I walked into the Ladies' Room marked 'White.' The women stared at me, but nobody said or did anything. I sort of liked the women staring at me. I felt very strong." Jack had misgivings about what she was doing, but he did not try to stop her.

Then, around ten o'clock, reality began to set in. They had been "bumped" from the eleven o'clock flight. Disappointed but calm, they accepted the promise of seats on a flight one hour later. Then that flight left without them, and without an adequate explanation. Angry now, they were also hungry. Jack went scouting for food. "Blacks could not eat in the coffee shop," he found out. "We asked where we could find a restaurant. We learned there was one that would prepare sandwiches provided we did not sit down and eat them there." He felt rage surging in him. "Jack almost exploded at this suggestion," according to Rachel. "The pride in both of us had rebelled, so under no circumstances would we accept food on this basis." Now they understood why Mallie Robinson, in her wisdom, had packed that shoebox for her children.

The black couple's pride mattered little or nothing to the airline authorities; the Robinsons should go into town and wait to be called when a flight became available. They agreed to go. From an earlier visit on a barnstorming tour, Jack was sure he knew of a hotel that would have them. A taxi driver then took them to a building of appalling shabbiness, a "dirty, dreadful place" of cobwebs and grime, Rachel recalled, and a bedroom with plastic mattress covers, from which she recoiled: "lying on the bed was like trying to sleep on newspapers." Hurt and degraded, she was further upset because Jack seemed satisfied. Meanwhile, no call came from the airline. When Jack finally telephoned, he was told to return at once to the airport. At seven in the evening, some twelve hours after their arrival, Jack and Rachel secured seats on a plane and left for Pensacola.

As they touched down at Pensacola, they heard themselves being paged: Jack and Rachel Robinson were to report to the ticket counter. When Jack left for the terminal, a flight attendant advised Rachel: "You'd better get off, too." To their indignation, they could not continue on the flight. First they heard that a storm was coming and the plane had to be made lighter, for extra fuel; next, after white passengers took their places, that the New Orleans authorities had not left room for persons booked out of Pensacola. Vigorously Jack argued their case, but he understood what was happening: whites wanted to fly and blacks had to wait. He was "ready to explode with rage," he later wrote, "but I knew that the result would mean newspaper headlines about an ugly racial incident and possible arrest not only for me but also for Rae." Rachel now understood, as she looked at Jack, what white power meant in the South. "I could see him seething. I thought he might hit somebody in his rage and then where would we be? I felt frightened now, I was scared, terrified."

When Jack revealed at last his link to the Dodgers organization, the officials became more solicitous; they offered the Robinsons a limousine into Pensacola. The white driver knew of no black hotels in the city; at a whites-only hotel, bellhops provided him with the address of a black family who rented out rooms. Stopping at a small frame house, he deposited their luggage on the front porch and sped off. Inside, the woman of the house was sympathetic, but Rachel could see that "the family was using the living room to sleep in, and it was obvious that there was no place for us." She and Jack made a decision. Giving up on the airline, they would take the next bus leaving for Jacksonville. After a hurried long-distance telephone call to the Dodger camp, they boarded the bus.

They were dozing in reclining seats to the rear, certain that they were complying with Jim Crow law, when at one stop the white driver, with a wave of his hand, ordered them back to the last, fixed row. Jack roused himself from sleep but was alert enough to keep himself under control. "I had a few bad seconds," he would recall, "deciding whether I could continue to endure this humiliation." By now, Rachel had lost all her nerve; "I made sure that we moved to the back." The bus ride lasted sixteen bitter hours. Jack fell asleep, but Rachel found that she could not. "I buried my head behind the seat in front of me and started to cry." She was crying more for Jack than for herself, but in the end she was crying for them both. She saw how Jim Crow customs sought to strip her black husband of his dignity and turn him into a submissive, even shuffling creature: "I finally began to realize that where we were going with Mr. Rickey's plan, none of us had ever been before. We were setting out on something we really didn't understand. And right in front of me, it was changing my life, changing who I was, or changing who I thought I was."

Just after dawn, the Jim Crow section of the bus began to fill up with black working men and women, many on their way to the fields, their dresses and overalls torn and soiled, heads wrapped in country bandannas. With many seats empty in the "white" section of the bus, the blacks took turns sharing the few back seats among themselves. What the laborers made of the strange couple—the man asleep in his rumpled suit and tie, the lady with her massed curls and her ermine coat and alligator bag—Rachel could only imagine. She could see clearly, however, their kindness to one another. In the humiliation she shared with these poor Southern blacks, "I really felt the beginning of a new understanding on my part. Now I understood about how black folks living under those terrible conditions really had to look out for one another, or we would all of us go down. I began to feel a great bond I had never felt before. I took comfort from those people, because I could tell they wanted to comfort me. And I needed comfort badly at that time."

When they pulled into Jacksonville, the bus station only added to their misery. The building was hot and fly-ridden, its Jim Crow section crowded and stinky as they waited for a connection to Daytona Beach to the south. Aside from apples and candy bars, once Mallie's shoebox was empty, they had eaten nothing on the journey by air and bus from New Orleans. Jack himself would have bought food from the holes in the wall where blacks were brusquely served, but Rachel refused to eat that way: "I wouldn't do it, and he said he would go along with me if I felt that way." Rachel remembered, "I had never been so tired, hungry, miserable, upset in my life as when we finally reached Daytona Beach." But she would also believe that her descent with Jack into the Jim Crow hell of the South "had made me a much stronger, more purposeful human being in a few hours. I saw the pointlessness, the vanity, of good looks and clothes when one faced an evil like Jim Crow. I think I was much more ready now to deal with the world we had entered."

On Saturday, March 2, in the late afternoon, after thirty-six hours of travel, Jack and Rachel at last stepped off the bus at Daytona Beach. On hand to greet them were three men sent by Branch Rickey. One was Wendell Smith, Jack's champion from the Pittsburgh *Courier;* another was Billy Rowe, an enterprising *Courier* photographer and writer who, the year before, had covered the Japanese surrender on the deck of the USS *Missouri.* In an agreement with the *Courier,* which thus had the inside track on the baseball story of the century, Rickey had put Smith and Rowe on the Dodgers' manifest, picking up their expenses. Their task was to stick with the Robinsons, to be protectors and advisors and friends, and a liaison with the local black community.

The third man was John Richard Wright, another black player signed by Rickey. In 1943, the quiet, lanky twenty-seven-year-old from New Orleans had won thirty games and lost only once in league play with the Homestead Grays of the Negro National League. In the Navy, he once beat a Chicago White Sox team and, in Ebbets Field, had pitched six shutout innings against a major-league all-star group.

Bitter, Jack reached Daytona Beach ready to return to California. "I never want another trip like that one," he told Smith and Rowe. But the writers worked quietly to bring his mind back to the job at hand. Jack could also see that his arrival had created a sensation in the bus station. Blacks and whites pressed forward to glimpse the man who had already rocked the world of white baseball, who would challenge Jim Crow in his own lair. In a phenomenon that would be repeated over the coming months and even years, few paid much attention to any other black ballplayer with him. The focus was on Jackie Robinson.

Luck is the residue of design, Branch Rickey had declared; and his design was almost everywhere in evidence, starting with the choice of Daytona Beach for the major phase of spring training. (To the press, Rickey had blamed Robinson's absence from camp on "bad flying weather in the vicinity of New Orleans.") After Jack and Rachel's harrowing experience, Daytona Beach, where the Halifax River flowed into the Atlantic, was a distinct lift. City leaders, including Mayor William Perry, seeing a financial windfall in having the Dodgers in town each spring, had agreed to welcome black players; Perry had known of Robinson's coming even before he signed with Montreal. "No one objects to Jackie Robinson and Johnny Wright training here," the mayor announced boldly. "We welcome them and wish them the best of luck!"

Compared with almost all other Southern towns, Daytona Beach was a liberal community. Here, some blacks were allowed to drive public buses and even to try on shoes—though not clothing—in local stores. One major reason was the influence of a black leader, Joe Harris, to whose home on Spruce Street Wendell Smith and Billy Rowe drove the Robinsons that afternoon. Harris, a pharmacist, was also an energetic organizer who could deliver the black vote on election day. A few steps from the home of Harris and his wife, Dufferin, was Bethune-Cookman College, whose founder and president, Mary McLeod Bethune, then seventy years old, was one of the best-known blacks in America. A tireless educator, Mrs. Bethune was a particular friend of Eleanor Roosevelt; after the President's death, his cane arrived as a gift to her. On Spruce Street, Duff Harris, "a dear, sentimental romantic," as Rachel recalled with affection, received them warmly. Squeezing the "love birds," as she liked to call them, into her idea of a honeymoon nest, a tiny room at the head of the stairs, she promised them their privacy. There Jack and Rachel unwound after their ordeal.

The following day, Sunday, according to plan, they moved forty miles south to the little town of Sanford for a week of spring training. Since February 1, Sanford had been the site of the Dodgers' baseball school, or "Rickey University," as writers had tagged it. More than 150 athletes, most of them returning soldiers, had matriculated; then, on March 1, the Dodgers and the Montreal Royals officially started spring workouts. In Sanford, Jack and Rachel again went to a private home, the spacious white house of a prominent local black couple, Mr. and Mrs. David Brock, while the white players stayed at the lakefront Mayfair Hotel, which would not accept blacks. Branch Rickey had checked out the Brock home in person. Before Jack and Rachel's arrival, he had lolled in a wicker chair on the verandah and pronounced the choice fine: "If we can't put them in the hotels, then they should stay some place that represents something. This is the type of home."

On Monday, March 4, Jack's first morning in Sanford, he dressed carefully at home in the gray baseball uniform of the Montreal Royals. Then he set off with Wright, Rowe, and Smith for the park. Rachel said goodbye on the porch: "I felt so protective I had to consciously restrain myself from following Jack to the car." As he entered the clubhouse, he felt a terrible sense of foreboding, a disquiet about how he would be received. In fact, the previous week Rickey had publicly warned the white players that he expected them "to be the gentlemen you have shown yourselves to be" when the two black men arrived; they should be seen as "two more baseball players" and given "the same treatment accorded all other players." At the same time, avoiding any impression that he was challenging the South on moral grounds, Rickey told the press that he had signed the blacks "because of my interest in winning a pennant." He went further. "If an elephant could play center field better than any man I have," he insisted, "I would play the elephant."

Jack's nervousness lifted a little when he saw the familiar smiling face of Clyde Sukeforth. His tremors returned, however, when he looked out over the green fields and saw some two hundred players, all white, going through their paces, running, fielding, throwing, "keeping up a constant barrage of the chatter," he would tell a writer, "that seems to go with Baseball." Then several of the players noticed him and Johnny Wright, and the chattering died. "It seemed that every one of those men stopped suddenly in his tracks and that four hundred eyes were trained on Wright and me." From affable Babe Hamburger, the Dodgers' equipment manager, they collected bats and balls and his advice to take it easy on the first day. But Jack found it impossible to relax; his stomach remained a knot. "Well," he told Sukeforth in the doorway, "this is it." At almost exactly 9:30, he and Wright stepped onto the field and, as the *Daily Worker* reported, "became the first two Negroes to crack modern organized baseball's Jim Crow."

Before the pair had gone far, reporters were on top of them. Most questions went straight to Jack; he was seen as the groundbreaker, the first. "Jack, do you think you can get along with these white boys?" "What would you do if one of these pitchers threw at your head?" Jack fielded the questions easily. "I've gotten along with white boys in high school, at Pasadena, at UCLA, and in the Army. I don't see why these should be any different." If a white pitcher threw at his head, why, "I'd duck!" Laughing, the reporters probed a little deeper. The most popular player on the Montreal Royals was the French-Canadian shortstop Stan Bréard: "Do you think you can win the shortstop job?" Jack stepped lightly: "I just mean to do the best I can." "Do you hope to play for Brooklyn some day?" Again, he was deft: "Of course I do, just like all these other players out here!"

Then the trap rattled. "So you're after Pee Wee Reese's job?" "I can't worry about Brooklyn," he feinted. "I haven't made the Montreal team yet."

With the newsmen, Jack acquitted himself well, as Rickey knew he would do. Next he met Clay Hopper, the new Montreal manager. In a deep molasses drawl redolent of magnolias and mint juleps, Hopper murmured pleasantries about the spring, but Jack heard mainly the undertone of a threat. In reality, Hopper was both a prisoner of history and a good soldier. The owner of a Mississippi plantation, he had opposed Rickey's signing of Robinson. To Hopper, Robinson's presence on the Montreal team would put the manager in a delicate position among friends and neighbors down home. But Rickey had prevailed on him, and Hopper greeted Robinson with an outstretched hand that was itself a good sign. "In those days," Jack would recall, "great numbers of southerners would under no circumstances shake hands with a Negro."

Robinson could hardly guess the depth of his manager's feelings. Some days later, after Rickey praised a particular play by Jackie as superhuman, Hopper was shocked. "Mr. Rickey," he asked, his lips quivering with emotion, "do you really think a nigger's a human being?" Rickey ignored him.

For two days, Jack practiced hard. One basic task was to lose some weight; he had reported at 195, at least ten pounds over his prime football weight. As he slimmed down, he also had to earn his spot on the Royals roster. He had to hit well, but he also had to find a place other than shortstop in the Royals infield.

Not only was his arm questionable at that position, but the Dodgers organization was deep in talent there, from Bréard in Montreal to the superb Reese, just back from the war, in Brooklyn. Montreal was weak at third base, but that did not seem to be Robinson's natural spot; and he had never seriously played second or first. Could he beat out seasoned players at those positions? "I never saw these fellows play so I can't say just how much chance I think I have," he conceded. "Certainly I would be willing to go to a lower class league, but I want to make this club."

Despite the pressures, his first two days in Sanford passed fairly smoothly. Then, suddenly, on March 5, Jack and Rachel, as well as Wright, were hustled out of town. According to later reports, they were at dinner with Wright, Rowe, and Smith at the Brock home when a series of phone calls to Smith from Rickey ended with a command: the Robinsons and Wright were to pack and leave at once. In fact, a large delegation of hostile local whites had called on the mayor of Sanford and demanded the ouster of the two black players. A march on the Brock home was rumored, and probably not to seek autographs. Exactly when Wright and Robinson had been scheduled to leave Sanford is unclear. The New York *Times* had reported they would stay until the weekend; the *Daily Worker* would report that they were to leave Sanford that day. In any event, the Robinsons fled Sanford for the safety of Daytona Beach.

Arriving in Daytona Beach, Jack was upset further when he and Rachel found themselves back in their tiny room at the Harrises' while the rest of the players (apart from Wright) stayed at the Riviera Hotel on the ocean. The Riviera was grungy after its wartime use, but he wanted to be with the other players. "We disliked this distinction," he later wrote, "almost as much as we resented being chased out of Sanford, but we knew that there could be no protest. Mr. Rickey had made it clear that, for the success of our venture, we would have to bear indignities and humiliations without complaint. He had said that I would have to be 'a man big enough to bear the cross of martyrdom.' "

At Kelly Field in Daytona Beach, where the Dodgers camped, he found it hard to field and hit. The cross he was carrying weighed him down as he tried to shine at shortstop with dazzling scrambles and accurate, quick, strong throws to first; it hampered him as he swung at pitches in his unorthodox batting style. Desperate to shine, he succeeded only in throwing his arm out; he awoke one day to find it burning and throbbing. The Dodgers' trainer applied hot compresses, Rachel, the trained nurse, applied cold; but only time would heal the arm. In these first few days, between Jack's injury and the pressures on him, he was unimpressive. Writing in the Montreal *Gazette,* the respected columnist Dink Carroll reported to Canadians what the sportswriters were murmuring in Florida: "that Mr. Rickey has played up Infielder Jackie Robinson but Pitcher John Wright is the better prospect of the two colored players." Roscoe McGowen of the New York *Times* openly doubted that either Robinson or Wright would make the Royals. Another, less courteous, white writer looked at Robinson, and at Rickey's experiment, and said: "If he was white they'd have booted him out of this camp long ago."

Away from the baseball field, in their temporary home on Spruce Street, Jack and Rachel worried a little but talked and played cards and made love and talked some more and made more passionate love as they waited for the month to unfold. (Jack loved and even studied card playing; Rachel was an indifferent player "except when I was playing him, and then I wanted to win.") On Spruce Street, their isolation was made worse because, despite Duff Harris's effusions, she would share her kitchen with nobody. Jack and Rachel had each other and their room; they had to take their meals in local black restaurants, all of them humble. They were seldom apart, since Rachel also attended practice every day. "Day after day," she recalled, "I would go out to the ball park and sit in the Jim Crow section to watch." She made it her business to be with Jack at the ballpark while he toiled; each morning, they set out for work together. (For the next twelve years, or until he retired from baseball, she would attend virtually every one of his home games. "How could I miss them?" she asked. "That's where the action was. That's where the drama was.")

With this closeness, Jack began to think and talk, as many observers would note over the years, not in terms of "I" but most often about "we"—as in "We hit a home run that day." Unlike Rachel, he had never been one to look inward, except in prayer, or to doubt himself, or to dwell on the past. Now, however, he found himself sharing more of his thoughts with her and starting to crave the experience. A sense of themselves as a couple, strong in unity and purpose, began to grow. As Rachel would say: "We began to see ourselves in terms of a social and historical problem, to know that the issue wasn't simply baseball but life and death, freedom and bondage, for an awful lot of people who didn't have the rewards that came to us. At the same time, we had to remember that we were only two young people, who didn't know much. Nothing in California had quite prepared us for what was happening, how we were growing."

Something else was growing. Before March was over, Rachel knew she was pregnant. Aware of what Jack was going through, she kept the news from him until June. "I was disappointed," she recalled. "Jack was delighted, thrilled, but I had hoped for a year of travel and freedom. I also knew what my mother would say, and she said it: 'Oh Rachel, I thought you would wait.' As the weeks passed, of course, I became very happy to be bearing our child; but Jack was happy from the start." Indeed he was. "My Dearest Darling," he would write to her later, while on the road,

> I just received your letter and I was so happy I nearly cried. Honest Honey I never felt like this before. When you said you had a surprise for me I couldn't even hope that what you told me was it but my Darling you won't be sorry. We will have loads of fun with Jr. . . . I won't tell a soul honey and don't worry I'll give Jr. something to read about later in his life. I am glad though

Honey so glad because I know we are going to be very happy. We can't miss. The way I love you and the way I can't help loving our child will really help to make us the envy of every married couple. . . . I get such a kick out of talking with you and Honey we are still courting. We will always court each other as long as we live. . . .

What a Christmas this is going to be. I'm going to have the greatest one of my life. A baby and for the first time. The sweetest wife in the world. I do love you with all my heart. I need you Darling you are my heart and Soul and certainly an inspiration that I need very much.

If Jack and Rachel were a couple, Rickey and Robinson were also a pair, as Sukeforth dubbed them. Rickey inspired confidence; he was a revelation. He yawned at questions about Jack's ailing arm; while it mended, as he knew it would, he stepped up work on the rest of the body. Deserting some of his other duties, he became Jack's personal coach and cheerleader. "Rickey would show up at the field wearing this odd little beat-up hat," according to Rachel, "and he would push and prod Jack: 'Go after that pitch! Take a lead! Be bold! Make them worry!' " Sensing Jack's need, Rickey did not waver; he was imperturbable in the face of lapses and miscues. "And Jack truly needed that support," Rachel remembered. "He was nervous and tense and needed the phone calls; and they came regularly. I was on the outside, but I didn't question it, because it was helping Jack beyond words. Rickey's relationship with Jack became very personal, very intimate. It was paternal—not paternalistic, but paternal. And it gave Jack deep support when he badly needed it."

To blacks, the intimacy of the relationship, the sense of two men, black and white, adrift on a raft together, touched a nerve. In the *Courier,* Wendell Smith noted its intimacy. Rickey "has been giving Jackie personal instructions and advice. Friday morning, for instance, Rickey took his 'baby' over to the sidelines and spent considerable time instructing him on how to stretch and how to tag." Facing doubters about Jack's place in the infield, Rickey was tough. If necessary, he made it clear, Robinson would play at first base: "Anyone with any mental capacity can handle first base. Robinson has shown that he is no dumb-bell. He is apt and learns things exceptionally fast. He may turn out to be Montreal's first-baseman." About this time, Mexican baseball was a real alternative for American players. But when a Mexican agent (a "swarthy señor," the *Courier* revealed) offered Jack a handsome sum to play ball over the border, an irate Rickey chased the man away, as the New York *Times* reported: "The Mahatma told the Senor to get out of his ball park, out of his hotel and out of the city." (Jack himself was cool to the offer: "I'm not interested. There's too much at stake here. These people are my friends.")

While his arm healed, Jack moved from short-stop to second to first, then back to second. He learned to play the new positions with a swiftness that amazed his teachers. "He had the greatest aptitude of any player I've ever seen," another Royals infielder, Al Campanis, later judged; "in one half hour he learned to make the double play pivot correctly." Jack had "some limitations," including his arm strength and his range to his left; but he "overcame both deficiencies because he was such a great athlete and applied himself to the game with such intensity."

Some white players were cool, but a few tried to help him. In the *Daily Worker,* Bill Mardo reported as "forever blasted to oblivion" the "hoary old lie" that white players wouldn't accept blacks. Although Jack felt isolated, some players reached out. Lou Rochelli, his leading rival at second base, worked hard to help Robinson there. "Lou was intelligent and he was a thoroughbred," Jack said later in tribute. Stan Bréard was also solicitous; at their first meeting, Jack posed for a picture between Bréard and his wife—a brave gesture on Bréard's part, given the situation. Campanis, too, was quite helpful.

On Sunday, March 17, as reporters noted, Jack made organized baseball history again. He became the first black man in this century to take the field alongside whites in a scheduled exhibition game for which admission would be charged. The game, at City Island Park in downtown Daytona Beach, was between the Royals and the Dodgers. Despite his progress, Robinson faced the game with some trepidation. How would the public receive him? How would he perform against major leaguers like Reese, Cookie Lavagetto, Gene Mauch, Pete Reiser, Gene Hermanski, Eddie Stanky, Dixie Walker, and Billy

Herman, all of whom would play that day? For once, he could not count on the support of Rickey, who refused to break the Sabbath even for his prize recruit. The game drew four thousand fans, one of the largest crowds ever for such a contest. Of these, more than one thousand were blacks drawn by the magic of history. Forced into the cramped Jim Crow section of the bleachers, they spilled onto the grounds and were then penned in beyond the right-field foul line. Jack's sensitive ears caught both their resolute cheering and "a few weak and scattered boos" when his name was first called. In five innings, he fielded flawlessly, stole a base, and scored a run; but he went hitless in three trips to the plate. "Playing under terrific pressure," the white Daytona Beach *Evening Journal* judged, "Robinson conducted himself well afield during his five-inning stint. He handled two chances aptly." Once on base, and "running like a scared rabbit," he scored easily.

He then fell into an awful hitting slump. Starting off fairly well in intersquad games, he struggled in his first two games against the Dodgers. He whiffed on the high outside fastballs that were his staple; he tripped over himself lunging at curves and change-ups. For Rachel, this was her introduction to the phenomenon of the slump, which only time ends. Jack knew about slumps, but now he had no way of knowing whether he was merely in one or finally out of his depth. "We were literally afraid that Jack simply would not make the team," according to Rachel, "that he would have to be cut in spring training. Every day without a hit made Rickey's experiment seem more risky." When the drought ended, an elated Rachel secured entry into Duff Harris's kitchen; with fresh chickens and vegetables donated by friends at Bethune-Cookman College, she served a victory dinner to a happy gathering of the inner circle, including Wright, Wendell Smith, and Billy Rowe. Exactly when this hit occurred is unclear; but a "perfect" bunt in the seventh inning of a game on March 30, against the St. Paul Saints, excited the *Courier:* "ROBINSON GETS A HIT; ROYALS LOSE." Rickey, parked in a box seat, was nonchalant: " 'He'll hit,' said Rickey, 'and he'll be quite a ball player. I'm sure of that.' "

To many blacks, watching Robinson struggle was deeply upsetting; they felt their race's suffering in his ordeal. That month, Sam Lacy of the Baltimore *Afro-American* wrote of him as "a man in a goldfish bowl." "Under these circumstances," Lacy confessed, "it is easy to see why I felt a lump in my throat each time a ball was hit in his direction in those first few days; why I experienced a sort of emptiness in the bottom of my stomach whenever he took a swing in batting practice. I was constantly in fear of his muffing an easy roller under the stress of things. And I uttered a silent prayer of thanks as, with closed eyes, I heard the solid whack of Robinson's bat against the ball." Lacy found himself "amazed at Jackie's total lack of self-consciousness." Jack was "easy-going, quiet, unaffected and intelligent. He makes friends easily."

His enemies were also legion. On March 21, word came that Jacksonville, about fifty percent black, forbade Robinson and Wright to play in an exhibition game at Durkee Field against the Jersey City Giants, a farm club of the New York Giants. An official of the Playground and Recreational Commission explained: "It is part of the rules and regulations of the Recreational Department that Negroes and whites cannot compete against each other on a city-owned playground." Clay Hopper, under orders from Rickey, declared his intention of playing Robinson there "unless I get official notice not to." When the notice came, he canceled the game—to the disappointment of the Giants, who wanted the Royals to leave Robinson home. "We lived up to our agreement," Rickey made clear. "The city of Jacksonville and the Jersey City Club are responsible for whatever happened."

A week later, on March 28, when Jacksonville canceled another Royals game, its decision stiffened the backbone of other cities. On April 5, the Royals announced that they had been forced to cancel three additional games—another in Jacksonville, one in Savannah, Georgia, and a third in Richmond, Virginia. In addition, a game planned for April 10 at De Land, Florida, had to be moved to Daytona Beach; local officials claimed that the stadium lights were not working. Jack mused: "What this had to do with the fact that the game was to be played in the daytime, no one bothered to explain."

The reaction spread further. On Sunday, April 7, at Sanford, which previously had chased out Robinson and Wright, the Royals began a scheduled game against the St. Paul Saints before about one hundred spectators. In the second inning, Jack singled, then scored on a base hit after stealing second. He was about to step onto the field for the third inning when the local chief of police ("Vicious old man Jim Crow," Wendell Smith wrote) ordered Hopper to remove Robinson or risk prosecution. Hopper replaced him.

The cancellations and disruptions were financially costly to the club and bad for team morale, but Rickey was ready to pay the price. According to the Pittsburgh *Courier,* he answered the offended cities with defiance: "Without Robinson and Wright, there'll be no games!" He insisted on official notification, on letterhead stationery, concerning all cancellations; he refused to take the initiative and stay away, or to find excuses to bench his black players. Instead, he pressed on. The Dodgers announced the signing of twenty-five-year-old Roy Campanella, the best-hitting catcher in the Negro leagues, and Don Newcombe, twenty-two, a tall, robust pitcher, and assigned them to Nashua, New Hampshire, in the New England League. (A barrier broke elsewhere. In March, the Los Angeles Rams signed Kenny Washington to break the color bar in football. "That's great," Jack told the press. "He's a great football player and Los Angeles will make a lot of money with him in the lineup.")

By this time, despite only fair hitting, Jack had won a place on the Royals, as had John Wright. Early on April 15, Jack and Rachel boarded a special orange-colored train carrying the Montreal Royals to New York City. Thus ended what Wendell Smith in

the *Courier* called "one of the most unique and sensational training sessions in the history of organized
baseball."

IN JERSEY CITY, NEW JERSEY, the Royals faced the
opening of the sixty-fourth season of the International League with only modest hopes. Although
Montreal had won the pennant the previous year,
1945, only three players remained from that squad.
The team seemed a hodgepodge of faded Dodgers
veterans and untested novices, some fresh from the
war. "Poor Hopper," mused Bruno Betzel, Hopper's
predecessor as manager of the Royals, who was now
in charge of the Jersey City Giants—"they've sure
handed him a wrecked team."

On April 18, under clear skies and in brilliant
sunshine at Roosevelt Stadium, before a capacity
opening-day crowd of just over 25,000, with jugglers
and tumblers and two marching bands and a seemingly endless parade lorded over by the ebullient
mayor, Frank Hague, and with the press box jammed
with reporters from every New York City daily and
black weekly, all eager to record the historic event,
Robinson made his debut.

For him, the moment was fraught with emotion.
"I remember the parades," Jack would recall, "the
brass band's playing 'The Star-Spangled Banner' and
the marvelous beauty of this 'day of destiny' for me.
Nothing else mattered now." He heard the strains of
the national anthem "with a lump in my throat and
my heart beating rapidly, my stomach feeling as if it

were full of feverish fireflies with claws on their feet." Meanwhile, Rachel roamed the stands, unable to sit still, elated by the setting but tingling with a free-floating anxiety. She knew that her anxiety was shared by the thousands of blacks who had crossed the river from Harlem or come from Newark and Philadelphia to be a part of history.

In his first at-bat, which came at 3:04 that afternoon, Jack felt weak in his knees and stomach as he heard the mild cheer that greeted his name. Working the pitcher to a full count, he then topped a weak grounder to the Giants' shortstop, who threw him out with ease. But the next time up, in the third inning, with two men on and the left-hander Warren Sandell expecting him to bunt, Robinson exploded on a fastball chest-high and down the middle. The ball jumped from his bat and carried high and far until it dropped into the left-field stands, more than 340 feet away. As he passed third base Jack beamed at Clay Hopper, who patted him on the back; George Shuba, moving in from the on-deck circle, pumped his hand vigorously as he crossed home plate.

Next, in the fifth inning, Jack set down a dainty bunt that stunned the Giants' infield, then flashed across first base steps ahead of the throw. He stole second, then went to third unexpectedly, on a groundout to third base. When a new pitcher, Phil Otis, entered the game, Jack teased him with feints toward home. Twice Otis threw to third; twice Jack scrambled back. Next, the catcher rifled the ball to third, but Jack was safe again. Then, as the now agitated Otis started another pitch, Jack feinted toward home again. Confused, Otis stopped suddenly. The umpire stepped in to call a balk, and Jack strolled home. "Now the crowd went wild," he recalled. "Not just the Negroes, but thousands of whites, including many Jersey City fans, screamed, laughed and stamped their feet." Mr. Rickey was right about the fans: "They liked daring baseball."

This was a day of near perfection for Robinson, a fantasy of a debut. In five at-bats, he hit safely four times, including the homer; he stole second twice and scored four runs, two of them on balks teased out of pitchers befuddled by his daring and quickness. One game was only one game, but Robinson had dealt a stunning blow to the notion of black physical and mental inferiority. Above all, his demeanor captivated the fans—his calibrated recklessness, his cheeky challenge to the white pitchers, the insolence of his base running, the grittiness of his base hits, the violence of the long ball. And, yes, Montreal had won the game, 14–1. (Unfortunately, Jack featured even in the Giants' scoring, with an error in the fifth inning when he threw low and wide trying to complete a double play.)

After the game, Robinson took no less than five minutes to reach the locker room, the New York *Herald Tribune* reported, "as he was mobbed trying to leave the field by fans of assorted ages, sizes and colors." He had "completely stolen the show and the hearts of 25,000 fans" in leading the Royals to victory. The clubhouse was "a mad scene," with "wellwishers fighting to get in" to congratulate him, according to another report. Jack was "so excited he had to tie his necktie three or four times but he was as happy as a kid on Christmas morning." Seizing the day, according to the New York *Times,* he had "converted his opportunity into a brilliant personal triumph." Two days later, the Montreal *Gazette* compared Jack's sense of drama with that of great stars like Babe Ruth, Red Grange, Jack Dempsey, and Bobby Jones: "Make no mistake, the man can play ball. He is big, abnormally fast for his size, and he can field." On a double play, "his feet were right, his hands were sure, his throw was perfect and all was accomplished in the minimum amount of time." Writing mainly for blacks, the New York *Amsterdam News* summed up: "Thus the most significant sports story of the century was written into the record books as baseball took up the cudgel for democracy and an unassuming but superlative Negro boy ascended the heights of excellence to prove the rightness of the experiment. And prove it in the only correct crucible for such an experiment—the crucible of white hot competition."

Opposing pitchers took note. Two days later, when the Royals beat the Giants to sweep the series, Jack drew three walks in five times at bat; he singled, drove in one run, stole two bases, and scored twice. The average attendance, twenty-two thousand, was excellent. Large crowds turned out again for the series against the Newark Bears in Newark, New Jersey, and the Syracuse Chiefs in Syracuse, New York, even as Jack's batting average dropped steadily. The true Royals hitting star was George Shuba, with six homers; the speedy Marvin "Rabbit" Rackley was stealing bases at a record clip. Still, Robinson had shown himself a potential mainstay, if not a star, of Montreal.

However, the next series, in Baltimore against the Orioles, was a setback. Baltimore was a Southern city, below the Mason-Dixon line; two years later, a group of whites and blacks would be arrested for playing tennis together in the city's Druid Hill Park. The local press warned about a hostile reaction to Robinson, even a possible riot, since a large influx of blacks was expected from Washington, D.C., Pittsburgh, and elsewhere. "While it's a ticklish problem with us," the Baltimore general manager declared, "we don't anticipate trouble, especially from the colored people." A Canadian reporter got the point: "He didn't say so, but the inference was that white hoodlums might cause some rancour." Only about three thousand fans attended the first game, where Rachel sat horrified in the stands while a man behind her shouted about that "nigger son of a bitch," Jackie Robinson. "There wasn't anything I could say," she recalled, "but I took it all personally. I couldn't be philosophical at all." The next day, over twenty-five thousand fans showed up for a doubleheader, with about ten thousand blacks crammed into segregated and inferior seating. Again Jack was subjected to abuse from white fans. The presence of thousands of blacks, who doted on every move he made, both elated and weighed on him. "It put a heavy burden of responsibility on me," he later wrote, "but it was a glorious challenge. On the good days the cries of approval made me feel ten feet tall, but my mistakes, no matter how small, plunged me into deep depression. I guess black, as well as white, fans recognized this, and that is why they gave me that extra support I needed so badly."

As the Royals headed home to Montreal, Branch Rickey's experiment was still alive but by no means a definite success. Once home in De Lorimer Downs, however, Clay Hopper's team began to come into its own. Its trademark turned out to be a smooth combination of speed and power, experience and youth. The team included former Dodgers stars such as Curt Davis, Herman Franks, and Lew Riggs, as well as younger players such as the left-handed pitcher Steve Nagy; the native-born darling Jean Pierre Roy, another pitcher; the fastest Royal, Rabbit Rackley— and Jackie Robinson. Clay Hopper was calm, authoritative, yet diplomatic. Steadily, the Royals began to overwhelm their opposition.

In Montreal, after about a month in a guest house, and despite an acute postwar housing shortage, Jack and Rachel found a nice apartment. Expecting the sordid resistance that would have come in virtually any white American neighborhood, she was stunned by the genteel response when she answered an advertisement to sublet half of a duplex apartment at 8232 Rue de Gaspé, in the traditionally French-speaking East End. Deliberately, Rachel had chosen the less affluent French-speaking district over its wealthier English counterpart, which she expected to be more exclusive. (Montreal had no distinctly black district.) On De Gaspé, almost everyone spoke mainly or only French, and a brown face was unusual; but the woman of the apartment received Rachel pleasantly, poured tea and talked, and quickly agreed to rent her apartment furnished, with all her own linen and kitchen utensils. Rachel was almost overwhelmed. "The woman didn't merely agree," she said; "she insisted that I use her things. She wanted me to be careful—no water on the hardwood floors, that sort of thing, but she was gracious. It left us euphoric, really. All the months in Canada were like that."

They moved in without incident. Later, when she began to show, an informal delegation of local women visited her to offer not only advice and friendship but also coupons from their ration books, so she could buy any scarce foodstuffs she needed or craved. With the language barrier and the demands of the Royals' schedule, Jack and Rachel could make very few friends in the neighborhood; but upstairs were the Méthots, with seven or eight children who brightened the house. Rachel and Jack came to know Edgar Méthot and his wife, who had just had a baby; twenty-seven years later, the Méthots would recall the Robinsons as "such good people." Their closest friends, however, were a Jewish couple, Sam and Belle Maltin. Sam, a Canadian and a socialist, wrote on sports for the Montreal *Herald* but was also a stringer for the Pittsburgh *Courier;* like Rachel, Belle was pregnant at the time. Knowing of Rachel's love of classical music, the Maltins took them to outdoor concerts on Mount Royal that reminded Rachel of visits to the Hollywood Bowl. Belle introduced Rachel to Jewish cooking and also knitted her a sweater she still wore fifty years later. The Maltins had another black friend, Herb Trawick, a football player with the Montreal Alouettes, and the Robinsons got to know him as well.

On the whole, however, the Robinsons aimed for a subdued life when Jack was home. Rachel's day was bound up in going to the ballpark to watch him. When he was away, sometimes she traveled with him (although the club frowned on wives on the road), but mostly she stayed home and sewed clothes for herself and the coming baby, or worked on a crochet tablecloth she was making for her dream home in California. She got to know some of the neighborhood children because they followed her on the street or carried her groceries home; she also tempted the children living upstairs by leaving a door open and a bowl of fruit in plain sight. Rachel could say little to most of the adults—she had taken Latin but no French—but they remained friendly and protective of her. She liked to watch them come out onto their balconies to take the sun in the lazy summer afternoons; they, no doubt, admired her brown-skinned beauty and grace. In May, an *Afro-American* woman reporter, recalling Rachel's night of abuse in Baltimore, wrote admiringly of her unusual calm and poise: "The only person I know who can equal her is that first citizen of the world, Mrs. Eleanor Roosevelt."

By early June, Jackie was an established presence in Montreal; on June 4, he was dubbed "the Colored Comet" in an illustration in the local *Gazette.* (His life story was also illustrated in April in *Picture News,* published by Comic Magazines.) His

.356 batting average led the league, and his only important setback was a leg injury that put him *hors de combat* for a week. Jack then spent several days at Joe Louis's training camp near Greenwood Lake, New Jersey, as Louis prepared for a title fight against Billy Conn at Yankee Stadium. Perhaps this visit was behind Jack's first tentative step, soon withdrawn, into political action—into placing his newfound national fame in service of progressive politics.

Jack's success on the field made him more than a passive symbol of integration; more and more people wanted to acknowledge, and share, or exploit it. Some calls on his time were about money, as the first of the sweet-sounding offers and deals arrived that would tease him for the rest of his life. Some calls were charitable, as when hundreds of wounded servicemen gave him a star's welcome on the grounds of the Montreal Military Hospital, where he helped to umpire a softball game between the Montreal Canadiens hockey team and an all-star YMHA team. Other invitations were more freighted. Appealing to his conscience, and thus possibly to his vanity, they sought to draw him away from the perceived shallows of sport toward a grander purpose. Late in May, the New York State organizing committee of the United Negro and Allied Veterans of America asked Jack to be its chairman; the national honorary commander of UNAVA was Joe Louis. On the committee, Jack would be associated with such popular political leaders as Congressman Adam Clayton Powell, State Assemblyman Hulan Jack, and Councilman Benjamin Davis Jr. Accepting the invitation,

Jack agreed to speak on June 9 at Abyssinian Baptist Church in Harlem with Powell, Jack, and Davis. "I consider it a great honor to serve as chairman," he wired the committee. "The burning problems of discrimination in housing, employment, education and on-the-job training facing Negro veterans demand an immediate solution."

On June 9, however, Jack was not at Powell's famous church in Harlem. In general, Branch Rickey forbade his players to deliver public speeches or attend public dinners during the season. More important, Rickey, a Republican and a strong anticommunist, would never have approved of the leftist source of Jack's invitation. That spring, Rickey had flown to Fulton, Missouri, to help give a hero's welcome to Winston Churchill at Westminster College, where Rickey was a trustee. On that occasion, Churchill had delivered his celebrated "Iron Curtain" speech about the evils of Soviet communism.

In any event, Robinson hardly needed a greater canvas than the ballpark to express himself politically. On the road, he was constantly aware of the price of being a martyr, as abuse came in forms from the subtle and patronizing to the crude and hostile, while he held his peace in compliance with his agreement with Rickey. At Syracuse, a rival player threw a black cat from the dugout onto the field as Jack waited to hit: "Hey Jackie, there's your cousin." Jack doubled to left, then scored on a single to center. As he passed the Syracuse dugout he offered his own taunt: "I guess my cousin's pretty happy now." He could count on a uniformly warm reception only at home, in De Lorimer Downs. "I owe more to Canadians than they'll ever know," he said later. "In my baseball career they were the first to make me feel my natural self." Robinson would write later about one French-accented rooter who "used to shout from the bleachers, if things were bad, 'Jackie, 'e's my boy!' The man had lungs of brass, a voice of iron, and a heart of gold."

But the support of the Montreal crowds, and the black crowds elsewhere, could not make up entirely for the hostility he faced; besides, Jack both liked and disliked being special—he longed simply to play ball like any other Royal. But he *was* different. In a mid-summer game at Syracuse, while one of the worst disturbances of the season raged at home plate, Jack rested stoically at second base. "I've reminded him several times," Clay Hopper told the press, " 'Jackie, you stay out of the arguments no matter what they are.' " Opposing pitchers threw repeatedly at his head; several base runners, according to Al Campanis and others, aimed their spikes at his flesh whenever they could. To the press, Jack offered hardly a murmur of complaint, but the Royals' general manager, Mel Jones, knew differently. "He came into the office more than once," Jones later revealed, "and he'd say, 'Nobody knows what I'm going through.' " At year's end one Montreal journalist looked back: "Because of his dark pigmentation Robbie could never protest. If there was a rhubarb on the field . . . he had to stay out of it. Otherwise there might have been a riot."

What he was going through would have brought many another man to explosions of rage and perhaps even patterns of psychopathology, and it did not leave Robinson utterly unscathed. The psychological and also the physical cost of so much pent-up indignation is hard to measure. Some things are certain. Anger, which can powerfully inhibit athletic ability, did not make Jack less effective as a player but seemed indeed to intensify his concentration and propel him to greater feats. Rage and hurt did not drive him to the usual, often destructive therapies—alcohol, tobacco, sexual adventuring: with Rachel's help, Robinson was able to stay on the straight-and-narrow course he had set for himself a long time before. But even such self-discipline carried its price and must have exacted a heavy toll in terms of inner peace and equilibrium of mind. Later, when Jack saw himself as released from Rickey's prohibitions, his response would sometimes seem excessive to some people, including some of those disposed to admire him. Such people perhaps underestimated or undervalued the depth of feeling he had dammed up in these early years in order to serve the greater cause of freedom and social equality.

The Royals stayed atop the league, but Jack continued to find his burden heavy. Writing of the infamous black-cat incident in Syracuse and the vile namecalling in Baltimore, he admitted that "the toll that incidents like these took was greater than I realized. I was overestimating my stamina and underestimating the beating I was taking. I couldn't sleep and often I couldn't eat." Rachel's pregnancy added to that pressure. It was both a disruption of their brief new life together and a source of anxiety when he took to the road without her. At some point, he began to find it hard to sleep; his eating, usually hearty, dropped off. Finally, a doctor examined Jack, found nothing wrong physically, and prescribed rest; even the sports pages were to go unread. The Royals granted him five days off. Three days later, when the team started to lose, he was back.

Meanwhile, Rachel had her own worries and problems but tried to keep almost all of them to herself. As she became bigger with child, the trips became more dangerous, but Rickey understood what she meant to Jack on the road. "Rachel's understanding love," as Jack later put it, "was a powerful antidote for the poison of being taunted by fans, sneered at by fellow-players, and constantly mistreated because of my blackness." She tried to shield Jack even when a mysterious problem crept into her pregnancy. Starting in her fifth month, she became feverish in the last two weeks of each month; her temperature soared as high as 103 degrees. Her obstetrician, baffled, took blood cultures but finally could only prescribe sulfur. She kept her illness to herself: "I never told Jack about the fever, I never told my neighbors, I couldn't risk upsetting him. He would call at night from the road and I would say, 'Everything's just fine.' When he got back, I would be better. I had to make the sacrifice, because I had begun to think that I was married to a man with a destiny, someone who had been chosen for a great task, and I couldn't let him down."

Protected in this way, Jack flourished on the field despite his periods of gloom. Typical was a game in

Baltimore when he led an injury-ridden Royals team to a 10–9 victory, after Montreal went ahead 8–0 only to have Baltimore tie the game. Jack not only got three of the Royals' seven hits but also stole home. Such feats made him a lion to his teammates, and to his manager, Hopper, who was now almost a complete convert to Rickey's view of Robinson. In *Newsweek,* Hopper saluted Jack as "a player who must go to the majors. He's a big-league ballplayer, a good team hustler, and a real gentleman." Race now meant less to other baseball men. "I'd like to have nine Robinsons," Bruno Betzel, the Jersey City Giants' manager, declared. "If I had one Jackie, I'd room with him myself and put him to bed nights, to make sure nothing happened to him."

"I've had great luck and great treatment," Jack told *Newsweek* modestly. "This is the greatest thing that has ever happened to me." By September, when the regular season ended, he had completely vindicated Rickey. Robinson became the first Royal to win the league batting crown; his average of .349 also eclipsed the Royals' team record, set in 1930. Hitting only three home runs, he nevertheless drove in 66 runs; he also scored more runs, 113, than anyone else in the league. His 40 stolen bases put him second only to his teammate Marvin Rackley's record-setting 65. At second base, he ended the season with the highest fielding percentage in the league. With one hundred victories, the highest number in team history, the Royals won the pennant by eighteen and a half games. They also played before the largest crowds at home and away—

·more than eight hundred thousand people—in the history of the club.

In the playoffs, the Royals won two tough seven-game series, first with the Newark Bears and then with the Syracuse Chiefs. Against Syracuse, in the deciding game, Jack went four-for-five. Then, late in September, the Royals traveled to Louisville, Kentucky, for the Little World Series against the Colonels of the American Association. For many of the Louisville players, officials, and fans, Robinson's presence was the most urgent single consideration; the series brought integrated baseball to Louisville for the first time. The Colonels, who had agreed only reluctantly to his playing, underscored their opposition by sharply limiting the number of seats for blacks, many of whom were left to mill about in confusion outside the park. Some who made it inside probably regretted their luck. "The tension was terrible," Robinson wrote, "and I was greeted with some of the worst vituperation I had yet experienced."

The series opened with three games in Louisville, during which Jack slumped, going one for eleven. His failure only fed the rage of many white fans in the cheaper seats. "The worse I played," he recalled, "the more vicious that howling mob in the stands became. I had been booed pretty soundly before, but nothing like this. A torrent of mass hatred burst from the stands with virtually every move I made." As Jack suffered, Montreal dropped two games after taking the first. The abuse was so great that the white Louisville *Courier-Journal* felt obliged to deplore the "demonstrations of prejudice against Montreal's fine second baseman, the young Negro, Jackie Robinson," as well as the "brusque refusal" of the park to accommodate more black fans. However, when the series moved to Montreal, the local fans repaid the Colonels. A storm of abuse, unprecedented at a Royals game, descended on the visitors. Down 4–0 at one point in the first home game, the Royals stormed back to win 6–5 in the tenth inning on a single by Robinson. In the fifth game, Jack doubled and, just after Louisville tied the game 3–all, hit a towering triple; then he laid down a bunt in the eighth inning "which really settled the fate of the Colonels," according to the Montreal *Daily Star.* "This was a really heady play, a beautifully placed hit." With Al Campanis, he also executed superb double plays to kill off Louisville scoring threats. Finally, on October 4, before an ecstatic crowd, the Royals defeated the Colonels once again, 2–0, to win the Little World Series. Robinson, who finished the series batting .400, also scored the last run.

Hustling to leave the ballpark in time to catch a plane, Jack made the mistake of stepping back onto the field before he could shower and change. Deliriously happy Montreal fans snatched him up in celebration. Previously, they had lifted Clay Hopper and a white player to their shoulders. Now, hugging and kissing Robinson, slapping him on the back, they carried him on their shoulders in triumph, singing songs of victory, until he was finally able to break away. Watching, the veteran writer Dink Carroll of

Mallie in her later years

Jack at five, 1924

Jack's mother, Mallie Robinson, with her children (from left): Mack, Jack, Edgar, Willa Mae, and Frank

Mack Robinson, Olympian, 1936

Jack a star at UCLA, 1939

Broad jumping, 1940

With Ray Bartlett (left) and another friend, Honolulu, 1941

Robinson works out with Private Joe Louis, Fort Riley, Kansas, 1942.

As a lieutenant in the cavalry, Fort Riley, Kansas, 1943

At the New Club Alabam, Central Avenue, Los Angeles, January 1944, with Rachel (left) and her friend Charlotte Robinson

Branch Rickey

With Satchel Paige on the Kansas City Monarchs, 1945

Signing with Montreal (from left): Royals president Hector Racine, Branch Rickey Jr., Jack, and Royals vice-president Romeo Gauvreau, October 23, 1945

**The marriage—
February 10, 1946,
Los Angeles,
the Reverend
Karl E. Downs
officiating**

**With Rachel,
leaving
Pensacola by bus
for Daytona
Beach, Florida,
1946**

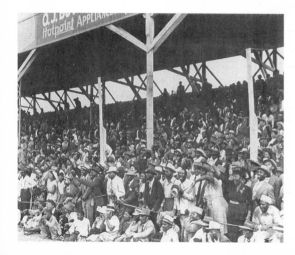

**Colored section,
West Palm Beach,
Florida, 1946**

With sportswriter Wendell Smith (left) and Hector Racine, 1946

Home run, Opening Day, April 18, 1946, Giants Stadium, Jersey City. George Shuba extends a hand.

With Dodgers coach Clyde Sukeforth, who brought Jack to Branch Rickey, 1947

Ebbets Field, April 11, 1947— before Jack's first game as a Dodger

Jackie Robinson Day, September 23, 1947: Jack's mother-in-law, Zellee Isum, holds Jackie Junior, as Jack Semel, a leading Dodger fan, presents an "interracial goodwill" plaque to Robinson.

With Jackie Junior, at a victory celebration in Brooklyn Borough Hall, September 1947

With Manager Leo Durocher, spring training, the Dominican Republic, 1948.

Manager Burt Shotton, with (clockwise) Carl Furillo, Pee Wee Reese, Jack, Roy Campanella, Duke Snider, and Gene Hermanski

Rachel and Jackie Junior, spring training, Florida, March 1949

Testifying before the House Un-American Activities Committee, July 19, 1949, Washington, D.C.

Most Valuable Player in the National League, 1949—Ford Frick presents the award.

**Happy Third Birthday, Jackie Junior, November 1949,
St. Albans, Queens; with Roy Campanella's son David
(in front of Rachel) and Sarah Satlow and her children.**

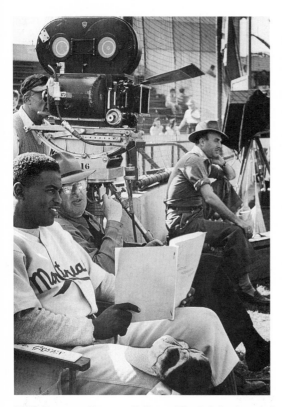

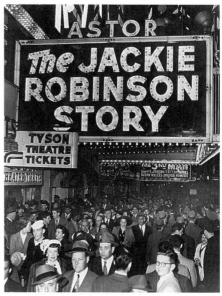

**Premiere, May 16, 1950,
New York City**

**With producer Mort Briskin on the
set of The Jackie Robinson Story,
Hollywood, 1950**

At the opening of the
Jackie Robinson Store,
1952, Harlem, with
(from left) Monte Irvin
of the Giants,
Ralph Bunche Jr.,
Ralph Bunche, and
Jack's teammate
Joe Black

With his favorite
manager,
Chuck Dressen

From left, Pee Wee Reese, Carl Furillo, Jack, Carl Erskine, Gil Hodges, Don Newcombe, Duke Snider, and Roy Campanella

Close play

With pitcher and friend Ralph Branca (center) and Pee Wee Reese, 1951

Hate mail

A familiar scene—down but not out, September 20, 1950, against the Pirates No. 6: Carl Furillo. Catcher: Clyde McCullough.

**Coming through
once again**

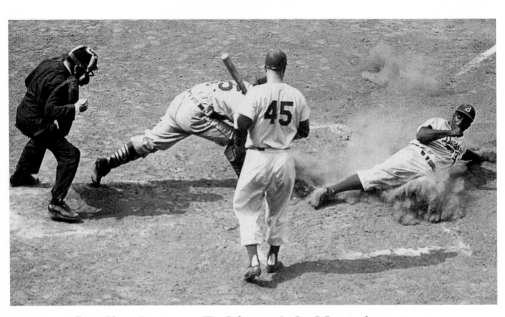

**Stealing home—Robinson's boldest signature.
At bat: Johnny Podres.**

the *Gazette* began to cry: "The tears poured down my cheeks and you choked up looking at it." Inside the locker room, Hopper warmly shook his hand. "You're a great ballplayer and a fine gentleman," he told Jack. "It's been wonderful having you on the team." When Robinson reappeared outside in street clothes, a large part of the crowd was still waiting. "They stormed around him, eager to touch him," the *Gazette* reported. Knowing exactly what he had accomplished over the season, they sang in tribute, "*Il a gagné ses épaulettes*"—He has earned his stripes; "they almost ripped the clothes from his back." In the *Courier,* his friend Sam Maltin wrote memorably of the astonishing scene: "It was probably the only day in history that a black man ran from a white mob with love instead of lynching on its mind."

From De Lorimer Downs, Jack and Rachel rushed to the airport and caught a flight to Detroit, where they parted ways. He went on to join a barnstorming team on a tour that would end in California. In the last month of her pregnancy, she returned directly to Los Angeles, to her mother's home on West 36th Place.

On November 18, Jack was at her side when their son was born at Good Samaritan Hospital in Los Angeles. The delivery was relatively easy; their baby boy was healthy in every respect. His parents named him Jack Roosevelt Robinson Jr. For Jack and Rachel, his coming was a miracle that left them euphoric. Jackie's birth capped the most tumultuous year of his father's life to that point. And yet Jack and others knew that the coming year, 1947, might yet surpass the astonishing year that had just ended. In Los Angeles, he waited for the call that might summon him to the Brooklyn Dodgers and the major leagues.

A Brooklyn Dodger

1946–1947

I know now that dreams do come true.
—*Jackie Robinson (1947)*

AT THANKSGIVING DINNER in Los Angeles, Jack was grateful for his new blessings, thrilled by the presence of his infant son, Jackie Junior, and surrounded by women who adored him: his wife, Rachel; his mother-in-law, Zellee; and Zellee's mother, Annetta Jones, who was now living with her daughter on 36th Place. With Jackie Junior the first child born into their family in twenty-five years, Zellee and Annetta doted on father and son. Jack and Rachel were living in cramped conditions, and the future was by no means certain; but Jack felt a substantial debt to God as he led his new family in prayer at Thanksgiving in November 1946.

He was happy, but also short on cash. Robinson's brief barnstorming adventure had yielded him nothing; according to Arthur Mann, Branch Rickey's assistant, "the promoters—Negro, at that—succeeded in swindling him out of his net profits." Jack had returned from the road with a fat bundle of checks totaling about $3,500, but almost all of them had bounced. With the aid of Thurgood Marshall of the NAACP he pressed his creditors, a Pittsburgh group, but the pressure yielded only promises. Unwillingly, he had then signed a contract for fifty dollars a game to play basketball with a local professional team, the Los Angeles Red Devils.

Here, as in baseball, Jim Crow was an issue. While the leading professional league, the Basketball Association of America, barred blacks, the Rochester Royals of the upstart National Basketball League, taking a cue from Rickey, had just signed their first black players, William "Dolly" King and William "Pop" Gates, both formerly of the elite all-black New York Renaissance team. (Because of racial friction, Rochester dropped both men the following season. Three years passed before another black played.) In Los Angeles, the Red Devils, seeking admission to the NBL, hired Robinson and two other black players for its otherwise white squad. Shifting gears smoothly from baseball, Jack played well. Against the visiting Sheboygan Redskins, he was the top scorer in a Red Devils victory; in a nonleague game, the Red Devils also defeated the Renaissance team. By early December, the Red Devils had won eight games and lost only once. To local blacks, this success was an important victory for racial integration. "Even if you don't care for basketball," a black sportswriter urged his readers, "see them anyhow, if only to get a real glimpse of a team that practices interracial harmony with real success."

Despite his solid play, Robinson's stint with the Red Devils ended suddenly in early December. Quite possibly, he was injured in a game and quit rather than risk a disaster. He had a particularly rough time against the Chicago American Gears, whose commanding center, George Mikan, would later be voted the most dominant basketball player of the half-century. Jack's friend Jack Gordon, present at these games, recalled how Mikan and the Gears "put a real hurting on Jack; they left him dizzy." But Jack may have quit basketball after a freak accident on a golf course in Los Angeles, when his back suddenly gave out in the middle of a swing. In addition, Branch Rickey, visiting Los Angeles early in December for a round of baseball meetings, met with Robinson and perhaps convinced him to give up basketball. Through a black boyhood friend and former teammate, Walter Worrill of the Pasadena YMCA, Jack then made several appearances as a speaker before groups of black, white, and Mexican youths in Los Angeles, Pasadena, and Phoenix, Arizona. In January, a journalist who watched him interact with his young audience reported that "to say that Robinson inspired the boys is to put it mildly."

Nevertheless, the thought uppermost in Jack's mind early in 1947 was his possible promotion to the Brooklyn Dodgers. On this matter, Rickey had been planning and scheming. Near the end of the Dodgers' season, claiming that Montreal needed Jack's services, he had rebuffed calls to bring Robinson up for the National League pennant race. Now, in January, an Associated Press poll of sports editors established that the major question of 1947 was whether or not Jackie Robinson would be promoted;

a symposium on this issue in the weekly *Sporting News* took up an entire page. Of the top ten hitters in the International League in 1946, only Robinson had not moved up to the majors. But Rickey refused to be rushed. "I have made every move with great deliberation," he reminded a reporter. "If Robinson merits being with the Dodgers, I'd prefer to have the players want him, rather than force him on the players. I want Robinson to have the fairest chance in the world without the slightest bit of prejudice."

Carefully, Jack followed Rickey's plan, as he told a reporter: "I guess Mr. Rickey wants to see if last season was just lucky for me, which I don't blame him." Rickey, if not Robinson, was aware of the deep opposition to Jack's promotion among the single most important group in baseball—the team owners, who in a secret ballot had voted fifteen to one (with Rickey alone dissenting) against integration. One year after Jack's historic signing, no owner had followed suit. Undeterred, Rickey took a significant step: he moved 1947 spring training for the Dodgers and Royals away from the Jim Crow South to the Caribbean, to Cuba and Panama. He also sought to channel and control the surging black interest in Robinson's future. This interest, Rickey believed, could wreck his plan if it served to antagonize whites. Consulting a number of black leaders, including Herbert T. Miller, the executive secretary of the Carlton Avenue branch of the YMCA in Brooklyn, Rickey arranged for Miller to invite more than thirty black New Yorkers to a working dinner. At that time, according to Miller's invitation, the group would discuss with Rickey "the things which are on his mind as well as ours, in connection with projection of what seems to be the inevitable."

On the raw, cold evening of February 5, after breaking bread with the group, Rickey laid out his brazen thesis that the major threat to Jackie Robinson's success—"the *one* enemy most likely to ruin that success—is the Negro people themselves!" Painting a garish picture of the worst scenario he could imagine after Robinson's promotion (just as he had done in his first meeting with Jack), he lashed out at his astonished audience. "You'll strut. You'll wear badges," he told the blacks. "You'll hold Jackie Robinson Days . . . and Jackie Robinson Nights. You'll get drunk. You'll fight. You'll be arrested. You'll wine and dine the player until he is fat and futile. You'll symbolize his importance into a national comedy . . . and an ultimate tragedy—yes, tragedy!" Above all, Rickey wanted nobody to use Jack's triumph as "a symbol of social 'ism' or schism," or, indeed, as "a triumph of race over race." Many in the audience, which included doctors and lawyers, must have been taken aback by such language, which Rickey himself called cruel; but his obvious sincerity, the directness of his appeal, and their pathetic lack of power within the world he represented won them over. Through the black press and churches, the word went out about the need for moderation at this crucial hour.

Around February 20, leaving Rachel and Jackie Junior behind, Jack flew to New York. There, according to Roy Campanella, he boarded an Atlantic Seaboard train headed south for Miami. With him were the three other black prospects, including Campanella, now in the Dodger organization. Campanella had been Jack's teammate in Venezuela in 1945, then had played with Nashua in 1946. At Nashua, under manager Walter Alston, Campanella was hailed as the outstanding catcher and voted the Most Valuable Player in the league, as his team won the league championship. Also at Nashua and now on the train heading south was the six-foot-four-inch pitcher Don Newcombe, who had won sixteen games. The last of the four players was a left-handed pitcher, Roy Partlow, a thirty-six-year-old former Negro-leagues star. Signed the previous season by the Royals after they demoted Johnny Wright in the Dodgers' farm system, Partlow had pitched inconsistently for Montreal. Sent down to join Wright, he had then overwhelmed the opposition and was now getting another chance with the Royals.

Once again, Jack reported to training camp seething about Jim Crow. Arriving in Havana, he was stunned to learn that the black players would be quartered away from not only the Brooklyn Dodgers, who were at the luxurious Hotel Nacional overlooking the Caribbean, but also the other Royals. While the white Royals would live and train at the National Military Academy, a spanking-new boarding school for the Cuban elite about fifteen miles out of the city, the four black players were to make do in a shabby downtown hotel. At first, Jack angrily blamed the Cuban government for insisting on Jim Crow; but the idea was Rickey's. "I was told that he felt his plans for us were on the threshold of success," Robinson wrote later, "and he didn't want a possible racial incident to jeopardize his program. I reluctantly accepted the explanation." Such a racial incident might involve white Cubans; more likely, white American tourists, many of whom insisted on segregation in local hotels and nightclubs, would cause trouble. "I can't afford to take a chance and have a single incident occur," Rickey informed Robinson. "This training session must be perfectly smooth."

Buttoning up his anger, Jack was soon complaining of various ailments. He had stomach trouble, which could be blamed, at least in part, on unfamiliar food and water, and was treated for dysentery; he needed minor surgery for a growth on one of his toes; and he saw a leading Havana doctor after his back seized up painfully in a recurrence of his golfing injury. On top of this catalog of troubles, he had arrived thirty pounds over his ideal playing weight. Working hard under the tropical sun, Jack began to shed this flab as he made ready for the crucial test: twelve games between the Royals and the Dodgers before the major-league season. Three games were to be played in Panama, seven in Cuba, and the last two at Ebbets Field.

As the Royals prepared to fly to Panama, the second baseman faced a new challenge. One day, without warning, the Royals' general manager, Mel Jones, paid a clubhouse custodian fifteen dollars for a used first baseman's mitt and tossed it to Jack. Taken aback by this move, Robinson balked; he had never played first base competitively. But when Jones informed him that the idea was Mr. Rickey's, Jack dutifully slipped on the mitt and caught a few throws. Did it fit? "I honestly wouldn't know," he answered. "I never had one on before. All I know is that the balls stick in there pretty good, and that's all that counts."

By this time, most likely, he had caught on to Rickey's reasoning. With the Dodgers, Pee Wee Reese was a fixture at shortstop; at second, Eddie Stanky ruled. The vacancy in the Dodgers' infield was at first. (In fact, Rickey had made the move after consulting with the Dodgers' manager, Leo Durocher.)

On March 15, the Royals flew to Panama. In this mainly black but white-dominated nation, Jack's arrival was a civic event. White Americans, especially the military, had brought Jim Crow, complete with separate drinking fountains and schools, to the Canal Zone; to most Panamanians, the four black Royals represented a significant rebuke to this insult. A large, excited crowd turned out for Jack's first game, against an all-black local team that had just beaten the Dodger stars. With Rickey sitting in the stands, and with the Panamanian fans praying for his success, Jack responded with a home run and a single and flawless play at first base. Campanella also homered, a reporter noted, "but the crowd came out to cheer for Jackie." His fine playing, including four hits in one game, continued against other local teams. Then, urged on by Rickey, he faced the Dodgers. "I want you to run wild," Rickey insisted, "to steal the pants off them, to be the most conspicuous player on the field." These games were crucial: "Not only will you impress the Dodger players, but the stories the newspapermen send back to the Brooklyn and New York newspapers will help create demand on the part of the fans that you be brought up to the majors."

Robinson's response was electric. In his first game against Brooklyn, before six thousand fans, he had two hits and thirteen put-outs, including a "startling" catch of a low throw at first base; three days later, he beat out two bunts and an infield hit for singles. A New York writer marveled at how brilliantly, in one at-bat, Robinson hoodwinked Dodger pitcher Ed Heusser as well as infielders Stanky and Ed Stevens. Feinting a bunt one way on a pitch, he then went the other way on the next: "The infield was made to look foolish." Calling time, Stanky picked up the ball and hurled it over the grandstand. Jack's play at first base amazed Herb Goren of the New York *Sun:* "Robinson's movements around the bag are graceful and amazingly precise for one strange to the position."

For Jack, facing the Dodger stars was no cakewalk. The sheer size and power of the pitchers Hugh Casey and Hal Gregg stunned him: "When they take their stride and come down with the ball you feel like they're standing right on top of you," he reported; "only time will tell" if he could hit such pitching consistently. Without comment, Jack noticed something else: almost to a man, the Dodgers were cold to him. Certainly no one was encouraging. In this respect, Rickey's plan was not working. Back in Havana, Dodgers coach Jake Pitler gamely lauded Robinson's amazing gifts. "It would be a crime not to let this boy come up because of his color," Pitler told the press. "Wait till you see him in action. . . . He's terrific." Leo Durocher also spoke up. "He's a swell ball player," Durocher had told Wendell Smith of the *Courier.* "He's my type of ball player. Jackie can hit, run and field. What more can a manager ask of a player?"

But, facing the Dodgers again, this time at the new Stadium del Cerro in Havana, Jack faltered. Stomach trouble kept him out of the first game. Diagnosing an inflamed colon, a doctor urged him to rest; but Jack insisted on playing, "because people might think I was quitting if I didn't." In the second game, he was "far off his usual brilliant form, being guilty of two errors," and he managed only one hit. He went hitless in the third game, sat out the next, then went hitless on his return. In the sixth game, perhaps delivering a message, the Dodger catcher Bruce Edwards stormed into first base as Robinson reached high for the ball, and knocked him out cold. Jack's teammates and the trainer rushed to his side; Al Campanis fanned the air about his face. Sore and battered, he watched the last game in Cuba from the stands.

To the press, Rickey remained noncommittal about a promotion. He would say only that Robinson would go to the Dodgers before the start of the season or not at all in 1947. Several reporters believed that Rickey wanted and even intended to promote Robinson. However, "there is also little doubt," one wired home, that "many Brooklyn players will neglect to welcome Jackie with open arms and mind." Jack, too, noted the chill and resented it. The previous year, he pointed out mordantly, the Royals "did not suffer by my presence." Then he shifted his point. The pennant had come from high team morale. "No, sir," he said, "morale is mighty important. If the Dodgers don't want me, there would be no point in forcing myself on them. I am in the Dodger organization and naturally I want to see them win. I wouldn't want to feel that I was doing anything that would keep them from winning." The reporter concluded: "The only thing keeping Robinson off the Dodgers now, plainly, is the attitude of the players."

But few outsiders knew the full extent of the players' opposition. Just before the start of the three-game series in Panama, a petition began to circulate seeking to keep Robinson off the Dodgers. At the center was a core of Southern veterans: the pitchers Hugh Casey of Georgia and Kirby Higbe of South Carolina; a backup catcher, Bobby Bragan of Alabama; and Dixie Walker, also of Alabama, not only an explosive hitter and outfielder but also the most popular player in Brooklyn—"the People's Cherce," in the local lingo. The outfielder Carl Furillo of Reading, Pennsylvania, also backed the revolt. At least three Southerners had balked at signing. Eddie Stanky, out of loyalty to Rickey and gratitude for a fat new contract, promised to smooth the way for his boss. After three years at war, eager to play and make money, Pee Wee Reese of Kentucky had rejected the petition. "I wasn't trying to think of myself as the Great White Father," he insisted—Robinson "had a right to be there too." Pete Reiser of Missouri had a different reason. Once, searching in a strange city for a doctor for his sick young daughter, Reiser had unhesitatingly entrusted her to a black physician; why would he sign such a petition? Then Kirby Higbe, unable to keep the plan a secret, shared its details with Harold Parrott, the Dodgers' secretary.

(Later, Walker and Bragan would deny knowledge of a petition. In his 1967 memoir, *The High Hard One,* Higbe declared that "there were five of us that went straight to Mr. Rickey" in opposition to Robinson: Walker, Bragan, Furillo, Higbe—and Pee Wee Reese. "As Southerners," Higbe wrote, "we had heard a lot of talk about how we abused and mistreated Negroes down South, and we knew we never had." Reese, Higbe wrote, then changed his mind about playing with Robinson. On May 3, Rickey traded Higbe to the Pirates.)

To put down the revolt, Rickey turned Durocher loose. Practically dragging the Dodgers out of their beds in the middle of the night, the explosive Durocher denounced the plot in a tirade studded with obscenities. "I don't care if the guy is yellow or black, or if he has stripes like a fuckin' zebra!" Durocher shouted, according to Parrott. "I'm the manager of this team, and I say he plays. What's more, I say he can make us all rich." Summoning the ringleaders to his suite at the Tivoli Hotel in the Canal Zone, Rickey blasted their stand against integration. He heaped scorn on Furillo, whose parents had come to America from Sicily in search of a better life. In Bragan's case, prejudice was ingrained. His father's black workers, he would explain, always

used the back door when they came to his home.
"When you're born and raised in that kind of atmosphere, you just have a different feeling." Bragan
readily accepted Rickey's offer to trade him. Rickey
was also tough on Walker. "He really reamed me
out," Walker conceded. "I didn't know if they would
spit on me or not," he said of his white Alabama
neighbors and his association with Jackie Robinson.
"I had a hardware and sporting goods store back
home."

Cracking the whip, Rickey was sure "that a little
show of force at the right time is necessary when
there's a deliberate violation of law." In response to
"an overt act of violence" or the "destruction of someone's rights," he declared, "it's no time to conduct an
experiment in education or persuasion." On March
26, Walker requested a trade. "Recently the thought
has occurred to me that a change of ball clubs would
benefit both the Brooklyn Baseball club and myself,"
he wrote to Rickey. "Therefore I would like to be
traded as soon as a deal can be arranged." He had
enjoyed his association with the Dodgers, but "for
reasons I don't care to go into I feel my decision is
best for all concerned." Rickey decided finally to
keep Walker, who in 1946 had hit .319 and driven in
116 runs, but he had made his central point. "No
player on this club," he declared, "will have anything
to say about who plays or does not play on it. I will
decide who is on it and Durocher will decide who of
those who are on it does the playing." (Eventually
Rickey forgave Bragan and Walker and even
employed them as coaches.)

If Robinson himself knew of the rebellion, it did not make him embittered or truculent; he kept his and Rickey's goals, their pact, in focus. In any event, he was struggling with insults from both inside and outside the Dodger organization. Once, he was forbidden to eat in the dining room of a major hotel in the Canal Zone, as local newspapers angrily reported. Controlling himself, Jack could barely stomach the easygoing attitude of his teammate Roy Partlow, who breezed into camp late and seemed ready to blow his big chance. In the first of two reports written for the *Courier,* Jack criticized Partlow, who was "one of the greatest left-hand pitchers in the game"; however, "at the present time he is discontented, and unless he gets the feeling that he wants to play, he may as well forget about the game . . . because it is a proven fact that a discontented player will never be as effective as one whose heart is in the game at all times."

(Before spring training ended, Partlow was gone, cut by the Royals. Some observers thought that both John Wright and Partlow were intimidated by the presence of white players—or appeared to have, as Wendell Smith put it, "a tendency to choke up while laboring among the Caucasians.")

Jack was also irritated by the way his friend Roy Campanella seemed to accept Jim Crow. To Campanella, there was no point in chafing at poor or even unfair conditions one couldn't change. This was a difference between the men that would only grow over the years; to many teammates, it also made Campy a better companion than the sensitive, even prickly Robinson. When Campanella at last protested, his complaint was that the ten-cent cigars he smoked at home cost thirty-five cents in Havana. "I tried not to notice the things that bothered Jackie," Campanella later wrote, alluding to Jack's stomach trouble in Cuba.

Jack's stomach was not helped by the absence of Rachel, whom he missed badly. Fighting against his loneliness, his anger at Jim Crow, and the uncertainty about his promotion, he was eager to see Rachel and Jackie Junior again. Thus he was happy early in April when he returned to New York with the Royals for the last two exhibition games against the Dodgers. On April 9, in the New York *Times,* Arthur Daley devoted his column to the Dodgers' return to Flatbush and "the most delicate question of them all, Jackie Robinson." Moving Robinson from one base to another smacked of "an old-fashioned runaround," Daley mused, but perhaps it wasn't. "Only Rickey knows and he ain't talkin'." Some reporters were sure Robinson would be called up, but "some are just as sure that he won't be—not if the Mahatma wants to keep peace in his baseball family."

But Rickey's baseball family was about to be rocked. That day, at the Dodgers' headquarters on Montague Street, Rickey, Parrott, and Durocher were meeting in Rickey's office when Rickey took a telephone call that shook him. Following a three-week inquiry into complaints by the New York Yankees about certain newspaper articles signed by Durocher, the commissioner of baseball, A. B. "Happy" Chandler, had decided to punish both teams. (The articles, ghostwritten by Parrott, had appeared in the Brook-

lyn *Eagle*.) Behind the Durocher columns was a running feud between the Dodgers and the Yankees—
between Rickey's predecessor with the Dodgers,
Larry MacPhail, now president of the Yankees, on
the one hand, and Rickey and Durocher, who had
managed the Dodgers under MacPhail, on the other.
In Cuba the previous month, Durocher had publicly
raised the issue of MacPhail's sitting with alleged
gamblers at a Yankees exhibition game there. After
MacPhail's bitter protests, and what the commissioner called "a series of publicity-producing affairs"
involving the colorful Durocher, Chandler had
decided not only to impose fines of $2,000 on the
Yankees and the Dodgers and a fine of $500 on Par-
rott, but to suspend Durocher for one year for conduct "detrimental to baseball."

Durocher's banishment shocked the baseball
world and overwhelmed the talk about Jackie Robinson. However, Rickey was determined not to seem
deflated or intimidated; while Chandler was making
waves, Rickey would make history. Early the next
day, April 10, a telephone call from a Dodger secretary roused Jack at his Manhattan hotel. He was to
come to a meeting with Rickey at 215 Montague
Street. Dressing quickly, he made the trip across the
East River. Later that day, in the sixth inning of a
game between the Royals and the Dodgers, just as
"several thousand Negroes" on hand groaned as Jack
bunted a pitch by Ralph Branca into a double play,
Rickey's assistant Arthur Mann strolled casually
through the press box. To each reporter he handed a

sheet of paper with a terse announcement that he himself had typed at home, in order to keep it a secret. The note was signed by Branch Rickey: "The Brooklyn Dodgers today purchased the contract of Jackie Roosevelt Robinson from the Montreal Royals. He will report immediately."

(On March 29, Wendell Smith had reported in the *Courier* that, according to "an unimpeachable source," Robinson would be promoted to the Brooklyn Dodgers on the night of April 10. The newspaper was off the mark, but only by a few hours. Arthur Daley of the New York *Times* also knew in advance, but Rickey forbade him to break the story. "My boy," Rickey told Daley, "I must hold you to your solemn word of honor. This is the most important thing I ever did in my life and a premature leak could destroy it.")

Reporting to the Dodgers' dressing room, Jack was handed a uniform bearing the number 42 and promised a locker as soon as one was free; meanwhile, a nail on the wall would suffice. Dapper in his new uniform, he beamed for a photograph shaking hands with his former manager, Clay Hopper. The next morning, at 215 Montague Street, Jack signed his contract with the Dodgers, which was for the major-league minimum salary: $5,000 for the year. Then, at noon, he reported at Ebbets Field to the interim Dodger manager, his old friend Clyde Sukeforth. Jack was in a daze, and barely listening to Sukeforth go over the strengths and weaknesses of the Yankee team, when the manager asked: "Robinson, how are you feeling today?" Jack replied that he was fine. "Okay," Sukeforth went on, "then you're playing first base for us today." Jack would remember his reaction: "I just sorta gulped."

"Next time I go to a movie and see a picture of a little ordinary girl become a great star," he wrote a few days later, "I'll believe it. And whenever I hear my wife read fairy tales to my little boy, I'll listen. I know now that dreams do come true." Before the game, a few Dodgers players, mainly former Royals teammates like Dixie Howell and Marvin Rackley, wished him well. "Then we went out on to the field," Jack wrote. "Gee it seemed big. Twice as big as the day before. I sat down in the Brooklyn dugout and started to think all over again. The game started and I found myself at first base. I was the Brooklyn first baseman. The day before I had been Montreal's first baseman. 'What a difference a day makes,' I said to myself. When the umpire said, 'Play ball!,' I finally started thinking baseball. I finally realized that I was a member of the Brooklyn Dodgers; that I had made the big leagues."

The three-game exhibition series against the Yankees was an extraordinary coming-out party as ecstatic black fans helped to swell attendance for the games at Ebbets Field to over eighty thousand, about double the record for any previous three-game exhibition series between the two teams. "He's certain to continue as a magnet," the *Times* noted of Robinson, "at least until the novelty of the situation wears off." On the field, under intense scrutiny, Jack held his own. In the first game, on Friday, April 11, he went hitless but drove in three runs with two deep fly balls;

at first base, he handled fifteen chances without an error. The next day, his single to left field drove in the only Dodger run in an 8–1 loss. On Sunday, he singled to right. Over the three games, he drove in five Dodger runs, and played error-free ball at first base.

The next day, Monday, Jack was at Idlewild Airport to meet Rachel and Jackie, who had flown in from Los Angeles to rejoin him. After a separation of almost two months, their reunion was profoundly sweet; the horrors of the previous year—the rude bumping from airplanes, the bus ride from Pensacola to Daytona Beach, the rout from Sanford, the lockouts at Jacksonville and the like—all seemed far in the past. From Idlewild, the Robinsons rode a cab into Manhattan to the McAlpin Hotel in the heart of Manhattan, where Sixth Avenue and Broadway cross 34th Street at Herald Square. (The Dodger organization regularly used the McAlpin.) Despite his promotion, the tenuousness of Jack's place on the Dodgers made a hotel room seem just about right. Jackie Robinson was now one of the more famous names in America, but many a flaming star of spring training had burned out before summer in the major leagues. "We were scared," according to Rachel. "One room was fine, really. We would have been terrified in a suite, because how would we keep it up?"

Again, as in setting out for spring training one year before, Jack faced the moment with confidence but also with a sense of foreboding. The brilliant year in Montreal had erased any doubts he had ever had about his ability to succeed ultimately as a player in the majors. Others had their doubts, but Jack had none, really. The opposition of whites, including his teammates, also had no immobilizing effect; Jack's boyhood among whites had given him a vision of the racial future, and he knew that it could be made to work. By this time, too, his faith in Rickey was set virtually in stone. Above all, this moment was more than an individual's opportunity, a passing gesture against segregation. It was the fulfillment of a prophecy that was not so much personal to Jack as rooted in the promise of American history—that blacks would one day be free, that the grand national ideals of equality and democracy would one day be writ so large as to include the grandchildren of slaves, of whom he was chosen to be the living embodiment. But the moment was not completely free of foreboding. His religion had taught him that the line between confidence and Satanic pride is a fine one; and chance—a twisted ankle, a turned knee—might yet intervene to reassert the inscrutable ways of Providence. The drama would unfold; he would be both spectator and the man at the plate; God would decide the outcome.

The next morning, Tuesday, April 15, Jack awoke early and set out for Ebbets Field. On a bitingly cold day, a large crowd turned out for the season opener against the Boston Braves. Rachel was in the stands, worried as much about Jackie Junior as about his father. "I was determined not to miss the game, after all we had been through," she recalled; but getting to Ebbets Field was hard. Jackie was sick with diarrhea from the change of water; getting him and herself ready to travel was an ordeal, as was finding a cab that would go to Brooklyn. Finally she made it to the park, where she found a hot dog vendor willing to heat her infant's formula. Settling into her seat, she suddenly realized that his light coat, fine for Los Angeles, was inadequate here. Then a black woman sitting next to her, whom she would remember as the mother of Ruthe Campanella, Roy's wife, took Jackie and placed him inside her fur coat. Rachel could turn her attention to the field.

Out there, Jack too had his problems. Today there would be no repeat of his fairy-tale opening in 1946 in Jersey City. Facing the Boston Braves and one of the most feared curve-ball pitchers in the major leagues, Johnny Sain of Arkansas, who had won twenty games in 1946, Robinson was baffled to the brink of embarrassment. "I did a miserable job," he wrote later. "There was an overflow crowd at Ebbets Field. If they expected any miracles out of Robinson, they were sadly disappointed." Called out at first base by an eyelash in his first at-bat, he never came close to a hit again. He flied out weakly to left field, hit into a double play, reached base on an error when his bunt was mishandled, and then was taken out for defensive purposes. "If they're all like this," he muttered unhappily about Sain's pitches, "I'm going to have a tough time making this league."

The next day, he managed his first hit in the major leagues, a "perfect" bunt off Glenn Eliot in the fifth inning. On Thursday, rain washed out play; but the Dodgers, sparked by Pete Reiser's brilliant hitting, had won both games.

Action then shifted on Friday across the river to the Polo Grounds in Manhattan for a series against Brooklyn's archrivals, the New York Giants. Now the Dodgers had a new manager. In a surprise move, Rickey had summoned out of his Florida retirement the sixty-three-year-old Burt Shotton, in baseball since 1913 and once the manager of the Phillies. While Shotton, who had arrived without knowing Rickey's intentions, quietly settled in, his team lost both games. But Jack's bat flashed into form with five hits in the series, including his first home run, off the left-hander Dave Koslo. In his first week in the major leagues he had played four games, gone six-for-fourteen, and scored five times; at first base he had made thirty-three put-outs without an error. Both on and off the field, Jack seemed sharp and poised. "Robby [Robinson] has supreme confidence he'll make the grade," Dick Young wrote in the *Daily News*—although, as Jack said, "you have to keep thinking and hustling every minute up here, or else you're lost." "The muscular Negro minds his own business," Arthur Daley noted, "and shrewdly makes no effort to push himself. He speaks quietly and intelligently when spoken to and already has made a strong impression. 'I was nervous in the first play of my first game at Ebbets Field,' he said with a ready grin, 'but nothing has bothered me since.' "

With blacks thronging the park and excitement among whites also high, attendance soared. More than ninety thousand fans saw the two-game series at the Polo Grounds; an overflow crowd of just over fifty-three thousand was the largest crowd ever to attend a single game there on a Saturday. "They came to see Jackie Robinson," the Dodger radio announcer Red Barber later asserted. "He became the biggest attraction in baseball since Babe Ruth." Fans, white and black, cheered when he stepped to the plate or took his position on the field (while scattered but unmistakable boos greeted Dixie Walker), and hundreds waited patiently after the games for Robinson to emerge from the dressing room, then mobbed him for autographs. After one Yankee exhibition game, Wendell Smith had written of "a thousand people" awaiting Robinson and of their "deafening roar" as they "surged upon him." Despite a squadron of police, Jack "was absorbed into a sea of slapping hands" as flashbulbs exploded with "machinegun" rapidity "and the whole world seemed to be screaming in unison: 'Jackie Robinson!' "

At the McAlpin, fishing for a fresh angle on the top story in baseball, writers stumbled over one another in the Robinsons' cramped room as Rachel strove to maintain order. Compounding her troubles was Jackie Junior's diarrhea; his diapers hung like pennants everywhere. A hot plate, stowed under the bed when not in use, warmed his meals, while Jack and Rachel took turns leaving the room to eat in a nearby cafeteria. "We never thought of room service," Rachel recalled; "it was just not something we thought we could afford to do." For the first time, she was on her own with a sick child and a husband in the limelight; she found the whole experience thrilling but also a burden. Jack, basking in his celebrity, turned down few requests from the press. With a woman reporter, he chortled about the fact that Rachel's father had opposed him as a suitor ("I don't know what you see in that great big ugly boy," Mr. Isum had said). Rachel tried gamely to respond but found it hard always to hit the right note. Her "restrained manner" and her "finishing-school poise and charm," the reporter decided, were not of "the Brooklyn baseball fan variety." Pressed about Dixie Walker and the opposition to her husband, Rachel kept cool. "Living and eating and traveling together will straighten that out. It's inevitable. And anyway, there's always a Dixie Walker."

As messages poured into Ebbets Field, Jack was gratified to find most white letter-writers friendly. "Hi, Black Boy!" opened a cute note from Portland, Oregon. "Glad to read that you have arrived. Had good idea that you had the stuff and would make the grade. You are a credit to your race—the human race, son. Very glad to see you in the big leagues. Good luck. Sincerely: WHITE BOY." A few messages were critical, but far more asked for Jack to attend dinners, parties, and the like. Rickey beamed in pleasure for a while, then exploded. "He's not a ballplayer!" he shouted at one news conference. "He's a sideshow attraction! If I had my own way, I'd place a cordon of police around him—give him protection so that he might be a ballplayer!" Lamenting Robinson's "5,000 invitations to attend all sorts of events," he barred any appearance not sanctioned by the Dodger front office.

Meanwhile, among his teammates, Jack's position was probably not helped by the booing of Dixie

Walker (who publicly denied that he had ever disapproved of Robinson). But the white players' opposition to his presence was embedded. Loud cheers from the stands and "I'm for Jackie" buttons blossoming on lapels were met in the clubhouse by a chill. Few players openly voiced their objections, although the *Daily Worker* reporter Lester Rodney said he heard Carl Furillo mutter more than once, "I ain't going to play with no niggers." But a few teammates backed Jack. The infielders stuck together almost from the start. The promotion of his Royals teammate at third base, John "Spider" Jorgenson, added an ally; Reese at shortstop was always polite; at second, Stanky knew that team unity was essential at the ballpark. But other players were snide and contemptuous. To the press, Jack revealed none of this coldness. The Dodgers were "a swell bunch. . . . We work together swell, all of them—Reese, Higbe, Stanky—they're wonderful guys to play ball with." Keeping to himself, he brooded and waited for whatever time would bring.

A two-game series in Boston, against the Braves, was lost to falling snow. The maddening weather and enforced idleness darkened his mood. Visiting him in his room at the Kenmore Hotel, a white writer found a somber scene, or described one: "Jackie is sitting on his bed. The room is dark, the shades are halfway and here is a lonely guy. His head sunk in his hands. He feels friendless." The two men talk about baseball but not at all about race. "Jackie smiles and seems to brighten. It's nice to talk to somebody even if it is only a baseball writer he never had met before." The writer leaves, satisfied to have his story "but concerned, too, because it's no fun to see a man fighting against odds that seem almost insurmountable." About this time, in an often-echoed line, Jimmy Cannon of the New York *Post* called Jackie Robinson "the loneliest man I have ever seen in sports."

On April 22, the Dodgers returned to Ebbets Field for three games against the Philadelphia Phillies. When they played the Braves and the Giants, the opposition had been so restrained that Rickey's warnings about the abuse that would be heaped on the first Negro player began to seem overblown, even unwarranted. Suddenly, with the Phillies, all that changed. The Alabama-born manager, Ben Chapman, had decided to make Robinson's color an issue and encouraged at least three of his men to do the same. On a bitingly cool day, with the temperature hovering near 45 degrees when play began, Chapman started in on Robinson. As Jack would later write, Tuesday, April 22, 1947, "of all the unpleasant days in my life, brought me nearer to cracking up than I ever had been."

> Starting to the plate in the first inning, I could scarcely believe my ears. Almost as if it had been synchronized by some master conductor, hate poured forth from the Phillies dugout.
>
> "Hey, nigger, why don't you go back to the cotton field where you belong?"
>
> "They're waiting for you in the jungles, black boy!"

"Hey, snowflake, which one of those white boys' wives are you dating tonight?"

"We don't want you here, nigger."

"Go back to the bushes!"

Those insults and taunts were only samples of the torrent of abuse which poured out from the Phillies dugout that April day.

Chapman's campaign brought Jack crashing down. Particularly pressing was the fact that it occurred at home, in New York City, and from a Northern team—not St. Louis, which he had feared, or Louisville or Baltimore, which he had endured in 1946. "I felt tortured and I tried just to play ball and ignore the insults," he would recall, in language overheated by his ghostwriter. "But it was really getting to me. What did the Phillies want from me? What, indeed, did Mr. Rickey expect of me? I was, after all, a human being. . . . For one wild and rage-crazed minute I thought, 'To hell with Mr. Rickey's noble experiment.' . . . To hell with the image of the patient black freak I was supposed to create. I could throw down my bat, stride over to that Phillies dugout, grab one of those white sons of bitches and smash his teeth in with my despised black fist. Then I could walk away from it all."

But Jack remembered his pact with Rickey, and his unspoken pact with his people, to do what was necessary to make the experiment work. In a 1–0 Dodgers victory, he singled, moved to third on an error, and scored on a hit by Gene Hermanski. (But on that same day, after forty-seven chances as a major leaguer, Jack also made his first error, in the eighth inning.) To his further relief, the next two games also went to the Dodgers for a sweep of the series. Gradually Jack pulled out of his gloom. A few days later, when he wrote about the episode in a column, "Jackie Robinson Says," in the Pittsburgh *Courier,* he was nonchalant. "The things the Phillies shouted at me from their bench have been shouted at me from other benches and I am not worried about it. They sound just the same in the big league as they did in the minor league."

By then, he had other reasons to feel better. Chapman's abuse had angered the white Dodgers. Eddie Stanky took up the challenge: "Listen, you yellow-bellied cowards," Jack remembered him screaming at the Phillies dugout, "why don't you yell at somebody who can answer back?" Even Dixie Walker was upset by Chapman, a good friend, and told him so. Pushed by the white players, writers picked up the story and revived charges of anti-Semitic remarks allegedly made by Chapman when he was a coach with the Yankees. In his national radio broadcast, the powerful journalist Walter Winchell chided him. In the *Daily Mirror,* Dan Parker hailed Robinson as "the only gentleman among those involved in the incident." In addition, the veteran Philadelphia infielder Jeep Handley, disgusted by his manager's behavior, apologized to Robinson. Rickey, who had anticipated both the abuse and the response, later commented: "Chapman did more than anybody to unite the Dodgers. When he poured out that string of unconscionable abuse, he solidified and unified thirty men. . . . Chapman made Jackie a real member of the Dodgers."

Surviving one assault, Jack encountered another, different challenge. After managing a few hits at the start of the season (he batted .225 in April), he began a streak of futility that saw him go zero for twenty at one point. Hanging over his head, despite his Montreal record, was the 1945 evaluation by perhaps the dominant pitcher then in baseball, Bob Feller, that Robinson would never hit major-league pitching consistently. Jack began to hear whispers of criticism behind his back—but not from his coaches, who remained unflappable. His manager, Burt Shotton, in his retiring style, shrugged off suggestions that he might bench Robinson. (With his white hair and steel-rimmed glasses, Shotton seemed to personify self-effacement; he even declined to wear a baseball uniform and thus could not set foot on the field during a game.) The coaches could see that Jack was hitting the ball hard but straight at fielders. In addition, his right shoulder was heavily taped, the result of an on-field collision. They waited for him to come around.

When the Giants arrived from Manhattan to clear the air after Chapman's departure, their manager, the future Hall of Fame player Mel Ott, was civil to Jack, as was his team. Better still, after rain washed out one game, the Dodgers beat the Giants twice to move improbably into first place in the standings. The mood in the clubhouse was now a little more congenial. At the second game, on Sunday, an incident showed how much the Brooklyn community itself was taking Jack to its heart. A buzz of approval greeted the arrival of Joe Louis as he took a seat in the stands, then burst into rich applause as Jack went over and shook Louis's hand. "Photographers sprang up around them like rain lilies after a cloudburst," according to Red Barber; following on the heels of the sordid episode with the Phillies, here was "a full ball park roaring approval" of two black men. "This was a turning point."

However, Jack was still in his batting slump. Some thought he was lunging at the ball, others that his bat was too heavy. He decided to change nothing. On April 30, he went hitless again in a loss against the visiting Chicago Cubs. But the next day, May 1, the slump ended when he lined a fastball from Bob Chipman, unbeaten thus far that season, into left field. Next, he sent the Cub outfielder Andy Pafko back against the wall with a sacrifice fly that drove in one run. The Dodgers won, to hold on to first place. Rain washed out two series against the visiting Cincinnati Reds and Pittsburgh Pirates, but the respite gave Jack's shoulder time to heal completely. Then Jack's confidence was tested again, when the defending World Series champion St. Louis Cardinals came to town.

Although he would deny its seriousness, Sam Breadon, the Cardinals' owner, had uncovered a plot among his players to go on strike on May 6 rather than play with Robinson; this action might then spread throughout the league, to turn back the clock on integration. On May 9 in the *Herald Tribune,* Stanley Woodward declared that Breadon had hurried to New York to confer with Ford Frick, the president of the National League (Woodward also revealed that the strike was the brainchild of a Dodgers player, never named). Without hesitation, Woodward wrote, Frick had then sent the following unequivocal rebuke, through Breadon, to the players: "If you do this you will be suspended from the league. You will find that the friends you think you have in the press box will not support you, that you will be outcasts. I do not care if half the league strikes. Those who do it will encounter quick retribution. All will be suspended and I don't care if it wrecks the National League for five years. This is the United States of America and one citizen has as much right to play as another. The National League will go down the line with Robinson whatever the consequences. You will find if you go through with your intention that you have been guilty of complete madness."

Although Woodward would be accused of overstating the crisis and putting words into Frick's mouth, the league president himself supported the story and stuck by the words. With this fierce attack by the National League president, which followed the chiding of Ben Chapman of the Phillies both in the press and by the office of the commissioner of baseball, Jim Crow in baseball had lost the war. Individuals and individual teams, such as the Yankees and the Boston Red Sox, could continue to fight on, in a protracted rear-guard action. But barring some unforeseen catastrophe, baseball would remain open to blacks.

Against the feared Cardinals, who had overtaken the Dodgers to win the pennant in 1946, Brooklyn won the first game, then dropped the next two to fall into a tie for first place in the league. For Rickey and Shotton, it was a time for stocktaking. Brooklyn had started the season well, but its pitching remained inconsistent and the team was obviously not yet unified. The season was young. The Cardinals, though, were still expected to be the team to beat as the season and the summer ripened. "We have a great squad," Rickey remarked to reporters, "but so far we haven't a great team." Hurt in part by poor weather, attendance at Ebbets Field was also off. By May 8, when lights went on for the first night game of the year, Ebbets Field had welcomed about fifty thousand fewer paying fans than in 1946 for the same number of games.

Next, the Dodgers headed to Philadelphia for their second series with the Phillies, starting on Friday, May 9. Now, stung by the criticism of his race baiting, Ben Chapman was a somewhat chastened figure. He defended himself by claiming that he had treated Robinson much as he treated players of Italian or Polish background, that the vile language was nothing but a form of initiation into the baseball fraternity. But actions by the Phillies management showed that Chapman was hardly without club support for his treatment of Robinson. First, in a telephone call, according to Harold Parrott, the Phillies' general manager, Herb Pennock, urged Rickey not to "bring the Nigger here with the rest of your team" (Rickey had invited Parrott to eavesdrop on the conversation); "we're just not ready for that sort of thing yet." Rickey, however, rebuffed Philadelphia; if it declined to play, Brooklyn would claim the games on forfeit. Then, in Philadelphia, the Dodgers arrived at the Benjamin Franklin Hotel, their usual haunt, to find the premises barred to them. "And don't bring your team back here," Parrott recalled the hotel manager snapping, "while you have any Nigras with you!" Scrambling for accommodations, Brooklyn was forced to stay at the more expensive Warwick Hotel.

At Shibe Park, too, the visit to Philadelphia was depressing. Several Phillies players kept up a modified but still offensive version of their earlier vile campaign; from the dugout, Jack recalled, some "pointed bats at me and made machine gun-like noises." Worse, the Dodgers lost three of the four games, including a Sunday doubleheader before a record-breaking crowd, and slipped out of first place. But one person had changed his tune: Ben Chapman, seeing his job in danger, asked Robinson, through Parrott, to pose for a photograph with him. Jack agreed at once. When Parrott offered to escort him to the meeting, Robinson demurred: "This is something I should do alone, not as if I'm being urged." Behind home plate, the two men held a bat for the cameras. Years later, Jack expressed his true feelings: "Having my picture taken with this man was one of the most difficult things I had to make myself do." And yet, in his *Courier* column a few days after the incident, he turned the other cheek, as he had promised Rickey he would do. "Chapman impressed me as a nice fellow,"

Robinson wrote, "and I don't think he really meant the things he was shouting at me the first time we played Philadelphia."

By this time, Jack also knew something more about the twisted spirit of a small section of the public. Among his voluminous mail were letters that sickened him, because they revealed levels of hatred triggered by what he, Rickey, and the Dodgers were doing in the realm of baseball. Harold Parrott recalled letters "scrawled and scribbled like the smut you see on toilet walls." Several emphasized a general rage against blacks, but more than one involved threats to do violence to Rachel and to kidnap Jackie Junior. After he showed these letters to Rickey, a police captain called on the Robinsons at MacDonough Street in Brooklyn, where they were now living. Rickey was not one to panic, but two letters were so vicious that he had turned them over to the police: "I felt they should be investigated." But the names and addresses of the senders turned out to be fake.

Despite these threats, insults, and humiliations, Jack was steadily growing in confidence and psychological strength when, near the middle of May, the Dodgers set out on the trip that would complete the first grand cycle of the season, out west to Cincinnati, Pittsburgh, Chicago, and St. Louis. The freak show that had been his presence a month before, at the start of the season, had slowly changed into something far more ordinary, more human, even as he strove to be an extraordinary player. At one level, Rickey's experiment was a success; at another, more personal level, concerning Jack's future, it was undecided. Whether or not he would take hold in the major leagues was still very much a question. His fielding and base running often seemed superior, his hitting less so. "I do not profess to be a finished first baseman yet," Jack wrote on June 7, "and I know that I have made a number of mistakes." In the New York *Times,* Arthur Daley, defending Jack's right to a fair trial in the major leagues, also allowed that "the Negro first baseman hasn't been any ball of fire."

No one was more keenly aware of the challenge than Jack. Away against Cincinnati, on May 13 and 14, with the stands jammed with his supporters, the Dodgers lost both games of their series even as he maintained an eight-game hitting streak. In this city, he could stay with the team at the Netherlands Plaza Hotel—but was not allowed to use its dining room or swimming pool. Next, against the Pirates, Brooklyn dropped two out of three to continue its slide. In the first game, some of the Pirates appeared to balk at taking the field against Robinson and the Dodgers, but quickly came to their senses. But for Robinson the series was a personal triumph, with six hits in thirteen at-bats for his best performance in a series thus far. He was also well received by some Pirate players and fans. In one play, hustling to beat out a hit, he collided with the massive first baseman Hank Greenberg, in his first season with Pittsburgh and his last as a player, after a league-leading forty-four home runs for Detroit in 1946, but the two players dusted themselves off and chatted amiably. Years before, Greenberg had endured nasty baiting from various players and fans as a Jew. "Stick in there," Jack remembered

Greenberg telling him. "You're doing fine. Keep your chin up." "Class tells," Jack commented to a reporter. "It sticks out all over Mr. Greenberg."

But not every Pirate was as nice. The pitcher Fritz Ostermueller, formerly of the Dodgers, almost beaned Jack, who threw up an arm but ended up in the dirt, writhing in pain. Some Pirates showed concern, but to Jack the response of his own teammates was far more gratifying; they rained imprecations on Ostermueller's head. "The guys on the team are all for him," Sukeforth commented happily about Robinson. "You could see that by the way they acted when he got hit. . . . Mr. Jackie Robinson's going to do all right." The second game had its own measure of drama. It featured the Pirates pitcher Kirby Higbe, traded by the Dodgers after his part in the move against Robinson. His first pitch to Pee Wee Reese, who had not joined the rebels, was at his head; getting up, Reese hit the next pitch for a home run.

In Chicago, a record Sunday crowd of 46,572 paying fans at Wrigley Field welcomed Jack, who now had hit safely in fourteen straight games. His streak ended that day—but the Dodgers won the game. In this series, Jack's patience was sorely tested when the Cubs shortstop Len Merullo kicked him after the two players became entangled at second base on a pick-off attempt. Jack's arm reared back to strike but he stayed in control. Merullo's act may have reflected the mood of many Cubs. According to one player years later, this team, too, had been ready to strike rather than play against Jack, until the position of league officials became clear.

Next, the Dodgers rolled on to St. Louis, where the Cardinals were in last place but, with hitters like the extraordinary Stan Musial (who was always friendly to Jack) and pitchers like Harry "the Cat" Breechen, still to be feared. Rain washed out the first game, at night; but Brooklyn beat Breechen to take the second. Off the field, Jack had to put up with being barred at the city's elegant Chase Hotel, where the Dodgers usually stayed. Instead, he registered unhappily at the black DeLuxe Hotel.

Although such humiliations drew no protest from the white players themselves, Jack's relationship with them steadily improved. In one play against the Cardinals, at first base, he stopped a hot smash with his glove, then comically lost sight of the ball between his feet while the infielders yelled at him to make a throw; later, his teammates, including veterans like Hugh Casey, ribbed him in a way that told him that they were now starting to see him as one of them. On the train, sometimes he played cards with Spider Jorgenson and Marvin Rackley, or Ed Chandler, a pitcher; sometimes he sat casually around the regular bridge game that included Sukeforth, Parrott, and Casey. At one of these games Casey almost curdled Jack's blood by breezily sharing with him his secret for changing his luck at cards down home in Georgia: "I used to go out and find me the biggest, blackest nigger woman I could find and rub her teats to change my luck." Casey then rubbed Jack's hair. In the shocked silence that followed, Jack swallowed hard, dug down deep, and said nothing. Ironically, Casey was one of the older players who liked to help Robinson in practice; he was also quick to back him more than once that season in rough episodes with opposing players. Dixie Walker had also come around. The same player who rudely rebuffed Duke Snider when the rookie outfielder asked for help in learning a certain play—"Find out for yourself, kid"—gave Jack tips about hitting.

At mealtime—the witching hour of race relations—Jack often ate alone, or with younger teammates like Snider. Growing up in Compton, California, Snider was in junior high school when he began to marvel at Jack's gifts: "I had been a Jackie Robinson fan long before most of the world heard about him." To other players, eating in public with a black man was an embarrassment not to be endured. Still, the clamorous interest of whites and blacks in Robinson only grew. Wendell Smith, who roomed with him on one trip, recalled the telephone jangling incessantly with invitations. "Robinson is now paying the price of fame, just as Joe Louis has been doing for years," Smith declared. "He seldom has a moment to himself. He is the target of well-wishers, autograph hounds and indiscreet politicians who would bask in his glory to win prestige for themselves." Late in May, the *Courier* complained about black fans who "displayed too much enthusiasm over Jackie, cheered every time he did so much as walk out on the field." Later, it confessed to "fears and apprehensions that some unlearned and untutored buffoons would attempt to put on their act and create a scene" over Jack. But to these fans, Robinson was their shining black prince, and they wanted him to know that he could count on their love and admiration in his time of struggle.

Roger Wilkins, a fifteen-year-old black boy in Grand Rapids, Michigan, would comment years later: "In 1947, Jackie Robinson was as important to me and other blacks, especially young blacks, as a parent would have been, I think. Because he brought pride and the certain knowledge that on a fair playing field, when there were rules and whites could not cheat and lie and steal, not only were they not supermen but we could beat 'em. And he knew what he was doing. He knew what the stakes were every time he danced off a base. If he failed, we failed. Every steal he made could have been a bonehead play: 'Stupid Nigger!' He was not a dumb man, doing what came naturally. He knew what he was trying to do. And this man, in a very personal sense, became a permanent part of my spirit and the spirit of a generation of black kids like me because of the way he faced his ordeal."

And an ordeal it was in those first few weeks, when many pitchers seemed determined to baptize the black rookie by fire. In the thirty-seven games played before the end of May, Jack was hit by pitches six times; in the entire 1946 season, no National League player had been hit by pitches more than six times. "But as he had promised Rickey," Red Barber noted, "he said nothing, just took his base, licked his wounds." While Robinson's color was almost certainly a factor in these blows, it only compounded the tendency of pitchers to throw at rookies. Robinson was hit by pitches but three more times over the rest of the season. He had passed a key test of courage, one that broke many a young ballplayer. Besides, hitting Robinson meant putting him on base, and few pitchers wanted him dancing and prancing on the base paths while they tried to do their job.

In the last week of May, after his first complete round of all the other teams in the league, he was happy at last to be back "in dear old Brooklyn." To celebrate his return he had three hits in four at-bats against the Phillies. His batting average rose sixteen points to a respectable .283; on May 25, he also hit his second home run of the season. He was learning the rhythms of the season, its constant demand for vigilance. If he had found out anything about the major leagues thus far, Jack wrote, "I have learned that you can never stop thinking and that all the time you're in the ball game you have to keep hustling." He was sure now that he was up to this challenge. On the last day of May, the Dodgers were only two games out of first place.

BY THIS POINT, Jack and Rachel were now living in Brooklyn itself. After about two weeks at the Hotel McAlpin, a woman had showed up unannounced with an offer to share with her an apartment in Bedford-Stuyvesant. They accepted the offer sight unseen, but soon regretted it. At 526 MacDonough Street, at the corner of Ralph Avenue, they found not the stylish building they had imagined but a tenement infested with roaches. The Robinsons rented a back bedroom, and their landlady had one to the front; but she had a regular visitor who parked himself every evening in the living room. Without a car, the Robinsons found their freedom sharply curtailed. For recreation, they often took the baby and rode the buses about the city. (Their arrangement was not so unusual; that year, Snider and Gil Hodges, then a backup catcher, were sharing a room in a private home in Flatbush and walked to work at Ebbets Field. "Times were simpler in 1947," Snider would explain.)

Under such pressures and the demands of a small child, the Robinsons' room inevitably pulsed with simmering little tensions that were not eased by the unwillingness of both Jack and Rachel to talk much about their most private needs, and by her wish not to add to Jack's troubles. In those months, according to Rachel, Jack's worries "were eating at his mind, for he would jerk and twitch and even talk in his troubled sleep, which was not like him." Sometimes he would raise his voice in anger, but anything more violent was out of the question. Aware of his ordeal, she tried hard to make their home a haven, which Jack appreciated; he had little interest in going out with the boys. Once at home, however, he felt both contentment and the usual irritations, which he understood only imperfectly, because he was not much given to doubting himself. Around the house he helped a little, but only a little; he had a traditional attitude to what was man's work and woman's work. With Jackie he would change a wet diaper but never one

soiled; he would feed his son but could not be scheduled to help. He expected peace and quiet as he
buried his head in his beloved newspapers, and
mornings he wanted a loving send-off as he headed
to the park.

For all the tensions, he was sure that he loved his
wife and that she loved him. One day in March, on
board a Pan American Clipper flying the Royals to
Panama, Jack had poured out his feelings for Rachel
and also hinted at the tensions between them. "Darling," he wrote in a short letter, "As we fly through the
air with what seems to be the greatest of ease my
thoughts as usual drift back to you and I am again
reminded that I love you so very much that life without you would seem empty indeed. I have never in my
28 years been so very happy and I feel that I have just
about all in my life a man can ask for." He knew well
enough, he admitted, that his temper was sometimes
sharp and that his edges were still rough. "I have
loved you very much," he insisted, "even the times I
was angr[y]. . . . I know I don't show it but darling
these last few weeks away from you proves that my
life when you are near is the closest to heaven I have
ever been. I have no desire to even look at anyone else
because when I do they all seem very sad and I get
disgusted." Now that they had a child, "it is really a
wonderful life. I can hardly wait to see you and show
you how much of your love I have missed."

The moments of anger had been relatively few.
One explosion had come in Los Angeles the previous
year, near the end of Rachel's pregnancy. Jack had
decided to go to his cousin Van Wade's wedding in

Pasadena but would not hear of Rachel's traveling in her ninth month. When he left the house, Rachel collapsed onto her bed and cried and cried. Of Jack's not showing his love, according to Rachel later, "he was not yet the kind of man he would become. He wasn't yet the man who would send me flowers at the least opportunity. He was still inclined to be closed and tight. And I had a certain reticence as well, because that's the way I had been brought up. But I always knew he loved me."

Rachel had other trials as she learned to be Mrs. Jackie Robinson. At first, she had no contact with the other Dodger wives; she waited outside the park for Jack and wondered where the other wives were. Then one day, Norma King, the young wife of the pitcher Clyde King, introduced herself and showed Rachel the usual gathering place, under the stands. Some tension among the wives was inevitable, since their husbands were often in competition with one another, sometimes for the same job. But slowly some friendships formed, especially with Gil Hodges's wife, Joan, and Pee Wee Reese's wife, Dottie. (Later, after Carl Erskine joined the club, his wife, Betty, would also be a good friend.) The wife of Vic Lombardi, the diminutive pitcher in his last Dodger year, was always pleasant. "I've met most of them now," Rachel gamely assured a reporter later that first season, "and they're all congenial. When they gossip I join right in and gossip with them. Of course, they're more intimate by themselves."

Far easier was the Robinsons' relationship with the local fans; both Jack and Rachel fell in love with

Brooklyn. "The feeling in Brooklyn was very support-
ive, very rich, and we loved it," she recalled. "Some
places on the road I hated, their total intolerance; but
Brooklyn was the opposite, and Jack loved it, too."
From the start he made it his business to be kind to
fans, especially at home. "He had his favorites, he
especially loved to talk with the little old ladies; he
would hug them and pat them and chat with them very
patiently. He would keep me waiting, and I would
wait, because it was important to him and it was nice
to see. We all waited for Jack." Aware that she needed
an interest outside baseball and beyond Jackie
Junior—and with an eye to the home they expected to
have one day in California—she completed a course
later in the year at the New York School of Interior
Decorating.

IN JUNE, A LONG home stand against St. Louis,
Pittsburgh, Chicago, and Cincinnati saw the Dodgers
fight back into a tenuous hold on first place in front
of record-setting crowds in Ebbets Field. Against
Cincinnati, after Rachel and Jackie Junior received a
thunderous ovation when the public-address system
announced their presence, Jack responded with his
fourth home run of the season. In another game he
went four-for-four, in his best hitting day thus far,
with two doubles, a triple, and a single. After losses
against the Cardinals, Brooklyn rebounded on the
strength of Shotton's cool managing, its splendid infield, and fierce hitting led by Robinson, who batted
.381 in June. In St. Louis, the Cardinals seemed

friendlier—or so Jack carefully chose to describe them. In the *Courier* he saluted Joe Medwick, Stan Musial, Joe Garagiola, and the manager, Eddie Dyer, as "a swell bunch of fellows. . . . They treated me so nice I was actually surprised."

Now Wendell Smith reported that Robinson was "definitely one of the Dodgers. He is 'one of the boys' and treated that way by his teammates." In Danville, Illinois, on an off day, Smith reported a remarkable sign of progress. Out on the golf course after lunch at a local club, Reese saw Smith and Robinson trailing his own foursome. "Why don't you two join us?" Reese asked. "There is harmony and unity on the Brooklyn club," Smith reported, "and Jackie is a part of it. He is no longer a player apart from the rest of them. He is no longer a curiosity."

With such gestures, Reese played an important role in Rickey's project. Perhaps his most telling single act was sensational, given the racism of that time: at one point, in full view of the public, he dared to put his white hand on Robinson's black shoulder in a gesture of solidarity. Exactly when and where this moment came is uncertain. It happened either in Boston (as Robinson recalled) or in Cincinnati, just across the river from Reese's native Kentucky (as others saw it). Robinson more than once placed it in 1948, but others remember it as happening in 1947. (In *Jackie Robinson: My Own Story,* published in 1948, Jack makes no mention of the incident.) Much later, Robinson would tell of Reese's hand touching him, but his earliest published account, filtered through a writer in 1949, does not include physical contact. Opposing players were abusing Reese "very viciously because he was playing on the team with me. . . . They were calling him some very vile names." Because Robinson knew that the nasty words were meant for him, each epithet "hit me like a machine-gun bullet. Pee Wee kind of sensed the sort of hopeless, dead feeling in me and came over and stood beside me for a while. He didn't say a word but he looked over at the chaps who were yelling at me through him and just stared. He was standing by me, I could tell you that." The hecklers fell silent. "I will never forget it." According to Joe Black and others, Reese over the years became Robinson's closest friend on the Dodgers, although Jack would also feel deeply about other players, including Carl Erskine, Gil Hodges, Ralph Branca, Billy Loes, Don Newcombe, Black himself, and— much later—Junior Gilliam.

In a Boston newspaper, Jack praised his team-mates: "I get all kinds of help from these fellows. I wouldn't be anywhere without it. Walker has mentioned several things to me. And Eddie Stanky is always positioning me for batters." To the newspaper, Robinson was now "far from the unhappy ballplayer of a couple of months back."

A new daring entered his game. On June 24, against Pittsburgh's Fritz Ostermueller, who earlier had thrown at his head, he stole home for the first time in the majors. That month, too, against the Cubs, he scored all the way from first base on a sacrifice fly. (In this series, after Stanky broke up Ewell Blackwell's historic attempt at a second consecutive no-hitter, Blackwell scorched Jack, the next batter, with an explosion of racist insults; Jack replied with a single to right.) On Sunday, June 29, four hits in the second game of a doubleheader saw his hitting streak reach sixteen games. To Branch Rickey, that was nothing. "You haven't seen Robinson yet," he assured reporters. "Maybe you won't really see him until next year. You'll see something when he gets to bunting and running as freely as he should. Just now he's still in a shell. It's only occasionally that he pokes his nose out and becomes adventurous."

On July 3, Rickey had another victory when Bill Veeck, the general manager of the Cleveland Indians, announced the signing of Larry Doby of the Newark Eagles in the Negro leagues. With Doby leapfrogging the minors, the rival American League now had its first black player. "He is a grand guy and a very good ball player," Jack wrote of Doby. "I'm glad to know that another Negro player is in the majors. I'm no longer in there by myself." Later in the season, the St. Louis Browns, also of the American League, signed Willard Brown and Henry Thompson, two former teammates of Jack's with the Kansas City Monarchs. (In August, both were cut; but Doby was soon a star.)

On July 4, Jack's hitting streak ended at twenty-one games (one short of the major-league rookie record), but he soon started another. For the All-Star Game at mid-season, he received more than three hundred thousand votes—"amazing for a rookie," as the Toronto *Star* noted, although not enough to make the squad.

Surging, the Dodgers swept the Cubs to open a lead, then later won seven in a row. At this point, the Cardinals at last began to move. Six Dodger losses in seven games and a seven-game Cardinal streak closed the gap. In the middle of August, the two teams met for a four-game series in Brooklyn. Each took two, but the series was marred by one of the more dangerous episodes involving Robinson. In the seventh inning of the last game, with Ralph Branca working on a no-hitter, Jack's career "came within an inch of being ended," as Red Barber and others declared, when Enos "Country" Slaughter, a Southern player thought to be one of the ringleaders of the Cardinals' aborted strike in May, came down hard with his spikes on Robinson's right foot as Jack stretched to take a throw at first base. Slaughter's spikes barely missed Jack's Achilles tendon; as Robinson writhed in pain, Slaughter trotted nonchalantly to the dugout. "Hate was running high in that first Robinson year," Parrott later wrote of the incident. Jack declared: "Slaughter deliberately went for my leg instead of the base." But Slaughter always denied trying to hurt him: "I know the truth and that is I never intentionally spiked Jackie Robinson."

In yet another incident, the Cardinal pitcher Harry Breechen, rather than throw Jack out easily at first, took the ball to the baseline clearly intending to block his path with a nasty tag. Jack stopped short of Breechen. "You better play your position as you should," he warned: the next time, he would not hesitate to knock him over.

On August 24, Rickey made major-league history again by signing the first black pitcher in the majors: Dan Bankhead, formerly of the Memphis Red Sox of the Negro American League. In his first at-bat, facing Fritz Ostermueller, Bankhead hit a home run. But he struggled on the mound. Some observers, including blacks, thought that he choked in facing white hitters.

In September, with sixteen games to go, the Dodgers arrived in St. Louis leading by only four and a half. Jack, who had missed some games with a bad back, was now moved in the batting order from the second spot to cleanup. In response, he got eleven hits in his next twenty-four at-bats. But the pennant race led to more nastiness. In the second inning of the first game, the St. Louis catcher, Joe Garagiola, hitting into a double play, stepped on Jack's foot at first base in a less dangerous reprise of the Enos Slaughter incident. When Robinson came to bat in the next inning, he and Garagiola exchanged angry words. The catcher threw down his mask, the stadium roared in anticipation, and Clyde Sukeforth stormed from the dugout. Quickly, the plate umpire, Beans Reardon, "broke up [the] incipient rhubarb," as the *Sporting News* reported. The next time at bat, Robinson hit a home run with a man on; Brooklyn won, 4–3. (Like Slaughter, Garagiola always denied spiking Robinson on purpose.)

In the last game, on September 13, another incident, of a radically different nature, also excited much comment. Catching a twisting foul ball, Jack was saved from tumbling into the Brooklyn dugout by the protecting arms of his teammate Ralph Branca. The sight of a black man in a white man's arms over-whelmed some watchers, but to Branca it was nothing. (The catch, coming in the eighth inning, helped Brooklyn win the game, 8–7.)

On September 22, a loss by St. Louis against the Cubs finally put the Dodgers over the top and sent the people of Brooklyn into paroxysms of delight. The next day was Jackie Robinson Day at Ebbets Field. Brooklyn had much to be grateful for. Only the ballpark's small dimensions held down the number of paying fans that season to 1,828,215, a Club record. (The Yankees, in their larger stadium, attracted 2,200,098.) Although Jackie Robinson Day was conceived by the *People's Voice* newspaper, it was soon taken over by others, including the borough president, John A. Cashmore, and the celebrated dancer Bill "Bojangles" Robinson, who saluted Jack as "Ty Cobb in Technicolor." ("I have tried to study Cobb's base running methods," Jack had acknowl-edged about Cobb, "and apply them this season in the National League.") A long list of gifts included cutlery, silverware, a television set, and a light gray Cadillac. To Jack's special delight, his mother, Mallie, had made her first airplane flight to help honor him.

Three days later, with the regular season ended, a motorcade took the entire team from Ebbets Field to a reception in front of Borough Hall that attracted a vast throng. On that day, J. Taylor Spink of the *Sport-ing News,* which had opposed the integration of baseball and derided Jackie Robinson as a prospect, handed him its first "Rookie of the Year" award. "The sociological experiment that Robinson represented, the trail-blazing that he did," Spink emphasized, "did not enter into the decision. He was rated and examined solely as a freshman player in the big leagues—on the basis of his hitting, his running, his defensive play, his team value." On September 22, taking a broader view of his success, *Time* placed Robinson on its cover.

But as a player he had done very well indeed. He led the Dodgers in several categories: runs scored (125), singles, bunt hits (14), total bases, and stolen bases (with 28, he led the league). In 46 tries at bunting, he failed only 4 times either to reach first base himself or to move runners along with a sacrifice. On his team, he tied Dixie Walker for the most doubles and Pee Wee Reese for the most home runs (12); he also drove in 48 runs. He hit well in Brooklyn (.290) but slightly better on the road (.304) for a season average of .297. Dixie Walker himself pronounced: "No other ballplayer on this club with the possible exception of [catcher] Bruce Edwards has done more to put the Dodgers up in the race than Robinson has. He is everything Branch Rickey said he was when he came up from Montreal."

"So we're in it and fighting those powerful Yankees," Jack wrote excitedly about the World Series. "It's really a thrill. I love it." In the first game, Jack captivated the sellout crowd with his daring on the bases, including an entertaining escape from a rundown; he also seduced pitcher Frank Shea into a balk. But the Yankees took that game, and the next. Brooklyn looked dead. In the third contest, at Ebbets Field, Robinson singled twice, scored a run, sacrificed once, and completed two double plays in a hard-fought Dodgers victory. The fourth game pulsed with drama as the Yankees' Floyd Bevins denied Brooklyn a hit until the bottom of the ninth inning. Then Cookie Lavagetto, pinch-hitting, crushed his famous two-run double off the wall; the Dodgers won, 3–2.

In the fifth game, when Joe DiMaggio's home run and Frank Shea's pitching helped the Yankees to victory, 2–1, Jack drove in the lone Dodger run. The sixth game would be remembered for Al Gionfriddo's relentless, game-saving pursuit and capture of a magnificent drive by DiMaggio ("I've played a lot of ball," Jack wrote the next day, "but I've never seen the likes of that"). Brooklyn won, 8–6. But the powerful Yankees would not be denied. They took the seventh and final game of a World Series many considered the most enthralling ever played.

Jack had played well but not spectacularly; he batted .296 (almost identical to his season average) and played error-free at first base.

After the last game, Jack made his way to each of his teammates. Disappointed to lose, he did not give up his poise. "It was a pleasure to play with you," was the gist of his farewell, according to a reporter. "Thanks for all you've done for me." In turn, "each one of them looked at him seriously. What he saw in their eyes made him feel good."

The 1947 baseball season had been a spectacular triumph for Robinson. His impact, and that of Branch Rickey's epochal experiment, had gone far beyond the baseball field. Indeed, Robinson's role in ending Jim Crow in organized white baseball hardly measured his achievement that year. Over a period of six months, from his first stumbling steps to the victories that closed the season, he had revolutionized the image of black Americans in the eyes of many whites. Starting out as a token, he had utterly complicated their sense of the nature of black people, how they thought and felt, their dignity and their courage in the face of adversity. No black American man had ever shone so brightly for so long as the epitome not only of stoic endurance but also of intelligence, bravery, physical power, and grit. Because baseball was lodged so deeply in the average white man's psyche, Robinson's protracted victory had left an intimate mark there.

Blacks, too, had been affected. "Many of us who went to the ballpark when Jackie played," the novelist John A. Williams would recall about his youth in Syracuse, "went there to protect him, to defend him from harm, if necessary, as well as to cheer him on." Slavery and Jim Crow had often sparked heroism in blacks, but also so much doubt and even self-hatred that many feared to demand justice for themselves. As their champion, Robinson had taken their hopes into the arena of baseball and succeeded beyond their wildest dreams. He had been stoical, but the essence of this story was the proven quality of his black manhood. To blacks, he passed now into the pantheon of their most sublime heroes, actual and legendary—the slave revolutionary Nat Turner and the abolitionist Frederick Douglass, the steel-driving John Henry and the roustabout Stagolee. Neither blacks nor whites would be quite the same thereafter in America.

— 9 —

A Most Valuable Player

1947–1950

He's entitled to all the rights
of any other American citizen.
—Branch Rickey (1949)

THE 1947 BASEBALL SEASON left Jackie Robinson not only the most celebrated black man in America but also one of the most respected men of any color. In November, a nationwide contest placed him ahead in popularity of President Truman, General Eisenhower, General MacArthur, and the comedian Bob Hope, and second only to America's favorite crooner, Bing Crosby. Among black Americans, he was even more revered. From a bellboy at the Eaton Hotel in Wichita, Kansas, who named his baby daughter Jackie (because Robinson was a "good sport" and a gentleman, "something our race needs as bad as they do a square deal"), to C. C. Spaulding, the insurance millionaire, who advised Jack that "the whole nation is looking to you," black Americans hailed him. In New York, Philadelphia, Washington, and Chicago, testimonial dinners sang his praises.

This was also a good time, Jack knew, to make some money. In certain newspapers, Branch Rickey was often ridiculed unfairly as "El Cheapo." Jack did not support this portrait of Rickey as a skinflint, but in 1947 the Dodgers had paid him only $5,000, the minimum amount allowed, while his presence had meant a windfall for the Dodgers and every club they visited (Walter White of the NAACP estimated the extra income for the league at $200,000). None of that money reached Jack; Happy Chandler, the baseball commissioner, had forbidden clubs from paying an end-of-season bonus to players. In addition, Rickey had barred Jack from taking money for endorsing products during his first season. "I was being watched critically by millions of Americans," Robinson wrote, "and, if I had allowed myself to be exploited commercially, I would have cheapened myself in their eyes." Thus he had lived with the irony of turning down hundreds of thousands of dollars, according to a reliable estimate, while living in a single hotel room and a tenement.

To Jack, time was of the essence. An injury could end his career at any time, but he was also becoming old for a professional athlete. "I've got to make it quick," he declared, "because I'm 28, older than most people think." At first he judged that he might play only two or three more years; then he revised his estimate: "I hope I've got six years of big-league ball ahead." Despite his success, Jack's interest in playing baseball at his age was limited once the Jim Crow barriers were truly broken. Thereafter, the game was mainly the means to an end, which was twofold: a solid financial foundation for himself and his family, and his long-term desire to help young people, especially the poor and black. He knew that now was the time to make money, while Jackie Robinson was a household name.

To exploit his fame, Jack reached an agreement with a Manhattan agent, Jules Ziegler, of General Artists Corporation (GAC). Soon he, sometimes with Rachel and Jackie Junior, was endorsing various commercial products, notably Homogenized Bond bread ("I get a double play in Homogenized Bond. It tastes grand and packs plenty of energy!") and Borden's milk. More dubiously, he endorsed Old Gold cigarettes, which moved the sportswriter Sam Lacy to warn that Robinson "should do something about clearing up [the] impression that he smokes." With advertisements that dwelt on Jack's handsome, athletic looks and brilliant smile, more history was probably being made. These were perhaps the first commercial messages aimed at the mass market using a black man or a black family as their spokespersons.

In October, the news broke that Robinson had been signed, with Rickey's approval, to appear in *Courage,* a motion picture to be made by a group called Producers Releasing Corporation. Behind this venture was a producer, Jack Goldberg, who agreed to pay Robinson $14,500 to take part in what was to be an all-black production. To some observers, this seemed ill-advised. Since Jackie had broken the color line in baseball, one black journalist asked, "why would he have to take a step backward and appear in an all-Negro moving picture?" Another contract, signed through GAC on October 10, 1947, called for an autobiography to be written by Wendell Smith of the *Courier* and published by a small New York house, Greenberg. Curiously, the contract offered no advance and only standard royalties. But probably the most questionable venture promised Jack $10,000 for about four weeks of work in vaudeville. Jack would make guest appearances in New York, Washington, D.C., Chicago, and Los Angeles as part of a show that featured comedians, singers, dancers, and an orchestra. Rachel had strong reservations about this latest gambit. It seemed risky, especially since "Jack couldn't sing, and he was only a fair dancer. I couldn't imagine what he was supposed to do."

But Jack liked the pay and accepted the challenge. On October 29, he made his debut, answering scripted questions about himself, at Frank Schiffman's Apollo Theater on 125th Street in Harlem, a major showcase of black talent. The critical response to the show was caustic. The Apollo, one reviewer wrote, hit "a new low" in its sloppy, inane buildup to his appearance; "the entire show, save Jackie, stank." Finally on stage, he seemed "disgusted and ashamed, looking completely out of place and character. . . . Everything Jackie had worked so hard to build, giving us an intelligent and capable ball player, was crumbled among those degrading surroundings." Another newspaper praised Robinson on stage as "a picture of dapper modesty, quiet dignity and class" but also loathed the show: "The thought grows on you as you watch, 'What the hell is Jackie Robinson doing in this?' " Clearly, "money" was the right answer, but "the idea persisted that there should be another way for him to earn the income he so richly deserves."

At the same time, Jack was ready to support charity. In Philadelphia, at the White Rock Baptist Church, he helped raise money for the church nursery. In October, Jack handed out silver medals to members of a boys' baseball team playing in the Police Athletic League in Manhattan—and received a medal himself "for his interest in the youth of the 32nd precinct." In California, where he lent support to the Beverly Hills Kiwanis Club, the comedian Red Skelton acknowledged Jack's "gracious, down-right big-hearted manner." Jack was also willing to make quiet visits to hospitals to comfort the sick, especially boys, as when he paid an unannounced visit to a badly burned youngster who seemed on the brink of giving up. In Malden, Massachusetts, outside Boston, he spent an hour visiting a sick Jesuit priest, a fan, who worked among blacks in Mississippi. When a ten-year-old Brooklyn boy, Milton Goldman, was gravely ill in Brooklyn Jewish Hospital and his doctors asked for a Dodger or two to visit him, Jack was the first volunteer. He arrived at the hospital bearing toys and a baseball autographed by his teammates. "Jackie took the boy's emaciated hand in his," one report went. "The boy tried to squeeze it. For several minutes Jackie sat talking to the boy, then out of a clear sky the lad muttered, 'Gee, Jackie Robinson, and he came here just to see me.'"

In November, after several weeks without Jackie Junior, who had gone to Los Angeles with Rachel's mother, Jack and Rachel drove home to California.

The news that Jackie was close to taking his first steps turned the trip into a race against time. "We'd pull off the road," Rachel said, "and Jack would tell me, 'We'll sleep a few hours.' Then I'd feel the car moving. Of course, we didn't make it. The day before we reached Los Angeles, the little guy decided to walk." In Los Angeles, they moved in with Rachel's older brother, Chuck Williams, and his wife, Brenda, at 1283 35th Street, the former home of Zellee's mother. Aside from his vaudeville stint at the Million Dollar Theatre, where he opened on November 18, Jack mainly relaxed and played golf in the balmy weather or passed hours at the race track, which he loved. But again, he found himself a frequent guest of honor at dinners. In Oakland, at the yearly dinner of the Alameda County branch of the NAACP, Jack received its Annual Merit Award as "the first man in the history of your country to grip the handle of a baseball bat and knock prejudice clear out of a Big League Ball Park!"

Just before Christmas, at Los Angeles General Hospital, under ether for about six hours, Jack underwent an operation for the removal of a bone spur in his right ankle. He left the hospital on crutches, discharged in time to enjoy a gala luncheon in his honor on December 31 at the Biltmore Hotel (where he and Rachel had their first date, seven years before), hosted by the Los Angeles Bruin and Varsity Clubs, booster groups for UCLA athletics. Wilbur Johns, Jack's basketball coach and now the university's athletic director, chaired the event; also attending were Babe Horrell, his former football coach at UCLA;

John Thurman, his baseball coach at Pasadena Junior College; his illustrious backfield partner in 1939, Kenny Washington; and Jack's former employers Bob and Blanche Campbell. After a moving eulogy, he was presented with a testimonial scroll and a sculpted bust of the late President Franklin D. Roosevelt. Then a poised, confident Jackie Robinson, no longer the hungry, disgruntled young athlete from Pasadena, responded with "a short but impressive speech."

Early in the new year, 1948, Jack had one firm engagement: at Branch Rickey's request, he was scheduled to fly east to take part, with Rickey, in a public rally in Virginia in January in support of a bond drive for a proposed World War II memorial stadium between the towns of Hampton and Newport News. However, pressed by Jack Goldberg, who insisted that production would start any day on their movie, he decided to stay in Los Angeles. Robinson then waited daily for the call from Goldberg, which never came; maddeningly, the movie project dissolved into nothing. Some time later, Robinson filed a suit against Goldberg for payment of the $14,500 promised him.

Jack had not informed Rickey that he wasn't coming; he simply failed to appear at the rally. "More than sixty thousand Negroes were disappointed," Rickey's assistant Arthur Mann wrote. So was Rickey, who was left to explain, as best he could, his black star's absence. Jack, who took pride in honoring his commitments, had thought he had sent word to Rickey through Leo Durocher, who was living in Los Angeles (his wife was the movie actress Laraine Day) and had attended the UCLA luncheon in Jack's honor; but Durocher, who was near the end of his suspension as the Dodger manager, refused to be blamed. (In February, Robinson made up for the missed date with a visit to Virginia that included a Chamber of Commerce luncheon, a radio interview, and a speech at a rally for the new memorial stadium.)

With almost two months left before training camp, Jack then decided to take his stage act on the road. Organized by a West Coast agent, Jimmie Daniels, the tour took in seventeen cities in the South, including Atlanta, Memphis, New Orleans, and San Antonio. In one way, the tour was a serious mistake; his body ballooned. In the segregated South, most meals were taken in private homes, and were lavish. His metabolism surrendered as Jack drank milk by the quart, indulged in huge breakfasts of eggs, potatoes, and grits; lunches and dinners of fried chicken, pork, and biscuits; and desserts of ice cream, cake, and other sweets, which he always craved. His weight jumped to around 230 pounds. "We ate like pigs," he confessed, "and for me it was disastrous."

On February 11, when Rickey and Robinson, accompanied by Rachel, finally met to settle his 1948 contract, an element of friction was present. The next day (the birthday of the Great Emancipator, Abraham Lincoln, as one reporter noted snidely), the two men signed Jack's contract. How much he would receive had been a subject of public speculation, especially after a poll of the Baseball Writers Association placed him fifth in the balloting for Most Valuable Player. "There's no question about it," Rickey had commented. "He deserves a substantial [raise] and will get it." One report even asserted that a contract had been signed, for $22,500. But the new figure was only $12,500, which left both Jack and Rachel disappointed. "I respected and respect Branch Rickey," Rachel said years later, "but the situation was pure plantation. There was no chance to negotiate, to discuss anything. It was no different for the white players, but I never thought it was right." The meeting so affronted her that when at one point Jack asked her a question, she simply made no reply. She sat quietly as Jack, Rickey, and Harold Parrott tried to interpret her silence. Arthur Mann, who was present, later wrote of a display of "considerable vehemence on both sides . . . a wholehearted confession of merits and demerits in the sphere of supply and demand." Before the press, however, Jack was loyal. "Mr. Rickey and I came to terms easily," he said. "I left it all up to him and he came through with a good contract."

Later that month, Jack was about to leave Los Angeles for the Caribbean and training camp when he received the most devastating news of his life since the death of his brother Frank in 1939. In Austin, Texas, the Reverend Karl Downs, Jack's most influential mentor in his late adolescence, was dead at the age of thirty-five. In September, Downs had come to Brooklyn for Jackie Robinson Day and stayed with the Robinsons. During his visit, he had taken ill with chronic stomach pain and gone with Rachel to a Brooklyn hospital. The Robinsons had urged him to stay there for further treatment, but Downs insisted on returning to Samuel Huston College in Austin, where he was still president. In Austin, on February 26, at the segregated Brackenridge Hospital, he had undergone an emergency operation at the hands of a white surgeon. "Complications set in," according to Robinson in his autobiography, but "rather than returning his black patient to the operating room or to a recovery room to be closely watched, the doctor in charge let him go to the segregated ward where he died." The death of the man who had brought Jack back to religion and given him a powerful sense of purpose tested Jack's faith: "It was hard to believe that God had taken the life of a man with such a promising future."

A few days after Downs's funeral on March 2, at Wesley Chapel Methodist Church in Austin, Jack reached Ciudad Trujillo in the Dominican Republic. There, tired and troubled, he checked into his hotel and joined the rest of the Dodgers for a month of training before a two-week exhibition tour of the southwestern United States. His inner turmoil was eased only a little by the fact that, unlike in 1947, he now stayed with his white teammates, at the luxurious Hotel Jaragua by the sea; and at the park, as he wrote from Ciudad Trujillo, "I met all the gang, Hugh Casey, Eddie Stanky, Pee Wee Reese, Tommy Brown, Ralph Branca and all the others I played with last season. They all seemed glad to see me and I certainly was glad to see them again." With him in the Dodgers camp was only one other black player, the pitcher Dan Bankhead. But some miles away, with the Montreal Royals, were Roy Campanella, on the brink of a call-up by the Dodgers, and Don Newcombe, who was still maturing as a pitcher.

Controversy surfaced at once. Stanky, the second baseman, was holding out for more money; but with Robinson waiting in the wings to claim second base, the Dodgers dawdled in negotiating. In 1947, Rickey had said openly: "The best second baseman in the world is now playing first base." Soon Stanky was traded to the Boston Braves. "I was sorry to see Eddie go," Jack wrote. "He was a great guy and a swell ball player." Second base was now open but he did not pounce. "Wherever they tell me to play, I'll play," he wrote, but "I like second base better than first . . . and hope I can do well enough to stay there all season."

A more serious controversy concerned Jack's weight, now about 215 pounds. Durocher, back in charge after his one-year suspension, was eager to reassert his authority on a club that had won the pennant and almost the World Series without him; he was perhaps also smarting from Robinson's charge that he had misled him about the Newport News engagement. Jack had taken the news of Durocher's return calmly. "I'm just a player," he declared, "I don't pick the managers. I'll give anybody the best I have." But in Ciudad Trujillo, Durocher took one look at Robinson and exploded. "What in the world happened to you?" he screamed (as Jack reported). "You look like an old woman. Look at all that fat around your midsection. . . . Why, you can't even bend over!" Feeling guilty but also humiliated, Jack offered Durocher excuses, "but he wouldn't listen. . . . All the newspapermen gathered around and gave me an 'army inspection.' " Durocher also offered another piece of criticism: Robinson hit too much to left field. "You've got to hit more to right this year," he lectured. "If you learn how to do that you'll hike your average by at least fifteen points."

"I think Durocher is right," Jack told a reporter. "I hit too many balls to left." As for his weight, Jack conceded that "my speed is a big asset—without that I would be lost." He gave a solemn promise that "I'm not going to blow up like that again. . . . I'm going to find something to do; something that will keep me down around playing weight." Durocher was not alone in criticizing him. In the Baltimore *Afro-American,* Sam Lacy bluntly challenged Robinson: "After an inexcusably 'easy' first week in training camp, Jack settled down to hard work." Tested furiously under the tropic sun by Durocher, Jack began to lose weight quickly, though a few excess pounds resisted his efforts. But his throwing arm went sore, and he was timid on the base paths. Only near the end of training did Jack seem to be rounding into form, when he hit two home runs against the Royals and a local all-star team.

He was buoyed, too, by his warm reception by people in the Dominican Republic and Puerto Rico, where the Dodgers also played a few games that month. In Ciudad Trujillo, he wrote, most locals were "conscious of their color and the things they have in common with colored people of America." Jack elicited the same reaction in Puerto Rico, where fans "pulled and tugged on his clothes, pleaded for autographs" and greeted his plate appearances "with spontaneous applause." Still, he was lonely away from Rachel and Jackie, and Karl Downs's untimely death overshadowed everything else. In the March 27 *Courier,* he devoted his entire column to Jackie Junior. "I miss him very much," he confessed freely. The "best thing" about being a major-league player "is that it gives you an opportunity to make a decent living and prepare for the future. . . . He's a grand little fellow and I want to be able to give him everything possible when he gets a bit older. . . . I want him to grow up in a good home, nice clothes, and some of the other things the average American kid enjoys."

The flight back to America from Ciudad Trujillo was a nightmare, as the Dodgers' DC-4 lost an engine and started misfiring on another. The pilot turned back. "Sure we were scared," Jack told reporters. A later flight took them to Vero Beach, Florida, to an old military facility acquired by Rickey as a permanent training center that would be exempt from Jim Crow. By this time Jack was down to about 200 pounds. "I'm in good shape," he declared gamely. "I'm ready for a big season. All I need is a little luck." And initially he seemed to have it. In his first game at Vero Beach, before the largest crowd (about half black) to see a baseball game there, he led off for Brooklyn and hit a home run. He also did fairly well on the tour, which started in Fort Worth,

Texas, and continued through Oklahoma, North Carolina, and Maryland, before ending in New York. Record crowds swollen by blacks, one reporter noted, made the turnstiles "click like a five and ten cent store cash register on bargain day." Encouragingly, whites seemed eager to support the black players, although along the way Robinson and Campanella, who was now a Dodger (although only temporarily), heard a few loud boos. At a luncheon in Dallas, three hundred local whites welcomed the black Dodgers. When Durocher declared that Brooklyn would not have won the pennant in 1947 without Jack, "the jam-packed room of Texans gave Robby a rousing round of applause."

JACK WAS OVERJOYED to reunite in April in New York with Rachel, who that month drove their Cadillac from Los Angeles in the company of her younger brother, Raymond, and little Jackie. At last, Jack, Rachel, and Jackie had decent accommodations. That month, they moved into the top floor of a two-family home at 5224 Tilden Avenue, near the Utica Avenue subway stop in Flatbush. A friend of a friend had bought the house and saved the top floor (at ninety dollars a month), with its two bedrooms and a charming, white-painted front porch, for the Robinsons. "We like it," Rachel told the press. "The only trouble is there's no real yard for Jackie to play in." She didn't mention that several residents in the overwhelmingly white area had opposed the sale of the house to a black. But a family two doors down, Arch and Sarah Satlow and their small children, Stevie, Paula, and Sena, had welcomed the Robinsons. Rachel and Sarah, the daughter of Russian immigrants, became instant friends. Fifty years later, with both Jack and Arch long gone, they were still close friends.

One day, an alarmed neighbor had called out to Sarah to warn her that a black family was moving into the neighborhood. "Oh, isn't that nice!" Sarah replied, without thinking. Her neighbor slammed the window shut. Then someone brought around a petition for Sarah to sign. "I said, 'Are you mad? Are you crazy?' We had a huge cherry tree in the backyard, that gave the most miraculous cherries. Arch and I picked a pail and took it over. From then on we were friends." Rachel and Sarah, who was only a few weeks younger than Jack, discovered they had things in common. Both had attended college and trained as nurses, and had a special interest in psychiatry, but had given up their careers to be wives and mothers; both loved the arts. Seeking precious free time, they helped one another by babysitting each other's children. "Rachel got the worst of the deal," Sarah recalled, "because she had only one and I had three. But it was nothing to her, she was such a kind and efficient person."

They were different in some ways. Sarah's family had been prosperous, but to her, Rachel seemed to the manner born. "She was a very demanding person, both with herself and others. Things had to be done right. In those days I dressed plainly, because everything was for the children; but Rachel dressed very well. She had discovered Saks and Bergdorf Goodman, and she had fabulous taste. She was fastidious; she had class and dash about her. She could sew; she was a wonderful cook; she baked beautifully. Her mother had taught her all these things." Once, helping Sarah learn how to bake, Rachel wounded her feelings. "She gave me this recipe for lemon meringue pie," Sarah explained. "It was my first meringue pie. It was a disaster, the crust turned out all soggy. I said to her, 'What do you think happened, Rachel?' She fell out laughing, she laughed and laughed. How was I supposed to know that you must bake the crust first? I didn't take it as a joke, I was so hurt. I never did it again, believe me, but I baked my head off!"

To cope with Jack's fan mail, which came by the laundry-basketful, as Rachel put it, she and Jack hired Sarah to prepare answers for Jack's signature; Jack would go over each letter and sign it. "I just loved Jack," Sarah said. "Because he had a gentle, bright, sharp mind, and it was always coated—the way I saw him—with a softness and a kindness, especially with children. He played so easily with children on the street, he visited Stevie in the hospital all by himself when Stevie was sick. It was something that was natural. What he did in the locker room with other men was another matter; in the twenty-five years I knew him, I always saw that softness about Jack. Of course, he could get angry, but I never heard a foul word in his mouth, except maybe once. I was in an office he was using at Rockefeller Center and he was taking a call and got disconnected. 'Oh, shit!' he said, and then he says, 'Oh, Sarah, I'm so sorry.' I said, 'I didn't hear you. I didn't hear you.' " To her, Jack was a man "with great vision, and strong emotional feelings."

With the Satlows nearby, Jackie Junior, who was about a week younger than Sena, the youngest Satlow, had a regular companion; one day a white sports reporter visiting the Robinsons was startled to see the two children, one black, the other blond, playing contentedly. Jackie at three was a warm, loving child, outgoing, easy to laugh, a charmer, showered with attention inside his family and outside, and especially as Jackie Robinson's son. In fact, as Rachel recalled, he was "our ambassador to the Flatbush community. He would be out on the sidewalk with his tricycle and then disappear into a backyard. Then he would reappear with cookies and pretzels. Once the people got over the shock of seeing this little black child suddenly appear, they were very nice and neighborly." Many of the neighborhood boys, including Stevie Satlow, were thrilled to have a genuine Dodger in their midst, although some had curious ways of showing it. Rachel remembered a boy of eight or nine who lived on an adjoining lot. "He clearly admired Jack, you could see that," she said; "but he took real pleasure in waiting for him to come home so he could taunt him about his playing. Jack took it all in stride. He might blow up on the field, at the ballpark, but not at home and not with young people. He actually liked the boy."

And yet the Robinsons did not feel entirely at home in the Flatbush apartment, where they did little entertaining. While they rented, and divided their year between the East and California, and while Jack's role in the baseball world unfolded, Jack and Rachel would continue to feel unrooted. Their sense of impermanence had little to do with the fact that Flatbush was unlike anything they had known before—a living, breathing Jewish community, complete with synagogues, yeshivas, kosher bakeries and butcher shops, delicatessens, and the like. Jack and Rachel liked this difference, this sense of being educated about the world, about the multiple richness of American life. "In California," Rachel said, "we knew nothing about Jewish culture. Particular names meant nothing to me, or physical types. We were innocent, or ignorant." So ignorant, in fact, that one Christmas they stunned the Satlows by giving them a Christmas tree. "We didn't know what to do," Sarah said. "What would my parents think? Then we decided to put it up. The children liked it, and Jack and Rachel meant well."

As the Robinsons gained more friends in the white world, they did not lose touch with the black. In fact, in 1947, as they endured life in their tenement room, Jack and Rachel had gained a satisfying complex of friendships rooted in black Brooklyn. Through Rickey and his memorable February 1947 dinner for prominent blacks, the Robinsons met another married couple, Lacy and Florence Covington, and Florence's sisters, all single at that time, Willette, Julia, Phyllis, and May Bailey. Originally from North Carolina, the Covingtons and the Baileys owned and shared two substantial brownstones on Stuyvesant Avenue near Fulton Street. Lacy Covington, a tall, handsome, courtly man, had been a brick-mason most of his life until, responding to an old ambition, he had studied for the ministry and been ordained. Lacy and Florence, a housewife, saw themselves as servants of the community; their home became a gathering place for a variety of people. On Sundays, Florence set a large table with china, silver, and linen, much of it shrewdly purchased in second-hand shops, and offered lunch to more than a dozen of their friends, many of whom, like Rachel, regularly brought dishes prepared at home. "There was a lot of good fellowship and good feeling in their home," Rachel remembered. "Whatever else was happening in our lives, we'd leave there feeling very good."

The Covingtons helped to make them see New York City as a community into which they could settle and be at ease; it was Florence who had secured for them their apartment in the Flatbush duplex. "Lacy and Florence and her sisters became like extended family to us, but true family nonetheless," according to Rachel. "Lacy was a lovely, lovely man among all those women, and he and Florence had a graciousness that made their home a special place." Best of all, in some respects, the Covingtons were happy to have Jackie Junior: "I could always take Jackie there and then go to the ballpark to be with Jack. And they would keep him all day until I got back, every day." From the start, also, the Robinsons hired Florence's sister Willette to help with Jackie. Eventually, Willette would become an important, beloved member of the Robinson household, living there but returning to her home on the weekends, with close ties to the children in particular.

The sense of tenuousness surrounding Jack's baseball career did not push Jack and Rachel apart; rather, it brought them closer, mainly because Jack had the sense to see and admit that he badly needed Rachel's help and advice and love as he moved into a future that was still uncertain. In public, he wanted her at his side as often as possible; she boosted his self-esteem with her reserved charm, easy intelligence, and striking looks. Jack could tell that Rachel impressed men he respected, including Rickey and Harold Parrott: "They evidently have high regard for you Darling," he wrote home. He had been chatting with Parrott by a swimming pool in Ciudad Trujillo, and "it pleased me to sit and listen because he spoke with respect when he mentioned your name. Darling you can't imagine how proud I am to be able to say you are my wife. I pride in the fact that I have a person who is capable of handling herself regardless of the crowd." On public occasions, many who came to honor Jack stayed to praise his wife. In Chicago, at a public dinner at the Savoy Ballroom, a reporter caught something of Rachel's appealing public personality when, accepting an award from a women's magazine, "she rose and in cultured, yet simple words voiced her appreciation of the honor paid her husband and her surprise at the award made to her."

Jack made a big point of giving Rachel full credit in public for his success. Rachel, he said in 1947, was "the one person who really kept me from throwing my hands up in despair many times"; she was "my strongest support during these trials. . . . She always had the wise suggestion, the comforting touch, the encouragement to go on which carried me through." "I can truly say," he told a gathering in 1948 at a high school in Madison, New Jersey, "that my rise to baseball fame is mainly due to my wife." She was obviously his main confidante and advisor, although Rickey also had a special place in Jack's life; in addition, she was the financial boss of the household. Jack turned over all sums to her, and she knew what was going out and what was falling into a reserve account about which Jack knew little. To be sure, the aura of perfection that hovered about Rachel sometimes annoyed him, but usually in little ways only. Knowing that Rachel was sensitive about her mother's opinion of her, he sometimes used that fact. "I hated it," Rachel said, "when he would tease me in front of her, or my brothers, about not being perfect, about spending too much on something, or making this or that mistake. I usually didn't mind what he was saying, but I did mind the company he said it in. Sometimes he got to me that way."

Jack continued, even with his growing fame in the aggressive world of male professional sports, to exert tight self-discipline about alcohol, tobacco, and sex. On the subject of affairs outside marriage he was rigid, as when he chastised a young admirer from Akron, Ohio, who propositioned him in a letter. "I want you to love me just once," she had pleaded. "Just once and then I might be satisfied. I know that you're [a] married man and that you have a son but you don't have to be an angel. . . . Your wife would never know about it." To which Robinson replied sternly: "When I married Mrs. Robinson, I exchanged vows to love, honor and cherish her for the rest of my life."

Although sex was a strong force in Jack, his principles and inhibitions probably prevented him from ever being completely comfortable coping with its demands. On the road, he burned with such longing for Rachel that he sometimes apologized for the steaminess of some of his letters—"but they are meant only for you to read and were written to let you know that regardless of how long I am away no one else can ever be seen." If sex was a strong drive, love and companionship were at least as important, and he was ready to say so. A roommate would remember with a sense of wonder the intensity of Robinson's frequent telephone calls home. "When he'd be on that phone talking to Rachel," Joe Black said, "I mean, you could feel the excitement exuding through his body. You could feel the love going from his voice to [her], flowing to her. I mean, he was trying to caress her with his voice." The weeks of separation, Jack wrote to Rachel from the Caribbean, had only "increased my love for you more than one could anticipate. I never dreamed I loved you so very much. I knew my love was very strong but until now I did not realize that I love you so very much that it hurts terribly to be away from you." Jack shared with Rachel his fear that they were too much the Puritans with one another. "We have not loved each other the way we are capable of loving or better than that we have not expressed our love as it should be. Both of us seem to wait for the other and as a result we are not able to get the most out of our love. Loving you Darling," he wrote, alluding specifically to his brother Mack and his wife, "makes me realize how awful it must be for two people to be married and not really be in love."

At times, Jack seemed to be on the verge of suggesting that Rachel was not as spontaneous as he wanted her to be; but finally he put it differently. "Darling," he wrote her, "if only you loved me as I love you then I would really be happy. I am satisfied with you loving me as you do now, however, because it would be impossible for two to be in love as much as I am with you. I wish there were ways I could prove it to you." For all these fine words, he was also well aware that he was not as mature and unselfish as he expected Rachel, as his wife, to be; he was a man, and in many things he did what he wanted and left her to clean up. What set him apart from many other men was his willingness, at least from time to time, to admit his failings and beg her to see that he truly loved her: "It seems my habits make you sometimes doubt me but there is no question in my mind that my marriage is the greatest thing that could have happened to me. All the other honors are really secondary and Darling someday I'll prove it. I hope it will be soon. I will do everything to prove it."

WHEN THE 1948 DODGER SEASON opened at the Polo Grounds, against the Giants, Jack was the picture of confidence. "We think we have a better club

now than we had this time last season," he proclaimed. But the Dodgers, including Jack, tripped
coming out of the gate. Although he was now installed at his preferred position, second base, a sore
right arm, a nagging back, and a tender knee made
him uncomfortable everywhere on the field.

He was still too fat to be truly effective, as
reporters quickly noted. He knew this was true, and
yet when he read one day that he had "waddled" after
a ground ball, he found the insult hard to take. With
his acutely pigeon-toed gait and top-heavy physique,
Jack usually walked with an odd, ducklike stride;
somehow, awkwardness fell away as the great body
accelerated or feinted sinuously or shuddered to a
swift stop. When he was not in shape, the oddness of
his stride was more pronounced. But the word "waddled" hurt him to the core. "He fought against tears,"
Arthur Mann stated (perhaps going too far). "No one
wrote of how he had worked and was working; how
he was undergoing the torture of hunger again in
order to diet. His temper flared." When Jack met Gus
Steiger, the author of the remark, his tongue "lashed
out in reprisal," according to Mann; the next day,
another newspaperman wrote that Robinson "was
developing a swelled head to match his midsection."

When Jack's bat stayed cold and his injuries
mounted, Durocher removed him from the lineup.
Some blacks were dismayed, but Jack would not
allow his skipper to be blamed for his own failings.
Durocher, he told his readers, was "a good manager
and a fine person. . . . I sat on the bench because of
my arm and not because he didn't like me." Then

Robinson seemed to return to form. On April 30, in a 2–1 victory, he drove in both runs with singles; the next day, he hit his first home run of the season. But something was not right. His flash and fire running on the bases, his unusual style and daring, were missing. Five weeks into the season, although he was now batting over .300, he had not yet stolen a single base. Late in May, he was sure he was back: "I think I'm ready for a rough, tough season." In June, however, as the club struggled, in a shocking but largely symbolic move Brooklyn placed him on waivers; technically he was available to other clubs. In the *Courier,* Wendell Smith, conceding that Robinson was no longer "the dashing, daring base runner of 1947," ventured wickedly that Rickey hadn't forgiven Jack "for his porky-pig appearance last spring." The New York *Daily Mirror* quoted Rickey on Robinson: "He has been overweight, sluggish and never has shown the abandon and speed on the bases that caused the opposition nervous spells." Stunned to be placed on waivers, Jack nevertheless brushed off its import in public. Yes, he wanted to stay in Brooklyn; but he would play just as hard for another club. As for his weight in the spring—"I'm not worried about that fat anymore. I'm fit as a fiddle and ready to go."

But by the middle of June, he had still not stolen a base, and his batting average was only .270. At last, on June 24, in a doubleheader at home against Pittsburgh, he pulled out of his slump. In the opener, with two men out in the bottom of the ninth, he broke a tie with a grand slam off Mel Queen, "the first time in my life that I ever hit a grand-slam homer anywhere."

In the second game, he had three more hits, as his batting average jumped from .279 to .306. He also stole his first base of the season. A few days later, after stealing home for the first time in 1948, he flashed his old speed with an inside-the-park home run against the Giants. Jack's reawakening helped to fire up the Dodgers just as Roy Campanella, who had been sent down to St. Paul in May, returned to Brooklyn with a vengeance. In his first three games, Campanella had nine hits in twelve tries, with two home runs.

Next, Rickey shook up baseball by completing an amazing deal that sent Leo Durocher to manage the Giants; Burt Shotton returned to the Dodgers. Despite the tension between them, Jack was sorry to see Durocher go. In the *Courier* he contrasted Durocher, "a human dynamo" who "loves nothing better than a fighting ball player," to the mild-mannered Shotton, but expressed no preference for one over the other. But Harold Parrott saw a loss: "What the black man needed behind him was Durocher's bark and brass and bellow—and in front of him too, to keep the umpires off him." To some observers, however, Jack's late-inning, three-run homer in a victory over Cincinnati seemed a celebration of Shotton's return. In last place on July 2, the Dodgers piled up seventeen victories in twenty-one games at one point as they pursued the league-leading Boston Braves. Late in August, Brooklyn edged into first place for the first time with a win in which Jack hit his eighth home run of 1948 and scored three runs; then the Dodgers slipped backward again. Another charge recaptured the top spot; in a doubleheader against St.

Louis, Jack hit for the cycle—a single, double, triple, and home run—in the first game and then went two-for-four in the second. However, the Dodgers' effort was in vain. Late in September, the Braves pulled ahead of the pack to claim the pennant. Brooklyn finished a disappointing third.

At the end of the season, Jack led the Dodgers in several categories, notably batting average (.296) and runs batted in (85). He also led in hits, doubles, triples, total bases, and runs scored; as a fielder, he was rated as the best second baseman in the National League, with an average of .979. "But deep in my heart I was miserable," he recalled, "because I knew that I should have done better—much better. I made myself a solemn vow to redeem myself and the Dodgers in 1949." An analysis of his 1948 performance by the statistician Allan Roth of the Dodgers praised him in several categories, including power hitting, overall offense, clutch hitting, bunting, and stolen bases. Adversely, Roth noted that Jack's hitting against left-handed pitchers "was only fair" and that his record in night games was ordinary. He was "exceptionally weak against the same two teams for the second season" (Boston and Chicago; he batted .221 as compared to .326 against the other clubs); and Jack had shown "disappointing all-around play the first part of [the] season" despite his decent batting average.

The season was by no means a total loss. Jack had survived his sophomore season, a noted jinx. He had also reached a new height of personal confidence; more readily accepted, he was also less willing to be meek. Two incidents in August underscored this change. Against the Chicago Cubs, he twice disputed an umpire's decision with a vehemence that would have been impossible in 1947. Now he was just another squawking ballplayer—or almost so. "Yes sir," he wrote happily, "when a Negro gets to the place when he can argue over a decision and no one makes anything of it, I begin to feel as though we have really arrived in the big leagues." His sense of arrival was tested again on August 24, at Forbes Field against the Pirates. Bitterly protesting the ejection of his teammate Bruce Edwards by umpire Butch Henline, Robinson was himself tossed by Henline—Jack's first ejection in the majors. "Jackie came rushing out of the dugout," according to one reporter, "as if he were possessed with the very devil itself and proceeded to give Henline a verbal lacing down that had all the characteristics of a three-ring circus." Just one year before, such behavior would have been unthinkable.

BETWEEN SEASONS, Jack made sure he did not repeat his patterns of the previous year, when he had eaten himself into trouble. Instead, he and Campanella went on a barnstorming baseball tour of the South and California with two teams sponsored by Alejandro Pompez, the veteran owner of the colored New York Cubans. After a month, the tour ended in Los Angeles with a series against Satchel Paige's All-Stars.

Back among the Negro leaguers, Jack was not always welcome. In July, he was elated when Paige, his former Kansas City teammate, made a belated but distinguished major-league debut with the Cleveland Indians. But the month before, in the popular black magazine *Ebony,* Jack had drawn on his mixed experience as a Monarch in 1945 to launch a devastating attack on the Negro leagues. Written "all by himself," as an astonished Wendell Smith (Robinson's main ghostwriter to this point) hastened to make clear, this essay sent the owners "into a frenzy." To them, Robinson seemed ungrateful and inconsiderate of the fact that integration was killing the Negro leagues. But Jack did not back down. "I certainly want to see Negro baseball continued," he insisted, but only after "a lot of house cleaning." The feud continued later in the year when Effa Manley, the mercurial owner of the Newark Eagles, comparing him to Larry Doby of the Cleveland Indians (formerly of the Eagles), sneered openly that Robinson "can't carry Doby's glove" as a player. Calling the statement "utterly ridiculous and childish," Jack reaffirmed both his admiration for Doby and his criticism of the leagues. To some blacks, Robinson was once again bravely speaking the truth; to others, he had gone too far and was forgetting where he had come from.

Jack himself had no fears about losing his place in the black world. When the tour ended in November, he reported for duty, along with Campanella, as a coach and counselor in the Boy's Work Department of the Harlem branch of the YMCA on 135th Street.

The pay was negligible, but the work was important. In October, the two Brooklyn stars had signed contracts with the branch director, Rudolph J. Thomas, one of Jack's closest advisors and friends in Harlem, to work during most of the off-season. To celebrate this coup, the Y honored the men on November 17 with a gala dinner. "Both Roy and I like this kind of work," Jack told the press, "and we are both crazy about children. . . . We are proud to be getting this chance to work at a job so near our hearts." The hiring was an experiment, but also a success; juvenile membership at the Harlem YMCA quickly doubled, and Jack began an association with the Harlem YMCA that would last the rest of his life. "We are very much encouraged by the results," he declared at the end of his stint. At first, the boys were awed, but soon found out that "we were just ordinary beings like themselves. Soon they were kidding and joking with us, but we had their respect, too. We were their pals."

That fall, he also experienced "a big thrill," as he put it, when WMCA, the largest independent radio station in New York City, signed him to conduct a fifteen-minute show on the air, six days a week. (Harold Parrott was his main writer.) From the start, in yet another breakthrough by a black American in the white world, Robinson looked forward to talking about more than sports. "During my broadcast," he wrote, "I will also get a chance to fight my pet peeve, juvenile delinquency." With more interviews scheduled than on any other show at the station, Jack proved adept as a radio personality. His voice was clear and resonant, if surprisingly high, and his diction excellent; he prepared well and asked solid questions. His favorite guest, late in December, was undoubtedly his old pal Joe Louis, now near retirement. "By his gentlemanly conduct and great sportsmanship," Robinson wrote that year, "Joe has made it easy for me and the other fellows now in baseball. . . . I have tried to follow his footsteps when it came to meeting the public and doing a good job."

Meeting the public and doing a good job were parts of an expanded sense of self, a growing sense of social responsibility. Another part of this change was the Robinsons' decision to drop anchor, as it were, and commit themselves to a new home, in the East. The winter of 1948 marked a turning point in Jack's life, as he and Rachel made no move to return to California as in the past. In the spring, Rachel had written to Jack in the Caribbean to ask that they stay in the East during the winter; he had agreed at once. They now owned a piece of land in Laurel Canyon in Los Angeles, where they imagined that one day they might build a home; but for the foreseeable future, New York would be home. Accordingly, Rachel began to house-hunt. By February she had found a place, in St. Albans, Queens.

In the late 1940s, the first signs of black migration into prosperous, all-white St. Albans had touched off massive white flight. One area in particular had attracted a number of black entertainers and other celebrities, including Roy Campanella, who had purchased a home and moved there. Jack and Rachel decided to follow Campanella's lead. The house, stucco, was old and rundown, with discolored walls and floors that needed sanding; but it sat on more than ten thousand square feet of land, with shady trees and an abundant lawn. White families were on either side, but they seemed friendly. "They are the kind of people," Jack wrote enthusiastically, "who, when the delivery man calls at your house and finds you out, will ask him to leave the stuff in their house until you come home." Only later would Rachel discover that one of her nicest neighbors had been vehement in opposing blacks on the street; slowly he had changed his ways and his friendship was genuine.

At some point later that year, but certainly by the middle of the baseball season, the Robinsons moved from their Flatbush apartment to the house on 177th Street in St. Albans.

EAGER FOR A MORE successful season in 1949, Jack was nevertheless determined to extract a large increase in salary from Rickey. He had a figure in mind—$20,000—which he saw as a reward for his own stimulating effect on the turnstiles. But when Jack mentioned inserting an attendance clause in his new contract, Rickey went deaf. "Mr. Rickey may have heard me," Jack reported later that year, but "he didn't give me a single sign of recognition. He just kept on talking about something else. I didn't have the heart to bring it up again." According to the Brooklyn *Eagle,* he settled for $17,500.

This was far below the league's best. That year, Cleveland's pitching star Bob Feller, who had led the league in wins from 1939 to 1941 and, after military service, from 1946 to 1947, would earn $65,000 (down from $82,000 in 1948, when he was the highest-paid player in baseball but also had one of his poorer years). In 1949, Lou Boudreau, the player-manager in Cleveland, reportedly would earn $75,000, following his MVP season in 1948. However, compared with other Dodgers, Jack was doing well. In 1948, for example, Jack's teammate Ralph Branca had earned $12,500. Offered $14,000 in 1949, he refused to sign. In 1948, Pee Wee Reese's salary, the Brooklyn *Eagle* claimed, had been $18,000; given a moderate raise (and appointed team captain, the first since Dolph Camilli in 1943), he accepted Rickey's 1949 offer without a quibble.

Setting the matter aside, and hungry to prove himself on the field after the Dodger failure of 1948, Jack reported on March 1 to Vero Beach. The camp was Spartan in its accommodations, but he was content with this austerity; his main concern was to lose weight, harden his body, and work on every facet of his game. Quickly, his sense of urgency landed him in the middle of a controversy. Two intersquad teams, one led by Reese and the other by Bruce Edwards, were playing a routine game when suddenly the mood turned nasty. After Robinson, playing under Reese, let an easy grounder roll through his legs, a "leather-lunged" rookie, Gale Wade, ridiculed him, as "the two teams let go verbal volleys back and forth." When a gangling minor-league pitcher, Chris Van Cuyk, came in, Robinson lined a single to left, then hooted at Van Cuyk as he headed to first base:

"You'll be a class D busher for twenty years." Van Cuyk began to bristle. During Jack's next time at bat, the pitcher raked him with a high inside fastball, then sent him hopping with a pitch that brushed his knees. Robinson was livid. "If you had hit me," he allegedly told Van Cuyk, "I would have punched you." The bad feeling did not last long. That evening, Jack took the lead as he and Van Cuyk shook hands, a reporter wrote, "and sheepishly admitted they had lost their heads."

It was more than that for some writers. A day or so before the incident, when asked about the coming season, Jack had told the writer Herb Goren about opposing players: "They better be rough on me, because I'm going to be rough on them." Goren had reported Jack's comment accurately, but other writers had picked it up and twisted it after the Van Cuyk incident. Commissioner Chandler then summoned Robinson (accompanied by Burt Shotton) to Miami to explain himself. When Jack pointed out that the two matters were not related, and that he meant no threat by his remark to Goren, Chandler accepted his word and dropped the matter. But Jack, seething with resentment at being singled out in this way, also blamed the press for distorting both the Van Cuyk incident and his innocent words to Goren. For the first time in his Dodgers career, Jack's relationship with the white press became ruffled.

His links to the black press were also disturbed. In his column "Sports Beat" in the *Courier,* Wendell Smith openly accused Robinson of ingratitude. "This, it seems, is time for someone to remind Mr.

Robinson," Smith wrote, "that the press has been especially fair to him throughout his career." Were it not for the press, Robinson would be "just another athlete insofar as the public is concerned. If it had not been for the press—the sympathetic press—Mr. Robinson would have probably still been t[r]amping around the country with Negro teams, living under what he has called 'intolerable conditions.' " Smith ended on a particularly crushing note: "Mr. Robinson's memory, it seems, is getting shorter and shorter. That is especially true in the case of the many newspapermen who have befriended him throughout his career."

(Perhaps Jack's relationship with Smith had become strained after the appearance of Robinson's autobiography, *Jackie Robinson: My Own Story,* as told to Wendell Smith, in May 1948. Of the many errors there, perhaps the most embarrassing had Jack declaring, "My family named me John Roosevelt Robinson"; he also gave his mother's name as "Mollie.")

A year before, in February 1948, after Jack failed to appear at the rally in Virginia and feuded with Durocher, Sam Lacy of the Baltimore *Afro-American* had also attacked him. Lacy had reminded Jack of his friend Joe Louis's record. In his ten years at the top of boxing, Lacy pointed out tartly, "he has NEVER had to deny having made a statement, he has NEVER criticized the people who gave him his chance, and he has NEVER blamed someone else for anything that happened." Lacy's advice to Robinson was to keep his mouth shut.

Unquestionably, Jack was becoming more assertive. He had now played three years in the Dodger organization. The idea would surface later, supported by Rickey, that at this point he formally released Jack from his 1945 agreement always to turn the other cheek and avoid fights. Rachel would deny that any special release was granted or sought; Jack had simply grown in stature and felt justified in asserting himself. "The idea that Branch Rickey had kept Jackie Robinson from exploding," Rickey's grandson Branch B. Rickey would say, "is nonsense. Branch Rickey was not on the field when someone spiked or hit Jackie. Jackie was not on a leash. It was Jackie Robinson who kept Jackie Robinson from exploding. He had given a pledge he believed in and he stuck by it—that's all." In any event, Rickey's response to the Van Cuyk affair, including Chandler's intervention, suggests that he now saw Robinson as his own man. "It was a tempest in a teapot," Rickey told the press, in his familiar rhetorical mixture of paternalism, condescension, loyalty to Jack, and a measure of insight into racism. "It's over the hill now and should be forgotten. Jackie's the same high-class boy he was the first year we brought him up. He's entitled to all the rights of any other American citizen. He's a great competitor and resents any violation of those rights. Perhaps he has lost his temper occasionally the same as any white player would do. But he's been sorry for it afterward and has used good judgment. . . . We couldn't have picked a finer boy than Robinson for our experiment of introducing a Negro into organized baseball."

Jack himself knew where blacks stood in the league. Perhaps black ballplayers were no longer seen as freaks, he told a reporter, but "one bad deed by one player right now can set the whole movement back, and I hope the boys coming up will be aware of that." (By May, Rickey had twelve blacks scattered through the Dodger system, including Robinson, Campanella, and Newcombe in the majors, Dan Bankhead and Sam Jethroe at Montreal, and Jim Pendleton at St. Paul.) Progress was coming, but slowly. By September 1, after almost three seasons of integration, only seven blacks played in the majors: three with Brooklyn, two (Paige and Doby) with Cleveland, and two (Monte Irvin and, formerly with the Browns, Henry Thompson) with the New York Giants. Nineteen blacks were queuing up in the minor leagues across the United States.

At Vero Beach, Robinson threw himself into his work. First he practiced his sliding technique, which Shotton considered limited; agreeing, Jack labored in the sawdust pit with "the Wild Horse of the Osage," Pepper Martin. Then, in a decisive move, Jack turned himself over to George Sisler, the Hall of Fame player (with a .340 lifetime batting average) hired by his mentor, Rickey, to teach hitting. With Jack spending hours hitting off a tee, Sisler followed up hard on Durocher's work of 1948 to teach Jack to hit to right field. "Sisler showed me how to stop lunging," Robinson wrote, "how to check my swing until the last fraction of a second. He showed me how to shift my feet and hit to right." Sisler also taught him how to prepare for the pitch, always looking for a fastball, never a curve; "I'll never stop being grateful to him." Immediately and in the long term, the results were spectacular. In sixteen games in the "Grapefruit League," Robinson hit .521 in 48 times at bat. "I feel right now I could hit Warren Spahn as if I owned him," Robinson said, reaching for his ultimate compliment. "That sure will be the big test."

Leaving Vero Beach, the Dodgers visited Oklahoma for a few games, then spent several days playing in Jack's native Georgia, with games in Macon, Valdosta, and Atlanta. Since January, this visit had been overshadowed by the vocal opposition of the Ku Klux Klan. Predicting trouble, Dr. Samuel Green, Grand Dragon of the Georgia Klan, vowed to invoke any and all laws that would prevent integrated baseball in Atlanta, where Brooklyn was to meet the white Atlanta Crackers on April 8, 9, and 10. But Rickey had reacted with scorn. "The only danger from mob violence," he predicted, "would come from people with pens in their hands." From cranks writing letters? "No, from autograph collectors."

Jack, too, was unintimidated. "I will play baseball," he declared, "where my employer, the Brooklyn Dodgers, want me to play." However, as the Georgia stage drew near, he felt a mixture of fear and loathing; he admitted that week that "I just hated the thought of putting foot on Georgia soil." But as he stepped off the plane in Macon, two white girls sweetly approached and in a honeyed drawl begged for his autograph; "I decided then that things weren't going to be so bad after all." Still, a volley of boos as he first stepped up to the plate chilled Robinson: "I was really paralyzed when I went up there." Frozen, he let two fat pitches go, then hit the third for a single. "After that, it was all right." In seventeen times at bat, he had seven hits, and stole home once; and the happy crowds, among the largest ever seen at Georgia ballparks, fully justified Rickey's confidence. Most had come to see Robinson. In contrast to him, Campanella seemed somehow to excite no special interest on the part of whites—or blacks—despite his brown skin and great talent. "Robinson, on the other hand," according to a writer, "was the center of every eye every minute he was on the field."

Confident about every aspect of his game, Jack opened the 1949 season on April 19, against the Giants. His confidence seemed well placed that day; he hit a home run and two singles. Then he sank into a trance at the plate, as the team itself struggled. With the splendid tandem of Reese and Robinson at shortstop and second, the reliable Gil Hodges at first, and the incomparable Billy Cox at third, the Dodger infield was perhaps the best in baseball; Carl Furillo, Duke Snider, and Gene Hermanski anchored a solid outfield; many people already called Campanella the best catcher in baseball. But the pitching was something else. Rex Barney, projected as the ace of the staff after an excellent close to 1948, was sometimes overpowering, sometimes wild. As quick as Barney, Ralph Branca, who had won twenty-one games for the Dodgers in 1947, when he was twenty-one, started well but then weakened. The devious Preacher Roe had not returned to the form that had made him the top strikeout pitcher in the National

League with the Pirates in 1945. Left-handed Joe Hatten, a dominant pitcher in 1947, was on the wane.

At first, Jack, too, seemed a shadow of himself; but although after thirteen games he was hitting around .200 (Campanella led the league with .463), he was confident enough to joke about his travails. "The Dodgers will have a great club," he predicted, "the day that Robinson joins them." At last, a month into the season, Robinson showed up. In a six-game span, he had ten hits in twenty-seven trips to the plate. Before the end of May he was hitting .311, with four home runs, twenty-eight runs batted in, and six stolen bases. Even against Boston, with their aces Warren Spahn and Johnny Sain, who had befuddled Jack into a dismal .159 average in 1948, he was a terror. In one series he had six hits in twelve tries, including a two-run homer against his nemesis, the left-hander Spahn.

Early June found Jack with a .344 average, second in the league; he led the league in runs batted in, and was tied for most stolen bases with his teammate Pee Wee Reese. Now the Dodgers were doing much better. Along with Robinson and Campanella, another "sepia" star stormed Ebbets Field: powerful young Don Newcombe, summoned in the middle of May from Montreal. Sent into action, Newcombe at first faltered; but he rebounded in his next game to pitch a shutout against Cincinnati. Newcombe had a reputation of being temperamental and even skittish; but Robinson, who saw true ability in the youngster, was determined to teach him how to win. Off the field, he could be cuddly with Newcombe. "This kid's going to be a great pitcher," he assured a reporter as Newcombe stood bashfully by. "All he needs to be sensational is a little more experience. He can win the pennant for us." On the field, however, Jack was often brutal. "I cuss him out from the beginning to the end," Robinson wrote. "I call him all the bad things I can think of. I got to, to keep him interested in the game." By the end of the season, with seventeen wins to his credit, Newcombe would be the premier pitcher on the staff.

By July 1, when Jack's average had soared to .361 and Newcombe's record was five wins and only one loss, all three black Dodgers were in contention to play in the All-Star Game, to be played that year at Ebbets Field. To Jack's deep satisfaction, it soon became clear that he would not only make the team but also be among the top vote-getters in the National League. In the end, he received 1,891,212 votes. Only Ted Williams of the Boston Red Sox, the finest hitter in baseball, received more.

On a rain-swept day, July 13, in Ebbets Field, Reese and Robinson started at their positions in the All-Star Game. Five other Dodgers saw action, including Campanella and Newcombe. Jack doubled in the first inning and scored three runs, but the National League fell, 11–7. Playing with or against some of the grandest names in baseball—Musial and DiMaggio, Williams and Feller—Robinson was at ease; he had earned his right to be there. He and the majestic DiMaggio, the ballplayer most admired by Robinson, were photographed together with a little girl as part of a drive to establish two new wings at a cancer hospital: one was to be named after DiMaggio, the other after Robinson. Seen together, Robinson seemed to embody the vital, changing future of baseball, as DiMaggio, hobbled by a foot injury, elegiacally represented its fading past.

The presence of the three Dodger blacks on an All-Star team was yet another sweet vindication of Branch Rickey's daring gambit; but it was a hard fact for even some locals to digest. "Negro Troops Fight Bravely in Flock Loss," went a headline in June in the Brooklyn *Eagle* over a story about a game between the Dodgers and Cincinnati; "Newcombe, Robinson, Campanella Fail to Put Skids Under Reds."

EARLY IN JULY, before the All-Star Game, a telegram arrived from Washington, D.C., to divert Jack's attention from baseball. To his astonishment ("I couldn't understand why they wanted me") a powerful congressional committee wanted him to come to Washington to testify before it. On July 8, John S. Wood, a Georgia Democrat, made the request public for Robinson to appear before the House Un-American Activities Committee, which he chaired, as it conducted hearings on the issue of black Americans and their loyalty to the nation.

Jack could not refuse the invitation easily; in some respects it was a command. Still, buffeted by conflicting advice from family, friends, and strangers, he pondered the wisdom of testifying in Washington. Rachel was guarded; Jack, she advised, should trust his instincts. Rickey, however, was sure that he should appear, to strike yet another blow for justice and equality. But most of the many letters and messages on the subject opposed Jack's testifying. An NAACP representative in Washington sent a telegram seeking to find out, with concern, if Jack had actually volunteered to speak: "As you know, over [the] years we have been critical of this committee's methods, activities, procedures, personnel and orientation." The NAACP man offered to help Jack in his response, but some of the messages made the mistake of threatening him. "I think it was that attempt to keep me quiet," Robinson wrote later, "that made me decide to go ahead and do it."

At the center of the controversy was Paul Robeson, one of the most famous and admired of living black Americans; the chairman of HUAC wanted Robinson specifically to refute statements by Robeson concerning blacks and the Soviet Union. But Jack had no special desire to join a fight against Robeson. An all-American football player and a brilliant student at Rutgers College and Columbia University Law School, Robeson had endured a host of indignities as a black in America before gaining international fame as a singer and a stage and motion picture star. Europe had received him warmly, but a visit to the Soviet Union in 1934, when he was treated with a humanity he had never known, started him down the road toward a commitment to radical socialism. After the war, his brave identification with radical causes, along with the growing enmity between the United States and the USSR, began to erode his popularity in America. Some concert halls were now denied him; pickets began to haunt his appearances. Then, according to news reports, on April 19 of that year, 1949, addressing a gathering of the leftist World Congress of the Partisans of Peace at the Salle Pleyel in Paris, Robeson had uttered his most controversial words. "It is unthinkable," he allegedly declared about the United States and the Soviet Union, "that American Negroes would go to war on behalf of those who have oppressed us for generations against a country which in one generation has raised our people to the full dignity of mankind."

Robeson's remark, as reported, was capable of two different interpretations: either that black Americans would never fight against the USSR or that such a fight would be horribly ironic, given the history of racism in America. But the second interpretation was given short shrift; the first, with its imputation of mass treason, carried the day. An informal poll of five hundred white Americans revealed a distrust of black American loyalty and patriotism. Robeson's remark was strongly criticized by a number of prominent black leaders, including Mary McLeod Bethune, the president of the National Council of Negro Women, and Walter White, executive secretary of the NAACP, who saw in the controversy a serious setback to the black cause at a critical juncture in American history. To the House Un-American Activities Committee, founded in the 1930s but freshly sparked by the intensifying cold war, the way was clear for a strike against the Communist effort since the 1920s to exploit Jim Crow and convert the black masses to radical socialism. HUAC invited testimony on this subject from several prominent Americans, most of them black but including also General Dwight D. Eisenhower, the former supreme commander in World War II, who sent a letter attesting to the devotion of black troops under him during the war.

Nevertheless, the spotlight was on Robinson. To many people, his brilliant career as a Brooklyn Dodger, capped by his popularity in the All-Star Game balloting, was further proof of the glory of American democracy. But Robinson was well aware of the ironies involved. He had never met Robeson, but knew that Robeson had stood up for ending Jim Crow in baseball. As Jack put it years later, "Now a white man from Georgia was asking *me,* a 'refugee' from Georgia, to denounce Robeson." In 1943, appearing before Commissioner Landis and the major-league owners, and riding a crest of personal prestige following his Broadway triumph in Shakespeare's *Othello,* Robeson had argued so powerfully for an end to Jim Crow in baseball that the owners gave him a "rousing ovation"—even as they tabled his plea. In 1945, while in Montreal for a concert, Robeson had hailed the Royals' signing of Robinson as "the greatest step ever taken by organized baseball on behalf of the American Negro."

Robinson knew that he could attack Robeson only at great risk to his own popularity with many blacks, to whom Robeson was both a glamorous entertainer and a black man of unusual courage;

among many whites, too, he was a highly respected, even revered figure. ("I felt so badly about it," Sarah Satlow, no radical herself, recalled. "I had a hero worship about Paul Robeson. I thought he was justified in every sense of the word. I couldn't believe that Jack was going to deal with that wretched committee about Robeson.") Nevertheless, Jack decided to testify; Robeson's alleged statement had put blacks in a poor position. He then set about preparing a statement to read to the committee, a statement he knew would be widely publicized. At first, Rickey was his main advisor as he sought words to capture his conflicted feelings about the subject; but soon it was clear to Rickey himself that someone else was needed, someone who had both keen insight into political matters and an intimate understanding of the black world. They then turned to Lester B. Granger, the executive director of the National Urban League, who himself testified before HUAC on July 14, when he dismissed the notion of significant Communist influence on black Americans. (In 1948, Robinson and Rickey had received the Urban League's annual Two Friends interracial award.)

Robeson's central assertion, as reported, struck Jack as almost willfully false. Whatever their reasons, black men from the American Revolution down to World War II had struggled at every point for the right to be warriors in defense of the nation. Robeson's statement was thus an implicit rebuke to these men, who included not only Jack himself, a commissioned officer whose patriotism had survived his court-martial, but also Rachel's older brother and her father, whose war wounds had only strengthened their patriotism. Moreover, Robinson was already, as he would remain, firmly anticommunist. The main issue for him, as it would be for many other blacks, was the Communist attitude to religion; for Jack, this was reason enough to oppose communism. In addition, he was well aware, as Robeson should have been, that the Soviet Union under Stalin was itself a harshly repressive society. Finally, America was home, and blacks would fight for home as most people everywhere were prepared to fight for home. Robinson recalled the wonderfully elliptical words about America spoken by Joe Louis in facing a similar irony in World War II. "There ain't nothing wrong with us," Louis had declared, "that Mr. Hitler can fix."

On the morning of July 18, dressed smartly in a tan gabardine suit, Jack flew with Rachel to Washington. They arrived at the House Office Building about forty-five minutes before his scheduled appearance. As they entered the crowded committee room, flash bulbs popped and movie and still cameras shot freely from every angle; for Robinson's appearance only, HUAC had waived its strict rules limiting photographs. As Jack read his statement in a clear, calm voice, Rachel sat nearby, her eyes fixed on him. She knew the speech by heart—as close observers of the newsreel version later could tell. "Intent on him, unconscious of the cameras," she told a magazine writer, "I was saying every word of his speech silently along with my husband!"

In homespun language, leavened only now and then by humor, Jack offered himself as both a humble man and one proud of his deeds; keenly opposed to racism in America but full of hope; alert to the dangers of communism but calm in facing them; aware that Communists were sometimes right but sure that communism was doomed; respectful of Robeson but dismissive of his alleged statement. Knowing little about politics, he said, he had hesitated to accept this invitation because his own field, baseball, "is as far removed as possible from politics as anybody can possibly imagine." Many people had urged him not to show up, so "why did I stick my neck out by agreeing to be present?" The answer boiled down to "a sense of responsibility." Although he was not an expert on much else, he was an expert on being "a colored American, with thirty years experience at it." He had been given a rare chance by baseball to be a star, but other blacks were starting to get a chance too.

Nevertheless, protesting against Jim Crow was important: "Every single Negro who is worth his salt is going to resent any kind of slurs and discrimination because of his race, and he's going to use every bit of intelligence, such as he has, to stop it. This has got absolutely nothing to do with what Communists may or may not be trying to do." Similarly, "because it is a Communist who denounces injustice in the courts, police brutality and lynching, when it happens, doesn't change the truth of his charges." Blacks were "stirred up long before" the Communists arrived and will be "stirred up long after the party has disappeared—unless Jim Crow has disappeared by then as well."

Turning at last to Robeson, Jack was light in his touch: "I haven't any comment to make, except that the statement, if Mr. Robeson actually made it, sounds very silly to me." Of course, Robeson had a right to express himself as he saw fit, even if there was nothing to his prediction, if prediction it was. In time of war, the few black Communists would probably act as most other Communists would act. But most blacks would act as blacks in general had acted in the last war: "They'd do their best to help their country stay out of war; if unsuccessful, they'd do their best to help their country win the war—against Russia or any other enemy that threatened us." People were wrong to think of radicalism "in terms of any special minority group." He could not speak for all blacks (and neither could Robeson) but he, and they, had too much invested in America "to throw it away because of a siren song sung in bass."

The arch comment about "a siren song sung in bass," an allusion to communism's seductive promises and Robeson's cavernous voice, was perhaps the only false note struck in the entire statement. Then, his part in the hearing over, Jack and Rachel hurried back to the airport to return home in time for him to play that evening at Ebbets Field against the Chicago Cubs.

If he had a single misgiving about his testimony, no one at the park could tell. In a 3–0 Dodgers victory before a roaring crowd of twenty-five thousand, according to the Brooklyn *Eagle,* "the Ebony Express went full steam ahead." In the sixth inning, Jack drew a walk, induced a poor throw that enabled him to scamper to third, then stole home after a series of impudent challenges to the pitcher. In the eighth inning, he tripled, then rattled a relief pitcher into committing a balk that sent him home. "Public speaking must agree with me," he cheekily remarked.

The next morning, and in the ensuing days and weeks, a deluge of congratulations poured over him—especially in the white press. Newspaper editorials and cartoons sang his praises, and the New York *Post* even offered an excerpt from his speech as an editorial entitled "Credo of an American." "Quite a man, this Jackie Robinson," the *Daily News* mused at the end of its own editorial. "Quite a ball player. And quite a credit, not only to his own race, but to all the American people." But the black press was more equivocal. To the New York *Age* newspaper, Harlemites were "split sharply on the issue." Robinson had come back from Washington "in the dual role" of leader of his race and "handkerchief head." The Baltimore *Afro-American* reported that HUAC's maneuver in summoning Robinson had "boomeranged," in that he had been much more severe on racism than on communism. Its headline read: "Jackie Flays Bias in Army."

From Lester Granger, Jack heard a far more favorable, if perhaps not altogether reliable, report on reaction on the streets of Harlem. After the first reports of Jack's testimony on the day of his talk, he had spent five hours sampling the opinions of strangers and friends, but in "not one single case" had he heard "anything but praise" for Robinson.

As for Robeson himself, he refused to denounce Robinson. "I have no quarrel with Jackie," he affirmed. "I have a great deal of respect for him. He is entitled to his views. I feel that the House Committee has insulted Jackie, it has insulted me, it has insulted the entire Negro race."

The patriotic aspects of Jack's speech clearly touched many white readers. One congressman, a former commander of the Veterans of Foreign Wars, cited Jack's testimony in nominating him for the VFW gold medal for good citizenship. Other honors followed from local organizations, including the Junior Chamber of Commerce of Philadelphia, the Rotary Club of Hudson, Massachusetts, and the Queens Catholic War Veterans, who in December named Robinson to receive a citation of praise. The patriotic Freedoms Foundation of Valley Forge, Pennsylvania, named him as an honoree in a group that included General Eisenhower. Not surprisingly, Jack was pleased but also a little defensive about the episode. "I have boxes of letters from many people regarding my testimony in Washington," he assured the public in August. "Ninety-nine per cent of them are friendly. I can show them to you." He still had not met Robeson but would like to ask him a question: "Can you sit down in Russia and say the head man is a louse?" The answer was obviously "No. Not unless you want to play centerfield in Siberia."

Within a few days, however, events in upstate New York, in the normally quiet community of Peekskill, shook Jack's sense of peace about his role in the HUAC affair. On Saturday, August 27, Robeson's scheduled appearance there at a benefit concert on behalf of the Civil Rights Congress, an organization denounced as subversive by the United States attorney general, brought out hundreds of angry opponents. They set up roadblocks, burned crosses, attacked buses and cars, demolished and torched the concert stage, and set off fights with concert patrons in which thirteen people were injured, including three with knife wounds. Friends of the singer, fearing for his life, spirited Robeson away.

The next day, Jack was sitting quietly in the Dodgers dugout, preparing for a game, when the *Daily Worker* sports editor, Bill Mardo, approached him with a newspaper account of the riot. Unaware until then of the events, Robinson read in shocked silence. Then he slowly lifted his eyes, as Mardo recalled, and with "anger written all over his face," gave his considered response: "Paul Robeson should have the right to sing, speak, or do anything he wants to. Those mobs make it tough on everyone. It's Robeson's right to do or be or say as he believes. They say here in America you're allowed to be whatever you want. I think those rioters ought to be investigated." Communism was not outlawed in the U.S.A., Jack pointed out; thus, "if Mr. Robeson wants to believe in Communism, that's his right. I prefer not to." He ended by expressing regret that in America, "anything progressive is called Communism."

Near the end of his life, in his autobiography *I Never Had It Made,* Robinson would write of eventually having grown "wiser and closer to painful truths about America's destructiveness," and of gaining thus "an increased respect" for Robeson and his sacrifice. To Mardo, however, Robinson's change had started with Peekskill. At that point, recognizing how much experience he and Robeson shared as blacks in America, "Jackie Robinson put his hand in Paul Robeson's, and together they fought the same fight. Each in his own voice, sure. But it was the same fight."

AFTER THE ALL-STAR GAME, Robinson's excellent play continued. Still batting above .360 in August, he became a contender for the Most Valuable Player award. Pee Wee Reese was having the season of his life; but Robinson, who publicly backed Reese as MVP, seemed more important to the Dodgers. "Without Robinson," Enos Slaughter declared, "they would be in the second division." In the New York *Post,* Jimmy Cannon, after listing the myriad troubles overcome by Robinson, from Jim Crow to changes in the infield, asked that Jack's baseball performance alone be considered. "You must admit," he concluded, "this is the Most Valuable Player in the National League."

To an almost uncanny degree for so talented a team, Brooklyn seemed to rise and fall according to Jack's playing. So Shotton thought. Early in August, when a badly bruised left heel seemed bound to keep Jack out of the next game, Shotton insisted that the Dodgers needed him against the Phillies. They did: in the ninth inning, with a man on base and the game tied, Jack hit his fourteenth home run of the season to lift the Dodgers to a win, 7–5. His heel injury persisted, and his overall fatigue was clear; but he kept playing. "They couldn't get me out of the lineup with a meat-axe," he insisted.

Late in August, the Dodgers lost six games out of eight but then righted themselves. On September 13, *Look* magazine hailed Robinson as "the Ball Player of the Year." In a tight race to the wire for the batting title with Musial and Slaughter, he prevailed with an average of .342 to Musial's .339 and Slaughter's .336. Second to Musial in singles, Jack tied for second place in doubles and was second in triples. He led the league in stolen bases. In November, a twenty-four-member committee of the Baseball Writers Association designated him the MVP for 1949 in the National League. Securing twelve first-place votes, he was mentioned on every ballot; Musial and Slaughter finished second and third respectively. "Well, what do you know," Jack piped modestly. "I ought to sleep well tonight. This is the nicest thing that could have happened to me."

The 1949 World Series was bad news for the Dodgers and Robinson himself, who had only three hits in a series swept by the Yankees. "What is there to say?" Jack asked in the *Courier.* "They beat us; in fact, they kicked heck out of us."

Then, he, Campanella, and Newcombe (who was declared Rookie of the Year in the National League by the *Sporting News*), joined by Larry Doby of the Indians, left on what was planned as a thirty-day barnstorming tour of the South. With the Jackie Robinson All-Stars playing against the Negro American League All-Stars, the tour drew well at first but ended prematurely, in part because three of the four major-league stars ceased to shine. Nervous about his arm, Newcombe declined to pitch; Doby, struck painfully on the elbow by a pitched ball, dropped out; and then Robinson himself withdrew from the lineup with what was called "a light case of the flu." Whatever the underlying reasons, the promoters halted the tour.

Jack had good reason to return to New York, where several new opportunities arising out of his MVP year awaited him. A New York City television station, WJZ-TV, signed him up to do two weekly sports shows. One, on Saturday afternoons, would aim at young people; the other, on Thursday nights, would feature Jack interviewing celebrities, especially from the sports world. He also agreed to host a daily radio sports show on the ABC radio network. In addition, there was the solid prospect of a Hollywood movie based on the biography of Jack written by Arthur Mann, in which Jack might play himself. "All this," he told the press, "means that I need somebody to handle my business interests. I can't do it myself. And I know it."

Most important of all, Rachel was pregnant, with their second child expected in January. Their home in St. Albans still needed work, including painting, much of which Jack wanted to do himself. Christmas 1949, celebrated by the Robinsons in a house of their very own for the first time, with Jack at the height of his career, Rachel awaiting the birth of their second child, and Jackie Junior happy and beloved, was a season of unusual joy and hope, abundance and the promise of greater prosperity to come. Then, on January 13, after a pregnancy free of the mysterious fevers that had plagued her in Montreal while she carried Jackie Junior, Rachel gave birth easily to their second child. Both Jack and Rachel had wanted a girl, and a girl the new baby was. They named her Sharon. The next morning, in front of the YMCA building on 135th Street, Jack handed out cigars and accepted congratulations and was the happiest man in the world.

— 10 —

Free at Last

1950–1952

He's the indispensable man. When he hits we win.
When he doesn't, we just don't look the same.
—Jake Pitler (1950)

SHARON'S BIRTH IN JANUARY 1950 was only the happiest event of a season filled with honors and awards, large and small, from the black world and the white, for Jackie Robinson. In Harlem, the Uptown Chamber of Commerce hailed him for his contribution to race relations. The United States Maccabi Association, perhaps the major Jewish athletic group, awarded him its Good Sportsmanship trophy. *Sport* magazine featured Robinson, along with the golfer Sam Snead, the tennis player Pancho Gonzales, and the boxer Sugar Ray Robinson, as among the "top performers" of 1949. The newspaper publisher Frank E. Gannett presented him with the gold medal of the George Washington Carver Memorial Institute, an honor previously accorded to Eleanor Roosevelt, William Randolph Hearst, and the movie producer Darryl F. Zanuck. "All America must applaud this award," Gannett declared. "It goes to a real All-American."

In the limelight, Jack tried to maintain a sense of balance. In an autobiographical series in the Brooklyn *Eagle,* he stressed his dependence on religion, his faith in God, his nightly habit of getting down on his knees at bedtime. "It's the best way to get close to God," he quipped, "and a hard-hit ground ball." Sunday games kept him from going to church, he complained; perhaps "a little chapel could be built at Ebbets Field, where the fellows of all religions could go and worship a little while." Jack talked, too, about the end of his career as if it might be close. By September, he revealed, his bat weighed heavily in his hands and his legs were often numb; but the worst pressure was psychological. "The strain of the last three or four years," he told the writer Dick Young, has "done something to me. Not that I have anything to worry about, but I'm jumpy and nervous all the time."

For all his success Jack felt unfulfilled; or his success stirred in him sharp feelings of guilt about the poor and the sick. His work with children at the YMCA, where he was now on the board of directors, was fine, but he wanted to do more. "This is too supervised for me," he told Lester Rodney of the *Daily Worker.* "I want to see the kids who can't even come into the Y. I want to try to help where it's needed more." He liked visiting the sick. Race seemed not to matter as he reached out; or perhaps it mattered that he reached out to whites as well as blacks, to set an example of interracial charity. Although Jack tried to avoid publicity on these occasions, his kindness to white children often made the news. At the Hospital for the Ruptured and Crippled in New York, he was photographed signing a ball for a fourteen-year-old Bronx patient, Carlo Accappicini, on Child Health Day in New York, for which Jack also raised money. When he (and other Dodgers) gave blood to help save the life of a four-year-old girl, Linda Pietrafesa, newspapers took note. Jack also went well out of his way, the press pointed out in admiration, to send a baseball signed by the team to a fourteen-year-old invalid, Johnny Nagelschmidt, of Cooperstown, New York.

Robinson clearly felt the urge to take his new fame and make something political out of it, something that more directly addressed broader questions of social injustice. About this time, he became fascinated by the efforts of the Anti-Defamation League, the most influential wing of the main Jewish community organization, B'nai B'rith ("Sons of the Covenant"). According to the ADL leader Arnold Forster, Robinson "heard me speak at a civil rights dinner, phoned and asked to meet. Jackie asked searching questions about fighting anti-Semitism. Satisfied that we Jews were on to something effective, Jackie helped intensify our cooperative relationship with black civil rights groups, determined that they use our techniques. In his speeches about racism, it became his custom to quote me by name on ADL methods, adding that when blacks succeeded in creating a duplicate operation for themselves, they would at long last be on the road to racial equality. And he worked hard to make it happen."

Jack's connection with the ADL was a natural outgrowth of the new circumstances of his life, of his move from California to New York. About half of Brooklyn's population was Jewish; among the Dodger faithful, Jews were probably far more ready than any other major group, such as the Irish or the Italians, to identify with the fight against Jim Crow embodied by Robinson. Both Jack and Rachel found themselves developing personal ties to Jews. "That may be so," Rachel would say years later, "but for us friendship was really a personal matter, as it should be. We made friends. For whatever reason, many happened to be Jewish. We didn't think of them as Jewish, unless we were dealing with a specific organization. They were simply interesting people who wanted to know us, just as we wanted to know them."

Almost certainly, the Robinsons found Jews far more ready than other whites to accept them socially. In addition to their friendship with the Satlows in Flatbush, they also grew close to Bea and Andre Baruch, a Dodgers broadcaster who also hosted the popular radio show *Lucky Strike Hit Parade.* Later, in Harlem, Jack fell in so easily with Frank Schiffman, the owner of the Apollo Theater, and his son Bobbie, that for some years the Harlem landmark was almost his private uptown office. Almost all of Jack's lawyers and financial counselors, as well as business partners, would be Jewish. Jack's friendship with a prosperous employer like Meyer Robinson, the head of Manischewitz Wines and an avid Dodger fan, was vital to him. In Chicago, he visited regularly with Caroline and David Wallerstein, who controlled a group of theaters and had been instrumental in Jack's 1948 vaudeville tour. Jennie Grossinger gave the

Robinsons (and other top athletes) virtual carte blanche at Grossinger's, her family's popular resort in the Catskill Mountains of New York, where over a number of years Jack was a great favorite and Rachel and the children also loved to go to rest, play, eat, and socialize.

Friendship with whites, no matter how easily developed, typically brought with it at least a small degree of tension. The shadow of race and racism, of white guilt and black and white doubt, fell over even the more intimate relationships. As blacks, the Robinsons had more freedom now than ever before, but the knowledge that in many instances the freedom derived mainly from Jack's celebrity took away some of the pleasure. In restaurants such as Lindy's in New York, where Jack was treated royally, the question that haunted him was how the same restaurant would treat an ordinary black. "One way we knew the answer to that," Rachel said, "was by looking at how I was treated when I was not with Jack—not with Jackie Robinson. Sometimes I was treated well, but very often, until or unless it came out that I was Jackie Robinson's wife, whites would be as rude to me as they were rude to other blacks. These things upset Jack pretty badly."

For both Jack and Rachel, as for many black couples, the worst part of Jim Crow was watching it begin to weigh, in one way or another, on their children. In November 1949, when Jackie Junior celebrated his third birthday at home in St. Albans, the published photograph of his little party, with ice cream and cake, created a stir in some circles; other than young David Campanella, all of the guests were white. One evening, as Rachel was putting him to bed after his bath, Jackie suddenly blurted out: "Mommy, my hands are still dirty." Stunned, Rachel quietly explained to him that his hands and her own were the same color, and clean. On another occasion, Jackie embarrassed her in a store by asking loudly, "Mommy, why are you lighter than I am?" One day, as she watched in horror, she saw youthful racism in action on her own lawn, where a "jungle gym," set up by Jack, had become a magnet for local kids. As Rachel watched, a little white girl who had been playing amicably with Jackie suddenly became cold to him when two white boys showed up. "Look," Rachel thought, "there's discrimination being practiced in our own yard!" When Jackie, in tears, came running to her, she was careful. "*Why* isn't she playing nicely with you now?" she asked. "Because I'm *different* from her," Jackie sobbed.

With integration, many blacks had both greater freedom and further reason for self-doubt; but Jack Robinson was not one of these. In 1954, a troubled black boy named Jimmie living in a Fort Wayne, Indiana, orphanage, shocked one of his mentors, a white man, by declaring: "I wish I was white." The man, who did not know Robinson personally, nevertheless asked him to help set the boy straight. In a letter that reached the newspapers, Robinson told Jimmie that while his desire to be white was "understandable for a boy your age," Jack himself did not share it; "I am so proud to be Negro that I feel really good." Jack's sense of the meaning of his black skin

derived mainly from his faith in God, not from admiration for the African past; whatever God does is
right, although we may not know God's plan. "I am
proud because God put us here on earth," he told
Jimmie, "and gave us a color that is distinctive, and
then put problems before us to see what would happen." Blacks, despite these problems, had achieved
much. "Because of some handicaps we are better
off," Jack argued; Jimmie must "look in the mirror at
yourself and be proud of what God gave you. I, too,
have felt the pains that you must feel, but I have
never been ashamed of what God has given me."

JACK BELIEVED IN CHARITY, but he also wanted to
capitalize on his fame; thus he jumped quickly at a
number of commercial endorsements. In one issue of
Ebony magazine, three advertisements featured him.
One endorsed the Jackie Robinson Official Baseball
Game ("Pitches Curves! Fast or Slow Balls! Hit
Home Runs Just as Jackie Does with the Dodgers!").
Another endorsed Chesterfield cigarettes (although
Jack still hated smoking). A third hawked a line of
Jackie Robinson shorts, sportshirts, and T-shirts
("Boys and Girls . . . I am proud to have you wear
them"). In Manhattan, Macy's department store of-
fered a line of Jackie Robinson jackets and caps;
elsewhere Jack endorsed a line of men's slacks. Thus
he was perhaps not altogether shocked in July when
a Chicago man, Stanley Kuttner, sued him for
$100,000 for allegedly violating an agreement about
the use of Robinson's name to sell clothing. In *The*

Saturday Evening Post and *Ebony*, and on subway billboards, Jack endorsed Wheaties, the breakfast cereal.

Searching for a financial advisor, Jack at last found one he liked in Martin Stone, a graduate of Columbia University and the Yale School of Law, and a pioneer of sorts in television. Tall, handsome, and urbane, Stone had helped to develop a number of popular television programs, notably the children's classic *The Howdy Doody Show*. One day in 1949, at the urging of a friend, he had gone out to St. Albans to visit the Robinsons about a specific legal matter. "Jack was mentioned to me," according to Stone, "by an agent who told me Jackie Robinson was so naive he would sign anything. After I met him, I agreed; I couldn't believe that the man could be so naive! He trusted everybody. In those days, he really had little idea what he was getting into half the time, or the kind of people he was dealing with; some of them were real crooks. My job, once we decided to work together, was to look closely at every deal when it came in, and then advise Jack how to proceed—to accept, to reject, to modify, and so on. I liked him from the start, and I think he and Rachel liked me. After all, we were still working together and good friends practically up to the end."

Stone's first challenge was extremely important; a financial windfall from Hollywood was at stake for the Robinsons. Stone had to get Jack out of his contract with the small New York publisher, Greenberg, that had brought out *Jackie Robinson: My Own Story* (written by Wendell Smith) in 1948. At issue now were the movie rights, because a motion picture of Jack's life was being planned in Hollywood. "It was a terrible deal," Stone recalled of the Greenberg contract, "just unfortunate from Jack's point of view. He had signed away everything for just about nothing." Stone settled the matter to Jack's advantage, and the new movie deal went forward.

The Hollywood story was complicated. Two years earlier, Lawrence Taylor, a screenwriter and baseball fan captivated by Jack's rookie exploits, had written a movie script about his life. Taylor quickly discovered that not one studio would agree to make a picture with a black leading man. "Two of the big studios were interested," Taylor said, "if the story could be changed to show a white man teaching Robinson to be a great ball player. Of course, that was out of the question." Then, as a result of Jack's HUAC appearance and his 1949 MVP season, and with Hollywood taking a decidedly liberal turn following films like *Gentleman's Agreement* (about anti-Semitism) and *Home of the Brave* (about blacks), Taylor at last had an interested producer. After several urgent telephone calls to investors, William J. Heineman of the Eagle-Lion studio found money for the project. Unfortunately, he found only $300,000, which would make *The Jackie Robinson Story* a low-budget movie. It also had to be a quickie, shot in about a month, to be ready to open early in the baseball season.

Brokered by Martin Stone, the deal called for Heineman to pay Jack $50,000 in two installments, from which Jack agreed to give Taylor and a collaborator, Louis Pollock, a total of $20,000. Also, Jack would receive fifteen percent of the net profits, out of which he would give the writers one-third. In addition, Jack would portray himself. Gary Cooper had been the doomed Lou Gehrig, and William Bendix had played Babe Ruth, but in this rare movie about an athlete still in his prime, Jack would play himself. At this point, Rickey stepped in—and almost killed the project. Reading the script, he became so enraged by its distortions that he flung it across the room. Recognizing the potential importance of the movie to his own reputation, Rickey assigned his assistant Arthur Mann to watch over it. Mann, aware of Jack's book with Greenberg, then decided to write his own biography of Robinson. Although "this might sound like 'muscling in,' " he wrote Rickey in November 1949, the draft of Mann's book would be the legal basis for fighting any claims by Greenberg or anyone else about infringement of copyright.

Once the deal was set, Rickey sent his private plane to bring Clay Hopper, Clyde Sukeforth, and Burt Shotton to Brooklyn to help with the script. In January, just before the start of shooting, Mann reached Hollywood with Rickey's final orders about the movie. Its basic structure was set. It would follow Jack's life chronologically, more or less, but would have its grand climax in his appearance before HUAC in Washington. Baseball would be integral to the story, and Robinson at its center, but ultimately it would be about the triumph of democracy and of Americans of goodwill, including both Robinson and Rickey.

On February 3, Jack flew to Los Angeles to begin shooting. Reporting to the set, he met the director,

Alfred Green, whose work included the highly successful movie *The Jolson Story;* the producer, Mort Briskin; the dialogue director, Ross Hunter, with whom Jack would work closely; and his fellow actors, including the beautiful and talented Ruby Dee, who would play Rachel. On every side, Jack heard the same advice: as an actor, be yourself. But the tight schedule made for a harried atmosphere on the set. "It took all of one day just to get him to relax," Hunter recalled. After talking on the telephone to Rachel in New York three times one day, Jack made a decision—she had to join him, to see him through this unusual challenge. Soon she was on a plane to Los Angeles.

Once Rachel was at Jack's side, everything went far more easily for him. "Jackie made a tremendous impression on everyone," according to Mann. Being a movie star did not make him temperamental; his sole demand had nothing to do with his own part. "He was a loyal guy," the producer Mort Briskin recalled. "He insisted, demanded" that some of his Pasadena and UCLA friends, including Kenny Washington, be written into the script. "Making the picture meant more to him the opening of doors, rather than the money." He kept his composure even when Al Green put the company on a day-and-night shooting schedule; Jack also put up calmly with the seemingly endless repetition required by the moviemakers. "The way they had me running bases, stealing second, running from first to third over and over again," he told a reporter, "I never had any spring training in which I worked any harder." But once over his nervousness, he showed a certain ease as an actor. "I simply explained what we wanted," Green recalled, "and he did it with all the feeling we asked." John Barrymore Jr., visiting the set, laughed at a suggestion that he give Robinson acting tips. "Are you kidding?" he asked. "He could teach me!"

Ruby Dee, playing Rachel, found Jack friendly but tense; most likely, he was flustered by their physical closeness as actors, and had no professional and little personal experience with other women to fall back on. "In one scene, I was to massage his back," she said. "So I put my hands on him and he jerked his head back over his shoulder and glared at me, and I realized my hands were so cold!" A magazine writer noticed Jack's clear embarrassment one day when, during "a mildly romantic scene" with Dee, Rachel strolled onto the set. Dee had an easier time with Rachel. Married to Ossie Davis, and even then pregnant with her own daughter, Dee was thrilled to be allowed to hold the infant Sharon. But she had one lasting regret: she had made Rachel too passive on the screen. "The moment I talked with her," Dee said, "I had the feeling I wasn't doing her justice. She was a much more outgoing person than I was portraying. She was twinkly-eyed, and I remember feeling, Gee, I wish I had known her before I took this part. She was a stronger woman than I portrayed. I had listened to too many directors about not undercutting the star. I hadn't imagined Rachel as she really was."

On the last day, Jack made it a point to thank in person everyone on the set. Workers inured to the vanity of stars were astonished to see him climb a catwalk to shake hands with an assistant electrician. Then, late for training camp, he hurried to catch a flight to Florida.

Opening on May 16 in New York, *The Jackie Robinson Story* was successful both at the box office and, within its limited scope as a low-budget film biography of a sports hero, with the critics. If its cheap production values disappointed some viewers, its patriotic theme (underscored by its repetitious use of the anthem "America the Beautiful") charmed many more—although the *Daily Worker,* affronted especially by its ending with Jack's HUAC testimony, found the movie "patronizing and offensive." Almost everyone agreed that Jack's acting was a pleasant surprise. As the influential columnist Louella Parsons put it: "Surprisingly, Jackie Robinson is just perfect playing himself. He has dignity and sympathy without ever being maudlin." The reviewer Bosley Crowther noted the hackneyed nature of the "pluck-and-luck" genre to which the movie belongs, but found elements of distinction: "Here the simple story of Mr. Robinson's trail-blazing career is reenacted with manifest fidelity and conspicuous dramatic restraint. And Mr. Robinson, commandeering that rare thing of playing himself in the picture's leading role, displays a calm assurance and composure that might be envied by many a Hollywood star."

The Jackie Robinson Story proved to be one of the more successful sports movies of the era, although the response at the box office was uneven and unpredictable. In Manhattan and even in Brooklyn, as well as in large cities such as Baltimore, Boston, and Washington, ticket sales fell well below expectations. But in Detroit and Chicago, in California and in Canada, and in many smaller midwestern towns, long lines formed to buy tickets. In the often mysterious way of Hollywood accounting, Jack made little additional money from the movie. However, almost fifty years later it had become both a period piece from Hollywood's darker days and a fascinating memento of a genuine American hero portraying himself on the silver screen.

IN VERO BEACH, the 1950 Dodgers were supremely confident. Burt Shotton, usually reticent, declared flatly that "we are going to win the pennant—and the World Series, too. We have more good ball players than anybody in baseball, so why shouldn't we?" Jack shared this confidence. He also started training with a plan designed to prevent his usual exhaustion near the end of the season. "I'm not going to steal bases merely to steal," he confided to a writer. "I will engage only in a minimum of pre-game practice, just enough to keep in shape." He would "run hard and be aggressive, but only when the game demands hard base running." This announcement was a mistake. A writer soon suggested that "Robinson's recently accumulated wealth has robbed him of his incentive"; he was no longer "the hungry player he used to be."

The snide reference had something to do with Jack's new salary. On January 26, after rumors swirled about a trade of Robinson to the Boston

Braves, Rickey made him the highest-paid Dodger ever. His 1950 contract called for $35,000, surpassing that of even the team captain, Pee Wee Reese. "Of course," Rickey declared, "in the case of Robinson, drawing power must be considered. I'm sure that other players are intelligent enough to realize that, and not be resentful."

Diligently Jack worked once again in camp on his hitting with George Sisler, whose spring tutoring had helped make 1949 a memorable season for Robinson. "Jackie is a better hitter right now than he ever was," Sisler commented. "He's just learning to hit." Then, still a little overweight but in good condition, Jack joined his teammates as they broke camp and headed north on their exhibition tour. Now, unlike in 1949, the presence of black players— Robinson, Newcombe, Campanella, and Bankhead—created little anxiety. The Klan leader, Samuel Green, who had caused trouble in 1949, was dead. Raw resistance to black players was simply fading; in Atlanta, a huge, congenial crowd filled the stands to watch Newcombe pitch against a Crackers team managed by Dixie Walker.

Returning to Ebbets Field, the Dodgers found themselves installed as heavy favorites to win the pennant. Early in the season they looked good; through May and June, they stayed atop the league. Their main strengths were superb defense and hitting; Hodges, Snider, and Campanella excelled in home-run power, and Robinson, Furillo, and Snider each batted over .300. But a shaky, immature pitching staff, despite solid performances by Preacher

Roe and Newcombe, kept Brooklyn shackled. Steadily, Philadelphia's brilliant young team, dubbed the "Whiz Kids," including Richie Ashburn, Del Ennis, Robin Roberts, Curt Simmons, and Jim Konstanty, took command of the pennant race. In September, the Phillies enjoyed an apparently insurmountable nine-game lead over the Dodgers. But Brooklyn, making a gallant late charge, won twelve of their next fifteen games as the Phillies dropped eight of their next eleven.

The last day of the season found the pennant still undecided, as Brooklyn faced Philadelphia in Ebbets Field, with Newcombe pitching against Roberts. In the bottom of the ninth, with the score tied, the Dodgers' Cal Abrams was thrown out trying to score from second in a memorable coaching blunder. Robinson then came to the plate with one out and runners on second and third. The Phillies, both unwilling to challenge him and hoping for the double play, decided to walk Jack; he watched helplessly as first Furillo, then Hodges, failed to drive in a run. The Phillies won on a home run off Newcombe by Dick Sisler, George Sisler's son, to secure their first pennant in thirty-five years.

For Jack, the season was a special disappointment because he had fallen short of the heights of his 1949 MVP season. As a hitter, he had gotten off to the best start of his career. When he continued to dominate through May, June, and July (with his batting average at one point reaching .380, well ahead of his main rival, Stan Musial), he seemed destined to win the National League batting title for a second consecutive year. (He would then have been the first player to do so since Rogers Hornsby in 1925.) But once again he wilted in August, when his average was a paltry .188 over twenty-eight games to make for his worst hitting slump as a Dodger. Musial, a hero even in Ebbets Field, breezed past Robinson to win his fourth batting crown (with .346).

In the end, despite his disappointment, Jack batted an excellent .328 overall. Nor had his value to Brooklyn lessened. As the Dodger coach Jake Pitler put it in June: "He's the indispensable man. When he hits we win. When he doesn't, we just don't look the same." Once again, Jack had the most doubles on the club, and his home-run total was on a par with past years. He drove in far fewer runs (81, compared to 124) than in 1949, but only because he had fewer opportunities to do so. Summarizing Jack's season at the plate, the team statistician, Allan Roth, noted his "consistency against all types of pitching and under all conditions, his ability to hit to left and to right depending upon how he is being pitched to, and his proven ability in the clutch"; Roth concluded that Robinson was "the best all-around hitter on the club." And Jack showed again and again how much winning meant to him. On July 6, when he failed to make the lineup because of injuries, he missed his first game in more than two years, or since June 2, 1948.

In other ways, he had weakened. On the bases, Jack had grown timid. In past seasons he had attempted an average of 41 steals; in 1950 he tried only 18 times (and was safe 12 times). If only to experts, his fielding also seemed in decline. Spectacular on double plays with Pee Wee Reese, and committing only eleven errors over the season, Jack was growing slower. His range moving to his right had shrunk—it was "definitely unsatisfactory," in Roth's opinion.

However, Jack had other reasons to be unhappy with the season. Stepping out more assertively as a player, he found himself again and again in controversies he could never win. Only passivity, even obsequiousness, could keep him exempt from criticism when he faced whites; almost any assertiveness was bound to be seen as a step out of line. But for Robinson, the statute of limitations in his 1945 pact with Rickey had certainly run out by this time. He was now on his own, and was a changed man.

On the Dodgers, Jack's conduct began to be compared unfavorably with Campanella's. Already seen as the finest catcher in baseball, except perhaps for the Yankees' Yogi Berra, Campanella played one way and lived another. Dominant behind the plate, he seldom challenged white men outside this sphere, and in general deferred to Jim Crow. His easygoing manner won him friends; their white teammates respected Jack and Roy, but also loved Campanella. Bubbling with enthusiasm, a quick-witted jokester, and fairly simple in his pleasures, Campanella knew his place and kept it. Harold Parrott would recall an evening in Florida when he took food out to Campanella and a seething Robinson from a roadside restaurant that would not serve them, even as their white teammates ate inside. "Let's not have no trouble, Jackie," Campy said, according to Parrott. "This is the onliest thing we can do right now, 'lessen we want to go back to them crummy Negro leagues." More than once, when Robinson complained of ethnic slurs hurled at him, Campanella denied hearing anything. When Jack one day asked Clyde Sukeforth, whom he trusted, if Sukeforth thought he was getting big-headed, Campanella broke in with some advice: "Better go easy, Jackie. Those buses in the minors aren't like the 20th Century or these big league air-cooled trains."

Campanella had his run-ins with umpires, but never dreamed of taking these disputes as far as Jack was prepared to go. In 1950, and the years to come, Jack battled with umpires over matters not simply of judgment but of ethics, in his growing belief that the umpires, all white, were abusing their power in order to put him in his place. Perhaps the worst incident of 1950 came during a game on July 2 at Shibe Park in Philadelphia. In the second inning, as Robinson walked testily away after taking a called third strike, the umpire, Jocko Conlan, suddenly piped up: "That strike was right down the middle." When Jack turned to face him, Conlan repeated the remark. Robinson then said something sharp to Conlan, who threw him out of the game. Jack exploded with a firestorm of abuse. Sure that Conlan and others were baiting him, Robinson wanted Ford Frick, the league president, to crack down on them. "Frick has given these guys too much power," he told the press. "Something's going to have to be done about it." Sukeforth supported Jack's position. "There is no question in my mind that the umpires are picking on Robinson," he declared. Sure, Jack liked to heckle—but "if Robinson were somebody else, no umpire would pay any attention."

Almost certainly, Jack's growing reputation as a troublemaker was behind his omission from the United Press news service's all-star team that year, when the Giants' Eddie Stanky was chosen at second base. Jack's superiority to Stanky in 1950 was clear: in batting average (.328 to Stanky's .300), hits (170 to 158), home runs (14 to 8), runs batted in (81 to 51), and stolen bases (12 to 9); nor was Stanky the superior fielder. And Stanky, called "the Brat," was no less aggressive than Robinson; in fact, his rage to win had exemplified Leo Durocher's most celebrated dictum "Nice guys finish last." But a double standard existed and persisted. What was feisty charm in a white player was often perceived as viciousness in a black, whose presence stirred conscious and subconscious reactions that only the most sensitive white observers recognized.

As his troubles mounted, Jack could take comfort in knowing that Branch Rickey stood solidly behind him; not a scintilla of tension had ever flared in public between the two men. But in July, Rickey's place in Brooklyn began to crumble. Exactly how it crumbled was to have a severe impact on Robinson's future with the Dodgers.

The death that month of one of the four Dodger owners, John L. Smith, a friendly pharmaceutical millionaire well liked by the players, set in motion a struggle for control of the club between Rickey and

Walter O'Malley, its vice-president and chief counsel. Like Rickey and O'Malley, Smith had owned a
quarter-interest in the Dodgers. Whoever gained control of Smith's block of shares would be in an excellent position to control the club. Increasingly critical
of some of Rickey's decisions over the years, and
ambitious to own the entire operation, O'Malley
decided to seek control. (The remaining block of
shares was owned by Dearie Mulvey, whose father
had run the club in the 1930s; but for some years
Mrs. Mulvey had taken no interest in its affairs.)
Securing John Smith's shares, O'Malley then moved
to acquire those of Rickey, whose days as general
manager were now numbered. Aware that Rickey's
capital was stretched thin, O'Malley offered to buy
his quarter-share for exactly the amount Rickey had
paid for it, about $300,000. Rickey's only recourse
would be to find a better offer elsewhere, which
O'Malley would then have to match, according to
board rules, in order to acquire the share.

Suddenly, in September, Rickey scored a financial coup. In "the biggest deal of his career," as a
newspaper put it, he accepted an offer to sell his
stock for $1,050,000 to William Zeckendorf, a rich
New York real estate speculator who had helped
assemble the parcel of land for the United Nations
headquarters in Manhattan. Of this sum, $50,000
was a premium that Zeckendorf exacted from
Rickey—or, in effect, from whoever matched the
offer—for tying up his money while the deal unfolded. (Behind Zeckendorf's serendipitous offer was
Rickey's great friend John W. Galbreath, the owner

of the Pittsburgh Pirates, where Rickey would soon be the new general manager.) O'Malley matched the offer. He also soon discovered that Zeckendorf had turned the premium of $50,000 back to Rickey. In O'Malley's eyes, Rickey had cheated him out of the sum. "That was a lot of money in those days," O'Malley's son, Peter, would say in 1972.

At a press conference in October, as he toyed with an unlit cigar, Rickey denied that a rift existed between himself and O'Malley; although his contract as general manager would expire on October 31, he would be delighted to stay on in Brooklyn. But Rickey was finished on Montague Street; O'Malley would soon exact a fine of one dollar from any employee who mentioned Rickey's name in his presence. At his own press conference, O'Malley let it be known that the club would take a new direction—away from Rickey. Rickey's old position would be subdivided, to prevent the abuse of power by any one man. Instead of the frequent sale of players to generate revenue (with Rickey taking a commission on each deal), the Dodgers would aim to win games and serve "the little guy."

Rickey's departure was a blow to Robinson. All his life, America had tested Jack's faith in religion, in idealism, in America, in himself; Rickey had justified that faith. With Rickey, Jack had not simply been a token of social change but a spearhead into the heart of bigotry. Only recently, that year, Rickey had appointed the first black scout in the major leagues, Elwood Parsons of Dayton, Ohio. Jack, and other blacks, could now dream not simply of playing in the major leagues but of becoming scouts, coaches, and perhaps even managers there.

Sometime in November, from Ciudad Trujillo, where he and Rachel were on vacation, Jack at last wrote Rickey about his departure. For "about a month" Robinson had been meaning to write, but "finding the right words come hard." Rickey's exit had been "tough on everyone in Brooklyn," but "much worse" for him. "It has been the finest experience I have had being associated with you and I want to thank you very much for all you have meant not only to me and my family but to the entire country and particularly the members of our race." As for the future: "I hope to end my playing days in Brooklyn as it means so very much but if I have to go any place I hope it can be with you." He and Rachel hoped that they could continue to count on Rickey's advice and counsel "regardless of where we may be." The letter was signed, "Sincerely yours, Jackie Robinson."

Instead of ending their relationship, Rickey's departure seemed to open the way to a deeper understanding between the two men. According to Rickey's grandson, Branch B. Rickey, "Sometimes my family believed that my grandfather really had two sons—my father and Jackie. We all accepted it as a fact of our lives; we knew that my grandfather loved Jackie, and we all respected Jackie. My own father knew how much Jackie meant to my grandfather and he was careful not to be resentful." This close relationship, maintained chiefly through telephone calls and infrequent reunions, would last until Rickey's death in 1965. "God brought these two men

together at this time in our history. If they had not
met, I am sure that baseball would have become integrated eventually—but never on the same plane,
never in the same way, because of the synergy that
existed between them. I think Branch Rickey was
simply overwhelmed by Jackie Robinson, the quality
of the man. Robinson was overwhelmed by my
grandfather, who was larger than life in his passion
for what he believed in."

Speculation now turned to Robinson's own
future with the Dodgers. In September the *Sporting
News* had inquired, with more prescience than it
knew, "Jackie Headed for Polo Grounds as a Giant?"
Jack waited for news that he, too, was gone. But if
O'Malley and E. J. "Buzzie" Bavasi, a veteran in the
organization who now took over as general manager,
ever discussed trading Robinson, no such move came
about. That winter, declaring himself completely satisfied with his pay, Jack signed a 1951 contract to
remain a Dodger. His salary was $39,750, up from
the 1950 figure of $35,000.

OCTOBER FOUND JACK once again barnstorming
through the South, for the promoters Ted Worner and
Lester Dworman. He did so reluctantly. In August, he
had accepted an offer to manage the Mayaguez club
in the six-team Puerto Rican League during the late
fall and winter. "I'll have my family down there with
me," he said, "and I positively will not play." Jack
also wanted the experience of managing, which he
hoped to do one day somewhere in the Dodgers or-

ganization in another historic step for a black man. At some point, he discussed his prospects with both O'Malley and Bavasi, who appeared to encourage him. "Nothing was promised," he said. "The idea intrigues me," he declared, "for the sake of my race." Pressed in March to say more, O'Malley himself allowed that there was "no reason why at some later date, Jackie could not become a manager of a triple-A club."

Instead of managing in Mayaguez, Jack found himself barnstorming after Worner and Dworman pointed out a clause in his 1949 contract that gave them the right to his services in 1950. In any event, barnstorming paid much more; according to one source, the 1949 tour had netted him over $15,000. Accordingly, in October he set off with Campanella, Newcombe, Larry Doby, and members of the black Indianapolis Clowns on a ramble through the South. In at least one place, Charlotte, North Carolina, blacks played against whites (a team of major leaguers) for the first time in local history. The tour continued uneventfully and profitably through the Carolinas, Georgia, Alabama, Mississippi, Tennessee, Arkansas, and Florida, before Jack took his vacation in the Dominican Republic, then returned with Rachel to New York.

Once again, Jack found himself, accompanied now by Rachel, doing a radio show each Saturday, but he also was appearing on television, where his charm and articulate speech made him a popular guest. He and Campanella found time to work with neighborhood youths at the Harlem YMCA and also to visit schools and youth groups across the city. With his name opening doors, Jack was also instrumental in soliciting funds for a proposed youth center attached to the YMCA. An appeal to John D. Rockefeller III, who sent the organization a gift of $2,500 in December, led a Rockefeller aide to note: "Because the call comes from Robinson, I think it would be nice if you could telephone him or see him briefly." That fall, Jack also started what would become an annual tradition for him—raising funds and gathering toys, clothes, and other gifts for the poor at Christmas. In 1950, raising about $9,000 for this purpose, he also hosted a party for some fifteen hundred needy youngsters in Harlem.

With Martin Stone's shrewd advice, he also sorted through the latest offers. For a while, they discussed with the producers of *The Jackie Robinson Story* a plan for Jack to do another movie for Eagle-Lion Productions; but nothing came of the idea. Stone looked hard into a proposal for Jack and Rachel to star in a husband-and-wife television show; however, this idea, too, fell through. The likelihood of such a show succeeding in 1951, even with Jackie Robinson involved, was slim indeed.

BY MARCH, when Jack reached Florida for preseason training, the post-Rickey regime had taken root. The Brooklyn offices had been renovated to purge all traces of Rickey; his fish tank and the portrait of Lincoln were now history. O'Malley had also dismissed Burt Shotton, who had been derided by Dick Young in the New York *Daily News* as aloof, indifferent to his players' problems, "a vain, proud and stubborn person." In his place, warmly welcomed by Robinson, who would later call him his favorite manager, was Charlie Dressen. Only five feet five inches but thickly built, outgoing, and confident to the point of egotism, the fifty-three-year-old Dressen had been a mediocre player but an aggressive coach or manager, first with the Reds, then with the Dodgers, before going on to the Yankees. In Brooklyn he had once served under Durocher; like Durocher and Robinson, he had an insatiable desire to win and the self-assurance that he could outsmart any opposition. Dressen made it clear who his ideal Dodger was: "I am counting on Robinson to be the most valuable player in the National League next year."

In Florida, O'Malley made other changes. The austere complex at Vero Beach would serve for basic conditioning; the team would then move to Miami for its exhibition games, in Miami Stadium. Most players welcomed the change, but for Jack and the other black players it meant a return to Jim Crow. They could not eat in, much less stay at, the luxurious hotel that would house the white players and staff. For Rachel, who came down to Miami with Jackie and Sharon and other team wives, the Jim Crow arrangement was humiliating. "It certainly did not help to bring us together," she said of the players' wives. "I remember sitting on a rickety old 'colored' bus with Jackie Junior and seeing some of the white Dodger women staring at us as we drove off to our colored and quite unequal hotel. Or waiting for the infrequent 'colored' taxi to come along, since white drivers could or would not take us. That was certainly not the best way to make friends."

Bottling up his resentment, however, Jack concentrated on getting in shape. Dieting had become a serious, if painful, part of his daily routine. Over the winter, at Dressen's urging, Jack had gone at least three times on a ghastly Mayo Clinic diet consisting mainly of eggs and grapefruit. "That dieting business is awful," he complained to reporters. "The main feature is no bread, and boy how I love that bread." At Vero Beach (joined by Newcombe and Campanella, who were even more seriously overweight) he put himself on another round of this diet. He also repudiated his 1950 strategy of restraint: "I'm going to open up on the bases this season." The other Dodgers were also eager for battle. The pitching corps of Roe, Newcombe, Erskine, Branca, and Clyde King was healthy; the home-run power of the Dodgers, tops in the league for the past two years, seemed assured. The outfield, especially Snider and Furillo, was fleet, the infield probably the best in the majors. And everyone seemed ready to follow Dressen. "We have a different attitude this year," Jack wrote. "I can tell that by the way the fellows talk and act. Last year at this time we thought we could take it any time we wanted. We knew we had the best team. . . . This year we feel we have the best team, but we know now we will have to scratch and fight to win every game. That's the way we are going at it."

For Jack, the scratching and fighting began in the exhibition season. Unfortunately, the enemy was not a baseball team but an umpire—Frank Dascoli of the National League, in a game at Asheville, North Carolina. Called out at first by Dascoli, Robinson lit into him with heated words that continued after Dascoli ejected him. Later, Dascoli accused him of using ethnic slurs—"wop," "dago," and the like—in his tirade. The charge shocked Jack. If Dascoli was seeking to discredit Robinson, he could hardly have picked a more clever way, even as Jack, adamantly supported by the Dodger coach Jake Pitler, denied using such language. "Jackie would *never* use an ethnic slur, never," Carl Erskine said. "And he was not a real umpire-baiter, compared to many other players. He disliked inconsistent umpiring, that was all. He was a superb, complete major leaguer, even when his skills were running down. He was a disciplined and spiritual person who would not have used ethnic slurs, period." Consciously or not, a trap was being set for Robinson. Both at home, from Rachel, and within the club, he heard advice to be quiet. Dressen warned him about the futility of antagonizing umpires. "I like aggressive play and want you to be that way," he assured Jack, "but lay off those umpires. If you get a reputation for questioning every decision they'll give you the works and it will hurt you as well as the club." Later in the month Dressen spoke out again: Jack "might be a little too aggressive for his own good. . . . I don't want to get the umpires mad at him. He's too valuable to get put out of games."

Lying low when he was sure that a conspiracy, formal or informal, existed against him was difficult for Robinson. At Ebbets Field, after clashing with umpires Babe Pinelli and Dusty Boggess, he flatly declared his belief that some umpires were abusing him: "Anything I do, they'll give me the worst of the breaks. I know what I am up against." Although he had promised to try and stay out of trouble, "I'm not blind. I think I know what's going on. Certain umpires are out to get me." Although he didn't want trouble, he told the Chicago *Tribune,* "I'm not going to be a sitting duck." Even to some of his allies, Jack's challenge to the umpires was ill-advised and even unseemly. To those disposed to dislike him, he was indeed a sitting duck. The *Sporting News,* now superficially in support of integration in baseball, criticized Robinson for his "umpire-baiting." In a haughty rebuke, the journal called upon him to be "the superb and stylish batsman, the deadly double-play dealer, the intrepid base-runner" he often was, which would "perhaps" take him one day to the Hall of Fame. However, "for the mean and petty practices of the chronic griper, there is no place, except in shabby, sordid memory."

As usual, such hostility served mainly to drive Robinson to new heights of brilliance. Early in June, his batting average stood at .412, tops in the majors. And despite uneven pitching, the Dodgers were off to a fine start. In contrast, the Dodgers' crosstown rivals, Durocher's Giants, staggered from the gate; by early May, the team had lost eleven straight games. When five losses to the Dodgers exacerbated the bitterness between the two teams, Jack found himself yet again at the center of a storm.

By this time, Durocher and Robinson, both driven to win, had spawned one of the more complicated personal relationships in baseball. Jack had never forgiven Durocher for humiliating him in Ciudad Trujillo in 1948 about being overweight; later that season, he was also not charmed when Giants fielders picked him off three times on the base paths. Yet Durocher had backed Jack's entry into baseball, and he had never allowed race to surface as a factor even when Robinson tested the limits of his tolerance. Jack did so by bringing Laraine Day, Durocher's film-actress wife, into their war and appearing to question the sexuality of the Giants manager, a noted clotheshorse given to dowsing himself with cologne. "Leo," Jack would announce loudly, as he sniffed the air, "I can smell Laraine's perfume." (Ms. Day, after watching Robinson play in the 1947 World Series, had told a reporter she was " 'amazed' by his catlike movements.") After Jack's first crack about perfume, according to Harold Parrott, Durocher sent him a case of Lifebuoy soap at the Dodger clubhouse; Leo wanted Jack to know he stank. "My dick to you," Durocher yelled at Robinson in another exchange. "Give it to Laraine," Jack shouted back, "she needs it more than I do." Perhaps these exchanges explain why Durocher at times seemed obsessed by Robinson. "You've got a swelled head," Durocher would scream at Jack. "Who are you to have such a big head?"

Late in the season, Laraine Day herself got into the act, mocking Robinson and the Dodgers as a bunch of sissies. "Did you notice," she asked reporters after a game in which he was hit by a pitch, "how Robinson rubbed his hand where he was supposed to have been hit? He kept rubbing it for a long time." No Giant player would have rubbed: "Our boys aren't cry babies." (Jack promised to fix Laraine good after the season, on his radio show.) The heckling between Robinson and Durocher continued on to the last game—that is, the last scheduled game—of the season, on September 9, even as Robinson denied hating Durocher. "I just don't like to be called big-headed and I don't care to be knocked down."

To Pee Wee Reese, the Robinson-Durocher war of words was mainly a comic spectacle. But it also had its violent aspect, mainly because Durocher expected his pitchers to intimidate opposing batters. In 1951, with the Robinson-Durocher feud still going strong, Jack and Sal "the Barber" Maglie, the saturnine Giants pitcher, clashed after Maglie, goaded by Durocher, sent the Dodger player down into the dirt with wicked inside pitching. Jack, setting down a bunt designed to lure Maglie over so that Jack could level him, ended up only bumping Maglie after he refused the bait. When Durocher denounced the play as "bush" league, Robinson assured everyone that Durocher himself had taught him the trick when he managed the Dodgers. As the series progressed and became more violent, with several Dodger players hit or menaced by Giant pitchers at Durocher's command, Robinson kept up an almost maniacally intense verbal barrage against the Giants. Hit by the pitcher Larry Jansen, he mocked him as he trotted to first: "You've got a nerve to try to scare a guy with that stuff. Try and do it again." His taunting rattled Jansen, who proceeded to yield a monstrous homer to Hodges, a double to Bruce Edwards, a single to Reese, and a double to Cox before he was hustled off the mound. Over six games, Jack hit three home runs, drove in eight runs, and averaged .409. While the Dodgers gloated in triumph, Durocher was left to mumble, unconvincingly, that "it's a long season."

Robinson's rare pugnaciousness helped to inspire his teammates, but won him few friends outside the Dodgers. In Philadelphia, he found himself heckled with an intensity he had not expected to find again. More seriously, he soon knew that he could not expect a fair shake from league officials. Complaining to a reporter that he was "tired" of Robinson's "popping off, and all that business," the National League president, Ford Frick, threatened to curb Robinson if the Dodgers would not. But the Dodgers management stood behind their controversial star. O'Malley declared: "I have no reason to be dissatisfied with Jackie Robinson, his conduct on the field, or his spirit. . . . He has the full support of this organization." Buzzie Bavasi, for whom Jack had developed an affection, insisted that Durocher and other Giants be called "on the carpet, too, to straighten out the whole deal."

Always loyal to Jack, Branch Rickey pointed out a fact: "Robinson always has been willing to take more than he has given." But in the Pittsburgh *Courier,* the black columnist W. Rollo Wilson reported the opinion of "many fans of both races" that Robinson "is becoming increasingly obsessed with his own importance. With them his name is a synonym for swelled-head." He recalled someone joking, apropos of President Truman's recent dismissal of his most famous general: "Who does General MacArthur think he is—Jackie Robinson?" Vincent X. Flaherty, a top columnist for the Hearst newspapers, chastised Jack both for his behavior and his hypersensitivity: "Robinson will read this and when he does, instead of smoldering into a rage, I hope he digests a little of it and looks to the future. I hope, in days to come, people won't point and say: 'There goes Jackie Robinson . . . what a guy he might have been!' "

This new level of hostility took an ominous turn on May 20, when Jack arrived at his hotel in Cincinnati to find two FBI men awaiting him. The Cincinnati Reds, the police, and the Cincinnati *Enquirer* had each received a letter containing a death threat against him: while he was out in the open at Crosley Field, someone with a rifle in a building across the street would shoot him. Each letter was signed "Three Travelers." Calmly, Jack brushed aside the idea that he should not play. He also joined his teammates in their grim joking. "I think we will all wear 42," Reese deadpanned, "and then they will have a shooting gallery." "That would be too much trouble for you fellows," Jack warned, "because you would have to darken up, too." But the death threat seemed to spur the Dodgers. Playing before a crowd aware of the letter, Brooklyn pounded out twenty-four runs to sweep a doubleheader. In the seventh inning of the first game, when Ewell Blackwell deliberately walked Duke Snider and pitched to Robinson, Jack hit a long homer over the center-field fence, in what seemed a magnificent riposte to the "Three Travelers." The Cincinnati team president, Warren Giles, no fan of Robinson's, called the fan response the most prolonged round of applause he had ever heard at Crosley Field.

Robinson gained more admirers the following week with his handling of another controversy. At Ebbets Field, in a game against the Phillies, he found himself stranded between third and home. Deftly eluding one trap after another, he then broke for home. Covering home plate, the pitcher Russ Meyer seemed to have an easy out. But Meyer dropped the ball when Robinson crashed into him and scored (the Dodgers won by one run). Enraged, Meyer had to be restrained from attacking Robinson, then loudly challenged him to a fight under the stands. Jack started out of the dugout, before his teammates stopped him. Later, Meyer visited the Dodger clubhouse to apologize to Robinson, who not only accepted the apology but also tried to share the blame: "If I hadn't started down to meet him, there would have been no trouble." (Meyer was fined $50 by the league.) Jack's gesture did not go unnoticed. The *Sporting News,* which praised him for facing the death threat "in a way that Americans like—lightly, and with wit"—also found his attempt to share the blame "American." Robinson "is a player to stir the spirit and admiration of all Americans, who, almost to a man, will respect quality and integrity of performance, allied with seemly deportment." Then the journal revealed its deep hostility to him: "However, they will resent and repel with all their force the agitator, the sharper with an angle, the fellow who is less than an American because he chooses to be a rabble rouser."

Despite the controversies, the Dodgers began to pull away from the rest of the league. Dressen lauded the team as better than the pennant-winning Dodgers of 1941; a Giants official called it the finest National League team since the 1929 Cubs. In August, the New York *World-Telegram and Sun* saw the Dodgers waltzing into the World Series; Philadelphia, the defending league champions, promised their fans a better effort in 1952. Near the end of the month, at home, Brooklyn steamrolled over the Cardinals with two tenth-inning victories. In the middle of September, responding to the public clamor for World Series tickets, Walter O'Malley announced that his team was willing to play the series in commodious Yankee Stadium.

Now, improbably, the Giants began to win. On August 11, they were thirteen games behind the Dodgers, with sixteen more losses than Brooklyn. Then, starting the next day, in a streak reminiscent of the 1935 Cubs, when Chicago won twenty-one games toward the end of the season to beat out the Cardinals, the Giants strung together sixteen straight victories. Steadily the gap closed between the two teams, even as the Dodgers assumed victory and Durocher seemed to concede defeat. When the Giants clinched at least second place—the best Giants finish in fourteen years—he said in contempt: "What good is that? You either win the pennant or you lose." Individual Giants players looked to their laurels in a lost season. On September 16, for example, Bobby Thomson tied his season mark for most home runs by hitting his twenty-ninth of the year.

The gap narrowed, although with ten games to play Brooklyn led the Giants by four and a half games, an apparently insurmountable gap. But at home, Brooklyn dropped two out of three to the Phillies, who were then swept by the Giants at the Polo Grounds. On September 25, in Boston, after dropping an afternoon game, the Dodgers committed three errors in one inning in a nighttime loss to the Braves. The lead was now one game. The next day, Robinson stole home for the first time in the season as Brooklyn won, to preserve the slim lead. (The run, coming in the eighth inning of what was already a rout, infuriated many Braves.) But the following day, September 27, a decision in the eighth inning by umpire Frank Dascoli (the same umpire who had accused Robinson of using ethnic slurs against him) gave Boston the game, 4–3. Fielding a sharp grounder, Robinson threw quickly to Campanella as a runner broke from third to home. Dascoli called him safe. When Campanella protested, Dascoli immediately ejected him from the game. "I'm not saying anything about the decision," an enraged Robinson told a newsman. "That was simply a matter of judgment. But I do say he had no right to throw Camp out. In a race like this, the umpires should expect tempers to be a little frayed."

After the umpires retired to their dressing room, a policeman reported seeing Robinson viciously kicking its door, splitting two panels as he cursed at the umpires. Backed by his teammate Preacher Roe, Robinson denied kicking the door. But despite his denials, the league fined him $100. (Roe had kicked in the door.)

At Shibe Park for the last three games of the regular season, Brooklyn was ahead 3–1 in the eighth inning of the opening game when Andy Seminick blasted a two-run home run off Carl Erskine to tie the score; in the ninth, the Phillies won. Brooklyn and New York were now tied for first place. The Giants then defeated Boston to move ahead, but the Dodgers, behind Don Newcombe's pitching, also won in Philadelphia. On the last scheduled day of the regular season, September 30, in Boston, the Giants edged the Braves in an afternoon game to move ahead once more. At 3:55 p.m., with the Dodgers trailing the Phillies 8–5, after trailing 6–1 (the one run driven in by a Robinson triple), the scoreboard at Shibe Park posted the Giants victory. But Brooklyn fought back to tie the game, 8–8, in the eighth inning. Three more innings went scoreless. Then, in the twelfth inning, near six o'clock, with the sunlight fading from the green, Newcombe pitching, and the bases loaded with two men out, Eddie Waitkus smashed a low drive to the right of second base. "The ball is a blur passing second base," Red Smith would write, "difficult to follow in the half-light, impossible to catch. Jackie Robinson catches it. He flings himself headlong at right angles to the flight of the ball, for an instant his body is suspended in midair, then somehow the outstretched glove intercepts the ball inches off the ground." The fall jammed his left elbow into his solar plexus so hard that he was knocked out. In the stands, word spread that a heart attack had felled him. To Roscoe McGowen of the New York *Times,* Jack's catch was "one of the greatest, if not the greatest, clutch plays I have seen in almost a lifetime of watching major league games." Red Smith would write of Robinson "stretched at full length in the insubstantial twilight, the unconquerable doing the impossible."

Two innings later, recovered, Jack drove a towering home run into the left-field stands off Robin Roberts to put the Dodgers ahead to stay, and preserve the tie with the Giants to end the regular season. "There's no stopping us now," Jack exulted later in the dressing room. "The breaks haven't been going our way during the past month, but now that we've gotten this far we aren't going to look back." In the three-game playoff series, the Giants took the first, at Ebbets Field, with home runs off Ralph Branca by Bobby Thomson and Monte Irvin; but the next day, at the Polo Grounds, the Dodger rookie Clem Labine shut out the Giants as the Dodgers scored ten runs. Robinson was a force: in the first inning, he hit a home run with Reese on base; he also drove in the third run.

Finally, in the deciding game on October 3, again at the Polo Grounds, Maglie faced Newcombe. In the first inning, Jack singled home a run off Maglie. After that, the pitchers dueled about evenly, but the Giants tied the game with a run in the seventh. In the eighth inning, when the Dodgers scored three times, a Brooklyn victory seemed certain. But in the bottom

of the ninth, the Giants' Alvin Dark and Don Mueller
singled off Newcombe. Monte Irvin, leading the
Giants in runs batted in, then popped out; but Whitey
Lockman doubled off Newcombe to drive in a run.
The score was now 4–2. Then, in one of the most
debated decisions in baseball history, Dressen
decided to replace the tiring Newcombe with Ralph
Branca. Branca's first pitch was a strike past Thomson. His next became the most famous home run in
major league history, as Thomson drove it into the
left-field stands to give the Giants their first pennant
since 1937.

The Dodgers had endured one of the most bitter
defeats in the annals of organized sports, but Robinson was calm. As Thomson circled the bases, Jack
watched him closely, making sure he touched every
base. Robinson was also one of the few Dodgers who
made the trip to the delirious Giants clubhouse to
congratulate the victors; he alone, according to
Branca later, consoled the heartbroken pitcher. Bob
Campbell, Jack's friend and former employer in his
UCLA days, was with Rachel when Robinson
emerged from the dressing room. They exchanged
wan smiles. "Well," Jack said, "we let the Brooklyn
fans down." Campbell told Jack that Rachel was
sorry for the Dodgers, because they had been counting on the money. "Yeah, that's true," Jack replied,
"but they have no business counting on it until the
season is over and the pennant is clinched."

However, some observers saw Dodger arrogance,
with Robinson a leading offender, behind the disaster. On August 9, according to the Giants' captain,

Alvin Dark, he and his teammates had listened grimly after a defeat to a stream of taunts coming from the Brooklyn dressing room. The Dodger team sang: "Roll out the barrels! . . . We've got the Giants on the run!" According to Dark, the "arrogant aria" was sung by four men in particular: Reese, Newcombe, Furillo, and Robinson. However, throughout Brooklyn, the brunt of criticism for the defeat fell on Charlie Dressen for his fateful decision to remove Newcombe. Robinson stoutly defended Dressen. During the game, Jack told a radio audience, Newcombe had twice warned the manager that his arm was dead. Robinson was sure his teammates did not blame Dressen: "We think he's a wonderful manager and just as great a fellow."

Disappointed, Robinson still saw the 1951 season as his best yet in the majors. His batting average was .338 (up ten points from 1950), with 19 home runs and 88 runs batted in. But the MVP award went to Roy Campanella. Despite injuries, Campanella hit .325 with 33 homers and 108 runs batted in. "He deserves every honor he can get," Jack said of Campy. "He kept us in the pennant race. . . . I'm convinced Campanella is the best catcher in baseball today." Jack himself came in sixth in the voting, behind Campanella, Musial, Monte Irvin, Sal Maglie, and Preacher Roe. The Baseball Writers Association also named him to their 1951 all-star team, as the best player at second base in either league. His .992 fielding percentage was the best in the league, and his seven errors set a record for fewest by a second baseman.

In the National League, the Rookie of the Year award, previously won by Robinson and Newcombe, went to a young black player, Willie Mays of the New York Giants. (Early in the next season, Robinson would marvel at a catch by Mays. "It was not only the best catch I've seen," he said, "but probably the best catch anyone has ever seen, because they just can't come any better.") In 1951, the project started in 1947 by Rickey and Robinson continued to grow, as fourteen black men played in the majors. No one could doubt the quality of their play; five were in the All-Star Game at mid-season. Only five teams fielded a black at any time that year, but those five teams finished in the first division of their league. In the World Series, in another landmark event, the Giants' Mays, Monte Irvin, and Henry Thompson formed the first all-black outfield in major-league history, when they faced the Yankees.

But Negro-league baseball, which had nurtured almost all of these players, was now virtually dead. Something else had happened. "Fans used to travel hundreds of miles to see Robinson and Doby," Walter O'Malley said in explaining a decline in Dodger attendance. "But they don't have to do that anymore. Negro players are all over the country." In the wake of Robinson's success, doors previously shut to black Americans were opening, however slowly. Althea Gibson became the first black woman to be invited to play at Forest Hills, New York, in the United States lawn tennis championships. The American Bowling Congress dropped its whites-only policy. And all but three teams in major-league baseball now had a black player under contract somewhere in their farm systems.

IN OCTOBER, in Wilmington, Delaware, Robinson started what he hoped would be his last barnstorming tour ever, a month-long ramble through some thirty towns and cities of the South, the Southwest, and California. "These trips are really tough," he complained. "The accommodations in the South are not good. You live on short-order food, have irregular hours and dress out of a suitcase." But a flood of letters "from my people in the South" (as well as the promise of good money) had made him play. Also encouraging was "the amazing overall change in attitude" of Southern whites to black players. "The reaction now," he said, "compared to when I first played down there in 1947 is unbelievable."

This time, Campanella led a rival team. He and Robinson jostled each other to claim the leading black stars—Larry Doby and the young first baseman Luke Easter of the Cleveland Indians and the veteran Sam Jethroe, sold by the Dodgers to the Boston Braves. With all three men joining Robinson, his team outdrew all other barnstorming outfits. "It's Robinson they come to see," the promoter Ted Worner knew; "I don't have any doubts about that." This was certainly so in California, where Oakland, Bakersfield, Los Angeles, and San Diego all honored him. November 4 was "Jackie Robinson Welcome Day" in Los Angeles, when fifteen thousand fans saw his team beat a group of West Coast all-stars led by Bob Lemon of the Cleveland Indians. The next day, before a UCLA homecoming crowd of fifty-five thousand in the Los Angeles Coliseum, Jack was honored before a football game against UC-Berkeley; a tumultuous reception greeted him when he rode with Rachel in an open, banner-draped car through the streets of Westwood as grand marshal of the Homecoming Day parade.

Back home in St. Albans, Jack faced so many engagements and tasks the New York *Journal-American* called him "the league's busiest non-working ball player." He continued to spend a great deal of his time at the YMCA facility on 135th Street in Harlem, and he accepted several invitations to speak at school assemblies. On December 4, for example, he addressed the history club at the elite Choate School in Wallingford, Connecticut. Gracefully he fielded questions about baseball but also tried to steer his remarks toward social problems. The next day, he played a leading role at a YMCA dinner at which Campanella and Sugar Ray Robinson won awards; Jack presented a plaque to Morris Morgenstern, a generous supporter of the Harlem branch. On December 28, at a function of the black Philadelphia Cotillion Society, he presented the Gold Cross of Malta to Branch Rickey—and received the Toussaint L'Ouverture Medal of Honor from the contralto Marian Anderson. On February 12, at its annual dinner, Robinson and Rickey were honored again, by the black Loendi Club of Pittsburgh. Accepting a plaque as the outstanding athlete of 1951, Jack emphasized the extent to which he had matured from his early days in the major leagues, when "I had a chip on my shoulder."

In the month before leaving for training camp, he took two more impressive steps beyond baseball. One solidified his place in television. On February 4, in Manhattan, the flagship stations of the NBC network, WNBC and WNBT, announced that they had signed Robinson to a two-year contract "unique in the field of broadcasting" as director of community activities, with the rank of vice-president. As such, he would not only perform on air but also supervise the development of youth programs, especially those involving sports, as well as work with organizations such as the Police Athletic League, the Catholic Youth Organization, the Boy Scouts, and the YMCA and YMHA. Jack's color was a major factor in the appointment. The general manager of the stations, Ted Cott, spoke of the appointment as "another trail blazing experience" by Robinson, one that would link the network to "the more than one million negroes" in the city area. Robinson would be concerned with combating juvenile delinquency and other "social service activities." To Jack, the new job pointed directly toward his retirement from baseball. "I have had to realize," he said, "that my baseball days will one day be over and, therefore, I've been thinking about a new turning point. This is it."

A few days later, he took another big step away from baseball, into the world of real-estate development. At this time, Robinson knew little or nothing about this field, but it would claim his attention, on and off, for the rest of his life. After discussions over the course of a year, he signed an agreement with a real-estate developer to construct a project, the Jackie Robinson Houses, on a site in or around New York City. The developer, Arnold H. Kagan, would supply the start-up funds, up to $250,000, and almost all the expertise; Jack's main contribution would be in using his fame to help secure a mortgage for the project under Section 213 of the U.S. Housing Act of 1949. (Kagan would get seventy-two percent of the profits, Jack would receive sixteen percent, and attorneys would get the rest.)

Although Jack hoped to make some money here, he had other motives as well. Perhaps equally important was his desire to help poorer blacks as they faced the postwar housing crisis in the New York area and elsewhere. The Housing Act of 1949 had set lofty goals; its central aim was to provide "a decent home in a suitable living environment for every American citizen." Under Title 1 of the act, developers could purchase slum property at drastically reduced prices; with this incentive, Congress expected them to build new housing for the poor and middle-class. Already the reality was proving to be somewhat different; many dilapidated dwellings were being razed by developers and replaced, all too frequently, by luxury apartments. The Jackie Robinson Houses, Robinson and Kagan hoped, would be built in the true spirit of the Housing Act of 1949.

(Ten years after its passage, in 1959, the number of housing units torn down under the provisions of Title 1 of the Housing Act far exceeded the number of new units. Taking the brunt of this imbalance in the major cities, including New York, were people of color, especially blacks. Easily displaced, they were also the least likely to find new housing. Less than two percent of new housing from all sources, including those sponsored under Title 1, would go to blacks.)

IN VERO BEACH, after the disappointment of 1950 and the disaster of 1951, the Dodgers faced the 1952 season with no bravado, only a feverish determination. "I think every player on the team," Robinson said, "will be putting out a little more this year because he feels that we let the fans down in bad finishes in the two previous years." This training camp was different in another way. Clyde Sukeforth, the veteran coach who had escorted Jack to Brooklyn in 1945 to meet Branch Rickey, was gone; unfairly, some people blamed him for the choice of Branca to relieve Newcombe in the last, fatal inning of 1951. Whatever the reason for Sukeforth's departure, Jack had lost his most reliable friend among the Dodger coaches, a man who had treated him from the start with decency and respect. Still, Jack's relationship with Walter O'Malley and, especially, Buzzie Bavasi remained sound. On January 9, when he signed his 1952 contract for $42,000, again the top salary on the team, he had declared himself "perfectly satisfied with my contract." O'Malley and the Brooklyn organization, Jack said publicly, "have treated me fairly."

At Vero Beach, a chastened Dressen, in greeting the team, openly thanked Robinson for his sturdy public support during the off-season. The Dodgers had nothing to be ashamed of, he told the club; they had been unlucky. But the bad luck seemed to continue when the Korean War claimed Newcombe, who entered the Army for a two-year stint. Fortunately, the Dodgers found two stellar pitching replacements. One was black—Joe Black, a handsome, six-foot-two-inch player from Plainfield, New Jersey, formerly with the Baltimore Elite Giants of the Negro leagues, then with St. Paul and Montreal in the Dodgers organization. A college man like Jack, Black was an alumnus of Morgan State with a degree in psychology and physical education. The other promising pitcher was white—Billy Loes, a young New Yorker of eccentric ways and an idiosyncratic curve ball. Roommates bonded further by race and education, Black and Robinson quickly became friends; but against all reasonable expectations, Loes slipped past Robinson's normal standards to become one of his favorites on the team.

Black was sitting in their room nervously waiting to meet Robinson when the star walked in. When Black asked Jack which bed he wanted, Jack brushed aside the question. Instead, he sized up Black's powerful body. "Can you fight?" he asked. "Yeah," Black answered. "But," Robinson insisted, "we're not going to fight." This was Robinson's reprise of Rickey's speech to him in 1945. Black must not strike back, Robinson warned. The first challenge came soon enough. Playing exhibition games in Montgomery and Mobile, Alabama, in particular, the heckling by whites was vicious. "I don't mind the booing," Robinson told a writer. "What got me was when some of them started to holler, 'Hit him in the head.' " But there were also signs of progress. In St. Petersburg, Florida, for example, blacks were finally admitted to the grandstand with whites. Another wall had fallen in a region of walls.

When the season opened, the Dodgers started slowly, in part because Campanella, for one, was mired in a prolonged slump, but also because Brooklyn had not yet discovered Joe Black. At first, Black seemed not much more than mediocre. If his fastball was impressive, his curve ball seemed modest; a wartime injury had damaged fingers on his right hand. And two pitches comprised his entire repertoire. But after Black pitched two excellent innings against the Cincinnati Reds in Brooklyn, to bring his record to seven innings without giving up a run, Dressen saw the light and announced that he would rely on Black in relief in the future. On June 1, when the rookie preserved a victory, the Dodgers also moved into first place for the first time in 1952. Eventually that season, as the heart of the Dodgers pitching staff, Black appeared in fifty-six games, won fifteen, saved fifteen, and lost only four.

The season was still young in May when Jack found himself embroiled again in controversy with umpire Frank Dascoli. After a report that certain Dodger players had taunted Dascoli, Warren Giles, the newly elected president of the National League, sent an official letter of rebuke to Chuck Dressen. Deploring ethnic slurs allegedly hurled at Dascoli, Giles singled out Robinson as "a greater offender than others." Upset by the charge, which he strongly denied, Jack protested to Giles in person. Giles ignored him. He then had both Martin Stone, his business manager, and O'Malley write formal letters of complaint to Giles about the error. Giles, no fan of Robinson, responded only to O'Malley. "I am satisfied that the matter is ended," O'Malley soon announced, "and that Jackie Robinson did not address anyone in uncomplimentary terms." But on May 13, visiting Brooklyn to present Campanella with the 1951 MVP trophy, Giles surprised his listeners by adding a brief, gratuitous bow to Jack to his praise of Campanella: "The National League is also proud of Jackie Robinson." This sly, patronizing response to his protests served only to annoy Robinson, who made it clear that he considered Giles's praise as an apology.

Apology or not, the Dascoli charge further damaged Jack's reputation. Although he was elected to the All-Star Game, where he and Campanella represented Brooklyn, some fans there booed him. July also brought a clash in Cincinnati, after an umpire declared a runner safe at second base and Robinson exploded. Leaping up and down, he threw ball and glove to the turf, then dispatched his glove with a vicious kick; the Associated Press photograph of Robinson punting his hapless glove was widely circulated. After the incident, as usual, Jack was contrite. "I know it's wrong for me to lose my temper," he confessed. "It doesn't do me any good and I really make an effort not to. The wife is after me about it all the time, too." But "when an umpire makes an obvious mistake it seems I automatically blow up. I just can't help myself."

He had other troubles. Earlier, when Joe Black entered a game in St. Louis, insults from certain Cardinals became so graphic that Robinson and Dressen protested to the league about the rabid use of the term "nigger," linked to obscene and other demeaning terms. (The targets were only Black and Robinson; Campanella made it clear that no one had insulted him.) When Eddie Stanky, now managing St. Louis, dismissed the nasty language as typical baseball teasing, and the team president, Fred Saigh, brushed off the protest as "too much fuss over nothing," Robinson disagreed. Race baiting, he insisted, had no place in the game. "You'd think that after six years they would cut that stuff out," he said. "I thought I had proved that those names don't hurt my play a bit."

And indeed, Robinson was once again leading the Dodgers in hitting; by the end of June his batting average was .327, with five home runs and eleven stolen bases. Once again, he was fighting with Stan Musial for the batting crown.

THROUGH THE SQUABBLES and skirmishes of the 1952 season, Jack found a refuge waiting for him at the end of most days at home in St. Albans, which the Robinsons now shared with Rachel's older brother, Chuck Williams; his wife, Brenda; and their son, Chuckie. At Jack's direct invitation, the Williamses had migrated from California; he saw them as the essential nucleus of the inner circle of his and Rachel's friends and supporters, who would make much easier their decision to live in the East. Through Jack, Chuck found a job with Schenley Liquors, where he eventually became a vice-president and, later, a member of the board of directors. In 1952, Brenda, a graduate of Xavier University in New Orleans, arrived from California pregnant with twins; to ease the transition, she and Chuck lived with the Robinsons for about a year. Later in 1952, Jack also invited his best friend and Pasadena Junior College buddy, Jack Gordon, to move east with his wife, Bernice, and their son, Bradley. Gordon would also find work through Jack, first in his clothing store, then with the Manischewitz wine company, where he too enjoyed a long career. Still later, Jack would convince Rachel to invite her mother to give up California and come to live with them.

In 1952, Rachel, too, was pregnant. On May 14, 1952, after the Dodgers lost a game to the Cardinals at Ebbets Field, Jack hurried to Doctors Hospital in Manhattan for the birth of his third child, a boy. Like the pregnancy itself, the delivery was uncomplicated. Rachel and Jack were ecstatic about the birth of their second son, David. She wanted to have at least four children, with as many boys as girls; Jack's idea of a family was probably even grander. But Jack's joy soon vanished when Rachel fell sick with nephritis, or an acute infection of the kidney, and had to remain in the hospital for several days. Needing help with David, Jack turned to Florence Covington's sister

Willette Bailey, who gladly took David home to St. Albans.

To Jack's relief—although her doctor warned her that because of the nephritis, she should probably have no more children—Rachel recovered quickly. Thus, a short time later, he was unprepared when, in St. Louis to play the Cardinals, a telephone call from New York brought troubling news of a medical emergency. Rachel was back in the hospital, awaiting an operation. She had discovered a lump in her breast; a surgeon, diagnosing the growth as probably malignant, ordered surgery as soon as possible. Stunned by the news, Rachel's main thought was to keep it from Jack. "I decided that with all he was going through," she said, "he didn't need to know about the operation." But the surgeon insisted. "He asked me right away, 'Where is your husband? Why isn't he here?' We argued a little but then he put his foot down. He wouldn't operate unless Jack knew about it."

In St. Louis, Jack hung up the telephone in the hotel room he was sharing with Joe Black and quietly told him that Rachel was ill. "I think I'm going to go home," he said. "And when he said that," according to Black, "water just came down his eyes, right down his cheek." By the time he reached the hospital he was in a state of nervous tension that only grew worse as the doctors talked to him. "They scared him to death," Rachel recalled, "with talk about how tumors have characteristics, about their size, their configuration, their mobility, and how certain factors suggest malignancy. They told him they thought mine did. I didn't think so, but they did." Jack took the news hard; he was not at his best waiting to find out the answers to possibly damaging questions. "I would never have told him any of that," she said. "Jack was badly frightened, because he was never, ever, able to tolerate anything being wrong with me. I had to be there, up and ready and able, managing. Anyway, it turned out to be not a tumor at all. I hadn't nursed, and the gland formed, became hard, and felt like a tumor. They just took it out and that was the end of it. Jack had been upset for nothing. He had come from St. Louis for nothing. But he wasn't angry about that. He just had a tremendous sense of relief."

Some teammates believed that Jack took a long time to recover fully from this scare. By July, although he had some good hitting days, he had slipped into a slump. At one point, he had only two hits in twenty-five at-bats, as his average fell below .300 for the first time since 1948. Astutely, Dressen made the connection between Rachel's surgery and the slump. "Before he left the club to see his wife, he was swinging just right," Dressen pointed out to the press, "and he hasn't been the same since." Gradually, however, Jack regained his form, in a reversal of his pattern of previous years. By late August he was back over .300; the Dodgers, behind the excellent pitching of Black and Preacher Roe, held on firmly to first place. Then, with nine losses in twelve games, Brooklyn seemed ready to fold again; but four straight defeats of the Cardinals set Brooklyn back on course. "Don't you worry," Jack assured a reporter, "we won't blow our lead this year. We're going all the way to the World Series. The Giants caught us last year but that won't happen again."

It didn't; Brooklyn won the pennant. Still, disputes continued to dog Robinson's steps. On August 13, when rain stopped a game between the Dodgers and the Cubs at Ebbets Field, he and Cubs manager Phil Cavarretta started a nasty shouting match conducted from their respective dugouts. The next day brought reports—completely false—that Jack and the Dodgers coach Cookie Lavagetto had to be restrained from punching Cavarretta. As usual, Jack's denials had little effect on the growing sense that he was out of control. His frustration on this score reached its peak on September 4 in Boston, with an incident that also involved Campanella and two umpires, Larry Goetz and Frank Secory. In the eleventh inning of a tied game, ruling that Johnny Logan of the Braves had been hit by a pitch, Secory awarded him first base even as Campanella angrily insisted that Logan had foul-tipped the ball. When Logan then scored the winning run, Dodger Rocky Bridges bitterly asked Secory if he had shaken Logan's hand as he crossed the plate. Robinson, too far away to hear the remark, then told Secory: "What he said goes double for me." He also told Goetz: "I didn't hear what he said, but he's right."

Acting on the umpires' complaint, Ford Frick, now the commissioner of baseball, then levied fines of $100 on Campanella and $75 on an incredulous Robinson, who flatly refused to pay up without a hearing. "Before I'll pay that fine," he told reporters,

"I'll take my spikes off and never play another game." His defiance, practically unheard of in baseball, was not well received by fans. Away from Ebbets Field, the booing of Robinson became intense even as he insisted on his right to a hearing. Apparently, only a trusted reporter's argument that Jack's inevitable suspension would be an unfair and perhaps a selfish blow to his teammates led Jack to back down. "I never thought of it that way," Robinson told the reporter. "I'll pay the fine."

In October, for the third time in Jack's six Brooklyn seasons, the Dodgers faced the Yankees in the World Series. For the third time, he failed to shine. In 1952, he was as eager as ever to do well. "The main thing is to beat the Yankees," he admitted. "But I'd like to come through with one really good World Series, and I know I'm not going to have many more opportunities." In the first game, Joe Black, after starting only two games all season, shocked the Yankees with a win. After the Yankees took the second, Preacher Roe then won in Yankee Stadium when the usually reliable Yogi Berra let a ball go by and two Dodgers scored in the ninth. Black pitched brilliantly again in the fourth game, yielding three hits and one run over seven innings; but Allie Reynolds was even better with a shutout. As a hitter, Jack touched bottom in this game; frozen by Reynolds's wicked curves, he was out three times on called third strikes. ("I couldn't argue about them," he conceded. "The umpire was right in calling them.") The fifth game went eleven innings before the Dodgers won, but the Yankees then tied up the series. The seventh inning of the seventh game found Robinson with an excellent shot at redemption: he came up to bat with the Dodgers down, 4–2, the bases loaded, and two men out. Redemption almost came. Jack swung hard; the ball skied over the pitcher's mound; the infielders seemed hypnotized. Then the Yankee second baseman Billy Martin, in a memorable play, stormed in to snatch the ball just before it hit the ground. Once again, the Yankees beat the Dodgers.

Proud to have helped bring another pennant home to Brooklyn, and happy for Black, who became the fifth black player to be named Rookie of the Year in the National League, Jack had performed well once again in Dodger blue. Still, as the season ended he was talking more and more about retiring from baseball. Would he quit? "I certainly might," he speculated on the radio in the course of an interview. "There's no getting around that. . . . Just say I'm considering it."

In Meridian, Mississippi, the previous fall, Jack had listened in horror to the reaction of a crowd at a baseball game to the news that Rocky Marciano had just knocked out the aging Joe Louis in a prize fight. To Jack's sorrow, many people there could feel no sympathy for the fallen former champion, once among the greatest heroes in America. Louis was washed up; he should face the fact and quit. "It made me stop and think," Robinson said, "what they might say about me if I started to go on the down grade. Like a good entertainer, I want to leave the stage with the audience asking for more."

— 11 —

Dodging Blows, Fighting Back

1952–1955

What do you think of the booing?
Why are they booing me?
—Jackie Robinson (1953)

DESPITE JACK'S GLOOMY talk about retiring, there
was really no chance in the fall of 1952 that he would
voluntarily step aside. Not only did he need his
salary; he also knew that his dream of making an
even larger impact on the world around him still depended in large part on baseball. He talked about
quitting but remained, late in 1952, determined to
carry on with the adventure launched in 1945 by
Branch Rickey and himself.

At the same time, that fall he branched out further
into the business world, this time as a retailer of men's
clothing. On the early evening of December 5, in
response to printed invitations, a small constellation
of celebrities, including Sugar Ray Robinson, Roy
Campanella, and the Hollywood character actor
Gabby Hayes (a rabid Dodgers fan), gathered at 111
West 125th Street for the "Grand Opening" of the
Jackie Robinson Store. Over the summer, Jack had
signed an agreement to do business in Harlem with a

Brooklyn businessman, Lou Oster, of Bedford Stores and Bedford Clothiers (of Bedford Avenue in Brooklyn). Jack intended his store to take its place alongside the other major businesses on 125th Street, Harlem's premier shopping and business strip: the Hotel Theresa, where virtually every important black visitor to New York stayed; Frank Schiffman's Apollo Theater, the nonpareil center of black musical and comedy entertainment; and Blumstein's department store, a retailing fixture in Harlem since at least the 1930s.

Robinson's name was on the business, but little of his own money was in it. Martin Stone had given only grudging approval to the plan. "I pointed out to Jack that he didn't know anything about the retail business," Stone said; "but he had made up his mind, and he was very excited about the prospect." Fascinated by Harlem and 125th Street, where he was always welcome at Schiffman's Apollo Theater, Robinson welcomed a chance to be a part of the black community there. The store also encouraged him to bring out from California his best friend, Jack Gordon. On his last visit to Los Angeles, Robinson had urged Gordon to think of moving east with his family. As the opening of the store drew near, Jack sent a letter to Gordon, air mail and special delivery, inviting him to move to New York to work at the Jackie Robinson Store—in effect, to be his eyes and ears there when Jack was away. "After the war, I had gone to tailoring school," Gordon revealed, "so Jack figured I was the man for the job. . . . Nothing was working out in California, and Jack was Jack, so we came in 1952 and we never left." The Harlem store was "a really fine shop. Our prices were lower than at the stores downtown, because our overhead was less; but nothing was cheap. The display windows were fantastic. The quality of the clothes was like Jack's own outfits, conservative but sharp."

Deliberately, because of his ethics and his pride, Robinson chose not to enter Harlem's business world selling cheap, inferior clothing at inflated prices to the poorest folk. He hoped his store would add to the quality of life in the community, not prey on it. But if his venture started promisingly, Jack soon faced certain realities about Harlem. Money was a grave problem, perhaps one more serious than he understood; attracting many buyers of quality merchandise would not be easy. Another factor, much harder to pin down, was also at work: would most blacks shop freely at a store owned, supposedly, by a black man, even if that man was Jackie Robinson? Sugar Ray Robinson warned Jack to expect the worst. The fighter's Harlem bar was well patronized; but his wife's lingerie shop next door, although well stocked, was not. Becoming aware of a degree of envy and suspicion he had not anticipated, Jack advised his partners not to put his name on garment labels. "Jack used to tell them," Gordon said, " 'I don't know whether it's a good idea. You know, some of these people are not exactly in love with Jackie Robinson. They buy where they want to buy. They like thinking of themselves as sophisticated New Yorkers.' "

Over the next six years, until he sold his share in 1958, the store made him hardly any money. "Whatever his deal was," Rachel said, "he saw very little income from it. I don't think Lou Oster himself was making very much, to begin with. But Jack made very little in return for what he put in—his time, lending his name and his contacts." Nevertheless, in the weeks before training camp, and whenever he was free thereafter, Robinson spent a great deal of time at his store. He liked meeting and greeting his customers there; in fact, he himself thoroughly enjoyed shopping—not for himself so much as for Rachel and, to a lesser extent, his children, especially Sharon. Loving a deal, as one woman friend put it, "Jack was an 'I can get it for you wholesale' man." ("He certainly was that," Rachel confirmed. "I'll never forget the day in St. Albans when a truck pulled up with an entire slaughtered cow Jack had bought from somebody in Chicago. The guys had a contract to bring it to the sidewalk and they wouldn't go a step further. Brenda and I, about eight months pregnant, had to lug it into the house. We ate a lot of beef that winter.")

Although the store was hardly making him rich, Jack's name was still a valuable entity, used to endorse a line of items from calendars and glassware to cocktail napkins and party favors. In addition, his real-estate partnership also seemed to be progressing nicely. About this time, he and his partner announced the acquisition of an eight-acre parcel of vacant land at the corner of Commonwealth and Story Avenues in the Bronx, on which they planned to erect what he was now calling the Jackie Robinson Apartments. The project, comprising eight buildings that would house 612 families, would serve mainly low-income tenants; but Jack was not coy about his financial interest in the project. "I'm no longer a young man," he said. "I'm trying to save money for when my legs give out."

In the off-season, Jack found himself embroiled in a dispute about baseball and racial discrimination. Appearing on a popular television program, *Youth Wants to Know,* he was asked by a girl whether he thought that the Yankees, still an all-white team, were anti-Negro. Behind the question was a small cloud hovering over yet another successful Yankee year in 1952—the failure of the team to bring up Vic Power, a fine-hitting black first baseman at Kansas City in their farm system. Jack's immediate answer was "Yes." He was referring, he stressed, not to the players, who were "fine sportsmen and wonderful gentlemen," but to the Yankee management: "There isn't a single Negro on the team now and there are very few in the entire Yankee farm system."

At Yankee Stadium, George Weiss, the general manager, reacted with outrage. The Yankees would field a Negro when it found one "who can play good enough ball to win a place on the Yankees," but would not hire a black "just for exploitation." Among insiders, Weiss was well known for being far more solicitous of his team's wealthy Westchester County fans than about abstract notions of fairness and democracy. Nevertheless, a number of writers gave Robinson a drubbing for the remark; even Wendell Smith in the *Courier* advised that "everyone should be very careful in these days and times about making such charges." Ford Frick, the commissioner of baseball, telephoned Robinson to request an explanation. Sending Frick a transcript of the show, Robinson pointed out that he had been asked a question: "I merely said what I honestly felt. Whether it's true I do not know, but that's the way I felt." According to Jack, Frick asked him "to avoid the issue in the future if I could do so and I said 'certainly.' But I also told him . . . I would give the same answer if I were ever asked the same question again."

If Jack regretted anything about the incident, it was probably the reactive nature of his part in it. Eager to speak out on questions of racism and justice, but lacking a proper forum, he had found himself once again on the defensive, forced to contribute to the debate on terms set largely by others. Seeking to alter that pattern, that winter Robinson became editor of a monthly magazine aimed mainly at blacks, *Our Sports.* In April 1953 the first issue appeared. According to Roger Kahn, who wrote for the magazine, the short-lived *Our Sports* was an offshoot of *Our World* (which had published pictures of the Robinsons' wedding in 1946). In May, the second number of *Our Sports* included articles by Joe Louis, Kahn ("What White Big Leaguers Really Think of Negro Players"), and Robinson himself ("My Feud with Leo Durocher"), ghostwritten by Kahn. In July, in the third number, Jack published his piece "The Branch Rickey They Don't Write About."

The sensitive, well-read Kahn was one of his favorite writers; Milton Gross was another. In February, *Sport* magazine published Gross's "Why They

Boo Jackie Robinson," perhaps the most provocative and complex essay written to date on the Dodger star. Jack himself had provided the title. Ridden harshly by Giants fans at the Polo Grounds in September after he refused to pay the fine imposed by Warren Giles, he had asked Gross almost plaintively: "What do you think of the booing? Why are they booing me?" Gross's article, for which he interviewed both Jack and Rachel at their home, searched for answers to some loaded questions about Jack's character and personality, as well as the apparent erosion of his popularity among whites: "Is Jackie overly aggressive? Is he getting too big for his pants? Is he a crybaby, a pop-off taking advantage of his position? Does he go looking for trouble? Is he much too prone to feel he is being singled out for censure? . . . Have the last two years begun to break down the good will and respect he built in his last four years in baseball?"

To Gross, Jack pleaded unselfishness in his actions, which were aimed at helping his team win. Of the fans he asked, "Do they think I do things deliberately to harm my popularity? I do them emotionally. I do them to win. I don't do them for Jack. I do them for the team." Giles's censure had stirred up the fans unfairly: "I think the adverse criticism, implied or otherwise, from the president's office had a lot to do with it." As a player, he was being held to a different standard. Matters involving him were "always magnified," he said, but "I do nothing that others on my club and on the other clubs do not do." Racial intolerance, he insisted, was the cause. "If the public will analyze it, they will see that those who have become opposed to me resent my success deep down inside only because I am a Negro." With no desire to be a martyr for black Americans, he still had a strong obligation to them. "I am not carrying the cross for the Negro people," Jack argued, "but I do have a sense of responsibility. I don't believe the people I'm trying to help would want me to walk away from trouble."

Perhaps the most fragile thread in this inquiry had to do with the relationship between the controversies and the health of his mind. If he was different from other players, he ventured, "maybe it's because I like to win more than some of the others. Maybe I take defeat harder." Why he was that way was another matter. Even less easily answered was the question about the extent to which his genuine ordeal both as a player and as a black man may have affected his mental stability. Unwittingly, Rachel raised the question in the article even as she defended him. "The very violence of Jack's reaction[s]," she argued, "shows they're spontaneous." This was a good defense of spontaneity, but not of clarity of vision, or mental health. Rachel and Jack were aware of this distinction; but the last thing he wanted was to be immobilized by it, to become passive out of the fear that he could not see correctly, from persistent self-doubt. Robinson had taken it upon himself to carry forward his people's struggle against injustice. At whatever cost to his happiness, he would continue to scream when he felt pain, lash back when unfairly attacked, shout the truth in the face of power.

In America, with its tragic history of race relations, this amounted, in a bizarre way, to progress. "People," Rachel told Gross, "are now recognizing the Negro as an individual. It's an endorsement of our American way of life. It's not as it should be yet, but it's progressing." Unfortunately, in 1953 few black celebrities were paying a higher price for this progress than Jackie Robinson.

In January, Jack and Buzzie Bavasi had agreed quickly on the terms of his new contract. "I've always been treated fairly by the Dodgers," he told the press, "and I knew I wouldn't have contract troubles this season." His salary was thought to be again around $42,000—about the same as Reese's, but probably still the highest on the club.

He reached training camp with one major personal goal for the 1953 season. Over the previous two years, his batting average had dropped thirty points, down to .308; he was determined to reverse this trend. "I hit a couple of homers late last season and suddenly went homer-nuts," he explained sheepishly; this year he would "forget the long ball and begin work at spraying my hits to all fields." He felt good about the club: "I don't see any team in the National League that compares with us in overall strength."

But even before the camp opened, trouble struck. On February 21, Charlie Dressen announced in Vero Beach that he would move the outstanding veteran Billy Cox from third base, where he was a benchmark player, and make him a utility fielder. ("That ain't a third baseman," Casey Stengel said about Cox. "That's a fuckin' acrobat.") Hearing about his move first from a writer, Cox became upset. His dismay turned to bitterness with the brilliant performance in camp of Jim "Junior" Gilliam, a black Montreal player who had won the MVP award in the International League in 1952. An excellent fielder, Gilliam had also batted .301 as a switch hitter and driven in 112 runs. Dressen wanted Gilliam for the Dodgers, and at second base, Jack's position. A better hitter than either Cox or Gilliam, Jack would move to third base. What was first mentioned to Cox as a springtime experiment now threatened to cost him his job. The fact that Dressen had not been frank with him disturbed Cox some; the fact that Gilliam was black may have rankled him. Although the club had come to accept Robinson and Campanella, the Dodgers were on the brink of fielding the first team in the majors with a black majority. (After what seemed like reluctance, they would do so in July 1954, with Robinson, Campanella, Gilliam, Sandy Amoros, and Newcombe.)

In the New York *Post,* Gross's story on the situation involving Cox, Dressen, Gilliam, and Robinson was ominously titled "Trouble on the Dodgers." Although Jack hated to cater to racism, he knew that the matter had to be settled soon. "I know Cox is upset," he admitted, "but I don't think it's anything personal. . . . I just hope he's not angry at me, and from what I've heard from some of the other fellows, he's not. Someone has moved him out of his position and he has a right to be upset. I don't think it makes any difference to him whether that some-one is white or Negro." Conceding that he was less gifted as a fielder than either Cox at third or Gilliam at second, he offered to play any other position. (However, Jake Pitler ridiculed a reporter's sugges-tion that Gilliam had run Jack off second base: "There isn't a guy in baseball who can run Robinson off second base if he doesn't want to go. He's still the best second baseman in baseball." Robinson had moved to help Gilliam, with whom he roomed for a while, and liked a great deal, and their club.) Mean-while, Bavasi met quickly with the veterans to re-solve the situation and preserve Dodger unity, even as Jack's good friend and club ally Carl Erskine, who would win twenty games that year, assured writers that Brooklyn was just fine: "You couldn't dream up a better relationship than that we have between the white and Negro members of our team."

The controversy had died down, with little resid-ual damage; the Dodger tradition of racial harmony, forged since 1947 in the fires of controversy, met its latest test well. The outstanding playing of the black Dodgers (Newcombe was still in the Army) could not be denied, although Joe Black, the stalwart Dodger reliever of 1952, fell into a slump from which he never fully recovered. But Gilliam, benched at one point for weak hitting, secured sec-ond base, and in the regular season Campanella would hit more home runs, 40, and drive in more runs, 142, than any other major-league catcher to date. Jack himself surprised with his versatility; that year, he fielded five different positions. From his accustomed second base, he made the transition to third smoothly; then, with Gil Hodges wallowing in a batting slump, Dressen moved Jack to first base, his 1947 spot. Next, on May 21, Jack ventured into left field and did so well that thereafter he alternated between left and third. Playing in left field was Jack's idea. "Our outfield wasn't going too good," he said, "and I figured they could get along without me in the infield. It doesn't make any difference to me where I play, so I figured I might as well be where I could do the team the most good." Most likely, he hoped to ease the pressure on Billy Cox.

Robinson's shuttling confused voters for the All-Star Game. "How do you vote Robinson onto the team?" Arthur Daley puzzled. "Is he a third-baseman or is he a left-fielder? The voter has to be specific." After Warren Giles ruled that Jack's proper position, for All-Star purposes, was at third, he came in second in the voting behind the dazzling young home-run hitter Eddie Mathews of the Milwaukee Braves (that year, the Braves had left Boston for Milwaukee).

Although Jack made few efforts to curb his tongue or his fighting spirit, he kept his temper ultimately in check. In July, for example, he and the Cardinals catcher Del Rice seemed ready to come to blows when Rice, irritated by Robinson's griping with an umpire, demanded that Jack "get up there and hit." The two men stood chest to chest, yelling at one another, until Eddie Stanky shoved them apart.

Robinson had a gift for laughing off incidents of this sort, for apologizing if he thought he was in the wrong, for shaking hands and moving on—if sometimes to the next collision. Afterward, he praised Stanky for stepping in, and teased Rice. "I knew there wasn't going to be any fight," he claimed, "because Rice kept his mask on the whole time. He's not going to fight with a mask on."

Not once in his twelve years in professional baseball would Robinson strike another player with his fist. Still, his reputation for violence grew, even as other players crossed the line but kept their reputations largely untouched. For example, Jack seldom went as far as the congenial Campanella went once that year. After being knocked down by two tight pitches from Lew Burdette of the Braves, who then allegedly called him a "black nigger bastard," Campanella advanced on the pitcher brandishing his bat before umpires and other players intervened. (Robinson claimed that Burdette called him, too, a "black bastard.") Nor did Jack ever go as far as his teammate Carl Furillo went on Sunday, September 6, in a game against the Giants. Infuriated at being hit by the pitcher Ruben Gomez, Furillo headed for the Giants' dugout to do battle with Durocher, the Giants' manager, the author of the injury, in Furillo's mind. Knocking Durocher over, Furillo seized his bald head in a viselike grip, then started to strangle him (even as umpire Babe Pinelli advised, "Kill him, Carl, kill him"). At worst, the incident added to Furillo's reputation as a hot-tempered knucklehead. Had Robinson done the same thing—wrestled a manager to the ground and punched him in the head—his career would probably have been in jeopardy.

Virtually all other players were seen as individuals; somehow, Robinson was always a symbol, both an individual human being and also a figment of America's guilty, shame-filled imagination. He was an exception even among the black players, whose conduct in facing the white world, during this first, tightly watched decade of racial integration, ranged mainly from congeniality, on the one hand, to rank obsequiousness, on the other. Only Jackie Robinson insisted, day in and day out, on challenging America on the matter of race and justice.

Not everyone criticized him. Many writers regretted the possibility of his retirement. (In August, when a knee injury benched him for several games, he talked of having "another two or three years to go as a full-time player.") Even a reporter who urged him to give up also saluted him: "He still compensates for his loss of speed with tremendous competitive spirit, lightning reflexes and a profound instinct for being at the right place at the right time." In the New York *Post,* Jimmy Cannon hailed Robinson in a lyrical tribute that stressed his uncanny indispensability to his team. Jack was not as prolific as Ralph Kiner, or a greater hitter than Ted Williams, or as "serenely dependable" as Stan Musial, or possessed of DiMaggio's "languid grace. But you can do more things than any ball player of your time. . . .

You had more ways to beat the other people than any man in your time."

Blessed with outstanding hitting and a balanced pitching corps of Erskine, Meyer, Loes, Labine, and Roe, Brooklyn cruised in 1953 to its most impressive pennant victory ever. Topping both leagues, the Dodgers clouted 202 homers; Snider and Campanella hit 41 and 40 respectively. Five Dodgers, including Robinson, hit above .300, with Furillo leading the majors with .344 and Snider not far behind with .336. On September 12, Brooklyn clinched the pennant by 13 games; they had more wins that season, 105, than any other Dodger team before them. Robinson, too, enjoyed an excellent year. Playing in 136 games, he succeeded in lifting his average from .308 in 1952 to .329 in 1953, with 12 home runs, 17 stolen bases, and 95 runs batted in. Except for his MVP season in 1949, this was his most productive year driving in runs.

For Robinson, as for many of the Dodgers, the World Series offered a challenge he faced with an almost bizarre mixture of confidence and resignation. "If we don't win it this time," he declared, "we'll never win it. We have the ball club this year, the kind of team it takes to beat the Yankees. We have the power, the kind of hitters who can belt the ball out of the park at any time, on any pitch." Brooklyn had all that, certainly; but the Yankees won the series in six games. Yankee power asserted itself in the fifth game, when Mickey Mantle hit a grand slam; and his pal Billy Martin sealed the series victory for the second straight year when he drove home the winning run in the ninth inning of the last game.

In November, joining Carl Hubbell, Stan Musial, and Rogers Hornsby as the only other two-time winners in league history, Roy Campanella won the 1953 MVP award (Gilliam was Rookie of the Year). In the voting for MVP, despite his good year, Jack received only 19 votes to Campy's 297, and he also failed to make the 1953 all-star team chosen by the baseball writers. In the Pittsburgh *Courier,* a gossip columnist took two shots at Robinson. For the second year in a row, he noted, Jackie Junior's birthday party on November 18 was an event "in which the juvenile guests were overwhelmingly members of the majority." Also, "the grapevine claims that a certain Negro star was more than a little agitated because Campanella won the MVP award a second time."

Another unsettling change hit the Dodgers. On October 14, Charlie Dressen, insisting on a two-year contract after three successful years as manager, was forced out by Walter O'Malley, who would not budge from a one-year deal. Dressen's departure sickened Robinson, who thereafter passed up few opportunities to proclaim Dressen the most intelligent and quick-witted skipper he had ever known. (However, the one-year contract would become a Dodger tradition, even as over the following forty-two years, ironically, the team employed only two managers.) Later that month, the popular Dodgers announcer Red Barber also left Brooklyn, to join the Yankees' broadcasting team. More talk was heard of a possible trade involving Robinson. This time, Jack allowed that he would accept a trade, provided that he could stay in New York. "If I am traded outside New York," he said, "I will quit baseball. All my business interests are in New York City and I have too much at stake to leave them."

DESPITE HIS EXPRESS wish never to barnstorm again, the World Series was barely over when Jack set off on yet another month-long tour promoted by Ted Worner. This time, Jack's team broke daring new ground by including three white players. Hodges of the Dodgers and Branca, formerly of the Dodgers and now with the Detroit Tigers, both signed up with Jack, as did second baseman Bobby Young of the newly formed Baltimore Orioles. (Willie Mays, on furlough from the Army, also played in one game for Robinson.) An average of about three thousand fans turned out for the first fifteen games, but twice that number were on hand in Memphis, Tennessee, when Jack found himself the center of an embarrassing dispute. There, as in Birmingham, Alabama, after city officials made clear their opposition to interracial play, his white players sat out the game. Soon, critics accused Robinson of caving in to Jim Crow, which he denied. "I had nothing to do with it," he asserted, "and I certainly didn't bench anyone." He was only the field skipper, he pointed out, not the manager of the team; the white players had stayed away on their own, so as not to disrupt the tour.

Later, in New York, speaking at the Harlem YMCA, Robinson was somewhat more forthcoming and accepted some responsibility for the decision. Conceding that he "may have been wrong," he explained that he had acted as he did "because I thought it was right." In benching the players, or condoning the decision to bench them, he had heeded the advice of blacks and whites alike. In Birmingham, many people were afraid that one candidate running for sheriff, Eugene "Bull" Connor, a race-baiter who would later play a major role in the civil rights movement, would exploit the issue to win the election (Connor was defeated). Clearly rethinking his actions, Jack promised to take another interracial team into the South—and give the entire proceeds to local charities. (Later that year, the ban on interracial play was rescinded in Birmingham.)

Fleeing the South and its benighted ways, Jack returned to the North in time to experience on the evening of November 23 what he freely called "one of the great thrills of my life," when he and Rachel attended a dinner in Washington, D.C., to mark the fortieth anniversary of the Anti-Defamation League of B'nai B'rith. The guest of honor was President Eisenhower, whose speech (noteworthy because it included his first clear criticism, albeit implied, of Senator Joseph McCarthy) was carried live by the four major television networks. In addition to many senators and other prominent politicians, a bevy of Broadway, movie, and television stars—including Lucille Ball and Desi Arnaz, Ethel Merman, Helen Hayes, and Eddie Fisher—lent further glamour to the occasion. For Jack, however, the most memorable moment came following the President's speech, when several of the stars walked up to the dais to shake Eisenhower's hand. Jack himself was supposed to join them but was somehow delayed; when he stood up, the President was already returning to his own seat. But when he saw Jack rise, the President turned around and, with all eyes trained on him, strode between the tables to offer his outstretched hand to a stunned Robinson.

"To think the President of the United States would come halfway across a room just to shake my hand!" Jack told a reporter. Two days later, he was still elated when he wrote to assure Eisenhower that for all the "great privilege" of dining with the President, "it was equally great for me to experience the warmth and sincerity of your handshake in the midst of such an illustrious group of Americans." Such events "make us certain our faith in democracy is indeed justified." The previous year, at a hotel in Chicago during the Republican National Convention, Jack had also met Richard M. Nixon, soon to be elected Vice-President, and had been impressed not only by his warmth but also by his evident admiration for Robinson, who had grown up not far from Whittier, Nixon's hometown. The Republican national leadership suddenly seemed far more attractive to a man who, on his Army induction statement in 1942, had declared his family to be inveterate Democrats.

Late in 1953, Jack's interest in party politics was still limited, but his interest in civil rights was starting to grow. Accordingly, in January 1954 he accepted the chairmanship of the Commission on

Community Organizations of the National Conference of Christians and Jews. Exactly how Robinson became involved in the NCCJ is not clear; but in the era before the bloodiest years of the civil rights movement in the South, the NCCJ offered an engaging profile to many Americans interested in working for religious and racial harmony. Founded in 1928, its first major program defended Alfred E. Smith, a Catholic, and the Roman Catholic Church against defamatory attacks sparked by Smith's run for the presidency that year. In 1934, the NCCJ started Brotherhood Week (usually held in February), which became so prestigious an event that the President usually served as its honorary chair. During the war, despite the global conflict, the NCCJ kept its basic goals in sight; afterward, in 1950, it launched a World Brotherhood organization. By 1954, the NCCJ had established a network of about sixty offices across the United States. That year, recruiting Jackie Robinson to its ranks was a major coup as the conference sought to adapt to an emerging redefinition of brotherhood, one that would emphasize racial justice in the age of desegregation.

In February, accompanied by Louis A. Radelet, an NCCJ official, Jack left New York on an extended lecture tour of a number of towns and cities from Pittsburgh in the East to Los Angeles in the West. For Jack, the tour offered a chance to speak to thousands of people, especially youngsters, about the importance of not only racial tolerance but also religion, education, and family life—his core beliefs. For his listeners, most of whom were white, he probably offered a heady mixture of novelty, glamour, and old-fashioned moral values articulated simply but with evident sincerity. "Education must begin in the home and church and then in the public institutions," Jack told his listeners, as he hammered away at the tragic rise of juvenile delinquency. Young people must practice self-discipline and learn a balanced approach to victory and defeat in sport as in life. "Americans have to learn to lose as well as win," he declared. "It is of utmost importance to learn the values of winning and losing and acquire the virtue of sportsmanship."

Tolerance, he preached, was crucial both to the nation and to each individual human being. "Brotherhood is a big word for a big idea," Jack wrote some time later in an editorial in an NCCJ magazine aimed at the young. "You should be learning to be a good human being and a good American. They're one and the same thing, really. You become a better human being by being a better American. . . . Begin by respecting the other person. Treat him fairly. . . . If you look down on him, you hurt yourself as much as you hurt him. . . . The Big Game is being played every minute of every day of our lives. . . . It requires teamwork, and the first step is for all of us to be the best person we can be."

Nothing he said was profound, but to many listeners Jack's visit was memorable. To one of his hosts, Robinson's "dedication to good human relations, his sincerity of purpose, and his charming and inspiring personality have contributed more to the spirit of brotherhood in Pittsburgh than anything which has happened in a long time." In Tulsa, where Jack also spoke to high-school students, a local official insisted that "I never witnessed more rapt attention to a speaker in a meeting." A Los Angeles leader, praising Robinson's "modesty and deep sincerity," noted the fact that "he is making a most significant contribution to the unity so essential to the survival of our democratic heritage."

Speaking for the NCCJ gave Robinson a sense of satisfaction matched by little that happened at the ballpark. It also exposed the hollowness of his position as a vice-president and director of community services at NBC. Despite a showy office in Rockefeller Center, he was accomplishing little. This was disappointing. The year before, 1953, he had drafted a letter proposing that the network make it possible for him to retire from baseball at the end of the season. Sometimes the network appeared to value him. "Jackie isn't just a ball player," the NBC general manager, Ted Cott, had declared in 1953. "He's a big draw, both as a person and as a symbol . . . and one of our best door-openers." And in December, just before Jack resigned, General David Sarnoff, the head of NBC, defended Robinson after someone complained about an article in *Jet* magazine where Jack appeared to criticize the network. Sarnoff pointed out that Robinson had in fact defended the company and its record in race relations. Robinson would resign, he had told the press, if he ever found NBC deficient in this way.

Nevertheless, on February 4, 1954, he tendered his resignation. Despite some pleasant memories, he knew now "that there is no future for me in the company." His duties were vague, he complained, "despite my willingness to work in whatever area you might assign. Projects which were once begun have long since been forgotten, so that I find myself assigned to individual tasks here and there but never to a job with continuing responsibilities." He did not hide his genuine regret; even as he said goodbye, Jack made a despairing appeal for a more substantial job with the network, which he saw as his ideal employer after baseball. "Nothing would please me more than to find a future with the company," he wrote; he was ready to "give up baseball should there be enough need for me at NBC now and were I certain that a future could be laid before me."

His appeal failed. Jack's resignation was accepted, although he would continue to work with the network from time to time in the coming years. Although his letter of resignation made no mention of Jim Crow, in 1954 it would have been difficult for a black man, even one with Jack's celebrity, to act with authority in an organization almost entirely white. Jack's part-time status also made it hard for him to be effective. But with NBC, as with other organizations, he was determined never to be a mere figurehead, no matter how generous his salary or prestigious the job.

About the same time, his hopes for another fling in Hollywood were dealt a hard blow when William J. Heineman, who had overseen *The Jackie Robinson Story* in 1950, responded negatively to the idea of a sequel to the movie. To the suggestion that Jack might star in a movie unrelated to his life, Heineman was equally cool. However, Jack received some consolation in connection with the screen world. Later that year, a court finally ruled in his suit against Jack Goldberg, the producer who in 1947 had signed a contract with Robinson that promised him $14,500 to make the motion picture *Courage*. After Jack testified about how he had languished in Los Angeles in January 1948 at Goldberg's request, while writers allegedly developed a treatment and a script, only to have the project fizzle, the court ruled in his favor and awarded him the sum of $14,500. Whether Jack ever received all, or indeed any, of this money is not clear.

AT DODGERTOWN IN VERO BEACH, a new manager, Walter Alston, as calm and unassuming as Charlie Dressen was brash and outspoken, awaited Jack and his teammates in training camp. Alston was a baseball journeyman. A former minor-league player in the Cardinal organization, he had followed Branch Rickey to the Dodger system as a farm club player and manager. In Nashua, St. Paul, and Montreal, Alston had helped develop at least fifteen of the current Dodgers, including every black player except Robinson. Campanella, in particular, had flourished under Alston, who once stunned the player by having him manage the Nashua team after Alston was tossed from a game (Campy won the game, with a pinch-hit home run by Newcombe). Robinson, hurt by the firing of Dressen, and calling for Pee Wee Reese as his replacement, was unmoved by such stories. When Alston was named, Jack had no choice but to accept him; but from the start he found the manager's personality flat, his thinking sluggish compared with that of Dressen and Durocher, and his loyalty to management bordering on the slavish.

As Alston would recall later (after Robinson described him as the worst manager he had ever had), their relationship eventually became cordial; but in 1954 Jack tested his new manager by often showing up late for morning calisthenics. "He had a way of finding somebody to stop and chat with," Alston recalled. "After several days, I talked with him about it privately. He didn't like being called on it, but he began to report with the others." Jack also irked him, Alston wrote, by sometimes insolently talking to other players while the manager was addressing the club. But in a contest of wills with his manager, Jack was at a disadvantage. He was no longer, at thirty-five, the magnificent athlete he once had been. His legs hurt now, his knees ached, and the extra pounds clung tenaciously to his midriff. Nipping at his heels was a corps of younger players, notably the twenty-four-year-old Cuban star Sandy Amoros, who had led the league in hitting at Montreal the previous year with .353, including 23 home runs. Jack was the second-oldest star on the club; only Preacher Roe was older, at thirty-nine. (Campanella, Reese, and Billy Cox were thirty-three; Furillo, thirty-two; Hodges, thirty; Newcombe, twenty-nine.)

Moreover, Alston knew that Jack had lost the support of some of his teammates, and had antagonized O'Malley and Bavasi no matter how politely they treated him. The low point of Jack's relationship with O'Malley, until Robinson's departure from the Dodgers, came when the owner not only summoned Robinson to his office in Miami for a dressing-down but also asked him to bring his wife along. Insisting on Rachel's presence was a blunder. If O'Malley expected her to take his side against Jack, to help in disciplining her husband the prima donna—as O'Malley called Jack during the meeting—he was mistaken. Rachel respected O'Malley and admired his wife, Kay; but calling Jack a prima donna lit a fuse in her. "I was pretty angry," she said, "and I told him in no uncertain terms that the charge was ridiculous, that Jack had always put the club above his own interests, that he had always played hurt if he could play at all. I told him that the finest thing about Branch Rickey was not that he brought Jack into baseball but that once he brought him in, Rickey stuck by him. He didn't snipe and carp at him, or allow others to attack him unfairly behind his back. Rickey backed Jack all the way."

Jack's eulogizing of Rickey in the July 1953 number of *Our Sports* widened the breach between himself and O'Malley. In particular, the article included an invidious, and inaccurate, comparison of the two men on the subject of money. Defending Rickey against an ancient libel that he was a cheapskate, Jack insisted that he was more generous than the new leaders in Brooklyn. They were "a fine group of men," but were paying him not "a cent more" than his last salary under Rickey. This charge angered

O'Malley and Bavasi, who assured reporters that Jack's current salary exceeded his last under Rickey by as much as a typical reporter's annual pay. Feebly, Jack conceded that he now earned more than in 1950—but denied that the difference was equal to a reporter's salary, which one source pegged at $6,500. In fact, the difference was probably $6,000; Bavasi's point was valid.

If this error was the fault of a ghostwriter, as Jack claimed, he should have corrected it. If he was underpaid, as perhaps he was (along with most of the other Dodgers under both Rickey and O'Malley), not once had he complained publicly, much less held out for a higher salary, as Doby, Furillo, Branca, and Newcombe, for example, all had done at one time or another with their respective teams. There is also evidence that O'Malley sought to preserve a balanced view of Robinson. When in November Jack played three games in Mexico at the end of a barnstorming tour, and someone wrote O'Malley to praise Jack's "actions, his attitude, and his willingness of cooperation," O'Malley replied scrupulously that "over the years Jackie Robinson has been big league in every respect." Only Robinson's ghostwriters, agents, and promoters had caused concern "on occasion."

Jack's unhappiness with the Dodger management was not softened by conditions in Florida, where the black players continued to stay at the "colored" Lord Calvert Hotel while the white Dodgers enjoyed air-conditioned, beachfront accommodations. In addition, Harold Parrott, the genial traveling secretary for years under Rickey, was gone; Lee Scott, his replacement, seemed less concerned with the griping of Negro players—as did O'Malley and Bavasi, compared with Rickey. On the road, the black players often had to search for a decent place to eat; once, they were reduced to buying a loaf of bread and slices of cold meat at a shop and eating in the streets. This was after white taxi drivers refused to pick them up and they were forced to lug their bags through the streets to a local black "hotel." "It was a dump," a player recalled. "I wouldn't have kept a dog there."

Martin Stone, Jack's manager, recalled trying to have an impromptu dinner with him at a Miami Beach hotel in the early 1950s. "I remember Jack sighing when I suggested it, meaning that we should not try," Stone said; "but I thought, Hey, I'm Jewish, this is Miami Beach, no problem! I called one hotel, very fashionable; I spoke to the manager, told him I wanted to bring Jackie Robinson. Silence. 'Anything wrong?' 'I'm sorry, Marty, but we have a problem.' I asked him if Sugar Ray Robinson hadn't been there with Walter Winchell. 'On the terrace,' he tells me. I hang up on him. I called Grossinger's, spoke to Paul, Jennie's son. 'Bring a black man here, Martin? I don't know what the help would do.' Now *he* hangs up on me! I tried several hotels and got nowhere. Finally I called a man named Walter Jacobs, who ran a hotel that the vaudeville people—Milton Berle, Sophie Tucker—liked. 'Walt,' I said, 'I have a problem. I want to take Jackie Robinson to dinner, but nobody will have us!' 'Give me an hour, Marty,' he says, 'and then come over. I'll see what I can do.' We get there, and the crowd is huge! Photographers everywhere! Walt Jacobs took advantage of the situation, but we got our dinner."

Rachel recalled her own first visit to a "white" Miami Beach nightclub: "Walter Winchell had arranged it. He literally led the way, parted the waters, as Jack and I, Sugar Ray Robinson and his wife, followed him like sheep to his table. It was more tense than fun, but it was another barrier broken."

When Rachel came down, usually with the children, Jack was happy. At the Lord Calvert, a haven for black notables visiting Miami, he proudly showed off his family, or slipped away with Rachel for long walks on the beach; on one stroll that year, he helped her dig up a huge piece of driftwood, which he later shipped north for conversion into a coffee table that she still owned forty years later. In March, he also traveled to Daytona Beach, the scene of their 1946 ordeal. This time, the local *Evening News* hailed the changes Robinson had wrought, "his tremendous contribution to this Nation by widening the racial basis of the sport which we call our national pastime." Jack revisited Bethune-Cookman College for "one of the biggest thrills I have ever had": accepting an honorary degree along with Dr. Ralph Bunche, the winner of the 1950 Nobel Peace Prize for his heroic work of mediation in Palestine for the United Nations. Like Robinson, Bunche had been a star basketball player at UCLA; a brilliant student, he had then gone on to earn a doctorate in history at Harvard. Like most black Americans,

Robinson was proud of Bunche, whose triumphs on the world stage would have been impossible with his own government. "Perhaps the most thrilling event of the entire evening for me," Jack wrote to Bunche, "was listening to your wonderful experiences."

The South was still Jim Crow, but there and elsewhere Jack found some signs of change. In St. Louis, the Chase Hotel finally agreed to permit the black Dodgers to register, if they did not loiter in the lobby, or use the dining room, or swim in the pool. Jack resented these rules, but on April 27, alone among the blacks on the club, he signed the register at the Chase. ("I'm not going to stay there," Campanella declared. "If they didn't want us before, they won't get my business now.") On the next trip to St. Louis, Jack approached Lee Scott and demanded to see the hotel manager. "I want it understood that I'm coming in here just like all the other players," Robinson told Scott. "If I want to have a visitor I'll have one. If I want to eat in the dining room, that's where I'll go." Scott then informed him that all barriers at the hotel were now down. Some time later, the other black players joined him at the Chase.

This breakthrough coincided almost precisely with the single most important event affecting racial segregation in the United States in this century: the decision of May 17 by the U.S. Supreme Court in *Brown* v. *The Board of Education of Topeka, Kansas* that "separate but equal" schools were a violation of the Constitution. That the Chase Hotel gave in before the Supreme Court ruled, and desegregated itself for a baseball team, suggests something about the deep significance of baseball, Rickey, and Robinson in the unfolding national drama about the passing of Jim Crow.

THE 1954 SEASON WAS both the worst by a Dodger team since 1947 and, for Jack, the most fractious and painful of his major-league career. That year, he admitted, "I lost my head more than I ever had in my eight years as a major leaguer." In April, he had announced some lofty goals—to win the National League batting title and MVP award again. Another goal was to break Ty Cobb's career record for stealing home (twenty-one times); Jack now had sixteen. For a while, he seemed on target with both objectives. After he hit two singles, a double, and a home run in a game against Philadelphia, the New York *Post* saluted him: "He ain't what he used to be, that's for sure, but Jackie Robinson can still make the wheels go 'round on occasion." On April 23, Jack stole home on a triple steal, with Amoros and Hodges, in a game against the Pirates that Brooklyn won by one run. In April, he hit .368; in May, .345; in June, .351. Then his season changed. In July, he hit only .211, and struggled as almost never before. In August he recovered, to bat .342. Then he slumped again, even as an assortment of injuries to his legs, ankles, and heels limited his at-bats. Ending the season above .300, he nevertheless drove in far fewer runs and stole far fewer bases than ever before in his career.

But for Jack, his growing notoriety was the main disappointment. Early in June, one of the most serious incidents of his career, at least as it affected his image in the white press and among fans, left him upset. With the Dodgers in Milwaukee to play the Braves, a bitter rivalry enveloped the two teams, not least of all because of a succession of Brooklyn wins in County Stadium. In the current series, one maniacal fan had been caught with a mirror trying to blind Russ Meyer, now a Brooklyn pitcher. Fans drenched Dodger fielders with paper cups full of beer, which was cheap in Milwaukee; the rival pitchers, especially Lew Burdette of the Braves, seemed on the brink of a beaning war.

On June 2, in the bottom of the fourth inning, an apparent counting error by umpire Lee Ballanfant gave a Brave hitter, Johnny Logan, first base on three balls. Jeered mercilessly from the Dodger dugout, an irritated Ballanfant ordered the bench cleared. In the top of the fifth, with Milwaukee ahead 6–2 and rain apparently about to end the game, Robinson, up to bat, felt free to taunt Ballanfant. "Can I get a walk on three balls the way Logan did?" he inquired sweetly. "Get in there and hit," Ballanfant said, "or get out of the game." When Robinson continued his needling, Ballanfant ejected him. Disgusted, Jack turned away and headed for the bench. Near the dugout, he flipped his bat forward, aiming for the dugout; but the bat, slippery and wet from the rain, carried into the stands, where it fell among Milwaukee fans.

Widely reported, the incident triggered a bitter reaction by white fans across the country, although Ballanfant himself assured the league office that Robinson had not acted deliberately or even in anger. According to initial reports, the bat injured no one. (However, almost a year later, on May 11, 1955, an enterprising couple filed a $40,000 damage suit in Federal Court against Jack and the Dodgers claiming that they each had suffered a brain concussion, nasty headaches, abrasions, and cuts after being struck by the bat.) Thereafter, throughout the summer, Jack was booed and jeered at every ballpark he visited; he became what *Sport* magazine later that year called "the most savagely booed, intensively criticized, ruthlessly libeled player in the game." According to *Sport,* "his every appearance on the field was greeted by a storm of boos, by cat-calls, by name-calling. No matter how hard others might applaud in order to balance the scales, Jackie's ears were filled with the roar of the crowd getting 'on' him, giving it to him, needling him, insulting him."

Eventually, Jack would try to give his side of the story in a three-part article called "Now I Know Why They Boo Me," in *Look* magazine early in 1955. This was his own provocative attempt to match Milton Gross's sympathetic essay "Why They Boo Jackie Robinson," published the previous February in *Sport.*

Early in August, Jack found himself in another fracas. This one came after his teammate Clem Labine knocked down the Braves' Joe Adcock with a ball to the head. In retaliation, the Braves' Gene Conley floored Robinson with a pitch that hit him; Jack then got into a confrontation with the Braves' third baseman Eddie Mathews. Again, while several players were involved, the harshest glare fell on Robinson, with the Milwaukee radio announcer Earle

Gillespie hotly denouncing him as "an agitator." This was a damaging remark, with overtones of Communist influence, for which Gillespie later apologized to Robinson privately; according to Jack, he "told me he was 'emotionally upset,' didn't know what he was talking about." (The blow from Conley marked the sixty-sixth time Jack had been hit by a pitch in the major leagues. "If that's a record," he said later, "I'm not proud of it.")

In Jack's battles, he could expect little support from Walter Alston. Their regard for one another, deteriorating through the season, hit bottom with an incident at Wrigley Field in Chicago. In a game against the Cubs, Duke Snider hit a ball that carried to the left-field bleachers, into the hands of fans there, before falling onto the turf. When the umpire ruled the hit a double, Jack stormed from the dugout, screaming that Snider had hit a home run. He was on the field, protesting vigorously, when it dawned on him slowly that no other Dodger was backing him— neither his teammates in the dugout nor Alston, who stood impassively in the third-base coaching box. "Out there alone, with the fans riding me more every second," Jack wrote, "I felt foolish. I wanted to find a hole and crawl into it. The Chicago players in the dugout were enjoying my predicament. One held up his hands to show that the ball had cleared the wall by two feet. If the umpire saw the signal, they gave no sign. I was ignored and they waved the game on." The next day, a photograph showed that Robinson was right; Snider had indeed hit a home run. When a contemptuous crack by Robinson about Alston "standing out there at third base like a wooden Indian" reached the Dodgers manager, the rift between the two men widened.

To many people, Robinson had no tender side worth noting. And yet the same Milwaukee stadium that witnessed the bat-throwing incident also saw the start that year of a warm relationship, entirely unpublicized, between Jack and an eight-year-old boy who brought little to their exchange beyond his hero worship of the ballplayer. The boy was Ronnie Rabinovitz, the adopted son of David Rabinovitz, an attorney and Democratic Party supporter from Sheboygan, Wisconsin. On his father's office stationery, he had written a fan letter to Robinson, who agreed to meet him if he should ever come to see the Dodgers play in Milwaukee, about fifty miles away. Outside the dugout after a game in the spring of 1954, as his father watched, the boy effusively greeted Robinson: "Hey Jackie, I'm Ronnie Rabinovitz. Remember me?" "Sure," Jack replied quickly. "I got your letter." Startled, David Rabinovitz gently objected. "You must get thousands of letters," he said. "You don't have to pretend you remember the one from my son." "I do," Jack responded. "It was the one that was on lawyer's stationery."

Thereafter, Ronnie and his father regularly attended Dodger games in County Stadium, with seats near the visitors' dugout and visits with Jack; less frequently, they met at public dinners, and once, as a grown man, Ron lunched with Robinson in Manhattan. Starting in 1954, also, Jack and Ronnie corresponded with one another, with Jack sending the youngster around twenty letters. Sometimes these letters touched on civil rights and politics, usually with light jabs at the Democrats (David Rabinovitz, an ardent supporter of John and Bobby Kennedy, was rewarded with a federal judgeship in Wisconsin). Mainly Jack wrote about what seemed important to his young friend—from Ronnie's struggle to lose weight to the happy occasions of his bar mitzvah and his graduation from high school. Underneath was a serious aspect; Jack knew that having accepted the boy's trust, he was now morally obliged to him. Once, Jack summed up for Ronnie, as simply and eloquently as he ever did, his own fundamental view of life. "I learned a long time ago that a person must be true to himself if he is to succeed," Jack wrote. "He must be willing to stand by his principles even at the possible loss of prestige. He must first learn to live with himself before he can hope to live with others. I have been fortunate. God has been good to me and I intend to work as hard as I can to repay all the things people have done for me."

This relationship, conducted away from the public eye, boosted Rabinovitz's confidence but also helped, if in a modest way, to sustain and reinforce Jack's own sense of self, his idealism and capacity for human sympathy, which many people did not want to see or would not acknowledge, or was obscured in the heat and dust of competition. To Rabinovitz, the core of their friendship was not its improbability but its solid, concrete nature. "The main thing," he said about Robinson, "is that he was a real man. He was an important big hero in my life and yet he had time to talk to a kid. He had time to visit. I don't know what it was. But right away he liked me and I liked him." In 1972, he would write to Rachel, who knew nothing of the correspondence, about the impact of Jack's courtesy: "I learned from Jackie the true meaning of being a man. I learned how cruel and full of hate some people are to others. I learned never to back down on a cause you truly believe in. . . . I will always cherish those memories and recall the friendship between a man and a boy."

This friendship was part of Jack's lifelong attraction to young people; but his kindness was not limited to youngsters. The writer Roger Kahn would tell of Robinson's immediate show of concern for a young journalist—probably Kahn himself—out of a job when his newspaper suddenly folded, and Jack's care in arranging for the man to be offered some work. Robinson was sensitive again in telephoning Kahn's wife immediately after he found out that she had suffered a miscarriage. "I hope my bringing this up doesn't upset you," he told her, "but I just want you to know that I'm sorry." "That was a particularly sensitive thing to say," she told her husband. "It was a lovely way to say something that I know must have been very hard for him to say at all."

But this aspect of Robinson was lost on many sportswriters, with whom Jack's relationship had now deteriorated badly. Among these was the powerful Dick Young of the New York *Daily News*. Once a Robinson supporter, Young now found much to criticize: Robinson was hypersensitive, too quick to see racism, too grand and independent. Kahn described a chilling scene between the two men, after Young had written an unflattering story about Robinson. In the Dodger clubhouse at Ebbets Field, Young was talking to someone when Robinson suddenly started shouting, "If you can't write the truth, you shouldn't write." As Young continued to speak, unaware that he was a target, Robinson persisted: "Yeah, you, Young. You didn't write the truth." Other players, embarrassed, stared away as the two men shouted at one another. "Ever since you went to Washington," Young screamed about Jack's 1949 HUAC testimony, "your head has been too big!" "If the shoe fits," Jack shot back, "wear it!" The shouting continued until, at last, it was time to play ball.

JACK HAD NOT BECOME ARROGANT, but undoubtedly he had risen in the world. September 1954 found him and his family living no longer in middle-class St. Albans but in a grand house in Connecticut. This house was not Jack and Rachel's, but had been lent to them; clearly, however, the once poor boy from Pasadena was now at home amid luxury. But Jack lived there with a clear conscience; if he was making good money, he had earned it.

About a year before, Rachel had decided that it was time for the family to leave St. Albans for the home they would live in after baseball. "Jack would have been satisfied staying in St. Albans," she said. "I wasn't. The public schools were going downhill, and

I wanted our three kids to go to public schools. I wanted more space, and a better social life for the children. I started thinking about Connecticut, about fresh air and ponds and lovely old stone walls. The whole notion of living in New England seemed good to me, a step up in upgrading our lives."

In moving to Connecticut, race was not an overwhelming factor. In St. Albans, the black presence, as the Robinsons experienced it, was still small. "Most of the black people near us," Rachel said, "had no children, or none the age of Jackie, Sharon, and David. Most of the kids were white. We could have joined a black church, but Sunday baseball made that difficult. So we were not leaving a strongly black environment for a white one. It was not so simple." To many blacks who could afford it, a belief in racial integration and social justice in the mid-1950s demanded precisely such a move. Integration meant living where one wished to live if one could afford to live there. The Robinsons knew they were taking a step that might profoundly alter their lives and those of their children, but were confident that the change would be all for the better.

Accordingly, Rachel began to comb the real estate section of the New York *Times.* "I wanted a view of water," she said. "I wanted beautiful trees. I wanted schools nearby, and good shopping, and a church. I had my dream place all clear in my mind." With a broker, a bubbly white woman, she began to take trips north into Connecticut. Jack never went along; picking a house was Rachel's business. But she soon realized that the task would be harder than she had imagined. A house in Port Chester, on the Connecticut border, seemed exactly right, even if some whites had stared coldly as she walked around the property. But when she boldly offered the asking price itself, the owner pulled the house off the market. In elite Greenwich, Connecticut, the owners of one house refused to show it to her. These snubs angered Rachel, and they riled her even more when she realized that her broker was probably colluding with the owners. The broker was also steering her away from one of the more desirable towns, Stamford, Connecticut. The broker herself lived there.

Then a reporter for the Bridgeport *Herald* got in touch with Rachel. Preparing a series on Jim Crow in housing, the newspaper had been told that Jackie Robinson's wife was meeting prejudice in her attempt to buy a house. "The *Herald* definitely did not hear about it from me," Rachel said. "When I was turned down, I just quietly went away. Brokers told the *Herald;* they also told the *Herald,* apparently, that I wasn't a serious buyer, that I was trying to start trouble—just like Jackie Robinson, I guess." The newspaper decided to target the town of Stamford— "which was unfair," she insisted, "because other towns had been just as tough to get into. But once Stamford was targeted, it had to respond, and it responded well." A group of concerned ministers got together, circulated pledges of nondiscrimination among their parishioners, and called a small meeting, to which they invited Rachel. The meeting was held at the country home of Andrea Simon, the wife of the publisher Richard Simon of Simon & Schuster. Telephoning Rachel, she arranged to meet her at an exit on the Merritt Parkway near Stamford.

Rachel liked Andrea Simon at once; Andrea, in turn, liked Rachel. Energetic, evidently strong-willed and yet sensitive, Simon promised to help Rachel with her house hunting. With four young children herself, she sympathized with Rachel's desire for a better life for her own. Following her to the meeting, Rachel turned up a driveway in front of a beautiful white mansion that sat on over fifty acres of land, with a flourishing apple orchard in the front yard. The meeting with the ministers was pleasant. Murmuring their apologies, the men promised to try to stir their flocks to do their Christian duty.

At the end of the meeting, as Rachel rose to leave, Simon asked her to stay. Next, to Rachel's surprise, a broker showed up, and the three women went off to look at houses. "I think Andrea herself thought that perhaps I was being difficult," Rachel said; "I think she wanted to see what sort of places I was turning down." They inspected five pieces of property. Each owner was willing to sell; but Rachel rejected them all. The broker then played her sixth card: a five-acre spread with the foundation of a small new house already in place. Here, the owner, Ben Gunnar, who was also a builder, was willing to sell. However, not long out of his native Russia and totally dependent on local credit, he feared he might be ruined, blackballed by every bank, if he sold to blacks. His fear seemed reasonable.

The plot of land, on rural Cascade Road, had a rugged look, green but pitted with countless granite boulders and the raw gougings of bulldozers. The parcel for sale was but one portion of an undeveloped tract also owned by the builder. The foundations for the proposed house were dug atop a small hill. Behind the house, at the foot of a slope, lay a pond that could be opened to join another, larger pond that ran the length of the tract. Protecting one flank of all this land was a serene lake, securely fenced off—the town reservoir. "It was perfect," Rachel said. "There and then, I said I wanted it."

A day or two later, Jack drove up with Rachel. "He took a good look at the property and he said, 'Yes, it looks nice. Let's do it.' He had no misgivings about moving. He knew I had a financial plan all worked out already, if we could get a mortgage, and he had no ties to St. Albans. He had no close friendships, no clubs he would miss. Our home was his favorite place, the only place that mattered, and if I could recreate that home somewhere else, and upgrade it, Jack was all for it." In the end, securing a mortgage was easy. "Two very nice brothers named Spelke—they were Jewish—owned State National Bank. 'If you bring the Robinsons here,' they assured Gunnar, 'we'll see to it that they get a mortgage.' We never had to shop around or suffer the indignity of being turned down."

The road was now clear for Gunnar to build the Robinsons a home. He and Rachel quickly settled on the basic design, a split-level contemporary with room for not only Jack, Rachel, and the three children but also Rachel's mother and Willette Bailey. From that point on, progress came slowly. Between

Rachel's soaring ideas about her dream house and Gunnar's own desire to make the house both a labor of love and a showcase for his talents as a builder, delay piled on delay, and expense on expense. The features included walls eighteen inches thick made of cinder block faced by local stone cut individually by hand on the property; a massive stone fireplace with a large headstone dug from the Simons' estate; paneling made of expensive African mahogany; a huge game room complete with a restaurant-size soda fountain; a room with sliding, internally illuminated glass cases to hold Jack's many trophies; and a "mother-in-law" apartment complete with its own kitchen.

By the summer of 1954, Rachel knew that the house would not be ready in time for Jackie and Sharon to start the school year in Connecticut. Then Andrea Simon again stepped in. Her relationship with Rachel had begun to grow and deepen. "She kept in touch with me," Rachel said. "She was fifteen years older but we made a connection across the years. She was instinctive, she felt things. She always wanted to know." Simon offered the Robinsons the use of their summer home over the fall and winter, when her family would be in their main home, in Riverdale in New York City. "Jack and I talked about it," Rachel said. "It seemed an odd way to start our new life. But we were very, very anxious to get the children into school by the start of their year. And Andrea was gracious about it. We accepted." Late in August, just in time for Jackie Junior and Sharon to enroll in schools in Stamford, the Robinson family left 177th Street in St. Albans and moved to Connecticut.

The house in St. Albans went on sale. As news spread of the family's move, and of the luxurious house being built in suburban Stamford, not everyone was happy for the family. In the Pittsburgh *Courier,* a mischievous columnist told his readers that "Jackie denies that he is trying to escape his own race."

BY THIS TIME, the Dodgers had lost the 1954 pennant to the Giants. One reason behind Brooklyn's fall was Roy Campanella; after an operation on his left hand, he had gradually lost all feeling in two of his fingers. He would end the season miserably, with a .207 batting average, 19 home runs, and 51 runs batted in, compared with .312, 41 homers, and 142 runs batted in the year before. The Giants cruised to victory by five games. Their new star, Willie Mays, prodigiously gifted but also the embodiment of boyish joy, hit .345 for the season and won the MVP award. Happy for Mays, Jack joined Durocher in hailing him, controversially, as the finest player now in baseball.

But where Robinson now stood as a player was itself a matter of debate. In some way, his 1954 record was an improvement over 1953. Playing in 124 games, far more than expected, he had batted above .300 (he finished at .311) for his sixth consecutive year, a feat equaled or surpassed by only two other active players, Ted Williams and Stan Musial. But Jack had flopped as a hitter in one crucial area:

he had driven in only 59 runs. "Overall it was his worst season," the Dodger statistician, Allan Roth, judged; "he failed to deliver in clutch situations, and in the clutch games. . . . He did not contribute to winning ball games as he had done in former years and he certainly wasn't the aggressive runner as in the past." That year, Robinson stole only seven bases, compared to seventeen in 1953 and twenty-four in 1952.

Nevertheless, according to Roth, a healthy Robinson could have a "good" year in 1955. But Andy High, the chief scout of the Dodgers, strongly disagreed. Robinson had clearly passed his peak and might drag the team down in 1955. "I would trade him," he wrote, "if he has any trading value."

Jack himself seemed ready to quit—except for the money. With expenses mounting on the house, he needed every penny he could earn. Still, he sometimes looked like a man on the way out. A reporter sent to learn Robinson's plans found the aging Dodger lion sitting in the locker room, fully dressed but gingerly, even daintily, wearing shower slippers on his feet, which were sore and battered from the impact of spiked baseball shoes. As usual, he was frank. "How can I think of retiring now?" Jack asked. "Only injuries could keep me from playing again next year. I couldn't afford it any other way. I've got more expenses now than I ever had before."

In September, the *Courier* predicted that come 1955, Robinson would either be a Pittsburgh Pirate, reunited with Rickey, or retired. (A year earlier, reports had Robinson and Reese on the verge of a trade to Pittsburgh.) Quite apart from Robinson's injuries, the *Courier* reported, Walter O'Malley "is said to be fed up with Jackie's insistence on getting into fights on and off the field, and is reported to have read the riot act to his star." Another newspaper published an account, embarrassing all around, of an incident in a Brooklyn bar in which several Dodger players were overheard deriding and berating Robinson. Gamely, O'Malley dismissed talk of dissension on his club, but Brooklyn seemed in disarray, with Robinson the most disruptive factor. In October, Wendell Smith, once Jack's bravest champion among newspapermen, wrote sadly about his decline. "It is tragic, in a way," Smith ventured, "that his Brooklyn career should end on such a sorry note." In the New York *World-Telegram and Sun,* Joe Williams was certain Robinson would be traded. "Hot or cold," according to Williams, "he goes this time.... Jackie Robinson has gotten himself an upper berth in the Bums' dog-house."

Robinson did not give up on himself. "I want to try and get back in the good graces of the fans next year," he confided to Dick Young. Pressed by Young to explain himself, Jack pointed elsewhere in the club: "I mean I've made my last argument for Brooklyn. I'm going to leave the arguing up to Alston from now on. I decided that in Chicago that day, remember?" Would he like to be a manager? Not really—"I worry about myself, the crowd, the other guys. Managing would give me ulcers." A black manager would come in the majors "eventually," but it probably wouldn't be him. Perhaps it would be Campanella:

"Roy knows the game and men like him. Campy loves the game, too. That's a big point." Jack's point seemed to be that men did not love him, and that he no longer loved the game, not as he was playing it, or not as it was being played.

Weary of playing and fighting, and with no barnstorming chore at hand for the first time in several years, Jack allowed himself to enjoy the glorious autumn of 1954 in New England. At the Simons' estate, the apple trees in the orchard between the white house and the road groaned with ripe fruit, and the air was crisp and clean. Golf had become his grand passion, and here he could play more easily, either as a guest at private clubs or on the municipal course in Stamford. The children, too, seemed to love their new life. Jackie Junior, eight years old that fall, was at Martha Hoyt, a quaint little elementary school with cobblestone walks; Sharon, not quite four, was at a nursery school; David, just past two, stayed at home. The Simons kept a courteous distance. Richard Simon made one impromptu visit, to see what was happening to his house, but Rachel passed the test with flying colors. After inspecting the house from top to bottom, Simon shook his head: "You really are a good housekeeper, aren't you?" "Yes," Rachel replied. "I really am."

A country squire in the making, Jack did not neglect his other commitments. In November, he and Rachel attended the annual meeting of the National Conference of Christians and Jews in Washington, D.C., and he committed himself to a tough two-week, cross-country NCCJ tour in the winter; in

Minneapolis, on January 25, for example, he gave several talks to high-school assemblies and a gathering at a YMCA branch. Jack accepted the cochairmanship of the New York Men's Committee of the United Negro College Fund; a fellow worker was John D. Rockefeller Jr., who praised Jack in November as "one who has himself been a good friend of the Fund for many years."

He was still in demand as a public speaker. At Howard University, at a football banquet, Jack took pains to praise Joe Louis as a hero who had opened doors for other black athletes, including Robinson himself; Louis had just turned in desperation to professional wrestling, as the once-wealthy former boxing champion continued a sad free-fall into poverty. At the invitation of the alumni association, Jack also spoke at Winston-Salem Teachers College in North Carolina. In December, in New York, he appeared on a television program, *Town Meeting,* to help answer the question "How Can We Break Down Community Prejudice?"

Meanwhile, through the fall and into the winter, as Jack kept his distance, Rachel dogged the builder Gunnar's steps, anxious for word that the house on Cascade Road was finished. But she also kept suggesting fresh touches, which Gunnar was only too happy to make; he also made several on his own. At last, on February 16, 1955, with construction still not complete, the various parties gathered with their lawyers in downtown Stamford for the formal closing. Jack and Rachel loved the house, but the event was not joyful. Jack, who had kept his eyes averted while Rachel toiled on the project, was shocked. The basic cost of the house was one thing; it was the long list of costly extras, presented for the first time at the closing by Gunnar, that took Jack's breath away. Unfortunately for Gunnar, his contract with the Robinsons severely limited added costs. "Jack's reaction was horror, horror that this could have happened," Rachel said. "Our lawyers also had a fit. They went after poor Gunnar. I myself got off rather easy, considering I was right there and knew that the costs were running up. But accounting just wasn't Gunnar's thing. We finished the closing, Gunnar looked sad, I felt sad, Jack was dumbfounded."

The base price of the house was $62,000. The extras agreed upon at the closing (only a portion of Gunnar's list) amounted to $28,500. By almost any ordinary standard in 1955, it was an expensive house. Withholding $4,000 for work still to be done, the Robinsons wrote the necessary checks and took legal possession of their home at 103 Cascade Road.

— 12 —

The Bottom of the Ninth

1955–1957

I could see the frustrations he had to endure,
and the battle scars.
—Don Drysdale (1990)

THE BEAUTIFUL NEW HOUSE in Stamford, the challenge of this move to the white suburbs—these factors both elated Jack and weighed on his mind as he left for Florida near the end of February 1955. "I have been proud many times in my life," he wrote Rachel from Vero Beach, "but never as much as when I noticed how happy you are about the house. It is going to be a big responsibility but I have no fear of the outcome." She had been ambitious but could count on his support: "I just want you to know I am with you all the way in the house and am sure you will have as much fun living in it as you had in building it." The children, too, seemed to love their new home, "and that's all any man could ask for." In another letter, about Rachel's health, he made clear how much he depended on her. "I am sure you know why I am so concerned," he wrote Rachel, "but I'll tell you anyway. I depend on you more than the children, Rae. . . . Without you I am nothing."

One reason for his frankness was the fact that, as he prepared for his ninth campaign with the Dodgers, his right to be a Dodger was in genuine dispute. The Dodgers were potent but aging. Over the winter, Bavasi had traded away to Baltimore both Billy Cox, who was Jack's age, and Preacher Roe, who promptly retired. At least one writer was now sure that "Jack would not be wearing a Brooklyn uniform in 1955"—that he, too, would soon be traded. In addition to his diminishing skills, his record of fomenting controversy had made him an uncomfortable presence within and outside the Brooklyn organization. In the winter, Jack's three-part memoir in *Look* magazine, "Now I Know Why They Boo Me," had provoked a storm of indignation. In an open letter to Robinson, J. G. Taylor Spink, editor of the *Sporting News,* accused him of ingratitude to baseball. "Wouldn't it be more fitting and gracious," Spink asked, "if you repaid the game, not only by your playing skill, but by words of good will instead of any bitterness?" Ben Chapman, the former manager of the Philadelphia Phillies, who had given Jack a vicious welcome in 1947, now took umbrage at the implication "that I was a bigot." Robinson was a whiner and a crybaby. "You don't see Furillo, Hodges, Reese and all those other great Dodger players," Chapman pointed out, "writing a story every two weeks on why they're being booed."

Nevertheless, Jack was still wearing Brooklyn blue when training camp opened on March 1— although one reason might have been his recent public announcement that he would retire if the Dodgers "traded him out of New York." With Cox gone, he arrived seeking to take over third base. Although in 1954 he had played seventy-four games in the outfield without an error, "I'd rather play third base than anywhere," he said to a writer. "That's where I'm best fitted, now, I think." But he faced stiff competition from Don Hoak, who was nine years younger than Robinson and at least as aggressive. Jack's position "could depend on Don Hoak," Walter Alston told the press, "if Don wins the job." But Hoak, who had never hit higher than .295 in his career even in the minors, inspired little fear in Robinson. He finished his first day of hard practice quietly optimistic. "I worked harder than ever," he wrote home to Rachel, "and will continue to do so until the training is over. None of my injuries bothered me and my legs had a lot of bounce. I was awful hitting but I'll not worry about that."

He worried, however, about the way his manager saw him. "Alston does not seem any better," he wrote home, "and I am sure he does not want to play me. I'll give him the benefit of the doubt and do the best I can until I see what is happening." In addition, Jack's efforts to be polite with Alston's wife were met with stony rebuffs. "Mrs. Alston still does not speak," he informed Rachel, "and I've made my last gesture. It will be her duty to speak first from here in and if she does fine, if not, who cares." But if he failed with Mrs. Alston, others received him well. "I am getting along with everyone," Jack reported home, "and am sure it will be a pleasant year all around." His strenuous efforts were being noticed. "I have never worked so hard in any training," he told Rachel, "and I am sure it will pay off. All the fellows are talking about it and I intend keeping the pressure up. If Alston has not already decided I am sure I'll be the third baseman. That's the position I am pointing for and must admit I look very good so far (smile)."

After a few days, even Alston seemed to be thawing out. In a private meeting, he assured Jack that "he has only had the very best reports on my condition and how I am working and I assured him all I want to do is help the ball club and will do whatever he pleases. I am sure this year will be much better than last and we will get along very well. I am to do my part and I promise whatever happens there will be absolutely nothing to worry about." Still, Jack found himself competing for playing time not only with Hoak but also with Don Zimmer, another promising prospect. Struggling to get in shape, Jack showed flashes of his old form. In Tampa, before more than five thousand fans (about two-thirds of them black), he got four straight hits, stole home, and befuddled a pitcher into a balk. Marveling at Robinson at thirty-six, a New York writer compared him to Tennyson's Ulysses, a warrior grown old but still restless and indomitable, "made weak by time and fate, but strong in will / To strive, to seek, to find, and not to yield."

But on April 1, in Montgomery, Alabama, Jack lost his poise. Snared in a despondent moment by Dick Young, Jack rashly vented his anger at his manager. "If Alston doesn't want to play me, let him get rid of me," he raged. "When I'm fit I've got as much right to be playing as any man on this team. He knows it—or maybe he doesn't." When a furious Alston asserted that Robinson was injured, Robinson denied that he was. "I've been in shape all spring," he insisted. "I just can't play one day and then sit on the bench for four days and do a good job." His frustration as he saw his career petering out in this way made him lash out. In the *Post,* Jimmy Cannon wrote that "the range of Jackie Robinson's hostility appears to have no frontiers. . . . He is a juggler of a sort, flashily keeping feuds in motion like Indian clubs." Robinson had gone "beyond the borders of competition," alienating "even Brooklyn partisans with his undisciplined protests."

This was an extreme view of Robinson, one promulgated in the newspapers by writers who often both exaggerated his aggressiveness and also refused to admit, much less investigate, the pervasive racism he alone seemed willing to fight in baseball. But to Harold Parrott, writing long after Jack's death about a similar assessment of his state of mind, "this was definitely not the Robinson I knew at all, at all. Or that Pee Wee Reese and Ralph Branca and Carl Erskine knew, and will talk about." To Parrott, Jack had no friends among the owners except for Rickey, and few friends, if any, among the umpires; but almost all the players liked and respected him as a man. Certainly, to new Dodgers, black or white, Jack was usually an embracing human presence, a man who lived the Dodger ideal of family unity. "Jackie Robinson is worth his salary to the Brooklyn Dodgers if he just sits on the bench," the pitcher Roger Craig remarked, shortly after joining the club from Montreal in July. "He took to me the first day I was there." When Craig returned to Montreal to fetch his wife, Robinson not only drove him to the airport but "on the way he talked to me and gave me a lot of confidence. He's as good as you'll find 'em." Such behavior was nothing new for Robinson. This was exactly the way he had welcomed Carl Erskine to the club in 1948. After playing against him in Fort Worth, Texas, when Erskine was in the minors, Jack had sought him out to praise his pitching. "I was totally suprised when he came over and asked for me," Erskine recalled. "It was such a fine thing for him to do, it really boosted my confidence." Then, when Erskine joined the Dodgers in the middle of 1948, Jack "bonded me to him by the enthusiastic way he greeted me the first day. He stuck out his hand and was very warm; he totally believed in me and my ability."

The pitching prospects Don Drysdale, Sandy Koufax, and Tommy Lasorda each would recall the warm welcome extended by the most embattled Dodger. In part, this was a Dodger tradition. "No matter who you were," Drysdale wrote, "if you had a Dodger uniform on, they made you feel like you were one of them—like part of the family, the Dodger family." But no one seemed to believe in this spirit more than Robinson did—although Drysdale recalled him also as "an awfully intense man. I could see the frustrations he had to endure, and the battle scars." Insulted everywhere, Jack had to walk a fine line: be aggressive, "because that was his style," but

At home, 1952, with (from left) David, Sharon, Jackie Junior, and Rachel

Relaxing on the road with (from left) Dan Bankhead, Don Newcombe, and Roy Campanella

Jack spoke often for the National Conference of Christians and Jews.

With nephew Teddy Walker, as Jack's mother, Mallie, looks on at her home, 133 Pepper Street, Pasadena.

With Reese, team captain and loyal ally

With Walter and Kay O'Malley at the Dodgers' pennant victory dinner, 1952

Farewell to Ebbets Field, January 7, 1957

Chock Full o' Nuts opening: with his boss, William Black, the company owner

Raising money for the NAACP

With NAACP leaders Thurgood Marshall (center) and Roy Wilkins

On the slopes at Grossinger's— Jack's first and only try

With close friend Marian Bruce Logan

An extraordinary greeting by President Eisenhower, November 1953

Campaigning with Richard and Pat Nixon, 1960

With (from left) Hubert H. Humphrey, Elston Howard of the Yankees, and champion high jumper John Thomas, at a Harlem YMCA awards ceremony

**As a special assistant to New York Governor
Nelson Rockefeller**

With Rachel, outside their home in Stamford, Connecticut

With (from left) boxer Floyd Patterson, Dr. Ralph Abernathy, and Dr. Martin Luther King Jr

With Branch Rickey at Jack's Hall of Fame induction ceremony, July 23, 1962. Mallie Robinson is in the background.

David (ten), Sharon (twelve), and Jackie Junior (sixteen) at Grossinger's, 1962

At a bombed black church, Georgia, 1962

After some contentious public debate, a truce: with Malcolm X and Harlem bookseller Lewis Michaux, at a Chock Full o' Nuts counter, Harlem, 1962

At the construction site of the Downstate Medical Center, Brooklyn, 1963

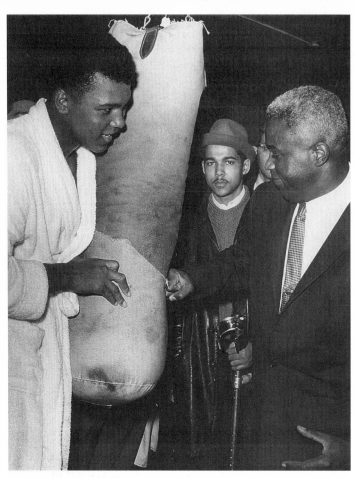

With Cassius Clay, later Muhammad Ali, March 11, 1963, New York City

Serenaded by an SCLC youth choir on an integration drive, June 15, 1964, St. Augustine, Florida

With Eleanor Roosevelt

Celebrity golfing with (from left) famed quarterbacks Otto Graham and Don Meredith, and Joe DiMaggio, March 1968

With boyhood friend and Los Angeles County Supervisor Warren Dorn and Willie Mays

At an antidrug block party in Harlem, August 10, 1970

With Jackie Junior, speaking out against drug abuse, April 1971

At the concert for Daytop, June 1971, a few days after Jackie Junior's death, with Daytop leader Kenny Williams and the Rev. Jesse Jackson.

Jack's best friend, Jack Gordon, and Bernice Gordon, with their grandchild Jill

Rachel's brother Chuck Williams and his wife, Brenda

With basketball star Bill Russell, 1971

Jack in tears, with Rachel at a testimonial luncheon, 1972

The last hurrah—in Cincinnati for the World Series, October 1972: with (standing, from left) Sharon Robinson Mitchell, Joe Mitchell, Rachel, and David; Zellee Isum is next to Jack.

At the World Series, 1972. From left: Joe Reichler, Bowie Kuhn, David's friend Patricia Hammock, and David; from right, Larry Doby, Joe Black, Peter O'Malley, and Charles Feeney; behind Jack: Sharon.

Jack's funeral cortege on 125th Street in Harlem, en route to Brooklyn, October 27, 1972

also "sit there and take a lot of crap. Try that some-time. . . ."

Jack's unhappiness with Alston continued right up to the start of the season. Robinson was hardly alone. Russ Meyer publicly complained about being ignored. Campanella, fighting back after his terrible 1954 season, revolted against being asked to bat at number eight. "That's fine encouragement he's giving me," Campy snarled to a writer, "having me hit with the batboy." But, miraculously, none of this squabbling mattered once the season started. Of their first twenty-five games, Brooklyn won twenty-two, including the first ten (a National League record); less than one month into the season, the Dodgers led by ten games. The heroes were numerous, including Carl Furillo, who hit seven home runs in the first two weeks; but Robinson also shone. On opening day, in the sixth inning, he prevented a sure double-play by craftily allowing a grounder (by Campanella) to hit him as he ran the bases. He was automatically out, according to the rules, but Campanella also had a hit, under the rules, and the double play was avoided. The cheeky shrewdness of the play was widely noted. "Robinson Can Still Do It All," the New York *Post* proclaimed. "I didn't think of it before," Jack said coolly. "It just happened and there's nothing in the rule book to prevent it."

The ten-game opening streak ended with victories by the Giants in games marked at times by brutal intensity. As usual, Jack was at or near the center of action. Beaned by a pitch in a game against the

Phillies, he was thrown at again first by Jim Hearn and then, on April 23, by Sal Maglie of the Giants. Looking for revenge against Maglie, Jack went perhaps further than he intended. Laying down a bunt, he hoped that Maglie would rush to cover first, where Jack would try to level him. Instead, when the second baseman, Davey Williams, raced over to take the throw, Jack barreled into him. Williams was hurt but Robinson was unrepentant. "I got nothing against Williams," he told the writers. "Maglie was the one I wanted to get even with." Sure, he had seen Williams come over, but decided, "Heck, I'm not going to get out of his way; let him get out of mine."

Although Jack would never admit that Alston was an astute manager, he was not above defending him. Early in May, he sided with the Dodger brass when a frustrated Newcombe, without a complete game in three starts, was suspended and fined by Bavasi for refusing to pitch batting practice. (A few days later, a contrite Newcombe tossed a one-hitter against the Cubs.) When a writer saw racial turmoil in the complaints of Robinson, Campanella, and Newcombe, Jack hurried to disagree. In a letter to a columnist, Bob Quincy, Jack was blunt: "Sportswriters in general have been very fair and I certainly hope they are not going to make any racial trouble on our club. I had my say but Walt Alston will tell you, I am sure, my first interest is the ball team and if I felt I could not help it win I would be the first to tell the manager." Elsewhere, he dismissed as "a lot of baloney" the charge that Dodger infighting was out of hand. "How can this club keep winning like it has if there is trouble?" He admitted "a great deal of scrambling for jobs," but saw it as "a healthy thing."

In May, Jack made good on his promise to tell his manager if he could not help the club. With his batting average at .244 and sinking, he asked Alston to bench him. "I'm doing as lousy as I've ever done," he conceded to reporters. "I can't seem to do anything right." Hoak replaced him, but also struggled at bat; Alston then decided to give Robinson his chance to nail down third base. Praising Jack's all-around play, he stressed his versatility as a hitter and his disruptive base running: "On top of it all, there is that terrific competitive spirit which keeps the entire club going." The move paid off; over the following month, Jack batted .328. Later, in the *Courier,* Ric Roberts spoke of Robinson's almost magical ability to inspire victory. As "the owner of psychic, spiritual force" that lifts his teammates, Robinson exemplified the "key guy, the very essence of truculence and heroism, whose reassuring presence paves the way to collective poise and confidence and eventually to a team victory." Roberts approvingly quoted another sportswriter, Bill Corum of the New York *Journal-American:* "Jackie is the pressure valve on the pressure cooker."

By mid-season, however, Robinson was back on the bench as often as not, hobbled by knee and ankle problems even as Brooklyn forged ahead. For the first time since 1949, he was not voted to the All-Star team. He was assuredly on the way out. But the following month, August, he took some consolation as a few sportswriters noted the tenth anniversary of his first interview in 1945 by Rickey. Now, almost forty black men played in the majors. The Boston Red Sox, the Philadelphia Phillies, and the Detroit Tigers still held out, but integration seemed irreversible, not least of all because of the high quality of these black players. With Campanella, Robinson, Doby, and Monte Irvin still epitomizing the brilliance of the pioneers, a number of sensational younger players, notably Mays, Henry Aaron, Ernie Banks, and the rookie Roberto Clemente, had built on that foundation. "The Negro player is no longer a novelty," the Chicago *American* noted. "The clubs that haven't any on their rosters are the novelties." (On the Yankees, Elston Howard, a catcher playing the outfield because of Yogi Berra's brilliance, had integrated the team.)

As the season drew to a close, Robinson enjoyed a stretch of inspired playing that helped forestall any notion of a Dodger collapse like that of 1951. "It's just that I made up my mind to go out there and hustle," he told the press. "I didn't expect to have the success that I did, but I felt if I started running, the others might take the cue. You know something? It worked." On September 8, leading the second-place Milwaukee Braves by eighteen games, Brooklyn clinched the pennant. No National League team had ever won the pennant at an earlier date.

Once again, they faced the Yankees in the World Series. Should Alston start Robinson? "Jackie Robinson was born to play and excel in the awful pressure of a World Series," Leo Durocher declared. "The Dodgers are not yet ready to win without him, no matter what the calendar says. Keeping the amazing leadership that is Robinson's on the shelf would be like pinch-hitting for Ruth in the clutch." Jack's physical gifts were fading, but his passion to win was as intense as ever. With an unflagging stream of chatter, with quips and barbs and taunts and insults, as well as a constant pushing forward of himself to center stage, he urged the Dodgers on.

In the first game, after the Yankees' Billy Martin was thrown out trying to steal home, Jack stole home himself (for the eighteenth time in his career). However, Brooklyn lost that game, and the next. Back at Ebbets Field, Jack again roused the crowd in the third game with his flashy base running; once, luring Elston Howard into throwing behind him, he turned a likely double into the most nonchalant of triples. With the same fierce hitting that had accounted for more than two hundred Dodger home runs for the second consecutive year, Brooklyn swept the three home games. In Yankee Stadium, the team lost the sixth to tie the series. Again the Yankees seemed poised to prevail. But in the seventh, behind the superb pitching of Johnny Podres and a fabulous running catch by Amoros followed by a relay via Reese to Hodges at first for an amazing double play, the Dodgers won the World Series for the first time in team history.

Although Jack did not play in the last game, veteran writers praised him lavishly. "His hair is gray," the Boston *Globe* noted. "His body is almost portly. And he can't run the way he did in his days in the Negro league." But "he showed his teammates, he showed his opponents, he showed a nation—that the Dodgers can beat the Yankees." "Aging Robinson Sets Dodgers Afire," headlined one newspaper after the third game. "Perhaps never in the history of the World Series," the broadcaster Harry Caray declared, "has one man played such a unique role as has Jackie Robinson this year." Through "the inspiration of his own play . . . his own daring and imagination," Robinson, as if carrying on "a personal crusade," had succeeded at last "in breathing life into a Dodger team which from the start of this series seemed destined for the embalmer." The Yankees, confident about beating Brooklyn, found out "they could never whip Robinson."

Just before quitting Yankee Stadium after the last game, Jack shook hands with Alston. If the two men had seen in one another "a competitor for control of the team's soul," as one writer put it, this was no time for recrimination. "I want to tell you I sincerely appreciate being with you this year," Robinson had assured Alston. "I've had my differences with Walt," he told the writer, "but I want to pay tribute to him. I've gotten a big kick out of the way he handled the series." Then, accompanied by the Dodgers announcer Andre Baruch and his wife, Bea, Jack and Rachel headed to Grossinger's in the Catskills for a vacation. Here Jack could unwind, play golf, and mull over his likely future, if he had any, with the Dodgers. Playing in only 105 games (19 fewer than in 1954, 51 fewer than his MVP year, 1949), he had hit a mediocre .256, forty points under his previous low, which was his rookie year of 1947. Driving in only 36 runs, he had stolen only twelve bases (although he had only seven in 1954). He was in no position to demand much from the Dodgers. "I'll talk with the ball club," he advised the New York *Post.* "It's up to the club. I'm going to do what they want. I want to play for them. With the world championship and all, they may not feel so badly toward the old boy."

Especially because of the new house, he needed the money (his World Series winner's share, $9,768.21, certainly helped here). Jack also wanted to benefit fully from a new player-pension plan that could mean, as he told Rachel, an extra $300 a month in his retirement checks if he played again. Still, at Robinson's prompting, his advisor Martin Stone was looking for the right job for him after baseball. But opportunities were severely limited for a man like Robinson. The columnist Jimmy Powers wrote the obvious: Jackie Robinson would probably make an excellent manager. In the *Post,* Milton Gross urged the Dodgers to hire him as a television announcer, paired with the outstanding Vin Scully; Robinson and Scully liked each other. But both jobs depended on O'Malley and Bavasi, and Jack probably knew that he could not expect their support.

RETURNING HOME, he looked forward to a relatively quiet winter. Despite his resignation as a vice-president, he now appeared twice a week on NBC's Channel 4 in New York. On Mondays at 6:30 in the evening he interviewed high-school students; on Friday nights his sports program followed the weekly fights. As always, he was a frequent visitor to the Harlem YMCA, and he also continued to work with the National Conference of Christians and Jews. On December 7, on behalf of the Canadian NCCJ, he arrived in Calgary for a two-day visit, including visits to high schools and a speech that night at an annual banquet. Dressed in a sleek charcoal-gray suit, his handsome dark face set off by silvery hair, Robinson was an impressive figure. He spoke easily and well, with just the right mixture of humor, sports talk, and somber commentary that ended in his righteous plea for social unity. To reporters, he gave frank answers. Who was the better manager, Alston or Dressen? Dressen, who "was always a couple of plays ahead of the other guy." Who was better, Mays or Snider, his teammate? "Willie is the best. No one can play with the kid. He does everything well." As for himself, he believed he had another year left in baseball. He would accept a trade, but "I won't play for any team in the American League unless the offer is very attractive."

A few days later, the local writers were startled to receive a gracious letter of thanks from Robinson. "Such a gesture proves what most of us thought," a journalist wrote in the Calgary *Herald,* "that Robinson is a high-class individual—for few athletes take the time to express their gratitude the way Jackie did." Jack had grown in graciousness, but he also had a special feeling for Canada that dated back to 1946. A few weeks later, Jack returned for the annual celebrity dinner of the Ontario Sports Writers and Sportscasters, to raise money for the Ontario Society for Crippled Children.

These visits, which forced Jack to talk before a foreign audience about race relations in the United States, came against a background of deepening crisis across the South, a crisis that troubled and challenged him. Six days before Jack's banquet address in Canada had come the first distinct act of community resistance by blacks in the South in the wake of the Supreme Court school desegregation decision of May 1954. On December 1, a middle-aged black woman named Rosa Parks, boarding a bus in Montgomery, Alabama, sat down quietly but by design in an empty seat toward the front of the vehicle. When she refused to yield her place to a white man, as the law required, the police arrested her. The next day, local black leaders called for a boycott of bus services by their community. Assigned to lead the boycott was the young, moderate pastor of the Dexter Avenue Baptist Church, Dr. Martin Luther King Jr. In charge of negotiations with the city was another pastor, Dr. Ralph Abernathy.

The blacks in Montgomery did not want much. They were not seeking an end to segregation on the buses. Seating for blacks and whites from the rear and the front, respectively, would continue, but with no restraint on the number of seats blacks could claim. They also wanted black drivers hired for routes serving their community. However, city officials, declaring these requests radical and impermissible, broke off negotiations. On February 26, 1956, almost one hundred blacks, including Dr. King, were indicted for conspiracy to promote an illegal boycott. On March 22, King was sentenced to prison, but avoided jail by paying a fine of $500. The NAACP, which hitherto had stayed out of the dispute because the boycotters condoned segregation, took the case to the federal district court. In June, the court ruled against the city, which promptly appealed to the U.S. Supreme Court. But in November, the Supreme Court upheld the district court ruling and declared bus segregation unconstitutional. The following month, a year after Rosa Parks's action, blacks ended their boycott when the city agreed to abide by the ruling.

"The more I read about the Montgomery situation," Jack wrote Rachel from Florida during the boycott, "the more respect I have for the job they are doing." The boycott mirrored almost exactly his own single most dangerous act of protest against Jim Crow—in July 1944, when he had refused to move to the back of the bus at Camp Hood in Texas. Without knowing it, at that moment he had placed at risk everything he would later become in life. Now, twelve years later, with his life utterly transformed, what was to be his role in the worsening crisis? Like most blacks and their liberal white allies, he hoped for a peaceful acceptance of the rulings of the Supreme Court and an orderly restructuring of the South. Some signs were positive. In February 1956, for example, just before reporting for spring training, he played in a celebrity golf tournament that marked the first time that blacks had been allowed on the Miami Springs Golf Course for more than one day at a time. And because of Robinson and Newcombe, another Miami course, the Bay Front Golf Course, opened its facilities to blacks for daily use for the first time in its history.

But such tokens of progress mocked the reality of Jim Crow for the masses of blacks. The previous year, 1955, had been a time of violence and terror, as well as of bitterly contested moves on the part of the NAACP to engage white power. Once again, lynching had become a feature of Southern life. In Mississippi, two black leaders involved in voter registration drives were killed as part of a campaign of terror designed to gut the electoral rolls of black voters. Also in Mississippi, in perhaps the most brutal incident of the year, a fourteen-year-old boy, Emmett Till, visiting from Chicago, was murdered by white men for allegedly whistling at a white woman. Across the South, several school districts agreed to try to desegregate; but intransigence ruled in many more places. In Jack's native Georgia, for example, the board of education voted to revoke the license of any teacher who belonged to the NAACP or who taught a class made up of different races.

Committed to working with the NCCJ, Robinson could not help recognizing that the conference was nowhere in the forefront of the fight that mattered most to him—the concrete struggle of blacks for their civil rights. Compared to that struggle, the moral and ethical goals of the NCCJ seemed almost flighty. He began to take a growing interest in the NAACP, whose lawyers, including men like Charles Houston and Thurgood Marshall, had led the fight against Jim Crow with skill and courage. In April 1955, even as he made ready for the new season, Jack denied a published report that he was in line to become executive secretary of the organization, following the death of his friend Walter White, the blond, blue-eyed Atlanta-born Negro who had led the organization since 1931. How such an idea came to be floated is unclear; as yet, Jack had only modest ties to the NAACP. But Robinson probably dreamed from time to time of having such a job, a position of authority in which he could bring to the civil rights struggle the bravery and dedication he displayed almost routinely on the baseball field. (White's successor was Roy Wilkins, a veteran NAACP journalist and executive long recognized as White's heir apparent.)

Sports provided Jack a bridge into the civil rights world. In Chicago in January, speaking to a black sports organization, he attacked the governor of Georgia for trying to pull Georgia Tech's football team out of a postseason game because its opponent, the University of Pittsburgh, had a black fullback. Jack called on other Southerners to speak out against such moves, to say "this is not what we want, that we don't share this belief." He had faith that most right-thinking white Southerners would stand alongside other Americans, black and white, against such bigotry. "I am awfully proud of the progress we have made," he declared, "and we are going to make our way, regardless of a few bigots. I don't believe the people who are responsible for this progress are going to let these few hold us back."

In training camp, Jack tried to set aside his deepening concern about the civil rights movement and concentrate on the main business at hand—the 1956 pennant race. Riding high from their World Series triumph, Alston and Bavasi took pains to make Robinson feel wanted. When Jack approached the general manager about securing a personal loan of $5,000 from the club, Bavasi agreed promptly to the request. "He then told me," Jack wrote Rachel, "that Walt talked with him and said how pleased he was with everything. He said the way things are going I am the most valuable man on the team and hoped everything would go on as it is now. I really felt good about it because he seemed so sincere and asked me to keep it going just as it is now. Of course I promised, because I felt things were going well and to hear Buzzie say it makes me feel all the better."

But Jack soon snapped out of this reverie. Challenging him now for the third-baseman spot was a potent threat, acquired over the winter: the former Chicago Cub Ransom "Randy" Jackson, who had hit twenty-one home runs in 1955. Jack greeted Jackson pleasantly but recognized the challenge. "I am not worried in the least about Jackson," he wrote home nervously to Rachel, "and I'll play as long as my legs and body hold out." Not everyone—he fretted about Duke Snider—was pulling his weight: "Duke has not worked very hard in training and is really out of shape. I hope he starts to realize this and decides to go to work. His condition can make the difference between a fast or a slow start." As for pitching, the loss of young Johnny Podres to the Navy meant "we

are in dire need of a left hander who can do a job."
The right-handers "have all looked good" but aside
from Sandy Koufax, still a promising prospect, "that
seems to me what we have. Thank goodness for
Labine and [Don] Bessent, they must have good
years again."

Clearly Jack was shaky about his own place with
the club. "Except for myself," he admitted to a
reporter, "I don't think any of the regulars is past his
peak." But his teammates seemed to be supporting
him. "I really have been hitting well," he wrote
home, "and all the fellows are on my side; at least
some have said as much." Robinson's sense of team
play was so strong that he was actually solicitous
about his rival Jackson—up to a point: "It is a shame
to see the way Randy has been playing but he's
surely a better ball player than he has shown." But his
main concern was himself: "I know that if I can keep
it as it is now there is no doubt as to who is going to
play. Of course a couple of games don't mean much
but at least it has given me a lot of confidence." Still
later, he admitted that his hitting needed to improve
but "I have been moving well as you probably have
heard and am really very satisfied with the progress I
have made. The club is just about ready. Duke is
beginning to hustle and the pitching seems to be
perking up some."

Although he tried to concentrate on baseball, a
number of distractions, from Jim Crow to some
teammates he now found tiresome, irked him. For
blacks, Vero Beach was a barren place; segregated
Miami, where blacks stayed at the mediocre, "col-

ored" Lord Calvert Hotel, was only slightly more diverting. Travel was often humiliating, with the black Dodgers barred from the team hotels, forced typically to sleep at night on Brooklyn's private train. Down south, both blacks and whites at times tried his patience. "This is one real bad town," he wrote at one point about a stopover in a segregated hotel. "There is absolutely nothing to do here. I have been to the movies once and am going again this afternoon. It's like the worst we saw in Daytona Beach and the odors are terrible. It seems the fable about Saturday bathing is true here because it would take at least that long to get as much of an odor as some carry." Folks seemed hopelessly backward: "It will take a tremendous educational job to get a lot of the people to understand just what is needed to get the ball rolling properly." During a game in Mobile, Alabama, whites assailed Jack with insults. "From the very first pitch the fans started," he wrote home; "one fellow right in back of our dugout said something about taking it to the supreme court and I looked up and said why not stop fighting the civil war and start being a real American. It went over well as nothing was said. The names we were called convinced me Alabama is no place for me because I would get into serious trouble. . . . The sooner we leave the south the better all around."

The charms of the locker room had also worn thin. Jack thought of his home in Stamford and had a hard time picturing some of his teammates there. "The fellows are all very nice," he wrote Rachel once, but "actually there are only a very few that I would like to socialize with." Sometimes he became "real disgusted with the attitude and actions" of his teammates. "I cannot for the life of me understand," he informed her, "why they use the floors of the club-house for a spittoon. It makes you wonder about their home life." Among his white teammates, whom he saw only sparingly outside baseball, Jack liked and admired Hodges, Branca (no longer a Dodger but still a friend), Erskine (perhaps "the most refined of the bunch"), Labine ("also very intelligent"), and Reese ("a fine team man"). But with several other white players he had little in common. As for the blacks—they were "really nice but I don't believe would make an evening very entertaining." Often fastidious about morals and manners, Jack detested womanizing and deplored sloppy personal habits. Overhearing a teammate telephone home, "I had to laugh to myself the other morning," he wrote Rachel. "He said hello and his wife asked who it was." The fellow spoke poorly but would not take the trouble to learn ("But he is really a nice kid," Jack continued. "I'll not say more about the others.").

He took pride in spanning the social and intellec-tual divide. Curiously warm to his fellow Dodger Billy Loes, who seemed interested mainly in cards and sex and little else, Jack was also proud of his more intellectual friends, including journalists like Edward R. Murrow, Roger Kahn, and Ed Sullivan, and the bridge master Charles Goren. Although he read few books, they did not intimidate him as they surely did many of his teammates, and Jack had grown adept at composing lucid little essays and speeches to reflect his simple but strong ideas about social justice. Not many professional athletes could claim the same interest or ability, or share Jack's sense of accomplishment in, for example, contributing an essay, "Free Minds and Hearts at Work," to Edward R. Murrow's 1952 volume *This I Believe: The Living Philosophies of One Hundred Thoughtful Men and Women in All Walks of Life.*

If one teammate, above all others, tested him, it was Campanella. As the Pittsburgh *Courier* once intimated, Jack may well have become envious of Campanella's spectacular success in baseball. (Coming back from a dismal season, in 1955 Campy won the MVP award in the National League for the third time.) Tension between the two men dated back at least to their barnstorming tour of 1949, when Campy discovered that Jack was earning more than he was. By 1955, the teammates had become estranged. That spring, when Campanella allegedly ridiculed Robinson to a visiting stranger, Robinson angrily appealed to Bavasi in order to avoid confronting Campanella. Little about his teammate off the field pleased Robinson, from Campanella's thriving liquor store in Harlem to his alleged weakness for women. (According to Martin Stone, "one major reason Jack wanted to quit baseball had to do with women. 'You know,' he told me, 'When I go out on the road, all these women are after me. I'm not interested in them. Get me something, I can't go on this way.' " To the Baltimore *Afro-American* writer Sam Lacy, Jack had "a cleanliness to his character that I admired. I remember once in the early days we were

playing cards in a hotel room in Miami, and somebody brought two white women in and Jackie just got
up and left right away. I suppose that was just his
nature.")

Robinson was sure that Campy begrudged him
his greater fame. Lacy agreed: "Campanella resented
Jackie. I think it was mainly because Jackie was dark
black, or smooth black, and Campy had the swarthy
Italian complexion. Whenever there was a group of
[black] people who came to circle around us, they
always went to Jackie. They'd run past Campanella,
and I think he resented it. Jackie was a symbol, Campanella was a maverick, a hybrid. They went to
Jackie, because he was theirs. Campanella was mar-
ginal, because of his name and skin color." Indeed,
this factor probably contributed to Rickey's choice of
Robinson over Campanella, who was at least as gifted
a player. Robinson, with his college career, his Army
commission, his record of protesting Jim Crow, and
his jet-black skin, was probably far more Rickey's
idea of what the first Negro player should look like—
and what he thought black Americans would want the
first to look like—than Campanella. In any event,
laboring under such unfair pressures, the two stars
came to resent one another. "It seems Campy has a
girl here," Jack wrote Rachel once, after the catcher
and Junior Gilliam almost came to blows, "and the
fellows keep kidding him about her and it has gotten
under his skin. . . . Camp is always kidding the other
guys but can't take it himself. I am sure one of these
days there is going to be some trouble. Thank God I
am not getting involved. The more you see of Camp

the less you like him. To me he's like a snake ready to strike at the best possible moment. Of course I am ready but am avoiding any fracas."

To Campy's son, Roy Campanella II (a student at Harvard College in the late 1960s, and a militant intellectual about whom Robinson would write admiringly), his father certainly detested racism as much as Robinson did. "Jackie Robinson was a bright, highly sensitive man," he said, "whose every fiber worked all the time in his outrage at the monumental injustices that black people faced because of the color of their skin. But it was more important to Dad to neutralize the rage, to turn bitterness into a productive and enjoyable life. Dad was always saying to me, 'Let's go fishing' or 'Let's go to the ballpark,' and I know that he was trying then to instill in me the idea that life was to be enjoyed no matter what happened. He always tried to be upbeat, and his motto in dealing with the injustices of the world was that living well was the best revenge. But he, too, felt the injustices keenly. You can be sure of that."

Careful also to avoid "any fracas" with the press, Jack bit his tongue in March when Dick Young wrote provokingly that Alston was playing Robinson and Jackson at third base, rather than young Don Zimmer, because the club had to justify their large salaries. Furious, Jack was careful not to explode. "I resented Dick Young's column but didn't say anything to him," he let Rachel know. "He probably noticed my coolness when he talked with me but nothing was said. . . . I did not mind him praising Don but did resent the reflections he cast as far as I am concerned. Say I am a lousy ball player but not that my salary keeps me on the job. As I said before let him write and if I can keep my weight and feel as I do now nobody will stop me."

Throughout the spring, his main relief from the sweat and strain of the hot days and the boredom and emptiness of the evenings and nights was the thought of his home in Connecticut, and especially Rachel there. In his letters, Jack's yearning for her had an unmistakably plaintive edge. "My Darling, I can't tell you how much talking with you eases my loneliness," he wrote once.

> It is so nice hearing your voice as it makes me feel you are closer to me and I don't feel so bad as I did before talking with you. I can hardly wait to be near you so I can hold you in my arms and love you like I have been wanting to do all the time I have been away. When you told me you were snowed in I [en]visioned our being together and loving each other as we so often do. I could feel your warmth and my darling I need to love and caress you tenderly as I have really missed being away. My only solution to this point has been my desire to get into as good a condition as possible and to try not to think too much about being away. It has worked to a certain extent but I miss you too much not to think about [you] every day all day. . . .

The 1956 season, Robinson's last, was both another triumph (Brooklyn's sixth pennant in his ten years with the team) and a sometimes somber, even depressing experience that hastened his departure from the game.

Hovering over the season was the specter of the demise of major-league baseball in Brooklyn. In 1950, Walter O'Malley had faced squarely the reality that Ebbets Field was, on the one hand, charming and saturated with nostalgia and, on the other, cramped, obsolete, and decrepit. The Dodgers were both the most lucrative franchise in the majors and the most threatened, as the repopulation of the borough by new immigrant communities was changing the peculiar culture that had long nourished the team. Shrewd and imaginative, O'Malley also faced political leaders and officials unwilling or unable to face either these facts or his own steely determination to do what he thought was best for himself and his family. "My father didn't want to leave Brooklyn," Peter O'Malley, who would succeed his father as president in 1970, said. "He wanted to build a ballpark in Brooklyn. He had a site, Atlantic and Flatbush Avenues, that he believed in. But he was not allowed to do it." In 1952, at Walter O'Malley's behest, the architect Norman Bel Geddes designed a domed stadium for the site. After that idea was met with general ridicule, the Dodgers president sold Ebbets Field to a real-estate developer, who then leased the ballpark back to the Dodgers on a five-year contract. In 1955, another O'Malley plan for a domed stadium, to be designed by the architect and visionary Buckminster Fuller, also elicited mainly scorn. In August of that year, the Dodgers announced that the team would play twenty "home" games, over a three-year period, in vacant Roosevelt Stadium in Jersey City.

When the Dodgers played their second game of the 1956 season on April 19 at Roosevelt Stadium, Robinson had come full circle; this was the scene of his grand debut as a Montreal Royal almost exactly ten years before. Then, on a sunny day in 1946, before an overflowing park, he had exploded the myth of Negro physical and mental inferiority in baseball. But this circle was not a harmony. Whereas more than twenty-five thousand people had watched that game in 1946, now only twelve thousand fans paid to view the opener in 1956, although the Dodgers were world champions. In 1946, the crowd had been respectful as it watched a black man, against the odds, break the color line; now, in 1956, many fans were openly hostile to Robinson although he was nominally playing at "home."

Stirring their anger were reports that Robinson had called Jersey City unworthy of a major-league team even on an interim basis; a fielding error charged to him only intensified the booing. He was clearly hurt and mystified by the response. "The way they acted," he said angrily about his error and the fans, "you'd think I did it on purpose." Pressed by reporters to explain his remark about Jersey City, Robinson grew more and more testy. Then, when Ed Brennan, a reporter with the local Jersey *Journal,* asked fatuously why he could not act like a gentleman, Jack exploded. A Dodger publicity man stopped him, allegedly, from going after Brennan. But Robinson's remarks about Jersey City had also angered his general manager. "Robinson doesn't have to worry about playing in Jersey City three more years," Bavasi snapped. "With the kind of playing he's been doing recently, he had better worry about the next three months."

The hostile reaction of Jersey City fans continued. A local bar owner, Jimmy Gallagher, explained that the town had been a Giants stronghold for thirteen years; besides, Robinson, great ballplayer that he was, "seems to have a gift for getting people riled up." Another factor, difficult to gauge, was perhaps the ethnic composition of the Jersey City audience, which probably included a far smaller percentage of Jews and blacks, Jack's most loyal supporters, than in Brooklyn. In any event, "it's the fans' privilege to boo," he conceded wearily to a writer. "I'm here to play ball, and if they want to come to the ball park to boo, that's their business. No ball player likes to be booed, but I'd be foolish to let it bother me."

On April 25, for the nineteenth and last time in a regular season in the majors, Jack stole home, against the Giants at the Polo Grounds. By mid-June, however, kept out by Alston in favor of Randy Jackson, he rode the bench and brooded on the dilemma he had become: Alston would not play him unless he looked sharp, but—especially at his age, thirty-seven—he could not be sharp unless he played consistently. Dangerously, he now and then flashed his rage against Alston for others to see. "I don't think the Dodgers would keep me at the salary they're paying me if they intended me to ride the bench," he told a reporter (a curious echo of an approach he had condemned when Dick Young expressed it). But more often he kept busy and hoped to catch Alston's eye. "I like Jack's attitude," Alston commented to the press. "He's been working hard, keeping in shape and I like the way he peps up the bench."

Sulking and silence were not Jack's way; by instinct, he remained a peppery, driving presence on the club even when he rode the bench. In July, he clashed once again with Warren Giles, the league president. Behind this new dispute was an incident in a game against Cincinnati, when Robinson and the umpire Augie Donatelli disagreed on a call. At bat, Robinson claimed he had foul-tipped a ball onto his toe; Donatelli ruled the ball fair (with Robinson thrown out at first base). When Jack threw down his batting helmet in disgust, Donatelli ejected him from the game. Later, to Jack's astonishment, Giles fined Robinson fifty dollars for making unspecified "remarks." Robinson was furious. "I'm fined for remarks?" he asked. "What remarks? I didn't swear. I didn't curse, except for maybe 'damn.' . . . If Donatelli says I swore he's a liar, but I don't think he did." To Jack, and some other observers, the fine was out of line; Billy Bruton of the Braves, for example, was fined the same amount for the far more serious offense of fighting with another player.

Unquestionably, racism played a role in such incidents; no supporter of racial integration or black players, Giles and many baseball administrators quietly detested a defiant Negro like Jack and sought ways to squash him. Jack, on the other hand, also brought to the ballpark in the summer of 1956 something that should have been irrelevant but was inescapable for a black man struggling in a white-dominated milieu: a keen awareness of the epidemic of violence aimed at blacks and white liberals in the South because of the civil rights movement. In communities across the South, blacks following the lead of Dr. King and his Montgomery bus boycott were arrested and jailed by local police, or subject to other random acts of brutality by whites. While some school districts complied with the Supreme Court ruling of 1954 on integration, in many places white mobs barred an end to Jim Crow. After Senator Harry Byrd of Virginia called for "massive resistance" to integration, more than one hundred Southern congressmen signed a manifesto supporting segregated schools, even as the reactionary White Citizens Councils reached a membership of over three hundred thousand persons. Autherine Lucy, a young black woman, was admitted to the University of Alabama by court decree, but removed in the face of white rioting and then expelled when she sued to be readmitted. In Birmingham, Alabama, the respected singer and pianist Nat "King" Cole was attacked on stage by a group of whites.

Cole's treatment in Birmingham, as well as other episodes in the intensifying civil rights struggle, was discussed in the Dodger dugout, where Robinson could count on players such as Reese, Labine, Hodges, and Erskine for sympathy. Other players were not always as understanding, even if they, too, struggled to preserve team unity. Beyond the team, Jack was often a visible target for whites venting their anger against blacks, as the nation underwent changes that had been unthinkable only a few years before. In July, one personal attack on Robinson, appearing first in the New Orleans *Times-Picayune,* expressed the rage felt by many whites against him as the symbol of the social and political changes that had overtaken America since World War II. Immediately behind the attack were two factors. The first was an essay by Jack, "The South After Ten Years in the Majors," commissioned by the Pittsburgh *Courier* and carried soon after in the *Sporting News.* The second factor was a new Louisiana law, approved unanimously by the legislature, that banned interracial sport.

In his article on the South, Jack was relatively mild. Essentially he found the South a paradox. Integration was growing, but racial tension was becoming worse. Many Southern whites were his friends, but in the South he still felt the raw force of white resentment. (Don Drysdale would recall a visit that year to Pelican Stadium in New Orleans, when the seats were close to the players "and Jackie got an earful. The fans called him the worst possible names, and about the most polite thing I heard was 'Gator Bait.' It was brutal, and I was always braced for an incident of some sort.") Jack wrote about the segregated hotels, but also about signs of progress, especially in Miami. Blacks were often intimidated, but some were standing up for their rights. In Mobile, Alabama, for example, he had seen "quite a bit of tension because of the Supreme Court decision. But in other cities I noticed Negroes helping in the fight."

Robinson's sense of balance got him nowhere with the *Times-Picayune* columnist, Bill Keefe, who both backed the new Jim Crow sports law and blamed it on Robinson, that "persistently insolent and trouble-making Negro of the Brooklyn Dodgers." Robinson had been "pampered and humored" by baseball officials until he thought he was "immune to discipline." Ending Jim Crow would bankrupt most hotels, Keefe wrote, because whites would stay away from them. "Sincere segregationists therefore should chip in and buy a plaque to present Robinson for his yeoman work."

Keefe's attack, which he subtitled "Enemy of His Race," hurt Jack deeply and drew from him one of the most incisive letters he had ever written. Scribbling a draft, ironically, on stationery of the once-segregationist Chase Hotel in St. Louis, he addressed Keefe "not as Jackie Robinson, but as one human being to another." Far from being a troublemaker, he was rather "an American who happens to be an American Negro and one who is proud of that heritage." Writing on behalf of black Americans, Jack insisted that "we ask for nothing special. We ask only that we be permitted to live as you live, and as our nation's constitution provides." Concerning segregated hotels, black ballplayers now stayed in "white" hotels in cities such as St. Louis and Cincinnati without these hotels losing trade, much less going out of business. "I wish you could see this as I do," he told Keefe, "but I hold little hope. I wish you could comprehend how unfair and un-American it is for the accident of birth to make such a difference to you."

As for being insolent, "I'll admit I have not been subservient, but would you use the same adjective to describe a white ball player—say Ted Williams, who is, more often than I, involved in controversial matters? Am I insolent, or am I merely insolent for a Negro (who has courage enough to speak against injustices such as yours and people like you)?" "I am happy for you, that you were born white," Robinson concluded. "It would have been extremely difficult for you had it been otherwise." (On August 7, for the third time in three weeks, Williams openly spat at fans at Fenway Park, some of whom had booed and insulted him. His club fined him $5,000, which he never paid, according to a Boston newspaper. The following month the state legislature itself acted: it approved a bill that would fine fans for using profanity.)

On the baseball field, when Jack's resentment of racism touched the pennant race, the potential for an explosion only increased. In Milwaukee, for example, as the Dodgers strove to catch the league-leading Braves, he came close to making one of the worst mistakes of his career. After he became convinced that Lew Burdette was aiming thinly disguised racial insults at him, Jack simmered and stewed and then retaliated with uncharacteristic violence. In the middle of a warmup session in the infield, he suddenly wheeled and fired the ball at Burdette, who was standing on the Braves' dugout steps. Barely missing Burdette's head, the baseball crashed into a wall behind him and rebounded onto the field. Astonished reporters found Robinson trembling with anger. Why had he thrown the ball at Burdette? "I threw it at him because I wanted to hit him right between the eyes," he responded. "He was calling me names, and I won't stand for that." Burdette had black teammates about whom he obviously cared little, and who were too intimidated or confused to stand up to him. "How do you think they felt?" he said. "I decided I'd have to say what [Henry] Aaron and [Bill] Bruton—a couple [of] kids—wouldn't say back to him. . . . He's nothing but a coward in my book." (When Burdette denied the remarks were racist, Robinson responded the way he normally did in such a case: he accepted the denial and ended the feud.)

Far more often, Jack channeled his anger into his play, or set his anger aside completely, in an act of will, as he concentrated on the task at hand. Early in August, when Alston returned him to the lineup against the front-running Braves after a spell in limbo, Jack responded with a two-run homer in the second inning, then won the game in the ninth with a long single to beat Milwaukee by one run. He continued to play an important role through September, as the Dodgers bore down in the home stretch on the faltering Braves. Leading the Brooklyn charge were Newcombe and the former Giants headhunter Sal Maglie, now a Dodger. Newcombe would finish with 27 wins for the finest season of his career (he was named MVP of the league). Maglie, acquired from the Indians in May to replace Podres, won 13 games himself. Although diminished compared to 1954 and 1955, Dodger hitting power was still formidable: Snider, about whom Jack had fretted in the spring, hit

43 home runs. On September 25, Maglie threw a no-hitter against the Phillies at Ebbets Field to keep the Dodgers only a half-game behind the Braves. Four days later, Brooklyn moved ahead of Milwaukee by one game with one game to go. On the last day of the season, the Dodgers won the pennant.

Robinson's inspired play down the stretch led Bill Corum in the New York *Journal-American* to salute him as "a one-man task force of the diamond," who was "still the most dangerous individual competitor in the game." In the World Series, once more against the Yankees, Jack played in all seven games and hit .250, with one home run and one game-winning hit. The Dodgers shone in the first two games at home, then dropped the next three in Yankee Stadium. The last game there, on October 8, saw Don Larsen, a physically imposing but hitherto mediocre pitcher, retire twenty-seven batters in a row to hurl a perfect game and defeat Maglie and the Dodgers, 2–0. (After the game, Jack called on Larsen to pay his respects.) Back at Ebbets Field, pitching dominated again, with both teams scoreless after nine innings. Then, in the tenth inning, when an aging Enos Slaughter misplayed Robinson's line drive to left field, Gilliam scored to give Brooklyn the win and tie the series; Jack's welcome in the Dodgers' dugout almost matched that accorded Larsen after his famous victory. But in the seventh and deciding game, the Dodger ace, Newcombe, lost in a rout.

By most accountings, Robinson had enjoyed a highly creditable series, to finish off a season that marked an improvement in many respects over 1955. Playing 12 more games (117), he had batted .275 (up from .256), with 43 runs batted in (instead of 36), 61 runs scored (up from 51), and 12 stolen bases (the same as 1955). His 10 home runs (up from 8) and 15 doubles (up from 6) helped to raise his slugging percentage to .412 (from .363 the previous year). Based on this performance (and his financial needs), he had little difficulty in deciding that he would play at least one more season in the majors.

But he would do so only reluctantly. His body clearly was not responding as it once did to exercise; now, despite stringent dieting, he gained weight routinely even during the season. His knees and ankles chronically hurt; his throwing arm often cried out for rest. Quite apart from the demands of his body was his urge to end his prolonged absences from Rachel and the children. Now, more than ever, Jack hoped for the chance in business that would allow him to move on to the next major phase of his life. But his own business ventures were only a mixed success, at best. On 125th Street in Harlem, his clothing store was barely alive. Thus far, his venture into housing construction had led nowhere, with no buildings erected—although in 1956 he was still using his name to open doors for his partners. Over the summer, a news item suggested breathlessly that he and a syndicate of investors were about to buy several radio stations in the South; but this deal, if it ever existed, fell through.

About managing in baseball, Jack was ambivalent, mainly because he wanted to be close to home in the future. His best chance, in any event, was a position outside the United States, where racism would be less of a factor. In Canada, Sam Bankhead, a brother of Dan Bankhead, the first black pitcher in the majors (with the Dodgers), had once managed at Drummondville in the Provincial League. To Jack, Montreal was ideal, if in the minor leagues; but the Royals job was not likely to be open to him, given his relationship with Walter O'Malley. ("Babe Ruth can't manage himself," a Yankee executive once snapped. "How can you expect him to manage twenty-five ball-players?" O'Malley had similar feelings about Robinson.) Talk was that Robinson would be offered the chance to manage the new Vancouver club, transferred from Oakland, California, in the Pacific Coast League; but the talk led nowhere. In October, another report again linked Robinson to the Montreal Royals. To an inquiring reporter, Jack confirmed that the offer was "strictly rumor"; however, "I'd like to manage a ball club. I'm thirty-seven years old now, and I've got a lot of gray hair."

Jack's weak joke about his gray hair was meant to deflect the pain he felt at yet another sign of the ironies of racism in America. In 1956, perhaps the best example of this perversity was the appointment of Bobby Bragan by Branch Rickey (as Rickey stepped down as general manager of the Pirates) to be field manager of the club. In 1947, refusing to play with a black man, Bragan was traded by Rickey from the Dodgers. Also ironic was the fact that Bragan had become, apparently, an excellent coach and manager of black players. In an article, "Why Can't

I Manage in the Majors?" (as told to Milton Gross), Robinson probed possible answers: *"Because I am a Negro? Because I am emotional? Because I can't get along with people, no matter what the pigmentation of their skin? Because white players would resent me and would be reluctant to take orders from me? Because baseball isn't ready now or never will be ready to accept a Negro as a manager at the major league level? Because I'm not qualified by experience or ability?"* Looking back, he knocked down each theory. From a boy, he had played well with whites, many of whom had remained his friends; as a player, he had been loyal and obedient, with a fine sense of team solidarity. "My managers know that I gave them everything I had as a player," he insisted. "I believe my players would give me everything they have if I were a manager. Maybe I wouldn't be a good manager, but the reason would come from what was inside me, not outside me, and inside my players."

WITH THE WORLD SERIES OVER, Jack temporarily set aside thoughts of business and left with the Dodgers on a twenty-game tour of Japan. For him, as for many of the Dodgers, the trip represented a financial sacrifice; as a barnstormer, certainly, he could have made more than twice the money. Several players went unwillingly; however, to the relief of the State Department, which viewed his participation as important, Robinson never hesitated about going. This would not be the first tour of Japan by an American team after World War II, but its diplomatic and cultural importance was obvious. "Your own presence in Japan will make a contribution," a government official had assured him, "the value of which cannot be estimated." Besides, all the Dodger wives were invited, and Rachel was eager to make the trip. After her mother came from Los Angeles to stay with the children, Jack and Rachel left on the longest journey of their lives together.

Columbus Day, October 12, found the team in Los Angeles. There, the Robinsons happily visited family and friends, and O'Malley happily took a helicopter ride. The helicopter was owned by the Sheriff's Department of the County of Los Angeles, and his host on board was Kenneth Hahn, a member of the County Board of Supervisors. From on high, O'Malley looked down speculatively at various parcels of land where, with the cooperation of the Board of Supervisors, a major-league ball club might build a new park. This was a crucial step in O'Malley's gestating plan to move the team west to California. Unknown to the players, Ebbets Field would be home for only one more year. Then the Brooklyn Dodgers would cease to exist. The club would be reborn, in California, as the Los Angeles Dodgers.

In Japan, after a few easy days in Hawaii, the Dodgers traveled all over the country, including Osaka, the ancient imperial city of Kyoto, Nagasaki with its ruins from the atomic bomb dropped on it in World War II, and the industrial city of Nagoya in central Honshu. For both Jack and Rachel, the tour was a grand experience. While Jack was at the ballpark, Rachel spent much of her time in the company of O'Malley's wife, Kay, a bright, engaging, cultivated woman who, like Rachel, liked museums and the theater. "Walter O'Malley had all sorts of Japanese friends," Rachel recalled, "so our welcome everywhere was very warm." But Jack was also probably the people's favorite in Japan, and he responded in kind. "What was unusual about Jack in Japan," Rachel said, "was that he tried new things eagerly, which was not always the case at home. There he was, dressing up in kimonos, trying gamely to eat all kinds of unfamiliar food. We had a lot of fun watching the geisha girls try to make him comfortable, because he literally could not sit down with his legs out, his leg muscles were so tight and large. But he tried; he was in high spirits most of the time. I think he saw the tour of Japan as a culmination of his Dodger career, especially after the World Series victory the year before. I think he knew the end was in sight."

On the baseball field, true to his fighting spirit, Robin-San became the first Dodger ejected by an umpire from a game in Japan (an American umpire, Jocko Conlan). Japanese baseball was then a decorous affair compared with its American counterpart, but the local fans understood what he had represented, including the samurai warrior spirit Robinson to some extent embodied in his career. But before Jack left Japan with the Dodgers, the United States ambassador, John M. Allison, sent him a special message of thanks for "what you have done while in this country." Allison praised Jack's "magnificent sportsmanship," which had helped to strengthen the ties "between the people of Japan and the people of America."

Returning to the United States, Jack took to the links with pleasure, but was soon on the road as a speaker, mainly for the NCCJ. The most important address came in late November, when he acted as master of ceremonies at a $100-a-plate dinner organized by the regional NCCJ at the Palmer House in Chicago, where Mayor Richard Daley also spoke. But Jack was also about to make a major change in the focus of his volunteering. Without breaking with the NCCJ or the Harlem YMCA, he decided to pay far more attention to the NAACP. Across the South, the association was under serious pressure and in desperate need of funds. In Alabama that year, for example, after it refused to allow hostile local officials to examine its books, the NAACP was fined $100,000 and forbidden by court order to operate within the state. In many other places, membership in the association was a dangerous business. Jack decided that this was where he should direct his efforts. Late in the year, accordingly, he agreed to become national chairman of the annual Fight for Freedom Fund campaign of the NAACP and to make an extended tour in the winter in that capacity.

The turning point for him probably was a notice he had received earlier in the year, in June, that the NAACP had decided to accord him its highest honor, the Spingarn Medal, given annually to a black American whose achievements had brought credit to the race. Robinson would be the forty-first person but the first athlete to win the medal, which in the past had gone mainly to artists, scientists, and civil rights leaders such as W. E. B. Du Bois, Marian Anderson, Richard Wright, Paul Robeson, A. Philip Randolph, and Ralph Bunche. To Jack, it was welcome evidence that he had transcended athletics in the course of his long career as a sportsman, and made the kind of lasting impression on American society to which he had long aspired. On December 8, at a gala luncheon at the Hotel Roosevelt in Manhattan, before a gathering of prominent civil rights leaders and their supporters, Jack proudly accepted his medal. On hand were the former president of the NAACP, Arthur B. Spingarn, and Amy Einstein Spingarn, whose late husband, Joel E. Spingarn, also a past president, had funded the award. Jack was introduced by his friend the network television star Ed Sullivan, and presented with the award by Channing H. Tobias, the chairman of the board of the NAACP. According to its citation, the medal came "in recognition of his superb sportsmanship, his pioneer role in opening up a new field of endeavor for young Negroes, and his civic consciousness."

In accepting the medal, Robinson thanked various individuals, including his mother, his wife, and Branch Rickey; but also mindful of the harsh criticism he had been receiving, he seized the moment to justify the correctness of his fighting attitude over the years in facing injustice. "I am now quite convinced," he declared, "that the way I have played and the way I have tried to conduct myself was the right way." Many people had advised him "not to speak up every time I thought there was an injustice. I was often advised to look after the Robinson family and not to worry about other people." Sometimes the "biting criticism" left him doubting himself. More-over, "many times I have been told that I should just let things work themselves out without involving myself in them. If I did so, many honors and awards would come my way." But if he had lost some prizes, "I am pretty certain now that what I have tried to do was in keeping with the spirit which the Spingarn Medal represents." The NAACP was "the tireless champion of the rights and well-being of the Negroes of America. It is even more than that, because its cause is the cause of democracy, which makes it the champion of all Americans who cherish the princi-ples on which this country was founded."

Then, within a day or two of the medal ceremony, his life took an even more decisive turn. Martin Stone's efforts to find the right job in business for Jack finally paid off. Around December 1, Jack received a telephone call from William H. Black, the president of a popular chain of coffee shops, Chock Full o' Nuts, asking that Jack join him for lunch in Manhattan. Within a week of their meeting, Black decided to offer Jack the job of director of personnel for the entire operation. At first glance, the proposed job seemed far removed from Robinson's interests and capabilities; but Black was convinced that he was the man for the position. Initially skeptical, Jack quickly became fascinated by the prospect of a posi-tion that would put him in charge of the welfare of more than a thousand people, most of them black.

Black's story was American to the core. An engineering graduate of Columbia University but with no job in the offing because of a recession, he had started out humbly around 1922, selling nuts at a stand under a staircase in a building at Forty-third Street and Broadway. Soon he had several small nut shops. Then, in 1931, with nuts suddenly a luxury in the Depression, Black converted several shops into "restaurants" specializing in a five-cent cup of coffee and a popular, five-cent nutted cheese sandwich made with whole-wheat raisin bread. By the 1950s, Chock Full o' Nuts was a city institution, selling its own line of roasted coffee and baked goods but noted also because of Black's humane rules of employment, which included generous annual holiday allowances, a day off with pay on each worker's birthday, a substantial Christmas bonus, and health, life insurance, and retirement plans at no cost to the employees. Black had also made sure that he employed both blacks and whites.

According to him, it was his idea to approach Robinson, whom he had never met, about coming to Chock Full o' Nuts after a vacancy suddenly arose in personnel. "From what I had read about Jackie," he said, "he was just the man for the job. I arranged to have lunch with him." The lunch went well, he told the press; "I was convinced he is the man for us." He then arranged for Robinson to make a day-long tour of the Chock Full o' Nuts empire. As Black had hoped, Robinson began to see himself in the position. Black probably did not share with Jack one of the main reasons for his interest in him: the owner's hope that Robinson would act as a buffer between his employees and the trade union movement, which Black feared as a businessman. According to Stone, who remembered the sequence of events differently, Black had mentioned to some friends of Stone "that he was having trouble with his employees over a trade union. He didn't want his work force unionized. In the shops, most of the employees were black. I went to see Black in the hope that he would select Jack to take charge of personnel matters."

In any event, on December 10, Black and Stone ("just about the best friend I have," Robinson declared happily the following month) met to negotiate terms. As vice-president in charge of personnel relations, Jack would be paid $30,000 a year along with a company car and stock or stock options. The initial agreement, commencing on March 4, 1957, would be for two years, at the end of which, if reappointed, Robinson would get a five-year contract— although, Black insisted, "I told Jackie that as far as I am concerned, this is a lifetime job." Stone and Black agreed that Robinson, if he agreed to the terms, would come to Black's office in Manhattan two days later, on December 12, to sign the contract.

For Jack, this was not a tough decision to reach; he was eager to accept the offer. As for Rachel, she "didn't try to influence me one way or the other," he insisted the following month. "She wanted this to be my decision."

Jack then faced two prime, possibly conflicting, obligations. One was to tell the Dodgers he would not be coming back; the other was to share the news with the weekly magazine *Look,* so as to comply with an agreement he had reached with the magazine two years before, in connection with his three-part article there, to give *Look* exclusive rights to the story of his retirement. In return, *Look* would pay Jack a fee of $50,000 (in reality, a two-year sports consultantcy at $25,000 a year).

Suppressing the story until *Look* could publish it guaranteed that Jack's departure from baseball would be controversial; but neither *Look* nor Robinson could have anticipated the next turn of events. On December 11, the day before Jack was due in Manhattan to sign his contract with Black, a Dodger employee called to say that Buzzie Bavasi wanted to see him in Brooklyn at 11:00 a.m. the next day. Robinson, who was scheduled to be at the *Look* office at that time, promised to telephone Bavasi. The next morning, at the breakfast table, he told his children what he was about to do. Jackie Junior burst into tears, and David followed suit; only Sharon, knowing that Dad would be home more, beamed. Jack and Rachel then drove from Stamford to the *Look* office in Manhattan. Around three o'clock, Robinson finally reached Bavasi on the telephone. Bavasi, evidently not free to talk, offered to visit Jack at home later. When Robinson said he was entertaining that evening, Bavasi then agreed to telephone him again. Around four o'clock, Jack and Marty Stone proceeded to the Chock Full o' Nuts headquarters at 425 Lexington Avenue. There, Bill Black greeted them warmly. While they were waiting to sign the contract, Bavasi tried to reach Robinson. According to

Stone, "I told Jack, 'Don't you dare answer that telephone until we are done with this contract!' " Around five o'clock, as soon as Jack signed the document, Stone gave the all-clear: "Now you can call Bavasi."

Stone listened in as Robinson made the call. "Jack, I have news for you," Bavasi said. "You've been traded to the New York Giants. It'll be in all the papers tomorrow. Congratulations!" In return for Robinson, Brooklyn would receive the left-handed relief pitcher Dick Littlefield, along with $35,000.

Jack heard Bavasi's message with a widening smile, because its timing seemed to confirm the wisdom of his decision to quit baseball. Still, the news rocked him, even as it soon rocked his family, his teammates, and legions of Dodger fans. The idea of their Jackie being traded was bad enough; the notion of him going to the archenemy, the Giants, was almost inconceivable. Even by baseball's chilly standards of conduct in such matters, the trade seemed arctic. "We made the deal," Bavasi would explain, "because we want to play one of our youngsters. As long as Jackie was on the club, the manager was going to play him. And you couldn't blame him." He and O'Malley had sent Robinson to the Giants because they felt "obligated to Jackie to trade him to a New York team." After all, Jack had long made it clear that he would not play away from New York. (Thirty years later, a New York *Times* writer, Dave Anderson, would offer as a theory long held that O'Malley had traded Robinson to avoid taking him home to Los Angeles, where Jack had been a hero.)

To some extent, Jack still had room to maneuver, even to change his mind. Although he had signed a contract with Chock Full o' Nuts, Black made it clear that he would release Robinson if Jack wanted to return to baseball. Jack probably also had time to cancel his deal with *Look,* where the story would not appear before January 8. But he apparently never wavered. However, to maintain the appearance that joining the Giants was possible, even probable, and thus to give a heavier punch to the *Look* exclusive, he masked his intentions. When the Giants' president, Horace Stoneham, telephoned Jack to express his delight with the trade, Robinson was gracious if also restrained: he would be delighted to play for the Giants, if he played for anyone. He also asked Stoneham to keep the news quiet for a while. That was impossible, Stoneham said. Too many people already knew.

Accordingly, Jack acted as if he might be joining the Giants. "I'll give the Giants everything I've got, just as I have the Dodgers," he allegedly told one reporter. "I've got no hard feelings against the Dodgers but I'm going to do everything I can to beat them next year." Certainly he seemed to enjoy the knowledge that O'Malley and Bavasi, without knowing it, were now chasing their tails. "There was a kind of revenge in it for us," Rachel admitted forty years later; "we felt that the top people had hurt us, and we were getting back a little at them." When the questions came too close to the truth, Jack set out for California; the idea came from *Look,* which paid for the trip.

Keeping up the charade, Jack was all humility in dealing with O'Malley, Bavasi, and Alston. In turn, their initial letters to him were gracious, even if their own main intention was to ease him off the premises quietly. On December 13, when Bavasi sent Robinson his "Official Release Notice," he took pains to assure Jack that he had acted reluctantly. Praising Jack for often helping the team to scout and sign certain players, Bavasi hinted at a possible management role for him. Baseball was more than playing—"I think you know what I mean." O'Malley, thanking Jack for his "courageous and fair and philosophical" response to the trade, also saw a possible "future intersection" of their paths. Alston, too, made sentimental noises. The press had exaggerated their differences; Alston had "always admired your fine competitive spirit and team play."

If there was duplicity here, it existed on both sides. For his part, Jack was misleading not only O'Malley and Bavasi but also his own innocent admirers, many of whom had rallied indignantly to his side with the news of the trade. Fans pointed out that Cleveland had kept its pitching hero Bob Feller on the payroll long after he ceased to be effective; why hadn't Robinson been accorded the same respect? His teammates paid their tributes, each in his own way. Erskine expressed his undying gratitude to Jack for welcoming him years before to the Dodgers; Campanella wondered what needling Robinson would be like now. Both players assumed that Jack would be a Giant, as did a popular columnist in penning a feverish but shrewd tribute to Jack.

"You are Jackie Robinson," Jimmy Cannon wrote, "who is consumed by rage and pride. You're a complicated man, persecuted by slanderous myths, using anger as a confederate. No athlete of any time has been assaulted by such an aching loneliness which created your personality and shaped your genuine greatness." As for reporting to the Giants: "It's a challenge and you won't back down.'

When the *Look* article, leaked by an employee, became public, sweetness vanished everywhere. Offended by Jack's refusal to die quietly, O'Malley privately dismissed him as a mercenary and an ingrate—curious charges, given Jack's record with the club. Earlier that year, O'Malley had told Roger Kahn that Robinson "is always seeking publicity. Maybe it's a speech he's about to make, or a sale at his store, but when Robinson gets his name in the headlines, you can be sure there's a reason." Angry at seeing his deal wrecked, Bavasi scorned the *Look* article as a ploy by Robinson to gouge more money out of the Giants. Robinson should have told him he was about to retire (Bavasi, apparently, had no obligation to tell Jack he was about to be traded): "There would have been no deal and I would have kept it in confidence if he asked me to. I knew of the *Look* deal for two years and I kept that in confidence."

Now it was Jack's turn to be insulted. No amount of money, he stormed, would make him play baseball again after Bavasi accused him of greed. "Million Dollars Won't Change My Mind," the *Daily Mirror* trumpeted: "Bitter Robinson Hits Bavasi for 'Insult' on Press Sellout." Jack was quitting the game "because of Buzzie Bavasi's unwarranted criticism in the press insulting my integrity. I am challenging those cracks and I intend to follow 'em up." Meanwhile, it is clear, he made sure that Bill Black knew that he was committed to him. On January 10, Black wrote Jack to say that he was "proud—very proud—to have you on my team."

Facing writers upset by his secrecy, Robinson argued that his deal with *Look* was common knowledge among them; but several begged to disagree. "Didn't you lie to your friends?" one man asked. "I did not lie," Jack replied. But some writers defended Robinson. After all, as one of them wrote in a Rhode Island paper, for an entire decade Jack had been "the bell-cow of the Dodgers, and it was almost ridiculous the way reporters made for Robinson's cubicle after the critical games. Others may have starred, but Robinson, all knew, was the one who talked." Robinson was often succinct and brilliant, and he never hedged; always reliable and good copy, he deserved his windfall from *Look*.

As for the Giants, they did not give up easily. On January 11, vice-president Charles S. "Chub" Feeney sent Jack a contract, as he was obliged to do by January 15 according to league rules, that would pay Jack $35,000 in 1957. But: "If you decide to play," Feeney wrote invitingly, "naturally financial terms will be open to discussion." (The Associated Press reported that the Giants were ready to pay Jack $65,000 for the season—more than any Dodger ever earned, although less than salaries paid to such contemporaries as DiMaggio, Williams, Musial, Feller, and Ralph Kiner.) But three days later, on Chock Full o' Nuts stationery, Robinson informed Stoneham that "after due consideration I have decided to request to be placed on the voluntary retired list as I am going to devote my full time to the business opportunities that have been presented." He assured Stoneham that his decision had "nothing to do with my trade to your organization." Stoneham then concluded their exchange with a pleasant note, handwritten, from Scottsdale, Arizona, wishing Jack success and happiness. However, he added, "I can't help thinking it would have been fun to have had you on our side for a year or two."

Now Jack's ten-year career in the major leagues and his eleven-year career in organized baseball were indeed over, although informal polls indicated that most fans across the city wanted him to continue playing, and although Rickey declared that Robinson had at least two good years left in him. The fighting over his *Look* contract clouded his exit, but not utterly. Many admirers, white and black, let him know that they understood the complex beast he had wrestled with for eleven years in the name of justice and baseball. Richie Ashburn of the Phillies assured Robinson that "both on and off the field . . . your tangible and intangible qualities made you the greatest player I had ever had the pleasure of playing against." Hank Greenberg, writing to praise "your long and illustrious career" and the "exemplary manner in which you have conducted yourself—both on and off the field," called Robinson "a credit to baseball and an inspiration" to youngsters "who will attempt to emulate your example." Cincinnati's Brooks Lawrence, a Negro National League pitcher who had become a major-league rookie at the age of twenty-nine in 1954, also paid tribute, but on behalf of a different group: "You opened the door for me and others who followed you and when you opened it you threw it wide open. You gave to us a new way of life for which we will be eternally grateful."

Not all the players felt the same way. Sal Maglie, only recently a Dodger, sneered that during the season Robinson had to be asked by Alston to play; Jack dismissed the remark as too ridiculous to answer. And Campanella took the lead in attacking Robinson, after the columnist Dick Young erroneously reported that Jack had declared the catcher washed up. ("I have never made such a statement!" Robinson insisted at the Chicago airport en route to San Francisco; he had said only that the Dodgers were "understandably concerned" about Campanella's hand following another operation.) "When it's my turn to bow out of baseball," Campanella let everyone know, "I certainly don't want to go out like he did. It just wasn't a dignified way to do it." Jack was always "shootin' off his mouth about everybody—and most of the time he doesn't know what he's talking about. He was always stirring up stuff like this in the clubhouse, too, making a lot of trouble. . . . Jackie should have left baseball with a lot of friends. Instead, he's got a lot of enemies. Instead of being grateful to baseball, he's criticizing it."

The veteran black sportswriter A. S. "Doc" Young, writing in the Los Angeles *Sentinel,* caught something of the precise flavor of Campanella's blast, and of the long feud between the two players: it "combined the bitterness of the Hatfields & McCoys with the tragic comedy of Amos 'n' Andy."

As Jack made his exit, yet another controversy flared up to light his way out. After a small church dinner, he let his guard down and ventured the opinion that Milwaukee had lost the 1956 pennant because a few of its players had been out carousing late at night instead of conserving their strength. The Braves and other baseball people were livid; Jack himself admitted making the remark but acknowledged that he had never meant it for publication, and that it should never have been published.

On January 18, seizing on the valedictory moment, Jack's friend Edward R. Murrow brought his popular live television show, *Person to Person,* to the house in Stamford to show America how Jackie Robinson now lived. America, watching the program, saw a graying but still potent lion at rest after his decade of labors, in a fairly opulent home that was tastefully decorated, shared with an attractive, assured wife and three happy children.

The children almost stole the show. "David, who liked to talk," Rachel remembered, "started to say something when he hadn't been asked a question. Jackie Junior, always more cautious, clamped a hand over his mouth. And we were terrified that David was going to bite him, right there, on the air! He didn't, but lots of people wrote in to say that was their favorite part of the whole program, because it reminded them of their own families."

The program was a success: Robinson's life seemed a very good life. In its typically manic style, *Variety,* the top magazine of the entertainment industry, praised his appearance: "Robinson happens to be gifted with the gab as a sidebar to his erstwhile baseball virtuosity. The well-known popoff and long-time star of the Bums . . . is a hep and happy guy, with a happy menage. The big athlete has always known where he was going."

One place the big athlete went, on a cold day in January, was out to Ebbets Field in Brooklyn, where he cleaned out his locker. A press photographer, seeking to capture the essence of this farewell to arms, caught the clubhouse cat looking on curiously as the onetime king gathered his things. Then, ten years after he had first walked nervously in, a black man breaking dangerously into the white world in search of a chance to show his talents, Robinson strode out of the Dodger clubhouse for the last time in his life.

Like Starting Over

1957–1960

Baseball was just a part of my life . . .
—Jackie Robinson (1957)

ONCE RACHEL AND THE three children got over the initial shock of Jack's retirement from baseball, they quickly fastened on the sweetest dividend it would provide: an end to the rigid baseball schedule that had kept him between March and October a sometime presence at home. No one was more keenly aware of the demands of baseball in this respect than Robinson himself. "I'll be very glad when this baseball is over and we settle down as a family," he had written to Rachel five years before. "I would rather not be away so much." The children obviously needed him. "When I would come home from a long trip," he confessed to one writer, "it was just like a stranger coming into the house. I lost a lot of contact with my kids that way and now I want to recoup. I want to have meals with them like every other father." To Rachel and their three children he was as lovingly committed as ever. "His devotion to them borders on the pious," one reporter noted. "His gentleness, from so powerful a person, is almost a shock."

Although Rachel had built the house, Jack had quickly fallen in love with it and their life in small-town Connecticut. The front lawn, a magnet for children up and down the road, was large enough to serve as the neighborhood softball field. Disinclined to join in much housework, Jack nevertheless took for himself the task of keeping the lawn in fine shape. His style was to race his commercial farm tractor at dazzling speeds up and down the expanse, then retire into the house to gaze out on his handiwork—acres and acres of shining green turf. In the summertime, the pond behind the house, to which the Robinsons added a strip of sandy beach, was a welcome respite from the heat. The family would picnic on its banks, and Jack and David, especially, loved to fish for sunnies, catfish, and small bass. The fall brought touch football games on the great lawn, and at Thanksgiving over the years an annual father-son football classic—Jack, Jack Gordon, and Chuck Williams against Jackie and David, Bradley, and Chuckie, with the females rooting on the sidelines. As winter came on, the pond was forbidden until Jack himself tested the ice (although he hated the cold and could not swim); then he would declare it officially open for winter games. From inside the warm house, where he often kept a fire going for his family's return, Robinson took pleasure in watching the kids at play.

Golf was his passion, and he practiced everywhere. In the game room he installed a floor-to-ceiling net and used it as a driving range. He putted on the living-room carpet; he chipped shots delicately on the expanse of lawn. Next to the huge stone fireplace was a cozy club chair where he read his beloved newspapers and magazines, wrote notes and drafts of speeches, or napped. He wanted to be where his family could see him, sit with him, or, as Rachel said, "give him a kiss as we passed by, or just watch him in peace."

"Jack was the sweetest man in the world," his sister-in-law Brenda Williams recalled. "He was very family-oriented, just intense about family. If he loved you, there were no boundaries. He was very sharing with good things that happened to come his way, always looking out for you to be included. He was also a big kidder—he and I had a really special relationship, one I treasured." They had one flash point of difference, but even there they remained friends. "I loved to argue politics with Jack," she said. "I was a complete liberal; he was a man from the right. We had some vehement discussions, loud, boisterous. Rachel and Chuck usually stayed out of our way when the debates got really hot. But we always made up in the end."

Willette Bailey, who lived with them during the week before returning to New York City on the weekends, was an important person in the home, from the time the Robinsons moved to Stamford until Rachel's mother came from California. She was not a housekeeper or a governess or a babysitter but in a real way all of these and a member of the family, although in fact their employee. Jack and Rachel trusted her, and she did everything to maintain that trust. A beautician until she assumed this role, Willette herself knew the real reason she was there. She loved Rachel ("a beautiful person") and Jack ("a wonderful man"), "but I was with them for the children. It was nice. It was home." With each of the three children she was able to establish a special bond, in part as a figure of authority, in part as an adult who was also a friend they would cherish for the rest of their lives.

All around the Robinson home were other growing families, all white, who formed a happy, moderately prosperous community that seemed to have banished racial prejudice. When the Robinsons arrived on the scene, one family had fled in terror; but that house had been snapped up by a genial CBS commentator, Harry Kramer, and his wife, whose younger son sometimes earned a little money babysitting for the Robinsons. Next door to the Robinsons was the Baco family (Mr. Baco owned the local gas station, on High Ridge Road), with eight children, for whom David became at one point a sort of den leader. Another friendly couple, Joe Mehan and his wife, had two boys themselves; the Dumbrowskis, also affable, had two boys. Directly across the street were the Joyces, with two sons and two daughters, including Christy Joyce, who for some years was Sharon's closest friend. Also living nearby were the Kweskins, Sydney and Ethel and their two sons; Syd became the Robinsons' trusted local attorney and close friend. In the summer, in addition, the Robinsons were often guests of Richard and Andrea Simon, who threw huge parties at which Jack almost inevitably found himself the center of some warm discussion of politics or sports. "The Robinsons were a fine, talented family," according to Joanna Simon, "and we were really fortunate to know them. They added something special to our lives. We were not there when they lived in our home but we got to know them well. My mother truly loved Rachel, and Rachel loved my mother, in spite of their differences in years and their other differences." Her brother, Peter, one of Jackie Junior's playmates, would recall Jack himself with special affection. "My own father was sick for a long time, before he died when I was twelve, and he didn't or couldn't do some of the things with me that I wanted him to do as a father. I remember Jack being very kind to me personally. My first set of golf clubs—I remember him taking me all the way to New Jersey to buy it, because he wanted to get me a special deal. He was always kind to me." Years later, a white neighbor, John Crosby, would recall the stories of Jackie Robinson's alleged combativeness and declare: "I never knew this Jackie Robinson at all. To us he was a shy, gentle giant of a man with an enchanting smile and huge hands that almost swallowed yours when he shook hands. He used to play softball with us and, even curbing his swing, could hardly refrain from knocking the ball clear out of Connecticut."

All of these close neighbors and friends were white, but the Robinsons also had a circle of black friends, both in Stamford and in New York City, which was their second home. When Rachel discovered a black professional family living not far away, she methodically set out to bring the children together. Thus Candace Allen, the straight-A daughter of a dentist, Dr. Edward Allen, and his wife, Dee, became Sharon's best friend as a teenager as well as the only other black girl in the fifth grade when she transferred to Martha Hoyt that year. Her brother, Eddie, became close to David. Edward Allen's sister, the theater director Billy Allen, and her husband, Luther Henderson, a well-known musician, also joined the inner circle around Jack and Rachel, as did Nat and Ellen Dickerson of Stamford (Nat had been one of the Mariners, a popular singing group). Holding on to one another, these blacks made Stamford a far more pleasant place for them all. Some white friends moved comfortably in both worlds. Sarah Satlow, in particular, was still a very good friend many years after meeting Jack and Rachel in Flatbush in 1948; and Howard Cosell, who revered Jack, often came up from Pound Ridge, New York, with his family to Sunday brunches and the like. It was Cosell who asked the Robinsons to invite the shy young boxer Floyd Patterson to their home, thus starting another friendship that Jack would cherish.

In New York City, the Robinsons' best friends were almost certainly Lacy and Florence Covington in Brooklyn and, in a far more urbane way, Arthur and Marian Logan, who owned a brownstone apartment house on West Eighty-eighth Street in Manhattan that was the premier salon in New York City for black professionals committed to the civil rights movement. Tall, handsome, and to the casual observer a white man, Arthur Logan was the most respected physician in Harlem, with a list of patients or former patients that embraced such renowned figures as Duke Ellington and W. E. B. Du Bois. A board member of King's Southern Christian Leadership Conference, Marian Logan (or Marian Bruce, as she was known in her days as a nightclub singer), was a sophisticated and yet earthy brown-skinned woman who dressed expensively but was every inch a race woman. Arthur loved to cook, liquor flowed freely, and with frequent guests such as Ellington and Billy Strayhorn, as well as Marian herself, the music was usually superb. At one time or another, almost every important civil rights leader, including Dr. King, stood on the impressive staircase of their duplex apartment and begged for support for some cause. Over the years since meeting in Montreal in 1946, Marian and Jack had become buddies. Irrepressible and artful, she broke through Jack's stout defenses against most women and became a confidante and valued ally as he sought a growing role in the movement.

Anchored in the black world but with strong ties to the white, Jack and Rachel moved with apparent ease as they lived out the misty dream of true racial integration in America in the 1950s. Nevertheless, they were almost always aware of those aspects of their lives that were perhaps illusory, of the extent to which racism often remained a reality despite signs of progress. Perplexed at times about how best to proceed, they also knew that their three children were among a few young blacks venturing into new social and psychological territory in America for which no one was fully prepared. Jack and Rachel could be firm, but they tried above all to protect their children from the various indignities, especially of racism, that they themselves had suffered growing up in California. Perhaps they went too far. "Unable to shield my brothers and me from the outside pressures," their daughter would write later, as a grown woman, "my parents' tendency was to overprotect and overindulge. At home, voices were rarely raised, spankings not used for punishment, and cursing considered inappropriate."

To broaden their children's experience beyond the overwhelmingly white Stamford world, their parents joined Jack and Jill, perhaps the premier black middle-class club for young people. But such a connection could go only so far in preparing the children for the world. The Robinsons' choice of a church exemplified the problem. Not far from the Robinson home was the North Stamford Congregational Church, serenely white in its austere New England elegance. Worshiping there seemed the natural thing to do; but while they were made to feel welcome, they also denied themselves certain valuable connections by being there. "Perhaps we should have sought out a black church," Rachel reflected some years later, "so the children would have had more black friends. But Jack's schedule as a ballplayer, with doubleheaders on Sunday, had drawn us away from churchgoing. Besides, I've always hated being preached at, and preaching was everything in most of the black churches. It was easier to join my neighbors and go to the church on the corner, as it were. It also seemed the right thing to do."

LESS THAN A MONTH after his retirement, Robinson's thoughts began to swing decisively away from baseball. "Don't get me wrong," he assured a gathering that month, "baseball has been wonderful to me and I owe everything to it." Nevertheless, in 1957 he would attend only two major-league baseball games; in 1958 and 1959, he would attend none, although he watched some contests on television. The disappointing way he had left the game had a great deal to do with this distance, but Robinson tried to offer a more positive perspective. "Baseball was just a part of my life," he explained. "Thank God that I didn't allow a sport or a business or any part of my life to dominate me completely. . . . I felt I had my time in athletics and that was it."

Instead, on January 20, accompanied by Franklin H. Williams, the secretary-counsel of the West Coast branch of the NAACP, he left New York for Baltimore and the start of a cross-country tour for the NAACP's Fight for Freedom Fund. Jack left New York on a happy note: Bill Black of Chock Full o' Nuts had sent him off with a check for $10,000 as a donation to the cause. At a press conference in Manhattan, Jack proudly presented the money to Arthur B. Spingarn, the president of the NAACP.

At this point, Jack knew little about the NAACP beyond its reputation as the top organization fighting for civil rights. Conceived in 1909 by three white liberals shocked by the lynching of a black man in Springfield, Illinois, the burial place of Abraham Lincoln, the NAACP had grown steadily because of its vigorous challenges to Jim Crow laws, its network of local and regional branches, and, especially in its first two decades, the crusading journalism of W. E. B. Du Bois, who edited its monthly journal, the *Crisis,* between 1910 and 1934. With its financial support always tenuous, and its leadership chronically nervous about being perceived as radical socialist, the NAACP by the mid-1940s had become a conservative group, apart from civil rights. However, the continuing challenges of its lawyers, in addition to the brutal reaction to these challenges by many white communities in the South especially, had kept it over the years the premier force for social justice for black Americans.

In 1953, caught up in increasingly costly legal battles, and with annual dues its main source of income, the NAACP had launched a ten-year program, the Fight for Freedom Fund, to raise one million dollars each year for a legal campaign to end segregation by January 1, 1963, the centennial of the Emancipation Proclamation. In 1956, the fund had collected $800,000. Assuming the chairmanship, Robinson was aware of this shortfall and determined not to repeat it; in a meeting with NAACP leaders, he had sought out precisely this kind of challenge. Asked at first simply to lend his name to the fund, "I said sure, that would be easy, but isn't there something concrete I can do?" When someone suggested a tour, Jack agreed at once. The NAACP now counted about

350,000 members and about 1,500 branches. Jack was determined to increase that number dramatically, and also to stimulate the sale of life memberships in the association, each of which brought in $500.

In fact, during his first year as chairman, membership in the NAACP would decline for the first time since 1944 (although Jack sold a record number of life memberships). He was not the cause. Many Southern states, including Texas, Arkansas, Georgia, Virginia, and Tennessee, took stern measures, especially the passage of prohibitive laws, aimed at destroying the association. Officials were arrested and some went to jail for offenses such as refusing to turn over records, including membership lists, to local authorities. That year, 1957, the NAACP found itself embroiled in at least two dozen separate cases involving its right to exist. Ironically, the Montgomery bus boycott, despite the assistance of the NAACP, led to yet another challenge to its future. Out of this turmoil came Dr. King's Southern Christian Leadership Conference, which sought to coordinate the efforts of nonviolent protest groups working for civil rights and racial integration. In some respects, the SCLC complemented the NAACP; in other ways, especially in fund raising, it became its direct competitor, not only for funds but also for the hearts and minds of black Americans and the growing number of their liberal white allies.

Despite his show of confidence and his experience speaking for the NCCJ, Jack could not have been sure that he was ready for the far more demanding task of raising funds for the NAACP. In turn, the

NAACP had no firm idea how this celebrity, known for his aggressiveness as a player, would respond to the mundane demands of the tour. (Indeed, as the tour started, the current issue of the popular black weekly magazine *Jet* asked on its cover: "Does Jackie Robinson Talk Too Much?") Accordingly, the association had paired Robinson with Williams, one of its most able administrators, with the two men meeting for the first time on the eve of the tour. Elegant, articulate, and shrewd, Williams (later the United States ambassador to Ghana under President Johnson) would serve as Robinson's tutor, in case he needed and would accept one.

Fears about Jack soon proved unjustified. In Baltimore, an overflowing crowd gave him a rousing welcome in the main auditorium of the Sharp Street Memorial Methodist Church, even as hundreds more listened downstairs over loudspeakers. (Baltimore was now the only city where black major-league players faced Jim Crow in hotel accommodations.) Over the following days, which were packed with press conferences, informal meetings, and appearances at schools and churches in addition to the main fund-raising presentation, Robinson and Williams traveled to a variety of cities, including Pittsburgh, Cleveland, Detroit, Cincinnati, St. Louis, San Francisco, Oakland, and Los Angeles. In some places the weather was poor and hampered their progress; in other places, weak local leadership achieved the same result. Still, the duo pressed on, taking their message from audience to audience, with Robinson proving both a star attraction and a brilliant spokesman for the NAACP. Now and then, they were joined by prominent local figures; in Pittsburgh, Branch Rickey astonished his audience by declaring that blacks must use every means short of violence to achieve their freedom. Most often, however, Robinson, aided by Williams, carried the show.

In one city, Robinson so dominated a church assembly that "they rose waving bills singing 'Jackie is our leader we shall not be moved,' " as Williams reported to NAACP headquarters. The core of Jack's appeal was the interplay between his baseball celebrity and his humble sense of duty to the cause. Delivering a prepared speech in "a low and well modulated voice," but also improvising, he used simple language to appeal to his audience but did not hesitate to show the passion he felt for civil rights and the NAACP. "I feel the NAACP and I believe in it," he insisted, "and I only hope I can get this feeling over to you." Freely he admitted that this was a new stage of his life. "There was a time when I erred in being complacent," he confessed. "I was tempted to take advantages I had received for granted. Then I realized my responsibility to my race and to my country." In Cleveland, where Rabbi Rudolph M. Rosenthal of the Temple on the Heights gave the invocation, Jack poignantly emphasized the fact that his efforts were not for himself but for the future. "It's too late for us now to reap the benefits," he conceded; "it's not too late for our children."

Most immediately, he was making this sacrifice in order to aid black people living under Jim Crow down south. "We can't let these people down. . . .

Let's all get out and vote and support the NAACP."
But the struggle was also for everyone, black and
white, in the United States. "If I thought the
NAACP was working only for Negro-Americans
and not for the good of the country," he said, "I
wouldn't be making this tour." "White people need
to support the NAACP as strongly as do Negroes,"
he declared, "because it means as much to them as
to colored people"; he also took pains to praise "the
contributions of the Spingarns and other white persons to the NAACP cause." The civil rights struggle
had global significance. "In the present world crisis," he said, "the colored peoples of the world have
their eyes on America to see how Negroes are
treated here." Would Negroes do what was needed
to win the fight? Again and again Jack told about an
incident on the Dodgers' tour of Japan, when an
American umpire started a game in Osaka in the
rain ("It was a dark, a dreary, a rainy day") and then
called it after six innings when the rain kept falling.
But the crowd of forty thousand refused to leave
their seats. Eventually, the umpires and the teams
gave in, and play resumed. To Robinson, it had been
an amazing display of collective willpower, of
effective silent protest. "We in the NAACP can
achieve the same thing," he insisted, "if we have
unity and determination."

The high point of the tour probably came on January 27 in Oakland, California, when almost ten
thousand persons filled the Oakland Auditorium as
the regional NAACP launched its annual membership drive and Jack gave one of the most inspired

speeches of the tour. Here, as elsewhere, there were light if profitable moments, when Williams gleefully sold off kisses from Jack, which many women in the audience snapped up; but here, too, Jack shamed his listeners with the sad fact—"a disgrace"—that out of a black national population of 17 million, the NAACP boasted only 350,000 members even as it fought to give "first-class citizenship" to all. Nothing was more important than full citizenship rights. The auditorium shook with the loudest, most sustained burst of applause when Robinson ended his speech by declaring: "If I had to choose between baseball's Hall of Fame and first-class citizenship I would say first-class citizenship to all of my people."

In Los Angeles, his welcome home brought out some of the top city leaders. For the County Board of Supervisors, Kenneth Hahn, who had escorted Walter O'Malley on his helicopter ride over Los Angeles the previous year, presented Jack with a scroll hailing him as "a living legend in the field of sports, one whose career has blazed the way toward better understanding between people, whose unique abilities as an athlete have commanded the respect and admiration of people the world over." At a testimonial luncheon on January 28, Wilbur Johns, Jack's former basketball coach and now the UCLA athletic director, was one of two co-chairmen, and the guest list included the mayor, various supervisors, including Jack's boyhood friend Warren Dorn, Charlie Dressen, now the manager of the Washington Senators, and Kenny Washington, as well as several members of Jack's family, including his mother, Mallie. (In a speech, Dressen called Jack the "smartest man in baseball" and offered him a job as a scout for the Senators.)

Jack's poise surprised some of his old friends. To Sam Maltin, a reporter and longtime friend, "When Jackie spoke, it was not a matter of a few fumbling, half-apologetic phrases to the effect that, Shucks, you do me too much honor. It was a full-bodied speech, warm with remembrances of his youth in this area, singing out names of people who had helped him along the rocky road . . . and then business-like in its devotion to his primary duty." Robinson also gave a glimpse of the resentment he still harbored against Pasadena, where he had first met Jim Crow. Would he, someone asked, return to live there? "Has Pasadena changed since I left it?" Jack asked in reply. "In Atlanta, I know what I can do. In Pasadena, I didn't know."

Robinson was "extremely easy" to work with, Franklin Williams reported to Roy Wilkins at the NAACP headquarters in New York, and found no request or assignment "burdensome." Coachable as always, Jack sought and used advice at every point. Williams had prepared a series of cards outlining ideas for Jack's speeches; Robinson not only read the cards but also sought suggestions on ways to improve his lecture. The inconveniences of travel and a tough schedule did not affect his spirit. According to Williams, summing up the tour, "From every standpoint, it was extremely successful."

If Williams had any criticism of Robinson, it was that "Jackie is completely frank—almost to the point of naivete." Specifically, in discussions with him, it was "imperative" to make "extremely clear" which matters "are confidential and which are for publication." Williams was struck, too, by Robinson's degree of certainty as a worker for the association; he was "extremely confident" that the main problem keeping black Americans from rallying to the side of the NAACP was, "as he puts it, our inability to get our story told." In other words, Robinson was to some extent an idealist and an enthusiast with a possibly unrealistic grasp of the multiple problems facing the organization.

This was a shrewd judgment. Whether there was room for a person as idealistic and passionate as Robinson in an organization like the NAACP, which was hidebound in many of its ways, remained to be seen. The tour, however, only intensified Jack's desire to help the association. He now proposed two fundraising ideas for which he would work. One was for a $100-a-plate dinner in New York; the association had never attempted anything so grand. The other called for a committee of artists and entertainers, including athletes, in support of the NAACP. For Jack, whose presence would sell tickets and attract other celebrities, these proposals were only a token of his zeal to offer something tangible to the civil rights struggle.

Returning to New York, Jack was soon on the road again for the NAACP, with trips to Boston, Philadelphia, Miami, and Atlanta before the beginning of March; for much of the year, he would travel almost every weekend on its behalf. His visit to Boston on February 1 showed his drawing power and zeal. He appeared at functions sponsored by the

NAACP, the NCCJ, and the Massachusetts Jewish War Veterans organization. He spoke at a breakfast gathering attended by the mayor, greeted several hundred cheering members of the Boy Scouts and other boys' clubs, visited eagerly with Ted Williams ("a fine person") at a sportsmen's show, and then spoke again for the NAACP at a church. In March, Jack appeared before four thousand persons in Memphis, Tennessee, and before three thousand more in Richmond, Virginia. As a speaker, he was the first choice of many NAACP branches. If he could not come, according to the New Britain, Connecticut, branch, then Dr. Martin Luther King Jr. or Thurgood Marshall would do.

By late June, at the 48th Annual NAACP Convention in Detroit, he spoke as a man transformed. "I sometimes find it hard to remember," he said, "what my life was like just a brief year ago." In those days, "the big thing in it was the National League pennant, with all its problems of team, and strategy, and injuries and the tough competition that go into big league baseball." Now he was concerned with more important matters.

These matters included his health. About this time, Jack discovered that he, like his brothers Edgar and Mack, was suffering from diabetes. Jack Gordon recalled that Robinson had been at the clothing store on 125th Street when he left for a physical examination by a doctor in midtown Manhattan. "He left in high spirits," Gordon recalled, "but when he came back a couple of hours later, he was very quiet. He said that the doctor had told him that for someone who had played sports for so long and didn't smoke or drink, he had never seen a body so badly deteriorated. Jack found out that he had diabetes. It was very, very sad."

In 1957, despite intense research, diabetes was a mysterious, often devastating disease that affected about two percent of the American population. As Jack was doubtless told, at its core is the inadequate production or utilization of insulin by the body. Insulin controls the amount of sugar in the blood system but somehow also affects protein and fat metabolism in addition to carbohydrates such as sugar. Diabetes seemed to lead in some way to early arteriosclerosis, with the increased danger of heart attacks and strokes. Unlike "normal" arteriosclerosis, this version typically affected smaller arteries, especially those in the nerves, skin, kidney, and eyes; blindness was a distinct eventuality, although many diabetics escaped it. Many diabetics also had trouble fighting bacteria in general. It remained now for Robinson to find out, over time, how his own case of the disease would proceed. Even with insulin, Jack had to know, the life expectancy of a diabetic around this time was less than two-thirds of that of a nondiabetic.

His first task was to learn to inject himself. "He practiced for a few days on a tomato, sticking in the needle and squeezing," Rachel remembered. "Then he started on himself. Pretty soon, it had become routine. But his diabetes was a huge shock to us all." He also had to abandon some of his eating habits. "Jack used to put away a pint of ice cream at one sitting," according to Rachel. "That stopped, along with the pies and cake." His weight soon dropped by about twenty pounds, in part because of the restrictions on his diet, in part because of diuretic drugs and the diabetes itself.

A year later, Jack was as comfortable with his regimen of injections as might be expected. "Taking the insulin has become pretty much of a habit," he wrote his Chicago friends David and Caroline Wallerstein, "and I don't really mind it at all. I am just thankful it wasn't any more serious."

ON MONDAY, MARCH 3, Jack drove from his home to Manhattan on the first day of his new career as a company vice-president. At 425 Lexington Avenue, with some trepidation as he entered a hitherto alien world, he took possession of his office and tried to settle into his job as principal personnel officer of the Chock Full o' Nuts corporation.

A month later, a visiting journalist found no trace of his storied baseball career on display, no indication that the new vice-president had been a star athlete. Eventually Jack's desk sported one memento from sports, a bronzed, size-13 football shoe from his glory years at UCLA. (Still later, in 1960, he would also display a small mahogany piece about the Emancipation, in the shape of a hand—Abe Lincoln's—clutching a scroll; this was a gift from Dick and Pat Nixon.) Quickly Jack was able to recite the precise location of each of the twenty-seven company restaurants, most of which he had visited in his quest to meet as many employees as possible. He had also toured a coffee-roasting plant in Brooklyn and a bakery in Harrison, New Jersey, that were crucial to the operation, which would gross $25 million in the coming year. He loved his work. "From the start to the end," Rachel said, "Jack devoted all the time he needed to do it well. At the end of every day we knew what had gone on in this office and that, at this shop or that. The details that bored other people seemed to energize him. He was very happy there."

On the job, Jack tried hard to set an amiable tone; he offered himself as a friend, a colleague, a teammate. A sign on his desk read "Mr. Jack R. Robinson Vice President," but he did not stand on ceremony. "The name Jackie has been part of me all my life," he said to a reporter, "and most people call me Jackie. Sometimes the employees call me Mr. Robinson, but if they call me Jackie, I don't mind. They like to kid with me, and I enjoy kidding them back." From years of playing team sports he knew the importance of helping employees to see themselves not as isolated individuals in a hierarchy but as a fluid group with common goals. "This is a team operation," he insisted. "To gain the confidence of employees, you must be willing to discuss their problems openly with them. Then, when you're looking for their cooperation, you find it working for you."

Clearly, he saw himself as an advocate for the employees. In June, he contacted a friend at the White House to seek help for a worker who wanted to bring his two sons, born out of wedlock, up from Jamaica. "He is one of our good men," Robinson wrote, "and I would like to help him if possible." At least once, Jack went to court to testify for an employee. In a case involving a coffee roaster who had slashed a man with a knife (the other fellow had a pitchfork, Jack pointed out), Judge Benjamin Gassman Jr. imposed a six-month sentence but then suspended it. Jack's presence was obviously a factor in the decision. "Your having left the Dodgers," Judge Gassman admonished him, "is the reason they're in last place now."

Robinson's desire to be liked also made him vulnerable. From the start, the worst part of the job was the fact that he had the last word on the dismissal of employees. A fierce competitor, he was known to teammates and friends as a soft touch (like his mother) for individuals in distress, for panhandlers, for the appealing poor. "The day when I had the worst butterflies in my stomach, far more than I ever had with the Dodgers, was the day I had to fire an employee," he told a reporter. "I felt like the governor who sends a man to the electric chair even though he believes that the verdict of the jury and the judge's sentence were just." But he soon found out, to his chagrin, that some workers were liars. "They looked right at you," Jack told a friend about many of the employees, "looked you right in the eye, and told you these things, and it wasn't true at all."

Another complicating factor on the job was race. Race had helped to land him the job, and race helped and hampered him on it. He came to believe that many black workers expected too much of him, especially when their work habits were questioned, but also that some white employees resented his authority. Bill Black did not help matters when he revealed that "I hired Jackie because a majority of the people who work for me are colored—and I figured they would worship him." The threat of unionization also persisted, with Robinson seeing himself as an obvious target. "They are going to attempt to discredit me in some way," he wrote a friend about the unions, "because they feel if they can intimidate me they will have a chance of getting into our shops. I feel pretty well set up defensively so I am not worried." After losing a vote about unionization overseen by the National Labor Relations Board, some workers filed a complaint that Robinson had warned certain black employees that a trade union would cost him his job, and had said that "the white employees were jealous of my position in the company." Robinson denied both allegations and the NLRB exonerated him.

Percy Sutton, a major Harlem political and business leader, and a lifetime union member who was once a radical socialist, would insist that Robinson was not antiunion. "Jackie Robinson wasn't anti-union. He was hired to represent his company, just as the union leader represents his union. One of the things Jackie had to do was negotiate with the union. He did that. He wasn't against the unions."

Such setbacks did not lessen his love of the job. "I feel fine in my new setup," he wrote to a friend, "and am looking forward to a long relationship with this company. I have certainly seen a great deal of difference in working with a man like Bill Black and his company than a Bavasi and the Dodgers. Frankly there's as much difference in character as day and night and I am proud to be away from baseball and the insecurity that goes with it." More than a year later he was still pleased, if more realistic. "My job is developing," he wrote, "but it really is a long hard struggle each day. I have a good idea about the company and personnel is interesting. Some of the things I run into make interesting work. It seems something different happens every day. . . . It will be nice if this develops into a lifetime job. . . . The help is pleased, I am not certain about Black."

If he was unsure about Black, possibly it was because Jack could not quite believe his luck in finding an employer so willing, whatever his reasons, to allow him the freedom he craved to speak out on civil rights. This generosity was even more important because Jack also knew that, as a black man, he was lucky to have the job at all. Black himself, a quiet man who saw himself as something of a maverick, heard protests about Robinson's activities even before he reported his first day. To one complainant he offered a stern rejoinder about Robinson: Black would not interfere with "his right to think and speak his mind." In the face of many other protests in the coming years, Black would maintain this position.

The importance of Robinson's efforts on behalf of the NAACP was emphasized the month of his first tour when, following the victory by the boycotters led by Martin Luther King Jr., bombs exploded in four black churches in Montgomery, as well as at the homes of two ministers, one black, the other white, who had supported the protest. Almost as disturbing was the ensuing silence of President Eisenhower— "our great President in the White House," Jack called him, without a trace of irony. Eisenhower's silence puzzled Jack, so certain was he of the President's decency. "Knowing President Eisenhower as I do," he declared in Los Angeles, "I am confident he will protest against the bombing in the South. Our struggle for civil rights is . . . the struggle of all Americans. We are losing prestige because of things like the bombings of churches and Negro homes in the South." Only slowly did it dawn on Jack that politics could overwhelm individual decency in Ike's case. "I have the greatest respect for President Eisenhower," Robinson insisted in Boston, "but he must step into the breach in this situation and show everyone that the U.S. government will not condone these bombings." The church bombings were particularly ominous because "the Negroes are being hit in the one place where they have felt safe."

These appeals by Jack were a token of his growing concern with the political aspect of the struggle, the extent to which elected officials, especially those at the highest levels, were responding to what he saw as their obligations. He seemed drawn not so much to the Republican Party as, at first, to the party's men in the White House, with his personal experience of Eisenhower and Nixon, the Vice-President, shaping his opinions. He had never forgotten Eisenhower's remarkable gesture of respect at the B'nai B'rith dinner in November 1953, when the President had crossed a room to shake his hand. Similarly, with

Nixon, he had been charmed by their first meeting, which took place in the lobby of a Chicago hotel during the Republican National Convention of 1952, when the Dodgers were also in town. Nixon was in the lobby, chatting with Harrison McCall, another party loyalist, when McCall asked him if he wanted to meet Jackie Robinson. McCall had noticed Robinson talking in a corner to Paul Williams, a delegate from California.

Introduced to Robinson, Nixon completely dazzled the ballplayer. Not only did they have a southern California boyhood in common, with Nixon a graduate of Whittier College, a frequent opponent in sports of Pasadena Junior College; congratulating Jack on hitting a home run that day, Nixon also recalled, in astonishing detail, a football game in which Jack had played for UCLA against the University of Oregon, probably in the fall of 1939 (because their annual game was played that year in Los Angeles). To Jack's delight, Nixon asked about a particularly intricate play that Jack had helped to execute that day, and which Jack himself remembered clearly and took pleasure in explaining to an apparently enraptured Nixon. "I said to Nixon as we walked away," McCall wrote, "that, while Robinson had undoubtedly met a lot of notables during his career, nevertheless I was sure there was one person he would never forget."

Jack's eventual support of Nixon in 1960 would seem to prove the astuteness of this judgment. For some time after Jack started working with the NAACP, a quotation from Nixon on race and America's international reputation would be a feature of many of his speeches. But flattery was not the only basis of Nixon's appeal to Robinson, who had been lavished with praise since his boyhood. He viewed Nixon not only as a champion of civil rights who might lead the country to a new high ground of tolerance but also as a potential friend. The meaning of Nixon's notorious smearing of opponents, notably Helen Gahagan Douglas in the 1948 race for the U.S. Senate, and his resolute support for the demagogue Senator Joseph McCarthy to the bitter end, had little adverse impact on Robinson. For one thing, Robinson was himself a fervent anticommunist. "Our country is engaged in a titanic struggle with a resourceful and powerful enemy," he insisted in 1957. "This conflict has not yet reached the shooting stage. It is now largely a struggle for men's minds." In the battle for the darker millions of the world, American segregationists "provide grist for the Soviet propaganda mill." Robinson's anticommunism was as heartfelt in 1957 as it had been in 1949, when he spoke out against Robeson. It also reflected official NAACP policy, which barred Communists from its membership. In 1958, the 49th Annual Convention would kill efforts to change the association's policy in this regard.

Although it is possible that he voted for the liberal Democrat Adlai Stevenson in 1952, in 1956 Jack was a solid supporter of the Eisenhower-Nixon ticket, and taken with the Republican Party especially after, in August, the Democratic Party Convention rejected a report on civil rights championed by Senator Herbert H. Lehman of New York, to whom

Jack dispatched a vivid telegram of support. In contrast, Robinson was heartened by Eisenhower's championing of the bill that would become the Civil Rights Act of 1957. At first, Eisenhower resisted a key provision that would allow the Department of Justice to file suit on behalf of blacks denied the right to vote, but he shifted his position in the middle of the 1956 campaign. The move won him Jack's endorsement, which the White House made clear it valued. On October 4, the only black appointee of any consequence in the executive branch, E. Frederic Morrow, who had visited the Robinsons in Stamford several times and was a champion of Vice-President Nixon in particular, wrote to assure Jack that the White House was in the Dodgers' camp in the World Series. The Dodgers lost, but Eisenhower did not, to Jack's obvious satisfaction. In January, Maxwell M. Rabb, the secretary to the cabinet, thanked him for his "very fine letter" about the President and civil rights.

Recognizing now the lukewarm nature of Eisenhower's approach to civil rights, Jack took comfort in statements attributed to Nixon and emanating from Addis Ababa in Ethiopia, where Nixon was on official business. Speaking out against Communist charges about the prevalence of racism in the United States, Nixon had made (according to a report in the *Herald Tribune*) a ringing endorsement of integration: "We shall never be satisfied with the progress we have been making in recent years until the problem is solved and equal opportunity becomes a reality for all Americans." This was precisely the kind of firm statement Robinson had been awaiting from the White House. Congratulating Nixon on the forthrightness of his pronouncement, Jack emphasized how important it was that the Vice-President had made this declaration about race and civil rights "in the heart of Africa." Hereafter, Robinson would fold this quotation from Nixon into most of his speeches on civil rights.

In turn, Nixon responded to Robinson's praise with warm words of his own. He had received several messages of commendation for his statements in Africa, but "none which meant more to me." It was a privilege, Nixon wrote, "to be working along with someone like yourself" for the goal of equal opportunity for all Americans. He hoped Robinson would continue to support him: "Your expressions of approval will be a constant source of strength and encouragement to me." In April, Jack was encouraged again about the administration when he read a speech delivered by Sherman Adams, a special assistant to the President, at a dinner in New York to mark the fiftieth anniversary of the American Jewish Committee. Robinson wrote to tell Adams, formerly the governor of New Hampshire, how encouraged he was "to know our national leadership is sensitive to and concerned about the remaining vestiges of discrimination here at home."

Seeking a larger political role involving civil rights, Jack saw his communications with the White House—almost perfunctory in reality, although he was genuinely admired—as evidence that he was succeeding. In April, his confidence was boosted

when he was invited to appear on the respected political interview program *Meet the Press,* to be questioned by four reporters including Lawrence E.
Spivak of NBC, who later congratulated Jack on having done "a superb job." Certainly Jack had taken his
appearance seriously. In preparation, he had written
Maxwell Rabb asking for a briefing at the White
House. Almost certainly, this meeting never took
place. However, a month later, Rabb welcomed Jack
to the White House on a visit to Washington, then
surprised him by taking him in to meet Eisenhower.
The President had given him "another big thrill,"
Jack wrote in thanks. Because of his talk with Rabb,
Jack went on, "I have a much better understanding of
your thinking in the field of race relations."

In turn, Eisenhower expressed his thanks in a letter that was gracious and yet unconsciously coded
with two ideas that would soon disturb Robinson and
other civil rights leaders. Thanking Jack for "your
approval of our efforts to achieve equality of opportunity," the President went on: "It is our hope that we
can continue to foster a moral climate within which
the forces of informed good will operate effectively
in an atmosphere of democracy." The first of the two
ideas was contained in the phrase "equality of opportunity," which marked with some precision the limits
of Eisenhower's commitment to racial change.
"Equality of opportunity" was a goal far more limited than the comprehensive integration that inspired
Robinson, King, and most liberal supporters, black
and white, of the civil rights movement. The other
idea, obscured by the President's notoriously awk-

ward syntax, was his emphasis on fostering "a moral climate" that would ease social change. Unmentioned here were factors such as vigorous executive leadership, strong new legislation, and the tough enforcement of laws, which Robinson thought necessary in the face of Jim Crow.

As the Republican-inspired civil rights package moved through the Senate, Robinson watched closely as Southern Democrats, in particular, tried to block it. Normally, the legislation would have gone to the Judiciary Committee, headed by Senator James Eastland of Mississippi, who fully intended to bury it there. Efforts to bypass the Judiciary Committee were opposed by several Democrats, including two senators who thereafter would find it hard to win Robinson's support: John F. Kennedy and Lyndon B. Johnson. The President, too, dismayed Robinson. As opponents targeted Title III of the bill, which gave the Justice Department the right to sue on behalf of civil rights, Eisenhower's support weakened. At a press conference early in July, after Senator Richard Russell of Georgia publicly questioned the President's understanding of the bill, Eisenhower played into the hands of the Southerners by conceding that there were indeed "certain phrases I didn't understand."

This admission, followed by the excision of Title III, upset Robinson. "I am really in a muddle, and I don't know exactly what to do," he wrote Rabb. He respected the President's previous statements on civil rights, but "then we are knocked spinning by his press conference at what appeared to be a complete about face." To such protests, Eisenhower and his associates, with one exception, responded with a shrug. That exception was Nixon, who privately characterized the bill as "watered-down" in promising Robinson that he himself would fight for more vigorous legislation. Eager to believe Nixon, Robinson heard several warnings about his record but dismissed the past as irrelevant. "What you do and say is the important thing," he assured the Vice-President. "We are all very proud of what you are doing. As far as I am concerned, a man's motives don't mean a thing as long as he is attempting to do good. We sincerely believe that is your intention, and we heartily endorse it."

Within a few days, Jack's respect for the White House was tested as never before. At the Robinsons' as in millions of American homes, the start of the school year in the late summer of 1957 was a time of mingled anxiety and joy. But Jack and Rachel's attention, and the nation's, was soon drawn to events surrounding the opening of school in Little Rock, Arkansas. They could not help seeing a link between events there and their own nervous negotiation of the hitherto all-white Martha Hoyt Elementary School when Jackie had enrolled there. In Little Rock, on September 2, the day before the start of classes, Governor Orval Faubus called in the National Guard, ostensibly to preserve order but in reality to bar the entry of nine black students. Backed by the Arkansas NAACP, the students were to integrate Central High School according to a plan set by the local school board and approved by the courts. Two days later, with a white mob yelling defiance—and worse—at the black children, the Guard prevented them from entering the school. In response, Eisenhower promised to uphold the Constitution but also called on all parties to be patient. The Justice Department then entered the case with a friend-of-the-court brief. On September 20, ruling against Governor Faubus, the presiding federal judge ordered the admission of the black students to Central High.

Jack responded indignantly to Eisenhower's call for patience. "We are wondering to whom you are referring," he sarcastically wired the White House, "when you say we must be patient." Blacks had been patient for hundreds of years; the time had come for action. Although Eisenhower did not respond directly to this message, a few days later Rabb spoke on the telephone to Robinson to try to explain the administration's position on the explosive situation. Whatever Rabb said hardly encouraged Robinson, who wrote his friend Caroline Wallerstein in Chicago that "as far as 'Ike' goes he has been a real disappointment." On Monday, September 23, three days after the ruling against Faubus, the nine black students, attempting to enter the school, found the guardsmen gone but city police present along with a vicious mob of about one thousand whites. At noon, on the orders of city officials, the students went home. Daisy Bates, the president of the Arkansas NAACP, then announced that they would not return "until they have the assurance of the President of the U.S. that they will be protected from the mob."

On Wednesday, to Jack's relief, Eisenhower finally acted. Placing ten thousand National Guards-

men on federal duty, he also sent one thousand paratroopers of the 101st Airborne Division to Little
Rock to protect the six black girls and three black
boys in one of the strongest assertions of federal
force against a local authority in the South since the
end of Reconstruction in 1877. The paratroopers
would stay in Little Rock until late November, but
some guardsmen were still on duty when the school
year ended. Eisenhower's action drew immediate
praise from civil rights supporters in the movement
and certainly transformed Robinson's opinion of the
President's performance. "Please accept my congratulations," he wired Eisenhower, "on the positive
position you have taken in the Little Rock situation. I
should have known you would do the right thing at
the crucial time. May God continue giving you the
wisdom to lead us in this struggle."

On October 17, with the situation in Little Rock
far from resolved, Jack joined Henry Lee Moon,
Herbert Hill, and Lucille Black of the NAACP in
New York for an open telephone conversation with
Daisy Bates and seven of the nine children who had
integrated Central High. With his typically warm
feeling for young people, Robinson was moved as he
chatted with each youngster in turn, praising them
and Mrs. Bates for their heroism in the face of mob
behavior that had shocked many Americans and gal-
vanized new support for civil rights. "I think you and
the youngsters are doing a tremendous job," Robinson told Mrs. Bates, "and it makes us swell up with
pride. . . . You certainly have the support of many,
many people and it is just wonderful."

A year after quitting baseball, Robinson had become a forceful, respected part of the civil rights debate, able to hold his own on programs such as *Meet the Press* or to field bristling questions from the journalist Mike Wallace about housing discrimination. At a commencement program, when Dr. King was also honored, Howard University in Washington, D.C., awarded him an honorary doctor of laws degree. The same day, Governor Abraham Ribicoff announced Jack's appointment to a new three-person board of parole of the Connecticut state prison system, effective September 1. Serving with him would be a Yale University professor of law and the chief justice of the state supreme court. This appointment moved Jack, because it seemed a tribute to his integrity and selflessness—the job carried no pay. Inexperienced about prisons, he would learn from the other men. "I'm not dumb enough to try to run things," he said. "I know I have a lot to learn." If he was "a little bit soft-hearted," he would aim to be judicious: "Sentiment is a good thing in its place, but when you're dealing with human lives then it seems to me that there are much more important considerations."

Almost everything he touched seemed to work well. At his $100-a-plate NAACP dinner, about fifteen hundred guests showed up to mark the end of the 1957 Fight for Freedom Fund drive. In his after-dinner speech, Jack talked of the pervasiveness of bigotry, of its power over money and fame, as exemplified by the recent failure of Nat "King" Cole to win a new national sponsor for his television show despite a successful season, and the rebuff of Willie Mays when he attempted to buy a house in San Francisco following the Giants' move there. "None of us," Jack ended in a theme he would repeat the rest of his life, "no matter how hard he has worked or how much money he has contributed, can afford to rest until this fight for freedom is won—and I assure you that it will be won. How, in my opinion, will be determined by the Negro himself. It is, indeed, a fight for survival, not alone for the Negro, but for the nation."

In January 1958, he denied a report that he would top off this new phase of his prestige and popularity by running for public office: "There just is not one kernel of truth to any such reports or rumors. I am perfectly happy with my job at Chock Full o' Nuts. I'm not entering politics. Period." Instead, he rededicated himself to the NAACP, the Harlem branch YMCA, and his other voluntary involvements. For the annual YMCA campaign, he raised $55,000 after challenging the official fund-raising committee to match every dollar he himself would raise independently. For these and other efforts, a flood of local honors—from the Young Adult Fellowship of the Salem Methodist Episcopal Church in Harlem to the Brooklyn chapter of the National Association of Business and Professional Women's Clubs—came his way. He was a popular graduation speaker, as in June at P.S. 111 in New York, when he urged parents not to dictate too sternly to their children. "These are swiftly moving times," he said, "and our children must move fast too. They have to stay with the times or otherwise be hopelessly left behind."

Recognizing his sterling work, the NAACP elected him to its board of directors. Later, along with the popular NAACP fund-raiser Kivie Kaplan, a wealthy Jewish manufacturer from Boston, Jack became a co-chairman of the Life Membership Committee. He then undertook perhaps his most dangerous assignment for the NAACP, with a trip through the South that included stops in Louisiana, Mississippi, and Florida. From Jackson, Mississippi, sending Robinson the names of prosperous blacks who might be approached for life memberships, the NAACP state leader Medgar Evers warned him: "Do not have N.A.A.C.P. on any part of the envelope. It is all right to be contained in the letter." On February 16, which the NAACP declared "Jackie Robinson Day" in Mississippi, he received a rousing welcome at a state conference of NAACP branches in Jackson. There, in an address called "Patience, Pride and Progress," Robinson challenged the notion that patience meant submission, or that impatience always meant radicalism. "Although we who struggle to secure civil rights deplore prejudice," he declared, "its elimination is not our goal. Containment is our goal. What we seek is the suppression, by law and the weight of public opinion, of the hostile manifestations of racial prejudice. We wish that the hearts of all men were filled with good will for their fellow human beings. But this goal is beyond our reach and we cannot wait until men's hearts are changed to enjoy our constitutional rights."

Jack's reception in Mississippi moved him. "We had an overflow crowd and they were very receptive," he wrote home to Rachel. "You would be amazed at how eager they are for someone to lend a helping hand and I must say I got a thrill out of the way they took to me."

Completing the tour in Florida, tired from his grinding schedule and on the strong advice of his doctor, Jack stopped off in Miami for a vacation. Drifting back into the past, he stayed at the "colored" Sir John Hotel, formerly the Lord Calvert, where he, Campanella, Newcombe, and other black Dodgers had lived over the years during spring training. No doubt he felt a twinge of nostalgia for his vanished days as a big-league star. "Miami isn't what it once was," he wrote home. In weather too cool for his liking he played some rounds of golf, but mainly he sought to rest after a grueling year in which he had often felt extreme fatigue. No one was sure how much his diabetes had to do with this condition, but his illness certainly did not help him as he kept up a dense schedule. "I needed this very much," he wrote Rachel from Miami, "and hope I don't allow myself to get this tired again. I was shot both mentally and physically when I arrived. I am coming around now and should be fine very soon."

As for baseball, Jack still had a soft spot in his heart for his former teammates, and even for the team. The previous year, in Woonsocket, Rhode Island, he spoke free of charge at a testimonial dinner for Clem Labine, one of his favorite teammates over the years with Brooklyn. Declining to join the chorus of outrage and recrimination in Brooklyn, Jack watched from a distance as the Golden Age ended and the Dodgers left a community that would never recover fully from this loss, and moved to Los Angeles. Most Dodger supporters heaped abuse on Walter O'Malley, but to his son, Peter, "it took a great deal of courage to move the franchise to Los Angeles without a place to play, until eventually a stadium could be designed and built. It was an extraordinary move. My father had believed in building a stadium in Brooklyn, and it didn't happen. He believed in the move to Los Angeles, and it did happen, and it proved to be very, very successful."

In January 1958, Jack heard with dismay the tragic news of the crippling of Roy Campanella in an accident at night, when a rented car he was driving skidded on an icy patch of road near his home on Long Island. The impact crushed the catcher's fifth cervical vertebra and left him, in mid-career, a quadriplegic. Despite Jack's clashes with Campanella, or perhaps because of them, he felt the tragedy of the accident keenly. In the years to come, he would be moved both by Campanella's indomitable response to his injury and by the unflagging devotion of Walter and Peter O'Malley to the welfare of the Campanellas.

In Los Angeles, awaiting the completion of their stadium, the team now played before huge crowds in the Coliseum, where Jack had starred in many a football game in 1939 and 1940. But when the stress of its transcontinental move, the uncertainty of a coming city referendum on its right to own and develop land in Chavez Ravine, and conditions in the Coliseum unsuited to baseball led to a dreadful record, he took no comfort in Dodger misery. "I root for them and wish them well," he said publicly in May. Jack was sincere. "I really feel sorry for the Dodgers," he wrote to a friend. "It seems they can't do a thing right and I am really hoping things break for them very soon." As for Campanella, "I am sorry to see him in this condition but feel he may pull out [of it] if he has any luck."

However, Robinson snapped when he heard that the Urban League of Los Angeles had given Walter O'Malley a plaque to mark his "enlightened leadership in opening the door to employment of Negro athletes in major league baseball." The report touched Jack in a tender spot; he could not bear to see Branch Rickey's glory given away so brazenly—especially since O'Malley, in a recent *Time* magazine cover story, had hinted that one reason for the Dodgers' move from Brooklyn was the rapid growth of its black and Puerto Rican populations. "That's preposterous," Jack said publicly about the citation. "O'Malley had nothing to do with it. It was all Mr. Rickey's idea, and I don't believe O'Malley even knew anything about it. In fact, he wasn't too keen about it in the first place." (On the defensive, the Urban League announced that the award was going to the Dodgers as an organization, not to O'Malley personally.)

The incident only deepened Jack's disappointment with baseball. In July, in Cleveland, when he ran into Bill Veeck and stopped to chat with the affable, progressive former owner of the Indians, Jack confessed that he had not bothered to watch the recent All-Star Game in Baltimore on television.

"Baseball has nothing for me," he told Veeck bitterly, "and I am damn sure I have nothing for it."

LATE IN THE SUMMER OF 1958, Jack and the entire Robinson home on Cascade Road endured a gentle but reverberating shock when Rachel, after several months of intense preparation, including study sessions starting at two in the morning, enrolled full-time at New York University in downtown Manhattan in a program leading to a master's degree in psychiatric nursing.

Rachel had decided to go back to school for two main reasons. One, the less important, was money. Jack's position at Chock Full o' Nuts, she knew, was hardly set in stone; in addition, their household expenses were mounting steadily and would only continue to climb as the three children approached college. Moreover, she needed to prepare herself in case anything untoward should happen to Jack. The second major reason had to do with her individual sense of fulfillment. After more than a decade spent in loyal support of Jack, she now wanted a career of her own, and in the profession she knew best, nursing, preferably as a teacher. She and Jack had many long discussions about his wish to see her remain at home and her desire to go back to school. "He was never adamant," she said later, "although he wasn't happy. I guess we both knew that the bigger problem would come later, if—or when—I took a job."

For several months, Jack watched curiously, perhaps hoping against hope that she would give up her plan, as Rachel became a diligent student again, just as she had been when he had first observed her in Westwood in the fall of 1940. Some eighteen years and three children later, uncertain of how she would fare, she had prepared for the Graduate Record Examinations, which were mandatory for admission to graduate school. "Rae is studying again," Jack wrote Caroline Wallerstein in Chicago. "She wants a masters in Nursing and the exam is rather hard. She spends most of her time (spare) with the books."

Helping to make Rachel's plans possible in 1958 was the presence in the Robinson home of her mother, Zellee. Following her own mother's death in Los Angeles, and at Jack's urging, Zellee had moved east. (With her coming, the Robinsons' live-in arrangement with Willette Bailey ended, although she remained like one of the family.) When the Robinsons bought her a car, she was able to help get the children, especially young David, to and from school; she could also prepare dinner when Rachel was away. On weekends, she would head for Brooklyn, where she had her own room at the Covingtons' and where she attended church and quickly developed a solid circle of friends, including Willette. For Zellee, the move was almost in every way a step upward. "I was less enthusiastic than Jack about having my mother live with us," Rachel said, "but she absolutely blossomed with the move. The children loved her, she made friends easily, and she took to East Coast life in a big way. And Jack, as always, adored her, just as she adored Jack. It freed me to make some changes in my life."

Changes in Rachel's life meant changes in Jack's life. Despite Rachel's astute handling of their finances, he was well aware of the tenuousness of his job, Bill Black's good intentions at Chock Full o' Nuts notwithstanding. Alertly, Jack continued to keep an eye open for new business opportunities, although nothing he attempted could be in conflict with his main job. But opportunities dwindled with each year away from baseball. That year he sold his share of the struggling Jackie Robinson Store on 125th Street; Jack's ventures in housing construction were still dormant.

Now and then he was teased by the prospect of another Hollywood film. Despite a show of nonchalance, when a telephone call alerted him that Kirk Douglas was doing a movie in which there might be a part for Jack, he hurried to explore his chances. "Frankly I don't care one way or the other," he wrote to the Wallersteins, who had very good movie connections, "but I heard it was to be filmed in Europe and you know how Rae has been dying for such a trip." Finally Jack confessed: "I guess I'm really a ham at heart because the call did excite me a bit." (The movie was probably *Spartacus,* released in 1960; if so, the coveted role went to Jack's statuesque teammate at UCLA Woody Strode, who still possessed the lithe physique that had entranced Bruin fans in the late 1930s.) Later, in Los Angeles, Jack had a chance to speak to the producer Sam Goldwyn Jr. about his proposed film version of *Adventures of Huckleberry Finn.* To Jack's disappointment, Goldwyn decided to look elsewhere for an actor to portray Mark Twain's noble slave Jim. "It's a pretty good script," Jack judged wistfully. "The last I heard Archie Moore [the boxer] was leading the field for the role. I just hope it turns out well."

Money, and Hollywood, were on Jack's mind again in signing a contract for a biography to be written by Carl T. Rowan, a veteran writer with the Minneapolis *Tribune* (later, he was ambassador to Finland and director of the United States Information Agency). Even more exciting for Jack was the rumor that Sidney Poitier and Harry Belafonte were eager to pick up the film rights. (In some ways, Poitier was the Jackie Robinson of Hollywood—the first man to be allowed consistently to play leading African-American roles with dignity in an integrated setting. That winter, as Poitier prepared to start his latest movie, he and his wife, Juanita, vacationed with the Robinsons in Mexico.) Above all, Jack saw the biography as a chance to show the world the brightest aspect of his story: not his triumph in baseball, but what he and Rachel, together, had been able to achieve in the face of adversity.

When Rachel seemed touchy about revealing private details, Jack urged openness. "I don't expect we should go into every aspect of our life," he reasoned in a letter to her, "but the things that we have accomplished together should be told to everyone. At least to me what your love has meant should be an incentive for others. Sharing this is something I like to do because there are few people that have done as much or gone through as much and still maintain the love we have." Properly written, the book could "do a lot of good. We have the story sweetheart if we aren't afraid to tell it."

EVEN AS HE LOYALLY served the NAACP, Robinson became increasingly bothered both by its conservatism and by its uneven support in the black world. Convinced that its conservatism bred apathy and even disdain, he looked at the timidity of many people under Jim Crow and placed some of the blame squarely on the NAACP leadership. In several places, he noticed how local blacks became excited by his bolder moves, as when he stood up to conservative white journalists in Jackson, Mississippi, or, in Denver, challenged the civil rights record of the governor of Colorado; and yet these same blacks, on their own, were fearful. He did not overstate his own militancy. In West Virginia, where he accepted a plaque honoring his efforts, Jack refused to strut. "As a Negro," he said, "I don't think I should be honored for going out and fighting for the rights we [should] have had many years ago." Much of the blame lay with educated blacks who turned their backs on the less fortunate. "Too many of our professional men," he went on, "achieve a certain amount of success and then forget the trials of their childhood."

Finally, gently at first, he began to criticize the NAACP and Roy Wilkins himself. In July, Jack boldly told a press conference before a meeting of the board of directors in Cleveland that he would "love to see a more aggressive stand by the NAACP" on civil rights. In the South, not without good reason, blacks were too scared to protest; but "in the North, what reason does a colored person have for not associating with the NAACP?" He cited a failure "as far as our leadership is concerned. I believe they have not done enough to gain the confidence of the little man in the street. The average person is waiting to see the leaders take an aggressive stand." Shortly afterward, he openly attacked Wilkins for suggesting that a seven-year delay in completing school integration in Prince Edward County, Virginia, apparently approved by a federal judge, "could be regarded as reasonable." "It is a tremendously unfortunate statement which will hurt the organization," Jack commented. "I was upset and angry when I read it." When Wilkins, who had been misled by a reporter's telephoned account of the judge's ruling, reversed himself, Jack did not let go. For the NAACP head to have agreed to any delay was "most unfortunate." Citing the struggle in Little Rock, Jack offered that "the leadership of the NAACP cannot allow the so-called little man down on the firing lines to feel he is being let down this way."

Although Wilkins could not afford to tangle publicly with Robinson on this issue, he resented Jack's public criticism, which smacked of self-righteousness once the NAACP leader had reversed himself. In September, Robinson antagonized Wilkins again. When A. Philip Randolph, the revered leader of the Brotherhood of Sleeping Car Porters and now a vice-president of the AFL-CIO trade union organization, called a meeting to discuss more aggressive moves against Jim Crow, Jack readily attended—but as an individual, not on behalf of the NAACP. At the meeting (where attendees worried over the fate of Dr. King, who was locked up in a Montgomery, Alabama, jail after city police violently arrested him), Jack threw his support behind Randolph's idea to stage a youth march the following month in Washington, D.C., to protest the brutality suffered by black children seeking integrated education in the South.

From the start, Robinson was perceived as point man for the march; he was designated its "marshal." Again, his presence helped to ensure a wide cross-section of support from groups as well as individuals for what was called the Youth March for Integrated Schools. Set at first at one thousand, the number of prospective marchers quickly multiplied. "3,000 to March on D.C.," the *Amsterdam News* proclaimed; "Jackie Robinson Will Lead Way." Included were representatives of the Protestant Council of Churches and the Jewish Labor Committee, as well as individuals such as the activist Stanley Levinson, who would be a major force in Dr. King's civil rights efforts, and Father John LaFarge, editor of the Catholic journal *America*. However, the NAACP was not officially among its number.

On the afternoon of October 25, joined by Rachel and Jackie Junior, as well as by several other prominent leaders and personalities such as Harry and Julie Belafonte and Coretta Scott King, Jack led about ten thousand students, black and white, on a march down Constitution Avenue to the Lincoln Memorial in the capital. The organizers had hoped to have some students present a statement to the President at the

White House, but Eisenhower and his advisors would not countenance it. Although the march might embarrass the administration, Jack had insisted that it was nonpartisan and definitely not a radical initiative, as some White House officials complained. Thus, Eisenhower's refusal angered him. "I have never been a Democrat in my life," he rashly told a reporter two weeks later, "—until October 25."

Wilkins and other leaders of the NAACP also had reservations about the march. In November, the president of the New York branch of the NAACP, Russell P. Crawford, undoubtedly spoke for more people than himself when he accused the organizers of diverting vital financial support from the NAACP with their venture into symbolism. In his column in the *Amsterdam News,* Crawford suggested archly of the event that its biggest beneficiary was probably the bus companies paid to drive the marchers to Washington. Incensed, Jack responded that such criticism "is causing groups to lose interest in the NAACP." Crawford published the text of a letter to him from Robinson but also his own reply, which indicated at least one underlying source of friction. Calling Robinson "the soul of sincerity," he urged him nevertheless to "discontinue the practice of attacking your teammates publicly as you did Mr. Wilkins because he made a perfectly human error."

Despite this friction, Jack was still ready to serve the Fight for Freedom Fund as master of ceremonies at yet another big dinner (honoring John H. Johnson of *Ebony* magazine and Rudolf Bing, general manager of the Metropolitan Opera, whose hiring of

Marian Anderson to sing in Verdi's *Un Ballo in Maschera* in 1955 had made her the Jackie Robinson of American opera). Two weeks later, however, Jack was peeved again when he addressed the Rhode Island Committee on Discrimination in Housing in Providence. With growing concern, he watched as the audience, at least half of them black, sat torpidly through the presentations. "You didn't seem interested," he scolded the gathering. "One of the things that's wrong with the Negro today is that they are so willing to sit back and let other people pick up the ball and run with it. . . . I think it's time for us to start pushing. This is the only way people respect you."

Seeking ways to make his own voice more influential, he finally landed the radio program he had been seeking for some time without success because of the lack of a sponsor. Starting early in January 1959, on Sundays at 6:30 p.m., listeners to WRCA in New York City could hear a half-hour interview program, *The Jackie Robinson Show*. Making the program possible, when other sponsors shied away, was Philip Liebmann of Liebmann Breweries of Brooklyn, makers of Rheingold Beer, reputedly the best-selling beer in the region. Liebmann and Rheingold Beer had led the way in sponsoring blacks on television, notably in the case of the landmark *Nat King Cole Show,* and in using blacks both to endorse products and as talent in commercial messages. Setting aside his scruples about alcohol, Jack gladly accepted this sponsorship. His guest list featured political figures such as former governor and senator Herbert Lehman of New York, Governor Abraham

Ribicoff of Connecticut, Mayor Robert Wagner of New York City, and Mrs. Eleanor Roosevelt. Without success, Jack even tried to attract the President and the Vice-President. Eisenhower was to read the Gettysburg Address—"all listeners would be thrilled by such a reading"—from his farm near the battlefield.

For Jack, the program was a perfect gift at an auspicious time. On January 31 that year, he celebrated his fortieth birthday.

WITHIN A FEW DAYS, he had more to celebrate. At Chock Full o' Nuts, where his two-year agreement was about to expire, Bill Black let Jack know that his contract would be renewed, for five years. Black continued to show solid support for his most controversial employee; in effect, the corporation was subsidizing Jack's civil rights work, but Black dismissed criticism on this score. "If anyone wants to boycott 'Chock' because I hired Jackie Robinson," he declared, "I recommend Martinson's coffee. It's just as good. As for our restaurants, there are Nedick's, Bickford's and Horn and Hardart in our price range. Try them. You may even like them better than ours."

More secure now, Jack used his job as a base for other activities, including another, larger Youth March for Integrated Schools. Early in April, he and Daisy Bates, the NAACP leader in Little Rock, addressed a spirited farewell rally at Friendship Baptist Church in Harlem. A week later, on Saturday, April 18, more than 130 buses left New York City for the capital, where over thirty thousand marchers, blacks and whites together, proceeded through the streets of the capital to the sound of drums and the singing of the civil rights anthem "We Shall Overcome." At the Washington Monument, to honor his crucial role in the event, leaders presented Jack with a scroll before a gathering that included celebrities such as Poitier, Belafonte, and Tom Mboya, the charming twenty-eight-year-old Kenyan labor leader, who seemed to personify the rich promise of the new Africa. The mood of this march, in contrast to the first, was far more upbeat; with A. Philip Randolph promising to lead marches again and again to Washington until the administration showed a proper concern for the issues involved, the White House itself was now more respectful. Although the President still hid out, a few aides met with march leaders to discuss its goals.

His strength sapped by diabetes, Jack nevertheless found it hard to resist appeals for help. He cut back in one place: he resigned his unpaid position on the Connecticut State Prison Parole Board. "I felt I wasn't being fair to the state," he explained, "and the state wasn't being fair to us." But he again denied rumors that he was clearing the deck to run for public office. "I'm going to have to stop doing a few other things," he explained, "because I just don't have the time." However, he found time for other activities: his radio program; helping to plan yet another Youth March for Integrated Schools in Washington, D.C.; fund-raising for the NAACP and the Harlem branch YMCA; organizing a major testimonial dinner for his friend Floyd Patterson after the traumatic loss of his heavyweight crown to Ingemar Johansson of Sweden; helping to launch Project Airlift Africa to bring African students to the United States; organizing another group, Athletes for Juvenile Decency, which sought to use well-known sports figures to fight juvenile crime and drug use; and testifying in Washington before the Senate Subcommittee on Juvenile Delinquency.

Respect for Robinson, especially among blacks, remained high. When he gave a splendid speech at the Polo Grounds (now deserted by the baseball Giants) to bring to a close the 50th Annual Convention of the NAACP, Roy Wilkins praised him for having done "a superb job of inspiring and instructing" the many delegates in attendance.

In April of that year, 1959, seeking an even more powerful forum for expressing his views than that offered by his radio program, Robinson became a columnist with the New York *Post*. One of the oldest newspapers in America (reputedly founded by Alexander Hamilton) and one of the most popular in New York, the *Post* identified with liberal causes. On April 24, James A. Wechsler, its editor, announcing Jack's appointment, informed readers that although the column, called simply "Jackie Robinson," would appear in the sports section (three times a week), Robinson would write freely "on any subject that he feels strongly about." The column would make history. With the *Post* offering it to other newspapers across the nation, this would mark the first time, in Wechsler's words, "that real national syndication has been attempted for a columnist who happens to be a Negro." Aiding him as a ghostwriter on the column was the talented young black playwright William Branch.

In his first column, on April 28, Jack promised to be bold in expressing his views, and to make the most of this unprecedented opportunity for a black voice. "For better or worse," he declared, "I've always thought it more important to take an intelligent and forthright stand on worthwhile questions than to worry about what some people might think." He would comment on sports but, he added, "I'll also express myself on the ticklish subject of politics." While he could not speak for all Negroes, he relished the chance "for one of us to speak to so wide an audience concerning just what we feel and think." In addition, "although I am no authority on international affairs," he would write on events in Cuba, Africa, Israel, Tibet—wherever events took place that he found of significance to his concerns.

On the whole, his column lived up to this prescription. It struck a balance between sports and other subjects but kept its author's sensitivity to racism and civil rights at the fore. Over the first year, baseball was the subject of the largest number of columns on any single subject. Jack also wrote several pieces on boxing; occasionally only, he wrote on football, basketball, golf, and tennis. But sport was perhaps the least inspired aspect of the column, which sparkled mainly when Robinson made civil rights, or some other aspect of the fight for social justice, his focus. Now and then, as in taking on the

Professional Golfers Association for its explicit "Caucasians Only" membership policy, sports and civil rights were coupled. In fact, Jack's columns attacking the PGA and the local Metropolitan Golfers Association, which abided by the PGA's Jim Crow rule, were a factor in the PGA's decision to grant membership to Charlie Sifford. Near the end of March 1960, Sifford became the Jackie Robinson of golf.

On the whole, Jack tried to express his views on a wide range of interrelated topics: politics in Harlem, juvenile delinquency, housing and school discrimination in New York and elsewhere, migrant workers, trade unions, and personalities who caught Robinson's fancy, including Belafonte and Poitier, the intelligent, socially conscious broadcaster and former attorney Howard Cosell, and the singer and actress Diahann Carroll. Modestly, Jack probed international affairs. He wrote a few columns on Africa, including South Africa and Southwest Africa, Liberia, and the Congo. After an erroneous report that Fidel Castro had invited him to dinner in Havana, Jack ("somewhat peeved by this report") sent Castro a letter urging him to build on the residue of American goodwill toward his revolution and act more responsibly. Castro should "stop now to see where he is going rather than continue to plunge along blindly. Passion and zeal are fine qualities. But a dose of foresight is a pretty good commodity to have along with them."

His real interest was America, and civil rights. In taut language, his second column described an incident that had occurred six days before, in Poplarville, Mississippi, when "a quiet, hooded, well-drilled group of men entered an unguarded jailhouse in southern Mississippi. And when they left, they took with them a screaming, beaten, bloody, human being." Jack's focus was the contrast between the terrible fate of the prisoner, Mack Charles Parker, a young black man who had been accused of raping a white woman, and the folly of those people who opposed civil rights legislation as being punitive of the South. In particular, Robinson criticized the delaying tactics of the governor of Mississippi, who claimed to oppose lynching but resisted laws to prevent it. "I can't really express my deep outrage," Jack wrote, "about this terrible incident. . . . The lynching of Mack Parker is but the end result of all the shouts of defiance by Southern legislatures, all the open incitement to disobey the law by Southern governors, and all the weak-kneed 'gradualism' of those entrusted with enforcing and protecting civil rights."

(Parker's body soon surfaced in the nearby Pearl River. The FBI, after investigating the lynching and deciding that it violated no federal law, turned over its findings, including the identities of the lynchers, to local authorities. But a grand jury of whites refused even to hear evidence against these men.)

On May 8, Robinson took an even bolder step in his column. Looking ahead to the elections the following year, 1960, he announced that his column would soon venture into the arena of politics. In 1959, this was a nervy step for a black man, a former professional athlete, publishing a column in the sports section of a newspaper. Nevertheless, Jack moved with some confidence, and his basic idea from the start was to sway voters. In 1947, he noted, players opposed to him had come around to his side because winning games meant more money; politics now "is somewhat similar to that situation—except that instead of money, it's votes." As 1960 approached, "all the politicians who have kept their distance since the last campaign are out in force now—each with a big smile, a warm handshake and a hatful of promises." He would try to find out the truth about each man.

For the presidency, the likely candidates included, among the Republicans, Richard Nixon and Nelson Rockefeller, the newly elected governor of New York. Among the Democrats were Rockefeller's predecessor as governor, Averell Harriman; Adlai Stevenson, twice defeated for the presidency; the liberal Senator Hubert H. Humphrey of Minnesota; and John F. Kennedy, the handsome, wealthy young senator from Massachusetts.

In his column, Jack positioned himself as belonging to neither party. "I guess you'd call me an independent, since I've never identified myself with one party or another in politics." He was, in fact, a registered independent. But already Robinson had shown a clear disposition to support the Republicans, and in particular Vice-President Nixon. His major motive for doing so was not personal gain. "I have no political ambitions," he would declare, "and want no job other than the excellent non-political one I already have. There are no rewards or payoffs that could ever make me sell out in my determination to fight for equal rights for all." Even with Eisenhower and Nixon, he was quick to strike when either man deviated from a firm commitment to civil rights. "How long, Mr. President," Jack asked after reading about the latest salute to democracy by Eisenhower, "must we continue to wait before you back up those fine and singing words with definite, positive action?"

But Robinson was a Republican at heart, albeit a liberal Republican on the key matter of civil rights. Flattered at their first meeting, he genuinely liked Nixon insofar as he knew him; perhaps Jack made a great deal of their common Californian roots. But he also had a good feeling about the Republican Party in general. He liked its toughness on communism, its image of moral austerity that was unsullied, unlike the Democratic Party's, by Southern bigotry or by the seedy corruption of some urban Democratic machines; he liked the Republicans' association with capitalism and business, an area Robinson was determined to learn and even conquer. Nevertheless, quite consciously, he also set out to achieve a difficult, perhaps impossible goal. Seeking to make his voice influential in both parties on the matter of civil rights, he aimed to influence both nominations for the presidential election. Each candidate would be measured by his ongoing record on civil rights legislation and his willingness to enforce laws to protect blacks. This refusal to pick a party and stick with his choice would be the defining factor in Robinson's politics for almost the rest of his life. It would make him often appear noble in his loyalty to principle, especially on civil rights; but it would also make him seem to some people self-righteous and even undependable.

In 1959, after Senator Hubert Humphrey addressed a formal dinner at the Harlem branch YMCA, Jack was sure that he had found his man among the Democrats. Humphrey's record as a liberal on race went back at least to 1946, when, as mayor of Minneapolis, he secured enactment of the first municipal Fair Employment Practices Act in the United States. In 1948, at the Democratic National Convention, in support of an uncompromising civil rights plank, he had called the delegates to action against Jim Crow. "Now is the time," Humphrey had urged, "for the Democratic Party to get out of the shadows of states' rights and walk in the sunshine of human rights." In July 1959, addressing the 50th Annual Convention of the NAACP in Minneapolis, he linked his chairmanship of the Senate Foreign Relations Committee to the matter of civil rights. With civil rights, "more than a question of law enforcement is involved," Humphrey argued; "at stake is a basic *moral* issue which underlies our very conception of democracy." Impressed by the breadth of Humphrey's vision, Robinson endorsed him. "This man and his principles must be supported," he told his *Post* readers. "For Humphrey's is the kind of leadership that brings pride and inspiration to people in all walks of life."

Jack's will to emphasize civil rights was only reinforced on October 25, when for perhaps the first time since his early days in baseball he came face to face with Jim Crow as enforced by armed white policemen in the South. Arriving at the airport in Greenville, South Carolina, for an NAACP event, he discovered that several people awaiting him had been forced out of the main or "white" waiting room by authorities. Returning to the airport for his flight home after a lively speech to some seventeen hundred people in Greenville, he decided to test the Jim Crow regulations there. Accompanied by Gloster Current, national director of NAACP branches, and a local supporter, Jack entered the main waiting room. Suddenly, "a disheveled, unshaven man in a jacket approached us. He was wearing a gun and told us he was a policeman. In halting, seemingly uneducated speech, he told us either to move on or be moved." No one moved. The airport manager then ordered the three blacks out of the main lounge. When they again refused, he summoned a uniformed policeman. "If they sit down," he told the policeman, "put them in jail." Jack and his friends, still refusing to budge, argued that the airport was a federally subsidized facility, operating under federal authority. Uncertain how to proceed, the officer quit the airport. Shortly afterward, Robinson boarded his plane without further incident.

This episode, mild compared to what blacks routinely faced in the South, only stiffened Jack's resolve to hold officials accountable about civil rights. Among the Republicans, he congratulated William Rogers, the attorney general, for deploring the miscarriage of justice in the Mack Charles Parker case; he strongly criticized Governor Nelson Rocke-

feller of New York for agreeing to return a black fugi-
tive to the South. (It was perhaps significant that
Rogers was known to be a Nixon man, and Rockefeller a Nixon adversary.) Robinson was increasingly
harsh on President Eisenhower, who in his travels
overseas mouthed "words of great hope and encouragement concerning freedom and independence" to
emerging nations such as India and Afghanistan but
preached patience to blacks at home. "If there had
been vigorous and uncompromising leadership from
the White House," he insisted, "America would never
have had the shame of a Little Rock or a Poplarville."
"Could it be," he asked of Eisenhower, "that his frequent trips for golf and hunting in Georgia bring him
in contact with people whose rigid opposition to
equal rights he is affected by? Or has he all along
adhered to the position he took before a Congressional committee in 1948 opposing the elimination
of racial segregation in the armed forces?"

When, at the close of 1959, Rockefeller
announced his decision not to seek the nomination
for the presidency in 1960, Robinson showed the rest
of his hand. Nixon, he argued with studied nonchalance, was not nearly as weak a candidate as many
Democrats supposed. "I've been following Nixon's
career for some time now," Jack wrote, "and I don't
mind admitting that generally I've liked what I've
seen and heard." Acknowledging Nixon's reputation
for unscrupulousness, he argued that the Vice-
President had grown much since his election in
1952—"grown more than any other person presently
in political life." His visit to Russia and his cele-

brated "kitchen" debate with Nikita Khrushchev showed this growth, but earlier trips, especially one to India and other "colored" nations in 1953, had deepened Nixon's understanding of racism. Nixon, Jack suggested, might yet prove attractive to voters "the Democrats consider safely in their pockets. And if it should come to a choice between a weak and indecisive Democratic nominee and Vice-President Nixon, I, for one, would enthusiastically support Nixon."

The hostile response by many *Post* readers to the column surprised Jack, as he wrote to Herbert Klein, an assistant to Nixon. "I thought I was controversial," Jack confessed, but he could see that Nixon "really has a battle to overcome some of his critics." Robinson now felt free to press Nixon at crucial times with telegrams calling for action, as on February 25, when he warned that events in Biloxi, Mississippi, where a "wade-in" by blacks at a Jim Crow beach led to gunfire that left ten blacks wounded, could lead to a general explosion. "The Negro is in an inflammable state," he wrote in pressing for a face-to-face meeting to discuss civil rights with the Vice-President. A major challenge for Nixon and all the other candidates, Jack knew, was the rising tempo of activism among blacks in the South. On February 1, in what would prove a historic step, four college students from North Carolina A&T sat down at a Woolworth's lunch counter in Greensboro, North Carolina, and kept their places after being refused service. This single action, barely premeditated, set in motion a wave of similar protests, mounted by blacks and whites, which began to roll across the South as segregated churches, restaurants, beaches, libraries, and other facilities found themselves under siege.

In March, in the middle of the Wisconsin primary, Robinson flew to Milwaukee to campaign for Humphrey. Earlier, through his friend Frank Reeves of Washington, D.C., a black lawyer active in NAACP and Democratic Party circles, he had startled Humphrey by offering to work for him as Humphrey wrestled with his main rival, John F. Kennedy, in a crucial stage of the race for the nomination; Robinson also helped to open the Humphrey for President office in Washington. These were significant steps for Jack; they marked his first direct involvement in a political campaign. Admiring Humphrey, he was perhaps even more eager to upset the candidacy of Kennedy, for whom he had taken a deep dislike. In particular, Kennedy's publicized breakfast meeting at his home the previous June with the segregationist governor of Alabama, John Patterson, and the president of the Alabama White Citizens Councils, Sam Englehardt, had led Jack to brand Kennedy an enemy of blacks. Robinson also knew of Kennedy's obstructionist role in the passage of the 1957 Civil Rights Bill, when only a concerted effort had saved the bill from death in the Judiciary Committee. In Milwaukee, when Robinson heard from a reporter that Robert Kennedy, who was managing his brother's campaign, had claimed that Humphrey had paid Robinson for the visit, he was livid. "I want right here to emphasize what I told that reporter," he wrote on March 16 in the *Post*. "Whoever originated such a story is a liar."

Despite Jack's efforts, Kennedy defeated Humphrey in Wisconsin. Early in June, his nomination practically assured, Kennedy finally responded to Robinson's attacks with a letter to the New York *Post* defending his civil rights record. In the same issue, however, Robinson accused the senator of making only token campaign appearances before blacks and only guarded statements of support for the sit-in demonstrations in the South. "I could go on," Robinson wrote, following a laundry list of Kennedy's errors and unfortunate associations. "When and if Kennedy firmly and vigorously repudiates the actions and policies of this crowd," he went on, "I will be happy to reevaluate my position. But as long as he continues to play politics at the expense of 18,000,000 Negro Americans, then I repeat: Sen. Kennedy is not fit to be the President of the U.S."

Meanwhile, Robinson and Nixon's relationship was strengthened by a luncheon meeting in Washington also attended by Attorney General Rogers. Later, Jack published the text of a cozy letter to him ("Dear Jackie") in which Nixon asserted the integrity of the American Negro vote and the "strength" of his position on civil rights, and offered two key reasons for supporting civil rights. The first had to do with foreign policy and the international reputation of the United States versus "atheistic communism." The second was economic; any denial of "the full talent and energies" of black America was an example of "stupidity of the greatest magnitude." Mentioning their luncheon meeting, the letter offered a sense of an easy intimacy between the men. Still, Jack took pains to appear independent. "Contrary to some published reports," his column concluded, "this corner thus far is still uncommitted to any candidate for the Presidency, now that Sen. Humphrey has withdrawn. I repeat, however, that I see no reason why Nixon should not be considered as seriously as anyone else." Because his "actual record and position" on important issues deserved support, "many of Nixon's critics will find themselves taking a second look, before making up their minds."

Deciding finally to do something about Robinson's opposition, Kennedy then invited him to Washington. Early in July they met at the home of Chester Bowles, the former governor of Connecticut, who, as chairman of the Platform Committee at the forthcoming Democratic convention, would help shape campaign policy on civil rights. Arriving at this meeting skeptical about Kennedy, Robinson left even less of an admirer. As he later complained, Kennedy was courteous but would not look him in the eye, which Jack considered a sure sign of insincerity; and the senator's candid admission that he did not know many Negroes, or "the Negro," angered Jack. "Although I appreciated his truthfulness in the matter, I was appalled that he could be so ignorant of our situation and be bidding for the highest office in the land." When Kennedy asked what it would take to get Robinson's support, Jack hurried to take offense. "Look, Senator," he recalled telling Kennedy, "I don't want any of your money. I'm just interested in helping the candidate who I think will be best for the black American."

On this antagonistic note, the meeting ended. A few days later, at Robinson's request, Kennedy sent him a written statement about civil rights. In it, the senator defended his meeting with Governor Patterson as an obligation of his office, and affirmed his desire to see "an end to all discrimination—in voting, in education, in housing, in employment, in the administration of justice, and in public facilities including lunch counters." As with Nixon's letter, Jack published this statement in full. However, he did not hide his doubts about Kennedy, "an impressive man" who admitted his "limited experience" with blacks but was "sincere" and "willing to learn." Making it clear that "this corner does not endorse his candidacy," Jack vowed to continue to scrutinize his record. "Sen. Kennedy is a little late in seeking to make himself clear, after 14 years in Congress. But if he is sincere, there is still time to catch up."

Soon after the meeting, Robinson received an invitation to join Chester Bowles on the Platform Committee but declined it. He then turned the senator's admission of ignorance against him by pointing to voting-rights abuses in Tennessee from which Kennedy might learn—if indeed he wished to learn. Later, when Jack congratulated the Democratic convention meeting in Los Angeles for adopting a bold program on civil rights, he barely mentioned Kennedy in giving "the lion's share of credit" to Bowles for "sticking to his guns" in the face of segregationists. When Kennedy chose as his running mate Lyndon Johnson, Jack struck again. Kennedy's choice was "a bid for the appeasement of Southern bigots." Asked to choose between a fence-sitting presidential nominee who had tied himself to "a proven segregationist," and a probable nominee (Nixon) with a "better-than-average" civil rights record who was unlikely to make such a choice, "I know how I, for one, shall cast my vote in November. I do not pretend to speak for anyone else. But I have a hunch I'm going to have plenty of company."

Robinson's picture of Johnson was in no way far-fetched; Johnson, who later would provide the most radical leadership on civil rights by a President since Abraham Lincoln, was widely perceived in 1960 as a segregationist. But many liberals were prepared to accept him and the support he would bring from the South, in order to aid Kennedy's election. Jack pounced again when the news broke that Kennedy had invited Governor Faubus of Arkansas to sit on the platform as he made his acceptance speech at the convention. Ignoring the senator's protest that he had invited every Democratic governor to attend, Jack denounced him. "It is now clearer than ever," he wrote in the *Post,* "that John Kennedy is first and foremost a cold, calculating political machine."

Robinson's condemnation of the Kennedy-Johnson ticket brought many protests from a wide cross-section of *Post* readers, including those who pointed out that the coming election was about more than civil rights. Dismissing most of these objections as patronizing, Robinson vowed to keep up his opposition even as he looked at other candidates—to wit, Nixon. However, Nixon's choice of a running mate (Henry Cabot Lodge of Massachusetts, the United States ambassador to the United Nations), in addition to his vigorous fight at the convention against conservative elements in his party, notably Senator Barry Goldwater of Arizona, settled the matter once and for all for Robinson: "The battle lines are now clearly drawn." The following month, when the Democrat-dominated Senate voted to table civil rights proposals advanced by Senator Jacob Javits of New York, Robinson laid the blame at Kennedy's feet: "Faced with this kind of continued fence-hopping from the Democratic nominee, is it any wonder that millions of American voters are wondering just where Kennedy—and under his leadership the Democratic party—really stands?"

The feeling between Robinson and the Kennedys, already sour, took a turn for the worse. At the center was an organization, the African-American Students Foundation, of which Robinson was a trustee, which sought to bring a group of about 240 African students to study at colleges and universities in the United States. The organization had grown out of the response by Robinson, Belafonte, and Poitier to a plea by Tom Mboya of Kenya for help in allowing young Africans to travel to the U.S.A. to attend school. In 1959, when Jack devoted a column to Project Airlift Africa, more than eighty students were able to come after Robinson, Belafonte, and Poitier wrote to a number of their friends and acquaintances. Now, in 1960, Robinson and others asked the State Depart-

ment for assistance, which was denied. John
Kennedy, on behalf of the Kennedy Foundation, controlled by his family, then offered the project a gift of
$5,000. At this point, Robinson moved to use his con-
nections to Nixon to make the State Department
reconsider its decision; clearly, he hoped to use the
project to burnish Nixon's image among blacks. But
Jack's attempt backfired.

On August 17, his *Post* column announced
brightly that "an aide to Vice President Nixon" had
just called with great news: the State Department
would pay for the transportation of the students from
Africa, at a cost of about $100,000. "Incidentally,"
Robinson went on, "it is no accident that an aide of
the Vice President was the one to call me about this."
Nixon, who had visited Africa "not long ago," had
expressed "immediate and deep interest" in the project. The column made no mention of the initial
response of the State Department, or of Nixon's pressure on State at Robinson's urgent request. But in his
next column, Jack made a baleful admission: "I don't
mind admitting it: I was wrong." The State Department would not be supporting the students. As Jack
explained, Sargent Shriver, Senator Kennedy's
brother-in-law, had boldly offered the African-
American Students Foundation more than $400,000
from the Kennedy Foundation, enough to support the
project for three years. The student organization had
then accepted the offer, and without consulting
Robinson. "Disappointed at not being kept abreast of
events," Jack was left to apologize to his readers for
having misinformed them.

Jack's embarrassment was still fresh a few days later when Robert Kennedy came to town. On a radio interview program, Kennedy launched a broad attack on Robinson's credibility. Kennedy accused Robinson of being William Black's antilabor tool at Chock Full o' Nuts, who "used his race to defeat a union shop there." Black himself, according to Kennedy, was a longtime Republican (in fact, Black was a registered Liberal). In return, flinging vitriol of his own, Robinson denounced Bobby Kennedy as a man "who will not hesitate to use lies, innuendoes and personal attacks on those who disagree with him to get his candidate into the White House." But Jack was on the defensive again when, on the floor of the Senate, John Kennedy questioned the propriety of the State Department's involvement in the African students project and possible interference in the election campaign. Kennedy, in a position supported (to Jack's consternation) by the African-American Students Foundation, argued that State had entered its bid only after his own foundation had pledged to support the airlift. In a column on August 29, hotly disputing this version, Robinson provided a detailed chronology that appeared to support his main point, that Nixon and State had offered their support before being aware of the Kennedy Foundation decision. In the process, however, Jack found himself admonishing a foundation on which he served as a trustee and accusing its leaders of "rewriting the sequence of events" with a "doctored version of what happened." The episode tarnished Jack's image and only added to Nixon's reputation for deceit. Even the *Post,* in an editorial, offered the opinion that Robinson "still seems to be confused about where to place the blame" for the controversy.

A week or so later, however, Robinson took twin steps to underscore his commitment to Nixon. Deciding to campaign fully on his behalf, he arranged with Chock Full o' Nuts for a leave of absence until the elections in November. Under pressure from the *Post,* he also set aside his column for the duration. On September 7, the *Post* carried, instead of Jack's column, "A Note on Jackie Robinson." The note read: "Jackie Robinson is on leave of absence from The Post while serving in Vice President Nixon's campaign organization."

Robinson knew that in taking this step into territory new to him he was also taking a risk. But as at other crucial moments in his life, when he found himself profoundly challenged to act, he could not sit on the sidelines but plunged into the fray. At whatever personal cost, he would throw his energies into supporting the Nixon campaign.

— 14 —

A New Frontier

1960–1964

I have never been so proud to be a Negro.
I have never been so proud to be an American.
—Jackie Robinson (1963)

FOR ROBINSON, the 1960 presidential campaign was an exhilarating but also a bruising affair, in which he worked hard and at times effectively as an unpaid volunteer for Nixon and Lodge but also endured some harsh attacks. At least once, he came to the brink of quitting; but in the end he remained loyal to Nixon. "After what the Democrats did to me and tried to do to me on the road," he told a reporter following Nixon's defeat, "I'm just about ready to became a Republican myself." Defeat did not change his views: "I still believe in Mr. Nixon and I still think he's the better man."

Beating the drum for Nixon across the country, from New York to California and even into the South, Jack showed a degree of dedication that surprised even Republicans. Everywhere he lauded the Vice-President for helping America make "more progress in the last seven years in civil rights than ever under the Democrats." At the same time, especially before blacks, he hammered at Senator Kennedy, who "wants us to put him in office so he can learn about us there. I think he'll learn about us from Johnson." True, Kennedy might make a good President one day; but "let him go out and learn about the American Negro first."

Joining Governor Nelson Rockefeller on campaign visits to four black churches in Brooklyn (including Nazarene Baptist, where the Robinsons' friend Lacy Covington was pastor), Jack's aggressiveness stood out. While Rockefeller himself never mentioned Nixon by name, Robinson unabashedly endorsed the Vice-President and struck at Kennedy and Johnson. In his zeal, Jack was not afraid to risk alienating local black Democratic leaders. At a rally in Memphis, Tennessee, he ridiculed those blacks who "champion the Negro cause until they are paid off—with a job or something else they want—and then the Negro is forgotten." After rousing appearances in Delaware and New Jersey, other campaign workers were "lavish in their praise" for "the almost superhuman effort" he was making; according to a high campaign official, "There are very few men in your position who would sacrifice so much for a cause and a conviction." Following a visit to Kentucky, the local chairman called Jack's effort "outstanding" and marveled at the evident "sincerity in your heart."

But criticism also came. The AFL-CIO, denouncing him as antilabor for his alleged role in union troubles at Chock Full o' Nuts, refused a request for $50,000 from the NAACP for a crusade to register a million black voters. ("I am not now, nor could I ever become, anti-union," Jack insisted, despite his support of William Black's efforts to block the unionization of his company. "But there are rotten apples in every phase of life.") More upsetting perhaps was the surge of opposition to Nixon from many of his friends. "So many people even tried to influence my wife," he told a reporter, "that she became quite worried and disturbed." ("I was not passive," Rachel said later, "and I disagreed with Jack's support of Nixon.") Worst of all, he was soon aware that, facing black voters, Nixon's managers were often ignorant and arrogant. To Jack's dismay, they declined to bring Nixon's caravan to Harlem in favor of trying harder to woo the white South. In this respect, Jack's friend E. Frederic Morrow, the only black on the White House staff (who also took a leave of absence without pay to campaign for Nixon), was appalled at the way he himself was treated: "The part given me to play was insulting." Val Washington, nominally the top black campaign manager, "was in a similar boat. . . . His urgent pleas for help fell on deaf and unsympathetic ears." It was left to the celebrity Jackie Robinson to carry most of the load. "He made a great personal sacrifice to help Nixon," Morrow recalled, "yet he, too, had a heavy heart from the ignorance with which the campaign was being conducted."

This ignorance eventually cost Nixon the election. The key moment of failure came in October, when a hostile local judge in De Kalb County, Georgia, sentenced Dr. King to four months in jail, to be served at hard labor on a road gang, for taking part in a sit-in demonstration. The sentence was so clearly a travesty of justice that King's family, including his pregnant wife, Coretta, feared for his life. At the almost frantic urging of Harry Belafonte, now a member of King's inner circle, Jack appealed to Nixon campaign leaders for a direct show of support for the civil rights leader. William Safire, an admirer of Robinson since his days at UCLA ("I used to holler myself hoarse at his exploits on the football field"), remembered him arguing vehemently at the midwestern hotel where they were staying that Nixon had to intervene. "He has to call Martin right now, today," Robinson pleaded with Safire. "I have the number of the jail." Safire took Robinson to see Robert Finch, who was managing Nixon's campaign. Finch, in turn, escorted Robinson into a meeting with the candidate himself. Ten minutes later, Robinson returned to Safire, "tears of frustration in his eyes." "He thinks calling Martin would be 'grandstanding,'" Jack blurted out. "Nixon doesn't deserve to win."

At this point, Jack was ready to abandon the campaign. He was further troubled when a close family friend, the psychologist Dr. Kenneth Clark (whose studies had influenced the 1954 Supreme Court decision *Brown* v. *Board of Education*), now not only switched from Nixon to Kennedy but joined others in urging Robinson to "come home." At the last minute, Robinson decided to stick with Nixon to the end. A telephone conversation with Branch Rickey, he said, made the difference. "Mr. Rickey reassured me that Mr. Nixon was still personally the fine man I thought he was," Jack told a reporter after the election. "And that I didn't want this one emotional thing to completely color my overall convictions."

Two years later, as Nixon prepared to run for the California governorship, Rickey would write to him about this watershed in the 1960 election, in which, Rickey insisted, "the Negro vote was determinative." Someone had alerted Rickey that the Democrats were mounting "a very strenuous effort" to have Jack pull out of his last four campaign appearances and disavow Nixon. Rickey had then tried frantically but without success to reach Robinson on the road. But Rockefeller had found him in a flash. Then, after a long conversation with Rickey, according to Rickey, "Jackie went manfully [on] with his schedule." Rickey had also spoken that day to Rachel, who was upset: both Carl Rowan and Bobby Kennedy had called her that morning to apply pressure. Recalling the opposition to Jack's 1949 HUAC appearance, she told Rickey: "This is worse. I am completely distraught. So is Jackie." Despite her own objections to Nixon, Rachel had helped a great deal to keep Jack on his course. ("By the way," Rickey confided to Nixon, "she's a lot of woman.")

Nixon's mistake, exploited by Kennedy's well-publicized telephone call of sympathy to Coretta King, as well as Bobby Kennedy's pressure on the judge who had sentenced King, which led to his release, cost him the election. The black vote, undecided until then, swung heavily to Kennedy, especially after King's father, a powerful pastor in Atlanta, openly threw his support behind the senator.

In at least three states that Kennedy carried narrowly (including Illinois, which he won by only nine thousand votes), the overwhelming support of black voters obviously made the difference.

Just before Election Day, when Nixon wrote to thank Jack for his "enormous contribution to our common cause"—by which he meant his campaign—he defended his decision in the King matter. Telephoning King or his wife would have been "what our good friend, Joe Louis, called a 'grandstand play' "; genuine progress in civil rights came from "the day to day, consistent application of the principles which we know are sound." In defeat, Nixon treated his leading black supporter with grace—letters of gratitude for Jack's efforts, the gift of a plaque signed by Richard and Pat Nixon, and an invitation to an emotional farewell dinner on January 17 that Jack called "one of the highlights of my life. What happened there convinced me more than ever that I supported the right man." (In return for the plaque, Robinson sent Nixon twenty-four pounds of Chock Full o' Nuts coffee.)

But Jack believed that the Republicans had thrown away a rare opportunity—and that blacks would suffer for this negligence. "I was terribly disappointed over the election," he wrote to a friendly party official, "and feel we are at a great loss. I only hope that Kennedy will prove to be a good president." Now Robinson heard snickering at his back, as perhaps when a respected *Amsterdam News* columnist ridiculed "the various self-styled Negro leaders" who in the recent election "suddenly became experts on advising Negroes on how to vote." But for Jack and his family, the most immediate concern was probably the reaction of William Black of Chock Full o' Nuts, who almost certainly had voted for Kennedy. But Black squashed any idea of firing Robinson. "It is my belief," he stressed, "that a publicly owned company has no right to take sides in a political campaign. An employee, however, has the right to speak out as he sees fit."

Black was sincere. A year later, he would take the initiative in Jack's appointment to the board of directors of the company. Jack would then be earning $42,500 a year, with only one other vice-president making more money.

But the New York *Post* was not so forgiving. Its editor, James Wechsler, writing the day of the election but before the results were known, fired Jack. Wechsler gave four reasons for his action. To Wechsler's embarrassment, he had found out that Robinson was going to work for Nixon only when someone at the New York *Times,* a major rival, called him about the matter. Also, Jack's behavior in the affair of the African students' airlift suggested that "partisanship played a larger role than journalism" in his thinking at that time. Making matters worse was Jack's sudden appearance as a columnist during the campaign in the black New York *Citizen-Call.* Last of all, Jack's use of a ghostwriter prevented his true personality from emerging in his columns.

A year later, this letter still riled Jack. Roughly, but not entirely convincingly, he rejected these reasons. "No one will ever convince me that the *Post* acted in an honest manner," he said. "I believe the simple truth is that they became somewhat alarmed when they realized that I really meant to write what I believed." Hinting vaguely at racial discrimination, he saw a "peculiar parallel" between some Northern liberals and "our outstanding Southern illiberals." Acting "magnificently" in many areas, the *Post* had become "uncomfortable" because it disliked his opinions.

Hurt to have been booted, Jack returned to Chock Full o' Nuts and also to the wide range of activities that placed his celebrity at the service of others in need. But the defeat of Nixon, and the punitive loss of his column, did not kill his interest in politics. Instead, Robinson realigned himself politically. In thanking him for his 1960 effort on behalf of Nixon and Lodge, an official in the Republican National Committee had offered a flattering remark: "Personally, it is my judgment that you could be a 'Messiah' for the Republican Party in the days ahead!" But within a week of Nixon's defeat, Robinson had already begun to look to another man as a potential political Messiah.

In October, as part of their efforts for Nixon, Jack had joined Nelson Rockefeller in a series of street-corner electioneering stops in Harlem that ended in a big Republican rally on St. Nicholas Avenue. In all these efforts, Jack was impressed by Rockefeller's ebullience and charm, his confidence and apparent sincerity in dealing with both the middle class and ordinary folks on the street. Later, at a luncheon in honor of Marian Anderson, Rockefeller confided to Jack details of his own efforts to convince Nixon to intervene in the King case. In addition, Jack was aware of the long association between Rockefeller money and black higher education through large gifts to schools like Spelman College, which was named after Laura Spelman, Nelson's grandmother. With Nixon's defeat, he began to see the governor, whose ambition to be President was well known, as poised to assume the leadership of the Republican Party and steer it toward the commitment to civil rights that Nixon had timidly shunned. Within days of Nixon's defeat, Robinson drafted a careful message to Rockefeller. "Please do not think me presumptuous because of this letter," he asked; "your family name is magic, but the lopsided Kennedy victory in New York City should be given careful study." Robinson offered to sit down "at some time" with Rockefeller's "representative" to discuss its implications.

Clearly Rockefeller welcomed this overture. In February, when Jack assured an *Amsterdam News* columnist that he would remain in politics, he ventured that he would "perhaps" be working closely with the governor. He again concealed his hand when he spoke the following month at a luncheon meeting of the Young Republican Club; but on Friday, April 7, he introduced Rockefeller at a meeting, unprecedented for a New York governor, that Jack helped to arrange with about a hundred other well-to-do blacks at the Dawn Casino on Seventh Avenue in Harlem. The meeting went well. Peppered with questions over an hour and a half, Rockefeller spoke smartly on issues of special interest to Harlem. After another meeting on June 12, this time in Brooklyn, Rockefeller thanked Robinson for his efforts in staging an event that was "most constructive and provided a wonderful opportunity for frank discussion."

Later that month, when Martin Luther King Jr. came to New York, he flew with the governor to the state capital, Albany, in Rockefeller's private plane, to fund-raising events for King's Southern Christian Leadership Conference. In Albany, Rockefeller escorted King to church rallies and in general threw his great prestige behind King. Rockefeller was laying the base for not only his reelection as governor in 1962 but also his expected challenge in 1964 for the Republican nomination and an expected showdown later that year with the incumbent, President Kennedy. Jack proposed to help him with this odyssey, and in the process strike a tremendous blow for black freedom and empowerment.

FEW PEOPLE WERE HAPPIER to see the 1960 campaign end than Rachel and the three children, for whom Jack's travels in support of Nixon, and the special pressures of the election, were a chilly reminder of Jack's old Dodger days, when from late February until October he was a sometime presence in their home. Jackie was now fourteen, Sharon ten, and David eight.

To the children, their father was a benign, beloved figure. David would remember him as "a tremendous physical presence, a big guy, so you were conscious of his size. But he was not one to raise his voice to us, certainly not his hands. There was none of that terror of their father some kids have. There wasn't ever a threat from him." Short of hugging and kissing, Jack showed them rich affection. "My father was very indulgent of me," Sharon said. "Perhaps too indulgent—to him I could do nothing wrong. He was so very loving without being touchy-feely; I never had any doubts that he loved me." David would remember various fishing trips, including one long, blissful outing to Canada, and hours on the links caddying for his dad. Sharon would never forget thrilling excursions into the city when she and her father, a man born to shop, went looking for clothes for her and Rachel in the garment district, where proprietors welcomed him like a rich cousin. Outgoing and popular, Sharon was also poised and responsible; and David was an amusing, inventive child confident enough to enjoy his own company. "My greatest love was fishing by myself," he recalled. All was not sweetness and mirth. Integrating New Canaan Country Day School, he had fought battles against "our small core of racists"; but he also made many friends and allies there and elsewhere. "I have extremely fond memories of my childhood," he said.

Jackie's experience was different. By 1960, his life was already pockmarked with setbacks in school and a stymied relationship with his father. Even to the most amateur of psychologists, the bane of Jackie's life was obviously the shadow cast by the famous father whose name he carried. Not yet five months old, Jackie had been present in 1947 when his father first stepped out at Ebbets Field. As Sharon would put it later, "Jackie was thrown into the noble experiment alongside our parents, and because of his name, there was no hiding place." To adoring fans, he was often more mascot than child; they showered him with so much intrusive attention that by three he was both exploiting and resenting it. A beautiful boy, whose large dark eyes set among long eyelashes and thick eyebrows added to his air of vulnerability, Jackie Junior drew people easily to serve him, and then became dependent on them. Sharon and David grew independent, but "Jackie was more dependent, pampered, and needy."

In some ways, the contrast between Jackie and Sharon was telling. Four years older than she, he was so afraid of the dark during one period that he would rouse her from sleep to turn on the light for him; she would drag a chair to the light switch to reach it, then go back to her own bed. Once, at a hotel swimming pool in Miami, in front of their parents and curious fellow guests, Jackie hung back timidly on a high diving board, then watched Sharon plunge recklessly into the water. Jackie had very good athletic ability, probably more than Sharon and David, who loved sports; but, she said, "we weren't afraid of our athletic ability, we weren't intimidated by it, as he was." She and David shared a horse, Diamond, that they rode with abandon into the woods and the pond; Jackie kept his distance. At school, where Sharon was a solid, dutiful student, and David sharp, Jackie had trouble reading and keeping still. Sharon came to think that, "feeling inadequate" in the face of his father's achievement, Jackie thought "that by acting out he could become the center of attention without meeting the demands of real achievement."

Entering Martha Hoyt in the fall of 1954, Jackie had done well at first. "I am really very proud of Jackie and I want you to tell him for me," his father wrote Rachel happily from Florida. "It's so rewarding seeing the great distance he has come and I hope he is on his way to go farther. The pride he has in his work is terribly important. I hope we can keep that in him. . . . I am very much in love with my family." To Jackie himself, Jack sent a tender message touched by guilt. "I know you sometimes wonder about me," Jack admitted, "and I hope you understand that I love you, Sharon and David very much. I know that if you wanted to, you could be one of the best students in the class and I hope you will try very hard. At times I may seem to get awfully angry at you but I hope you are never afraid of me. My love for my family is as big as anything and I am proud of the progress you have made. . . . I want you to come to me anytime as man to man and ask anything you want. . . . I am already very proud of you, will you make me more proud? Please try, Jackie."

He wanted to see his son do better. "I am right proud of my little family," he assured Rachel another time, "and if all works well we are sure to be proud of the Robinsons. Jackie to me is as fine a boy as I have seen." But Jackie, unlike Sharon ("my little sweetheart") and David ("my little man"), almost always elicited implied criticism along with compliments. A notice about good grades "makes me know you are again working. I hope to hear of many more good reports." As the end of baseball drew closer, Jack vowed to tighten the family bonds. "I know I haven't given the children the attention I should have," he confessed to Rachel. "I am sure I'll be able to make it up to them without changing our course as far as discipline is concerned. I am sure you know how fortunate I feel in having such a family and I have no doubts about them growing into outstanding youngsters."

"The Jackie Junior I knew as a child," Peter Simon said, "was sweet, loving, and very talented as an athlete. We went to camp together, including my first sleep-away, in Vermont. He was a genuinely nice, bright, caring child." To Jack Gordon's son, Bradley, who lived in Manhattan but spent almost all his vacations at the Robinson home and became Jackie's best friend, Jackie was not quite the child his father saw. "I saw a different side of Jackie," Bradley said. "He was very bright, very brave, a daredevil. Dealing with other kids, he had high self-esteem. But his self-esteem around his father was a lot lower; with his mother, it was higher. He wanted his father to be proud of him, but a lot of times Jackie was befuddled about how to approach him. Eventually he became fed up with being Jackie Robinson's son. He didn't resent it in the sense of hating his father. Jackie had all the respect and love for him in the world. But he just couldn't find a way to have his identity and to have his father be proud of him, too."

If Jackie as a boy truly disappointed his father in one area, it was in athletics, especially baseball. But the trouble was not that his father wanted a star but that Jackie, clearly gifted, soon showed little desire to succeed. In 1957, his first year of retirement, Jack took pleasure in coaching the Stamford Lions Little League team, to which Jackie belonged. (As a local reporter watched in amazement, Jack showed his "remarkable memory" by "rattling off" the name of each team member as he hit the ball to him.) The next year, Jack reported on Jackie's first game as a pitcher (he was left-handed), in which he gave up three runs in the first inning, then settled down, but lost 3–2. "It was exciting and Jackie took it well," Jack wrote. "I am not at all satisfied with his hitting. . . . I hope to influence him to change but he is a bit stubborn." A year later, in 1959, Jack was still pleased by his son's efforts. "Jackie is developing fine," he wrote to the Wallersteins in Chicago. "His ballplaying is coming a lot faster than I had expected. . . . He loves it and with his natural ability should go places. Of course this is a father looking at a son but we are proud of his play." And at Christmas that year: "We have so much fun with the kids. Jackie will probably be an athlete, Sharon can't wait to get married and David is always teased because he likes to play with puppets and the piano and not much on athletics. However, at seven who cares?"

Despite all setbacks, Jack remained optimistic about Jackie; even a stay at summer camp, he hoped, might be a turning point in the boy's life: "I have a hunch however it is going to do him a world of good." But at some point, Jackie stopped trying. At Martha Hoyt, working under one teacher he loved, a

Mrs. Carlucci, he did fine; with less skilled or less caring elders he sank again. At Dolan Junior High School, where he clashed with a strict principal, his record remained poor, and his troubles continued during his first year at Stamford High School, which he entered in the fall of 1960, just as his father became entangled in the Nixon campaign. Rachel withdrew temporarily from NYU to watch out for him. He had also lost interest in baseball. For a while he showed promise in football—"Jackie could really play some ball," Bradley Gordon said. "He was a defensive end and a very good one." Soon, however, he turned away from football also.

Jack tried to put the best face on the situation. "Jackie is trying to find himself," he wrote Caroline Wallerstein. "We think he is about ready to do so but we'll just wait and see." About this time, despite Robinson's skepticism about psychiatry, Jackie underwent counseling at the hands of Dr. Kenneth Clark, who suggested that he should be sent to a special boarding school. After some reflection, Jack and Rachel agreed. "We hope sending him away to school will spur him on," Jack wrote, as he sought to minimize his eldest child's crisis. "Sharon and David get as much mileage out of their ability as they can," he declared, "but Jackie is a bit on the lazy side."

As SIT-INS AND other demonstrations began to sweep across the South, and hundreds of students found themselves in jail for defying Jim Crow laws, Robinson and Marian Logan founded the Student

Emergency Fund early in 1960, with money solicited in letters sent to several hundred persons. Although the fund probably never exceeded $5,000, starting in 1960 they were able to send small sums of money as well as books, cigarettes, and candy to boost the morale of protesters in Virginia, Florida, Louisiana, and elsewhere in the South. In July, after watching a fund-raising program on television hosted by James Farmer of the Congress of Racial Equality and the folksinger Theodore Bikel, Logan and Robinson sent $500 as a gift. The sum of $1,000 went to a child development center headed by Dr. Mamie Phipps Clark and her husband, Dr. Kenneth Clark. In December, when they sent over $1,000 to an embattled New Orleans couple, Robinson and Logan admitted that while the money could not compensate "for the insults, embarrassments and economic reprisals you are suffering," it was meant as "a gesture and more tangible proof of our admiration and respect."

Jack sought other ways to show his concern for the student movement. When the lawyer and civil rights leader Floyd McKissick invited him to address a citywide rally in Durham, North Carolina, where students had just launched a statewide "stand-in" of segregated theaters, Jack agreed to go at once. But his major effort that spring was as part of the continuing voter-registration drives by the NAACP in the South. In some places, blacks had been forced off the voter rolls recently; in other places, they had not voted since Reconstruction. On April 16, in Decatur, Georgia, he stirred a crowd at the Thankful Baptist Church on Atlanta Avenue in connection with a voter-registration drive organized in De Kalb County; the next day, more than one thousand persons heard him in Chattanooga, Tennessee. "We are going to get our share of this country—we are going to fight for it," Robinson insisted to the crowd. "We must take it step by step." Older blacks should rely on the spirit of the youngsters and support the effort of "these kids in their stand-ins and sit-ins."

At the same time, Jack's relationship with the Kennedys improved a little. Although disappointed that no black was appointed to the cabinet, he was encouraged by other gestures by the White House. On February 9, clearly still doubtful, he sent the President a conflicted letter. Opening with praise for "your obviously fine start as our President," it soon lapsed into a muddle of skepticism and defiance about civil rights: "We are going to use whatever voice we have to awaken our people." Jack was starting to see the administration in a more positive light. A genuine turning point came in May; that month, a dramatic phase of the movement started when members of CORE embarked on a Freedom Ride by bus from Washington, D.C., to Mississippi in order to test new anti–Jim Crow laws and regulations put in place largely through the efforts of Robert Kennedy, now United States attorney general. At various stops, angry whites brutally beat riders and at least one federal official. On May 6, an outraged Robert Kennedy, standing tall in the lions' den of the University of Georgia, pledged to enforce strictly all civil rights laws and regulations. Elated, Robinson rushed to congratulate him. "Your actions demonstrate your sincere desire to support the principles of your important office," Jack declared. "I had grave doubts about your sincerity. In this case, I find it a pleasure to be proven wrong."

For Robinson, Robert Kennedy's decision later that month to send six hundred U.S. marshals to protect the riders in Montgomery, Alabama, confirmed his new opinion of the attorney general. "You are doing a capital job, and we applaud you," he wrote Kennedy in a second message. "Your department, under your dynamic leadership, shows that it means business." In return, Kennedy politely invited Jack to "stop in to say hello" when next he was in the capital. But Robinson recoiled from a friend's suggestion that he was turning Democratic. "Not so fast," he admonished her. "I have not by any means 'seen the light.' I just feel that when anyone does the right thing it must be recognized. . . . President Kennedy has given moral leadership but runs when someone suggests he support legislative action. . . . I had grave doubts, some have been eliminated but until he takes a firm stand for legislative action one must wonder."

In the coming years, Jack's admiration for Robert Kennedy would mainly grow. The element of passion in the attorney general, which verged at times on moral fanaticism, touched Robinson when it flared in the service of civil rights for blacks—about which the President himself, often ironical and aloof, seemed to be almost heartless. That summer, after Jack took a major role in a Freedom Awards rally in Brooklyn in which Robert Kennedy was among those honored, he defended this choice against critics affronted by Kennedy's recent call for a "cooling off" in the Freedom Rides. Robinson, who also opposed any "cooling off" period, was sure the idea had come from someone else in the Administration, probably the President. "I am firm in my belief," he wrote, "that, if the Attorney General is left alone to carry out his own will, we will see glowing history made by the Justice Department in the cause of real democracy."

A few days later, Jack felt quite comfortable taking part in a conference staged by the State Department to help bring racial diversity to the thirteen-thousand-member organization. In fact, several people he knew personally were now of some prominence at State. Chester Bowles was now under secretary of state; Carl Rowan (Jack's biographer, whose *Wait Till Next Year* had appeared in 1960) was now a deputy assistant secretary for public affairs; and Franklin Williams of the NAACP was also drawn to State. Joining freely in discussions, Jack pronounced himself very impressed by the effort, as he told several people, including Harris Wofford, perhaps the main architect of John Kennedy's civil rights policy and the man behind his telephone call to Coretta King. "Williams reports that Jackie is in high spirits about the Administration at present," Wofford reported.

No doubt Jack looked on a little wistfully as Rowan and Williams found dignified niches in Washington, as each became a sort of Jackie Robinson in his chosen area, but in an America significantly changed since 1947, when he was the one and only

Jackie Robinson. Instead, he was on the outside. Nevertheless, Robinson was also far more interested in the civil rights movement than in the perquisites of high office. For him, every call for help was validation enough, as when late in July, Medgar Evers, the valiant NAACP leader in Jackson, Mississippi, invited him to address a mass meeting there in the fall. Disapproving of the hostile attitude of some in the NAACP to other civil rights groups, he was eager to work for both SCLC and CORE. Early in September, for example, he strongly endorsed CORE at an Interracial Action Institute it sponsored in Miami. At least once he sent out a letter on CORE stationery requesting donations to the group. "My children and your children," he declared in Miami, "won't have to fight the same battles we did—that's why I support CORE." The sit-ins had "helped to make America a better country for my children. I am impressed by the speed with which non-violent, direct action has achieved results all over the South." Lunch counters had been integrated, "but more important is the new dignity and greater self respect which have come from the sit-ins."

BY THE END OF that summer, 1961, life at home was altered again when Rachel took up a full-time job in the Bronx. Late in May, at the age of thirty-nine, she was graduated from New York University with a master's degree in psychiatric nursing. With pride and also curiosity, Jack had watched the last frantic weeks of her studying. "She gets her degree next week," he wrote Caroline Wallerstein, "and for what seems to be months has kept her head in her books. Almost like being without a wife. Thank goodness she is about finished. Of course she goes into teaching, that may be just as bad. It's good to see the joy she gets from her work. I can only hope she continues to enjoy it."

Almost immediately, she landed a position in the Bronx as a clinical nurse in the First Day Hospital, which served acutely ill psychiatric patients. This facility, connected to Jacobi Hospital, was staffed by residents of the Albert Einstein College of Medicine. Soon Rachel was head of psychiatric nursing at Albert Einstein. Now she was gone from home five days a week. On a typical morning, determined to maintain her former role at home, she rose to make breakfast and help the children prepare for school. (On the weekends, Jack made breakfast, with waffles and pancakes his specialties.) Around seven-fifteen, Rachel left home; shortly afterward, Jack pulled out in his gray Cadillac for his typically swift drive to Manhattan. Rachel's mother made sure that the children got off to school on time.

Despite Rachel's efforts, her job altered the old routine at home. Jack was glad to see her flourishing at work, but he also had trouble adjusting to the change. "Rae has been so busy lately," he wrote the Wallersteins, "we haven't been able to do many of the things we like doing but she is so wrapped up in her work she doesn't mind at all." Her professional zeal, insofar as he could judge it, both impressed and chastened him. "I don't know when I have seen her any happier," he went on. "I believe before she is finished there will be many changes in our system of nursing."

Both in those sour-sweet words and in the earlier reference to "almost like being without a wife," Jack showed his lack of ease with the new order. But slowly he began to accept Rachel's new life, and his own. In addition, there was another, far more serious source of concern at home. Jackie Junior continued to be a question mark, although Jack, ever hopeful, saw the bright side. Jackie was now at the Stockbridge School in Massachusetts, where the headmaster was said to be good with kids in trouble. In October, a visit to see Jackie in Stockbridge encouraged Rachel and Jack, who found the trip "very exciting," as he wrote the Wallersteins. Jackie was "very happy there although he won't admit it. Every one of his teachers feels he has great potential but his background may cause him trouble. Our only concern is how he tries. We see already a change in what is important. His sense of values has changed completely and even if he does not do well in his grades we believe the overall change is for the best."

THE NEW YEAR, 1962, started on two high notes. One was Jack's selection to the Baseball Hall of Fame. The news broke late on January 23. With a shriek of joy, Rachel heard it before he did, when a *Daily News* reporter called. "I am so grateful," Jack told the press. "I have had a lot of wonderful things

happen to me in my life. . . . But to make the Hall of
Fame on the first go-around, where do you put that
on the list?" Quickly he placed telephone calls to
Branch Rickey and to his mother, Mallie. Arriving at
the Boston airport on January 25, on his way to the
annual dinner of local baseball writers, Jack waited a
half-hour for the plane bringing his fellow inductee
and dinner guest Bob Feller to land. In 1945, Feller
had predicted failure for Robinson. Now Jack held
no grudge. "It is a pleasure," he told Feller, "to go
hand in hand into the Hall of Fame with you." His
own excitement was clear. "I've been up on Cloud
Nine for about forty-eight hours," he told reporters.
"I hope I never come down."

Also that month, Jack became a columnist again.
In the New York black weekly *Amsterdam News,*
published by C. B. Powell, he started a column called
first "Jackie Robinson Says," then "Home Plate." In
his first column, he rehashed his parting quarrel in
1960 with the New York *Post* and reaffirmed his
motive for writing. "We feel deeply indebted to the
Negro masses for their loyalty," he wrote. "That is
why we have the compulsion to be vocal on issues
about which we are deeply concerned." On this job,
Jack's ghostwriter was Alfred Duckett, a former
newsman who would work with Robinson in this
capacity for the rest of Robinson's life. (Jack continued to take pains to ensure that the column represented his ideas precisely. "We have been working
together a long time," he wrote in 1963 about Duckett, "and I am pleased to have a person who is able to
capture my thoughts so well on paper!")

Printed on the editorial page, his column now paid only slight attention to sports. Politics and civil rights remained its heart. Picking up where his *Post* writing left off, Jack bore down again on the President. In his third column, Robinson praised Bobby Kennedy but criticized John Kennedy's record. Bob Kennedy was "a champion scrapper and a man of very deep convictions," Jack declared. "I like his personal approach. I like the statements he has made and appointments he has made. But I do not think our President is straight down the line on civil rights like Bob Kennedy is." A week later, just after the President indicated he would delay making good on his campaign promise to issue an executive order outlawing discrimination in public housing, Robinson attacked him again. "I am now convinced that President Kennedy really doesn't understand the Negro problem," he declared. "I am afraid, too, that I am going to have to revise my opinion about his sincerity."

Kennedy's failure to make civil rights a major feature of his 1962 State of the Union address, and the ongoing delay in the Senate confirmation of Robert Weaver as the first black cabinet member, further alienated Robinson. When Kennedy angrily confronted barons of the steel industry over the price of steel, Robinson countered with an open letter: "Mr. President, don't you believe that the explosive situation in the South and the sneaky, covered up prejudice in the North are as damaging to the public interest, to democracy and to world peace as a $6 raise in steel prices?" Still later, as Kennedy hesitated to act on a proposal by Dr. King for an executive order banning all discrimination, in a kind of second Emancipation Proclamation, Robinson jeered at Kennedy. "We think the President is a fine man, like we said," Jack wrote. "But an Abraham Lincoln he ain't." In August, Kennedy offended Robinson again. This time, he had declined to greet more than one hundred ministers who marched on the White House in support of Dr. King, who was in a jail in Albany, Georgia, as part of the massive civil rights action there by a united NAACP, CORE, and SCLC and its youthful offshoot, the Student Non-Violent Coordinating Committee, or SNCC. The President's inaction, Robinson declared, was "an insult to the national Negro community."

Not surprisingly, President Kennedy rejected an invitation to serve as honorary chairman of Robinson's Hall of Fame testimonial dinner in July in Manhattan. "It is not going to be possible for him to accept," Kennedy's black deputy press spokesman, Andrew Hatcher, informed the sponsors. In the end, Kennedy sent a telegram of praise to be read at the dinner; but by this time the Kennedy camp had probably given up any hope of ever winning Robinson over. The two sides were irreconcilable. The Kennedys never betrayed much interest in what Jack had achieved in baseball (perhaps too plebeian a game for Camelot); Robinson remained largely unimpressed by all the talk about the New Frontier. Not until December did Robinson find something complimentary to write about the President; and then, when Kennedy finally signed the executive order on housing, Jack was somewhat arch: "I have to say in all honesty that the President has shown courage and that it is heart-warming to note that he has finally kept his promise."

Throughout this year, 1962, the civil rights movement commanded Jack's attention and loyalty, even as his standing as a celebrity was recharged mightily in January by his selection to the Baseball Hall of Fame. On February 9, he helped to kick off the annual NAACP fund-raising at a rally in Washington, D.C. Then, accompanied by Floyd Patterson, he headed further south to other venues. (Patterson's eagerness to help the movement touched Jack. "I always get sort of choked up," he confessed, "when I try to express the way I feel about him.") Next, after a respite in Miami, where Jack again played in the annual black North-South golf tournament, they arrived on February 25 in Jackson, Mississippi. Joining them there were the former boxing champion Archie Moore and, from baseball, young Curt Flood of the St. Louis Cardinals; Jack's old dream of drawing other top athletes or former top athletes into the struggle at last became a reality. (Facing the selfishness of some athletes, Jack once asked angrily: "Is there a medal anywhere which is worth a man's dignity?") In Jackson, more than four thousand persons, a record for an NAACP rally there, turned out to greet them. Elated by what he called "our advent in the cradle of segregation," Archie Moore vowed to be a regular speaker for the NAACP.

As his Hall of Fame induction in July approached, honors and awards showered down on

Jack, as well as invitations to speak on radio and television and at gala dinners, graduation exercises, and the like. On May 6, an NAACP Freedom Day rally of more than twenty-five hundred persons in Raleigh, North Carolina, saluted him. Later that month, he flew to Los Angeles, where, on May 19, the Alumni Association of UCLA hailed him as its "Man of the Year" in a ceremony he called "one of the most touching days of my life." Finally, on July 20, came one of the grand evenings of Robinson's life, the testimonial dinner in his honor at the Waldorf-Astoria Hotel. That Dr. King had a central role in organizing the dinner touched Jack deeply. "Dr. Martin King is giving it at the Waldorf," he wrote with obvious pride to a friend. Although the fact that all proceeds were to go to the SCLC rankled NAACP leaders, Robinson made no apology about his wish to aid King's organization, or the pride he felt in being thus honored by its leader.

Suddenly, a nasty controversy boiling over on 125th Street in Harlem threatened to ruin Robinson's hour of glory. The trouble started when Lloyd Von Blaine, the owner of a neighborhood restaurant, Lloyd's Steakhouse, at 217 West 125th Street, reacted sourly to the news that competition was coming to 125th Street. The new restaurant would be part of a nationwide chain of steakhouses owned by Sol Singer, and was scheduled to open at a site leased from the owner of the Apollo Theater, Frank Schiffman. With Singer's steaks likely to sell for only $1.19, Lloyd's saw a distinct threat to its existence. The fact that Singer and Schiffman were white and

Jewish, and Blaine black, quickly became an issue in a community supersensitive to the mixture of Jim Crow and economic exploitation; many people remembered when blacks could not be hired as clerks on 125th Street. When Lewis H. Michaux, a local bookstore owner and the president of an unabashedly black nationalist group called the Harlem Consumers Committee, decided to picket the Apollo, Singer's and Schiffman's religion became an issue. After years as a popular Harlem business leader, Schiffman now found himself taunted as, among other things, "the Merchant of Venice." Some picketers chanted: "Jew go away—black man stay!"

Except for the veteran labor leader A. Philip Randolph, who denounced the pickets as "inflammatory," most black leaders were silent as the pressure mounted. After a meeting with Michaux arranged by Randolph, Schiffman agreed to release Singer from the lease if he wished to go. Singer then announced that he would sell his interest without profit to a black buyer; but no one stepped forward to buy. On July 14, Robinson entered the fight. In a sharply worded column, "Strange Happenings on West 125th St.," he pointed out that Schiffman had advertised the disputed space for rent for months without success, and that Singer's offer had not been accepted. Robinson took aim squarely at the anti-Jewish rhetoric of Michaux's supporters. "Anti-Semitism is as rotten as anti-Negroism," he argued. "It is a shame that, so far, none of the Negroes of Harlem have yet had the guts to say so in tones which could be heard throughout the city." (He had thought of bidding on the new restaurant, he revealed, but "lost interest because the proposed store offers steaks only in the $1.19 category. We feel Harlem needs a restaurant where both the low-priced steaks and better steaks are offered.")

Michaux's group quickly retaliated. It launched a "hate Jackie Robinson campaign," as Jack himself put it. Telegrams protesting his column reached the *Amsterdam News* and the Chock Full o' Nuts headquarters. On July 17, pickets sprouted outside the chain's coffee shop at the corner of Seventh Avenue and 125th Street. Dutifully, a worker recorded some of the signs. One declared: "Jackie is a classified so called Negro." Another: "The Jackie of all trades and master of only one. His mouth is too big." Some picketers chanted: "Old Black Joe—Jackie must go." Uneasily, Robinson reported to Bill Black on the situation. "Is there anything you would want me to do about this?" he asked. "I am sure you know I personally will never retract my statement because, regardless of what these people threaten, I feel that they are wrong and someone should speak out against them."

If some people defended the protesters, support for Robinson was also strong. On behalf of the NAACP, Roy Wilkins sent a telegram backing him "one hundred percent"; blacks could not use "the slimy tool of anti-Semitism or indulge in racism. . . . We are lost if we adopt Klan methods in the name of exalting black people." "It was beautiful," Arnold Forster of the Anti-Defamation League declared about Jack's column, "and I congratulate you." Whitney Young, the new director of the National Urban League, denounced "all who mask bigotry under the false mantle of nationalism or the hooded robes of the Klansmen." "Bigotry is intolerable," Ralph Bunche wired Jack, "whether the bigots are white or black." The progressive young pastor of Antioch Baptist Church in Brooklyn, the Reverend George Lawrence, an old friend of the Robinsons', alerted Black that he would ask the four thousand members of his congregation each to go to lunch at Chock Full o' Nuts and to purchase two pounds of the firm's coffee every time they needed it, to support Robinson's "magnificent stand against anti-Semitism."

The controversy seemed about to escalate after pink-and-black handbills announced a "mass rally" sponsored by the Nation of Islam, aimed at the "moral elevation of our community." Led by the Honorable Elijah Muhammad, the Nation of Islam combined major elements of orthodox Islamic traditions with a dogmatic faith in the inherent evil of whites. Behind the rally was Elijah Muhammad's Mosque No. 7, located on West 116th Street in Harlem. The event was to take place on July 21 on the corner of 125th Street and Seventh Avenue—outside the Chock Full o' Nuts restaurant. The main speakers, according to the handbill, would include both Lewis Michaux and the controversial leader of Mosque No. 7, Malcolm X.

For a while the picketers continued to impede customers entering the restaurant. Then, following a heated debate between Jack and Michaux over the radio station WWRL, and an informal talk between Jack and Malcolm at another point, tempers began to cool. In a strange about-face that was evidence of the sometimes surreal nature of Harlem life, Michaux not only attended Jack's testimonial dinner at the Waldorf Astoria but also sat at Schiffman's table. Warmed by the praise heaped on Robinson, he soon declared himself forever one of Jack's fans. In the end, Michaux denied that his group had voiced anti-Jewish chants, while Robinson upheld the right of the group to picket, as long as it expressed no race hatred. Michaux then called upon his followers to put away their signs. A few weeks later, he announced that his group, Blaine, and Singer had reached an agreement on all issues concerning the restaurant, which would open in the fall.

To some ultranationalist blacks, however, Jackie Robinson was a traitor. Hostile letters reached the offices of the *Amsterdam News.* "You have banished yourself from the Black Race," one informed him. "You are no longer one of us. You are a man without a race. . . . We can never destroy the white race with rattle snakes like you." But such letters did not intimidate him. "Jack had been attacked so often for so long," Rachel said, "that nothing they wrote could upset him. He shrugged the words off." In fact, he faced accusations of being a white man's Negro by offering columns in defense of white friends such as Pee Wee Reese, under fire in Louisville for allegedly owning a segregated bowling alley, and the television star Ed Sullivan, attacked by a young black dramatist for allegedly keeping serious black drama off his nationally popular weekly show. But he also defended blacks, including those in the Nation of Islam. On August 25, he published a column chastising the head of the House Un-American Activities Committee, Francis E. Walter of Pennsylvania, after Walter announced that he was thinking of launching "a very intensive investigation of a Negro group known as the Black Muslims." Jack was indignant. What about an investigation of white supremacist groups, including the White Citizens Councils?

In any event, unbowed by attacks on him because of the steakhouse episode, he moved to his testimonial dinner and his Hall of Fame induction confident that he had done the right thing in standing up to racial and religious hatred. The outpouring of respect and love at the dinner and the induction ceremony in Cooperstown, New York, healed whatever wound the episode had inflicted.

EVEN IN THE DOG DAYS of August, Robinson remained busy. On August 16, he was the main speaker in Springfield, Massachusetts, at a dinner marking the hundredth birthday of Amos Alonzo Stagg, the "Grand Old Man" of football, so called because of his long career as a coach, including forty-seven years at the University of Chicago, and his many innovations in the sport.

Some days later, he left home on an even more important task: a visit, at the request of Dr. King, to speak in Albany, Georgia, at the dangerous height of the concerted civil rights action there known as the Albany Movement. On the morning of August 26, Jack was at the Atlanta airport, en route to Albany, when he heard the news of the destruction by fire of two black churches near Albany that had been involved in voter registration. About two weeks before, another black church, the Shady Grove Baptist Church in Lee County, had also burned. Accompanied by Dr. King's executive assistant, Wyatt Tee Walker (who had delivered King's speech at Jack's Hall of Fame dinner the previous month), he flew south to Albany. There, he delivered a rousing address to an overflow crowd. Then, with some trepidation ("There was fear in the voice of someone," he said, "who thought it might not be wise to go"), he joined Walker and other figures in the Albany Movement who headed south in three cars to the small town of Sasser to view the still-smoldering ruins of the Mount Olive Baptist Church. There, its pastor, the Reverend F. S. Swaggot, wept openly as he walked with them about the grounds. "It really makes you want to cry deep down in your heart," Jack told a reporter. When Walker insisted that something should be done in response, Robinson knew at once that the churches had to be rebuilt. To that end, he pledged one hundred dollars on the spot. Later that day, Dr. King telephoned to ask him to serve as national chairman of the rebuilding fund. Jack agreed to do so.

"Jackie Robinson had long been a hero to me," Walker later recalled, "and it was like a dream come true to work with him. His presence in the South was very important to us. I have said a number of times that Jackie Robinson's entrance into the big leagues did more for race relations than all the work of the so-called forces of Christ combined. We worried about his safety in Albany and later in Birmingham, and we had a small group of people, bodyguards really, to look out for him. He was brave—he had already proven his bravery, but he showed it again in the South at a very bad time in our history."

Returning home, Jack boldly launched the Church Fund to rebuild the Shady Grove, Mount Olive, and Mount Mary Baptist Churches. The fund netted $6,000 in its first hour, with Bill Black of Chock Full o' Nuts giving $5,000 and C. B. Powell of the *Amsterdam News* donating $1,000. At Jack's invitation, five hundred of his fellow employees pledged to donate a dollar a week for twenty weeks to raise an additional $10,000. Governor Rockefeller, a Baptist, contributed $10,000. Frank Schiffman gave $1,000 and stopped performances nightly at the Apollo Theater to take up a collection. Floyd Patterson agreed to turn over a share of his purse from his upcoming title fight with Sonny Liston. On radio and television and in the newspapers, Robinson appealed for checks from the public made out to King's SCLC but mailed to him for conveyance to King. "Let's rebuild these churches," he urged. "Let's do it ourselves."

To Jack's disappointment, the Church Fund soon bogged down. Some blacks flatly refused to give anything. "It is sad to think," he wrote in his column, "that any Negro would refuse to give even a coin to show how he feels about race-haters who burn down Negro churches which are trying to help the Negro to vote in the South. Thank God, those kind of people are in the minority, and the overwhelming majority of Negro people recognize their own responsibility." Eventually, almost two years later, he was able to announce that he had collected $50,000 and that all three churches had been mostly rebuilt. He was glad that white Georgians had also helped. Donations came from the Atlanta *Constitution* Fund and various white church groups, including the Georgia Council of Churches, the United Citizens of Christ, and a Trappist monastery in Georgia that provided stained-glass windows free of charge to the new buildings.

On September 24, he was back in the South, invited by King to address the sixth annual convention of the SCLC in Birmingham, Alabama. At the airport, police stopped an attempt to form a motorcade that would escort Robinson into town. Nevertheless, he delivered a stirring speech even as the focus of national attention to civil rights swung sharply to the University of Mississippi, where an Air Force veteran, James Meredith, was seeking to attend classes as the first black student at "Ole Miss." (After rioting that left two dead and more than one hundred injured, a force of three thousand federal troops restored order.) In Birmingham, however, the SCLC convention took an important step. Emphasizing the role of Jim Crow in employment, SCLC leaders decided to open a new front, in addition to voter registration. Jack supported this expanded role for the SCLC even as leaders at the NAACP saw its own powers being usurped. To Robinson, the common goal was greater freedom for blacks. Two days later, back in New York, he gladly served as the central figure at a mammoth NAACP voter-registration rally at

Metropolitan Baptist Church at 128th Street and Seventh Avenue in Harlem.

The fall of 1962 was dominated by important local elections, including races for the United States Senate and the governorship. To Jack's satisfaction, the Republican Jacob Javits won easy reelection to the Senate. Governor Rockefeller's task was harder, and Jack was active in his support. On August 29, Robinson was prominent in a reception honoring Rockefeller for "his continued and sustained interest in behalf of the Harlem community." Jack also helped smooth the way in various campaign walks by Rockefeller in Harlem and Brooklyn; in October, he presented a Baptist layman award to the governor at Antioch Baptist Church in Brooklyn. However, in one election race Robinson stirred up antagonism from many other blacks. In the race for state attorney general, he openly opposed the Democratic Party candidate, Edward Dudley, who was seeking to become the first black to hold statewide office in New York. (Dudley was the president of the Borough of Manhattan; he was also the NAACP official who had corresponded with Robinson in 1944 about his court-martial.) But Robinson endorsed Dudley's Republican opponent, Louis Lefkowitz. "Do you turn your back on a white candidate for re-election," Jack asked, "who has built a reputation for being one of the most dedicated, militant and conscientious public servants in the nation and who has steadily batted 1,000 percent on the civil rights issue? Do you turn your back on him because he is a white man and you are a Negro who would like to see another Negro move up to a high office?" On Election Day, most black voters answered yes. They voted for Dudley— but Lefkowitz won.

One other election of special concern to Robinson took place on the other side of the country. In California, where Jack had campaigned for him, Richard Nixon lost the race for the governorship. Bitter and exhausted, he then unloaded on the press and declared himself done with politics forever. But Robinson hurried to console him. "I hope that you will reconsider, Dick," Jack wrote, "because it is the great men people attack. You are good for politics; good for America. . . . I urge you to remain active. There is so much to be done and there are too few qualified people to do the job now. Your loss would be an added blow to our efforts."

CHRISTMAS 1962 WAS AS usual a happy time in the Robinson home, a season of giving and celebration; but it was also overshadowed a little by Jack's nervous expectation of surgery early in the new year. His left knee was the problem. For some time he had been playing tennis again, but finally had to give it up because of chronic pain from arthritis and a torn cartilage that needed repairing.

On January 7, Jack underwent surgery at Mount Vernon Hospital in Westchester County near New York City. His doctors, Dr. Robert Rosen and Dr. Arthur Sadler, pronounced the operation successful. With his left leg in a cast from ankle to thigh, Jack was wheeled back to his fifth-floor room, where he expected to stay two or three days before returning home. But two weeks later he was still there. Complications set in: staphylococcal bacteria had infected his knee, which became almost unbearably painful, and spread poisonously into his blood system; the septicemia also threw his diabetes wildly out of control. Treated with massive doses of penicillin and insulin and fed intravenously, Robinson slipped in and out of consciousness. "One day, early in the morning, I came into his room as I did every day," Rachel recalled, "and he did not know who I was. He was delirious, completely out of it. The poison was systemic, and it wasn't clear right away that the antibiotics would work in time."

After a while he began to recover. Certainly the ordeal disturbed him. Lavished with attention by the hospital staff, he could only wonder what might have happened to him otherwise. "I was not afraid," he wrote from the hospital, even as he joked nervously about not being quite ready to "steal home." He was "deeply concerned" mainly about the effect on his wife and children "if I were taken away at this time. I like to believe that God has a lot of work left for me to do and wants to give me time to do it the best I possibly can."

Flowers, cards, and letters poured into the hospital, as well as a stream of visitors that included eighty-two-year-old Branch Rickey, who had almost stolen home a few times himself because of chronic heart problems. Chastened, Jack looked forward to returning to Stamford and the comfort of his home, with his family about him. Rachel's daily visits had meant a lot to him, but the children, too, had been attentive. Lying in his hospital bed, he had been deeply moved by a Christmas gift they had given him and Rachel—a loving cup, engraved with the words "To the Best Parents" and, underneath, the children's names. The cup, Jack told his readers, was worth more to him than all the trophies he ever received. "Like any other family, we have our problems," he confessed. "Up until this Christmas, we haven't been sure we were even on our way to solving some of our problems." But things were better now; the cup symbolized the new unity of the Robinson family.

Mainly, if not exclusively, Jack was referring to Jackie, who had failed again at boarding school. Refusing to honor the dress code and other rules and ignoring his schoolwork, he had also been involved in fights. The school asked him not to return. Back in Stamford, where he enrolled in Rippowam High School, he fell back into some of his old ways but also seemed to be trying hard to improve. That November, he turned sixteen. By Christmas, he seemed a much more contented person than in the past. To Jack, the loving cup was the final touch in what he was sure was Jackie's emerging maturity.

Jack's first day back home was a pleasure. Hobbled by bandages on his left leg and supported by crutches, he could not move about much. But he could look through the window out onto the snowy ground strewn with granite boulders, and the pond he had come to love and the green willows his family had planted on the banks. Above all, he looked forward to his first dinner with his family since the first week of January. But near dinnertime, no one could find Jackie. Urgent telephone calls to his friends brought no news. "Then someone called us from the bank," Rachel recalled. "Jackie had stopped by and withdrawn all of his money and stuffed it into a paper bag. Something didn't seem right, and the bank thought that maybe we ought to know. Sooner or later we realized that Jackie had run away. Jack just crumbled. He started to cry. It was the first time the family—Sharon and David, my mother, all of us— had seen him break down and cry. What he had just been through at the hospital had something to do with it, but he was deeply, deeply hurt."

Jackie and a fellow Rippowam High student, a white youngster whose family was also left in the dark, had taken off by bus for California. They ran out of money in Texas but somehow made it to California, where they expected to find jobs picking fruit—except that the fruit harvests were some months away. Finally, in frustration, Jackie called home from Los Angeles, where local police soon picked him up along with his companion. After about two weeks away, they returned home to Stamford.

For Jack and his son, this was a turning point in their relationship, from which they would not recover for several years.

FORCED NOW TO USE A CANE, his full head of hair gone gray, Jack was a sobering sight to old friends who recalled him in his athletic prime. For the first time in years, his traveling to raise money for the

NAACP fell off; he was not up to taking long trips in cramped airplanes. Staying close to home, however, he did what he could to help. At the Harlem branch YMCA, he became a co-chairman of a drive to raise $137,000 to renovate the decaying main building on 135th Street and the boys' department across the street.

His column showed no loss of vigor. In March, Jack startled readers by an open letter blasting the most powerful and beloved elected official in Harlem, Adam Clayton Powell Jr., the pastor of Abyssinian Baptist Church and a veteran congress- man. To Robinson, Powell had long been a hero. A brilliant civil rights leader in Harlem during the Depression, Powell had entered Congress in 1945. There, his aggressive civil rights leadership, as well as his flamboyant personal style, had made him stand out; admired and even beloved by most blacks, he was also criticized by many whites. Scrutiny of Pow- ell's record only increased after 1960, when his seniority gave him the chairmanship of the important House Committee on Education and Labor, the first House chairmanship held by a black. By 1963, Pow- ell was the center of controversy over charges of cor- ruption and absenteeism from the House. His absenteeism was clear; having lost a libel suit in the amount of more than $200,000 brought against him by a Harlem woman, Powell now kept his distance from New York to avoid paying up. In 1963, when Robinson attacked him, Harlem had just answered the charges against Powell by reelecting him by a landslide.

To this point, Jack had avoided any public criticism of Powell; in fact, at a recent appearance at Howard University, a student had berated him for not speaking out against Powell. But Jack had been provoked by a widely reported speech, "One Thousand Tomorrows," delivered by Powell first at the Capital Press Club in Washington, then at a rally on 125th Street. Behind the speech was Powell's anger at the major black civil rights organizations for failing to come to his defense. Much of the speech was familiar stuff—a call for black racial unity, an attack on the black middle class for evading their duty to the race, and resentment that liberal whites were offering mainly charity when blacks wanted a fair shake. Now, however, Powell came close to urging a boycott of the leading civil rights groups, because they included too many whites among their leaders. "We have got to have organizations where Negroes control the policy," he told the crowd. "How many Negroes sit on the Board of Directors of the American Jewish Congress or the Italian societies?" Naming the NAACP, the National Urban League, SCLC, and CORE, he insisted now that "we must consider boycotting those organization we don't control."

At the NAACP and the National Urban League, Roy Wilkins and Whitney Young reacted with outrage. Robinson's own reply was an open letter to "a friend in the wrong." His tone was a mixture of regret and censure: "I write it because it is my sincere belief that you have set back the cause of the Negro, let your race down and failed miserably . . . as an important national leader of the Negro in this nation." Defending the role of white veterans of the NAACP such as its president, Arthur Spingarn, and its life-membership chairman, Kivie Kaplan, he also attacked Powell's benign views of Malcolm X and the Nation of Islam. Powell knew that "the answer for the Negro is to be found, not in segregation or in separation, but by his insistence upon moving into his rightful place—the same place as that of any other American—within our society." As for Powell's personal troubles, it was "pretty obvious that you had placed yourself in a vulnerable position to be condemned by many people with many different motives."

The open letter enraged some blacks, and especially Malcolm's supporters. One of them offered three messages: "To Jackie Robinson: 'Shut your mouth, go away.' To Adam Powell: 'Welcome home brother, you've been gone too long.' To Malcolm X: 'I'd be lost without you.' " "We as black people," another letter suggested, "must get rid of fellows like Jackie Robinson, who can be purchased by our number one enemy." "I was one of your admirers, Jackie," still another warned, "but you must remember that you are not on the ball field now. You are playing with the destinies and freedom of your people in America." Although the response was intense, Jack would not budge. "If I have to give up my right to say exactly what I believe to earn popularity and admiration," he declared, "you can keep the popularity and admiration." He was "deeply proud" of his link to men like Black and Rickey. (In fact, in the middle of the controversy he published a column in praise of a veteran white civil rights lawyer, David

Levinson, in Philadelphia.) As for Powell: "Adam was my friend and if he so chooses, he still is. Sometimes it takes a friend to say the things other people won't say."

Jack's antipathy to President Kennedy about civil rights helped to close the distance between himself and Powell, if only to some degree. When, in April, Powell broke a truce between himself and Kennedy over the issue of discrimination in public housing, Robinson praised Powell: "This kind of forthright action is exactly what we meant when we wrote that Adam could once again exert leadership if he so desired." On July 8, the second speaker in a lecture series on the "Black Revolution" at Abyssinian Baptist Church was Jackie Robinson.

In April, still leaning on his cane and eager for the tropic sun, Jack and Rachel flew to Venezuela as the guest of the Sheraton chain for the opening of one of its hotels there; they also attended the inauguration of Rómulo Betancourt as president of the country. This baseball-loving country, where Jack had played in 1945 as a barnstormer with a Negro leagues team, welcomed Jack as a hero, and he and Betancourt even shared a press conference. Rested, he returned to the United States prepared to resume his traveling for the civil rights movement. The center of attention was now, once again, Birmingham, Alabama, where that month Martin Luther King Jr. announced a campaign to breach its thick walls of segregation. Commanded by the infamous police chief Eugene "Bull" Connor, officers arrested over two thousand demonstrators and jailed more than one thousand; but the most harrowing stage of the action began on May 1, when King summoned black schoolchildren to join the desegregation campaign. Filmed images of police dogs and fire hoses turned on demonstrators, including women and children, sickened much of the nation and swept around the world.

On May 7, after a briefing by Al Duckett and Noel Marder, a wealthy young white publisher from Yonkers committed to the movement, who had just returned from visiting King in Birmingham, Jack sent out a flood of telegrams announcing an emergency meeting at Sardi's restaurant in Manhattan to discuss the crisis in Birmingham. He also dispatched an impassioned telegram to President Kennedy protesting the sluggish pace of civil rights progress and calling for federal support of the protesters. "The revolution that is taking place in this country," Robinson insisted, "can not be squelched by police dogs or high power hoses." A host of leaders and celebrities, from A. Philip Randolph, Arnold Forster, and Louis Lefkowitz to Diahann Carroll, Ruby Dee, and Juanita Poitier, turned out for what Jack described as the organizing meeting of a new support group, "Back Our Brothers," of which Marder and Robinson were co-chairmen. The luncheon netted more than $8,000 for Dr. King, as well as a pledge to raise $20,000 more at a dinner in June.

With news cameras rolling, Jack also announced that, at King's invitation, he would soon fly to Birmingham to join the protest. This news brought a flood of calls from friends eager to support the Birmingham effort. Ella Fitzgerald sent a check for

$1,000. Floyd Patterson, training doggedly for his rematch with the new heavyweight boxing champion, Sonny Liston, telephoned to ask if he could accompany Jack. "I can't stay in jail but three days," he told Robinson, who hoped not to go to jail at all, "but I'll go down and stay that long with you." Never one to offer himself as a martyr, Robinson downplayed the courage involved in his decision. "I don't like to be bitten by dogs," he confessed, "because I'm a coward. I don't like to go to jail either, because, as I say, I'm a coward. But we've got to show Martin Luther King that we are behind him."

On May 10, in Birmingham, Dr. King announced an agreement reached with the Senior Citizens Committee, a group of leading white businessmen, for desegregating the city. But euphoria about this victory was soon shattered. On May 13, at one o'clock in the morning, an urgent telephone call from Wyatt Tee Walker in Birmingham awakened Jack with the news that a bomb had shattered part of the black-owned Gaston Motel, which King used as his headquarters there. Walker needed to reach White House officials who might intervene to protect King from another assassination attempt. Jack was able to reach a presidential advisor and inform him of their concern. Later that day, Robinson, Patterson, and eleven others in their party left Newark Airport. That evening, just after 7 p.m., they reached Birmingham. There, Walker, whose wife had been clubbed savagely in her head with a rifle butt by a police officer, greeted them with a warning about new threats of violence against them in particular.

With a police escort, Robinson, Patterson, and their party drove to the Fifth Street Baptist Church, where Dr. King, his associate Ralph Abernathy, and other top leaders warmly greeted them. Inside, a capacity crowd of some two thousand persons were singing a movement anthem when the two celebrities made a dramatic entrance, Robinson gray-haired and leaning on his cane, Patterson young and vigorous but with a bandaged right hand from a training-camp accident. The assembly erupted in joy at the sight of two men so closely identified over the recent years as symbols of brave black manhood. In his speech, Robinson attacked President Kennedy for not sending troops into Birmingham and also excoriated the Alabama State Police and Bull Connor in particular for their response to protesters. Then he and Patterson went to Pilgrim Baptist Church, where hundreds of participants at a youth rally gave them another wildly enthusiastic reception. At the end of a long evening, after uneasily inspecting the bombed-out section, they went to bed at the Gaston Motel.

The next morning, Robinson and Patterson were joined by the Reverend Fred Shuttlesworth, the most prominent local protest leader and a veteran of many clashes with the police, who had been hospitalized after being struck by high-pressure hoses. Accompanied by the Reverend A. D. King (Martin's brother), Robinson then returned to New York in time to take a major role in an NAACP rally on Seventh Avenue in Harlem to commemorate the ninth anniversary on May 17 of *Brown* v. *Board of Education.* If he was a hero to many for having visited Birmingham at this time, he was not a hero to all. The New York *Daily News* questioned the wisdom of the trip, as did the former star athlete Jesse Owens; they saw Robinson and other Northerners stirring up trouble rather than ending it. (In an exchange of messages, Robinson rebuked Owens.) Also critical of the Birmingham effort was Malcolm X: Robinson and Patterson had gone there at the behest of white liberals, to defuse black rage. Moreover, Malcolm argued, no self-respecting black man would send his children to be abused by police dogs and fire hoses, as the protestors had done.

The danger facing blacks protesting in the South was tragically underscored on June 12 when, near midnight, a gunman shot and killed thirty-seven-year-old Medgar Evers in the driveway of his home in Jackson, Mississippi, as he returned from a civil rights meeting. At least twice, Evers had welcomed Robinson to Jackson in support of the NAACP. Robinson did not attend the funeral but sent an impassioned telegram to President Kennedy pleading for protection for Dr. King, who attended the event on June 15. If King were harmed, Robinson declared, "the restraint of many people all over this nation might burst its bonds and bring about a brutal bloody holocaust the like of which this country has not seen." Ironically, the murder occurred only a few hours after another extraordinary moment, when the President finally threw his full support behind the movement. Pressed by King and other civil rights leaders to take a moral stand against Jim Crow in addition to signing legislation, President Kennedy had just delivered a television address, some of it improvised, of surpassing eloquence and insight. After hearing the address, Jack at once sent a telegram to the White House: "Thank you for emerging as the most forthright President we have ever had and for providing us with the inspired leadership that we so desperately needed. I am more proud than ever of my American heritage."

A few days later, "Back Our Brothers" held its second event, a $100-a-plate fund-raising dinner in honor of the "Four Horsemen" of SCLC and the movement—Martin Luther King Jr., Ralph Abernathy, Fred Shuttlesworth, and Wyatt Tee Walker. Jack personally presented an award to Walker, Ed Sullivan to Dr. King. Then, on the last Sunday in June, in what would become an annual event, Jack and Rachel hosted an "Afternoon of Jazz" on the grounds of their home. The concert, which featured musicians such as Dave Brubeck, Cannonball Adderley, and Dizzy Gillespie, attracted about five hundred patrons and raised more than $15,000 for SCLC.

The concert for SCLC put a new strain on Jack's tense ties to the NAACP, which was now often overshadowed in the news by SCLC and its aggressive student offshoot, SNCC. In July, in the *Amsterdam News,* Jack criticized Roy Wilkins for "casting disparaging remarks against other civil rights agencies." At the same time, Robinson also sniped at Whitney Young of the National Urban League for a similar reason, after Young, like Wilkins on another occasion, ridiculed the crucial strategy of SCLC in Birmingham and elsewhere of filling the city jails in a direct challenge to Jim Crow. Jack saw no justification for Young's comment when, as he put it, "the course of history and the shape of current events are being altered by young and old all over this nation who are making this kind of sacrifice." He made it clear that he did not wish to deny Wilkins or Young, only to acknowledge King's rare bravery and effectiveness. "I do not say this as a would-be leader," he went on. "I do not think I have the ability and know that I do not have the inclination for leadership. . . . I say this as Robinson."

Behind the new signs of disunity Jack saw, ironically, the effect of the murder of Medgar Evers, which by its savage boldness had made the rival leaders more antagonistic to one another—as if the confrontational style of SCLC and SNCC were ultimately to blame for the NAACP leader's death. "Disunity," Jack argued, "is no proper memorial to give to a courageous man who died in order that we might win freedom." Robinson was even more appalled when supporters of the Nation of Islam pelted Dr. King with eggs when he arrived at Salem Methodist Church in Harlem to preach an evening sermon. Although Malcolm denied that his followers in the Nation were involved, Robinson ignored his denial. Conceding to Malcolm X's organization the right to free speech, Jack insisted on its marginality among blacks despite its prominence in the white press (especially after the airing of a television program, *The Hate That Hate Produced*, about the Nation of Islam, by Mike Wallace). To Robinson, it was "very odd that the power structure in journalism, television and radio keeps promoting the Muslims." Could it be, he asked, that pro-segregationist groups "outside the race" formed the basis of the Nation's support? "Where do the Muslims get their money? Who finances them?"

In contrast, Jack was full of praise for "the magnificent role the organized white clergy of America has begun to play in the civil rights struggle." He was moved to this paean after a visit a few weeks before to address the Fourth General Synod of the United Church of Christ, which he lauded for its decisive support of the movement. Unlike other major religious denominations that cowered on the sidelines despite the concern of individual members, the United Church of Christ had taken a bold collective stand. At the synod, it had adopted a credo that recognized the morality of racial integration, including intermarriage. Partly as a result of his successful speech here, Jack was elected in November to a three-year term, starting January 1, 1964, as president of United Church Men, which represented some ten million churchmen as one of the major departments of the National Council of the Churches of Christ in the United States. The National Council, which united all major Protestant and Orthodox religions in America, had also come out in strong support of civil rights for blacks, including support of sit-ins and boycotts.

Conveniently for Robinson, the headquarters of the United Church Men was in Manhattan, in the Riverside Church complex.

ALL THESE ACTIVITIES, some highly publicized, were not without an effect on Jack's main job, as a vice-president at Chock Full o' Nuts. Although he still found much satisfaction in his work there, and although Bill Black still seemed fully behind him, changes were occurring that had undermined his place in the company. That summer, after a golfing vacation in Puerto Rico, where Jack served as honorary chairman of a golf tournament at the Dorado Hilton, he returned to New York to find his place at Chock Full o' Nuts in jeopardy. As Jack knew well, his second contract (for five years) with the company would expire early in the next year, 1964.

For some time, the company had been vexed by problems involving worker efficiency and morale, on the one hand, and trade union organizing, on the other. Standards of service at the restaurants, where tipping was forbidden, were breaking down even as the United Mine Workers sought to organize the workers. As the head of personnel, Robinson was in a crucial position concerning these matters, but increasingly his performance was found wanting. Although he did his job conscientiously, his efforts on behalf of civil rights and related matters probably were at the expense of Chock Full o' Nuts. At least some of his colleagues wanted the company's name and image separated more distinctly from his other activities; Robinson did not help matters by often using company stationery for civil rights and other political correspondence. In addition, instead of cracking down on delinquent workers, Jack's instinct from the start was to defend them.

At some point, Robinson found himself assigned an assistant in the personnel office over whom he had little control. This assistant, a black man named Herb Samuel, who had trained as a fighter pilot during the war and attended Tuskegee Institute and Cornell University, had evidently been imposed on him although, as Jack put it to another executive, "we don't see eye to eye and neither of us have much respect for the other"; Samuel was "to be my assistant whether I liked it or not."

On July 13, while Jack was away from the office for about a month, the company fired six employees who had been involved, apparently, in some form of trade-union recruiting. Normally, Robinson, as the head of personnel, passed on all firings of nonsupervisory staff; but he found out about the dismissals only on his return. He then sent a sharply worded memorandum to Samuel. On August 13, in words at least as tough, Black reprimanded Jack for his message to Samuel, and for expecting the company to refrain from acting while he was away. Black and another executive had reviewed the firings: "Don't you have any respect for our judgments?" Black's tone shook Jack. The next day, in a reply, Robinson stuck to his position that as head of personnel he should be involved in all dismissals, but was careful not to offend Black. "I hope you will accept this as I write it. It has nothing to do with my personal high regard for you, but it certainly has a great deal to do with what I think of myself." The next day, Jack drafted an even more conciliatory letter, although he continued to insist that his letter to Samuel was in order. Black had not hired Jack in 1957 as a figurehead; "I'm sure, today, that you wouldn't want me and don't want me to be a figurehead."

As Jack mulled over his options, he was grateful for the huge, elevating distraction provided by the March on Washington, when a coalition of all the major civil rights groups and their supporters, black and white, descended on the capital in an unprecedented show of solidarity. To Jack, who attended the march with Rachel, Jackie, Sharon, and David, the day was an unparalleled triumph. Instead of the fights and rioting that some predicted, the mood was one of self-confidence and shared humanity. "I have never been so proud to be a Negro," he wrote. "I have never been so proud to be an American." The sight of thousands of blacks and whites marching together for a common cause stirred him: "One had to be deeply moved as [one] stood, watching Negroes and whites, marching hand in hand, singing songs of freedom," he wrote. He was proud, too, of his family. Jack watched Rachel's eyes moisten as, spellbound, she listened to Dr. King's "I Have a Dream" oration. He saw Jackie, who was usually bored by politics, join in the singing and handclapping and heard him talk of doing more for the movement. Hand in hand, he walked proudly with eleven-year-old David, explaining to him this or that facet of the struggle. A passing scare came when Sharon, overcome by the heat, fainted and had to be taken to a Red Cross station. The only lasting regret was watching "the decadent, ignorant philosophy" of three reactionary Southern senators as they offered on television their poisoned opinions of the day's events.

Buoyed by the joyful spirit of the march, on September 9, with Marian Logan directing the effort, the Robinsons hosted their second "Afternoon of Jazz" of the year at their home in Stamford, this time in aid of both the SCLC and the NAACP. With both Roy Wilkins and Martin Luther King Jr. as honored guests, the response was even greater than before; more than thirteen hundred people heard the music of Horace Silver, Herbie Mann, Billy Taylor, and Joe Williams.

A week later, on the morning of September 16, joy turned to horror and sorrow when a bomb thrown into the Sixteenth Street Baptist Church in Birmingham, Alabama, killed four girls at Sunday school and wounded twenty other persons. Behind the bombing Jack saw the evil hands of Bull Connor and Governor George Wallace. "God bless Dr. Martin Luther King," he mused bitterly in his column. But if his child had been one of those killed, "I'm afraid he would have lost me as a potential disciple of his credo of non-violence."

Meanwhile, his place at Chock Full o' Nuts was crumbling. On September 7, Jimmy Booker, who published a column of inside political news and gossip in the *Amsterdam News,* offered this squib: "Friends say that Jackie Robinson is considering leaving the restaurant business and taking a job with Gov. Rockefeller." Later that month, word came that the alleged job was as the next chairman of the New York State Athletic Commission (on which no blacks sat). On September 18, Robinson and the governor indeed met to discuss this move. Coincidentally, Jack and Rachel had rented a small unit in the brownstone owned by the Logans on West Eighty-eighth Street, so that he now had a residence in New York State. On October 5, Booker announced that the appointment would come within a few days. Again it failed to materialize.

The state job carried a salary of $20,475 a year, which would mean a severe cut in Jack's pay. But he would soon need a position. Increasingly he stayed away from Chock Full o' Nuts, even as the six dismissed workers, who ironically blamed Robinson for their situation, filed a formal complaint with the City Commission on Human Rights. Early in October, the National Labor Relations Board set a hearing for later in the month of a charge by the United Mine Workers concerning unfair labor practices. Within the company, Jack heard very little about this matter. Then, around eleven in the morning on October 29, someone asked him to come to the front office; the company and the union were about to sign their agreement. This was Robinson's first notice that the union had won the war.

The next day, Robinson sent another executive, Sam Ostrove, a letter that spelled out his estrangement. In addition to the gnawing presence of Samuel was his loss of face in the trade-union struggle.

While he had been complying with the unofficial company policy of discouraging the union, behind his back his company had been negotiating a change. The six employees had attacked Robinson although he had not been involved in their firing; now they were to be rehired without his consent. Robinson felt the loss of face keenly. His ability to be head of personnel was irreparably damaged, as he saw it. "People are saying," he complained, "He not only can't hire, but he has no voice." He also faced up to the criticism that he was "away from the office frequently. This is without question, but it started only in the last few weeks. It should be obvious why this has happened."

His crisis at work did not curb his fighting spirit. On the road, he made speeches for the Anti-Defamation League and the NAACP, at the University of Pennsylvania, and in Detroit for the Trade Union Leadership Council. In his newspaper column, Robinson went on the offensive following an attack by Adam Clayton Powell and Malcolm X on Ralph Bunche, who had spoken scathingly of the Black Muslims. As a UN official, he pointed out, Bunche was supposed to be aloof from the internal affairs of the United States, but he had spoken out repeatedly in the South against Jim Crow. In contrast, Powell, "once a friend of mine," had deserted blacks in the current civil rights crisis. "When we have heard from him," Robinson wrote, "it has usually been in the form of some grandstand, publicity-conscious barrage of wild promises which the Congressman failed to keep." Malcolm, "whose intelligence and articulateness I respect deeply," was not much better: "Malcolm is very militant on Harlem street corners where militancy is not dangerous." Neither man possessed "one twentieth of the integrity and leadership" of Bunche.

Powell rolled with these punches; but Malcolm, who had a gift for taunting, heaped scorn on Robinson as a toady of one big white man after another: Rickey in his attack on Robeson in 1949, Nixon, Black, and now Rockefeller. "We hear," he reminded Jack, "that you are about to be appointed Boxing Commissioner of New York State by Governor Nelson Rockefeller. Does this have any bearing on your efforts to get Negroes into Rockefeller's camp? Just who are you playing ball for today, good Friend?" Stung by the imputation of cowardice in Robinson's letter, Malcolm spitefully imagined Robinson himself shot down, like Medgar Evers, at the hands of whites—the same white "friends" to whom he was now so obsequious. This kind of malice was beyond Robinson, who countered with another harsh letter to Malcolm. "Coming from you," he told Malcolm, "an attack is a tribute."

Now a barrage of letters hostile to Robinson added to the din. A Brooklyn man regretted the sad spectacle of black men attacking one another in public—"but then I do not consider Mr. Robinson a true black man. Rather he is a white mind covered by a black skin." But on November 22, in the middle of this controversy, came the assassination of President

Kennedy, which muted it. Within a few days, Malcolm was silenced further. On December 1, at a rally in Manhattan, he gave this reaction to the President's death: "Chickens coming home to roost never made me sad. They always made me glad." Repudiating the comment, Elijah Muhammad announced Malcolm's suspension in telegrams sent to various news organizations.

Jack had just returned with Rachel from Pasadena, where a public park had been dedicated in his name, when the news about the assassination broke. "When the tragic news first hit," he wrote in the *Amsterdam News,* "I gasped with disbelief that here in America in 1963, a President could be murdered simply because he was a man of courageous conviction." Although "this was a man whom I often criticized," Kennedy had "done more for the civil rights cause than any other President." Remorseful about his constant criticism of the President on civil rights, he emphasized now that he had begun to admire him. One of Kennedy's top aides had said to Robinson recently: "Jack, you are certainly in his corner now, aren't you?"

However, even in mourning for Kennedy, he was looking ahead. His column about the assassination ended with a call for Republicans to line up behind Rockefeller as a candidate for the presidency in 1964. His reasoning was easy to follow, at least while observers still assumed that Lyndon Johnson was at heart a segregationist unlikely to pursue the civil rights policies initiated by the Kennedys: "If the Democratic Party chooses President Johnson as its standard-bearer in 1964," he wrote, "and if the Republicans select Barry Goldwater, where will the Negro stand?"

ON DECEMBER 26, at the end of one of the most wrenching years in American history, Jack headed for Jamaica in the West Indies on a vacation he badly needed. The guest of Hugh Shearer, the second-in-command in the government of Prime Minister Alexander Bustamante, he relaxed at the luxurious Runaway Bay Hotel on the North Coast of the island with Rachel, David, David's friend Eddie Allen, and Jack's ghostwriter, Al Duckett. Independent only since 1962, Jamaica seemed in stark contrast to the United States on the question of race. With its motto "Out of Many, One People," it seemed to epitomize true democracy and effortless racial integration. After a touch of rain on their first day, the tropical skies were clear and blue and the nights heavenly. Jack and Rachel loafed in the sun and tried to think as little as possible about Chock Full o' Nuts.

In his first column of the New Year, 1964, Jimmy Booker in the New York *Amsterdam News* offered a prediction: "Jackie Robinson and Chock Full o' Nuts will part company whether he gets that state post or not." By the first week of February, Robinson was indeed out, with his resignation to take effect officially on February 28, almost seven years to the day after he joined the company. Ostensibly, his departure was amicable. Jack was leaving to join Rockefeller's presidential campaign as one of six deputy national directors. "We'll miss Jackie," Black told the press, "but it was his wish to enter politics. . . . Our 1,500 employees and I wish him good luck." At first, Jack, too, put a bright face on his leaving. But a few weeks later, when he at last commented on it directly, he was terse: "I did not want to be in any job where I would be a figurehead." Scarcely mentioning Black's name, he said nothing that could be construed as praise but also lashed out at no one. He seemed more baffled than angry by what had transpired. But given the range of Jack's activities, and the nature of his political sympathies, the leeway Black had granted him for seven years was extraordinary.

Now, in the middle of his life, two major roads lay ahead. Each had its own peril. One involved his continuing work in politics, and especially his relationship with Rockefeller. That way was uncertain, ill defined; in any event, it seemed intrinsically limited. The other—more dangerous, because his ability to earn a livelihood was directly at stake—involved business. His prospects here were slim. In the late winter of 1964, Robinson was now truly on his own.

— 15 —

On the Killing Ground

1964–1968

*Every dire development which I had
envisioned . . . is coming to pass.*
—Jackie Robinson (1964)

ON JANUARY 31, 1964, Jack passed his forty-fifth birthday well aware that he was at a watershed in his life. His seven-year career as a company executive was drawing to a close without a similar job anywhere in sight. The civil rights movement, in which he had invested much of his hopes, and which was once united, was coming apart in ways that threatened to leave him more and more isolated. His future in electoral politics, which was increasingly tied to Nelson Rockefeller, was also uncertain. At home, his relationship with his son Jackie had soured into distrust and silence. Worst of all, although he had recovered from his brush with death in Mount Vernon Hospital the year before, the decline in his health was beginning to accelerate. Diabetes was placing a growing strain on his eyes and his legs, and ultimately on his heart.

Feeling the danger but ever optimistic, Robinson put on the brightest face he could muster as he weighed his chances in business. "The time is ripest now," he insisted in his column, "for the Negro to gamble and go into serious business for himself because the opportunities are greatest today." In the coming years, Jack would find himself caught up in a wide variety of ventures. Some were a continuation of old interests, others were new. At one time or another, he would launch or help to launch serious projects involving banking, public relations, life insurance, real estate development and construction, books, radio and television broadcasting, and professional football. He also found time for an array of other related activities—from serving on the board of directors of the New York State World's Fair (scheduled to open in the spring of 1964) to working as elected treasurer of the Negro Actors Guild of America, which he did in 1963 and 1964. According to J. Bruce Llewellyn, who would become one of the most powerful blacks in the American financial world, "Jack had what I would call a pioneering competitiveness. But that makes the road doubly harder. It's tough enough to be a good competitor, but it's really tough to be a pathfinder, making your own way through the woods, so to speak. And he was always doing that, making new paths, as a black man who wanted to be an entrepreneur."

But politics was foremost in his mind even as he cleaned out his office at Chock Full o' Nuts. On January 3, Senator Barry Goldwater of Arizona had announced his candidacy for the Republican nomination for President of the United States. Jack's view of the Republicans was complicated. The previous

August, in the *Saturday Evening Post,* he had bared his central anxiety with a controversial article, "The G.O.P: For White Men Only?" Robinson saw "a striking parallel" between the Black Muslims and Goldwater Republicans: "Both groups want to detour from the highway to racial integration. Both groups feel they can reach their goals by traveling the road of racial separation." Goldwater, by adhering to a rigid states'-rights position and by appearing to court the extremist John Birch Society and even the Ku Klux Klan, had become the Devil incarnate for Robinson. Other leading Republicans also failed the crucial civil rights test, including Everett Dirksen, the silver-haired, oracular, but reactionary senator from Illinois; the former actor Ronald Reagan, once a liberal and now a rising conservative star in California; and Richard Nixon himself, stirring again after declaring himself dead in 1962. "The danger of the Republican Party being taken over by the lily-whiteist conservatives," Jack had argued once in the *Amsterdam News,* "is more serious than many people realize." That the Republicans had targeted the South with "Operation Dixie" was well known. But, he asked, "is Operation Dixie calculated to corral Negro as well as white votes—and if not, why not?"

Increasingly, even as many pundits wrote off Rockefeller's chances of being nominated, especially following his recent divorce and remarriage, Jack saw him as the sole hope of the party. "I am proud of Governor Rockefeller," he proclaimed. "He has once again displayed his deep concern for justice and human rights." The zeal Jack brought to his new role as a deputy director of the Rockefeller campaign surprised some observers. On January 29, the fierceness of his speech at a fund-raising dinner and his sheer hard work for the event earned the gratitude of one party loyalist for "the most effective work which you did in that capacity." Impressive with black voters, Jack also attracted younger voters, black and white. On February 28, the New York Young Republican Club, resisting Goldwater's spell, presented Jack with its annual War Memorial Award for humanitarian service. A month later, he scored with a youthful audience again when he took part in a mock Republican Convention at the Perkiomen School in Pennsburg, Pennsylvania. There he spoke grimly of the results of the Wisconsin Democratic primary, where George Wallace swept twenty-five percent of the vote. "What can they possibly think of us in Africa?" Jack asked his audience, incredulous. "When a man—a crazy man like Wallace—can go into a Northern state and draw 25 percent of the vote, then there is something very seriously wrong."

On cross-country trips to campaign for Rockefeller in primaries, Jack hit hard at Goldwater— harder in most ways than Rockefeller himself ever struck. In Portland, Oregon, Jack left little unsaid. "If we have a bigot running for the presidency of the United States," he said, "it will set back the course of the country. Rockefeller must beat Goldwater in the primary." He even urged Democrats in the audience to switch party affiliation temporarily in order to vote against Goldwater in the primary: "If you want to go back being a Democrat after the election that's your privilege." (In an upset, Rockefeller won in Oregon.) In May, as the featured speaker at a gala dinner at Concordia College in Minnesota, he spoke of the election in almost spiritual terms. "This is a struggle to redeem the soul of America," Robinson insisted, as he warned of a possible race war resulting from the extremism of Birchers and Klansmen. "The Negro is not interested in avenging the past, but in enriching the future. How fatal it would be if we came face to face with each other in armed camps of white versus Negro." The rising popularity of Wallace in the North, and of Goldwater across the nation, was a catastrophe. "I feel sorrow," he said, "when Gov. Wallace can come into a northern liberal state and pile up hundreds of thousands of votes. It is tragic that a madman can do this."

By early May, polls showed a dead heat between Goldwater and Rockefeller among voters in general; but a Gallup poll taken of Republican Party members told a different tale: Rockefeller had barely nine percent of the party faithful behind him. For Robinson, this was a grave disappointment. He would also support Henry Cabot Lodge of Massachusetts or William Scranton of Pennsylvania; but under no condition would he vote for either Goldwater or Nixon, against whom Robinson had turned decisively once Nixon had declared his support of Goldwater. On June 2, Jack was thus in a difficult spot when the California primary wrote finis to Rockefeller's hopes and assured Goldwater of the nomination. "I never could nor never will buy Goldwater," Jack stated unequivocally. "In my opinion he is a bigot, an advocate of white supremacy and more dangerous than Governor Wallace." Senator Jacob Javits of New York also refused to support Goldwater, because, he said, he was an American first. "I am a Negro first," Robinson said; supporting Goldwater was out of the question. On June 15, speaking to an overflowing crowd of restless blacks in still-segregated St. Augustine, Florida, Jack urged them to march for their rights— "This is the time for action"—and to vote Democratic if Goldwater won the nomination.

On June 27, he flew to Harrisburg, Pennsylvania, to meet with Governor Scranton, who had attracted most of the anti-Goldwater forces. Robinson left the meeting assured only that Scranton would try hard to influence the party platform away from right-wing views and toward a liberal position on civil rights for blacks. The next day, Jack was in Sasser, Georgia, along with Martin Luther King Jr., for the rededication of the three black churches rebuilt, largely through Robinson's fund-raising efforts, after their torching in 1962. A few days later, taking the last vacation they would ever have as a family, the Robinsons drove west from Connecticut to San Francisco, the site of the convention. They went by way of the finest natural sights in America, the Grand Canyon in Arizona and the Grand Tetons in Wyoming, where they were guests of Nelson Rockefeller at the family ranch there. "We had a beautiful time on the way out," Rachel recalled, "and an entertaining stay at the Rockefeller ranch. Jack was never one to love the wilds, and he hated mosquitoes. But I noticed that he sat on the Rockefeller porch with the insects eating him alive and never said a word. He was thrilled to be there, to help plan the convention fight."

In San Francisco at the Cow Palace, the site of the convention, Jack quickly united with the few blacks accredited as delegates or alternate delegates; out of 1,303 delegates, they accounted for slightly more than a dozen. Their plight reflected the unpopularity of any liberal presence at the convention. A move to condemn the Klan and the John Birch Society also foundered, and lofty talk about the "neighborhood school" concept made it clear that many delegates favored segregation. But Jack would not surrender quietly. When local church and labor groups sponsored a Freedom March to the City Hall plaza, he gamely joined a throng of about thirty thousand people despite the fact that he had trouble keeping up. "Jackie Robinson looked," one reporter wrote, "as though he was having some trouble with his old knee injury as he marched. At one point he was limping along until he sat for some minutes on the hood of an NBC radio car. Evidently the rest did the trick because he came swinging into the Plaza under his own steam."

Inside the convention, he did his best to make his presence felt. He helped bring together most of the black delegates and alternates in meetings to plan strategy in the face of the wholesale defeat of Scranton's liberal amendments and Goldwater's sweep of entire state delegations, such as that of Ohio. Out of this group would come the National Negro Republican Assembly, which sought to advance black interests within the party. In San Francisco, Robinson was "undoubtedly the leading light and spirit," according to one reporter, "in a relentless fight for the party and the principles he believes in." But for Jack, the highlight of the convention was Rockefeller's doggedly noble performance in addressing the convention, when a torrent of boos, taunts, and jeers by Goldwater supporters all but drowned out his speech. Finding himself behind the Alabama delegation, Robinson became such a vocal one-man cheering section that he almost got into a fist fight with another delegate after someone allegedly threw a lighted cigarette or some sort of corrosive on the jacket of a Rockefeller supporter. For Jack, Rockefeller's courage would remain vivid. Two years later, he would write that it had been "a classic and splendid sight to observe this man standing tall in a hostile atmosphere, fighting with all the vigor and eloquence at his command."

Goldwater won nomination on the first ballot. In his acceptance speech, he offered his dictum that "extremism in the defense of liberty is no vice" and "moderation in the pursuit of justice is no virtue." These words further alarmed his opponents, including Robinson. Thus when, after the convention, Goldwater reached out to him, Robinson was not receptive. On July 25, he sent Jack a letter that was half conciliatory, half a rebuke. Robinson had attacked him "rather viciously on several occasions" publicly without seeking to ascertain in person the senator's views. Now Goldwater "would deem it a great pleasure," he assured Jack, "to sit down and break bread with you sometime" and explain his positions.

But if Goldwater expected a friendly response to this letter, which he made clear would soon be public, he did not get it. In a reply that Jack also made public, he offered a long, scathing list of questions that Goldwater might answer in the private meeting he proposed. These included queries about his opposition in the Senate to the Civil Rights Act of 1964, his silence on certain brutal crimes against civil rights workers that summer, his ties to the John Birch Society, and the treatment of Rockefeller at the convention. No rapprochement was possible between the two men. "Is it unity you seek or uniformity," Jack asked rhetorically, "compromise or conformity, cooperation or complaisance?"

For Jack, his duty was now clear. Acting once again as an apparent renegade in party politics, he swung his support to Hubert Humphrey of Minnesota in the Democratic Party. He did so even though he understood that Johnson would be nominated for the presidency. Humphrey's vigorous efforts throughout the spring to move the Senate to pass the Civil Rights Act of 1964 had earned for him Robinson's continuing support, which in turn moved Humphrey: "Your understanding and support mean a great deal to me." When, after the San Francisco convention, Humphrey wrote Robinson to lament that it was "truly a great national tragedy" to see extremists capture the Republican Party, Jack volunteered to campaign on behalf of the Johnson-Humphrey ticket.

Jack did not understand how any right-thinking American could support Goldwater, and his severity on this matter embraced even Rockefeller. On October 7, after the governor set aside the memory of his humiliation at the Cow Palace and came out for Goldwater, Jack rebuked him in a stinging letter. "You know and I know," he wrote, "that a Goldwater victory would result in violence and bloodshed. His candidacy reeks with prejudice and bigotry. . . . It seems to me that to support him is to reject the ideals and principles for which the Rockefeller name has always stood. Your doing so is one of the most disappointing things that has ever happened to me." Robinson became national chairman of the Republicans for Johnson Committee.

In November, Johnson and Humphrey crushed Goldwater and his running mate, William E. Miller. But to Jack's disappointment, Robert Kennedy, despite Jack's vigorous support of the incumbent, Kenneth Keating, a liberal Republican, won election to the Senate from New York. It was "inconceivable to this writer," Robinson had written, "that New Yorkers will be so blinded by the Kennedy glamour that they will forget the splendid job" done over the years by Keating. In fact, blacks and whites alike rushed to support Kennedy. Robinson continued to hope for a revival of inclusiveness and compassion among the Republicans, and to believe that the African-American future depended on having a black presence on both sides of the party divide. "We must have a two-party system," he insisted. "The Negro needs to be able to occupy a bargaining position." Or, as he put it else-where, "A split ballot can mean a united nation."

EARLY IN 1964, Robinson was also haunted by the fear that the March on Washington and the killing of Evers and Kennedy, among others, had been a terri-ble watershed in the nation's history. Growing gloomy about America, soon he was talking about a white backlash in response to "the Negro Revolution of the summer, fall and winter of 1963." But he also saw a new bitterness among young blacks. "I am no race leader, no social scientist," he admitted to a re-porter, "and claim no special wisdom as a spokesman or analyst. Yet, every dire development which I had envisioned . . . is coming to pass." In large part, he was alluding to an epidemic of crime in the black communities, including violent crimes against whites fueled by racial rage. Lamenting "the atmo-sphere of hate which seems to be spreading through-out the land," he traced much of it to Kennedy's death, which had demoralized the nation. "We were a saddened people, shaken up by the naked exposure of hatred"; yet now there was "more disunity among Americans today than ever before."

No two black figures disturbed him more than the boxer Muhammad Ali (formerly Cassius Clay) and his mentor, Malcolm X. "I thought he would be good for boxing," Jack said sorrowfully of Ali, whom he still called Clay. "I never in my life suspected he would hold these extreme views." While he defended

Clay's right to be a Muslim, he opposed the Muslims "because they advocate the separation of the races." The spectacle of Malcolm X capturing the mind of the handsome, charming young boxer oppressed Robinson, who found Malcolm's appeal a mystery. "Malcolm has big audiences," he pointed out to reporters, "but no constructive program. He has big words, but no records of deeds in civil rights. He is terribly militant on soapboxes, on streetcorners of Negro ghettoes. Yet, he has not faced Southern police dogs in Birmingham . . . nor gone to jail for freedom." Writing about the possibility of a "deliberate and evil design in the schizophrenic policy of the white press," he attacked newspapers that seemed to glamorize "on their front pages the very persons they condemn in their editorials." A report in the New York *Journal-American* that Malcolm was now poised to lead the civil rights movement angered Robinson, who dubbed him "the fair-haired boy of the white press."

Jack was also growing despondent about many young blacks, although he continued his youth work. In July, for example, he was the guest of honor at the annual Youth Banquet held at the NAACP national convention. But he feared the forces that were making even heinous crimes routine, and often in the name of politics. "I wish I could have a heart-to-heart, man-to-man talk with some of the youngsters who, by their blindly reckless acts, are endangering the freedom struggle," he wrote in the *Amsterdam News*. "I do not believe there is an organized hate movement among the

Negro people. . . . I do know that there are resentments and despairs and fears and frustrations which drive some of these youngsters to lash out and seek revenge. But I would say to them, man to man, that you don't win like this."

Meanwhile, he continued to urge tougher stands on civil rights by organizations like the NAACP. In February, just after he was honored by the NCCJ at its annual Brotherhood Banquet, he went to Florida for the NAACP. There, posing the question "Is the Negro Ready?" he tried to shake up the members of local branches in towns like Tampa, St. Petersburg, Ocala, and Clearwater, where Jim Crow was still strong. Jack's message was that militancy and race pride must be welded to a strong sense of morality; to be ready, he stressed, blacks need not be docile. The basic rights "which belong to each white infant born into this nation should and must belong to every black infant," he said. "These rights are no gift to be patronizingly doled out by some benefactor if we 'behave ourselves.' " In Frankfort, Kentucky, when he joined Dr. King and addressed a rally of ten thousand persons marching in support of a bill to end Jim Crow in public accommodations, Robinson sounded one of his constant refrains, that no Negro would have it made until "the last Negro in the Deep South has it made."

The violence unleashed by the civil rights movement flared again in June in Neshoba County, Mississippi, when three civil rights workers disappeared after local police let them go after arresting and jailing them for allegedly speeding. James Chaney, twenty-one, of Meridian, was a black CORE staff worker at the Freedom Center there. Andrew Goodman, twenty and white, was a student volunteer from New York on the same project. Michael Schwerner, twenty-four and also white, was a graduate of the New York School of Social Work who had organized the Meridian Center for CORE. Eventually, the FBI recovered their battered bodies. Together, the three young men wove together contrasting threads of race, religion, class, money, and education that left many observers, including Jack, heartbroken at their fate. To him, the three slain young men were "classic prototypes of the new breed of valiant American youth which has been carrying on the struggle." In addition, Goodman's parents, Robert and Carolyn Goodman, were friends of Marian Logan's. In August, Jack announced that he would chair the Chaney-Goodman-Schwerner Planning Drive, to raise $250,000 to build a new community center in Meridian in their memory. To this end, he and Rachel hosted another jazz concert at their home in Stamford. The concert raised $20,000 for the cause.

Violence in the South spread to the North. A new, aggressive spirit, part militant, part cynical and fatalistic, swept the northern cities in the summer of 1964. In July, after the shooting of a fifteen-year-old Harlem boy, James Powell, in the white Yorkville section of Manhattan by an off-duty police officer, Harlem erupted into nights of violence that saw blacks hurling "Molotov cocktails" against white businesses; one person died and several hundred were arrested in the worst riot there since 1943. A few days later, blacks in Brooklyn also struck; the era of the "long, hot summer" had begun. That year saw disturbances in several other cities in the Northeast, including Rochester, New York; Jersey City and Paterson in New Jersey; and Philadelphia. In the Chicago suburb of Dixmoor, armed blacks defiantly battled state troopers. Confusion began to claim the once resolute civil rights movement. While the NAACP, the National Urban League, and SCLC held fast to old values, other groups such as CORE and SNCC became militant. Robinson found himself somewhere in between. Finding himself in San Francisco when Harlem exploded, he at first lamented the "tragic coincidence" of black civil disturbances with the Goldwater nomination; soon, however, after telephone calls to friends in New York, he was pointing to the "Gestapo" tactics used by the police in repressing protest.

Early in the new year, 1965, violence claimed another black victim, Malcolm X himself, gunned down by Nation of Islam supporters on February 21 at the Audubon Ballroom in upper Manhattan. Malcolm's death shocked Robinson but elicited no eulogy from him. He was not among the more than thirty thousand persons who filed past the coffin, in which, swathed in white linen robes and with its head turned devotionally toward Mecca, Malcolm's body lay. But Robinson and Malcolm X were linked figures. It was left to the actor Ossie Davis, eulogizing Malcolm at his funeral, to invoke the crucial terms that would make those links visible. Malcolm was "a Black Shining Prince who did not hesitate to die because he loved us so," Davis declared; he "was our manhood, our living black manhood. . . . Harlem had no braver, more gallant champion than this Afro-American who lies before us now—unconquered still."

Jack had claimed not to understand Malcolm's appeal; but with Malcolm's death an era had passed, in which the definition of black manhood epitomized by Robinson in 1947 had given way to a new interpretation, one epitomized by Malcolm—or the idealized memory of Malcolm—even as Malcolm's model of black manhood itself rested on the precedent of Robinson. In 1947, black and handsome, athletically gifted but also cool and astute in his play, stoically enduring insult and injury, Robinson had revolutionized the image of the black man in America. He had supplanted the immensely popular image projected during World War II by Joe Louis, that of the physically powerful but uneducated, perhaps even weak-witted, black man uplifted by humility and patriotism—a modern, African-American version of the noble savage. But history was not static. The revolution Robinson had helped to set in motion now demanded a new image. Gone was the ideal of patient suffering; gone, too, was the underlying ideal of an integrated America in which justice would prevail for all. The new black man cared little for stoicism, and less for integration. Instead, power was the great goal; and justice seemed to demand an element of retribution, or revenge.

On one thing Robinson and Malcolm agreed: they, too, would be superseded. Two years after Malcolm's death, Robinson would invoke his memory in looking into the future. "Jackie," Robinson quoted Malcolm as saying, "in days to come, your son and my son will not be willing to settle for things we are willing to settle for."

AS A WOULD-BE ENTREPRENEUR, Jack liked to quote the words of Malcolm X, of all people, to the effect that he was interested in integrating lunch counters only because he wanted to own the cup he drank from, and the counter on which his coffee rested, and the building in which the business was housed. In business, Robinson, too, was seeking not a simple "job integration," as he put it, but an entrance into commerce "from the standpoint of becoming a producer, a manufacturer, a developer and creator of business, a provider of jobs." "For too long," he insisted, "the Negro has been only the consumer."

In 1964, Jack's most ambitious project was the development of a bank located in Harlem, and owned mainly by blacks, to serve the community there. This project was first the dream of Dunbar McLaurin, a Harlem businessman with a good knowledge of finance, who knew that the name Jackie Robinson would open many doors otherwise closed to him. Slowly Jack came around to accepting the challenge. The need for such a bank was real. In 1963, black Americans had a commanding stake in only thirteen banks and thirty-four federally insured savings and loan associations nationally. The assets of the average black bank came to just under $6 million; the national average was over $25 million. In Harlem, Carver Federal Savings and Loan Association was flourishing, but full-service banking was provided only by branches of banks with centers outside the community. Historically, banking and Jim Crow went hand in hand. "When it came to mortgages to buy homes," Jack would write, or "business loans to enable blacks to become entrepreneurs, blacks were discriminated against. Yet they faithfully and religiously deposited their savings in white banks."

In 1963, Robinson and McLaurin, working closely with one of the black community's most honored lawyers, Samuel Pierce, a Cornell University graduate and former judge and now an associate in the midtown law firm of Battle, Fowler, Stokes and Kheel, began to move in earnest. Putting together an organizing committee, they included three whites: Frank Schiffman of the Apollo Theater; Jack Blumstein of Blumstein's department store, another fixture on 125th Street; and Irving B. Altman, a retired banker slated to be the chief administrative officer. The committee also included Herbert Evans of the Housing and Redevelopment Board of the City of New York, who would supply expertise about housing and mortgages, and Alvin C. Hudgins, whose father, William Hudgins, was chairman of the board of Carver Federal Savings and Loan and a close friend of Jack's. Later, three other members would be added: William Hudgins himself; Lloyd Dickens, a New York State assemblyman; and Rose Morgan, whose nationally organized Rose-Meta System of

Beauty had made her perhaps the best-known woman entrepreneur in Harlem.

With Robinson and McLaurin as co-chairs of the committee, the project moved ahead smoothly in 1963. A site was found: offices on 125th Street about to be vacated by another bank, which was relocating. In September, James Saxon, the Comptroller of the Currency, the federal authority who regulated most banks in the nation, gave approval to Jack's group to proceed with their plans. Robinson was now designated chairman of the board. In that capacity, he oversaw the offering of sixty thousand shares of common stock for sale at twenty-five dollars a share. By agreement, this offering was aimed at the larger Harlem community; to encourage democracy, each individual could buy a total of only one thousand shares and the committee itself would own only twenty percent of the offering. Robinson's offering letter appealed frankly to Harlem's pride; the new bank would be "a community enterprise which will in every way belong to the people it is to serve."

To Jack's surprise and disappointment, selling stock proved a tough task in Harlem, where money was scarce and many people were wary of ambitious ventures. Worse, a clash of personalities soon threatened to abort the project. Dunbar McLaurin, who was expected to serve as president, had begun to act in ways that Robinson found dictatorial and self-serving. Proclaiming his "proprietorial" interest in the enterprise and scorning questions about his expenses, McLaurin demanded the loyalty of any organizer who hoped to serve as a director. When Jack offered to withdraw from the project, "I had hardly got my words out of my mouth," he later wrote, "when McLaurin produced resignation papers for me, already drawn up, indicating my withdrawal from the organizing committee and the proposed board of the bank." But other organizers prevailed on Robinson not to resign. The matter was then referred to Saxon, the Comptroller of the Currency. In December, after a meeting in Washington, Saxon ruled against McLaurin on every major point; in fact, the project could not proceed with him as president.

Having briefly appeared to accept this ruling, McLaurin then challenged it. Withholding important documents in his possession, he also exploited the primal fears of black Harlem concerning white power and black subservience. According to an affidavit filed by Samuel Pierce in federal court, McLaurin "issued press releases to Negro newspapers stating that white people had taken over the Bank. He made statements in the Harlem community to the effect that the three white members of the Organizing Committee had been allowed to take control of the Bank, which was untrue." The three whites on the committee, Pierce asserted, were not dominating the proceedings. "The only real struggle was the one Mr. McLaurin created between himself and the other Organizers."

Despite these setbacks, and benefiting from two ninety-day extensions from the Comptroller, the sale of stock went on. About six hundred investors had bought shares, but about one-third of the offering remained unsold when seven members of the committee, including Robinson, stepped in to purchase the remaining shares at a cost of about $500,000. At least on paper, the bank project had reached its goal of capitalization at $1.5 million. On March 10, 1964, the Comptroller declared Freedom National Bank of New York a corporate entity. But the internal struggle was not over. Two days later, leading a dozen disruptive supporters into a meeting attended by three of the organizers (Jack was not present), McLaurin proceeded to "appoint" his supporters to the board, which then "elected" him president. While confusion reigned, someone changed the locks on the main office door.

The next day, the original committee met and expelled McLaurin. But he was not done fighting. Now, the committee had to weather a lawsuit filed against it in the United States District Court for Southern New York aimed at restraining its activities. However, on April 15, stockholders met and elected ten directors of Freedom National Bank. Bill Hudgins was now president of the bank; Robinson was confirmed as chairman of the board.

Confidently, Jack announced that the new bank would open "on schedule, probably June 1." In fact, it would not open for business until noon on December 18. As the operation settled in, a stream of curious visitors, including many of its now twelve hundred stockholders and its hundred-member advisory board, quickly deposited about $400,000. Three weeks later, on January 4, 1965, Freedom National Bank was officially dedicated when Alex Quaison-

Sackey, the first African president of the United Nations General Assembly, cut a gold ribbon across the doorway of its offices at 275 West 125th Street. Among a flood of telegrams of congratulations was one from Vice-President-elect Hubert H. Humphrey to "my good friend, Jackie Robinson." Humphrey hailed the bank as "a symbol of the advances" of black Americans.

For an elated Robinson, this bank was merely a start. "In my humble opinion," he declared, "Freedom National is not just another local bank. It is symbolic of the determination of the Negro to become an integral part of the mainstream of our American economy." If Freedom National succeeded, other banks would rise elsewhere—"banks which are color blind and banks which have as resources, not only their reserve funds, but also the support of the masses of the Negro people." And with Bill Hudgins working tirelessly to promote it, the bank flourished. Aided by cash deposits from a variety of individuals and organizations—from Martin Luther King Jr., who deposited his Nobel Prize check there, to labor unions, state and city bodies, and the Ford Foundation—its assets jumped to $2 million by mid-March, $5 million by May, and almost $10 million on its first anniversary in 1966. Five years after opening, it was the top black bank in the nation even as Robinson appealed publicly "for more cash to aid the growing need for rehabilitation of the black community."

As chairman of the board, Jack was no figurehead. "I have been getting myself a real business education," he wrote privately just as the bank opened. "The years I had with 'Chock' seem to have stood me in good stead. I am pretty much able to hold my own in our meetings. I still need some help on parliamentary procedure but I'll overcome that." He now pressed forward with more confidence into other business ventures. One of these was housing. After almost a decade as a front man here, Robinson had little to show for his pains; but he had renewed his efforts. In 1963, he finally had a measure of success, in a joint venture with his friend Floyd Patterson. In May, at a press conference at Mama Leone's restaurant in Manhattan, the men announced the founding of a company to build low-income housing in integrated communities. Already their company held title to about 130 acres of land upstate, near the town of Wurtsboro in Sullivan County; with about $250,000 already invested, the first group of homes was now being built. "We believe," Jack declared, "that the building of homes in integrated communities can be profitable for the community, for the buyer, for our country and for one another. We intend to prove this."

Robinson was right about the need for such housing. In October, when the first five model homes were opened to the public, visitors overran the site. But for reasons that are unclear, this project soon lost its luster; the Robinson-Patterson venture into housing quietly folded. Jack began to look overseas, and especially in the Caribbean, for sites. Over the following years, on visits to Puerto Rico and Jamaica, he would hold talks with local officials about building low-income housing there. Puerto Rico quickly proved impossible to crack; in 1963, Governor Luis Muñoz Marín respectfully turned down as far too expensive Jack's proposals to build some units there. In Jamaica, where he had the ear of Hugh Shearer, who later became prime minister, Robinson and his partners made some progress; but this project, too, went nowhere.

Another major venture, but one that ended more painfully for Jack, was into the field of life insurance. Around 1963, about fifty black-owned insurance companies existed nationally; for the most part, however, blacks were served by white insurance companies that had little interest in the long-term goals of the community. As with Freedom National Bank, Robinson hoped both to make money and to provide blacks with an economic lift. In 1964, along with Arthur Logan and Sam Pierce (who that year became the first black director of the powerful Prudential Life Insurance Company of Boston), he set about securing a charter for a life insurance company. On November 17, 1964, the state insurance department approved a charter for the Gibraltar Life Insurance Company.

The following June, Jack and his partners, who now included whites, filed a stock-offering plan for Gibraltar, as required, with the Securities and Exchange Commission in Washington, D.C. The offering was of six hundred thousand shares at five dollars a share; following the sale, the company would open for business on July 1. But, as with the bank, selling stock proved to be a problem. In December, after a renewed effort, the *Amsterdam*

News reported that Robinson was "readying the sale of stock for his new insurance company next month." But this second attempt also flopped.

Then, in June 1966, a squib in the same newspaper announced that Robinson had "an offer to merge his life insurance company with an already existing white company." Earlier, at least four white companies had offered a merger. The winning company was a sensation: Hamilton Life Insurance Company, barely seven years old but with reported sales of about half a billion dollars. Behind Hamilton was the dynamic figure of young Philip J. Goldberg, who now presented Jack with a rare opportunity. In the proposed merger, Goldberg would name Robinson co-chairman of Hamilton, allow him to appoint three new directors, and give him enviable stock options. "I am deeply impressed," Jack told his readers, "by the talent, dedication and sincerity of Philip Goldberg." At a press conference, the two men pledged to join forces not only to build the company into a billion-dollar firm but also to "pay just as much attention to the Negro market as we are to the white market."

Jack then took a step he was to regret. He sank $25,000 of his own money, which he could ill afford, into the purchase of stock in Hamilton Life; at some point he and Rachel's brother Chuck Williams acquired 14,000 shares. Jack would see little of this money again. Within a year, the news broke that Hamilton Life was in deep financial trouble, $800,000 in debt. On February 2, 1968, the Securities and Exchange Commission suspended over-the-counter trading in Hamilton stock. The next month, the state superintendent of insurance barred it from writing new policies. Jack's son David would recall the bitterness he felt as a youth at the loss of his parents' money, which he blamed on one man at Hamilton Life. "I could never understand how this man could have taken our money. We knew where he lived, on the East Side, we knew the building and I would go by it, and it was all I could do not to kick the door in and demand it back."

On February 2, 1965, not long after Lyndon Johnson's inauguration, Jack and Rachel attended a dinner at the White House for Vice-President Humphrey, House Speaker John McCormack, and Chief Justice Earl Warren. For Rachel, the highlight of the evening was probably a whirl around the floor with Johnson, who danced only three times before withdrawing for the evening. Although Jack still had misgivings about Johnson, he also believed that now, unlike in 1961, he had a genuine friend in the White House in Humphrey. A few days later, Humphrey assured Jack that the President had asked him to make certain that the Civil Rights Act of 1964, which forbade discrimination in employment and public accommodations, and gave the Justice Department means to enforce the law, was "fully implemented."

Soon, events at the Edmund Pettus Bridge in Selma, Alabama, vividly caught on television, tested Johnson's nerve. In Selma, on March 7, a force of state troopers and deputies, using tear gas, whips, and clubs, crushed a march led by Dr. King and John Lewis of SNCC in protest against the killing of a civil rights worker and the jailing of hundreds of demonstrators taking part in a voter-registration drive. Dispatching a furious telegram to the President demanding "immediate action" in Selma, Robinson warned that "one more day of savage treatment by legalized hatchet men could lead to open warfare by aroused Negroes. America cannot afford this in 1965." But by the time the White House acknowledged receipt of this message, Johnson had taken a historic step. Summoning a joint session of Congress, he proposed a civil rights bill that would end all impediments to voter registration based on race. The United States, he insisted, "must overcome the crippling legacy of bigotry and injustice." He then closed his speech by invoking the most sacred slogan of the civil rights movement, "We shall overcome."

Especially after the Voting Rights Act of 1965 was passed, Robinson came to see Johnson as a true ally of the civil rights movement; but he and the President never became friends. Clifford Alexander, a black White House aide and later secretary of the army, put Robinson's 1964 dalliance with the Democrats in perspective in 1965: "While it is true that Jackie Robinson supported the President with his right hand, he was doing everything with his left hand to defeat a variety of Democratic senatorial and congressional candidates across the country." To the Democrats, as indeed to many Republican loyalists, Robinson was a loose cannon, a force the party could not count on, and perhaps even a showboat. Following another stern missive to Johnson from Robinson about race relations, Alexander dismissed it by suggesting that it was probably "one of his grandstand political plays." Humphrey was more careful with his celebrated black ally. After receiving yet another tart note from Jack, Humphrey replied soothingly. "A true friend is one who speaks the truth," he wrote patiently, "and I always look upon Jackie Robinson as a true friend."

Elsewhere, it was clear in 1965 that, probably because of his key role in Freedom National Bank, some people now looked on Robinson with new respect as a spokesman on topics such as poverty, urban development, and youth problems. He was the keynote speaker at a conference on young people called by the office of the governor of Illinois; he spoke in Tucson, Arizona, to the National Conference on Poverty in the Southwest; in Philadelphia, he was the cheerleader at a gathering of an organization established by a visionary local black minister, Leon Sullivan, who would later be influential in shaping American business practices in South Africa. Sullivan's hope was to teach various skills to inner-city blacks as a way of lifting the quality of their lives. To Sullivan's group, Robinson was the epitome of success: a black man who had conquered the worlds of baseball and business.

In March, Jack crowned what seemed to be his new prosperity after Chock Full o' Nuts by returning to baseball, albeit only as a television commentator. At a news conference at Toots Shor's restaurant, a noted sports hangout, Roone Arledge of ABC-TV Sports announced that he had hired Jack for twenty-seven weekly baseball games for the network's East schedule (Leo Durocher would handle the West), starting April 17. Just after playing in the annual black North-South golf tournament in Miami, Jack traveled to Clearwater, Florida, to begin practicing for his on-air stints. Robinson, hurt at being shut out of organized baseball, had claimed to have lost interest in the game. But his love had returned. "Jack didn't go to the ballpark," Rachel said, "but he watched baseball on television and absolutely loved it. He would get up and talk to the hitters and the fielders and the pitchers and he argued with the managers and he hooted and yelled and had a good old time usually." In fact, the previous fall, watching a thrilling Los Angeles Dodgers game, Robinson's heart had beat so quickly that he had to turn the set off for relief. He was grateful for his chance with ABC. "If it hadn't been for sports, I doubt I would have accomplished much in life," he told a reporter. "Maybe God would have given me some other ability, I don't know. I do know what athletics have meant to me. It's nice to be able to repay debts, and I have paid mine, but it's good to be back in sports."

Almost certainly, Jack also needed the money from ABC, which amounted to $13,500, or $500 per game.

His renewed interest in baseball had resulted in two books. One was *Breakthrough to the Big Leagues,* aimed at a younger audience. The more provocative volume had come the previous year, 1964: *Baseball Has Done It,* which the New York *Times* called "one of the year's most significant and interesting collections of autobiographical sketches."

This book emphasized the effects of desegregation on baseball, with chapters by a variety of players, black and white, including Jim Gilliam, Billy Bruton, Bobby Bragan, and Alvin Dark. Jack was moved by the testimony of a once hostile white player like Bragan, who had opposed him in 1947 but now was a champion of integration in the game. He also expressed "my delight at the uncompromising stand" taken by Roy Campanella; once wary of protest, Campy was now ready, in Jack's words, to "hit hard at the immoral and unjust practices" of Jim Crow.

By this time, too, Jack had tried to make peace with Walter O'Malley. In 1962, in the evening before the Hall of Fame ceremony in Cooperstown, he was having dinner at the Otesaga Hotel with his family when Kay O'Malley, Walter's wife, came in with their son, Peter. Jack had gone over at once to talk to her. Although they had chatted about various matters, Jack wrote O'Malley a few days later, "I really wanted to talk with her about you and I." The idea that "I was entering the Hall of Fame and I did not have any real ties with the game" had made him sad. Who was to blame for the souring of their relationship? "Being stubborn, and believing that it all stemmed from my relationship with Mr. Rickey, I made no attempt to find the cause." Now Jack wanted to talk things out with O'Malley. "Of course, there is the possibility that we are at an impasse, and nothing can be done. I feel, however, I must make this attempt to let you know I sincerely regret we have not tried to find the cause for this breach." A few days later, in Los Angeles, Robinson called O'Malley's office to see if they could meet.

It proved impossible. In his memoir, *Off the Record,* Buzzie Bavasi would write that O'Malley had taken Jack's departure in 1956 "as a personal affront" and "an embarrassment" to the Dodgers: "You don't do things like that to O'Malley. I don't think he and Jackie ever spoke to each other again." But some years later Peter O'Malley would say: "I think my dad, like all of us, had extraordinary respect for Jackie, what he had accomplished as a man and what he accomplished for our team, and how he had helped our team win. In all our conversations at home about Jackie and Rachel, I never sensed anything other than that respect and admiration." In any event, Robinson had no regrets about his attempt to heal the wound opened with his refusal to be traded to the Giants.

As JACK PRESSED AHEAD in business, he was proud of the fact that Rachel, too, was advancing. In 1965, she became director of nursing at the state mental health center in New Haven as well as an assistant professor at the Yale University School of Nursing there. Associated with colleagues renowned in the field of psychiatry and psychology, she found much satisfaction in her work. She also knew that her chances of further advancement were limited because of her family commitments, especially her obligations to Jack. "It was something I accepted," she said. "He and I reached an agreement and I stuck by it. Jack needed me at home and I had to be there. The children needed me, too."

Jackie certainly needed her. He was now barely speaking to his father. "Jack felt completely baffled and helpless in the face of Jackie's growing aloofness," Rachel later wrote. "He had worked earnestly at being a good man and father, a man his son could be proud of, and he was tormented by Jackie's plight." Then, one day in March 1964, she ran into Jackie on a street in downtown Stamford. "With an air of confidence that I hadn't seen in him for a long time," she wrote, "he told me he was headed for the army recruitment office and said he had a lot of learning to do and needed discipline as well." About four months past his seventeenth birthday, he was going to enlist. "In a panic, I tried to talk him out of it," Rachel recalled, "but then I went with him to the recruiting office. The men there were very good at talking about the chances for education in the Army, how he would be able to learn and so on. We believed them."

On March 30, 1964, Jackie enlisted in the Army. For basic training, he was sent to Fort Riley, Kansas—where his father had trained under Jim Crow during World War II. Jackie's departure saddened Jack; but he, too, believed that the Army could teach his son a great deal. At Christmas, when Jackie returned home on leave, he seemed a much more mature young man. "Jackie has grown a great deal," his father informed friends. "He seems to be developing into a real man and I am certain his Army stint will be a blessing. He is a real handsome boy." Still, Robinson could not help noticing, disapprovingly, that "his entire vacation has been used at parties. He still needs to develop but we are proud of the achievements he has made."

When Jackie returned to the Army, life at home was quieter, less stressful. On the brink of fifteen that Christmas, Sharon was still a delight to her father. "Sharon is everyone's girl," he wrote his friends, "wherever she goes she makes a real impression. She is a beautiful girl, looking and acting more like Rachel every day." Doing well in high school, careful in her friendships, and steering clear of trouble, she seemed as solid and promising as Jackie Junior was shaky and a question mark. What was true of Sharon also seemed to apply to David, who at thirteen was an excellent student-athlete at the elite New Canaan Country Day School, able to handle with apparent ease many of the privileges and challenges that had upset his brother. "David keeps amazing us," Jack wrote. "He learned football fast and seems to be potentially good. He learns quick and is one of the hardest workers I have seen. It's something how he has adjusted to his school and in spite of being over his head in some areas holds his own with the best."

Then, late in June 1965, Jackie Junior was suddenly out of the country. He had been shipped to the jungles of Southeast Asia in the first massive escalation of the war in Vietnam. The swiftness of the move stunned his parents. At that time, as with most Americans, neither one opposed the American presence in Vietnam for purely political reasons; for some time, indeed, Jack would defend the war, when pressed, on anticommunist grounds. But their prime concern was their son's life. The thought of Jackie, a grown man in some ways, still a boy in others, thrust suddenly into deadly combat thousands of miles from home was heart-wrenching to them both. In response to the American escalation, the Viet Cong and the North Vietnamese had shown themselves to be a formidable enemy. From Hubert Humphrey and his wife, Muriel, as from other friends, came letters of sympathy; the Humphreys were "praying for the safety of your son in Vietnam."

IN JULY, JUST AFTER Jackie arrived in Vietnam, Jack and Rachel vacationed in Jamaica. Robinson returned home to pleasant duties—his television work for ABC-TV Sports, but also to flattering appearances such as one at Antioch Baptist Church on July 22, when he was honored at a "Night of Champions" service; or, drawing toward the end of his three-year appointment as head of United Church Men of the National Council of Churches in Christ, as a major speaker at a gathering in New York City of Catholic, Protestant, and Jewish leaders. But such events did little to still Jack's growing sense of disquiet about the way his life was going, and about the country as a whole. Increasingly, the civil rights struggle and explosions in the cities of the North offered younger blacks and whites an ominous counterpoint to the bugle call of patriotism. In August, the Los Angeles suburb of Watts, well known to Jack and Rachel, was shattered by one of the most violent riots in the history of the United States. Thirty-four persons died, more than a thousand were injured, some four thousand arrested, and almost a thousand businesses either destroyed or severely damaged. Lesser explosions followed in several other cities, including Chicago and Philadelphia.

Speaking for the NAACP, Roy Wilkins expressed his dismay at the futility and self-abuse of this urban rioting. The "most tragic picture" on television, he declared, was that of several Negro children trying to pry open "a cash register that had already been looted"; the "most frightening" riot cry was that "this is the Negro Revolution!" Riots, Wilkins insisted, "benefit no people, help no cause." Jack shared Wilkins's sentiments but he also felt a more restless desire to empathize with the poor and the young. In October, returning to Los Angeles, he went to Watts to view the still-graphic remains of the riot. The sight of gutted businesses and the stories of inhumanity cast a pall over the main reason for his visit: to be honored at homecoming ceremonies at Pasadena City College, formerly Pasadena Junior College, where several of the records he had set between 1937 and 1939 were still standing, including his national junior-college long-jump record of 25 feet 6½ inches. Sitting in an open car beside the homecoming queen, Jack rode around Horrell Field to the applause of spectators, then later delivered the keynote address at a banquet in the main student dining hall.

In November, nominated by UCLA, he received an honor that even more directly acknowledged the success he had made of his life since then. At the tenth annual Silver Anniversary All-America Awards presented by *Sports Illustrated,* Robinson was one of twenty-five former college football stars saluted twenty-five years after their senior season for their effective blending of athletics and education. At a nostalgic gathering of the former stars, nobody could wonder for long which one among them had put his college career to the most enduring use. And yet these honors hardly soothed Jack's growing anxieties about his present life: his declining health, the fragility of his business ventures, his fears about Jackie and about young blacks in general, the deepening national crisis in civil rights and race relations, and his own lack of a sharply defined role in helping to solve these problems.

November and December brought further disquieting news. In Vietnam, on November 19, 1965, the day after his nineteenth birthday, Jackie Junior and his platoon of soldiers were caught in a terrifying ambush. Jackie came close to death; two buddies, one on either side of him, were cut down; he was wounded in the left shoulder. Heroically, he had dragged one of the men from the field of fire, but when the fight was over both his friends were dead. Devastated, Jackie spent about one week in the hospital, then returned, by his own choice, to active duty. The Army awarded him the Purple Heart.

Jack and Rachel had hardly absorbed this news when the next month, on December 9, at the age of eighty-four, Branch Rickey died. Almost a month before, Rickey had collapsed in Columbia, Missouri, where he had gone to be inducted into the state Hall of Fame. Jack took the news of his mentor's death hard. "He filled a void for me and I for him," he explained quietly to newsmen. "Here was a man who had lost a son, and myself who had never had a father." (Rickey's eldest son, Branch, a diabetic like Jack, had died in 1960.) For Robinson, absorbing Rickey's death was a trial to compare to his 1947 ordeal: "I tried to prepare myself emotionally the same way I had for that first year." His deep feeling for Rickey, Jack made clear, was only in part owing to the fact that Rickey had chosen him to be the first black player. Far more, he loved Rickey because Rickey had been loyal to him. He had been loyal during their four tumultuous years in the Dodger organization, but, more important to Jack, loyal when the cheering had died down, and especially after Jack retired from the game. To Robinson, the "wonderful communication we had with each other" after baseball made him feel now "almost as if I had lost my own father." Rickey had treated him "like a son."

The world had changed since 1947; what was revolutionary then was taken for granted now. When Jack looked around at the funeral in St. Louis, he saw only two other black players. The lack of respect hurt Jack. To the veteran black journalist A. S. "Doc" Young, writing about Rickey, "The bigots who hated his guts because he integrated a sport and the chief beneficiaries of that integration movement were all together in absence." The absent black players were "too busy to attend the funeral," Young surmised. "Too busy as in . . . playing golf, selling booze, or counting money."

JACK'S HEALTH CONTINUED to decline. After a battery of tests early in January 1966 at the French Hospital in New York, where his physician, Dr. Cyril Solomon, had privileges, he was warned to slow down.

Instead, Robinson stepped up his activities a few days later by heading into the South. "I owe a great deal to a lot of people," he explained. On January 14, he spoke in Greensboro, North Carolina, at North Carolina A&T College, where he honored the crucial civil rights role played by the four students who had started the first sit-in there in 1960. Presenting the school with a plaque on behalf of Freedom National Bank, he urged his audience to recommit itself to that earlier spirit. "Our big lesson," he declared, "is that no intelligent, self-respecting Negro can afford to remain aloof from the struggle. . . . There is a wealth of personal satisfaction in being able to say that you played a role, took a part—participated in the drive to help free yourself and your fellow man." In Selma, Alabama, at a YMCA dinner, he also pressed his audience to cast their ballots wisely: "Vote for the man who will do the most for the greatest number of people."

Ironically, with each passing year the South seemed a more encouraging region than parts of the North, as the reputedly immovable walls of Dixie segregation came down almost smoothly in many places. "A miracle is unfolding in the Deep South," Jack wrote. "The very people who were fighting the hardest to keep the Negroes from exercising the right to vote are wooing the Negro for his vote." In the North, blacks seemed to care less about the vote; they also seemed, in the absence of the brutal physical threats that had often flared in the South, self-destructive. In Westchester County, New York, a black CORE leader, enraged by his white opponents in a civic dispute, hotly declared that the problem was not that Hitler had killed many Jews but that he had not killed enough of them. The remark shocked Robinson, as well as Dr. King and other leaders, black and white. "There are black bigots as well as white bigots," Jack observed in his column. He was further dismayed when James Farmer, the director of CORE and "a decent man," seemed to equate the remark, which Farmer condemned, with the opposition that had inspired it. "There can be no such honest equation," Robinson insisted. "For, to pose it is to excuse or alibi the depths of bigotry from which the statement arose." Robinson was blunt: "The man did not attack the Jews, he attacked God, he attacked you and me."

Jack's return early in 1966 to the *Amsterdam News* after an unexplained one-year hiatus allowed him to resume his open strife with other leading figures. To many people, his eagerness to fight was a source of some wonder; one New Year's wish of his fellow columnist James Booker was for Robinson to get "a machine to end all feuds." But unpopularity mattered little to Robinson. "I'm not in a popularity contest," he said flatly. "That is not my purpose in life. I simply stand up for what I think is right." In fact, early in 1966 Robinson was gearing up to plunge further into the fray. In a year in which Nelson Rockefeller, who still harbored dreams of being President, was up for reelection as governor of New York, Jack decided to throw in his lot decisively with the governor.

By this time, Rockefeller's confidence in Robinson, and his affection for him, were firmly established. Occasionally, over matters such as the state minimum wage and the number of black appointees in the government, Jack had criticized the governor. But far more often, he sang Rockefeller's praises as a visionary leader committed to securing justice for all. They had grown closer after October 17, 1965, when Jack had flown in Rockefeller's private plane to lend support during a crucial venture: a quasi-state visit by Rockefeller and his wife, Happy, to the Kings in Atlanta, to preach a sermon in "Daddy" King's Ebenezer Baptist Church and dine at the home of Dr. King. This visit clearly sought to recapitulate but also trump John Kennedy's celebrated phone call to Coretta Scott King in the fall of 1960; it acknowledged the importance not only of the black vote but also of Dr. King's influence on it. Black voting power was proven again that fall in New York City when Republican Congressman John V. Lindsay, running on a fusion ticket but with strong black support in Harlem and Brooklyn, trounced his Democratic opponent to win the mayoralty. Appearing with him on a stroll down Fifth Avenue near Forty-second Street as Lindsay shook hands with voters, Robinson had helped him to win an upset victory.

The election had brought Jack one wickedly articulate foe: William F. Buckley Jr., the sharp-tongued editor of the conservative *National Review,* who also ran for mayor that year. In April, Buckley angered Robinson and other blacks when, in a speech at a policemen's breakfast, he appeared to criticize the actions of some black demonstrators in Selma. A nastier episode came near Election Day. On an interview show on WINS radio, Robinson had laid out the allegedly dire consequences for blacks if Buckley became mayor; it would be a disaster for which blacks should prepare. Pouncing, Buckley then denounced these remarks as "a direct call to violent illegal action [by blacks] to subvert the democratic process." Informed of Buckley's charge, Robinson completely lost his poise. "He's a liar and a bigot and that's just what he is," he stormed to a reporter. "What we're advocating is preparedness."

EARLY IN 1966, Robinson in his column endorsed Rockefeller for reelection: "I think he will fight very hard to win—and I hope he will win BIG." A message had to be sent to the National Republican Committee, to Goldwater, and to Buckley. To Jack, Rockefeller was not above criticism. After several barbs in the black press about the absence of Negroes in the state government, Robinson sent the governor a stern letter, "one of the most difficult letters I have ever had to write." He was bold: "While I believe there is not a more dedicated politician on the scene, your record toward the Negro regarding political appointments cannot be accepted by any self-respecting Negro." Without a change, Robinson would speak out publicly, and soon. "I hope you understand my position," he told Rockefeller. "I do not put personal feelings above the feeling I have for the masses of our people."

On February 8, at a press conference in Albany, Rockefeller personally announced Robinson's appointment to the position of special assistant to the governor for community affairs. His home base would be New York City, Jack told reporters, "but we will get around to every nook and cranny in the State. We want to talk to people. We want to try to unite as many people as we possibly can. . . . I am tickled to death that we've got the guidance of Governor Rockefeller, because I know we're going to get the right kind of leadership here." This appointment was private; Robinson was paid from the governor's personal funds. Jack's salary was probably around $25,000 a year, or roughly half of what Chock Full o' Nuts had paid him.

Not long afterward, Rockefeller also hired Evelyn Cunningham, the veteran Pittsburgh *Courier* journalist, to be Jack's assistant. Soon, other blacks augmented what Robinson called his "team," including his ghostwriter, Al Duckett; the Reverend Wyatt Tee Walker, now special assistant to the governor for urban affairs; and Grant Reynolds, an attorney and prominent Republican. Robinson saw himself in charge of this group. "I have rolled up my sleeves and gone to work," he explained, in part to further the two-party system for blacks, in part because "I want to see liberal, progressive Lindsay and Rockefeller Republicanism triumph."

"I was brought in," Cunningham revealed later, "to help Jackie Robinson stay on track with the governor's program. Some of the governor's people obviously thought he fired too often from the hip, and Jackie himself was worried about this. I remember him calling me early one morning, upset at a story of the front page of the *Times* saying that he had criticized the governor. 'That's not what I said!' he kept telling me. 'Should I call the *Times?*' I said, 'No, why don't you call the governor?' The governor told him, 'Try to calm down, Jackie, because I'm really not upset. If I'm not able to take care of little things like this, I shouldn't be governor. This is nothing for me to worry about and certainly nothing for you to worry about.' But Jackie remained upset for quite a while. He didn't intend to be quiet but he did not want to harm the governor."

For Cunningham, who had also been one of the organizers of Rockefeller's introduction to Harlem at the Dawn Casino in 1961, Robinson and Rockefeller "went through a big love affair with one another. They had such respect and admiration for one another, it was really like love. Rockefeller was convinced that Jackie really cared about him despite the fact that he was a rich, powerful man. He wanted to be loved by everybody, but he was never certain and he would never be certain that it wasn't for his money and power. But he believed Jack. And in the meantime, he loved Jackie over and beyond his being a baseball hero. He was always puzzled and pleased that Jackie supported him and was his friend."

Percy Sutton, the influential Democratic leader in Harlem, saw both the value of Jack's relationship to Rockefeller and its sterling character. "Jackie got things done," Sutton said, "and he helped us across party lines. When Medgar Evers's brother Charles was elected mayor in Mississippi and we wanted a plane to fly down to see him sworn in, to see history, Jackie arranged it. And you only had to watch Rockefeller and Robinson together to know the genuine affection and respect they had for one another. It was real. Rockefeller, once he embraced you, was real. He gave you access and opportunity and contacts, and he didn't abandon you. And he embraced Jackie."

Operating in quarters adjacent to the governor's New York offices at 22 West Fifty-fifth Street, Jack threw himself into his job. "Jackie was usually the first one in the office every day," according to Cunningham. "He was a zealous worker. If there was nothing to do, he'd try to create something." To her, Robinson was not always confident about his intelligence, but "Rockefeller had no dummies around him, not one mediocre person. Jackie maybe was out of his element in electoral politics, but he was not out of his depth." Soon, as part of his job, Jack was testifying before the State Investigation Commission on middle-income housing; descending on the offices of the Queens district attorney to discuss citizens' complaints; standing in for the governor and reading a speech to the Ohio Republican Council in Cleveland, Ohio. He could stand in easily for the governor because he was the greater celebrity; when the two men strolled in Manhattan, someone pointed out, taxi drivers usually yelled out greetings to Robinson and ignored Rockefeller.

Driving Jack and his team was the knowledge that in the major New York cities Democrats outnumbered Republicans by almost a million voters. Thus, the black vote was crucial to the governor's chances. On April 7, when Jack attended a key planning meeting, it was emphasized that in contrast to 1962, the 1966 campaign needed a much more intense effort. Rockefeller would have to "go into areas he has never been before," including "trouble areas" like the poor Bedford-Stuyvesant district of Brooklyn, with Robinson "as close to him as possible." For greater effect, Jack was urged to use his title "Special Assistant to the Governor" more and to deemphasize his role as a campaign official. Although "he was not to concern himself exclusively with minority affairs," he was a crucial figure in wooing the black vote. The importance of that vote was underscored in the governor's almost gaudy gesture later that month when, with Robinson taking a prominent role, he launched his third gubernatorial campaign at the offices of the New York *Amsterdam News* in Harlem.

But Jack was also effective with white voters, especially men. Cunningham remembered a trip with him to Staten Island. "We faced a very conservative group," she recalled, "and not very nice people either, definitely antiblack and not real fond of women either. But for Jackie, they turned out in droves; the halls were packed, and Jackie was the key. It was like, Okay, okay, enough, we'll vote for Rockefeller—now, Jackie, how about that play in that game? And so on. They adored him, and Jackie was very good, very outgoing, laughing a lot when they asked funny questions. At the end, sheepishly, he started signing autographs, and graciously too. We got the votes."

On some points, however, Jack would not yield. When talk arose that Rockefeller might use William E. Miller, Goldwater's running mate in 1964, in the fall election, Jack put his foot down. Unaccustomed to being crossed, the governor nevertheless accepted such resistance from Robinson. "I like a man," Jack wrote later, "who can look me in the eye and say to me—as Governor Rockefeller has done—'Jackie, I agree with you that you should always say what you feel you must say. Don't worry about upsetting me or upsetting anyone else. I believe in a man's right to be true to himself.' " In turn, Jack was loyal to the governor, unless he thought the welfare of blacks was at risk. When a reporter counted only about two dozen blacks among almost thirty-five hundred guests at a state Republican dinner in New York, Jack was defensive; the reporter was "nit-picking" and "looking for trouble." But Robinson kept alive his special interest in black Republicans; on May 21, in Detroit, he delivered the main address at the first national convention of the Negro Republican Assembly. The *Amsterdam*

News noted that inside the party, Robinson "is proving to be a real pro in the political infighting and is getting some key recognition for Negroes."

Fishing for black votes in strange, sometimes treacherous waters, Rockefeller often needed Robinson's help. But sometimes even Jack was not enough. That summer, as a perspiring, shirt-sleeved Rockefeller tried to open a campaign office in Harlem, about one hundred heckling black nationalists led by Roy Innis of CORE shouted rude questions about the Rockefeller family's holdings in South Africa and almost broke up the event. As Robinson, buttoned up in a dark suit and tie, watched helplessly, it was left to Eddie "Pork Chop" Davis, a Harlem street-corner orator, to seize the microphone from the beleaguered governor, shout down the hecklers, and restore order.

By this time, another long, hot summer was playing out across the nation. "One of the most terrible tragedies of our times," Jack wrote, "is being acted out in the streets of our big cities. It is both frustrating and frightening to see the hordes of Negro people, so many of them the restless young, exploding into the most sickening kind of violence." The tension in New York was made worse by a prolonged public dispute between forces favoring a strong civilian review board, which Jack supported, and backers of police independence, of whom William F. Buckley Jr. was perhaps the most provocative spokesman. As so often happened, Robinson quickly turned a political dispute into something personal, as in rebuking a popular liberal WMCA radio personality and longtime friend, Barry Gray, who had sided with the police. "I hope I am wrong, Barry," Jack chided Gray in his column. "I would not in good conscience call you a bigot. But you know the logical conclusion about the man who lies down with hogs. The hogs do not end up smelling like men." The idea of Gray and the reactionary Buckley uniting on this issue "would be ludicrous if it were not tragic."

Making the situation more volatile was the increasingly fierce rhetoric about Black Power. On May 26, 1965, in a commencement speech at Howard University, Adam Clayton Powell Jr. had introduced the term; in the audience was Stokely Carmichael of SNCC, who then used it to galvanizing effect in rallies later that year. To Robinson, the slogan encouraged demagogues and even crime by lending them an aura of political legitimacy. Meanwhile, he said, "the white power structure builds into giant visibility the slightest pip squeak who comes along with something incendiary or radical to say." Late in August, a new ingredient was added to the brew. With Carmichael in the chair and all whites banished, a large crowd of SNCC supporters warmly welcomed a spokesman for a new militant group, the Black Panthers, while six Panthers, dressed in black berets, black shirts, and black slacks, stood guard. SNCC, born out of the efforts of Dr. King's SCLC, had moved some distance away from its source. Later that year, Robinson issued his own definition of Black Power: "When we use our ballot and our dollars wisely, we are exercising black power without having to define it."

In November, Rockefeller swept to victory in New York by four hundred thousand votes. While his plurality was somewhat less than in 1962, his support among blacks had grown. For Jack and his team, this was a personal triumph, underscored when he and Rachel were among twenty-five guests who spent the evening awaiting the election results at the governor's Fifth Avenue apartment. Writing before the results were known, Jack called his effort in the campaign, in which he had served, he said, as "a day to day, sometimes almost around the clock worker," one of the "most rewarding experiences of my life." He was "proud to have made whatever contribution I made because, in my book, the Governor is tops."

Although Jack could not have known it, this would be the crowning moment of his career as a political operative. Other election victories also encouraged him. In Massachusetts, Edward Brooke, a Republican, became the first black elected to the United States Senate since Reconstruction. To Jack, this was "the most resounding reply which could have been given" to those who wanted or expected a white backlash. In Alabama, a black ex-paratrooper was elected sheriff of Macon County over two white opponents, to become the first black sheriff in the South since Reconstruction. In California, on the other hand, Ronald Reagan was elected. "In my book," Robinson wrote, "Ronald Reagan is as bad news for minority people as Governor Rockefeller is good news."

IN JUNE, JACK AND RACHEL were overjoyed when Jackie Junior finally returned from Vietnam. However, they soon saw that he was in bad shape. The racism of the white military and the horrors of warfare had left him a demoralized version of the sweet, confused young man who had gone into the Army more than two years before, looking for a place to grow up. He returned to a nation where many young people, and even many older people, black and white, had grown sick of the American effort. This disapproval of the military left Jackie, as it did countless other returning soldiers, baffled and hurt. In addition, if Jackie now seemed almost out from under his father's shadow, he had also lost the umbrella of protection Jack had provided all his life. But his father's fame was still a problem, as when Rockefeller, with the best of intentions, wrote to praise Jackie for a job well done in Vietnam, which had added "a lustre of your own to the famous name you bear."

Not long after his return, when Rachel and Jackie accompanied Jack on a visit to Montreal, Rachel saw that something was not right with him. "Jackie was behaving just a little strangely," Rachel recalled. "Almost by instinct he would drift away from me as we walked, and he seemed to want to walk as close to the buildings as possible, almost hugging them. He told me that this was Vietnam taking over; he was keeping close to cover. I began to get a better sense of what he had gone through and how it was affecting him." Soon Jackie was living in Colorado, where the Army had released him, as his parents puzzled over what he was doing there. While he was in Vietnam, a girlfriend of his from Connecticut, Penny Pankey, gave birth to their child, Sonya. She was Jack and Rachel's first grandchild. "I know I have a large responsibility to Penny and the Baby," Jackie had written his father; but he was also sure that marriage was out of the question, given his state of mind.

The gap between father and son grew wider. In his column, Jack wrote about the grave troubles that youths faced—and his own sense of powerlessness to help them: "As I look around today and observe how lost and frustrated and bitter our youngsters are, I find myself wishing that there was some way to reach out to them and let them know that we want to try to understand their problems; that we want to help. I confess I don't know the way."

In most other ways, he seemed to know what he was doing and where he was going. A reporter trailing him to Freedom National one morning described a man of energy and verve, although his eyes were failing. "His step was brisk, his calendar was crowded, he had no time for philosophic pause," the reporter noted. Entering the bank's conference room, which he used as an office, Jack flung his overcoat on a swivel chair and pointed toward a corner. "That telephone," he declared, "is going to be humming today." In three hours, Robinson made or took twenty-one calls, with many of them ending in new tasks for him. "As his obligations pyramid," the reporter noted, "he will complain that someday he'll have to learn to say no, but he will continue to say yes. He will swivel in his chair, swing his legs left, pluck hard at his cheek. Then, at a moment of intense exasperation, he will abruptly smile."

To Evelyn Cunningham, he was a man of some complexity. "Jackie was not too close to many people," she observed. "He was embarrassed by adulation. On the other hand, he wanted desperately to be liked. And he knew not everyone liked him. Some people would say, 'Oh, he's a cold turkey. I don't like Jackie Robinson. He's cold.' " They respected him but they didn't like him. "I was never sure he liked me," she said. "To this day, I don't know for sure. But I admired him. He had great respect for women. I don't think he was a real feminist but he respected women and he worshiped Rachel. He was also a little shy about us. I remember once he brought back a big box of clothes and started to show me what he had bought for her—gorgeous underwear, bras, panties. And then, all of a sudden he got embarrassed. He covered up the box and turned away. Another time, a black man, a stranger, came in with a sculpture he had carved to give to Jackie. It was a nude torso of a woman. Jackie took it, but once the man left he said, 'You want it?' I said yes. He seemed embarrassed, with me looking at the nude with my eyes, and he's standing there. I took it before he changed his mind. I still have it."

"There must have been something way back in his life," she decided, "that had frightened him about people. I was one of the people who absolutely worshiped him, but I knew that I could only show it to him by making a joke about it. He was a very good man, but in many ways he was a sort of mystery."

ONCE THE GUBERNATORIAL election of 1966 was over, Jack and Rachel headed for a much-needed vacation in the Bahamas, where Jack was quickly caught up in local election fever. The British-ruled, traditionally white-dominated Bahamas seemed about to elect its first black government, and Jack met the most prominent of the rising local politicians, Lynden O. Pindling, of the Progressive Liberal Party. Both as Jackie Robinson the race hero and as a special assistant to Governor Rockefeller, he was warmly received by the younger politicians. The rise of blacks to power in the Caribbean was linked to the growing freedom of blacks in the United States. In addition, the Bahamas could be fertile ground for an American with Robinson's background and connections.

Over the New Year holiday, Jack and Rachel were back in the Bahamas, just in time for the elections that swept Pindling and his party into power. Soon Jack was holding discussions with a senior official of the powerful Grand Bahama Port Authority about its interest in "a small personalized hotel project" to be run by Robinson or Sidney Poitier or "in partnership together." He was still in the Bahamas a few days later when fifty leaders of the black American press arrived as guests of the Ministry of Tourism. In addition to bracing rounds of golf (including at least one round with Joe DiMaggio, another celebrity visitor), Jack met Pindling and discussed with him ways in which Robinson might assist the Bahamas in pursuing its interests in the United States. The men agreed that Jack would pave the way for Pindling's first official visit to the United States.

Returning home, Jack officially registered under Section 2 of the Foreign Agents Registration Act of 1938 as an agent for the Bahamas in the United States. On February 26, when Pindling reached New York, Jack supervised his news conference and also saw to it that he met both Mayor Lindsay and Governor Rockefeller. However, this turned out to be just about all that Robinson did for Pindling, who eventually would be accused of corruption. "Jack discovered he had backed the wrong candidate," according to Rachel.

About this time, Jack had another disappointment as he came close to realizing one of his persisting dreams: organizing a golf and country club where his family and other black families, and their white friends, could feel at home. "I can hardly describe," Rachel said, "what golf meant to Jack and his buddies. Since he didn't drink or run around, it was really the one time when he could socialize fully with other men, and he loved golf with a passion."

"Jack absolutely loved golf," according to his friend Warren Jackson, who was part of a group of black men who organized an annual golf tournament—with Robinson as official host—that drew hundreds of players to courses across the United States and overseas. "He was a terrific competitor, pretty fierce once he got out there on the course. At the sponsored golf tournaments he was an excellent host. He used all the old Robinson charm—but he could become real testy if you approached him the wrong way once he started playing. His mind was on his game and he wanted to win, and that was that."

Despite his solid citizenship, the private High Ridge Country Club in Stamford, where he played often as a guest, refused him as a member. (According to one report, a member had complained to another that he was having Robinson as a guest too often. "Too often? I'll bring Ralph Bunche next week, maybe he's O.K." "Yeah," came the reply. "You bring Ralph Bunche and I'll bring my maid.") According to another report, the male members relented but their wives stopped them. The women did not want blacks, any blacks, as members. Jack was left to wake up as early as 4:30 a.m. some Saturdays to stake out a good starting time on the overcrowded municipal course.

As far back as 1963, Jack and Bill Hudgins had been hunting for a piece of suitable property; the *Amsterdam News* reported then that the two men "were looking over an upstate site for a golf course." Two years later, in 1965, they found their spot: the 136-acre Putnam Country Club in Mahopac, New York, some fifty miles from New York City. The club, predominantly Jewish in its membership, had fallen into financial trouble and was on sale for $1.4 million. A real estate broker arranged for a visit by Robinson, Hudgins, and a few of their friends to play the course. But when the group showed up on November 21, officials of the club at first denied that any appointment had been made, then reluctantly allowed Jack's party to tee off. However, before their round was over a miracle occurred: the club's finances were in much better shape than previously thought. The club was definitely not for sale. In January 1966, alleging racial discrimination, the NAACP filed charges on behalf of Robinson and his friends with the State Commission on Human Rights; but the club prevailed.

That summer, Robinson and Hudgins tried again, this time bidding for a 216-acre parcel of land in Lewisboro, New York, on the Connecticut border. Acting on behalf of several dozen prospective club members, Jack headed a small group that presented plans to the Lewisboro Zoning Board for the Pleasant Valley Golf and Country Club, complete with an eighteen-hole golf course. Membership would be limited to 250 persons, including local residents; the actress Colleen Dewhurst, who lived nearby, and her husband, the actor George C. Scott, would be members. After hearing a variety of complaints from local residents about the effect of the course on water supply, drainage, errant golf shots, traffic flow, and the like, the zoning board finally gave permission for the project, but with strict conditions. For example, members had to be American citizens but politically neither to the far right nor the far left of the spectrum; they could not build homes or live on the club property, or even stay there overnight.

Jack and his partners were preparing to move forward when two owners of adjoining land took the case to the State Supreme Court. Early in January 1967, the court ruled in favor of the plaintiffs. Once again, Robinson and Hudgins found themselves appealing to the State Commission on Human Rights. Once again, they lost. The NAACP promised to continue the fight, but by this time—to Jack's dismay—many of the black investors had lost heart. In a column months later in the *Amsterdam News,* Jack wrote off his dream of an integrated country club. He blamed his fellow blacks, mainly. "They told me in effect," he said, " 'We're not ready for this.' They didn't say it in so many words, but the defeatism was there. . . . I must confess that I became disgusted. . . . I don't want to give up. But it gets to be like bumping your head against a brick wall. You bump and bump and all you get is a headache."

At least Freedom National Bank was flourishing. On January 9, 1967, it opened its first branch office, in the predominantly black Bedford-Stuyvesant district of Brooklyn. In ceremonies to mark the opening, Jack made much of what he called his return to the borough that had embraced him in 1947. "Coming back as a banker," Jack said, "will give me an opportunity to attempt to repay some of the people of that Borough for all the good which has come my way." In fact, this was Jack's second major attempt to "return" to Brooklyn. The previous May, he had taken on yet another job, albeit one that proved more illusory than real. At a press conference, he accepted the post of general manager of the Brooklyn Dodgers football team of the fledgling Continental Football League. Although the team, sponsored by a group of Brooklyn-based investors, had neither players nor an arena, Robinson spoke aggressively about its plans. "We want to build a stadium in Brooklyn for both football and baseball," he announced, "and we hope to bring back major league baseball. Brooklyn is starving for a sports team."

(With yet another job title to his name, Robinson found himself lampooned by a cartoonist in the *Amsterdam News*. Jackie Robinson "oughta be tired of firsts," one character comments; "what *does* he need all those jobs for?" Another quips: "Baby, *I* dig *that* completely! If he hangs around the house, his wife'll really put him to work!!")

THE GALA OPENING of the Brooklyn branch of the bank was overshadowed by upsetting news: the House of Representatives had stripped Adam Clayton Powell Jr. of his chairmanship of the Labor and Education Committee. The next step would be to oust him from Congress altogether. Like many other leading blacks, Jack had severe misgivings about Powell's ways. "I am not an Adam Powell fan," he admitted. Powell had said and done many things "absolutely distasteful" and had been "offensively arrogant" to both blacks and whites and "made a joke out of his office." But Jack stood solidly behind him in this fight—especially because Powell had been an effective committee chairman, praised by President Johnson for expediting legislation. Robinson saw Jim Crow at work against a black man with power. "It's the same kind of conspiracy," he wrote, "used to defranchise the Negro during Reconstruction." Meanwhile, he pointed out, perhaps irrelevantly, whites in Georgia had just elected the demagogue Lester Maddox, who was infamous for wielding an ax handle to bar blacks from his restaurant, as governor of the state.

On March 1, the House voted to expel Powell and call a special election to replace him. When Powell indicated that he would contest the election—although he would not actually return from the Bahamas to campaign for himself—Robinson continued to defend him. Jack reacted with outrage when white Republican Party leaders tried to push forward the candidacy of James Meredith, the black man who had briefly integrated the University of Mississippi, against Powell. This plan was quickly dropped. In the special election on April 11, Harlem spoke: Powell won eighty-six percent of the vote. But some people speculated, not for the first time, that Jackie Robinson was about to run for public office. In the *Amsterdam News,* the columnist James Booker observed: "Jackie Robinson and his wife have purchased a cooperative apartment on 96th Street and will move back to Manhattan later this year. Any special political plans, Jackie?"

In fact, Jack and Rachel had bought two apartments, not one, and both were in a building on Ninety-third Street. They had bought them for pleasure and convenience and as a financial investment—not with any possible political office in mind. (Rachel and a friend had found the building and negotiated the financial structure for a takeover by a group of owners. The building was in a "redeveloped" section of the Upper West Side, and she was able to purchase the two apartments on very favorable terms.)

Robinson had no interest in running for office. He supported Powell now because of principle, just as he also defended Muhammad Ali, arrested for refusing to enter the military because of his religious convictions. When Ali was finally convicted, Jack drew attention to "the heroism and the tragedy" of Ali's case. "He, in my view, has won a battle by standing up for his principle. But will he lose the war in terms of the greater contribution he could have made, based on his splendid career and prospects?"

Principle also led to another troubling feud, this time with the sixty-six-year-old Roy Wilkins. Once again, Wilkins had beaten back a challenge to his leadership of the NAACP and overseen the reelection of ancients to the board of directors. Robinson had seen enough. Now, threatening to quit the board, on which he had served for almost a decade, he fired two broadsides. First came a speech that asked, "Is NAACP Contracting Infantile Paralysis?" Next, in a column, Jack published the attack: "I am forced to say sadly that I am terribly disappointed in the NAACP and deeply concerned about its future." He had watched "the brave but unsuccessful efforts of younger, more vibrant, more aggressive, well-prepared insurgents to inject new blood and new life into the Association. But Mr. Wilkins and his Old Guard always seem to stomp these efforts down." In addition, Jack accused the NAACP of being too dependent financially on white organizations like the Ford Foundation.

But Wilkins, a masterful debater, seemed to demolish Jack's arguments. The column, he said, came from either "gross misinformation or deliberate distortion." The NAACP was structurally far more democratic than any other major black civil rights group; only the NAACP elected its board in a democratic process. The previous year, moreover, it had raised eighty-two percent of its income from its almost five hundred thousand members while all other civil rights groups had depended upon "the general public (which means white people) for their funds." Wilkins ended with a blast of his own: "One of these days before you are seventy, some down-to-earth wisdom will find its way into your life. . . . If you had played ball with a hot head instead of a cool brain, you would have remained in the minors."

Although there was more than an element of truth in his criticism of Wilkins, Robinson managed only a sputtering response to this counterattack. "I am so sorry you cannot accept honest criticism," he wrote Wilkins. "I saw for years, first hand, what was going on and it is obvious things have not changed. I don't intend to remain silent when I see things I believe to be wrong. I have to laugh when you talk about down-to-earth wisdom. When I speak it's because I know what I am doing. I am sorry the truth hurts so much. I don't really have to answer to you for what I have done and I certainly will not apologize. . . . I don't intend to get into a further hassle with you. Whenever I feel criticism of you, the N.A.A.C.P. or any other organization is justified—expect it." Five days later, he wrote Wilkins again. "I am not proud of the progress we have made and cannot see why you should be. The Association needs new blood. It needs young men with new ideas and a mind of their own. Unfortunately I don't think this is true of the present Board."

Jack continued to work with the NAACP and other major civil rights groups, but also continued to have serious reservations about their leaders. In 1967, as word spread that Dr. King might run for the presidency on an anti–Vietnam War ticket, Robinson turned his attention to him. On April 8, Robinson made his first, gentle criticism of King, "an idol of mine" but a voice now largely silent about civil rights. Carefully Jack laid out his objection: "It happens that I do not agree with Dr. King in his stand on Vietnam." America was crying out for leadership on civil rights: "Let us hear from Dr. King on the DOMESTIC crisis." When King did not reply at once, Robinson raised his voice. "Confused" by King's record, he called on "Martin" to end his unilateral criticism of United States policy in Vietnam: "Aren't you being unfair when you place all of the burden of blame upon America and none upon the Communist forces we are fighting?" King should not demand that the United States stop bombing North Vietnam without also insisting that the North Vietnamese cease their own attacks. "Why is it, Martin, that you seem to ignore the blood which is upon their hands and to speak only of the 'guilt' of the United States?"

But as much as he supported Johnson's Vietnam policy (and lauded his domestic moves, as in that year nominating Thurgood Marshall to the Supreme Court), Robinson did not want to break with Dr. King. Thus he was utterly relieved late one night when the telephone rang and King was on the line, ready to have a long talk and defend his efforts in the antiwar movement. Robinson's sense of relief was almost palpable when, in his next column, he bowed to King as "still my leader—a man to whose defense I would come at any time he might need me. This is a personal commitment and a public pledge." Despite their differences about Vietnam, Jack made clear, he revered King: "If ever a man was placed on this earth by divine force to help solve the doubts and ease the hurts and dispel the fears of mortal man, I believe that man is Dr. King."

BETWEEN BLACK POWER and the antiwar movement, the summer of 1967 was a season of turmoil. As a special assistant to the governor, Jack found himself trying to chill one overheated situation after another across the state. Rockefeller understood Jack's importance in the trenches, as when in June he helped to resolve a "potentially explosive situation," as Rockefeller called it, in Rochester; or in Buffalo, where Jack roamed the hot streets speaking to people and preaching calm after days of unrest in which more than two hundred youths went to jail. Jack was a shield again when he and the governor attended an acrimonious meeting on racism in the state civil service; or again when, at a "town meeting" in Harlem, the local firebrand Charles Kenyatta, head of a group called the Mau Mau Society, fulminated before Rockefeller against the sinister control of crime and drugs in the ghetto by "the men behind you."

Faced by demagogues, Robinson would not back down. In his column, he attacked black leaders who "chickened out" in the face of trouble "for fear of criticism and attack from that noisy minority which seeks to inflame, to urge burning and hate." A certain statement sent out by Roy Wilkins was fine, but "it should have nailed down issues and called names. It should have identified H. Rap Brown [who had replaced Stokely Carmichael as the leader of SNCC] for what he is—a sensationalist, dangerous, irresponsible agitator who has a talent for getting fires ignited and getting himself safely out of the way." Brown and Carmichael did not intimidate Robinson. "Stokely Carmichael's version of Black Power," Jack declared on television, "can only get us more [George] Wallaces elected to office." Despite "the frustrations that our young people have had over the years," street violence served no useful purpose. Black Power should mean "the wise use of our dollar, the wise use of our political strength. . . . But if we are talking about getting in the streets, resorting to violence, creating disturbances, this cannot help anything." And yet, asked if he believed with Adam Clayton Powell Jr. that an "obscene distinction" existed between justice for blacks and whites in America, he replied: "There's no question about it. I agree with him 1,000%."

Nevertheless, that November, 1967, Jack called on the unregenerate Powell to resign his seat. In major cities that month, including Gary, Indiana, and Cleveland, Ohio, blacks won office as mayors; Powell was out of step with black progress. And yet

Jack's position also seemed to some people out of step with reality in its linkage to the political fortunes of Rockefeller. This connection offered Jack a measure of authority, as when, in Albany late in November, he addressed a state Conference on Critical Health Problems; or in December, when he and Rachel filled in for Nelson and Happy to host a function at the governor's mansion. Fundamentally, however, Robinson was in a dependent position. In the superheated political and racial climate of 1967 he had to endure accusations that he was an Uncle Tom.

Early in 1967, at a gathering of black Republicans in Albany, Jack had fended off unspoken charges that their activity was somehow shameful and compromised. "We will not be traitors to principle," he insisted. "We will not sell out for personal advantage or gain. We will not become the creatures of either great white fathers or black uncle toms." But by year's end he had to deal with two separate public charges by younger blacks that he had indeed become an Uncle Tom. Robinson stood his ground: "I feel perfectly secure in saying that I have not been an Uncle Tom to him and happy to say that the Governor neither wants me as an Uncle Tom nor believes I could become one."

Not for the first time in his life, but now from a source he had never expected, Jack had also become the target of much hate mail—and even death threats. Authorities had just uncovered an alleged black nationalist plot to kill Roy Wilkins and Whitney Young. Again Robinson refused to yield. "I don't seek to be anyone's martyr or hero," he pleaded, "but telling it like I think it is—that's the only way I know how to be me." Accustomed to attacks, he would not bow to these threats. "I am human," he wrote. "I like public approval as well as anyone else. But, if I have to be misunderstood and misrepresented because I follow my convictions and speak my mind, then so be it. . . . In the long run, I'm the guy I have to live with. And if I ever become untrue to myself and to the black people from which I came, I wouldn't like myself very much."

But the new year, 1968, would only further test his courage and resolve. It would be a year largely of death and disappointment, as he and his family, and the nation itself, endured a series of blows for which no one, including Robinson, was well prepared.

— 16 —

Rounding Third

1968–1971

I can't imagine what else can happen to us this year.
—Jackie Robinson (1968)

FOR ROBINSON, 1968 OPENED on a promising note. A new business venture offered an opportunity to succeed where other schemes had stagnated or failed. On January 4, Sea Host Incorporated, a subsidiary of Proteus Foods & Industries, both of Manhattan, hired him to help launch its main project: the sale of franchises for "fast food" restaurants specializing in fish and other seafood. Jack's main role would be to publicize the project. In addition to seeking out and encouraging potential franchisees, he would secure as much publicity as possible on radio, television, and other media for Sea Host. In return, he would be paid $10,000 a year, $500 for each franchise sold "through your personal contacts," as well as stock options and a tiny fraction of the gross sales of each franchise in the operation. Finally, if he wanted to take part in the 1968 presidential elections, he was guaranteed a "sabbatical" without pay.

For Jack, this job represented a hope not only for himself but also for cash-starved blacks eager for a chance to break into business on their own. If in 1968 franchising was still in its relative infancy in the United States, it accounted nevertheless for about ten percent of the gross national product, with almost $90 billion in total sales. With Sea Host, a would-be franchisee needed only about $16,000 to go into business—$2,500 for capitalization costs, $10,000 for the franchise fee, plus an additional sum for equipment and miscellaneous expenses. The franchisee then had a chance to earn between an estimated $10,000 and $18,000 a year in profit. "Our aim is to help people help themselves," Robinson declared. "With the company's training program and support, almost anyone prepared to work for his income can become a successful Sea Host franchisee."

Robinson offered a rosy picture, but in almost every way this job was a step down for him. His pay was about a quarter of his last Chock Full o' Nuts salary. Between him and the president of Sea Host, Wah F. Chin, there was little of the mixture of idealism and practicality that had sparked Jack's relationship with William Black. Formerly, Jack was the head of personnel; with Sea Host, he was more or less a front man, a "shill" for the product. An internal memorandum laid out the company's hopes in this respect. In general, the opening of franchises would be trumpeted as something far more significant, "particularly for ghetto or ethnic areas." In particular, Robinson's work with black investors would bring highly favorable publicity.

The "utilization" of Robinson's prestige in the black community was needed because by 1968, the franchising industry was already plagued by accusations of fraud and deception at the expense of gullible or powerless franchisees. In fronting for a corporation that sought to attract black investors, Robinson was placing his own reputation on the line. "I think the masses of black people know," he declared more than a year later, "that Jack Robinson is not going to sell them out for anything. . . . I have the feeling that the black community, while they don't always agree with me, at least know I'm not going to sell them out."

JACK'S NEW BUSINESS did not prevent him from giving his time generously, as always, to help others. On January 26, in Los Angeles, he addressed a fund-raising dinner to help endow a professorship in memory of Karl Everette Downs, his former pastor and guide in Pasadena and employer at Samuel Huston College in Texas in 1945; at the dinner, Jack presented the fund with a check for $5,000, a gift from Nelson Rockefeller. In February, still loyal to the National Conference of Christians and Jews, Jack served as national chairman of its Brotherhood Week. He also spoke out on certain issues of the day. In a short letter to the New York *Times,* he praised the paper for its editorial sympathetic to the singer Eartha Kitt, who was under fire for noisily disrupting a White House luncheon with a protest against the Vietnam War. He joined the national debate about whether or not black athletes should boycott the Olympic Games later that year. While the boycott struck him as unwise, "I do support the individuals who decided to make the sacrifice by giving up their chance to win an Olympic Medal. I respect their courage." As spokesman for a large group of current and former athletes, he pressed the conservative American Olympic Committee to vote not to readmit the Union of South Africa (barred from the 1964 games) to the Olympics because of its commitment to apartheid. Many Americans, he knew, resented mixing sports and politics; but they should try to "understand the reasons and frustrations behind these protests, and the causes involved, and not just react unfavorably to the mere fact of protest." He went further. Today's young athletes, he told the writer Robert Lipsyte, insisted on being heard. "It was different in my day; perhaps we lacked courage."

On March 4, Robinson was absorbed in work at his Rockefeller office on West Fifty-fifth Street when a newspaper reporter reached him on the telephone. Did Robinson have any comment? Comment on what? On the news that the police in Stamford had arrested his son Jackie and charged him with possession of marijuana and heroin, as well as a .22-caliber revolver. Early in the morning, narcotics officers had broken up a drug sale in front of the Allison-Scott Hotel in downtown Stamford. Shots were fired both by the police and by Jackie, who fled the scene but was apprehended not far away, on South Street. He was now in the Stamford jail, held on $5,000 bail.

Since returning to the United States, Jackie had been a mysterious, troubling figure to his parents, adrift and aimless in Colorado, where he was honorably discharged by the Army in 1966, or at home in Stamford, unable to remain in a regular job, a shadowy presence in and out of their house. From Colorado Springs one day, a policeman had called to alert them that Jackie might be heading for trouble; when police stopped his car one day for a traffic offense, they had found inside it drug paraphernalia, which Jackie said belonged to a young woman riding with him. Late one night, a local judge in Stamford had called Jack and Rachel to warn them that the police were about to arrest Jackie. Nevertheless, the charge of possession of heroin came as a shock; the idea that his elder son might be a dope addict, or a dope pusher, or both, stunned Jack. Jackie's sister, Sharon, would recall first hearing the news on her car radio in Stamford: "I felt hot. Sick. I wanted to scream at someone. Cry out. Blame the faceless-thankless voice on the radio. Smash the dashboard. Crawl into a hole."

With their local attorney and friend Sydney Kweskin, Jack and Rachel, accompanied by Sharon, went to the gloomy red-brick prison building to post Jackie's bail. (David was away at a boarding school, Mount Hermon, in Massachusetts.) On the telephone, Rachel had already arranged for Jackie to be accepted at Yale–New Haven Hospital, where she worked, for detoxification and psychiatric evaluation. Outside the station, reporters peppered Jack with questions and snapped photographs. Roger Kahn, gathering material for *The Boys of Summer,* saw "a bent gray man, answering questions in a whisper, and drawing shallow breaths, because a longer breath might feed a sob."

"Sir, are you going to stick by your son?"

"We will, but we'll have to take the consequences."

"Were you aware he had certain problems, Mr. Robinson?"

"He quit high school. He joined the Army. He fought in Vietnam and he was wounded. I've had more effect on other people's kids than on my own."

"How do you feel about *that,* sir?"

"I couldn't have had an *important* effect on anybody's child, if this happened to my own." After answering another question "at length, as if in relief, as if in penance," Jack continued to speak to the reporters but pressed through their ranks with Rachel and Sharon.

Downstairs they found Jackie slumped in a cell. Rachel and Sharon broke down in tears; Jack was more stoical.

"Are you all right, son?" he asked, as Rachel reached through the bars to take Jackie's hand. Eventually Jack posted bail and, with Jackie in tow, left the prison for New Haven. There, Jackie entered the hospital for an extended period of observation and treatment.

On April 7, Jackie's case was heard before Judge George DiCenzo. No doubt because Jackie was a first offender, and a veteran, and perhaps also because he was Jackie Robinson's son, he was given a choice of jail or entering a strict rehabilitation program. Judge DiCenzo ordered that charges against Robinson be delayed for two years, during which time Jackie was to undergo treatment and rehabilitation under state supervision. Two court-appointed psychiatrists, Dr. Herbert Kleber and Dr. Robert Willis—both colleagues of Rachel's at Yale—testified that for about six months before his arrest, Jackie Junior had been addicted to heroin.

At the time of Jackie's arrest, Jack informed reporters that his son had started smoking marijuana in Vietnam; this was Jackie's story to him. Gradually the truth came out. Two years later, Jackie would come clean before a United States Senate subcommittee about his drug abuse, which had started in earnest under the abnormal pressures of Vietnam, then accelerated in the United States. "In Colorado I started getting involved with a lot of the camp followers," Jackie admitted. "These are people that are prostitutes, gamblers, thieves, drug users and pushers that kind of follow Army towns." In Colorado, he used mainly marijuana, pills, and cough syrup on a daily basis; then, back in the New York area, "I started using cocaine, heroin, occasionally LSD" and amphetamines; "I was using all types of drugs at this point." He fell also "into about every type of crime that you could get into in order to support my habit at this point." He would steal from other soldiers, or sell marijuana; "I was breaking into houses and after a while I was selling heroin and cocaine." He now carried guns routinely, as in Vietnam: "I think it was something I got obsessed with over there and fit very well into the image of what I thought was a man . . . the image of being tough and fighting and this whole thing being what manhood was all about."

Once Jack and Rachel knew these facts, they were able to put Jackie's letters from Vietnam into sharper perspective and understand the murderous forces that had driven him over the edge. At first, those letters were simple missives from a young man venturing into the great world, seeking to be all that he could be. Then the letters began to reveal the terrifying pressures on him and the other young American soldiers ordered to Vietnam. If one incident set the tone, it came early, when some other soldiers killed a Viet Cong sniper. "They tied him to the front of their jeep like a deer," Jackie wrote his father, "then drove through the village with a loud speaker & had the interpreter tell the people that this is what would happen to all Viet Congs and people who support them. It was a horrible sight."

Horror soon became routine. His platoon sergeant from Fort Reilly, a man he liked—"he always gave me a fair break"—was killed. In another action, "We lost six men this week, including our executive officer. We also had eleven wounded." By this time Jackie was sick to his stomach about the war. "This is the most miserable place in the world," he wrote his father. "I can't see why we're fighting for it. When you see somebody get shot you think about what a waste this all is." Bradley Gordon remembered Jackie telling him later: "Man, you talk to a guy in the morning, and you're putting him into a body bag in the afternoon. Or you're grabbing parts of him, putting them in a body bag. . . . Man, how can I tell my parents this? How can I tell anyone? No one really understands. Everyone tells me I'll get over it, I'll get over it. Man, I have nightmares at night."

But in Vietnam, military violence was not the only force that shattered ideals. After his relatively congenial years in Stamford, the bitterness between blacks and whites in the U.S. Army over there devastated Jackie. Now he warned Rachel about having his brother, David, grow up in a mainly white world, as he himself had done: "If he doesn't learn to talk like he's colored and get in the groove with *at least* the low-middle class Negro he's going to get a shock soon." For one thing, David must learn to dance the way blacks danced. "I didn't know how to dance," Jackie wrote, so "I'd get a bunch of hardheads together" and "break up dances." In fact, the sweep of history had already made David much more aware of race and his African ancestry than Jackie had ever been. "Jackie had come from a world of acceptance by whites," Bradley Gordon said, "but a place where he was an oddity, a famous black man's son. And then he left that sanctuary and found out that it was a horrible world out there. It got to the point where he couldn't bring himself to explain one more time what he was about, why he liked anonymity so much. He came back from Vietnam, and he was not the same person. He said, 'Man, it's crazy. We're over there fighting this war, and the racism stinks.' He was angry. No one understood, he couldn't talk to anyone." (Gordon himself would soon understand. Commissioned as an officer in the Air Force at nineteen, he fought in Vietnam and was wounded in the Tet Offensive of 1968.)

By the time Jackie's orders came to return home, he was a changed young man—how much so, his parents were to find out only after his arrest. But his last letters from Vietnam gave an ominous hint of the change. "I'm going to need some time to myself," he warned his mother. "I know I wouldn't be up to anyone hollering at me or trying [to] force [a] decision on me." He knew that he was a different person now, and more dangerous. "I'm in perfect control of myself but strange things aggravate me and I can't guarantee how much I can take. When somebody over here is pushed too far he's capable of anything."

After Jackie's arrest, a flood of sympathetic messages poured in, many of them including offers of help for the Robinson family. Jack and Rachel declined virtually all these offers; they would face the situation as a family and do what they could to help Jackie. "We know the only real solution," Jack wrote the Wallersteins, "is the love and understanding we as a family give our son. While your offer of help is appreciated, I have faith that our family ties are strong and that with God's help we will come through this crisis."

JACKIE'S ARREST DEEPLY upset his father but did not disable him. Later in March, along with the writer James Baldwin and others, he testified before a congressional subcommittee in favor of a proposal by a New York congressman, James H. Scheuer of the Bronx, to establish a presidential commission on black American history. He also stepped up his efforts to affect the presidential election coming in the fall. Despite Vietnam, Johnson seemed likely to be renominated by the Democrats; among the Republicans, Nixon had inherited much of the old Goldwater support, and also seemed certain of nomination. Robinson, dismayed, continued to fret at the attitude of the Republican Party to blacks. Writing to Clarence Lee Towns Jr., the leading black on the Republican National Committee, he warned that blacks, who had made up only six percent of the voters for Goldwater, would not support Nixon: "I suspect that unless the party shows a desire to win our vote, it may rest assured that I and my friends cannot and will not support a conservative."

Ironically, Robinson and the Arizona senator now enjoyed a far more cordial relationship than in 1964. Attending a public banquet in Arizona, Robinson had listened in amazement as Goldwater voiced his outrage at examples of racial prejudice he had seen on a recent trip into the South. After the dinner, the two men met and chatted amicably. Later, Goldwater invited Robinson to join him at lunch in New York City. "This time, I accepted," Jack told his *Amsterdam News* readers in March 1968, alluding to his public refusal of a similar invitation in 1964. "In person, the Senator is a charmer. . . . I must confess that, although we still disagree sharply in some areas, my personal anti-Goldwater feelings have ebbed considerably." But this thaw with Goldwater had nothing to do with Nixon: "I have my right to remember that I am black and American before I am Republican. As such, I will never vote for Mr. Nixon."

In a memorandum of March 8, four days after his son's arrest, Jack solemnly laid out for Rockefeller his thinking on the 1968 campaign. "Speaking from the heart of Jackie Robinson," he began, "I must tell you several of my strong beliefs." This was a critical moment in history. "I believe that each man is placed upon this earth with a destiny to fulfill. I feel strongly that you were meant to lead in world councils, in national affairs and domestic problems and within a political party which was born slanted towards freedom, but which in recent times has turned its back on its own heritage." Robinson himself could not support Nixon. "The people who rejected the black man in 1964 and carried the Goldwater standard are the identical people who desire the all-things-to-all-men phoniness of a Richard Nixon and his crowd." Rockefeller had a duty to run. "I believe overwhelmingly that you are THE Republican with a decent chance to win over Mr. Johnson. . . . I believe you have no alternative but to go firmly forward to acceptance of your rightful role in our society."

But the presidential race soon became even more complicated. First, Senator Robert Kennedy announced that he would pursue the Democratic nomination. Then, on March 31, beaten down by opposition to the Vietnam War, President Johnson stunned the nation with the news that he would neither seek nor accept renomination. In April, Vice-President Humphrey, preparing for his own entry, formally sought Robinson's support. However, Jack made it clear that "Governor Rockefeller's desires dictate my actions. I fully expect he will be the Republican nominee and I will do everything I can for him. I find him to be a man of great integrity and ability." Should the Rockefeller candidacy fail, Jack would then "be happy" to help Humphrey. Although Robinson had developed a sincere respect for Robert Kennedy, he would not support his candidacy over that of Humphrey.

Then, the day after Jack wrote this letter, a calamitous blow descended. On April 4, in Memphis, Tennessee, where he had gone to the aid of striking sanitation workers, Dr. Martin Luther King Jr. was assassinated. Leaving Jackie's hospital room in New Haven, where they were visiting, Jack and Rachel sorrowfully drove down from Connecticut to New York to join a group of mourners gathered at the home of Arthur and Marian Logan, then flew south to Atlanta for the funeral. Few deaths had ever touched Jack more intimately. Perhaps he had seen in King a reincarnation of the selfless black spiritual leader, attuned to the reality of politics but also humble and loving, he had experienced crucially in his early life with Karl Downs in Pasadena and later in Austin; in any event, Robinson had come to see Dr. King as the embodiment of the finest traditions of black manhood, a figure who could lead by the power of personal moral authority as well as eloquence, a man Jack was proud to follow. In his weekly column, he hailed the martyred minister as "the greatest leader of the Twentieth Century."

The death of Dr. King and the ugly disturbances that followed in Harlem and in a hundred other cities across the nation cast a somber spell over the following days and weeks. On April 10, sad and demoralized by this terrible blow to the civil rights cause and to his own liberal ideals, but striving to be upbeat, Jack presided over the "Hollywood-style" opening of the first Sea Host restaurant in Harlem, located at the corner of Lexington Avenue and 138th Street, near the Harlem Hospital. His heart was elsewhere, but Jack said what he had to say. "Our people have always been enthusiastic about seafood," he announced. "Now we can offer fine quality at sensible prices."

His many involvements away from Sea Host offered more in the way of dignity. Later that month, for example, he traveled to Louisville, Kentucky, for an NCCJ Brotherhood dinner attended by a thousand guests at Bellarmine College there. On May 2, he was co-chairman of the annual gala awards dinner of the National Urban League. The next day, in Austin, Texas, he was the main speaker, on "The Church and the World," at the 81st Annual Assembly of the Texas Association of Christian Churches. One week later, in Boston, Jack addressed Northeastern University's fourth annual national police seminar, which that year asked the question "Is Justice a Myth?"

But another event, bittersweet at best, troubled the family and especially Jack and Rachel. Sharon, now eighteen, had decided to marry her boyfriend, a high-school basketball star from nearby Norwalk, Connecticut. To her parents, her decision was a grave disappointment; neither bride nor bridegroom seemed prepared for the challenges of marriage. Nevertheless, on April 27, leaning on her father's arm and beautiful in a white bridal gown and veil, she walked down the aisle of the North Stamford Congregational Church near the Robinson home on Cascade Road. "Dad smiled reassuringly," Sharon recalled, "but I sensed his reluctance as he handed me over." His reluctance was justified. Although Jack did not know it, Sharon's husband had more than once struck her in fits of rage. Almost exactly one year later, the couple would be divorced.

A month later, Jack was hammered again. On May 21, his mother, Mallie, now seventy-eight years old, was walking up the driveway at 121 Pepper Street, with her eldest son, Edgar, watching her from his porch, when she collapsed. Uncertain about her state, Jack took the first plane he could find to Los Angeles, but Mallie was dead when he arrived. In Pasadena, Jack found it hard to look at his mother's face. Mallie's power to command his attention, to charge and recharge his conscience and his sense of duty, shame, and guilt, was still strong. "I felt I couldn't go into the room where she lay," he wrote. "Somehow I managed to and I shall always be glad that I did. There was a look, an expression on her face, that calmed me. It didn't do anything about her hurt, but it made me realize that she had died at peace with herself."

June brought another terrible death. In Los Angeles, on the evening of his victory in the California primary, Robert F. Kennedy was shot dead by Sirhan Sirhan. The blow was complicated for Jack by the fact that the issue of the *Amsterdam News* that featured news of the death included a column by Jack critical of Kennedy, written before his death. Jack had to emphasize his genuine sorrow concerning the assassination; Kennedy had shown an unmistakable passion for social justice, and he was deservedly a hero to most black Americans. Speculation quickly arose, in both the black and the white press, that Governor Rockefeller might choose Robinson, or some other leading black, such as Whitney Young of the National Urban League, to complete Kennedy's unexpired term in the Senate. (Eventually, the governor chose a white politician from upstate New York.) Certainly Rockefeller and Robinson now seemed as close as ever. On June 15, at the governor's request, Jack spoke on the importance of civil liberties at an Elks convocation in Grand Rapids, Michigan. Then, on June 23, Rockefeller made a spectacular entrance, in a helicopter, as Jack and Rachel hosted a luncheon for a powerful group of about seventy members of the black National Newspaper Publishers Association, which had just ended its annual convention in New York City. Dressed in a hound's-tooth jacket and black slacks, Jack suavely introduced the governor. After some brief remarks by Rockefeller and an informal question-and-answer session, Robinson seized the chance to blast Nixon. "If Nixon is elected President, we as Negroes are in serious trouble; we would, in my opinion, be going backward."

Jack was again busy as a host and in the news the following Sunday, when he and Rachel welcomed about two thousand patrons to another "Afternoon of Jazz" on the grounds of their home. The event was in part festive, in part somber: this concert would raise funds for the support of Dr. King's children. Under a searing sun, a green-and-white-striped tent gave a measure of relief to an honor roll of musicians, including the Modern Jazz Quartet, the Cannonball Adderley Quintet, Thelonious Monk, Billy Taylor, Dave Brubeck, Gerry Mulligan, Lionel Hampton, and Duke Ellington, all eager to take part in the event. The concert raised about $30,000 for its cause.

These hectic events, coupled with the more intimate, multiple blows and strains of the preceding year, almost ended in disaster for Jack himself. On June 24, the day after the publishers' luncheon, Jack visited his physician, Dr. Cyril Solomon, with complaints about a mild discomfort in his chest. Dr. Solomon sent him to have an electrocardiogram. Hearing nothing from the cardiologist, Robinson and Dr. Solomon assumed that Jack's heart was in good shape. Then, on June 28, at a dinner, Jack fell ill and almost collapsed. On July 1, after a strenuous day at the jazz concert, he finally consulted again with Dr. Solomon, who decided to telephone the cardiologist. To his astonishment, Solomon learned that the EKG showed that Jack had suffered a mild heart attack. Fortunately, he had sustained no tissue damage to his heart; rest would probably take care of the problem.

Death was in the air, and Robinson could hardly avoid brooding on his own. "I guess the good Lord has a job for me," he wrote a friend, "or else I could or would have had some serious heart damage. . . . I have not been too disturbed and know when it's time nothing will prevent any of us going. I don't know what it is but the good Lord has one more job for me or else I would be a lot sicker than I am. I am heeding his warning and am really doing well, getting plenty of rest and reading." He was well aware of all that he had gone through in the preceding year, from the deaths of his mother, Branch Rickey, Dr. King, and Robert Kennedy to the arrest of Jackie and Sharon's unpromising marriage. "I can't imagine what else can happen to us this year. We had our share of problems but as has been said frequently if we can stand the test all will come out fine. I am sure we have the courage. I pray we have seen the last of trouble for a while, anyway."

The summer of 1968 became a time mainly of rest and recuperation. No longer at the hospital in New Haven, Jackie was now a resident at the Daytop Rehabilitation Program in Seymour, Connecticut, highly recommended by experts in the field of narcotics treatment; its hard discipline was enforced by the reformed drug addicts who made up its staff. Residents had to prove themselves again and again, in a highly structured format, before they would be seen as cured. "This is a tough period," Jack wrote about his son's ordeal; "only God knows how he will do. He swears he'll be O.K. but it's not that easy. We can only hope and pray, for Jackie has lots of problems and only he can solve them. We will know in a matter of time. We are hopeful but we know how tough it is."

Barely a month later, Jackie fell again. On the night of August 23, police arrested him in a hotel room in Stamford along with a nineteen-year-old woman from Manhattan. Jackie's companion was charged with "loitering for the purposes of prostitution," he with "using females for immoral purposes." The police would say no more. Jackie's bond was posted at $7,000. His arrest could have ended fatally; according to the police, he had pointed a handgun at an officer. Again, somehow, he was able to avoid jail. He was sentenced to a suspended term of two to four years in prison and ordered back to Daytop.

As Jack and Rachel knew now, there would be no easy cure for their son. He would make progress, then falter; but as long as he returned to Daytop, they could still hope for his eventual recovery. In the meantime, his parents, as well as Sharon and David, stayed resolutely in touch with him. They visited him in Seymour, welcomed him home when he returned, sent him cards and letters and homemade cookies and cakes—whatever they could do to assure him that he was wanted and loved.

As for the Republican National Convention that summer, Jack made no effort to go to Miami Beach early in August to attend it. As expected, the party chose Nixon to run for President. To Jack's disgust, Nixon then chose as his running mate the governor of Maryland, Spiro Agnew, a man of impressive looks but little substance, and known in Baltimore to be hostile to blacks. Thus Robinson was eagerly responsive when Humphrey, struggling with Senator George McGovern of South Dakota and Senator

Eugene McCarthy of Minnesota for the Democratic nomination, set out to win over the most influential black supporters of Rockefeller, Martin Luther King Sr. and Robinson himself. On August 11, Jack announced that he was resigning as Rockefeller's special assistant for community affairs to campaign for the Democrats, "if they will have me." He was especially incensed by reports that Nixon had apparently given the South, in the person of the segregationist Senator Strom Thurmond of South Carolina, veto power over his choice for Vice-President. "Now he's sold out," Robinson said contemptuously of Nixon to a reporter. "He's really prostituted himself to get the Southern vote."

The harshest counterattack came from William F. Buckley Jr., in an essay, "Robinson Strikes Out," in the New York *Post.* "It is surely time," Buckley argued, "to put an end to the mischievous national habit of taking seriously this pompous moralizer who whines his way through life as though all America were at Ebbets Field cheering him on against the big bad racist St. Louis Cardinals." Robinson's habit of describing himself as "first a black man, second an American, third a Republican" was itself racist. (And indeed, Robinson once would not have ordered things in this way; but he understood now, in the wake of the social turbulence of the preceding years, that for most Americans his skin color was more defining of his identity than his citizenship ever could be.)

"If that is racism, so be it," he responded in the *Amsterdam News.* "I am proud to be black. I am also embattled because I am black; but for white Americans of the Buckley ilk, I am only one of millions of blacks who are tired of it!" On August 14, two weeks before the Democratic convention, he roused himself from rest to be present in Harlem for an official visit by Humphrey. At the offices of the Freedom National Bank, standing beside Humphrey, he announced that he was formally endorsing the Vice-President. But this choreographed visit did not go smoothly. On 125th Street, behind wooden barricades, most of about one thousand Harlem folk gave Humphrey a cheery welcome; but others turned on him and on Robinson. "Get him out of here!" one man shouted as Humphrey stepped grinning out of the bank. "Uncle Tom!" another yelled at Robinson.

Two weeks later, in Chicago, at one of the most tumultuous political conventions in American history, Humphrey was nominated for the presidency. But most Rockefeller supporters, including James Farmer, the former director of CORE, declined to follow Jack's lead in supporting Humphrey; Senator Jacob Javits of New York called the decision "precipitate and to be deplored." Robinson knew well that he was taking a fateful step. In handwritten drafts of a letter to Rockefeller, he pleaded with him for understanding. "This is perhaps the most difficult moment of my life," Jack began, before amending the sentence to read "These are difficult times." His two years as a special assistant had been "personally rewarding"; moreover, he had also seen "a possible breakthrough" in race relations because of the governor's leadership. But the atmosphere of unity at the Republican convention had been achieved at the expense of blacks; he had to fight it. As for his job as a special assistant, "I would expect to return to my position with you when the campaign is over. I am aware however [of] the politics involved and can only ask if you were Black and searching for dignity could you do any different?"

But this time, Robinson had gone too far. As a top Republican leader, Rockefeller could hardly employ a lieutenant who campaigned for the opposition. Robinson was an exceptional figure, but reappointing him was probably out of the question. Over the next few years, Robinson continued to support Rockefeller; but he never again held a full-time position with the governor. Perhaps Jack would not have resigned if the job itself had been more rewarding. "Whatever it was at first, it was no longer rewarding," Rachel insisted. "Jack had an office and a title but no power at all. Everything had to be referred to people higher up; Jack was simply a possible way to reach the governor, and more and more not a very clear or open way. He had enjoyed much more power at Chock Full o' Nuts. I think he was ready to go."

On January 22, 1969, following Nixon's inaugural address, Robinson sent him a formal letter that made only scant reference to Jack's earlier support. Accepting the election result, "we all pray that your years in Washington will be most successful." Although blacks had not supported him, Nixon should set aside that fact and work for national unity. "For Mr. President, Black people cannot afford a racial conflict; White people cannot afford one. And it's a fact that America cannot afford one. If we are to survive as a nation, we must do it together. Black people will work for one America if we are given hope. Without hope, the present feeling of despair will lead to worse problems."

Victorious at last, Nixon ignored this missive. He also ignored a group of about thirty black leaders, including Robinson and Floyd McKissick, who showed up at the White House gates soon after the inauguration to request a meeting with him; the group was kept waiting for about half an hour, then turned away. Nixon still admired Robinson the former Brooklyn Dodger, but he was no longer interested in, or had need for, Robinson as a political player. In this regard, the previous autumn, Jack had suffered another major setback when the New York *Amsterdam News* quietly dropped his column. The loss of this forum, in addition to the severance of his formal ties to Rockefeller, made him truly a private citizen once again.

A few days later, on January 31, Jack celebrated his fiftieth birthday. "We had a nice party one afternoon," Rachel recalled, "with lots of family and friends—my brother Chuck and his family, Lacy and Florence Covington, Willette Bailey of course, and the Kweskins, and the Logans with Chipper, their little son, and Marty Stone, Howard Cosell and his family, I think, and others. It was a beautiful day, very cold but clear and bright, with snow crusting on the ground and the pond iced over. We had a big fire going and a nice buffet and drinks for those who wanted them. Then the most amazing thing happened. Suddenly Jack turned away and opened the glass sliding doors that looked over the hillside. Before we knew it he was at the top of the slope and getting onto the kids' toboggan. Then all of a sudden he was sliding down the slope, heading for the pond. We held our breath because he really couldn't steer the bobsled, and there was a big bump at the edge of the lake, but he went over the bump beautifully and out onto the ice and then he just slid all the way across the pond to the foot of the trees on the other side, and he sat there in the bobsled, laughing his head off like a happy kid. We were shocked, he hadn't been at all well. But it was wonderful to see him be so physical, to do something so daring, so reckless. He was very pleased with himself."

MEANWHILE, SEA HOST SEEMED to be making some progress. However, in its ability to attract and sign black and Puerto Rican franchisees, the venture was struggling; by the middle of 1969, Harlem had only two restaurants. Once again Jack had proof, if he needed it, of the scarcity of money among black folks. To stimulate sales of franchises to minorities (and make some money for themselves) Jack and a small group of other businessmen, including his brother-in-law Chuck Williams, founded Jackie Robinson Associates. "We don't want the company to own stores in the black and Puerto Rican areas," Robinson said flatly. "We want blacks and Puerto Ricans to own these stores." Seeking funds from various agencies, JRA then sought to funnel this money in the form of loans to prospective franchisees. Eventually, JRA struck a deal with the Interracial Council for Business Opportunity (ICBO), which was itself funded by the Ford Foundation, for this purpose. JRA, led by Robinson, then began to choose minority prospective franchisees for support.

Within Sea Host, however, Jack was not growing comfortable. A wall separated him from the principals, who were mainly Asian or Asian-American and seemed uninclined to share confidences with him. "All I know," Rachel said, "is that Jack complained early that whenever anything important had to be decided, the Asian principals would draw apart—go into a closet, he said, which could not have been literally true—and come to a decision without consulting him. He really had little idea what was going on." On at least one occasion, when Rachel went with Jack to visit a potential franchisee, she saw the consequences of this distancing. "There were questions Jack couldn't answer," she recalled. "He had been left out of the loop within the company. He found it very frustrating." There were other problems. "Several of us wanted to be a part of franchising," Jack's friend Warren Jackson said, "and we even went to meet with Wah Chin, the head of Sea Host, at his posh office on Park Avenue—Jack was there, and other friends. But really none of us was ready or able to provide hands-on leadership, which is what you need in franchising. I mean, we just knew that we wouldn't be in every day, kneading dough or mixing batter. We all went on to other things."

The combination of his discomfort within Sea Host and his unhappiness with governmental attitudes to blacks made Robinson pessimistic about race relations. Although he was often hard on black leaders, as in calling on Harlem voters the previous fall to dump Adam Clayton Powell Jr. (who was reelected by the usual landslide), Jack was harder still on the inaction or indifference or malevolence of most urban, state, and federal authorities where blacks were concerned. "I'm afraid we are going to have a conflict such as this country has never seen," he declared. "I think we're just a rumor away from it, unless there is concrete action—not by the black community, but by the federal, state, and local governments. The black community has no confidence in the leadership of this country today. . . . The waiting period is over as far as the black community is concerned. They're tired of waiting."

This did not mean that Robinson now endorsed the more radical young black leaders. Openly he talked about his contempt for many of the new celebrity militants. "My daughter had a picture of Eldridge Cleaver in her room," he told a reporter, "and I objected to it. She said, 'But it's my room.' I said, 'But it's my house, and I want that picture down.' I caught the devil from my sons. But we sat down and talked about it. You know, if a guy goes out and shoots and kills a policeman, in too many areas he's a hero. Too many of our people don't care whether or not a guy has committed a crime." (The picture was actually one of Huey Newton.) On the other hand, he also loathed the symbols of the American right wing, especially those sponsored by support of the Vietnam War. That summer, Robinson flashed into the news when he launched an attack on the increasingly popular habit, pushed by *Reader's Digest* and the Gulf Oil company, of displaying decals of the Stars and Stripes. He was still for the war, but the decal, he declared, was an ominous sign. "I wouldn't fly the flag on the Fourth of July, or any other day," he said. "When I see a car with a flag pasted on it, I figure the guy behind the wheel isn't my friend."

Nevertheless, Jack remained quietly loyal to the United States military effort. On August 21, 1969, he was the guest speaker at a luncheon in connection with the annual Command Chaplains' Conference at Fort Meyer, Virginia. In his audience, in addition to the chaplains, were various other high-ranking members of the armed forces, including the Army chief of staff and Vietnam military leader William Westmoreland.

AWARE OF TIME RUNNING OUT, Jack pressed ahead with plans for another book on his life, this time an autobiography written with Alfred Duckett. At one point, publishers would have come to him; now he had to go to them. Accordingly, in June or July he found himself having a business lunch in New York with a young black woman who had just been appointed a senior editor at Random House and was eager to acquire good black authors. (Her first novel, *The Bluest Eye*, was about to appear.) Encouraged by Charles Harris, another black senior editor, Toni Morrison had invited Jack, whom she had never met, to lunch to talk about the project. "We met at a bistro near Random House on the East Side," she recalled. "He didn't eat much. He explained that he had diabetes, he had to watch his diet. He was quiet at first, but it took him just a little while to decide that, yes, he was in smart company. Then he relaxed and became comfortable and informal. He seemed very intelligent and knowledgeable; he had sophisticated views of life, he was warm, funny, and forthcoming." Morrison found herself enjoying the lunch more than she had expected.

"I already knew a great deal," she said, "about the way many black men in that position often talked to black women who had a little power, which was to show the women that they really had none. Robinson was totally unlike that. He made no gestures to say, 'I'm more important than you; you know, you have to accommodate me because I am a man; aren't you really a secretary?' He played none of the usual gender games. He respected me, felt comfortable with me. In hindsight, he was one of the few black men I had business dealings with in those days with whom I didn't have to watch myself all the time."

Later that afternoon, buoyed by their meeting, Morrison took Robinson in to meet her superiors, all white men, and make a pitch for the book. "By now I was very enthusiastic, I was ready to edit the book myself." At first it was pleasant, Robinson sitting there among the men, trading stories about baseball. "I felt at a disadvantage," Morrison said, "because I didn't know baseball; but Robinson seemed such a fascinating person. He said that he wanted his book to be about more than baseball. He wanted it to be about the larger picture, about society and the times he had lived through. I knew what he meant, but I could also feel the interest ebbing from the room. The white men became cool, indifferent. They wanted something more exotic, something more voluptuous than he was prepared to offer. When he left, they complained that the book was going to be too political, too much social studies, it wouldn't sell. They turned us down."

To have his autobiography turned down by Random House was a rude slap—not least of all because in 1960 the company had eagerly published Carl Rowan's biography of Jack, *Wait Till Next Year.* Nevertheless, the new book was soon placed with another publisher, Putnam, and Jack began work on it with Duckett.

With the New Year, 1970, Robinson had one unequivocal victory to celebrate. With its fifth anniversary in January, Freedom National Bank, where he was still chairman of the board, was firmly established as the most successful black-controlled bank in the United States. But at Sea Host, business was bad. On January 20, appearing in Washington, D.C., before the Senate Small Business Committee's Subcommittee on Urban and Rural Development, which was investigating the franchising industry, Jack defended franchising as a partial solution to black economic problems. He blamed the Nixon administration for many of those problems. "The very poor relations between black America and the present Administration are causing a serious rift in this country," he insisted. The Nixon efforts seemed to be aimed mainly at creating a few black millionaires, not helping the mass of blacks. Late in 1969, after United States Secretary of Commerce Maurice Stans met with black business leaders, including Robinson and Bill Hudgins, at Freedom National Bank, Jack praised Stans's efforts but also criticized his call for patience. "I don't think anyone can ask us for patience," he declared. "Black people have shown a tremendous amount of patience."

He then made a bold move of his own, one that reflected both his continuing search for a business enterprise he could pass on to his family and his longtime belief in the premier role of housing as an issue in the black world. (Told once by a friend that schooling was the top need for any young black, Jack strongly disagreed: "Housing is the first thing. Unless he's got a home he wants to come back to, it doesn't matter what kind of school he goes to.") After much discussion, Jack reached an agreement with three young but highly successful real estate men, Arthur Sutton, Mickey Weissman, and Richard Cohen, who put up $50,000 to launch the project, to form the Jackie Robinson Construction Corporation. Although all his partners were white, Jack's aim was both profit for the principals and a long-term benefit to the black community through the construction of low- and middle-income housing (an emphasis new to Jack's partners). Robinson's hope, Sutton said, "was that it would be a truly interracial company dedicated to training contractors who had never worked on big projects." In addition, "we had to keep

the payroll money in the community we were working in." "There is enough profit," Jack himself
insisted, "so that we can share it with the community
we are building in." The construction company
would support the Robinson family for many years
after Jack died.

Soon, he had settled into what became his main
business office: the headquarters of the company at
560 Sylvan Avenue in Englewood Cliffs, New Jersey,
across the George Washington Bridge from Manhattan. There, he had an able assistant, Merlyn White; a
popular Harlem man-about-town, Kiah Sayles,
served as his boon companion and gofer. A letter on
his new company stationery to his good friend and
golfing partner Andre Baruch, now living in Beverly
Hills, California, echoed Jack's optimism: "As you
can see we are in another business and it's very exciting. For really the first time we have a potential that
is great. . . . As things have not worked out in other
ventures I am trying to hold down my enthusiasm.
However, with each passing day things look better."

In setting up the company and then helping it to
develop, Jack depended a great deal on the efforts of
a young lawyer who quickly became a close advisor
and friend. He was Martin Edelman, educated at
Princeton and Columbia Law School, who met
Robinson not long after joining the law firm of Battle, Fowler, the counsel for Freedom National Bank.
Sent uptown to a bank meeting for the first time, he
had met Robinson. "It was January or February," he
recalled, "and the meeting was over. It was six-thirty,
cold and dark. I went downstairs and was standing in

front of the bank, on 125th Street, trying to decide whether to take a cab or the subway, when this enormous hand touched my shoulder from behind, and Jack said, 'I bet you would like a ride.' We talked all the way downtown. Because of bank business, we saw a fair amount of one another, and after meetings he would drive me home to Rye, on the way to Stamford. I wasn't looking for a mentor; but I suppose I found one. We sort of 'clicked.' When the chance came for him to incorporate and go into construction, he asked me to be his lawyer. I agreed at once."

Respecting Robinson, Edelman began to make a habit of calling him almost every weeknight around ten o'clock to go over the business of the day. He found Robinson not only grateful but also a spirited partner in their exchanges. "Both with the bank and with the corporation," according to Edelman, "some people clearly imagined that Jack was a figurehead, that he was there for celebrity value only. It was not true at all. He had a very searching and determined intellect, a fine instinct for sensing that something was wrong, even if he couldn't put his finger on it. He brought to his business, day in, day out, an incredible sense of determination, a sense of morality, and a value system that people he did business with felt was very special."

Gradually, Edelman's role expanded within Jack's business affairs; the vetting of proposals once reserved for Martin Stone now passed to him. "It's very convenient for people to say that Jack was naive and that he wasn't that smart," Edelman said.

"Jack was plenty smart; there can be no issue here. You could explain something to Jack and he remembered it, and it became a part of his analytical framework. He was not one to command the absolute small details, but he mastered the implications, he had an understanding of the financial impact, and he moved on." If Jack was prone to any mistake, Edelman ventured, "it was in trusting people he happened to like. . . ."

As THE JACKIE ROBINSON Construction Corporation slowly established itself in the spring of 1970, Jack and Rachel were conscious of a mending in their lives, at least in some respects, after the horrors of 1968 in particular.

At Mount Hermon, David was doing very well; a recruiter from Stanford University had given him a top rating as a prospect, and he was admitted there for the fall. Sharon was happy again. On Christmas Eve, she had remarried; Jack liked and respected her new husband, Joe Mitchell, a former SNCC member who was eleven years older than Sharon. They had met at Howard University in Washington, D.C., where she was now studying to become a nurse and he was studying to become a doctor.

At Christmas, too, Jackie had come home from Daytop, where his record had been inconsistent at best. Back in his old environment in Stamford he quickly backslid, according to his own reckoning. But after a while he headed back voluntarily to the discipline of Daytop. "It makes us happy," Jack wrote his friends the Wallersteins, "for it indicates he really understands his problem."

Certainly Jack himself had come a long way toward understanding Jackie's problems, and the menace of drug addiction in general. Earlier in the year, Robinson had spoken publicly about his experience as the father of an addict to a meeting called by the group Ministers Against Narcotics at the Holiday Inn at La Guardia Airport, attended by Governor Rockefeller and other high-ranking officials. He said that his decision to "stick by my son" had been "tremendously rewarding." That month, on a Harlem street corner, he also addressed some two hundred people at an antidrug block party on the subject of the epidemic sweeping the city. "I'm here because I'm concerned about it," he said. "I hope most of you will be concerned enough to go home and do something about the evil effects of this problem."

And in a letter to Jackie, he had expressed both his love and his determination to balance love with sternness and vigilance. "I know how difficult it is for you and realize as best I can what you are going through," Jack wrote his son.

> I hope also you realize what we are going through. We have been so proud of what appeared great progress and you must know the disappointment we felt when you didn't have the strength to resist the damaging urge you felt. I am happy you went back when you did for we

didn't know what to do but felt you would not be helping your future by staying away. Daytop seems to be your answer and if you have any chance for a decent future it will happen only if you understand yourself and become determined to succeed. Mother, Sharon, David, Grandmother and I are with you. We know how it is but pray you have learned your lesson. . . . We feel you will make it and we'll be a family again. It seems much depends on you. We're with you and while we are not completely satisfied we are confident.

The turning point, in many respects, came in May of that year, 1970, after Jack and Rachel decided to host a picnic on the grounds of their home for about fifty members of Daytop as a way of thanking them for what they were doing for Jackie. The event, meticulously planned by the Daytop members themselves, led enthusiastically by Jackie, was a great success. In beautiful, warm spring weather, Jackie's friends enjoyed an afternoon of fun and food. When it was time to leave on their bus, they lined up to thank Jack and Rachel for having them. At the end of the line, proud and happy, was Jackie himself. In 1964, when his parents had seen him off at the train station as he left for the Army, Jackie had embraced Rachel emotionally but had stopped his father when Jack tried to hug him. Now, at the end of the picnic for his Daytop friends, he embraced Rachel again but this time included his father. "I stuck out my hand to shake his hand," Jack wrote, "remembering the day of his departure for the service. He brushed my hand aside, pulled me to him, and embraced me in a tight hug. That single moment paid for every bit of sacrifice, every bit of anguish, I had ever undergone. I had my son back."

Increasingly Jackie became attentive not only to his family on Cascade Road but also to his young daughter, Sonya Pankey, for whom he had developed a strong affection. Jack himself could see the difference. Jackie, he told the Wallersteins that summer, seemed finally to be "on the right track. He understands and communicates a great deal more but the most important thing is his concern for others. I think he has learned a valuable lesson and we now await his leaving Daytop to see what happens once he drops his crutch. While we are not positive we are confident."

Early in June came one of the most satisfying moments of Robinson's life, when he delivered the commencement address at Mount Hermon before David's graduating class. After a brief stay at home, and before leaving for Stanford in the fall, David was off to Springfield, Massachusetts, for a summer of social work. There, as his father wrote proudly, he was living frugally with a Puerto Rican family who spoke little English, and "eating rice and beans for every meal."

IN HARLEM THAT SUMMER, the old order changed. On June 23, 1970, Adam Clayton Powell Jr. was defeated in the Democratic Party primary by Charles

Rangel, who would go on to win Powell's seat in Congress. Robinson had joined a broad group of black and white leaders backing Rangel, but his role was not small. Percy Sutton, then Manhattan borough president and young Rangel's main champion, later praised Robinson both for himself and as a conduit to Rockefeller. "When you see Charlie Rangel today as a congressman," he said, "you have to appreciate that Rockefeller, a Republican, gave me the first money to put behind Rangel. And it was Jackie who made that possible; it was through him we were able to get Connecticut people with money to support us, and a lot of them were Republican. Jackie also got the Republican Party to endorse Rangel. And there were other things Jackie did for us over the years, right to the end of his life."

But all the news was not good that summer. In July, the ax fell at Sea Host. Jack was at a Holiday Inn hotel in Coral Gables, Miami, when he received a letter dated July 17, air mail and special delivery, from the acting president of Sea Host, Samuel N. Rubin. Because of serious problems in cash flow, marketing, and general operations, Sea Host was now on an emergency footing. As of that day, July 17, Robinson was fired. The letter, almost certainly the same as sent to virtually all the employees, offered vaguely to help with finding another job but made no mention of compensation. Later that year, on November 19, Sea Host filed for bankruptcy in federal court in New York.

Jack now had no regular source of income other than a small salary from his construction company.

But even with his worsening illness, he and Rachel had no overriding sense of financial danger. Rachel and Jack had been careful in their planning. For many years, at the insistence of an accountant, Jack's life had been heavily insured, as was the mortgage on the house in Stamford. In Manhattan, they owned two apartments that would yield a very nice profit when sold. But Jack also had high hopes for his construction company. "We are still struggling with business," he wrote the Wallersteins, "but like the civil rights struggle are seeing the light at the tunnel's end. We have a chance to develop something good but we have seen other chances fade so we will continue to do our job wherever we are and grab the opportunity to make it good if the chances come."

Still, with Jack's failing health, Rachel could see the dark closing in. In the fall of 1969, she had resigned her position with the mental health program in New Haven and taken a one-year, unpaid leave of absence from Yale. "I told everyone that the idea was for me to study," she said, "to read the mountain of books I had wanted to read but could never find time for. I really did spend a fair amount of time in the library. But I was also more available for Jack and Jackie." Happy to see Jackie and Sharon turn around their misfortunes and David stay on course, she was nevertheless in growing pain herself because of Jack's physical deterioration. By this point, she understood that he was dying. Examining Jack's body, Arthur Logan could not discover a pulse in his legs. In two or three years, he told Rachel, Jack would be dead. "I was very angry at Arthur," she recalled. "I did not want to hear such news. Jack definitely did not want to hear such news. He would not talk about death. Denial was his greatest prop, and he denied that he was dying. But after a while I knew I had to do something, so I went into therapy in order to learn how to cope with this terrible fact."

As her sabbatical year drew to a close in the summer of 1970, she seemed to Jack "like a caged lion with too much spare time."

In August, Jack felt well enough to join Jesse Jackson, the national director of Operation Breadbasket, and Fannie Lou Hamer, vice-chairman of the Mississippi Freedom Party, in helping to judge a Miss Black America beauty pageant at Madison Square Garden. He and three other members of Jackie Robinson Associates also met with Rockefeller family aides to seek a loan of $150,000 toward the purchase of a black-owned office building in Washington, D.C. But a few days later Robinson was back in the hospital. Chronically tired, with his feet aching and pain throbbing through his legs, he had visited his doctor. Tests revealed Jack's diabetes in a new, frightening stage; his weight had dropped notably, but his blood pressure and blood sugar were high. He had also suffered a mild stroke. In fact, that month he suffered two mild strokes, the first on his right side, the second on his left. Deceptive in that their effects were hard to see, the strokes left Robinson's physical strength and his speech virtually unaffected but caused an unnerving loss of balance as well as a substantial loss of sensation on his left side. Most distressingly, they also ruptured blood vessels in his eyes, with episodes of hemorrhaging that seriously damaged the retina and diminished his sight. Jack seemed on his way to blindness.

In September, on what she called one of the most harrowing days of her life, Rachel and Jack watched as their last child, David, left home. Behind the steering wheel of a little yellow English sports car, a 1969 MG Midget, David headed down the driveway, turned left on Cascade Road, and set out alone for Palo Alto, California, to begin his freshman year at Stanford. Now, after fifteen years, the big house on Cascade Road was a lonesome place. "It was so traumatic for me, to see David go," Rachel recalled, "that I took off for Cape Cod and spent three days looking out at the water as I tried to come to terms with what was happening in our lives."

She returned in time to join Jack on September 14, when he received an honorary doctorate of civil law from Pace University at the dedication of its Civic Center Campus in lower Manhattan, and Terence Cardinal Cooke, the Roman Catholic prelate, was also honored. A week or so later, Governor Rockefeller announced that Robinson would be a deputy manager in his campaign for reelection that fall, when his main opponent was Arthur Goldberg, a former United States Supreme Court justice and ambassador to the United Nations. But Jack's thoughts were mainly about his failing health. In October, after a persistent wheezing and coughing at night and an oppressive shortness of breath, he went to Minneapolis for a consultation at the celebrated Mayo Clinic. There, mysteriously, despite evidence of severe hypertension and congestive heart failure, with a blood pressure reading of 185 over 115, he was told, apparently, that nothing was wrong with him. Back home, his nighttime coughing and wheezing became worse, as did shortness of breath and an increasingly painful pressure in the middle of his chest. Twice his shortness of breath had become almost unendurable. In these moments of stress, as he told his doctor, his main relief was to lean forward, or to kneel down by his bed and rest his arms helplessly on the side of the bed.

Still, an ailing Jackie Robinson had more energy than most other people. On a sunny Saturday afternoon in October, he and Rachel welcomed about three hundred guests to the grounds of their home for a cocktail party in support of Rockefeller in his bid for reelection. With Rachel striking in a tiger-striped gown matched by a flowing cape of the same material, lately purchased at an African boutique in Harlem, Jack made a bright speech to his guests and urged them to build a better, more purposeful Republican Party.

Above all, he took comfort in his children's growing sense of fulfillment. Earlier in the fall, Jack and Rachel had visited David in California. The antiwar mood of student life across the nation had reached Stanford, where David greeted his parents dressed in a preppy blue blazer, white shirt, and white cotton trousers—but with the American flag sewn across his bottom. In Washington, D.C., Sharon was happy with her husband, Joe Mitchell, and her studies at Howard. Most profoundly gratifying of all, on November 4, in an informal but unforgettable ceremony in Seymour, Connecticut, attended by the entire family, Jackie graduated from Daytop. In the eyes of even the hard-boiled former addicts who ran the facility, he was now clean. Indeed, he showed promise of becoming an outstanding leader within the organization. Earlier that year, he had testified frankly and in detail about his drug experience before Senator Thomas Dodd of Connecticut's Subcommittee to Investigate Juvenile Delinquency in the United States.

To Jack, as he faced the growing ravages of his heart and lung disease and the specter of his increasing blindness, this was a source of sublime comfort as he looked ahead to the few years left to him.

Heading Home

1971–1972

I always thought I'd be the first to go.
—Jackie Robinson (1972)

FEBRUARY 10, 1971, was a special day for the Robinsons, their twenty-fifth wedding anniversary. Jack surprised Rachel, who loved fine cars, with something special. She had given her 1969 MG Midget to David to drive to Palo Alto. Now Jack gave her, in its place, a sporty convertible two-seater Mercedes Benz 280SL. It was only a token of the gratitude he felt for her love and support of him over the years.

A few days later, he was a patient in the French Hospital again. Feeling poorly, he had gone on February 12 to the New York offices of Dr. Eric Cassell, whose mentor before and after medical school had been Jack's physician of many years, Dr. Cyril Solomon. Examining Robinson, Dr. Cassell found him in alarming condition and ordered him into the hospital for a series of tests. On February 17, also at Cassell's insistence, Jack underwent a cardiac catheterization at St. Vincent's Hospital. A catheter was passed through the groin up into the heart; dye was then pumped into the heart to measure its performance. Dr. Cassell found clear evidence of advanced heart disease caused both by hypertension and by severe blocking of the arteries; he also diagnosed chronic, obstructive lung disease. Cassell put Robinson on strong medication for his heart and his lung troubles and increased his daily dosage of insulin. Jack was also given diuretics that dropped his weight by several pounds.

Once, working for Dr. Solomon, Cassell had gone to the New Yorker Hotel to draw blood from Babe Ruth, who was living there. Although Ruth's body was wasted, as he slowly succumbed to lung cancer, he had seemed immense to Cassell. Robinson was like Ruth in that way. "Meeting Robinson," Cassell recalled, "I thought, 'This is a big man.' My response had nothing to do with how much he weighed; it was that he and Babe Ruth were men who inhabited their own authority, who inhabited themselves to the fullest. They knew who they were and what they were about." Nevertheless, Robinson was also "modest. He was relaxed, he didn't make a big fuss about things. He certainly did not advertise his celebrity. He was who he was." He would remain Cassell's patient for the rest of his life.

After six days at the French Hospital, Jack was discharged. Sending him off, Dr. Cassell pressed on him the need to stick to his medications, to watch his diet, and to walk at least a half-mile every day, to try to force blood into his deteriorating legs. Back home, Robinson tried to keep up his exercising but found the going tough. Physical discomfort was one reason; another reason was psychological. "Every time I go to do what you want me to do," he told Dr. Cassell, "all I'm aware of is what I cannot do." Walking was now painful. Then Jack tried riding a stationary bicycle and found that he liked it better. The circulation in his legs seemed to improve. Over the coming year, his blood pressure would drop from 180 over 110 to 125 over 80, or normal.

Jack's hospitalization early in 1971 and his growing weakness did not stop him altogether. In January, he had gone to Chicago to speak on behalf of a young political leader in whom he was becoming more and more confident, as he looked for bold, far-sighted new black leaders. His man in Chicago was the Reverend Jesse Jackson, a former disciple of Dr. King in SCLC and now with a firm political base in Chicago through his grass-roots organization Operation Breadbasket, on which Jack had been serving as a board member for some time. Out of this venture, following Jackson's resignation from SCLC (when he could no longer work amicably with Dr. King's successor at SCLC, Ralph Abernathy), would come, in December 1971, Jackson's PUSH—People United to Save Humanity—which he would announce with Jack standing beside him in New York City. "I have hopes for Jesse Jackson," Robinson would write. "I think he offers the most viable leadership for blacks and oppressed minorities in America and also for the salvation of our national decency. I think Jesse's leadership is potentially one of majestic proportions. He is totally dedicated and if we are to arise out of this deepening pit between us as a people, it will be by supporting the kind of leadership Jesse Jackson offers."

Also in January, Jack had joined other black bankers vigorously protesting the charge by Andrew Brimmer, a black economist on the Federal Reserve Bank, that black banks, because of their high costs and economic isolation, could contribute little to black economic empowerment. Even so, Robinson was well aware that Freedom National Bank might be in some trouble. Over the preceding three years, he had heard whispers about alleged irregularities in some of its loans, leading to bad debts that now threatened its stability. Once, a respected Wall Street figure had warned Jack, without much explanation: "If you want to save Freedom National Bank, the only way you are going to be able to do it is to take it over and clean house. You are in serious trouble." Later, Jack had begun to see that officers of the Comptroller of the Currency appeared to be holding Freedom National to a lower standard of efficiency, because it was a black bank, than most other banks. For Jack, this kind of paternalism, with its tacit presumption of black inferiority, was galling. Late in February 1971, as he himself wrote, "I began really digging in." He also consulted friends who understood the world of finance, such as J. Bruce Llewellyn. "Jack was a man of deep integrity," Llewellyn said. "As soon as he knew that something was wrong, he took action to stop it."

Relying on inside information from a few employees willing to jeopardize their jobs, including the head of the mortgage department, Madeline Walburg, he began his investigation of Freedom National. The result was an extended period of arduous, sometimes contentious work as he found himself pitted against William Hudgins, the president of Freedom National, whose skill and energy had built the institution over the past six years. On May 7, after a particularly acrimonious meeting of the mortgage loan committee, Robinson wrote to Walburg to say that he had been "particularly impressed with the way you stood firm in your conviction." Slowly Jack began to convince other members of the board about the gravity of the situation. But he was doing so at some cost to his own health, as he wrote. "I found myself losing sleep nights and involved in a great deal of activity at the bank trying to make certain that I had a strong basis for making a move. . . . The more involved I got with the bank problems, the sicker I became." Walburg, too, became increasingly nervous and upset; when she suddenly died of a brain hemorrhage in the middle of the bank dispute, Jack took the news hard.

The relationship between him and Hudgins reached a point of no return. Drawing the support of most of the rest of the board, Robinson finally won out; in August, Hudgins announced his resignation as president of Freedom National Bank. With Jack's consent, and in the interest of stability, Hudgins agreed to stay on as vice-chairman of the board. The change went smoothly. "At 64, I need more time to spend with my family," Hudgins told the press. "His contacts and knowledge will mean much to the future capital growth of Freedom," Robinson added. A new president, approved by Jack, arrived: Robert Boyd, a former professional football player with the Los Angeles Rams and an experienced businessman.

As the struggle at the bank grew more intense and his health suffered, Jack was heartened that spring mainly by his son Jackie's continuing progress. Steadily, Jackie was emerging as a respected, quietly eloquent leader in the Daytop community; he had become assistant regional director of Daytop. In March, Jack and Jackie appeared together on a program about drug abuse sponsored by the New York State Narcotics Addiction Control Commission for the Scotia-Glenville school district. Father and son worked so well together, with Jackie speaking of the personal trauma of drug abuse, and Jack telling of the importance of family support based on love and discipline, that they began to plan other joint engagements. Jack and Rachel also decided to make Daytop the beneficiary of the next "Afternoon of Jazz" on the grounds of their home, on the last Sunday in June.

This decision worked to inspire Jackie further; he took on the main task of organizing the concert even as he kept up his activity at Daytop, including his growing schedule of speeches against drug abuse. On June 13, for example, he spoke about the menace of narcotics to the congregation at the Nazarene Congregational Church in Brooklyn, where Lacy Covington was assistant pastor. As the concert drew near, Jackie found himself working long hours as he lined up not only the musicians but also the various support staff that could make the "Afternoon of Jazz" a financial bonanza for Daytop. He now had the help of David, who was home for the summer after his freshman year at Stanford, having driven back across the country in his MG.

Early in the morning of Thursday, June 17, with Rachel away at a conference on group relations at Holyoke in Massachusetts, Jack was asleep at home after a dinner out with Sharon and David when the sound of the doorbell ringing awakened him. By the time he reached the door Sharon was already there. In the doorway was a policeman, who gently broke the news that Jackie was dead. Driving home in David's car on the Merritt Parkway from New York City around two o'clock in the morning, he had lost control of the MG. Spinning wildly, the little car had crashed into an abutment, demolished various guard-rail posts, then come to rest. Jackie was pinned in the wreckage, his neck broken.

By this time David had roused himself and also come to the door. Shocked himself, he could also see the terrible effect of the news on his father. "I had gone weak all over," Jack would write. "I knew that I couldn't go to that hospital or morgue or whatever and look at my dead son's body."

While David, thrust suddenly by the crisis into authority, went to the morgue to identify his brother's body, Jack and Sharon drove to Holyoke to break the news to Rachel. They found her in her hotel room, about to go to breakfast. Hearing the news, she collapsed into almost violent crying. Marian Logan was at the Robinsons' home when Jack, Sharon, and

Rachel returned. "You could hear Rachel screaming, screeching like a banshee," she said; "all the way up to the house, she screamed, screamed, screamed. When she got out of the car, she began running around the house, up and down the fields and everything." Watching her, Jack himself broke down into tears.

On June 21, more than fifteen hundred persons attended Jackie's funeral at Antioch Baptist Church on Greene Avenue in Brooklyn. The pastor and long-time family friend, George Lawrence, conducted the service, accompanied by Lacy Covington; a choir from Daytop sang hymns. David again stood strong; for many people, the most memorable moment would be his reading of a long, imagistic prose narrative he had written that seemed to capture his brother's lifelong wrestling with demons, and the ecstatic freedom Jackie had finally achieved in death. Draped with flowers, the bronze casket was taken to Cypress Hills Cemetery for burial.

Six days after Jackie's funeral, the "Afternoon of Jazz" planned for the benefit of Daytop took place as scheduled. Roberta Flack sang, and Dave Brubeck, Billy Taylor, Herbie Mann, and Clark Terry were among the other musical stars in a concert haunted by sadness but lifted by the fine music and the inspirational words of Jesse Jackson, Bayard Rustin, and Marian Logan, who read a poem she had written for Jackie's funeral. Then Jack himself spoke, in "a moving and dramatic talk that reached the hearts of all there," according to one reporter. Quietly Robinson explained that the concert had gone on despite his son's death because Jackie had worked so hard to make it a success. Aided by many extra donations, the event raised more than $40,000 for Daytop.

Not long afterward, having shown himself to be possessed of an almost uncanny strength and calm, but hurting from the tragedy of his brother's death, David left the United States to travel for the rest of the summer. First he went to the Netherlands and to Scotland, to Loch Ness, then to Africa, where his traveling ended in Tanzania on the Indian Ocean. He made up his mind not to return to Stanford University.

When David came back later that year to the United States, he stayed near home so as to be close to his father in particular. Soon he began to dream about Africa. After a while, he said, "four or five nights every week, I would dream about Tanzania. I would dream about leaving the United States and going to live there."

Jackie's death deeply affected Jack, but it devastated Rachel. For weeks she was inconsolable, and virtually silent; laughter and lightness went out of their lives. Jack had a strong element of religious faith and fatalism to fall back on; Rachel's sense of God was different from Jack's, and provided little comfort now as she struggled with the banality of Jackie's death, the pain of having had her son sink so low, rise again, then be snatched away just when he was whole and healed, ready at last for life. In turn, her withdrawal into grief had a chilling effect on Jack. In 1941, the death of her father, and the depth of Rachel's pain in response to it, had helped to bring them together as young people moving forward with their lives. Thirty years later, they could see little or nothing to be salvaged from this death, no redemptive lesson that needed to be learned, no sense of a bright, mysterious, but life-affirming future that would one day give meaning to the terrible present loss. She blamed no one for Jackie's death—not Jack, not herself—but her sense of having failed Jackie, of having failed to rescue him, was overwhelming and profoundly painful. Increasingly, she withdrew into herself at home.

A degree of serious tension entered their lives for the first time since they were married. As Jack's illness became more oppressive, he began to return home earlier than ever. On a strict diet, he craved an early evening meal, but refused to touch any food unless Rachel was there to share it. As a gesture of love, this restraint was touching; but it also amounted to blackmail, and Rachel saw it as such. "What made it worse," she recalled, "was that I discovered that my mother was also moving against me. She was working with Jack to make me feel guilty for being away at work. One way was to prepare the meal well ahead of time. I would come in the house and smell the cooked food and become angry. Even the vegetables she had already done and were now soggy. And Jack would be waiting, hungry and fuming, and I would walk in as the villain of the piece."

One evening after supper, when Sharon happened to be back visiting, she was walking from her old bedroom to the kitchen when she heard something that made her freeze. "As I neared the entrance to the living room I stopped, startled by the sound of muffled sobs," she wrote. "I stood still listening for a minute trying to identify the source. I looked into the living room. There was a shadowy figure silhouetted by the light coming into the room from a full moon. As my eyes adjusted, I realized that the slumped body sitting on the couch was my father. Dad was sitting alone in the darkness crying." Sharon, unaccustomed to seeing her father break down, was unsure what to do. But then she decided to speak to him. "Dad, why are you crying?" she asked. In a trembling voice, her father answered: "First Mr. Rickey and my mother, then your brother. Now I wonder if I am losing my wife."

Still afraid she might be intruding, Sharon left him and tapped on her parents' bedroom door. Rachel heard from Sharon what was happening, put down the book she was reading, and hurried to Jack. Slowly, over the coming weeks and months, they began to get over the raw pain of Jackie's death.

As Jack waited for his construction company to gain momentum, he kept himself busy with other, smaller entrepreneurial ventures that brought in little money but also scarcely taxed his remarkably abundant energy. Two ventures were in the West Indies. Once he sank some money into a Chicken Shack fast-food franchise restaurant in St. Martin, in partnership with an old friend, the singer Jimmy Randolph. With a partner, he also visited Port of Spain, Trinidad, seeking a deal that would permit the production of gold and silver commemorative coins on behalf of an Italian company. In yet another move, after talking Rachel out of $12,000 she had squirreled away, he invested in a cosmetics-distribution scheme in partnership with Marian Logan. But while the products piled up at her home, she and Jack neglected to develop a sales force to distribute them. At one point, Jack also joined two associates in bidding for a license to operate a radio station in Stamford.

A former associate, Peter Bienstock, remembers a business venture involving Robinson as chairman of the board of a company that would produce radio spots about black culture for sale to radio stations. "Jackie indeed opened doors in the financial community," Bienstock said. "Everyone leapt at the idea once they heard Jackie was involved. This was not mere greed; these people were like little boys, eager to meet Jackie, to be in a room with him and to talk with him." Unfortunately, baseball dominated the meetings, "and we took forever to get to the business at hand." Also, Jackie, while charming, "wanted to organize Wall Streeters to fund [civil rights] work, and he would go on at great length about this, to the point that eyes glazed over and people started to look at their watches."

He was not always so serious. Marian Logan portrayed his part in their cosmetics venture as "almost cavalier," as a writer put it. "Jackie put me in charge," she said, "set me up, and then he'd go off laughing, you know. I got mad one time; I said, 'Jack, you know I've lost eight thousand dollars in this venture so far,' and he would just laugh." He was very serious, however, about his construction company. Thus he was very pleased when his group at last broke ground on its first major effort: Whitney Young Manor, a development of 197 units in Yonkers, New York, named after the former National Urban League director, who had drowned tragically on a visit to Nigeria.

Despite this success, and the sound underpinnings of his personal finances, Robinson remained interested in finding a salaried job not unlike his previous position with Rockefeller; but he could not bring himself to ask the governor for another job. At one point, Rachel made the move herself. "I asked Arthur Logan to speak to Nelson Rockefeller about a job for Jack," she recalled. "But Arthur had his own problems by that time and I think he spent the time talking with Rockefeller about something for himself. In any case, Rockefeller did nothing for Jack. I was deeply disappointed. I thought he owed Jack something. I think Jack felt the same way, too, although he wouldn't admit it." But Evelyn Cunningham, a Rockefeller stalwart, believed that the governor never understood Jack's need. "He would not have wanted to insult Jackie by offering him a charity job," she believed. "He assumed Jack was well taken care of." In fact, when a gubernatorial appointment finally came for Jack, it almost mocked his need. On May 27, following confirmation by the state senate, Jack was sworn in to a two-year term on the New York State Athletic Commission, which oversaw boxing and wrestling. But the job carried no salary. Members received $100.33 for each working day.

However, on September 13, 1971, Jack was probably happy not to be working still as a special assistant to Rockefeller. Protesting conditions at Attica State Prison in upstate New York, inmates there had engineered a mass uprising and taken hostage twenty-eight correction officers. Tense negotiations followed, with a demand by the prisoners that Rockefeller meet with them to discuss their grievances. Instead, heeding advice not to give in, he ordered an assault that claimed the lives of thirty-two prisoners (twenty-three blacks and nine whites) and ten prison guards. Jack's longtime friend Wyatt Tee Walker, special assistant to the governor for urban affairs (in addition to being pastor of Canaan Baptist Church in Harlem), had counseled patience but had also become caught up in the emotional and political complexities of the situation. "If I had been an inmate at Attica," Walker declared after the killings, "I would have joined the liberation front because there was no other alternative." Governor Rockefeller "had scarred his illustrious political career" forever.

To Rachel, the massacre at Attica was the last straw in her relationship with Rockefeller. Jack's response is not clear; he no longer had a public forum from which to express his opinions. He sent a telegram at once to Rockefeller, to which an aide responded: "To use your own words, no one has had a finer friend than you." Robinson was in touch with Rockefeller again later in the year, when a grand jury began a probe of the affair. In December, Jack wrote to suggest a meeting between the governor and Jesse Jackson as a way perhaps of clarifying the situation. On the whole, he appeared to remain loyal to the governor despite his severe misgivings about the horrifying events at Attica.

Attica was only the most gory single manifestation of the violence that seemed endemic to race relations and life in general in big American cities in 1971. In Harlem, Robinson found himself in at least two dangerous scrapes. Once, he stepped boldly in to rescue an elderly white man, an office worker on 125th Street, from a group of menacing young blacks. On another occasion, in the tense aftermath of the killing of two police officers in Harlem, a white plainclothesman roughly barred Jack's way as he tried to enter the lobby of the Apollo Theater, then grabbed him and drew a gun when Robinson protested being manhandled. The policeman backed off only after excited bystanders told him who Robinson was. "Thinking over that incident," Jack wrote, "it horrifies me to realize what might have happened if I had been just another citizen of Harlem."

For about two or three months, Jack was happy to have as a sort of chauffeur and traveling companion his son David, who drove him around to various engagements in New York and New England and as far south as Washington, D.C. For Jack, grieving still for Jackie, this was an important passage in his life, as it was for David, who was aware of his father's worsening illness. "I saw more of my father than I had seen in a long time," David said, "and I got a chance to hear people speak about him, introduce him before his speeches, and so on. It was moving to see how people looked up to him, and how much he meant to them. But the happiest time, I think, was when we'd go upstairs at the Apollo in Harlem and shoot the breeze with Dad's friends. That's when my father was most relaxed, not in the public glare, not having to put on any kind of image. It was good to see him so happy and relaxed."

After David was hired away by a New York film company, Jack resumed his own driving. Then, after he almost caused a terrible accident, because his peripheral vision was just about gone, Rachel hired a driver for him. The man, thoroughly resented by Robinson, took him every day to 560 Sylvan Avenue in Englewood Cliffs, New Jersey, the headquarters of the Jackie Robinson Construction Corporation. By this point Jack had given up golf; his last public pleasure was the race track, where he loved to bet on the horses. But he was not about to sit at home in silence. In October, when A. Philip Randolph and Governor Rockefeller were honored at a gala benefit for a New York hospital, Jack was in attendance. Later that month, he addressed a major gathering of the restaurant industry on the matter of civil rights. He continued to plan an event of great personal importance to him: a salute to Dr. Ralph Bunche, whose health was now failing rapidly, and from the same ailments that dogged Robinson: a deadly combination of heart trouble, diabetes, and hypertension. On December 6, Jack himself was honored at Mama Leone's Restaurant at the twenty-fifth anniversary celebration of *Sport* magazine. Also honored were some of the greatest figures in sports, including Arnold Palmer, Bill Russell, Rocky Marciano, Gale Sayers, Rod Laver, Johnny Unitas, and Gordie Howe; but among them all Robinson was selected as "The Man of 25 Years in Sports," the single most important athlete of the previous quarter-century. The evening brought him close to tears several times, especially when towering Bill Russell of the Boston Celtics, recently appointed the first black coach in the NBA, showed his respect and affection for Jack with a warm embrace. When Jack rose to speak, his voice quavered, and he went unerringly once again to the memory of his mother, Mallie, and of Branch Rickey as he praised those people who had stood by him and helped to give his life its rich meaning. As for Rachel, "she has been a warm and understanding mother, and without a doubt, a wonderful wife. Her strength gave me strength, and I question how far I would have come without her. Everything I have done, has been because of her."

Shortly after the event, to Jack's sorrow, Ralph Bunche died, before Robinson's tribute could take place.

Christmas found Jack and Rachel, as well as Sharon and David, on a beach in Jamaica. That year, because of Jackie's death, they had not celebrated Thanksgiving. Rachel decided to gather the family for a vacation at Dragon's Bay on the north coast of the island. The warm weather lifted everyone's spirits, although Christmas itself was painful and sad. Impulsively, they decided to telephone Marian Logan and Zellee and invite them to come down and join the party. For Jack, this vacation marked two curious rites of passage. At the suggestion of Dr. Cassell, he had the first alcoholic drinks of his life; Jack chose a mixture of vodka and orange juice, which he swallowed in one gulp, like medicine. Also, he ventured into the sea for apparently the first time in his life. Jack, who had never learned to swim and had kept a nervous distance from the water on previous vacations, now started in, as if on a mission. "I grabbed Dad's hand," Sharon remembered. "Marian and Mom started jumping up and down cheering my father on. They acted like high school cheerleaders." David, navigating, led them out farther from shore. "We slowly descended deeper and deeper into the sea. When the water reached Dad's waist, he tugged at my hand. We had gone far enough."

A few days later, in New York, he underwent experimental laser surgery on his eyes, in an attempt to stop retinal bleeding by cauterizing broken blood vessels that had taken a severe toll on his sight. Vision in Robinson's right eye was just about gone; the left eye was also failing, although doctors hoped it would revive. His insulin dosage was increased. His legs were now in worse shape; walking was sometimes utterly painful. He could not hurry. But Jack refused to give in to self-pity, as Dr. Cassell had noted in his files after one visit: "The patient, as always, says he feels great."

Refusing to dwell on his own miseries, Jack fastened on those of the nation, which seemed to him early in 1972 to be in a critical state. Late in January, when he traveled to California to address the

National Restaurant Association, he spoke pes-
simistically about race relations. "We're definitely
on a collision course between the races," he insisted.
More and more whites know what must be done, "but
if we don't have it we could collide in a very short
time, which would be the greatest tragedy this country ever had." The year would see another presidential election but with an apparently foregone
conclusion. Curiously, Robinson seemed less hostile
to Nixon than in the past. "I'm not opposed to Mr.
Nixon," he declared. The President was only the prisoner of the odious deals and moral compromises
worked out at the 1968 Republican Convention,
which had brought him to power. The men about
him, however—especially Strom Thurmond, Attorney General John Mitchell, and Vice-President
Agnew—were more to be despised. "I just don't
think they are friends of the black community."

However, Robinson was present early in the year
for a remarkable event in Washington, D.C.—a sold-
out tribute to Robert Brown, a black special assistant
to Nixon, that turned into a spectacular public relations success for President Nixon when he showed
up unexpectedly and received a tumultuous standing
ovation from the many powerful blacks present,
including Robinson, the entertainer Sammy Davis
Jr., Senator Edward Brooke, Vernon Jordan, Floyd
McKissick, and James Farmer. And in the spring,
Jack was present at a highly organized "Kick-Off
Campaign" dinner put on by the Black Committee to
Re-Elect the President that raised more than
$150,000 for Nixon's campaign, according to one

report. Probably it was this event, to which David Robinson escorted his father, that so upset David—as it disturbed the many blacks who detested Nixon—that he became almost physically sick in his outrage.

Apart from a sally of this sort, Jack was no longer even a small force in national politics. He would attempt no intervention in either the Republican or the Democratic primaries. Hubert Humphrey had been reelected to the Senate in 1970 and was now challenging for the Democratic nomination; but Robinson was in no position, physically or politically, to help him. However, Jack's support of young Jesse Jackson continued. Through the winter he did what he could to assist Jackson's PUSH. On March 26, he and Rachel were prominent in a "Tribute to Black Heroes" organized as a fund-raiser at the 369th Armory in Harlem. Later, they were honored at PUSH headquarters in Chicago.

April 2 brought twin disasters. One was the death in California of Jack's cousin Ralph Wade, who had come out with him as a child from Georgia in 1920 in the intrepid band of migrants led by Mallie Robinson and Ralph's parents, Sam and Cora Wade, Mallie's sister. But that same day, in addition, the baseball world was stunned at the news that Gil Hodges, one of the Dodger immortals, had died of a heart attack in West Palm Beach, Florida. Hodges was only two days shy of his forty-eighth birthday. "It's shocking and saddening," Robinson told the press. "I feel a great deal for the family." At Hodges's funeral in New York, mouths dropped open at the sight of a frail

Jackie Robinson moving slowly to find a place among the mourners. Seated next to Pee Wee Reese, Jack could not recognize him. "Gil always was a calming presence," Jack told Roger Kahn softly. Then, "suddenly, tersely: 'I always thought I'd be the first to go.' "

On May 15, Robinson was in Daytona Beach, Florida, to deliver a commencement address at the graduation exercises at Bethune-Cookman College, when he also received an honorary doctorate. In 1946, the campus and its people had been perhaps his main solace as he and Rachel, newly married, struggled with his ordeal of breaking into white baseball. Five days later, he received another honorary degree, Doctor of Laws, at Sacred Heart University in Connecticut. And on May 24, at Flushing Meadow Park in Queens, in a touching ceremony that brought back searing memories of Jackie, Jack was honored as "Parent of the Year" by RARE, or Relatives Alerted to Rehabilitation through Education, a support group for drug addicts and their families connected to the New York Boulevard Youth Center in Jamaica, Queens. One year before, Robinson had spoken at the annual dinner-dance of RARE about Jackie's heroic conquering of his addiction; a few days later, Jackie was dead. Now Robinson accepted an award named after his son.

These awards all testified to the fact that many people understood that Robinson's life was coming to an end. He himself was still ready to do battle, if the cause was right; but he also appreciated the healing of wounds. Perhaps few were as important as his strife with the men who controlled baseball. In 1970, Jack had joined Hank Greenberg in testifying in federal court against baseball's reserve-clause system, which had been challenged by the black player Curt Flood. "Anything that is one-sided is wrong in America," Robinson offered. "The reserve clause is one-sided in favor of the owners and should be modified to give the player some control over his destiny." (Flood lost his case, but change eventually came.) Late in 1971, Jack had angered many observers when, resentful at the continuing bias against hiring a black manager, he had ridiculed the notion that Casey Stengel of the Mets, formerly of the Yankees, was a great manager. He closed one breach, with Buzzie Bavasi, after Bavasi came out strongly against admitting former Negro-league stars to the Baseball Hall of Fame in a separate, segregated area. "Your action justifies the way I thought about you before the 1957 misunderstanding," Jack wrote to Bavasi, who was now running the San Diego Padres.

But the one unhealed wound was with the Dodgers, where the presidency had passed from Walter O'Malley to his son, Peter, who was far more sympathetic to Robinson. The younger O'Malley reached out with an invitation to Jack to come to Dodger Stadium on June 4 for Old Timers Day. At first Robinson resisted, but an old teammate, at O'Malley's urging, convinced him to break his rule about not attending Old Timers Days. "If it hadn't been for the good feeling I had for Don Newcombe," Jack declared, "I doubt very much I'd have come to this one." On June 4, three numbers were retired:

those of Sandy Koufax, who had been elected to the Hall of Fame in January, the youngest person ever to be voted in; Roy Campanella, inducted in 1969; and Jackie Robinson—number 42. (Ironically, Casey Stengel was also honored at the game.)

In the end, Robinson was happy that he had come. "This is truly one of the greatest moments of my life," he told the large crowd, with genuine feeling. In a long talk with Peter O'Malley, Jack unburdened himself about various matters. Later, tired and stretched out on his bed in his downtown hotel, he spoke to a reporter about their conversation. "I told Peter I was distressed at the way baseball treats its black players after their playing days are through. I was very much impressed by Peter's attitude. I don't know what he can do about it, but first of all there has to be a sensitivity to it." Robinson saw the younger O'Malley and Mike Burke, the president of the New York Yankees, as representing a new, more enlightened breed of baseball leaders. As for his feud with the Dodgers: "The problem was never between Jackie Robinson and Walter O'Malley," Jack insisted. "It was between Walter O'Malley and Branch Rickey."

To Peter O'Malley, the circumstances of Jack's departure from the Dodgers and baseball (when Peter himself was only twenty-two) were hard to fathom. "It's not something I understand, and it wouldn't happen now," he said later, "to a star like that at the end of his career, for all that Jackie stood for and accomplished, and with his popularity. Why not go to him and say, 'Jackie, we really think your playing days are over. How about retiring as an active player, and maybe consider another job in the organization, or not?' But to trade him at the end of his career, it's unheard of today. I was very glad that he came to see his number retired, to be a part of a great day." As for Robinson as a manager: "He was so bright, quick, and natural to baseball, so good on strategy, I think he would have made a great manager."

Robinson's physical condition shocked many people, including the black writer A. S. "Doc" Young. "When he walked out on the field to be introduced to the wildly cheering crowd," Young wrote of Robinson, "he walked like a man of 80." Young related a story of someone tossing a baseball underhand to Robinson; the ball hit Jack in the head and knocked off his Dodger cap. "Oh, it was sad! So sad!" Also shocked at Jack's state was Ray Bartlett, his former teammate throughout virtually his entire youth in organized sports. At Jack's request, Bartlett had brought together between twenty-five and thirty minority contractors to hear Robinson speak about the possibilities of building low-rent housing. "He walked in," Bartlett recalled, "moving with difficulty and very slowly. I remembered the days when he was such a tremendous athlete. . . . I felt inside that he was forcing himself to keep going, he had too much determination to stop. I just felt bad, real bad. I can't even describe it."

The following month, on July 18, Jack was honored with a gala luncheon sponsored by the government of the U.S. Virgin Islands, ostensibly to recognize the ways in which Jack's breakthrough in baseball had paved the way for various Virgin Islands players to make their way in his footsteps. Roger Kahn was the master of ceremonies, and among the guests were familiar names from Jack's baseball past, including Clyde Sukeforth, Joe Black, Ralph Branca, and Sandy Amoros.

One of Jack's pleasures now was listening to Rachel read from the galleys of his autobiography with Alfred Duckett, *I Never Had It Made.* He himself could not read the pages. His right eye was blind; the left eye was dim and strained. Still he was upbeat: "I've gotten tremendous thrills," he wrote, out of the pages he had heard.

To all inquirers, Jack gave a most cheerful answer about the state of his health. "Health is a progressive thing," he told a writer for the Los Angeles *Times,* "but I've felt a lot better in the last four or five years." What Robinson meant by this statement is not clear. His physician, Dr. Cassell, saw Jack's continuing optimism and also a mature graciousness that perhaps implied Jack's new understanding of his mortality. "One day," Cassell related, "he had come to the office and was walking down the hallway. And this man, who was my contemporary, saw him and just blurted out: 'Jackie Robinson! You've been my hero for my whole life!' Now, most people, when others say that to them, are very diffident. They say, 'Oh, well . . .' But Robinson said, 'What a wonderful thing to say to somebody!' He meant, 'What a great gift to give me!' I thought, Wow, if I could only do that. I wanted to learn; I tried never to behave the other way again. Somebody gave him a gift and he took the gift and said Thank you! instead of giving the gift back, which is what most people do."

But Cassell also knew the truth about Jack's physical condition: "His legs had to go. They had to be amputated. I was getting him ready for that step. He was having increasing pain in his legs, when there's not enough blood supply even when you're not doing anything. What follows usually is gangrene and things like that. Amputation seemed on the horizon. I was relatively straight with him. He didn't like bad news; most people don't."

Robinson forged ahead with his plans. On September 5, he proudly announced that his construction company would erect a $17 million apartment complex in the Bedford-Stuyvesant section of Brooklyn. Making the project possible was a forty-year mortgage secured from the New York State Urban Development Corporation. Later that month, he was also prominent in a group of investors who announced plans to build a thoroughbred and harness race track on 430 acres of land in Newtown, Connecticut.

On September 6, he took part in a memorial service at the headquarters of the Anti-Defamation League in New York City to honor the Israeli athletes slain by terrorists in Munich at the Olympic Games that summer.

Meanwhile, pressured by his former Dodger teammate Joe Black to do something, anything, to honor Jackie Robinson on the twenty-fifth anniversary of his historic step into the major leagues, the office of the commissioner of baseball, Bowie Kuhn, invited him to make the ceremonial throwing out of the first ball at a game at Riverfront Stadium, Cincinnati, during the upcoming World Series. Again, Robinson first resisted the invitation. Reached by Joe Reichler, the chief publicist in Kuhn's office, Jack made it clear that he would use the occasion to criticize baseball—especially for its tired excuses as to why no black manager had yet been hired in the majors. Pointing to the potential of former players such as Frank Robinson, Jim Gilliam, and Elston Howard, Jack had assailed the owners and top executives on this score. "As long as they keep digging down and hiring guys who have already failed in one city," Jack said in Miami, "I'm not encouraged." (In October 1974, with the Cleveland Indians, Frank Robinson would become the first black manager in the major leagues.)

The World Series, Jack knew, with the Oakland Athletics playing the Cincinnati Reds, would be a bully pulpit for this message. "If you people expect me to change my thinking, or my speech, you're mistaken," he said to Reichler, "because I'm simply not going to do it." Then baseball offered an inducement Jack could not resist: the event would also pay tribute to the memory of Jackie and to the Daytop organization. "How can a man say no to a dead son?" Dick Young asked in the *Daily News.*

The entire family gathered for the occasion. In a loving, protective spirit, Rachel and Zellee; Sharon and her husband, Joe Mitchell; and David and his girlfriend all accompanied Jack to Cincinnati for his moment of glory. After a happy dinner at their hotel the night before the game, they crowded together for a group picture snapped by a magazine photographer. As they waited for the shutter to click, Rachel heard Jack murmur: "The last hurrah." On October 15, the day after Oakland won the first game against Cincinnati, Robinson threw out the first ball of the second game before a record local crowd and an estimated television audience of some sixty million viewers. Accepting a plaque marking the twenty-fifth anniversary of his entry into the majors, Robinson was brief. "I am extremely proud and pleased," he declared. But "I'm going to be tremendously more pleased and more proud when I look at that third base coaching line one day and see a black face managing in baseball."

(Daytop received a luxury station wagon, a gift from the Chrysler Corporation, and a double-decker bus, a gift from Greyhound. Major-league baseball, someone noted sardonically, donated the plaque.)

Entering the Oakland dugout, Jack was warmly greeted by the A's manager Dick Williams, who embraced and kissed him. The black pitcher Blue Moon Odom also reacted effusively to Jack's presence. But to at least one observer, Odom was the only player, black or white, to show any particular interest in Robinson. "I was surprised by their indifference, especially the blacks," Dick Young wrote. "There seems to be a feeling among the current black players that they owe Jackie nothing."

Roger Kahn was with Jack at the game when a fan offered Robinson a baseball to autograph. "I'm sorry," Jack said, "I can't see it." Jim Murray, a nationally syndicated columnist with whom Jack had feuded at various times, called out to him. "Who's that?" Robinson asked. "Oh, Jim! I'm sorry I can't see you any more." But Jack was not looking for sympathy. "I've lost the sight in one eye," he told Kahn, "but they think they can save the other. I've got nothing to complain about."

His love of horse racing remained strong. "On Columbus Day," Brenda Williams, Jack's sister-in-law, said, "Jack called me and asked if I would go to Belmont to the racetrack with him. Chuck came along, and we had a good time, although Jack misplaced a bet one time, because of his bad eyesight, and he became embarrassed. But the people at the track were wonderful to him, as usual. Rachel joined us afterward for dinner in Manhasset. It was the last time we were all together."

On October 23, Jack went into work at the office in Englewood Cliffs. Later that day, as he often did, he had his driver take him around to various wholesalers, where he collected a load of meat and some boxes of canned goods and other foodstuffs. Then they drove out to Brooklyn, where Jack left his donations at Lacy Covington's Nazarene Baptist Church for distribution to the poor.

The next day, at 6:26 a.m., Rachel called the police, saying that Jack would need an ambulance. Two policemen arrived within a few minutes and administered oxygen to him. Shortly afterward, an ambulance arrived. At 7:10 that morning, on the way to the hospital, Robinson died. He was declared dead on arrival at Stamford Hospital.

On October 27, between 1 p.m. and 9 p.m., Robinson's body lay in state at Duncan Brothers Funeral Home at 2303 Seventh Avenue in Harlem. On the two following days, viewing was at Riverside Church on Riverside Drive at 122nd Street, near Grant's Tomb. With Reverend Wyatt Tee Walker's help, the family prepared for the funeral. In lieu of flowers, contributions were to be sent to Daytop, Inc., in care of the Jackie Robinson Construction Corporation.

Tributes to Robinson poured in from the famous and the ordinary. President Nixon, who announced that he would not attend the funeral but would send an official delegation of some forty persons, lauded him. "His courage, his sense of brotherhood and his brilliance on the playing field," Nixon declared, "brought a new human dimension not only to the game of baseball but to every area of American life where black and white people work side by side." The civil rights leader Vernon Jordan hailed Robinson as "a trail-blazer for all black people and a great spokesman for justice." Red Smith, the New York *Times* columnist, declared: "The word for Jackie Robinson is 'unconquerable.' . . . He would not be defeated. Not by the other team and not by life." The old Yankee catcher Yogi Berra, offering some plain words, spoke another kind of truth: "He could beat you in a lot of ways."

The funeral took place at noon on October 29, at Riverside Church. Some twenty-five hundred mourners heard the Reverend Jesse Jackson deliver the eulogy; Jackie Robinson had stolen home. Rockefeller was there, and Dick Gregory, Roy Wilkins, and A. Philip Randolph; Peter O'Malley, Hank Greenberg, and Joe Louis, too. Campanella was in his wheelchair; Sargent Shriver, Bill Veeck, Larry Doby, Henry Aaron, and Vida Blue. Outside, hundreds of ordinary folk awaited the end of the service.

Six former athletes carried Jack's coffin, silver-blue and draped with red roses, out of Riverside Church and into the waiting hearse. One, Bill Russell, was a Boston Celtic; but the others were old Brooklyn Dodgers: Newcombe, Black, Gilliam, Reese, and Branca. Then the funeral cortege, stretching several city blocks, rolled slowly across Manhattan toward Brooklyn and Jack's final resting place, Cypress Hills Cemetery, where his son Jackie was also buried, only a few blocks from vanished Ebbets Field.

One mourner at the funeral was Jack and Rachel's friend Robert Campbell, of Campbell's Bookstore near UCLA. He had flown overnight to attend the funeral and would return that night to Los Angeles. "The service was excellent," he would recall, "except it was so sad." Heading downtown after the cortege had left, he shared a cab with someone who said he was from the National Urban League. "We talked all the way back about Jack and what a fine person he was. We were all glad that he didn't suffer longer, but we were sorry he had to go so young."

The day before, on October 28, in Pasadena, almost three hundred persons had gathered on the steps of City Hall to pay tribute to Robinson. A choir was on hand, from John Muir High School, as well as a trumpeter from the bugle corps at Pasadena City College. After the choir sang some songs a cappella, the trumpeter sounded taps.

Epilogue

1997

IMMEDIATELY AFTER JACK'S DEATH in 1972, Rachel resigned from her job at Yale University. For about two months she lived alone, at her insistence, in the house in Stamford. Then, finding it too painful to remain there with Jack gone, she moved to one of her two apartments on West 93rd Street in Manhattan. She lived there for about two years before returning home.

In the meantime, soon after Jack's death, she became president of the Jackie Robinson Construction Corporation. Along with Mickey Weissman and Richard Cohen, as well as Joel Halpern, another young real estate developer, she renamed the company the Jackie Robinson Development Corporation. Over the next few years, JRDC was responsible for building some sixteen hundred units of housing. Later, she formed a successful real estate management and training corporation, of which she was also president.

In 1973, she formally registered the Jackie Robinson Foundation. The other founders were Martin Edelman, her brother Charles Williams, and Franklin Williams. Through the foundation, she hoped to assist students from poor and minority backgrounds to attend college by giving them tuition grants. In 1977, the foundation awarded its first scholarships. By 1997, it had awarded more than five hundred scholarships to students whose graduation rate of almost ninety-two percent is thought to be the highest of all organizations with a similar mission in the United States. In 1997, 142 Jackie Robinson Scholars were attending colleges and universities across the United States. (The foundation offices are at 3 West 35th Street, New York, NY 10001.) Rachel resigned as chair of the board of directors late in 1996, but Sharon and David remain active directors.

In 1986, Rachel sold her house in Stamford and bought a sixty-acre farm located about two hours north of Manhattan, where she still resides. (About one year after the sale of the Stamford house to a popular young musician, it was resold to a developer who then destroyed it and erected a new house in its place.) In 1996, Rachel published an illustrated narrative, *Jackie Robinson: An Intimate Portrait.*

In 1973, Sharon Robinson graduated from Howard University with a degree in nursing, then earned a master's degree at Columbia University in midwifery. She practiced for about twelve years before joining the Reverend Jesse Jackson's Operation PUSH as one of its top officials. After five years, she returned to midwifery; at one time she held the rank of assistant professor in the School of Nursing at Yale University. In recent years she lived again in Stamford, and now owns a home in the neighboring town of Norwalk, Connecticut, where she lives with her husband, Molver Fieffe. In 1996, she published *Stealing Home: An Intimate Family Portrait by the Daughter of Jackie Robinson.*

David Robinson, who did not return to Stanford University following his brother Jackie's death, worked for some years in Harlem. Mainly through United Harlem Growth, a company he helped to form, he led efforts to rehabilitate decayed housing stock there in a "sweat equity" plan that helped local residents acquire property from the government in return for their labor. In the 1980s, he left the United States and emigrated to Tanzania. However, he returns regularly to the United States, and his mother has visited him at least once a year in Africa. In Tanzania, he first helped to form a fishing cooperative near Dar-es-Salaam, then moved deep into the interior, to Mbeya, where he acquired and cleared about one hundred acres of land for a farm. He now grows coffee and assists in a cooperative arrangement that exports coffee overseas, including to the United States.

In 1995, David's daughter, Ayo Robinson, born in the United States but reared in Tanzania, enrolled as a first-year student at her father's old prep school in Massachusetts, Mount Hermon, where she is still a student. Her older sister, Susan Thomas, works for the City of New York in the area of prisoner rehabilitation. Sharon's only child, her son, Jesse Martin Simms, became a student at King and Low-Heywood Thomas

School in Stamford. (The school occupies the former summer home of Richard and Andrea Simon, where the Robinsons had lived on first moving to Stamford in 1954.) An outstanding prep-school football player, Jesse committed himself late in 1996 to enrolling as a freshman the following year at UCLA. Sonya Pankey, Jackie's daughter, has been for many years a member of the Ralph Lauren organization. Her own daughter, Sherita, Rachel's only great-grandchild, works as a volunteer at the Jackie Robinson Foundation.

In 1997, Jack's older brother Mack Robinson and his sister, Willa Mae Robinson Walker, until her death in June 1997, were still living in Pasadena. Mack, however, is severely incapacitated by a stroke suffered a few years ago. He lives at home with his wife of more than thirty years, Delano Robinson. Their daughter Kathy Robinson, who has worked hard to recover and preserve the Robinson family's history, also lives in Pasadena.

In various ways since his death in 1972, the nation has officially honored the memory of Jack Roosevelt "Jackie" Robinson. On March 26, 1984, President Reagan gave him the nation's highest civilian award, the Medal of Freedom. In 1996, in an even rarer honor, a bill approved by both houses of Congress and signed into law by President Clinton authorized the minting of gold and silver coins of the realm to commemorate the fiftieth anniversary of Robinson's entry into major-league baseball in 1947. And on April 15, 1997, came the announcement that his Brooklyn Dodgers number, 42, would be retired from major-league baseball for all time to come.

Jack and Rachel

Notes

ABBREVIATIONS

AMP	Arthur Mann Papers, Library of Congress
BE	Brooklyn *Eagle*
BRP	Branch Rickey Papers, Library of Congress
CDB	California *Daily Bruin* (UCLA)
I Never	Jackie Robinson (as told to Alfred Duckett), *I Never Had It Made* (New York: Putnam's Sons, 1972)
JR	Jack Roosevelt "Jackie" Robinson
JRP	Jackie Robinson Papers, Jackie Robinson Foundation, New York City
LC	Library of Congress
NAACPR	National Association for the Advancement of Colored People Records, Library of Congress
NYAN	New York *Amsterdam News*
NYP	New York *Post*
NYT	New York *Times*
PJCC	Pasadena Junior College *Chronicle*
PP	Pasadena *Post*
PSN	Pasadena *Star-News*
PC	Pittsburgh *Courier*
Rachel Robinson, Interview	Interviews with author, 1994–1997
RRP	Rachel Robinson Papers, in her possession
SN	*Sporting News*
WP	Washington *Post*

PROLOGUE

I wanted to see everything!: Ron Gabriel to author, interview, Oct. 13, 1996. / **supreme, a model athlete**: New York *Daily Mirror,* Jan. 25, 1962. / **What I remember**: Ron Gabriel, interview. / **I feel inadequate**: New York *Daily News,* July 24, 1962. / **I could not be here**: SN, Aug. 4, 1962. / **who was as a father**: NYT, July 24, 1962. / **are all here today**: ibid. / **I'm positive I won't**: *Newsweek,* Jan. 23, 1962. / **If I had been white**: ibid. / **He has a talent**: New York *Daily News,* Jan. 6, 1962. / **The aggressive Robbie carried**: NYT, Jan. 5, 1962. / **Jackie, I know**: Philadelphia *Inquirer,* Jan. 7, 1962. / **a hero of the struggle**: NYT, July 21, 1962. / **There are days when**: Richard Nixon to JR, Jan. 23, 1962, JRP. / **He has demonstrated**: John F. Kennedy to Chairman, JR Testimonial Dinner, July 18, 1962, JRP. / **He has the right**: Martin Luther King Jr., Address, Hall of Fame Testimonial Dinner, July 20, 1962, JRP. / **You are the richest**: "Brock" [L. I. Brockenbury?] to JR, July 25, 1962, JRP. / **I'm a tremendously**: JR, Address, Hall of Fame Testimonial Dinner, July 20, 1962, JRP. / **I thanked Rickey**: Ron Gabriel, interview. / **Brooklyn N.L. 1947**: Baseball Hall of Fame, Cooperstown, N.Y. / **To see Robinson's career**: Roger Kahn, "Jackie Robinson: Man of the 25 Years," *Sport,* December 1971, p. 86. / **Again, Robinson was like**: Ron Gabriel, interview.

CHAPTER 1

the Egypt of the Confederacy: W. E. B. Du Bois, *The Souls of Black Folk* (A. C. McClurg, 1903), p. 122. / **a period of broken**: Harold Henry Spangle, *The History of the Black Community of Thomas County, Georgia from 1827 to 1909* (Thomasville, Ga.: Thomas College Press, 1994), p. 25. / **Although there were white**: Spangle, p. 54. / **the interesting fact**: *Cairo and Grady County* (Board of Trade, Cairo, Ga., 1911–12), unpag. / **We were living just**: "Mrs. Robinson's Notes," misc. ms., n.d., JRP. / **It's true, my grandmother**: Olin Faulk to author, interview, May 13, 1996. / **You're about the sassiest**: "Mrs. Robinson's Notes." / **a**

tall, rawboned man: William J. Vanlandingham to author, interview, May 12, 1996. / **You might as well**: "Mrs. Robinson's Notes." / **If you want to get**: ibid. / **In those days**: Charles Copeland to author, interview, May 13, 1996. /

CHAPTER 2

the most beautiful sight: "Mrs. Robinson's Notes," misc. ms., n.d., JRP. / **really very much a loner**: Willa Mae Walker to author, interview, Feb. 10, 1995. / **"Mattie" Robinson**: Pasadena City Directory, 1921–1922, Pasadena Public Library, Pasadena, Cal. / **the richest city**: *California: A Guide to the Golden State* (Works Progress Administration of the State of California) (N.Y.: Hastings House, 1939), p. 247. / **a civic pride running**: Delilah L. Beasley, *The Negro Trail Blazers of California* (L.A., 1919), p. 143. / **Sophisticated and wealthy**: Ann Scheid, *Pasadena: Crown of the Valley* (Pasadena: Windsor Publications, 1986), p. 96. / **the beginning of the transition**: Earl L. Cartland, "A Study of the Negroes Living in Pasadena," M.A. thesis, Whittier College, California (June 1948), p. 13. Pasadena Historical Society. / **to come together and**: *California Eagle,* Feb. 28, 1919. / **You couldn't live east**: Ernie Cunningham to author, interview, Feb. 10, 1995. / **a single policeman**: *California Eagle,* Aug. 1, 1940. / **The condition of affairs**: *California Eagle,* Nov. 7, 1924. / **We had apples**: Willa Mae Walker, interview. / **Sometimes there were only**: *I Never,* pp. 16–17. / **We went through a sort**: Willa Mae Walker, interview. / **The police were there**: ibid. / **My mother never lost**: *I Never,* p. 18. / **Nigger! Nigger!**: Willa Mae Walker, interview. / **My mother divided**: ibid. / **Mallie loved to sit**: Rachel Robinson, interview. / **We knew that we**: Willa Mae Walker, interview. / **I remember sitting**: WP, Aug. 22, 1949. / **God watches what you do**: "Mrs. Robinson's Notes." / **Prayer *is* belief**: Arthur Mann, *The Jackie Robinson Story* (N.Y.: Grosset & Dunlap, 1951), p. 33. / **I was Jack's little mother**: Willa Mae Walker, interview. / **When I was eight**: WP, Aug. 21, 1949. / **but it was only**: Sid Heard to author, interview, Sept. 10, 1995. / **would get to school**: Willa Mae Walker, interview. / **always had a kind word**: WP,

Aug. 21, 1949. / **a deep, embedded friendship**: Willa Mae Walker, interview. / **they put all of**: Eleanor Peters Heard to author, Feb. 10, 1995. / **Gardener**: Transcript of grades, Washington Elementary School, Pasadena. / **He was a special**: Willa Mae Walker, interview. / **We used to play**: Sid Heard, interview. / **When I was in**: WP, Aug. 21, 1949. / **a constant user**: Unidentified clipping, n.d., JRP. / **I used to be**: Ray Bartlett to author, interview, Sept. 8, 1995. / **I guess I was**: WP, Aug. 24, 1949. / **to tell the truth**: ibid. / **didn't have the things**: Van Wade to author, interview, Feb. 10, 1995. / **because some of us**: Willa Mae Walker, interview. / **We didn't know him**: Mack Robinson, interview, c. 1985, JRP. / **My father's will and spirit**: JR, ms., fragment, speeches, JRP. / **I could only think**: *I Never*, p. 16. / **she wasn't going to**: Willa Mae Walker, interview. / **somewhat sickly sometimes**: WP, Aug. 21, 1949. / **Edgar was mentally retarded**: Ray Bartlett, interview. / **There was always something**: WP, Aug. 21, 1949. / **tall and thin**: ibid. / **I remember going**: ibid. / **In many places they**: PP, July 2, 1938. / **When it was a cold**: PSN, April 7, 1987. / **I think he thought**: PSN, April 7, 1987. / **we was right there**: Mack Robinson, interview, c. 1985, JRP. / **I will take care**: Jack Gordon to author, interview, Feb. 21, 1995. / **soured him on life**: WP, Aug. 21, 1949. / **Many times I felt**: Cited in PSN, April 7, 1987. / **Through some miracle**: WP, Aug. 23, 1949. / **At that time Jackie**: Ernie Cunningham, interview. / **Our gang was made up**: *I Never*, p. 18. / **There was no drugs**: Ray Bartlett, interview. / **We never got into**: *I Never*, p. 18. / **Hardly a week went by**: ibid. / **About nine feet tall**: Ernie Cunningham, interview. / **He was always ready**: WP, Aug. 22, 1949. / **to his office "often"**: "Mrs. Robinson's Notes." / **I think he did**: Ray Bartlett, interview. / **He made me see**: *I Never*, p. 19. / **He also organized**: Sid Heard, interview. / **I always thought Pasadena**: WP, Aug. 21, 1949. / **At the Kress soda fountain**: Bernice Gordon, interview, Feb. 21, 1995. / **The Robinson the world**: L.A. *Times,* April 4, 1977. / **The only curse word**: Sid Heard, interview. / **exceptionally good**: John Muir Technical High School Yearbook, 1935. / **You [toe] the line**: WP, Aug. 22, 1949. / **much ability**: Muir High School Yearbook, 1936. / **mainstay**: ibid. / **the nucleus of the squad**: John Muir Technical High School Yearbook, 1936. / **Jack**

was always very: Eleanor Peters Heard, interview. / **He was a hard loser**: Ray Bartlett, interview. / **snake-hipped**: PP, Oct. 11, 1936. / **dusky . . . sped around**: PP, Oct. 25, 1936. / **Then the fun started**: PP, Nov. 12, 1936. / **three Glendale boys piled on**: PP, Nov. 22, 1936. / **Robinson was all over**: PP, Jan. 30, 1937. / **for two years has been**: PSN, Jan. 29, 1937.

CHAPTER 3

created a sensation: PP, March 27, 1937. / **one of the most**: PP, May 24, 1937. / **the greatest athletic season**: PSN, May 29, 1937. / **Jack was kind of shy**: Jack Gordon, interview. / **I hear you got**: ibid. / **I remember he used**: WP, Aug. 22, 1949. / **Say we are at**: Jack Gordon, interview. / **Someone told my mom**: ibid. / **It was there**: WP, Aug. 22, 1949. / **in almost every game**: PP, July 10, 1937. / **the most beautiful**: PJCC, Sept. 3, 1937. / **Jack Robinson, the dashing**: PJCC, Sept. 14, 1937. / **fumbled the ball**: PP, Nov. 14, 1937. / **dark-hued phantom**: PP, Nov. 25, 1937. / **I had found out**: Jack Gordon, interview. / **the three colored players**: PP, Dec. 8, 1937. / **Pasadena will lose**: PJCC, Dec. 17, 1937. / **I wouldn't join it**: Ray Bartlett, interview. / **We wore our official**: Jack Gordon, interview. / **I remember we had**: Warren Dorn to author, interview, Sept. 9, 1995. / **Sure, I socialized**: Ray Bartlett, interview. / **A lot of the time**: Shig Kawai to author, interview, Feb. 10, 1995. / **I felt left out**: Ray Bartlett, interview. / **You can't eat in here**: Jack Gordon, interview. / **a slurring remark**: WP, Aug. 23, 1949. / **The Oklahoma boys**: Jack Gordon, interview. / **I called a little**: Roger Kahn, "Does Jackie Robinson Talk Too Much?" *Our World,* April 1953, p. 13. / **Coach Mallory laid down**: Carl T. Rowan with Jackie Robinson, *Wait Till Next Year* (N.Y.: Random House, 1960), p. 42. / **I decided that Bartlett**: Rowan, p. 43. / **Jack had the ball**: Jack Gordon, interview. / **the stormy petrel**: PJCC, Jan. 30, 1938. / **The next moment**: PP, Jan. 23, 1938. / **There is a story**: PSN, April 4, 1987. / **All that left**: ibid. / **had busted many**: Mack Robinson, interview. / **We didn't have face masks**: Ray Bartlett, interview. / **They didn't regard Jack**: Henry Shatford to author, interview,

Sept. 6, 1995. / **Is Jack Robinson here?**: Jack Gordon, interview. / **elder members objected**: *I Never,* p. 20. / **He looked half his age**: Eleanor Peters Heard, interview. / **fearless, rational, comprehensive**: Karl E. Downs, "Timid Negro Students!," *Crisis* (June 1936), pp. 171, 187. / **He really was a sort**: Ray Bartlett, interview. / **but no matter how**: *I Never,* p. 20. / **When I talked with**: ibid. / **there was somebody else**: WP, Aug. 23, 1949. / **instead of stopping**: PJCC, March 27, 1938. / **the greatest base runner**: PJCC, May 20, 1938. / **Geez, if that kid**: L.A. *Times,* April 4, 1977. / **a rather skinny kid**: CDB, Feb. 28, 1941. / **what struck me then**: PSN, Jan. 30, 1987. / **I couldn't get over**: L.A. *Times,* April 4, 1977. / **the greatest all-around**: PJCC, June 4, 1938. / **It is doubtful**: PP, June 16, 1938. / **I never did understand**: PSN, April 7, 1987. / **mainly because the barbers**: PP, June 1, 1938. / **directly responsible for**: PP, Sept. 24, 1938. / **another scintillating exhibition**: PP, Oct. 1, 1938. / **after squirming out**: PP, Oct. 23, 1938. / **phenomenal**: PP, Oct. 28, 1938. / **reversed his field**: Duke Snider and Bill Gilbert, *The Duke of Flatbush* (N.Y.: Zebra, 1988), p. 22. / **Have you ever seen**: PP, Oct. 30, 1938. / **Gift from Heaven**: PP, Dec. 4, 1938. / **a number of colleges**: *I Never,* p. 22. / **We all knew USC**: Ray Bartlett, interview. / **a real good scholarship**: Henry Shatford, interview. / **my greatest fan**: *I Never,* p. 21. / **high class, cultured**: Woody Strode and Sam Young, *Goal Dust* (N.Y.: Madison Books, 1990), p. 84. / **Don't bet any money**: PP, Dec. 13, 1938. / **He made a decided**: PP, Dec. 21, 1938. / **Compton's old bugaboo**: PP, Jan. 7, 1939. / **The phenomenal Negro athlete**: PP, Feb. 4, 1938. / **outstanding service**: Pasadena Junior College Yearbook, 1939. / **To them he was**: L.A. *Times,* April 4, 1977. / **a free-for-all scuffle**: *California Eagle,* Jan. 12, 1939. / **we don't allow Negroes**: ibid. / **of flagrant discrimination**: ibid. / **If my mother, brothers**: PSN, April 7, 1987.

CHAPTER 4

the wild rumors that: CDB, Feb. 16, 1939. / **one of the greatest**: ibid. / **the Black Panther**: *California Eagle,* March 9, 1939. / **his**

wickedly unorthodox style: *California Eagle,* July 6, 1939. / **Mama was living**: Willa Mae Walker, interview. / **I was very shaken**: *I Never,* p. 22. / **the biggest argument**: *California Eagle,* Aug. 17, 1939. / **swimming offered**: *California Eagle,* July 27, 1939. / **use and occupancy**: James E. Crimi, "The Social Status of the Negro in Pasadena, California," M.A. thesis, University of Southern California (June 1941), p. 72, Pasadena Historical Society. / **and the man said something**: Ray Bartlett, interview. / **he turned pale**: WP, Aug. 21, 1949. / **between 40 and 50**: PSN, Sept. 6, 1939. / **So I withdrew**: Ray Bartlett, interview. / **I found myself**: WP, Aug. 21, 1949. / **an attorney prominent**: PSN, Oct. 17, 1939. / **another Negro youth**: PSN, Oct. 18, 1939. / **the police court had**: ibid. / **that the Negro football**: ibid. / **I got out of that**: WP, Aug. 22, 1949. / **I understand**: Ray Bartlett, interview. / **Didn't the newspapers come**: WP, Aug. 22, 1949. / **This thing followed me**: ibid. / **my first personal experience**: ibid. / **There were really two**: Henry Shatford, interview. / **UCLA was the first**: CDB, Feb. 2, 1979. / **Gold Dust Trio**: CDB, Sept. 29, 1939. / **Pasadena and Westwood faithfuls**: CDB, Registration Edition, Sept. 1939. / **We've never run**: CDB, Oct. 2, 1939. / **the prettiest piece**: *California Eagle,* Oct. 12, 1939. / **were unanimous**: CDB, Oct. 9, 1939. / **Three thousand Bruin rooters**: CDB, Oct. 16, 1939. / **Jackrabbit Jackie Robinson**: CDB, Oct. 23, 1939. / **Mr. Robinson took**: Oct. 30, 1939. / **the greatest ball-carrier**: *California Eagle,* Oct. 26, 1939. / **Bruin stock went all**: CDB, Nov. 2, 1939. / **snaked his way down**: CDB, Dec. 1, 1939. / **Jackie was well past**: *California Eagle,* Dec. 7, 1939. / **past our secondary**: Woody Strode and Sam Young, *Goal Dust* (N.Y.: Madison Books, 1990), p. 101. / **Jack Robinson—Better than**: CDB, Oct. 27, 1939. / **"White man, you're"**: Henry Shatford, interview. / **Kenny is a really**: *California Eagle,* Oct. 5, 1939. / **the greatest athlete**: CDB, Oct. 10, 1940. / **Jackie was a very**: Strode, *Goal Dust,* pp. 86–87. / **It was a real treat**: Henry Shatford, interview. / **was always eager to cooperate**: Westwood *Home Press,* Oct. 6, 1955. / **They had loaned me**: Ray Bartlett, interview. / **When the Headman saw**: CDB, Nov. 9, 1939. / **Jack Robinson, who is**: CDB, Jan. 10, 1940. / **a very willing worker**: Robert Campbell to John B. Jackson and Joel Gardner, interview, 1980, UCLA Oral

History Program, UCLA Archives. / **He encouraged me**: WP, Aug. 25, 1949. / **Easily the best man**: CDB (Registration Edition, Sept. 1940). / **the best individual performance**: CDB, Feb. 26, 1940. / **On one series**: CDB, Feb. 22, 1940. / **Robinson has more natural**: CDB, Feb. 27, 1940. / **the speed and shooting**: CDB, March 1, 1940. / **Schools cannot teach that**: Arthur Mann, *The Jackie Robinson Story* (N.Y.: Grosset & Dunlap, 1951), p. 62. / **The phenomenal Negro athlete**: CDB, March 11, 1940. / **I can't see**: CDB, March 12, 1940. / **colder than Jackie Robinson's**: CDB, April 22, 1940. / **the kind of a behind**: CDB, April 29, 1940. / **a long, sad afternoon**: CDB, May 2, 1940. / **provided he met**: CDB, May 14, 1940. / **"I Do Not Choose"**: CDB, May 8, 1940. / **He talked about this**: Ray Bartlett, interview. / **My father was sick**: Rachel Robinson, interview. / **He needed me**: ibid. / **She had nothing**: ibid. / **All my sorrows**: ibid. / **I remember**: ibid. / **I was the aggressor**: ibid. / **He was Zellee's dream guy**: ibid. / **Rachel's father didn't like**: David Falkner, *Great Time Coming: The Life of Jackie Robinson, from Baseball to Birmingham* (N.Y.: Simon & Schuster, 1995), p. 63. / **Jack's color would not**: Rachel Robinson, interview. / **Mallie was very gracious**: ibid. / **colossalness is almost**: CDB, Aug. 9, 1940. / **and went all the**: CDB, Sept. 30, 1940. / **a wild and woolly**: CDB, Nov. 18, 1940. / **A lot of it**: Rachel Robinson, interview. / **the greatest of all**: Mann, p. 59. / **viciously treated**: CDB, Feb. 17, 1941. / **long, weary basketball season**: CDB, Feb. 25, 1941. / **Robinson Fails to Make**: CDB, March 4, 1941. / **flagrant bit of prejudice**: CDB, March 5, 1941. / **I was aghast**: Rachel Robinson, interview. / **honorable dismissal**: CDB, March 4, 1941. / **very fine letter**: John B. Jackson to JR, May 7, 1941, UCLA Archives. / **I was indeed serious**: JR to John B. Jackson, n.d., UCLA Archives.

CHAPTER 5

I had offers: Frank Waldman, *Famous American Athletes of Today* (Boston: L.C. Page, 1949), p. 244. / **I could see no**: *I Never*, p. 23. / **that their free time**: JR, Personnel Placement Questionnaire, U.S. War Department, Nov. 23, 1942, U.S. Army

Records, JRP. / **fortunate, indeed**: Unidentified clipping, n.d., JRP. / **something that I have**: JR to John B. Jackson, n.d., UCLA Archives. / **the biggest kid of all**: WP, Aug. 25, 1949. / **loved and appreciated**: ibid. / **it took one scrimmage**: Carl T. Rowan with Jackie Robinson, *Wait Till Next Year* (N.Y.: Random House, 1960), p. 65. / **a soft-spoken, dark-skinned**: Rowan, p. 66. / **The only time**: PSN, Oct. 26, 1977. / **The construction job**: Ray Bartlett, interview. / **Century Express**: Misc. clipping, n.d., JRP. / **See the Sensational**: ibid. / **When he found out**: Ray Bartlett, interview. / **Robinson, almost entirely**: Frank Ardolino, "Jackie Robinson and the 1941 Honolulu Bears," *The National Pastime: A Review of Baseball History* 16 (1996), p. 70. / **discrimination in the employment**: John Morton Blum, *V Was for Victory: Politics and American Culture During World War II* (N.Y.: Harcourt Brace Jovanovich, 1976), p. 188. / **If Jack and his mother**: Rachel Robinson, interview. / **I wasn't thinking**: ibid. / **Rae's deep grief**: *I Never,* p. 23. / **My father's death**: Rachel Robinson, interview. / **It's a wonder**: ibid. / **Like all men**: *I Never,* p. 24. / **Personally, I would welcome**: *Daily Worker,* March 23, 1942. / **has been proven satisfactory**: Lee Nichols, *Breakthrough on the Color Front* (N.Y.: Three Continents Press, rev. ed. 1993), p. 103. / **There is a consensus**: Jack D. Foner, *Blacks and the Military in American History: A New Perspective* (N.Y.: Praeger, 1974), p. 146. / **on the score that**: Foner, p. 140. / **expert . . . excellent**: JR's U.S. Army Records, JRP. / **The men in our**: *I Never,* p. 24. / **Leadership is not imbedded**: Blum, p. 185. / **I'll break up**: Rowan, *Wait,* p. 74. / **Negro athletes such as**: Ruth Danenhower Wilson, *Jim Crow Joins Up: A Study of Negroes in the Armed Forces of the United States* (N.Y.: William J. Clark, 1944), p. 7. / **We gon do our part**: Chris Mead, *Champion: Joe Louis, Black Hero in White America* (N.Y.: Charles Scribner's Sons, 1985), p. 218. / **was the quickest fellow**: Arthur Mann, *The Jackie Robinson Story* (N.Y.: Grosset & Dunlap, 1951), p. 87. / **one of the sharpest**: JR, misc. speeches, n.d., JRP. / **I got this telephone**: Rachel Robinson, interview. / **I'm sure if it**: ibid. / **stupid nigger**: Mead, *Joe Louis,* p. 227. / **Joe gave the general**: Truman K. Gibson to author, interview, Feb. 25, 1996. / **at Fort Riley**: Wilson, p. 27. / **I was at headquarters**: Jack Gordon, interview. / **I had come to realize**: Rachel Robinson, interview. / **Jack began**: ibid. / **Tell her to either**: ibid. / **Do you have a sable**: ibid. / **One day we were**: Peter Golenbock, *Bums: An Oral History of the Brooklyn Dodgers* (N.Y.: Simon & Schuster, 1984), p. 152. / **because we know of**: William J. Neal to Commanding Officer, 372nd Infantry, Camp Breckenridge, KY, October 12, 1944, Army Records, JRP. / **had lost confidence**: Foner, p. 159. / **Lieutenant, let me**: *I Never,* p. 26. / **made it quite clear**: *I Never,* pp. 28–29. / **arthritis, chronic**: JR, Army Records, JRP. / **physically disqualified**: ibid. / **I shook with rage**: *I Never,* p. 25. / **I told him I was**: Rachel Robinson, interview. / **Stubbornly I vowed**: *I Never,* p. 25. / **"New" Gonorrhoea, Acute**: JR, Army Records, JRP. / **Seek, Strike**: Odie B. Faulk and Laura E. Faulk, *Fort Hood: The First Fifty Years* (Temple, Tex.: Frank W. Mayborn Foundation, 1990), p. 69. / **Segregation there**: Mary Penick Motley, ed., *The Invisible Soldier: The Experience of the Black Soldier, World War II* (Detroit: Wayne State University Press, 1975), p. 328. / **One day Jackie was**: Motley, p. 163. / **Our boots were shined**: David Falkner, *Great Time Coming: The Life of Jackie Robinson* (N.Y.: Simon & Schuster, 1995), pp. 73–74. / **Men, I know nothing**: WP, Aug. 25, 1949. / **He was kind of**: Falkner, p. 75. / **who tended to pick**: ibid. / **in very high regard**: JR, Transcript of Court Martial, August 2, 1944, Army Records, JRP. / **I said I'd be**: ibid. / **to determine the physical**: Army Records, May 25, 1944, JRP. / **type of duty**: Lt. Robert W. Gilmore to Commanding Officer, Camp Hood, June 21, 1944, Army Records, JRP. / **a bony mass**: ibid. / **fit for limited**: Proceedings of Meeting of Disposition Board, June 26, 1944, Army Records, JRP. / **I said that's all**: The complete record of Robinson's court-martial trial, August 2, 1944, including a transcript of the trial and a copy of all depositions, are in U.S. Army Records, JRP. / **This is a very**: "Summary of Telephone Conversation," Colonel E. A. Kimball, Commander of the 5th Armored Group, to Colonel Walter D. Buie, Chief of Staff of the XXIII Corps, July 17, 1944, Army Records, JRP. / **seeking your help**: JR to NAACP, July 24, 1944, NAACPR, LC. / **We will be unable**: Edward R. Dudley to JR, Aug. 3, 1944, NAACPR, LC. / **this incident is only**: Anon. to NAACP, July 20, 1944, NAACPR, LC. /

that God would take: Rachel Robinson, interview. / **The accused stated**: Army Records, JRP. / **told me the NAACP**: Hal Davis, "The Court-Martial of Lt. Jackie Robinson," *National Law Journal,* Sept. 19, 1994: A12. / **a young Michigan officer**: *I Never,* p. 34. / **behaving with disrespect**: Trial transcript, JRP. All quotations here are from the transcript, unless otherwise noted. / **The provost marshal didn't**: Davis, p. A12. / **He was handcuffed**: David J. Williams, *Hit Hard* (N.Y.: Bantam, 1983), pp. 126–127. / **Jackie said**: Mead, p. 227. / **No . . . permanent**: Army Records, JRP. / **I was told there**: JR to Adjutant General, U.S. Army, Aug. 25, 1944, Army Records, JRP. / **would only further aggravate**: JR to Adjutant General, Army, Army Records, JRP. / **inasmuch as Lieutenant Robinson**: Adjutant General to Commanding General, Eighth Service Command, Sept. 26, 1944, Army Records, JRP. / **revert to an inactive**: Special Order No. 249, Fifth Service Command, Oct. 17, 1944, Army Records, JRP. / **I had almost made**: WP, Aug. 24, 1949. / **honorably relieved from active**: Army Records, JRP.

CHAPTER 6

I believe that my: Karleen Downs Berthel to author, interview, March 12, 1996. / **The college was**: Galveston *Voice,* Feb. 28, 1948. / **Bringing Jackie Robinson**: Dr. John Quill Taylor King to author, interview, July 7, 1995. / **top team from**: JR, " 'Your temper can ruin us!,' " *Look,* Feb. 15, 1955, p. 82. / **everybody, *everybody***: Janet Bruce, *The Kansas City Monarchs: Champions of Black Baseball* (Lawrence: University Press of Kansas, 1985), p. 24. / **a Monarch never had**: Buck Owens to Janet Bruce, cited in John B. Holway, *Blackball Stars: Negro League Pioneers* (Westport, Conn.: Meckler Books, 1988), p. 341. / **I inquired about my**: JR, "What's Wrong with Negro Baseball?" ms., n.d., pp. 116–137, JRP. / **the rooms were dingy**: ibid. / **lopsided game**: JR, " 'Your temper can ruin us!,' " p. 82. / **seeing the best type**: ibid. / **Jackie was able**: Sammie Haynes to Spike Lee, interview, Dec. 29, 1994, JRP. / **a very smart ball**: Bruce, p. 106. / **an average fielder**: Donn Rogosin, *Invisible Men: Life in Baseball's*

Negro Leagues (N.Y.: Atheneum, 1983), p. 203. / **He didn't have that**: ibid. / **instead of the outside**: Rogosin, p. 204. / **perhaps the best curve**: David Falkner, *Great Time Coming: The Life of Jackie Robinson* (N.Y.: Simon & Schuster, 1995), p. 121. / **All the time I**: JR as told to Wendell Smith, *Jackie Robinson: My Own Story* (N.Y.: Greenberg, 1948), p. 11. / **Quickly the old-time**: Rogosin, p. 85. / **give Robinson a base**: Rogosin, pp. 85–86. / **He did not fit**: Rogosin, p. 203. / **I could never figure**: JR, " 'Your temper can ruin us!,' " p. 82. / **Well, have you been**: Haynes to Spike Lee, interview. / **I was in the outfield**: Boston *Herald,* April 16, 1987. / **I'm telling you**: ibid. / **What a ballplayer**: ibid. / **He said to me**: ibid. / **I wish I could**: Chicago *Tribune,* July 28, 1994. / **He went home**: Toronto *Sun,* Aug. 1, 1994. / **Could we, by any chance**: Carl T. Rowan with Jackie Robinson, *Wait Till Next Year* (N.Y.: Random House, 1960), p. 97. / **Negroes are not barred**: Chicago *Defender,* July 25, 1942. / **brandish sharp spikes**: Rowan, p. 101. / **Frankly, we were met**: Chicago *Tribune,* July 28, 1994. / **Why not?**: Rowan, p. 104. / **Damned skin**: Arthur Mann, *The Jackie Robinson Story* (N.Y.: Grosset & Dunlap, 1951), p. 30. / **That scene haunted me**: Rowan, p. 106. / **the most humiliating**: Robert W. Peterson, *Only the Ball Was White* (Englewood Cliffs, N.J.: Prentice-Hall, 1970), p. 185. / **trying to assume**: Peterson, p. 187. / **the ideal Negro star**: Montreal *Gazette,* Oct. 24, 1945. / **I knew most**: Harold Parrott, *The Lords of Baseball* (N.Y.: Praeger, 1976), p. 187. / **carefully, and when I**: Donald Honig, "When Baseball Grew Up," *Reader's Digest,* August 1975, p. 151. / **Player fell on shoulder**: Mann, p. 26. / **Hello, Jackie**: Mann, p. 29. / **I was thrilled, scared**: *I Never,* p. 43. / **Jack waited, and waited**: L.A. *Times,* April 9, 1990. / **I know you're a good**: *I Never,* p. 43. / **my race, my parents**: *I Never,* p. 46. / **I had to do it**: ibid. / **the most stupefying**: Giovanni Papini, *The Life of Christ,* trans. Dorothy Canfield Fisher (N.Y.: Harcourt, Brace, 1923), pp. 104–105. / **On the telephone**: Rachel Robinson, interview. / **I was told I would**: JR, "What's Wrong with the Negro Leagues?" / **and make one break**: Wesley Rickey to Arthur Mann, Oct. 7, 1945, AMP, LC. / **Of course, I can't**: NYT, Oct. 24, 1945. / **undoubtedly will be criticized**: Montreal *Gazette,* Oct. 24, 1945. / **a fine way**: NYT, Oct. 24, 1945. / **very few players**:

ibid. / **They didn't make**: NYT, Oct. 26, 1945. / **It is those of**: Rowan, p. 121. / **will not make the grade**: Rowan, pp. 122–123. / **couldn't foresee any future**: Rowan, p. 123. / **We won't take it**: NYT, Oct. 24, 1945. / **Rickey is no Abraham**: Rogosin, p. 207. / **The Negro league is**: ibid. / **There is no Negro**: Holway, p. 342. / **and who are being**: Montreal *Gazette,* Oct. 24, 1945. / **I feel that I speak**: Montreal *Gazette,* Oct. 27, 1945. / **it all came down**: Rogosin, p. 214. / **We'd get 300 people**: Holway, p. 326. / **did not like being**: Rogosin, p. 86. / **One day Felton Snow**: ibid. / **just a swell person**: Falkner, p. 121. / **It was my mother's**: Rachel Robinson, interview. / **It was a lovely wedding**: Robert Campbell, interview, UCLA Archives. / **I could feel**: Rachel Robinson, interview.

CHAPTER 7

I also compulsively spent: Rachel Robinson, interview. / **that piece of ermine**: ibid. / **I couldn't be sure**: Carl T. Rowan with Jackie Robinson, *Wait Till Next Year* (N.Y.: Random House, 1960), p. 131. / **Blacks could not eat**: *I Never,* p. 52. / **Jack almost exploded**: Rowan, p. 132. / **dirty, dreadful place**: ibid. / **You'd better get off**: Rachel Robinson, interview. / **ready to explode**: *I Never,* p. 53. / **I could see him**: Rachel Robinson, interview. / **I had a few**: *I Never,* p. 53. / **I made sure that**: Rachel Robinson, interview. / **I wouldn't do it**: Rowan, p. 135. / **I never want another**: PC, March 9, 1946. / **bad flying weather**: Montreal *Gazette,* March 2, 1946. / **No one objects**: PC, March 9, 1946. / **a dear, sentimental romantic**: Rachel Robinson, interview. / **If we can't put**: PC, March 9, 1946. / **I felt so protective**: Rachel Robinson, interview. / **to be the gentlemen**: Montreal *Gazette,* March 1, 1946. / **because of my interest**: NYT, March 1, 1946. / **keeping up a constant**: Rowan, pp. 137–138. / **Well, this is it**: Clyde Sukeforth to Rachel Robinson, March 18, 1987, RRP [dated 1976]. / **became the first two**: New York *Daily Worker,* March 5, 1946. / **Jack, do you think**: See Rowan, p. 138. Not verbatim. / **In those days**: Rowan, p. 139. / **Mr. Rickey, do you**: Rowan, p. 145. / **I never saw these**: Montreal *Gazette,* March 5,

1946. / **We disliked this distinction**: Rowan, p. 142. / **that Mr. Rickey has played**: Montreal *Gazette*, March 6, 1946. / **If he was white**: Rowan, p. 144. / **Day after day**: Rachel Robinson, "I Live with a Hero," *Negro Digest*, June 1951, p. 4. / **How could I miss**: Rachel Robinson, interview. / **We began to see**: ibid. / **I was disappointed**: ibid. / **My Dearest Darling**: JR to Rachel Robinson, n.d., RRP. / **Rickey would show up**: Rachel Robinson, interview. / **has been giving Jackie**: PC, March 30, 1946. / **swarthy señor**: PC, March 23, 1946. / **I'm not interested**: PC, March 30, 1946. / **He had the greatest**: Philadelphia *Daily News*, Oct. 27, 1972. / **forever blasted**: *Daily Worker*, March 17, 1946. / **Lou was intelligent**: *I Never*, p. 57. / **a few weak**: *I Never*, p. 58. / **Playing under terrific pressure**: Daytona Beach *Evening Journal*, March 17, 1946. / **We were literally afraid**: Rachel Robinson, interview. / **ROBINSON GETS A HIT**: PC, April 6, 1946. / **a man in a goldfish**: Baltimore *Afro-American*, March 16, 1946. / **It is part of**: Montreal *Gazette*, March 22, 1946. / **We lived up to**: PC, April 6, 1946. / **What this had to**: *I Never*, p. 61. / **Vicious old man Jim**: PC, April 13, 1946. / **Without Robinson and Wright**: PC, April 13, 1946. / **That's great**: PC, March 30, 1946. / **one of the most**: PC, April 13, 1946. / **Poor Hopper**: Montreal *Standard*, April 4, 1946. / **I remember the parades**: Rowan, p. 149. / **Now the crowd went**: Rowan, p. 154. / **as he was mobbed**: New York *Herald Tribune*, April 19, 1946. / **a mad scene**: Montreal *Gazette*, April 19, 1946. / **converted his opportunity**: NYT, April 19, 1946. / **Make no mistake**: Montreal *Gazette*, April 20, 1946. / **Thus the most significant**: New York *Amsterdam News*, April 27, 1946. / **While it's a ticklish**: Montreal *Standard*, April 28, 1946. / **He didn't say so**: ibid. / **nigger son of a bitch**: misc. clipping, n.d., JRP. / **It put a heavy**: *I Never*, pp. 59–60. / **The woman didn't merely**: Rachel Robinson, interview. / **such good people**: Edgar Méthot to Jack and Rachel Robinson, July 10, 1972, JRP. / **The only person**: Baltimore *Afro-American*, May 11, 1946. / **the Colored Comet**: Montreal *Gazette*, June 4, 1946. / **I consider it a great**: JR to New York State Organizing Committee, United Negro and Allied Veterans of America, n.d. [1946], JRP. / **Hey Jackie, there's**: *I Never*, p. 62. / **I owe more**: Toronto *Star*, March 16, 1957. / **I've reminded him**: Montreal *Gazette*, Oct. 5, 1946. /

He came into the office: Montreal *Gazette,* Oct. 7, 1946. / **Because of his dark**: ibid. / **the toll that incidents**: *I Never,* p. 62. / **Rachel's understanding love**: *I Never,* p. 67. / **I never told Jack**: Rachel Robinson, interview. / **a player who must**: *Newsweek,* Aug. 26, 1946, p. 72. / **I'd like to have**: Rowan, p. 161. / **I've had great luck**: *Newsweek,* Aug. 26, 1946, p. 72. / **The tension was terrible**: *I Never,* p. 63. / **The worse I played**: *I Never,* p. 63. / **demonstrations of prejudice**: Louisville *Courier-Journal,* Oct. 6, 1946. / **which really settled**: Montreal *Daily Star,* Oct. 4, 1946. / **The tears poured down**: Montreal *Gazette,* Oct. 6, 1946. / **You're a great ballplayer**: *I Never,* p. 65. / **They stormed around him**: Montreal *Gazette,* Oct. 6, 1946. / **It was probably**: *I Never,* p. 65.

CHAPTER 8

the promoters: Arthur Mann, *The Jackie Robinson Story* (N.Y.: Grosset & Dunlap, 1951), p. 158. / **Even if you don't**: Susan Rayl, "Jackie Robinson and Basketball: Excellence on the Court," address, Bethune-Cookman College, Fla., March 15, 1996. / **put a real hurting**: Jack Gordon, interview. / **to say that Robinson**: PC, Jan. 25, 1947. / **I have made every**: PC, Feb. 1, 1947. / **I guess Mr. Rickey**: ibid. / **the things which are**: Mann, pp. 160–161. / **the *one* enemy most**: Mann, pp. 162–163. / **I was told that**: *I Never,* p. 68. / **I can't afford to**: Roger Kahn, "The Ten Years of Jackie Robinson," *Sport,* October 1955, p. 12. / **I honestly wouldn't know**: SN, April 2, 1947. / **but the crowd came**: SN, March 26, 1947. / **I want you to run**: *I Never,* p. 69. / **startling**: SN, March 26, 1947. / **The infield was made**: SN, April 2, 1947. / **Robinson's movements around**: ibid. / **When they take their**: PC, March 29, 1947. / **It would be a crime**: SN, March 26, 1947. / **He's a swell ball**: PC, March 1, 1947. / **because people might think**: NYT, March 30, 1947. / **far off his usual**: SN, April 2, 1947. / **there is also little**: SN, March 26, 1947. / **did not suffer by**: SN, April 2, 1947. / **I wasn't trying**: NYT, July 17, 1977. / **there were five of**: Kirby Higbe, *The High Hard One* (N.Y.: Viking, 1967), pp. 103–104. / **I don't care if**:

Harold Parrott, *The Lords of Baseball* (N.Y.: Praeger, 1976), pp. 208–209. / **When you're born**: *Daily News* (Philadelphia), April 14, 1987. / **He really reamed me**: NYT, Dec. 10, 1981. / **that a little show**: *I Never*, p. 68. / **Recently the thought**: Dixie Walker to Branch Rickey, March 26, 1947, BRP. / **No player on this**: NYT, April 1, 1947. / **one of the greatest**: PC, March 22, 1947. / **a tendency to choke up**: PC, April 5, 1947. / **I tried not to notice**: Roy Campanella, *It's Good to Be Alive* (Boston: Little, Brown, 1959), p. 131. / **the most delicate question**: NYT, April 9, 1947. / **detrimental to baseball**: NYT, April 10, 1947. / **several thousand Negroes**: NYT, April 11, 1947. / **an unimpeachable source**: PC, March 29, 1947. / **My boy, I must**: NYT, Oct. 26, 1972. / **Robinson, how are you**: PC, April 19, 1947. / **Next time I go**: ibid. / **He's certain to continue**: NYT, April 12, 1947. / **We were scared**: Rachel Robinson, interview. / **I was determined**: Rachel Robinson, interview. / **I did a miserable**: *I Never*, p. 70. / **If they're all like**: New York *Daily News*, April 17, 1947. / **perfect**: NYT, April 18, 1947. / **Robby has supreme confidence**: New York *Daily News*, April 17, 1947. / **The muscular Negro**: NYT, April 16, 1947. / **They came to see**: Red Barber, *1947—When All Hell Broke Loose in Baseball* (N.Y.: Doubleday, 1982), p. 155. / **a thousand people**: PC, April 19, 1947. / **We never thought of**: Rachel Robinson, interview. / **I don't know what**: PC, April 26, 1947. / **Hi, Black Boy!**: ibid. / **He's not a ballplayer**: New York *Daily Mirror*, April 17, 1947. / **I ain't going to**: Lester Rodney to Paul Buhle and Michael Fermanowsky, transcript of interview, 1981, UCLA Oral History Program, UCLA Archives, p. 66. / **a swell bunch**: Marty Solow, "Meet Jackie Robinson," *Union Voice*, April 27, 1947. / **Jackie is sitting**: Boston *Globe*, Jan. 24, 1962. / **the loneliest man**: May 10, 1947. / **of all the unpleasant**: *I Never*, pp. 71–72. / **The things the Phillies**: PC, May 3, 1947. / **Listen, you yellow-bellied**: *I Never*, p. 73. / **the only gentleman**: ibid. / **Chapman did more than**: *I Never*, p. 74. / **Photographers sprang up**: Barber, p. 162. / **If you do this**: New York *Herald Tribune*, May 9, 1947. / **We have a great**: NYT, April 29, 1947. / **bring the Nigger here**: Parrott, p. 193. / **And don't bring your**: ibid. / **pointed**

bats at me: *I Never,* p. 76. / **This is something I**: Parrott, p. 217. / **Having my picture taken**: *I Never,* p. 75. / **Chapman impressed me**: PC, May 17, 1947. / **scrawled and scribbled**: Parrott, p. 190. / **I felt they should**: Philadelphia *Inquirer,* May 10, 1947. / **I do not profess**: PC, June 7, 1947. / **the Negro first baseman**: NYT, May 13, 1947. / **Stick in there**: PC, May 24, 1947. / **Class tells**: NYT, May 18, 1947. / **The guys on the team**: PC, May 24, 1947. / **I used to go out**: *I Never,* p. 78. / **Find out for yourself**: Duke Snider and Bill Gilbert, *The Duke of Flatbush* (N.Y.: Zebra, 1988), p. 21. / **I had been**: ibid. / **Robinson is now paying**: PC, May 31, 1947. / **displayed too much enthusiasm**: ibid. / **fears and apprehensions**: PC, June 7, 1947. / **In 1947, Jackie**: Roger Wilkins to author, interview, May 16, 1995. / **But as he had**: Barber, p. 200. / **in dear old Brooklyn**: PC, May 31, 1947. / **I have learned that**: PC, June 14, 1947. / **Times were simpler**: Snider, p. 20. / **were eating at his**: Parrott, p. 199. / **Darling, As we fly**: JR to Rachel Robinson, n.d., RRP. / **he was not yet**: Rachel Robinson, interview. / **I've met most**: misc. clipping, n.d., JRP. / **The feeling in Brooklyn**: Rachel Robinson, interview. / **a swell bunch**: PC, June 21, 1947. / **definitely one**: PC, June 28, 1947. / **very viciously**: WP, Aug. 28, 1949. / **I get all kinds**: Boston *Daily Herald,* June 28, 1947. / **You haven't seen Robinson**: misc. uniden. clipping, June 25, 1947, JRP. / **He is a grand**: PC, July 12, 1947. / **amazing for a rookie**: Toronto *Star,* July 7, 1947. / **came within an inch**: Barber, p. 277. / **Hate was running high**: Barber, p. 278. / **Slaughter deliberately went**: *I Never,* p. 80. / **I know the truth**: NYT, Sept. 29, 1996. / **You better play your**: Roscoe McGowen, "If You Were Jackie Robinson," *Sport,* September 1947, p. 41. / **broke up [the] incipient**: SN, Sept. 24, 1947. / **Ty Cobb in Technicolor**: Christopher Jennison, *Wait 'Til Next Year: The Yankees, Dodgers, and Giants, 1947–1957* (N.Y.: Norton, 1974), p. 22. / **I have tried to**: PC, Aug. 23, 1947. / **The sociological experiment**: Rowan, pp. 193–194. / **No other ballplayer**: *I Never,* p. 81. / **So we're in it**: PC, Oct. 4, 1947. / **I've played a lot**: PC, Oct. 11, 1947. / **It was a pleasure**: misc. clipping, Jan. 6, 1948, JRP. / **Many of us who**: John A. Williams to author, interview, April 17, 1997.

CHAPTER 9

good sport: anon. to JR, n.d., AMP, LC. / **the whole nation**: C. C. Spaulding to JR, Oct. 3, 1947, AMP, LC. / **I was being watched**: JR, misc. fragment, ms., n.d., JRP. / **I've got to make**: ibid. / **should do something**: Baltimore *Afro-American,* Oct. 25, 1947. / **why would he have**: NYAN, Oct. 25, 1947. / **Jack couldn't sing**: Rachel Robinson, interview. / **a new low**: Baltimore *Afro-American,* Nov. 1, 1947. / **a picture of dapper**: NYAN, Oct. 25, 1947. / **for his interest**: ibid. / **gracious, down-right big-hearted**: Red Skelton to JR, Feb. 19, 1948, JRP. / **Jackie took the boy's**: misc. clipping, uniden., JRP. / **We'd pull off the**: Rachel Robinson, interview. / **the first man in**: Oakland *Tribune,* Dec. 2, 1947. / **a short but impressive**: PC, Jan. 3, 1948. / **More than sixty thousand**: Arthur Mann, *The Jackie Robinson Story* (N.Y.: Grosset & Dunlap, 1951), p. 202. / **We ate like pigs**: *I Never,* p. 83. / **There's no question**: NYAN, Dec. 6, 1947. / **I respected and respect**: Rachel Robinson, interview. / **considerable vehemence**: Mann, p. 202. / **Mr. Rickey and I**: PC, Feb. 21, 1948. / **Complications set in**: *I Never,* pp. 82–83. / **I met all the gang**: PC, March 13, 1948. / **The best second baseman**: Baltimore *Afro-American,* March 13, 1948. / **I was sorry to see**: PC, March 20, 1948. / **Wherever they tell me**: PC, April 17, 1948. / **I'm just a player**: Baltimore *Afro-American,* Dec. 6, 1947. / **What in the world**: PC, March 13, 1948. / **I think Durocher is**: New York *Daily News,* March 29, 1948. / **After an inexcusably**: Baltimore *Afro-American,* March 27, 1948. / **conscious of their color**: PC, March 13, 1948. / **pulled and tugged**: PC, March 20, 1948. / **I miss him**: PC, March 27, 1948. / **Sure we were scared**: PC, April 10, 1948. / **I'm in good shape**: ibid. / **click like a five**: PC, April 17, 1948. / **the jam-packed room**: ibid. / **We like it**: misc. uniden. clipping, n.d., JRP. / **Oh, isn't that nice**: Sarah [Satlow] Cymrot to author, interview, June 14, 1995. / **our ambassador**: Rachel Robinson, interview. / **We didn't know what**: Sarah Cymrot, interview. / **There was a lot**: Rachel Robinson, interview. / **They evidently have**: JR to Rachel Robinson, n.d., RRP. / **she rose and in**: Baltimore *Afro-American,* Nov. 15, 1947. / **the one person**: ibid. / **I can truly say**: Madison (N.J.) *Eagle,* Dec. 30, 1948. / **I**

hated it: Rachel Robinson, interview. / **I want you to love**: anon. to JR, Oct. 6, 1947, AMP, LC. / **When I married**: JR to anon., n.d., AMP, LC. / **but they are meant**: JR to Rachel Robinson, n.d., RRP. / **When he'd be on**: Joe Black to Spike Lee, interview, Oct. 27, 1994. / **increased my love**: JR to Rachel Robinson, n.d., RRP. / **Darling, if only**: JR to Rachel Robinson, n.d., RRP. / **We think we have**: PC, April 17, 1948. / **waddled**: Mann, p. 205. / **He fought against tears**: Mann, p. 206. / **a good manager**: PC, May 15, 1948. / **I think I'm ready**: PC, May 22, 1948. / **the dashing, daring base**: PC, June 5, 1948. / **He has been overweight**: New York *Daily Mirror,* May 26, 1948. / **I'm not worried about**: PC, June 5, 1948. / **the first time**: NYT, June 25, 1948. / **a human dynamo**: PC, July 24, 1948. / **What the black man**: Harold Parrott, *The Lords of Baseball* (N.Y.: Praeger, 1976), p. 204. / **But deep in my**: Carl Rowan, *Wait Till Next Year* (N.Y.: Random House, 1960), pp. 198–199. / **was only fair**: Allan Roth, "1948 Brooklyn Dodgers: Complete Statistical Data, Team and Individual Batting and Pitching Record, Individual Player Analysis [Jackie Robinson]," Los Angeles Dodgers Archives. / **Yes sir, when a Negro**: PC, Aug. 14, 1948. / **Jackie came rushing out**: PC, Sept. 4, 1948. / **all by himself**: PC, June 5, 1948. / **I certainly want**: PC, June 12, 1948. / **can't carry Doby's glove**: PC, Nov. 13, 1948. / **utterly ridiculous**: ibid. / **Both Roy and I**: *The New Sign* (Harlem Branch YMCA), Sept. 18, 1948, p. 1. / **We are very much**: PC, March 5, 1949. / **a big thrill**: PC, Oct. 9, 1948. / **By his gentlemanly conduct**: PC, July 3, 1948. / **They are the kind**: WP, Aug. 30, 1949. / **Mr. Rickey may have**: PC, Oct. 22, 1949. / **leather-lunged**: PC, March 19, 1949. / **They better be rough**: New York *Sun,* March 6, 1949. / **This, it seems**: PC, March 19, 1949. / **My family named me**: JR, *Jackie Robinson: My Own Story* (N.Y.: Greenberg, 1948), p. 7. / **he has NEVER had**: Baltimore *Afro-American,* Feb. 14, 1948. / **The idea that Branch**: Branch B. Rickey to author, interview, Feb. 27, 1997. / **It was a tempest**: BE, March 19, 1949. / **one bad deed by**: PC, March 5, 1949. / **Sisler showed me how**: PC, April 9, 1949. / **I feel right now**: BE, March 28, 1949. / **The only danger from**: BE, April 7, 1949. / **I will play baseball**: BE, Jan. 16, 1949. / **I decided then**: PC, April 16, 1949. / **Robinson, on the other**: PC, April 16, 1949. / **The Dodgers will**

have: PC, May 7, 1949. / **This kid's going to**: PC, June 25, 1949. / **I cuss him out**: PC, Aug. 16, 1949. / **Negro Troops Fight Bravely**: BE, June 23, 1949. / **I couldn't understand why**: misc. fragment, ms, n.d., JRP. / **As you know**: Leslie Perry to JR, July 11, 1949, BRP, LC. / **I think it was**: misc. fragment, n.d., JRP. / **It is unthinkable**: NYT, April 21, 1949. / **Now a white man**: Rowan, *Wait*, p. 203. / **rousing ovation**: Ronald A. Smith, "The Paul Robeson–Jackie Robinson Saga and a Political Collision," *Journal of Sport History* 6 (Summer 1979), p. 14. / **the greatest step ever**: Montreal *Gazette,* October 24, 1945. / **I felt so badly**: Sarah [Satlow] Cymrot, interview. / **There ain't nothing wrong**: misc. clipping, n.d., JRP. / **Intent on him**: Rachel Robinson, "I Live with a Hero," *Negro Digest,* June 1951, p. 10. / **is as far removed**: Hearings Regarding Communist Infiltration of Minority Groups, Hearings Before the Committee on Un-American Activities, House of Representatives, Eighty-first Congress, July 18, 1949, pp. 479–483. / **the Ebony Express**: BE, July 19, 1949. / **Public speaking must agree**: ibid. / **Credo of an American**: NYP, July 19, 1949. / **Quite a man**: New York *Daily News,* July 20, 1949. / **split sharply**: New York *Age,* July 23, 1949. / **boomeranged**: Baltimore *Afro-American,* July 23, 1949. / **not one single case**: Lester Granger to JR, July 19, 1949, BRP, LC. / **I have no quarrel**: BE, July 21, 1949. / **I have boxes**: WP, Aug. 30, 1949. / **anger written all over**: Bill Mardo to the *Nation,* May 5, 1995; courtesy of Bill Mardo. / **if Mr. Robeson wants**: *Daily Worker,* Aug. 29, 1949. / **wiser and closer**: *I Never,* p. 98. / **Jackie Robinson put his**: Bill Mardo to the *Nation,* May 5, 1995. / **Without Robinson**: PC, Aug. 13, 1949. / **You must admit**: cited in PC, Aug. 13, 1949. / **They couldn't get me**: PC, Sept. 10, 1949. / **Well, what do you**: PC, Nov. 26, 1949. / **What is there to**: PC, Oct. 15, 1949. / **a light case of**: PC, Nov. 12, 1949. / **All this means**: PC, Nov. 26, 1949.

CHAPTER 10

All America must applaud: misc. clippings, n.d., JRP. / **It's the best way**: WP, Aug. 23, 1949. / **The strain of the last**: New York

Daily News, Nov. 19, 1949. / **This is too supervised**: *Daily Worker* clipping, n.d. [1949], JRP. / **heard me speak**: Arnold Forster, *Square One: A Memoir* (N.Y.: Donald I. Fine, 1988), p. 97. / **That may be so**: Rachel Robinson, interview. / **One way we knew**: ibid. / **Mommy, my hands**: ibid. / **Look, there's discrimination**: Jack Harrison Pollack, "Meet a Family Named Robinson," *Parents' Magazine & Family Home Guide,* Oct. 1955, p. 111. / **I wish I was white**: misc. clipping, n.d., JRP. / **Pitches Curves!**: "The Jackie Robinson Story," *Ebony,* June 1950, p. 83. / **Jack was mentioned**: Martin Stone to author, interview, July 14, 1995. / **Two of the big**: "The Jackie Robinson Story," *Ebony,* p. 91. / **this might sound like**: Arthur Mann to Branch Rickey, Nov. 18, 1949, BRP. / **It took all**: "The Jackie Robinson Story," *Ebony,* p. 92. / **Jackie made a tremendous**: SN, May 10, 1950. / **He was a loyal**: Los Angeles *Herald-Examiner,* Oct. 26, 1972. / **The way they had**: "The Jackie Robinson Story," *Ebony,* p. 92. / **I simply explained**: ibid. / **Are you kidding?**: SN, May 10, 1950. / **In one scene**: Ruby Dee to author, interview, July 20, 1995. / **a mildly romantic scene**: "Jackie Robinson's Double Play," *Life,* May 8, 1950, p. 131. / **The moment I talked**: Ruby Dee, interview. / **patronizing and offensive**: Carl E. Prince, *Brooklyn's Dodgers: The Bums, the Borough, and the Best of Baseball, 1947–1957* (New York: Oxford, 1996), p. 35. / **Surprisingly, Jackie Robinson**: misc. clipping, n.d., JRP. / **Here the simple story**: NYT, May 17, 1950. / **we are going to**: PC, Feb. 11, 1950. / **I'm not going to**: PC, Feb. 4, 1950. / **Robinson's recently accumulated**: PC, April 1, 1950. / **Of course, in the case**: New York *Daily News,* Jan. 26, 1950. / **Jackie is a better**: PC, April 29, 1950. / **He's the indispensable man**: PC, June 17, 1950. / **consistency against**: Allan Roth, "1949 Brooklyn Dodgers," Los Angeles Dodgers Archives. / **Let's not have no**: Harold Parrott, *The Lords of Baseball* (N.Y.: Praeger, 1976), p. 218. / **Better go easy, Jackie**: SN, Aug. 29, 1951. / **That strike was right**: SN, July 12, 1950. / **Frick has given these**: ibid. / **There is no question**: PC, July 15, 1950. / **the biggest deal**: SN, Oct. 4, 1950. / **That was a lot**: Los Angeles *Times,* June 5, 1972. / **the little guy**: SN, March 7, 1951. / **about a month**: JR to Branch Rickey, n.d., BRP, LC. / **Sometimes my family**: Branch B. Rickey to author, interview, Feb. 24, 1997. / **Jackie Headed for Polo**: SN, Sept. 27, 1950. / **I'll have my family**: PC, Aug. 12, 1950. / **Nothing was promised**: SN, Nov. 21, 1951. / **no reason why**: PC, March 31, 1951. / **Because the call comes**: memorandum to John D. Rockefeller III, Dec. 27, 1950, JRP. / **a vain, proud**: SN, Aug. 16, 1950. / **I am counting on**: PC, Dec. 9, 1950. / **It certainly did not**: Rachel Robinson, interview. / **That dieting business**: PC, March 10, 1951. / **I'm going to open**: PC, Feb. 10, 1951. / **We have a different**: SN, March 28, 1951. / **Jackie would** *never*: Carl Erskine to author, interview, Feb. 10, 1997. / **I like aggressive play**: PC, April 7, 1951. / **might be a little**: PC, April 21, 1951. / **Anything I do**: SN, May 2, 1951. / **I'm not going to be**: SN, May 23, 1951. / **umpire-baiting**: SN, May 2, 1951. / **Leo, I can smell**: Prince, p. 49. / **"amazed" by his catlike**: Baltimore *Afro-American,* March 13, 1948. / **My dick to you**: Roger Kahn, *The Boys of Summer* (N.Y.: Harper & Row, 1972), p. 97. / **You've got a swelled**: PC, June 13, 1950. / **Did you notice**: SN, Sept. 19, 1951. / **I just don't like**: ibid. / **You've got a nerve**: SN, May 9, 1951. / **it's a long season**: ibid. / **tired ... popping off**: ibid. / **I have no reason**: ibid. / **on the carpet**: ibid. / **Robinson always has been**: SN, May 16, 1951. / **many fans of both races**: PC, May 5, 1951. / **Robinson will read this**: PC, May 19, 1951. / **I think we will**: SN, May 30, 1951. / **If I hadn't started**: SN, June 6, 1951. / **in a way that**: SN, June 13, 1951. / **What good is that**: SN, Sept. 26, 1951. / **I'm not saying anything**: SN, Oct. 10, 1951. / **The ball is a blur**: NYT, Oct. 25, 1972. / **one of the greatest**: SN, Jan. 2, 1952. / **stretched at full length**: NYT, Oct. 25, 1972. / **There's no stopping us**: PC, Oct. 6, 1951. / **Well, we let**: Robert Campbell, interview, UCLA Archives. / **Roll out the barrels**: SN, Oct. 10, 1951. / **We think he's**: SN, Oct. 17, 1951. / **He deserves every honor**: SN, Nov. 7, 1951. / **It was not only**: PC, June 7, 1952. / **Fans used to travel**: PC, Nov. 22, 1952. / **These trips are really**: SN, Nov. 21, 1951. / **It's Robinson they come**: PC, Dec. 8, 1951. / **the league's busiest**: SN, Feb. 20, 1952. / **I had a chip**: PC, Feb. 23, 1952. / **unique in the field**: "News from NBC" (press release), Feb. 4, 1952; JRP. / **a decent home**: NYP, Sept. 23, 1959. / **I think every player**: SN, Feb. 20, 1952. / **perfectly satisfied**: PC, Jan. 19, 1952. / **Can you fight?**: Joe Black to

Spike Lee, interview, Oct. 27, 1994. / **I don't mind**: SN, April 16, 1952. / **a greater offender**: PC, May 24, 1952. / **The National League is**: Milton Gross, "Why They Boo Jackie Robinson," *Sport,* Feb. 1953, p. 96. / **I know it's wrong**: PC, July 26, 1952. / **too much fuss over**: PC, June 21, 1952. / **I decided that**: Rachel Robinson, interview. / **I think I'm going**: Joe Black to Spike Lee, interview. / **They scared him**: Rachel Robinson, interview. / **Before he left**: PC, Aug. 2, 1952. / **Don't you worry**: PC, Sept. 6, 1952. / **What he said**: Gross, p. 96. / **Before I'll pay that**: ibid. / **I never thought**: ibid. / **The main thing**: PC, Oct. 4, 1952. / **I couldn't argue**: PC, Oct. 11, 1952. / **I certainly might**: PC, Sept. 27, 1952. / **It made me stop**: SN, Nov. 21, 1951.

CHAPTER 11

I pointed out: Martin Stone, interview. / **After the war**: Jack Gordon, interview. / **Whatever his deal was**: Rachel Robinson, interview. / **Jack was an "I . . ."**: Evelyn Cunningham, interview, June 19, 1995. / **He certainly was**: Rachel Robinson, interview. / **I'm no longer**: St. Louis *Post-Dispatch,* April 8, 1953. / **fine sportsmen and wonderful**: PC, Dec. 27, 1952. / **who can play good**: ibid. / **everyone should be**: ibid. / **I merely said**: ibid. / **What do you think**: Milton Gross, "Why They Boo Jackie Robinson," *Sport,* Feb. 1953, p. 95. / **Do they think**: Gross, p. 97. / **maybe it's because**: ibid. / **The very violence**: ibid. / **I've always been treated**: PC, Jan. 24, 1953. / **I hit a couple**: PC, March 14, 1953. / **I don't see any**: PC, Jan. 24, 1953. / **That ain't a third**: Mike Shatzkin, ed., *The Ballplayers: Baseball's Ultimate Biographical Reference* (New York: William Morrow, 1990), p. 229. / **Trouble on the Dodgers**: NYP, March 23, 1953. / **I know Cox is**: PC, March 28, 1953. / **There isn't a guy**: PC, June 20, 1953. / **You couldn't dream up**: PC, March 28, 1953. / **Our outfield wasn't going**: PC, June 6, 1953. / **How do you vote**: NYT, July 3, 1953. / **get up there**: PC, July 25, 1953. / **black nigger bastard**: PC, Aug. 15, 1953. / **Kill him, Carl**: Carl E. Prince, *Brooklyn's Dodgers* (N.Y.: Oxford, 1996), p. 45. / **another two or three**: PC, Aug. 15, 1953. / **He still compensates**:

Newark (N.J.) *Evening News,* July 16, 1953. / **serenely depend-able**: NYP, Sept. 7, 1953. / **If we don't win**: PC, Sept. 26, 1953. / **in which the juvenile**: ibid. / **the grapevine claims that**: PC, Jan. 23, 1954. / **If I am traded**: PC, Nov. 28, 1953. / **I had nothing**: PC, Nov. 7, 1953. / **may have been wrong**: PC, Dec. 5, 1953. / **one of the great**: JR to Dwight D. Eisenhower, Nov. 27, 1953, JRP. / **To think the President**: misc. clipping, n.d., JRP. / **great privilege**: JR to Dwight D. Eisenhower, Nov. 27, 1953. / **Education must begin**: JR, misc. speeches, n.d., JRP. / **Brother-hood is a big**: JR, "The Big Game (An Editorial)," *Read,* March 1, 1956, p. 2. / **dedication to good human**: Russell L. Bradley to NBC, Feb. 9, 1954, JRP. / **I never witnessed**: Hastings Harrison to NBC, Feb. 18, 1954, JRP. / **modesty and deep sincerity**: William Lindsay Young to NBC, Feb. 16, 1954, JRP. / **Jackie isn't just**: misc. clipping, n.d. (1953), JRP. / **that there is no**: JR to Ernest de la Ossa, NBC, Feb. 4, 1954, JRP. / **He had a way**: Anaheim (Cal.) *Bulletin,* Feb. 24, 1972. / **I was pretty angry**: Rachel Robinson, interview. / **a fine group of men**: JR, "The Branch Rickey They Don't Write About," *Our Sports,* July 1953, p. 63. / **actions, his attitude**: Howard F. Klein to Walter O'Mal-ley, Nov. 11, 1953, JRP. / **over the years Jackie**: Walter O'Mal-ley to Howard F. Klein, Nov. 17, 1953, JRP. / **It was a dump**: PC, May 8, 1954. / **I remember Jack sighing**: Martin Stone, inter-view. / **Walter Winchell had arranged**: Rachel Robinson, inter-view. / **his tremendous contribution**: Daytona Beach (Fla.) *Evening News,* March 17, 1954. / **one of the biggest**: JR to Richard V. Moore, March 18, 1954, JRP. / **Perhaps the most thrilling**: JR to Ralph Bunche, March 18, 1954, JRP. / **I'm not going to**: PC, May 8, 1954. / **I want it understood**: misc. clip-ping, n.d., JRP. / **I lost my head**: PC, Jan. 22, 1955. / **He ain't what he**: NYP, April 19, 1954. / **Can I get a walk**: JR, "Now I Know Why They Boo Me," *Look,* Jan. 25, 1955, p. 24. / **the most savagely booed**: cited in PC, Nov. 6, 1954. / **an agitator**: JR, "Now I Know Why They Boo Me," p. 24. / **If that's a record**: PC, Jan. 22, 1955. / **Out there alone**: JR, "Now I Know Why They Boo Me," p. 23. / **standing out there**: *I Never,* p. 130. / **Hey Jackie, I'm Ronnie**: Chicago *Sun-Times,* April 5, 1987. / **I learned a long**: JR to Ron Rabinovitz, n.d., in Minneapolis *Star* *and Tribune,* April 12, 1987. / **The main thing**: Chicago *Sun-Times,* April 5, 1987. / **I learned from Jackie**: Minneapolis *Star Tribune,* April 12, 1987. / **I hope my bringing**: Roger Kahn, "The Ten Years of Jackie Robinson," *Sport,* Oct. 1955, p. 13. / **If you can't write**: ibid. / **Jack would have been**: Rachel Robinson, interview. / **Most of the black people**: ibid. / **Jackie denies**: PC, Jan. 22, 1955. / **Overall it was**: Allan Roth, "1954 Brooklyn Dodgers: Complete Statistical Data [Jackie Robinson]," Los Angeles Dodgers Archives. / **I would trade him**: Andy A. High, note, n.d., in Roth, "1954 Brooklyn Dodgers," L.A. Dodgers Archives. / **How can I think**: misc. clipping, n.d., JRP. / **is said to be**: PC, Sept. 18, 1954. / **It is tragic**: PC, Oct. 16, 1954. / **Hot or cold**: PC, Oct. 16, 1954. / **I want to try**: New York *Daily News,* Nov. 21, 1954. / **I worry about myself**: PC, Feb. 26, 1955. / **You really are**: Rachel Robinson, interview. / **one who has himself**: John D. Rockefeller to JR, Nov. 3, 1954, JRP. / **Jack's reaction was horror**: Rachel Robinson, interview.

CHAPTER 12

I have been proud: JR to Rachel Robinson, n.d., RRP. / **I am sure you**: JR to Rachel Robinson, n.d., RRP. / **Jack would not be**: SN, Jan. 5, 1955. / **Wouldn't it be more**: SN, Feb. 2, 1955. / **that I was a bigot**: SN, March 2, 1955. / **traded him out**: SN, Feb. 2, 1955. / **I'd rather play third**: SN, May 4, 1955. / **could depend on Don**: SN, March 9, 1955. / **I worked harder**: JR to Rachel Robinson, n.d., RRP. / **Alston does not seem**: ibid. / **I am getting along**: JR to Rachel Robinson, n.d., RRP. / **he has only had**: JR to Rachel Robinson, n.d., RRP. / **made weak by time**: SN, April 6, 1955. / **If Alston doesn't want**: misc. clipping, n.d., JRP. / **I've been in shape**: SN, April 13, 1955 / **the range of Jackie**: NYP, April 7, 1955. / **this was definitely not**: Harold Parrott, *The Lords of Baseball* (N.Y.: Praeger, 1976), p. 211. / **Jackie Robinson is worth**: PC, Feb. 28, 1956. / **I was totally surprised**: Carl Erskine to author, interview, Feb. 25, 1997. / **No matter who**: Don Drysdale (with Bob Verdi), *Once a Bum, Always a Dodger* (New York: St. Martin's Press, 1990), p. 29. / **an**

awfully intense: Drysdale, p. 62. / **That's fine encouragement**: misc. clipping, n.d., JRP. / **Robinson Can Still Do**: NYP, April 14, 1955. / **I got nothing against**: SN, May 4, 1955. / **Sportswriters in general**: misc. clipping, May 18, 1955, JRP. / **a lot of baloney**: PC, May 21, 1955. / **I'm doing as lousy**: SN, May 25, 1955. / **On top of it all**: PC, June 20, 1955. / **the owner of psychic**: PC, Aug. 27, 1955. / **The Negro player is**: misc. clipping, n.d., JRP. / **It's just that I**: PC, Sept. 10, 1955. / **Jackie Robinson was born**: misc. clipping, Oct. 1, 1955, JRP. / **His hair is gray**: Boston *Globe,* Oct. 1, 1955. / **Aging Robinson Sets Dodgers**: misc. clipping, Oct. 1, 1955, JRP. / **Perhaps never**: Harry Caray, *KMOX Sports Digest,* Oct. 2, 1955. / **a competitor for control**: NYP, Oct. 5, 1955. / **I'll talk with**: ibid. / **was always a couple**: Calgary *Herald,* Dec. 8, 1955. / **Such a gesture proves**: Calgary *Herald,* Dec. 17, 1955. / **The more I read**: JR to Rachel Robinson, n.d., RRP. / **this is not what**: Chicago *Daily News,* Jan. 21, 1956. / **He then told me**: JR to Rachel Robinson, n.d., RRP. / **I am not worried**: JR to Rachel Robinson, n.d., RRP. / **Except for myself**: misc. clipping, n.d., JRP. / **I really have been**: JR to Rachel Robinson, n.d., RRP. / **I have been moving**: JR to Rachel Robinson, n.d., RRP. / **This is one real**: JR to Rachel Robinson, n.d., RRP. / **From the very first**: JR to Rachel Robinson, n.d., RRP. / **The fellows are all**: JR to Rachel Robinson, fragment, n.d., RRP. / **I had to laugh**: ibid. / **one major reason**: Martin Stone, interview. / **a cleanliness to**: Sam Lacy to author, interview, May 17, 1995. / **It seems Campy has**: JR to Rachel Robinson, n.d., RRP. / **Jackie Robinson was**: Roy Campanella II to author, interview, Oct. 8, 1996. / **I resented Dick Young's**: JR to Rachel Robinson, n.d., RRP. / **My Darling, I can't**: JR to Rachel Robinson, n.d., RRP. / **My father didn't want**: Peter O'Malley to author, interview, Sept. 7, 1995. / **The way they acted**: PC, April 19, 1956. / **Robinson doesn't have to**: ibid. / **seems to have**: NYT, June 25, 1956. / **I don't think**: PC, June 23, 1956. / **I like Jack's attitude**: ibid. / **I'm fined for remarks**: PC, July 7, 1956. / **and Jackie got an earful**: Drysdale, p. 63. / **quite a bit**: PC, May 12, 1956. / **persistently insolent and trouble-making**: New Orleans *Times-Picayune,* July 18, 1956. / **not as Jackie Robinson**: PC, Aug. 4, 1956. / **I threw**

it: PC, Sept. 8, 1956. / **a one-man task**: New York *Journal-American,* Oct. 2, 1956. / **Babe Ruth can't manage**: NYT, April 15, 1987. / **strictly rumor**: Honolulu *Star-Bulletin,* Oct. 15, 1956. / *Because I am a Negro*: JR, as told to Milton Gross, "Why Can't I Manage in the Majors?" misc. clipping (1956), JRP. / **Your own presence**: Russell L. Riley to JR, Sept. 14, 1956, JRP. / **Walter O'Malley had**: Rachel Robinson, interview. / **what you have done**: John M. Allison to JR, Nov. 5, 1956, JRP. / **in recognition**: misc. clipping, n.d., JRP. / **I am now quite**: "Acceptance Address by Jackie Robinson at Special Luncheon Honoring Him on Presentation of 41st Spingarn Medal," ms., Dec. 8, 1956, JRP. / **From what I had read**: PC, Feb. 9, 1957. / **that he was having**: Martin Stone, interview. / **just about the best**: JR, "Why I'm Quitting Baseball," *Look,* Jan. 8, 1957, p. 90. / **I told Jackie**: PC, Feb. 9, 1957. / **didn't try to influence**: JR, "Why I'm Quitting Baseball," p. 91. / **I told Jack, "Don't . . ."**: Martin Stone, interview. / **We made the deal**: NYP, Dec. 13, 1956. / **I'll give the Giants**: New York *Newsday,* Dec. 14, 1956. / **There was a kind**: Rachel Robinson, interview. / **I think you know**: E. J. Bavasi to JR, Dec. 13, 1956, JRP. / **courageous and fair**: Walter O'Malley to JR, Dec. 14, 1956, JRP. / **always admired**: Walter Alston to JR, Dec. 18, 1956, JRP. / **You are Jackie Robinson**: New York *Newsday,* Dec. 14, 1956. / **is always seeking publicity**: Roger Kahn, "The Ten Years of Jackie Robinson," p. 15. / **There would have been**: misc. clipping, n.d., JRP. / **Million Dollars Won't Change**: New York *Daily Mirror,* Jan. 7, 1957. / **proud—very proud**: William Black to JR, Jan. 10, 1957, JRP. / **Didn't you lie**: Kahn, *The Boys of Summer* (N.Y.: New American Library, 1971), p. 354. / **the bell-cow**: Providence (R.I.) *Evening Bulletin,* Jan. 8, 1957. / **If you decide**: Charles S. Feeney to JR, Jan. 11, 1957, JRP. / **after due consideration**: JR to Horace C. Stoneham, Jan. 14, 1957, JRP. / **I can't help thinking**: Horace C. Stoneham to JR, Jan. 12, 1957, JRP. / **both on and off**: Richie Ashburn to JR, n.d., JRP. / **your long and illustrious**: Hank Greenberg to JR, Jan. 7, 1957, JRP. / **You opened the door**: Brooks Lawrence to JR, Jan. 18, 1957, JRP. / **I have never made**: San Francisco *Examiner,* Jan. 27, 1957. / **When it's my turn**: Los Angeles *Sentinel,* Jan. 31, 1957. / **combined the bitterness**: ibid. / **David,**

who liked: Rachel Robinson, interview. / **Robinson happens to be**: *Variety,* Jan. 19, 1957.

CHAPTER 13

I'll be very glad: JR to Rachel Robinson, n.d., RRP. / **When I would come**: Leonard Gross, "*Pageant* Listens to Jackie Robinson," *Pageant,* May 1957, p. 141. / **His devotion to them**: ibid. / **Give him a kiss**: Rachel Robinson, interview. / **Jack was the sweetest**: Brenda Williams to author, interview, March 1, 1997. / **a beautiful person**: Willette Bailey to author, interview, June 28, 1995. / **The Robinsons were**: Joanna Simon to author, interview, July 27, 1995. / **My own father**: Peter Simon to author, interview, Aug. 10, 1996. / **I never knew this**: *Observer* (London, England), Nov. 5, 1972. / **Unable to shield my**: Sharon Robinson, *Stealing Home: An Intimate Family Portrait* (New York: HarperCollins, 1996), p. 87. / **Perhaps we should have**: Rachel Robinson, interview. / **Don't get me wrong**: Baltimore *Sun,* Jan. 21, 1957. / **Baseball was just**: transcript of *Viewpoint,* Mutual Broadcasting Company, Dec. 14, 1957, JRP. / **I said sure**: transcript of speeches of JR and Franklin H. Williams, NAACP Fund Rally, Oakland, Cal., Jan. 27, 1957, JRP. / **Does Jackie Robinson**: *Jet,* Jan. 31, 1957, pp. 52–55. / **they rose waving bills**: Franklin H. Williams to NAACP, Feb. 15, 1957, NAACPR, LC. / **a low and well**: Baltimore *Afro-American,* Jan. 22, 1957. / **There was a time**: Detroit *Times,* Jan. 24, 1957. / **It's too late**: Cleveland *Plain Dealer,* Jan. 23, 1957. / **We can't let these**: Baltimore *Afro-American,* Jan. 22, 1957. / **If I thought**: PC, Feb. 2, 1957. / **White people need**: Detroit *Chronicle,* Jan. 22, 1957. / **We in the NAACP**: Cleveland *Plain Dealer,* Jan. 23, 1957. / **a disgrace**: Oakland *Tribune,* Jan. 28, 1957. / **a living legend**: Los Angeles *Tribune,* Jan. 30, 1957. / **smartest man in baseball**: Los Angeles *Examiner,* Jan. 29, 1957. / **When Jackie spoke**: Los Angeles *Herald & Express,* Jan. 30, 1957. / **Has Pasadena changed**: Los Angeles *Tribune,* Jan. 30, 1957. / **extremely easy**: Franklin H. Williams to Roy Wilkins, Feb. 15, 1957, NAACPR, LC. / **a fine person**: Boston *Sunday Advertiser,* Feb. 3, 1957. / **I sometimes find**: JR, address, Olympia

Stadium, Detroit, June 30, 1957, JRP. / **He left in high**: Jack Gordon, interview. / **He practiced**: Rachel Robinson, interview. / **Taking the insulin**: JR to David and Caroline Wallerstein, [May 19, 1958], JRP. / **From the start**: Rachel Robinson, interview. / **The name Jackie**: NYT, March 9, 1958. / **This is a team**: ibid. / **He is one**: JR to E. Frederic Morrow, June 28, 1957, JRP. / **Your having left**: New York *Daily News,* May 21, 1958. / **The day when I**: NYT, March 9, 1958. / **They looked right at**: Robert Campbell, interview, UCLA Archives. / **I hired Jackie because**: Gross, p. 140. / **They are going to**: JR to Caroline Wallerstein, n.d., JRP. / **the white employees**: misc. clipping, n.d., JRP. / **Jackie Robinson wasn't antiunion**: Percy Sutton to author, interview, July 18, 1995. / **I feel fine**: JR to David and Caroline Wallerstein, n.d., JRP. / **My job is developing**: JR to Caroline Wallerstein, n.d. [May 19, 1958], JRP. / **his right to think**: William Black to Ray Grody, Feb. 4, 1957, JRP. / **our great President**: Los Angeles *Tribune,* Jan. 30, 1957. / **Knowing President Eisenhower**: Los Angeles *Mirror-News,* Jan. 29, 1957. / **I have the greatest**: Boston *Sunday Herald,* Feb. 3, 1957. / **I said to Nixon**: Harrison McCall, memorandum, Jan. 3, 1959, JRP. / **Our country is engaged**: JR, speech to American Friends Service Committee, April 6, 1957, JRP. / **very fine letter**: Maxwell M. Rabb to JR, Jan. 4, 1957, JRP. / **We shall never be**: JR to Richard M. Nixon, March 17, 1957, JRP. / **in the heart**: ibid. / **none which meant more**: Richard M. Nixon to JR, March 22, 1957, JRP. / **to know our national**: JR to Sherman Adams, April 7, 1957, JRP. / **a superb job**: Lawrence E. Spivak to JR, April 15, 1957, JRP. / **another big thrill**: JR to Dwight D. Eisenhower, May 15, 1957, JRP. / **your approval**: Dwight D. Eisenhower to JR, May 21, 1957, JRP. / **certain phrases I didn't**: Peter M. Bergman, *The Negro in America* (New York: Harper and Row, 1969), p. 551. / **I am really in**: JR to Maxwell M. Rabb, July 19, 1957, JRP. / **watered-down**: Richard M. Nixon to JR, Aug. 8, 1957, JRP. / **What you do**: JR to Richard M. Nixon, Aug. 28, 1957, JRP. / **We are wondering**: JR to Dwight D. Eisenhower, Sept. 13, 1957, JRP. / **as far as "Ike"**: JR to Caroline Wallerstein, Sept. 23, 1957, JRP. / **until they have**: Bergman, p. 550. / **Please accept**: JR to Dwight D. Eisenhower, Sept. 25, 1957, JRP. / **I think you and**: transcript of telephone conversation between JR and Mrs. Daisy Bates and others, Oct. 18, 1957, NAACPR, LC. / **I'm not dumb enough**: Waterbury (Conn.) *Sunday Republican,* June 16, 1957. / **None of us**: JR, ms., Nov. 22, 1957, JRP. / **There just is not**: NYAN, Jan. 18, 1958. / **These are swiftly moving**: NYAN, July 5, 1958. / **Do not have N.A.A.C.P.**: Medgar Evers to JR, Dec. 27, 1957, JRP. / **Although we who struggle**: JR, "Patience, Pride and Progress," ms., Feb. 16, 1958, JRP. / **We had an overflow**: JR to Rachel Robinson, n.d., RRP. / **Miami isn't what**: ibid. / **it took a great**: Peter O'Malley, interview. / **I root for them**: Newark *Star-Ledger,* May 9, 1958. / **I really feel sorry**: JR to Caroline Wallerstein, May 19, 1958, JRP. / **enlightened leadership**: New York *Daily News,* May 3, 1958. / **That's preposterous**: Newark *Star-Ledger,* May 9, 1958. / **Baseball has nothing**: Cleveland *Call-Post,* July 19, 1958. / **He was never adamant**: Rachel Robinson, interview. / **Rae is studying again**: JR to Caroline Wallerstein, July 11, 1958, JRP. / **I was less enthusiastic**: Rachel Robinson, interview. / **Frankly I don't care**: JR to David and Caroline Wallerstein, n.d., JRP. / **It's a pretty good**: JR to David and Caroline Wallerstein, n.d., JRP. / **I don't expect we**: JR to Rachel Robinson, n.d., RRP. / **As a Negro**: Charleston (W. Va.) *Gazette,* April 18, 1958. / **love to see**: Cleveland *Call-Post,* July 19, 1958. / **could be regarded**: NYAN, Aug. 9, 1958. / **3,000 to march**: NYAN, Oct. 25, 1958. / **I have never been**: Providence (R.I.) *Journal,* Nov. 6, 1958. / **is causing groups**: NYAN, Nov. 29, 1958. / **the soul of sincerity**: ibid. / **You didn't seem interested**: Providence *Journal,* Nov. 6, 1958. / **all listeners would be**: JR to Dwight D. Eisenhower, Jan. 15, 1959, JRP. / **If anyone wants to**: NYP, June 26, 1959. / **I felt I wasn't**: NYAN, Aug. 15, 1959. / **a superb job**: Roy Wilkins to JR, Aug. 3, 1959, JRP. / **on any subject**: NYP, April 24, 1959. / **For better or worse**: NYP, April 28, 1959. / **somewhat peeved by this**: NYP, Jan. 13, 1960. / **a quiet, hooded**: NYP, April 30, 1959. / **is somewhat similar to**: NYP, May 8, 1959. / **I guess you'd call**: ibid. / **I have no political**: NYP, July 25, 1960. / **How long, Mr. President**: NYP, June 12, 1959. / **Now is the time**: NYP, Aug. 3, 1959. / **more than a question**: ibid. / **This man and his**: ibid. / **a disheveled, unshaven man**: NYP, Oct. 28, 1959. / **words of great hope**: NYP, Dec. 14, 1959. / **Could it be**:

NYP, Jan. 20, 1960. / **I've been following**: Dec. 30, 1959. / **the Democrats consider**: ibid. / **I thought I was**: JR to Herbert Klein, Jan. 10, 1960, JRP. / **The Negro is in**: JR to Richard M. Nixon, Feb. 25, 1960, JRP. / **I want right here**: NYP, March 16, 1960. / **I could go on**: NYP, June 3, 1960. / **Dear Jackie**: NYP, June 10, 1960. / **Although I appreciated**: *I Never,* pp. 149–150. / **an end to all**: NYP, July 6, 1960. / **the lion's share**: NYP, July 15, 1960. / **a bid for**: ibid. / **It is now clearer**: NYP, July 18, 1960. / **The battle lines**: NYP, July 29, 1960. / **Faced with this kind**: NYP, Aug. 15, 1960. / **an aide**: NYP, Aug. 17, 1960. / **I don't mind admitting**: NYP, Aug. 19, 1960. / **used his race**: NYP, Aug. 26, 1960. / **who will not hesitate**: ibid. / **rewriting the sequence**: NYP, Aug. 29, 1960. / **still seems to be**: ibid. / **Jackie Robinson is on**: NYP, Sept. 7, 1960.

CHAPTER 14

After what the Democrats: PC, Nov. 20, 1960. / **more progress**: Dayton (Ohio) *Journal,* Oct. 29, 1960. / **champion the Negro cause**: Memphis *Commercial Appeal,* Oct. 27, 1960. / **lavish in their praise**: Val Washington to JR, Oct. 24, 1960, JRP. / **outstanding ... sincerity**: Sidney Rosenblum to JR, Oct. 21, 1960, JRP. / **I am not now**: New York *Citizen-Call,* Oct. 15, 1960. / **So many people even**: PC, Nov. 20, 1960. / **I was not passive**: Rachel Robinson, interview. / **The part given me**: E. Frederic Morrow, *Black Man in the White House* (New York: Coward-McCann, 1963), pp. 295–96. / **I used to holler**: PSN, April 14, 1987. / **come home**: NYAN, Nov. 5, 1960. / **Mr. Rickey reassured me**: PC, Nov. 20, 1960. / **the Negro vote was**: Branch Rickey to Richard M. Nixon, Feb. 1, 1962, BRP, LC. / **enormous contribution**: Richard M. Nixon to JR, Nov. 4, 1960, JRP. / **one of the highlights**: JR to Richard M. Nixon, Jan. 18, 1961, JRP. / **I was terribly disappointed**: JR to A. B. Hermann, Nov. 14, 1960, JRP. / **the various self-styled**: NYAN, Nov. 12, 1960. / **It is my belief**: PC, Nov. 20, 1960. / **partisanship played**: James A. Wechsler to JR, Nov. 8, 1960, JRP. / **No one will ever**: NYAN, Jan. 6, 1962. / **Personally, it is my**: A. B. Hermann to JR, Nov. 23, 1960, JRP. / **Please do not**

think: draft, JR to Nelson A. Rockefeller, Nov. 15, 1960, JRP. / **perhaps**: NYAN, Feb. 11, 1961. / **most constructive**: Nelson Rockefeller to JR, July 6, 1961, JRP. / **a tremendous physical presence**: David Robinson to author, May 12, 1995. / **My father was very**: Sharon Robinson to author, July 10, 1995. / **My greatest love**: David Robinson, interview. / **Jackie was thrown**: Sharon Robinson, *Stealing Home* (N.Y.: HarperCollins, 1996), p. 86. / **Jackie was more dependent**: Sharon Robinson, *Stealing Home,* p. 87. / **we weren't afraid of**: Sharon Robinson, interview. / **feeling inadequate**: Sharon Robinson, *Stealing Home,* p. 88. / **I am really very**: JR to Rachel Robinson, n.d., RRP. / **I know you sometimes**: JR to Jackie Robinson Jr., n.d. RRP. / **I am right proud**: JR to Rachel Robinson, n.d., RRP. / **my little sweetheart**: JR to Jackie, Sharon, and David Robinson, n.d., RRP. / **I know I haven't**: JR to Rachel Robinson, n.d., RRP. / **The Jackie Junior**: Peter Simon to author, Aug. 10, 1996. / **I saw a different**: Bradley Gordon to author, interview, March 13, 1996. / **remarkable memory**: misc. clipping, 1957, JRP. / **It was exciting**: JR to Caroline Wallerstein, n.d. (May 19, 1958), JRP. / **Jackie is developing**: JR to David and Caroline Wallerstein, n.d. (1959), JRP. / **We have so much**: JR to David and Caroline Wallerstein, n.d. (Dec. 22, 1959), JRP. / **I have a hunch**: JR to David and Caroline Wallerstein, n.d. (July 11, 1959), JRP. / **Jackie could really play**: Bradley Gordon, interview. / **Jackie is trying**: JR to Caroline Wallerstein, n.d. (May 16, 1961), JRP. / **We hope sending**: ibid. / **for the insults**: JR and Marian Logan to Mr. and Mrs. James Gabrielle, Dec. 8, 1960, JRP. / **We are going to**: Chattanooga (Tenn.) *News–Free Press,* April 17, 1961. / **your obviously fine start**: JR to John F. Kennedy, Feb. 9, 1961, JRP. / **Your actions demonstrate**: WP, May 12, 1961. / **You are doing**: JR to Robert F. Kennedy, May 25, 1961, JRP. / **stop in to say**: Robert F. Kennedy to JR, June 2, 1961, JRP. / **Not so fast**: JR to Caroline Wallerstein, n.d. (May 16, 1961), JRP. / **I am firm**: NYAN, Aug. 12, 1961. / **Williams reports**: Harris Wofford to Richard Goodwin, Sept. 5, 1961, JRP. / **My children and your**: press release, Congress of Racial Equality, Sept. 5 (1961), JRP. / **She gets her degree**: JR to Caroline Wallerstein, n.d. (May 16, 1961), JRP. / **Rae has been**: JR to David and Caroline Wallerstein, n.d. (Oct. 26, 1961), JRP. / **very exciting**: JR to David and Caroline

Wallerstein, n.d. (Oct. 26, 1961), JRP. / **I am so grateful**: New York *Daily News,* Jan. 24, 1962. / **It is a pleasure**: Boston *Globe,* Jan. 26, 1962. / **We feel deeply indebted**: NYAN, Jan. 6, 1962. / **We have been working**: JR, marginalia on letter, Ed Kaiser Jr. to JR, Aug. 25, 1963, JRP. / **a champion scrapper**: NYAN, Jan. 20, 1962. / **I am now convinced**: NYAN, Jan. 27, 1962. / **Mr. President, don't you**: NYAN, May 5, 1961. / **We think the President**: NYAN, May 26, 1962. / **an insult**: NYAN, Aug. 18, 1962. / **It is not going**: Andrew Hatcher to Alfred Duckett, May 11, 1962, JRP. / **I have to say**: NYAN, Dec. 1, 1962. / **I always get**: NYAN, Aug. 24, 1963. / **Is there a medal**: NYAN, March 3, 1962. / **our advent**: Archie Moore to JR, March 16, 1962, NAACPR, LC. / **one of the most**: Dan Blumenthal to William Black, May 23, 1962, JRP. / **Dr. Martin King is giving**: JR to Caroline Wallerstein, n.d. (May 2, 1962), JRP. / **the Merchant of Venice**: NYAN, July 28, 1962. / **Jew go away**: NYT, July 13, 1962. / **Strange Happenings**: NYAN, July 14, 1962. / **hate Jackie Robinson**: NYAN, July 28, 1962. / **Jackie is a classified**: Dan S. Blumenthal to Isidore Lapan, July 17, 1962, JRP. / **Is there anything**: JR to William Black, n.d., JRP. / **one hundred percent**: Roy Wilkins to JR, July 16, 1962, NAACPR, LC. / **It was beautiful**: Arnold Forster to JR, July 18, 1962, JRP. / **all who mask bigotry**: Whitney Young to JR, July 17, 1962, JRP. / **Bigotry is intolerable**: Ralph Bunche to JR, July 19, 1962, JRP. / **magnificent stand**: George Lawrence to William Black, July 15, 1962, JRP. / **mass rally**: NYAN, July 21, 1962. / **You have banished yourself**: NYAN, July 18, 1962. / **Jack had been attacked**: Rachel Robinson, interview. / **a very intensive investigation**: NYAN, Aug. 25, 1962. / **There was fear**: NYAN, Sept. 22, 1962. / **It really makes you**: Albany (Geo.) *Herald,* Sept. 9, 1962. / **Jackie Robinson had**: Wyatt Tee Walker to author, interview, March 25, 1997. / **Let's rebuild these churches**: NYAN, Sept. 15, 1962. / **It is sad**: NYAN, Oct. 6, 1962. / **his continued and sustained**: NYAN, Aug. 25, 1962. / **Do you turn**: NYAN, Oct. 20, 1962. / **I hope that you**: JR to Richard M. Nixon, Nov. 12, 1962, JRP. / **One day, early**: Rachel Robinson, interview. / **I was not afraid**: NYAN, Feb. 9, 1963. / **Like any other family**: NYAN, Jan. 19, 1963. / **Then someone called us**: Rachel Robinson, interview. / **We have got to have**: NYAN, March 30, 1963. / **a friend in** the wrong: NYAN, March 30, 1963. / **To Jackie Robinson**: NYAN, April 6, 1963. / **We as black people**: NYAN, April 13, 1963. / **I was one**: ibid. / **If I have to give**: NYAN, April 20, 1963. / **This kind of forthright**: NYAN, May 11, 1963. / **The revolution that is**: JR to John F. Kennedy, May 7, 1963, JRP. / **I can't stay**: NYAN, May 11, 1963. / **I don't like to**: misc. clipping, United Press International, May 8, 1963, JRP. / **the restraint of many**: JR to John F. Kennedy, June 15, 1963, JRP. / **Thank you for emerging**: NYAN, June 22, 1963. / **casting disparaging remarks**: NYAN, July 6, 1963. / **the course of history**: ibid. / **Disunity is no proper**: NYAN, July 6, 1963. / **very odd that**: NYAN, June 13, 1963. / **the magnificent role**: NYAN, July 27, 1963. / **we don't see eye**: JR to Sam [Ostrove?], Oct. 30, 1963, JRP. / **Don't you have**: William Black to JR, Aug. 13, 1963, JRP. / **I hope you will**: JR to William Black, Aug. 14, 1963, JRP. / **I'm sure, today**: JR to William Black, draft, Aug. 15, 1963, JRP. / **I have never been**: NYAN, Sept. 7, 1963. / **God bless Dr. Martin**: NYAN, Sept. 28, 1963. / **Friends say that Jackie**: NYAN, Sept. 7, 1963. / **People are saying**: JR to Sam [Ostrove?], Oct. 30, 1963, JRP. / **once a friend**: NYAN, Nov. 16, 1963. / **We hear that you**: NYAN, Nov. 30, 1963. / **Coming from you**: NYAN, Dec. 14, 1963. / **but then I do not**: NYAN, Dec. 7, 1963. / **Chickens coming home**: ibid. / **When the tragic news**: NYAN, Nov. 30, 1963. / **If the Democratic Party**: ibid. / **Jackie Robinson and Chock**: NYAN, Jan. 4, 1964. / **We'll miss Jackie**: NYT, Feb. 1, 1964. / **I did not want**: NYAN, March 28, 1964.

CHAPTER 15

The time is ripest: NYAN, Feb. 15, 1964. / **Jack had what I**: J. Bruce Llewellyn to author, interview, July 24, 1995. / **a striking parallel**: JR, "The G.O.P.: For White Men Only?" *Saturday Evening Post,* Aug. 10–17, 1963, p. 10. / **The danger**: NYAN, Aug. 10, 1963. / **I am proud**: NYAN, Aug. 17, 1963. / **the most effective work**: Winthrop W. Aldrich to JR, Jan. 30, 1964, JRP. / **What can they possibly**: Philadelphia *Inquirer,* April 9, 1964. / **If we have**: Portland (Ore.) *Reporter,* April 14, 1964. / **This is a**

struggle: Moorhead (Minn.) *Concordian,* May 22, 1964, p. 1. / **I never could**: NYAN, July 4, 1964. / **I am a Negro**: NYAN, July 4, 1964. / **This is the time**: NYT, June 16, 1964. / **We had a beautiful**: Rachel Robinson, interview. / **Jackie Robinson looked**: NYAN, July 18, 1964. / **undoubtedly the leading light**: ibid. / **a classic and splendid**: NYAN, Jan. 8, 1966. / **extremism in the defense**: *Encyclopedia Americana* Vol. 13 (Danbury, Conn.: Grolier, 1992), p. 38. / **rather viciously**: Barry Goldwater to JR, July 25, 1964, JRP. / **Is it unity**: NYAN, Aug. 15, 1964. / **Your understanding and support**: Hubert H. Humphrey to JR, April 24, 1964, JRP. / **truly a great national**: Hubert H. Humphrey to JR, Aug. 5, 1964, JRP. / **You know and I know**: JR to Nelson A. Rockefeller, Oct. 7, 1964, JRP. / **inconceivable to this writer**: NYAN, Sept. 19, 1964. / **We must have**: NYAN, Nov. 21, 1964. / **A split ballot**: NYAN, Sept. 19, 1964. / **the Negro Revolution**: NYAN, April 11, 1964. / **I am no race leader**: New York *Herald Tribune,* April 26, 1964. / **the atmosphere of hate**: NYAN, May 16, 1964. / **I thought he would**: Los Angeles *Times,* March 22, 1964. / **because they advocate**: Portland (Ore.) *Reporter,* April 15, 1964. / **Malcolm has big audiences**: New York *Herald Tribune,* April 26, 1964. / **deliberate and evil design**: NYAN, April 11, 1964. / **the fair-haired boy**: NYAN, July 18, 1964. / **I wish I could**: NYAN, June 12, 1964. / **which belong to each**: JR, "Is the Negro Ready," misc. speeches, n.d., JRP. / **the last Negro**: NYT, March 6, 1964. / **classic prototypes**: NYAN, Aug. 22, 1964. / **tragic coincidence**: NYAN, July 25, 1964. / **a Black Shining Prince**: NYAN, March 6, 1965. / **Jackie, in days**: NYAN, Dec. 16, 1967. / **job integration**: NYAN, June 20, 1964. / **When it came to**: *I Never,* p. 196. / **a community enterprise**: *I Never,* p. 197. / **I had hardly got**: *I Never,* p. 198. / **issued press releases**: NYAN, April 18, 1864. / **on schedule**: NYT, March 26, 1964. / **my good friend**: Hubert H. Humphrey to JR, Jan. 4, 1965, JRP. / **In my humble opinion**: NYAN, Jan. 2, 1965. / **for more cash**: NYAN, June 18, 1966. / **I have been getting**: JR to David and Caroline Wallerstein, n.d. (Dec. 23, 1964), JRP. / **We believe that the building**: NYAN, May 18, 1963. / **readying the sale**: NYAN, Dec. 18, 1965. / **an offer to merge**: NYAN, June 25, 1966. / **I am deeply impressed**:

NYAN, July 2, 1966. / **I could never understand**: David Robinson, interview. / **fully implemented**: Hubert H. Humphrey to JR, Feb. 11, 1965, JRP. / **immediate action**: JR to Lyndon Baines Johnson, March 8, 1965, JRP. / **must overcome the crippling**: NYT, March 16, 1965. / **While it is true**: Clifford L. Alexander to Bess Abell, Nov. 22, 1965, JRP. / **one of his grandstand**: Clifford L. Alexander, memorandum, April 20, 1967, JRP. / **A true friend**: Hubert H. Humphrey to JR, Oct. 25, 1965, JRP. / **Jack didn't go**: Rachel Robinson, interview. / **If it hadn't been**: Los Angeles *Herald-Examiner,* April 1, 1965. / **one of the year's**: NYT, May 2, 1964. / **my delight**: NYAN, May 30, 1964. / **I really wanted**: JR to Walter O'Malley, July 25, 1962, JRP. / **as a personal affront**: Buzzie Bavasi with John Strege, *Off the Record* (Chicago: Contemporary Books, 1987), p. 37. / **I think my dad**: Peter O'Malley, interview. / **It was something**: Rachel Robinson, interview. / **Jack felt completely baffled**: Rachel Robinson (with Lee Daniels), *Jackie Robinson: An Intimate Portrait* (New York: Harry Abrams, 1996), p. 194. / **Jackie has grown**: JR to David and Caroline Wallerstein, n.d. (Dec. 23, 1964), JRP. / **Sharon is everyone's**: ibid. / **praying for the safety**: Hubert H. Humphrey to JR, July 30, 1965, JRP. / **most tragic picture**: NYAN, Aug. 21, 1965. / **He filled a void**: Greensboro (N.C.) *Daily News,* Jan. 10, 1966. / **wonderful communication**: NYAN, Dec. 18, 1965. / **The bigots who hated**: Los Angeles *Sentinel,* Dec. 18, 1965. / **I owe a great**: misc. clipping, n.d., JRP. / **Our big lesson**: North Carolina A&T College *Register,* Jan. 14, 1966. / **Vote for the man**: misc. clipping, n.d., JRP. / **A miracle is unfolding**: NYAN, April 30, 1966. / **There are black bigots**: NYAN, Feb. 19, 1966. / **a decent man**: ibid. / **a machine to end**: NYAN, Dec. 25, 1965. / **I'm not in a popularity**: New York *Herald Tribune,* March 6, 1966. / **a direct call**: NYT, Nov. 2, 1965. / **He's a liar**: ibid. / **I think he will**: NYAN, Jan. 8, 1966. / **one of the most**: JR to Nelson Rockefeller, Jan. 12, 1966, JRP. / **but we will get**: transcript, news conference concerning appointment of Jackie Robinson, Feb. 8, 1966, JRP. / **I have rolled up**: NYAN, Feb. 26, 1966. / **I was brought in**: Evelyn Cunningham, interview. / **Jackie got things done**: Percy Sutton, interview. / **Jackie was usually**: Evelyn Cunningham, interview. / **go into areas**: misc. memorandum, n.d., JRP. / **We faced a very**: Evelyn Cunningham, interview. / **I like a man**: NYAN, Aug. 13, 1966. / **nit-picking**: NYAN, June 18, 1966. / **is proving to be**: NYAN, June 25, 1966. / **One of the most**: NYAN, July 30, 1966. / **I hope I am wrong**: JR to Barry Gray, Aug. 17, 1966, JRP. / **the white power structure**: NYAN, July 30, 1966. / **When we use our**: NYAN, Oct. 22, 1966. / **a day to day**: NYAN, Nov. 12, 1966. / **the most resounding reply**: NYAN, Nov. 26, 1966. / **In my book**: NYAN, Nov. 19, 1966. / **a lustre**: Nelson Rockefeller to Jack Robinson Jr., June 23, 1966, RRP. / **Jackie was behaving**: Rachel Robinson, interview. / **I know I have**: Jackie Robinson Jr. to JR, n.d., RRP. / **As I look around**: NYAN, Aug. 5, 1967. / **His step was brisk**: New York *Herald Tribune,* March 6, 1966. / **Jackie was not too**: Evelyn Cunningham, interview. / **a small personalized hotel**: C. G. Bernard to JR, Jan. 3, 1967, JRP. / **Jack discovered**: Rachel Robinson, interview. / **I can hardly describe**: ibid. / **Jack absolutely loved**: Warren Jackson to author, interview, March 20, 1997. / **Too often?**: uniden. notes, n.d., JRP. / **were looking over**: NYAN, July 6, 1963. / **They told me**: NYAN, Dec. 30, 1967. / **Coming back**: NYAN, Jan. 7, 1967. / **We want to build**: New York *Daily News,* May 3, 1966. / **oughta be tired**: NYAN, May 21, 1966. / **I am not an Adam**: NYAN, Jan. 21, 1967. / **It's the same kind**: NYAN, Jan. 14, 1967. / **Jackie Robinson and his wife**: NYAN, April 11, 1967. / **the heroism**: NYAN, Nov. 14, 1967. / **I am forced to say**: NYAN, Jan. 14, 1967. / **gross misinformation**: Roy Wilkins to JR, Feb. 2, 1967, JRP. / **I am so sorry**: JR to Roy Wilkins, Feb. 15, 1967, NAACPR, LC. / **I am not proud**: JR to Roy Wilkins, Feb. 20, 1967, JRP. / **an idol of mine**: NYAN, April 8, 1967. / **Confused**: NYAN, May 13, 1967. / **still my leader**: NYAN, July 1, 1967. / **potentially explosive situation**: Nelson Rockefeller to JR, June 26, 1967, JRP. / **the men behind you**: NYAN, Dec. 9, 1967. / **chickened out**: NYAN, Aug. 26, 1967. / **Stokely Carmichael's version**: transcript of interview with Theodore Granik, "Youth Wants to Know," April 1967, JRP. / **We will not be**: NYAN, May 27, 1967. / **I feel perfectly secure**: NYAN, Jan. 20, 1968. / **I don't seek**: NYAN, Oct. 7, 1967. / **I am human**: NYAN, Jan. 20, 1968.

CHAPTER 16

through your personal contacts: Wah F. Chin to JR, Jan. 4, 1968, JRP. / **Our aim is to help**: NYAN, April 13, 1968. / **particularly for ghetto**: Shura Bary to Randall Jones, Jan. 3, 1968, JRP. / **I think the masses**: "Sea Host Inc.: Toward a Black Middle Class," *Fast Food: The Magazine of the Restaurant Business,* Nov. 1969, unpag. / **I do support**: NYT, Feb. 9, 1968. / **understand the reasons**: ibid. / **It was different**: NYT, Feb. 10, 1968. / **I felt hot**: Sharon Robinson, *Stealing Home* (N.Y.: HarperCollins, 1996), p. 128. / **a bent gray man**: Roger Kahn, "Jackie Robinson: Man of the 25 Years," *Sport,* Dec. 1971, p. 65. / **Are you all right**: Sharon Robinson, *Stealing Home,* p. 131. / **In Colorado I started**: Hearings Before the Subcommittee to Investigate Juvenile Delinquency of the Committee on the Judiciary, United States Senate, Ninety-First Congress, March 24–25, Aug. 18–20, Oct. 30, 1970 (Washington, D.C.: U.S. Government Printing Office, 1971), p. 6903. / **They tied him**: Jack Roosevelt Robinson Jr. to Jack and Rachel Robinson, n.d., RRP. All letters cited here are from RRP. / **Man, you talk**: Bradley Gordon, interview. / **If he doesn't learn**: Jack Roosevelt Robinson Jr. to Rachel Robinson, n.d., RRP. / **Jackie had come from**: Bradley Gordon, interview. / **I'm going to need**: Jack Roosevelt Robinson Jr. to Rachel Robinson, n.d. / **We know the only**: JR to David and Caroline Wallerstein, March 14, 1968, JRP. / **I suspect that unless**: JR to Clarence L. Towns Jr., Feb. 29, 1968, JRP. / **This time, I accepted**: NYAN, March 23, 1968. / **Speaking from the heart**: JR to Nelson Rockefeller, March 8, 1968, JRP. / **Governor Rockefeller's desires**: JR to Hubert H. Humphrey, May 3, 1968, JRP. / **the greatest leader**: NYAN, April 13, 1968. / **Our people have always**: ibid. / **Dad smiled reassuringly**: Sharon Robinson, *Stealing Home,* p. 137. / **I felt I couldn't**: *I Never,* p. 275. / **If Nixon is elected**: NYT, June 24, 1968. / **I guess the good Lord**: JR to Caroline Wallerstein, July 20, 1968, JRP. / **I can't imagine what**: ibid. / **This is a tough period**: ibid. / **loitering for the purposes**: NYT, Aug. 25, 1968. / **if they will have me**: NYT, Aug. 12, 1968. / **Now he's sold out**: NYT, Aug. 12, 1968. / **It is surely time**: NYP, Aug. 15, 1968. / **If that is racism**: NYAN, Sept. 7, 1968. / **Get him out of here!**:

NYT, Aug. 15, 1968. / **precipitate and to be**: NYT, Aug. 20, 1968. / **This is perhaps**: JR to Nelson Rockefeller, fragment, n.d., RRP. / **Whatever it was**: Rachel Robinson, interview. / **we all pray that**: JR to Richard M. Nixon, Jan. 22, 1969, JRP. / **We had a nice**: Rachel Robinson, interview. / **We don't want**: "Sea Host Inc.," unpag. / **All I know**: Rachel Robinson, interview. / **Several of us**: Warren Jackson to author, interview, March 20, 1997. / **I'm afraid we are**: "Sea Host Inc.," unpag. / **My daughter had**: ibid. / **I wouldn't fly**: NYT, July 4, 1968. / **We met at a bistro**: Toni Morrison to author, interview, Nov. 19, 1996. / **The very poor relations**: NYT, Jan. 20, 1970. / **I don't think anyone**: NYT, Dec. 4, 1969. / **Housing is the first**: NYT, Oct. 25, 1972. / **was that it would**: NYT, July 30, 1972. / **There is enough profit**: ibid. / **As you can see**: JR to Andre Baruch, n.d., JRP. / **It was January**: Martin Edelman to author, interview, July 7, 1995. / **It makes us happy**: JR to David and Caroline Wallerstein, March 26, 1970, JRP. / **stick by my son**: NYT, Aug. 5, 1970. / **I'm here because**: NYT, Aug. 10, 1970. / **I know how difficult**: JR to Jackie Robinson Jr., June 17, 1969. / **I stuck out my**: *I Never,* p. 238. / **on the right track**: JR to David and Caroline Wallerstein, July 9, 1970, JRP. / **eating rice and beans**: ibid. / **When you see Charlie**: Percy Sutton, interview. / **We are still struggling**: JR to David and Caroline Wallerstein, July 19, 1970. / **I told everyone**: Rachel Robinson, interview. / **like a caged lion**: JR to David and Caroline Wallerstein, July 9, 1970. / **It was so traumatic**: Rachel Robinson, interview.

CHAPTER 17

Meeting Robinson: Dr. Eric Cassell to author, interview, June 26, 1995. / **Every time I go**: ibid. / **I have hopes**: *I Never,* p. 279. / **If you want to save**: *I Never,* p. 203. / **Jack was a man**: J. Bruce Llewellyn to author, interview, July 24, 1995. / **particularly impressed with**: JR to Marilyn Walburg, May 7, 1971, JRP. / **I found myself losing**: *I Never,* p. 205. / **At 64, I need**: NYAN, Aug. 21, 1971. / **I had gone weak**: *I Never,* p. 256. / **You could hear Rachel**: David Falkner, *Great Time Coming: The Life of*

Jackie Robinson (N.Y.: Simon & Schuster, 1995), pp. 337–38. / **a moving and dramatic**: NYAN, July 3, 1971. / **four or five nights**: David Robinson, interview. / **What made it worse**: Rachel Robinson, interview. / **As I neared the entrance**: Sharon Robinson, *Stealing Home* (N.Y.: HarperCollins, 1996), p. 182. / **First Mr. Rickey**: Sharon Robinson, interview. / **Jackie indeed opened**: Peter Bienstock to author, March 1, 1997. / **almost cavalier**: Falkner, p. 332. / **I asked Arthur Logan**: Rachel Robinson, interview. / **He would not have**: Evelyn Cunningham, interview. / **If I had been**: NYAN, Oct. 30, 1971. / **To use your own**: Ann C. Whitman to JR, Sept. 29, 1971, JRP. / **Thinking over that incident**: *I Never*, p. 281. / **I saw more of my**: David Robinson, interview. / **she has been a warm**: NYAN, Dec. 11, 1971. / **I grabbed Dad's hand**: Sharon Robinson, *Stealing Home,* p. 189. / **The patient, as always**: JR, medical records (Sept. 27, 1971). / **We're definitely**: Long Beach (Cal.) *Independent Press-Telegram,* Jan. 23, 1972. / **I'm not opposed**: ibid. / **It's shocking and saddening**: NYT, April 3, 1972. / **Gil always was**: Roger Kahn, *The Boys of Summer* (N.Y.: New American Library, 1971), p. 401. / **Anything that is**: NYT, May 22, 1970. / **Your action justifies**: JR to E. J. Bavasi, Feb. 11, 1971, JRP. / **If it hadn't been**: Los Angeles *Times,* June 5, 1972. / **This is truly**: ibid. / **I told Peter**: ibid. / **It's not something**: Peter O'Malley, interview. / **When he walked out**: misc. clipping, April 1977, JRP. / **He walked in**: CDB, Feb. 2, 1979. / **I've gotten tremendous thrills**: JR to Alfred Duckett, July 22, 1972, JRP. / **Health is a progressive**: Los Angeles *Times,* June 5, 1972. / **One day he had come**: Eric Cassell, interview. / **As long as they**: NYT, Sept. 9, 1972. / **If you people expect**: Torrance (Cal.) *Daily Breeze,* Oct. 25, 1972. / **How can a man**: New York *Daily News,* Oct. 25, 1972. / **The last hurrah**: Rachel Robinson, interview. / **I am extremely proud**: Transcript of ceremony, Oct. 15, 1972, JRP. / **I was surprised**: ibid. / **I'm sorry**: Los Angeles *Times,* Oct. 26, 1972. / **On Columbus Day**: Brenda Williams to author, interview, March 1, 1997. / **His courage, his sense**: NYT, Oct. 25, 1972. / **a trailblazer**: ibid. / **The word for Jackie**: ibid. / **He could beat you**: ibid. / **The service was excellent**: Robert Campbell, interview, UCLA Archives.

Acknowledgments

This project began soon after Rachel Robinson and I, following some prompting by my friend William C. Rhoden, agreed that I should attempt a biography of her late husband to be published, if possible, in 1997, the fiftieth anniversary of his entry into the major leagues. Mrs. Robinson promised me her full cooperation, including access to most of the personal letters and other material in her possession as well as to the archives at the Jackie Robinson Foundation.

From the outset, we understood that I could not proceed unless she waived her right to approve the manuscript before its publication. Mrs. Robinson did so readily, and has stood by our agreement despite the fact that, in certain places, my interpretation of aspects of her husband's life is somewhat different from her own. I thank her for many things, but above all for bringing a fierce integrity and intelligence to her part in this project, combined at all times with graciousness of spirit.

Once again I am grateful to Jonathan Segal of Alfred A. Knopf, Inc., whose interest in a biography of Jackie Robinson goes back many years. His zeal in acquiring this book has been matched by his sensitivity to the various dimensions of Robinson's story. As with our work together on Arthur Ashe's *Days of Grace,* I have benefited from his sound advice at every point.

I am indebted to everyone at the Jackie Robinson Foundation, but especially to its president, Betty Phillips Adams. I thank her and professor Michael Lutzker of New York University, who have worked hard over the years to develop the archives at the foundation. Emma Roberson, Sonnie Humphries, Claudette Rose, Holly Cooper, Judi Beville, Jermaine Smith—everyone there has helped me in various ways. Spike Lee, whose research for a movie about Robinson (also with Mrs. Robinson's support) coincided at one point with my own digging, was generous in sharing with me his findings, especially the texts of more than forty interviews he conducted with various baseball personalities. Michelle Forman, who assisted him in his research, was also helpful.

At Princeton University, I thank Lee Clark Mitchell, the chair of the Department of English, for his support and understanding. Bruce Simon brought his keen intelligence and industriousness to the task of assisting my research; he also read and criticized the manuscript in helpful ways, as did Hilary Herbold when we prepared it for publication. Stuart Burrows, too, helped me find new material. Judith Ferszt of American Studies transcribed most of my interviews, and Jean Washington and Hattie Black of African-American Studies also made my task easier.

In Los Angeles, Elston Carr of UCLA was diligent in helping me gather material pertaining to Robinson's early years in California. In Pasadena, Kathy Robinson, the daughter of Mack Robinson and niece of Jackie Robinson, has worked hard to recover the history of her remarkable family; I thank her, too, for her generosity. Ray Bartlett, Jack Gordon, and Henry W. Shatford, all friends of Jackie Robinson in his youth, were unstinting in their attempts to help me understand him.

In Cairo, Georgia, Dr. Linda Walden and her family, including her mother, Lula Walden, and her uncle, Jack Hadley, all relatives of Jackie Robinson, welcomed Rachel Robinson and me and facilitated my research into Robinson's Georgia roots. Joseph P. Lee also sent me useful material about Jackie Robinson and Georgia.

Among librarians, I thank Lois Nase and Patricia Pon-
zoli of Princeton University; Adrienne Canon of the Library
of Congress; John Vernon of the National Archives; Joellen
Elbashir of the Moorland-Spingarn Research Collection;
Esme Bhan, formerly of the Moorland-Spingarn; Alan L.
Kaye of the Roddenberry Library, Cairo, Georgia; Tom Hill
of the Thomasville Historical Society; at UCLA, Dennis Bit-
terlich of the University Archives and David Zeidberg and
Susan M. Allan of Special Collections. I also thank Bill Bib-
biani of the Pasadena Unified School District; Steve
Gietschier of the *Sporting News;* Tania Rizzo of the
Pasadena Historical Society; Mary Ann Laun of the
Pasadena City College Library; J. Kevin O'Brien, Chief of
the Freedom of Information Section, Federal Bureau of
Investigation, U.S. Department of Justice; Patricia Quarter-
man of Huston-Tillotson College, Austin, Texas; John
Olguin, archivist of the Los Angeles Dodgers; Sarah Cooper
of the Southern California Library of Social Studies; and the
staff of the Firestone Library of Princeton University. At the
National Baseball Hall of Fame and Museum in Cooperstown, New York, I thank Donald Marr Jr. and also James L.
Gates Jr., the librarian of the Hall of Fame, and his colleague, Timothy J. Wiles.

Needless to say, I owe much to previous writers on
Jackie Robinson, from newspaper reporters such as Shav
Glick and Henry Shatford in his youth to such stalwarts as
Red Smith and Roger Kahn and to David Falkner, whose
recent book about Robinson, *Great Time Coming,* seeks, as
my own book does, to broaden our understanding of Robinson beyond baseball. My account of Robinson's early years
draws on the fine work of Carl T. Rowan in his *Wait Till Next
Year.* Of course, all serious scholarly work on Jackie Robinson builds on Jules Tygiel's landmark study, *Baseball's
Great Experiment: Jackie Robinson and His Legacy.* Among
other scholars and researchers, some individuals stand out.

Professor Robin D. G. Kelley of New York University generously lent me his notes from an extended research project about blacks in Pasadena. Also at NYU, I thank Professor Carl Prince, author of the recently published *Brooklyn's Dodgers,* and Professor Jeffrey Sammons, who, as always, was a source of invaluable insight and encouragement. At UCLA, Professor Richard Yarborough was once again someone I could count on. Jonathan Mercantini, Susan Rayl, and Frank Ardolino, as well as Chris Lamb, Glen Beske, and Marc Bona, were among the several other scholars who shared their work with me.

Ralph Schoenstein of Princeton read the manuscript near its completion and offered sage advice based on his many years as a writer and as a fan of the Brooklyn Dodgers. Martin Edelman also read the manuscript at a crucial point and provided invaluable commentary.

I thank all the other people who shared with me their knowledge of Jackie Robinson or in some other tangible way helped me to complete this project. They include Willette Bailey, Robert Behn, Peter Bienstock, Peter Bjarkman, John Bracey, Gene Budig, Roy Campanella II, W. Bliss Carnochan, Dr. Eric J. Cassell, Leonard Coleman, Charles Copeland, John Crowley, Ernest Cunningham, Evelyn Cunningham, Sarah and Ben Cymrot, Ossie Davis, Ruby Dee, Phil Dixon, Larry Doby, Winston C. Doby, Phyllis Dorn, Warren Dorn, Raymond Doswell, Karleen Downs Berthel, Robert Downs, Dorothy Duckett Joseph, Carl Erskine, Olan Faulk, Ron Gabriel, Truman Gibson, Steve Gietschier, Bernice Gordon, Bradley Gordon, Enid Gort, Ronnie Hall, Roland Harden, James Hatch, Tommy Hawkins, Sidney Heard, Tom Hill, Larry Hogan, Russia Hughes, Lonnie Jackson, Warren Jackson, Shig Kawai, David Kelly, Taylor King, Michael Kronish, Sam Lacy, Harlan Lebo, Joseph P. Lee, Beverley LeMay, Leonard Lempel, J. Bruce Llewellyn, Warren Logan, David Lurry, Willa Mae Lurry, Bill Mardo, Terri

Bond Michel, Rose Morgan, Don Newcombe, Peter O'Malley, Eleanor Peters Heard, Samuel Pierce, Sean Presant, Brad Pye Jr., Dr. John Quill, Mark Reese, William C. Rhoden, Branch B. Rickey, David Robinson, Delano Robinson, Sharon Robinson, William Rowe, Julia Sandy-Bailey, Clarence Seniors, Joanna Simon, Peter Simon, Wynella Smith, Martin Stone, Clyde Sukeforth, Percy Sutton, William H. Sword, William J. Vanlandingham, Van Wade, Willa Mae Walker, Reverend Wyatt Tee Walker, Morris Weissman, Roger Wilkins, John A. Williams, Shirley Broyard Williams, Bob Williamson, Jesse Wills, Liz Withnell, and Richard Yarborough.

I thank my agent on this project, Fifi Oscard, and Kevin McShane of the Fifi Oscard Agency for their advice and assistance. Last but by no means least, my wife, Marvina White, provided aid and comfort, as always, throughout the writing of this book. I'll be eternally grateful.

Index

players' petition against
   Robinson, 290
Robinson's war of words
   with, 419–21
suspension from baseball,
   293–4
Dworman, Lester, 412, 413
Dyer, Eddie, 323
Dykes, Jimmy, 93–4, 155

Easter, Luke, 431
Eastland, James, 581
Ebbets Field, 2, 521
Edelman, Martin, 779–81, 824
Edwards, Bruce, 288, 329,
   360, 365
Egan, Dave, 210
Egan, Wish, 209–10
Eisenhower, Dwight D., 377,
   575, 577–8, 580–2, 583–4,
   597–8, 600, 607, 610
Robinson's handshake with,
   463–4
Eliot, Glenn, 299
Ellington, Duke, 765
Elwood, George A., 180, 188
Englehardt, Sam, 612
Ennis, Del, 404
Erskine, Betty, 321
Erskine, Carl, 324, 417, 426,
   456, 500, 516, 525, 544
Evans, Herbert, 700
Evers, Charles, 726
Evers, Medgar, 587, 641, 669,
   671

Farmer, James, 637, 721, 769,
   809,

Farrell, Herbert, 113
Faubus, Orval, 582, 583, 616
Faulk, Olin, 22
Feeney, Charles S. "Chub,"
   546
Feller, Bob, 3, 228, 307,
   364–5, 544, 644
Fieffe, Molver, 825
Finch, Robert, 624
Fitzgerald, Ella, 666–7
Flack, Roberta, 798
Flaherty, Vincent X., 422
Flood, Curt, 647, 812
football, integration of, 260
Forster, Arnold, 391, 650, 666
Fort Riley, Kansas, 156
Foster, Andrew "Rube," 201
franchising industry, 750; *see
   also* Sea Host Incorpo-
   rated
Franks, Herman, 266
Freedom National Bank,
   699–704, 733, 739, 777,
   794–6
Freedom Rides, 638–40
Fresno State University, 99
Frick, Ford, 309, 407, 421,
   443, 451
Fuller, Buckminster, 521
Furillo, Carl, 289, 290, 371,
   403, 404, 416, 429,
   458–9, 460, 470, 501

Gabriel, Ron, 2, 4, 9–10,
   11–12
Gabrielino Indians, 30
Galbreath, John W., 409–10
Gallagher, Jimmy, 523

Anthony Calvacca, New York *Post*: Section Two, page 4 (middle)

Wagner International Photos: Section Two, pages 4 (top), 9 (middle)

Sepia magazine: Section Two, page 15 (top)

Barney Stein: Section One, pages 9 (bottom), 10 (top), 15 (top); Section Two, page 2 (bottom)

Darnell C. Mitchell: Section One, page 12 (bottom right)

Cecil Layne: Section One, page 13 (top); Section Two, page 6 (bottom)

Roger Kahn: Section One, page 14 (top)

Monroe Samuel Frederick II: Section Two, page 14 (bottom)

Bob Weyer: Section Two, page 8 (middle)

Herb Scharfman: Section Two, page 15 (bottom)

Peter Simon: Photo facing the last page

Source unknown: Section One, pages 5 (top left), 7 (top), 16 (bottom); Section Two, pages 1 (bottom), 6 (top), 11 (bottom)

(continued)

Guest, Judith, *Errands*
Hailey, Arthur, *Detective*
Halberstam, David, *The Fifties* (2 volumes)
Hepburn, Katharine, *Me*
James, P. D., *The Children of Men*
Koontz, Dean, *Dark Rivers of the Heart*
Koontz, Dean, *Icebound*
Koontz, Dean, *Intensity*
Koontz, Dean, *Sole Survivor*
Koontz, Dean, *Ticktock*
Krantz, Judith, *Lovers*
Krantz, Judith, *Scruples Two*
Krantz, Judith, *Spring Collection*
Landers, Ann, *Wake Up and Smell the Coffee!*
le Carré, John, *Our Game*
le Carré, John, *The Tailor of Panama*
Lindbergh, Anne Morrow, *Gift from the Sea*
Ludlum, Robert, *The Road to Omaha*
Mayle, Peter, *Anything Considered*
Mayle, Peter, *Chasing Cezanne*
McCarthy, Cormac, *The Crossing*
Meadows, Audrey with Joe Daley, *Love, Alice*
Michaels, Judith, *Acts of Love*
Michener, James A., *Mexico*
Mother Teresa, *A Simple Path*
Patterson, Richard North, *Eyes of a Child*
Patterson, Richard North, *The Final Judgment*
Patterson, Richard North, *Silent Witness*
Peck, M. Scott, M.D., *Denial of the Soul*
Phillips, Louis, editor, *The Random House Large Print Treasury of Best-Loved Poems*
Pope John Paul II, *Crossing the Threshold of Hope*
Pope John Paul II, *The Gospel of Life*
Powell, Colin with Joseph E. Persico, *My American Journey*

(continued)

Puzo, Mario, *The Last Don*
Rampersad, Arnold, *Jackie Robinson*
Rendell, Ruth, *The Keys to the Street*
Rice, Anne, *Servant of the Bones*
Riva, Maria, *Marlene Dietrich* (2 volumes)
Salamon, Julie and Jill Weber, *The Christmas Tree*
Shaara, Jeff, *Gods and Generals*
Snead, Sam with Fran Pirozzolo, *The Game I Love*
Truman, Margaret, *Murder at the National Gallery*
Truman, Margaret, *Murder on the Potomac*
Truman, Margaret, *Murder in the House*
Tyler, Anne, *Ladder of Years*
Tyler, Anne, *Saint Maybe*
Updike, John, *Rabbit at Rest*
Updike, John, *Golf Dreams*
Whitney, Phyllis A., *Amethyst Dreams*